CONSUMING BEHAVIOUR

JOHN DESMOND

DBS Arts

99006513

D0718327

DBS Arts

RECEIVED
2 1 OCT 2002
ARTS Library

Dawson
£24.99 Stg

DBS Arts Library

palgrave

© John Desmond 2003

All rights reserved. No reproduction, copy or transmission of this publication may be made without written permission.

No paragraph of this publication may be reproduced, copied or transmitted save with written permission or in accordance with the provisions of the Copyright, Designs and Patents Act 1988, or under the terms of any licence permitting limited copying issued by the Copyright Licensing Agency, 90 Tottenham Court Road, London W1T 4LP.

Any person who does any unauthorized act in relation to this publication may be liable to criminal prosecution and civil claims for damages.

The author has asserted his right to be identified as the author of this work in accordance with the Copyright, Designs and Patents Act 1988.

First published 2003 by
PALGRAVE
Houndmills, Basingstoke, Hampshire RG21 6XS and
175 Fifth Avenue, New York, N.Y. 10010
Companies and representatives throughout the world

PALGRAVE is the new global academic imprint of
St. Martin's Press LLC Scholarly and Reference Division and
Palgrave Publishers Ltd (formerly Macmillan Press Ltd).

ISBN 0–333–94992–7

This book is printed on paper suitable for recycling and made from fully managed and sustained forest sources.

A catalogue record for this book is available from the British Library.

A catalog record for this book is available from the Library of Congress

10   9   8   7   6   5   4   3   2   1
12   11   10   09   08   07   06   05   04   03

Printed and bound in Great Britain by
J.W. Arrowsmith Ltd, Bristol

CONTENTS

List of Tables and Figures   vii
Acknowledgements   ix
Introduction   xi

CHAPTER 1   **CONSUMING TALES**   1

Learning objectives   1
1.1   Introduction   1
1.2   Two tales of consumption   2
1.3   Norbert Elias: the civilizing process   9
1.4   Discussion of Elias's civilizing process   16
1.5   Postmodernism and the neo-tribes: return to community?   18
1.6   Discussion of postmodernism and the neo-tribes   22
1.7   Applicability to other cultures   25
1.8   Chapter summary   26
End-of-chapter review questions   27
References and further reading   27
Notes   27

CHAPTER 2   **CONSUMING SPACE AND TIME**   29

Learning objectives   29
2.1   Introduction   29
2.2   Consumption: space and time   30
2.3   The place of community versus the space of society   30
2.4   Max Weber: modernity as rational ordering of space   32
2.5   Karl Marx: melting modernity   56
2.6   Discussion   72
2.7   Conclusion   73
2.8   Chapter summary   74
2.9   Case study: Down on the old factory farm   74
End-of-chapter review questions   77
References and further reading   77
Notes   79

CHAPTER 3	**CONSUMING POWER**	**81**
	Learning objectives	81
	3.1 Introduction	81
	3.2 Sovereign power	82
	3.3 Disciplinary power	121
	3.4 Chapter summary	129
	3.5 Case study: Global resistance – turning the heat up	129
	End-of-chapter review questions	130
	References and further reading	130
	Notes	134

CHAPTER 4	**CONSUMING NEEDS AND VALUES**	**137**
	Learning objectives	137
	4.1 Introduction	137
	4.2 Forms of exchange	138
	4.3 The issue of needs in commodity exchange	147
	4.4 Consuming values	161
	4.5 Chapter summary	174
	4.6 Case study: What's in a community?	175
	End-of-chapter review questions	178
	References and further reading	178
	Notes	180

CHAPTER 5	**SEMIOTICS: CONSUMING MEANING**	**181**
	Learning objectives	181
	5.1 Introduction	181
	5.2 The semiological tradition of Ferdinand de Saussure (1857–1913)	184
	5.3 Are other sign systems like language?	189
	5.4 How do products come to generate meaning?	195
	5.5 Structuralism	198
	5.6 The semiotics of C.S. Peirce (1839–1914)	209
	5.7 Signs: identity and difference	212
	5.8 Signs can tell the truth and . . . signs can lie	213
	5.9 The scope of semiotic research in marketing	218
	5.10 Chapter summary	219
	5.11 Case study: Ways to get laid	219
	5.12 Case study: Marketing the past – Norkunas's study of tourist sites in Monterey	220
	End-of-chapter review questions	222
	References and further reading	222
	Notes	223

CHAPTER 6	**CONSUMPTION AND IDENTITY**	**225**
	Learning objectives	225
	6.1 Introduction	225

6.2   Inside-out approaches to identity   227
6.3   Outside-in approaches to identity   236
6.4   Psychoanalytic theory: in-between approaches to identity   249
6.5   The extension of self   265
6.6   Constraint or freedom? Identity and fashion   269
6.7   Chapter summary   271
6.8   Case study: Hot Topic   272
End-of-chapter review questions   273
References and further reading   274
Notes   275

CHAPTER 7   **THE CONSUMING BODY**   **276**

Learning objectives   276
7.1   Introduction   276
7.2   Falk: identity and the body   278
7.3   Transition to the disciplined body   280
7.4   Modern identity   283
7.5   Bodily strategies: self-protection – self-fulfilment –
          self-expression   285
7.6   Self-fulfilment   292
7.7   Self-expression   293
7.8   Chapter summary   300
7.9   Case study: Just how beautiful is big?   300
End-of-chapter review questions   301
References and further reading   301
Notes   303

CHAPTER 8   **CONSUMING 'DISORDERS'**   **304**

Learning objectives   304
8.1   Introduction   304
8.2   Starvation disorders: anorexia nervosa and bulimia nervosa   305
8.3   Explanations of anorexia nervosa and bulimia nervosa   306
8.4   A discursive 'Foucauldian' interpretation of anorexia   323
8.5   Summary on eating disorders   331
8.6   Obesity   333
8.7   Summary on obesity   341
8.8   Case study: Now eat this! Olestra, the fat-free fat   341
End-of-chapter review questions   343
References and further reading   343
Notes   345

CHAPTER 9   **CONSUMING BRANDS**   **347**

Learning objectives   347
9.1   Introduction   347

9.2   Brand values   348
9.3   Managerial discourses of brands   354
9.4   Popular brand discourses   361
9.5   Discourse and brand identity   366
9.6   And finally – a word of caution   370
9.7   Chapter summary   371
9.8   Case study: Barr's Irn-Bru   371
End-of-chapter review questions   374
References and further reading   374
Notes   375

CHAPTER 10   **CONSUMING ADDICTION**   **376**
Learning objectives   376
10.1   Introduction   376
10.2   What are drugs?   377
10.3   Drugs and society   378
10.4   Drugs and popular culture   381
10.5   Legal issues   383
10.6   Consuming addiction   390
10.7   Chapter summary   407
10.8   Case study: Scotland Against Drugs   408
End-of-chapter review questions   414
References and further reading   414
Notes   416

INDEX   **417**

LIST OF TABLES AND FIGURES

TABLES

1.1   Development of economic and cultural individualism,
        confidence in democratic and authoritative institutions,
        and tolerance towards ethnic groups and deviant behaviour   24

2.1   Global brand power   43
2.2   The global economy: growing disparity and flux   61

3.1   Some modern hazards   105

4.1   Summary of principal differences between gift exchange
        and commodity exchange   147

8.1   Age-standardized prevalence (percentage) of raised BMI
        social class – men and women aged 16+   335

9.1   Brand affiliations – M.J. Deene   367

FIGURES

I.1   Scheme for periods of European history   xvii

1.1   A scheme for the movement from premodernity to
        modernity and postmodernity   22

2.1   The annual calendar of the Kabyle, according to Bourdieu
        (1977)   31
2.2   Consuming space as a resource for the construction of
        identity   45
2.3   Annihilation of space through time: a firm's view   62

3.1   System of disciplinary power   124

5.1   Map of relations between concepts and theorists   184
5.2   Relations between signifier and signified   185

5.3	Beware of the dog!	186
5.4	Syntagmatic and paradigmatic relations	188
5.5	Syntagmatic and paradigmatic relations for potential advertising copy	191
5.6	AutoTrader advertisement	193
5.7	Collage Board for 'freedom'	194
5.8	Referent system for perfume products	196
5.9	Denotation and connotation	199
5.10	Peirce's trichotomy of signification	210
5.11	Ways to get laid	220

6.1	Map of relations between theorists cited in this chapter	226
6.2	Some important brain centres	228
6.3	Details of a neuron within an array of neurons	229
6.4	Excitation/inhibition of a neuron by a neurotransmitter	230
6.5	Erikson's stages in the development of personality	256
6.6	The infant in 'bits and pieces' in the order of the real	262
6.7	Identification with image in the mirror stage: jubilation and emptiness	263
6.8	Modernity: freedom and identity	269
6.9	Fashion: adoption and rejection	271

7.1	The primitive 'eating community'	279
7.2	The emergence of the modern self	284
7.3	About-Face commentary on Gucci ad	290
7.4	Marketing images as body-armour	292

8.1	The media and body-image	308
8.2	The serotonin system	315
8.3	Jo Spence/Dr Tim Sheard (1989): Greedy	321
8.4	Can only the male body be positively portrayed as being fat?	326

9.1	The 'Lazy S' brand mark	351
9.2	Two well-known petroleum brands	351
9.3	The evil and the cure	354
9.4	A crude typology of brand-related discourses	361
9.5	Flaunting authority through brand use	364
9.6	Branding the skin	369
9.7	New-style Irn-Bru ad	373

10.1	A terrible beauty: Van Gogh, *Skull with burning cigarette*	407
10.2	'Paranoid Instamatic' ad from SAD Youth Campaign	410
10.3	Parent Campaign for SAD	411
10.4	Media schedule for SAD (excluding television)	412

ACKNOWLEDGEMENTS

Thanks to the students of 312FM.2 at Heriot-Watt, and MN3124 at St Andrews, for their contribution. Hazel Loeb was not only a good researcher but provided 'critical' commentary and guidance on 'political correctness' (whatever that may be). A debt is also owed to Geraldine and Laura for the drawings. David Marshall and Stephanie O'Donohoe gave much of their (rare) spare time in looking over earlier drafts and in passing comment on these and Ian Munro kindly looked over some later drafts. Thanks to Amanda Henderson and Tim Poots for providing the photos. Issues concerned with morality which are discussed in Chapter 3 were developed as part of a dialogue with Andy Crane. Patrick Hetzel's use of the Greimas square has been borrowed for use in Chapters 2, 6 and 9, to facilitate the discussion of aspects of consumer identity. Thanks also to Liz who lent me the use of her faster printer and Barbara who helped package this up on at least one occasion. And Finally to F for her patience.

Thanks also to Roy Leitch of Heriot-Watt University for allowing the reproduction of chunks of Chapters 1, 4, 5, 6, 7 and 8 of the 312FM.2.

The following sources for Tables and Figures are also gratefully acknowledged:

Table 1.1 reproduced with permisson of and thanks to Andries van den Broek. Adapted from Table 4.1, page 76, Chapter 4, of Andries van den Broek and Felix Heunks, 'Political Culture: Patterns of Political Orientations and Behaviour', in Ester, Peter (ed.), *The Individualizing Society: Value Change in Europe and North-America*, 1994.

Figure 2.1, the annual calendar of the Kabyle, according to Bourdieu (1977), reproduced from Figure 3, page 134 of *The Farming Year and the Mythical Year*, by permission of Cambridge University Press.

Figure 5.6, AutoTrader ad, with permission of AutoTrader and Faulds Advertising Edinburgh; thanks to Andrew Barnett.

Figure 5.7 reproduced with kind permission of John Nolan and the Collage Board Shop.

Figure 5.11 with thanks to the Leith Agency and Barr's Ltd.

Figure 6.3 with thanks to Thomas Gittins.

Figure 6.4 thanks to John Sell.

Figures 6.6 and 6.7 with thanks to GMT.

DBS Arts Library

Figure 6.9 is based on Figure 6 of Hetzel, Patrick (1993) *The Role of Fashion and Design in a Postmodern Society*, IAE de Lyon, Recherche URA CNRS 1257, No. 24, reproduced with kind permission of the author.

Figures 7.1 and 7.2 are reproduced from Figures 2.3 and 2.2, respectively, from Pasi Falk (1994) *The Consuming Body*, with kind permission of the author.

Figure 8.1 is reproduced with permission of GMT.

Figure 8.2, the serotonin system, is reproduced from Borne, R.F. (1994) Serotonin: The Neurotransmitter for the 90's, *Drug Topics*, October 10th: 108, by kind permission of the author.

Figure 8.3 is reproduced from Figure 28 of *Cultural Sniping* (1995) by Jo Spence, Jo Spence/Dr Tim Sheard, Copyright Jo Spence Archive, c/o Terry Dennett, 152 Upper St, N1 IRA, by permission of copyright holder.

Figure 8.4 by permission of Associated Press.

Logos in Figure 9.2 reproduced with permission of Shell and ExxonMobil.

Figures 9.5 and 9.6 with thanks to Amanda Henderson and Tim Poots.

Figure 9.7 reproduced with permission of Barr's Irn-Bru; thanks also to Keli Smythe of the Leith Agency, Edinburgh.

Figure 10.1 reproduced with permission of Van Gogh Museum.

Figures 10.2, 10.3 and 10.4 reproduced with permission of Alistair Ramsay of Scotland Against Drugs; thanks also to David McGlone of Faulds Advertising.

Every effort has been made to contact all copyright holders, but if any have been inadvertently omitted the publishers will be pleased to make the necessary arrangements at the earliest opportunity.

INTRODUCTION

Aim:

- To provide an interesting, topical and relevant course which meets the demand for a reflective, comparative and critical approach to consumption behaviour and the role played by marketing processes in relation to it.

Topicality and relevance: To bring important contemporary concerns into the marketing classroom. This is difficult moral terrain. With respect to issues such as eating disorders or addiction, readers should be aware that this is an academic text and not a prescriptive manual. It in no way seeks to equip the reader as being competent to provide advice or guidance. If they or a friend has a 'problem' they should bring this to the attention of a counsellor.

Comparative approach: The text seeks to achieve this in different ways in different areas. For example:

- economic, psychological, social and anthropological approaches to exchange are considered in Chapter 4;
- two different approaches to semiology/semiotics are discussed in Chapter 5;
- biological, psychological and social explanations are discussed in relation to identity formation, the body and eating disorders.

Critical approach: With a small 'c' in adopting a questioning approach; with a capital 'C' in introducing ideas from Critical Theory and beyond.

Critical discussion of marketing: This is a marketing text to the extent that it is designed to fill the slot currently occupied by the 'typical' consumer behaviour course. Marketing processes are central to any understanding of consumer culture or consuming behaviour. This is a typical marketing text to the extent that:

- it explores issues concerned with the construction and implementation of marketing strategy;
- it is concerned to explore how marketers encode meaning into ads and how consumers decode them;
- it considers a number of topics which have appeared in major marketing journals – for example issues concerned with exchange, community,

identity and the body, which have appeared in the *Journal of Consumer Research* and in other marketing journals in recent years.

The principal differences between this text and a typical consumer behaviour text are twofold:

- This text is not intended as a guide for the manager who wishes to learn how best to lure and capture customers. Instead it is intended as a guide for the person who is interested in understanding the role played by marketing, among other forces, in the creation and sustenance of consumption contexts.
- The text does not seek to replicate the cognitive/psychological/theoretical template employed in consumer behaviour texts. Because of its individualist focus, the traditional approach tends to highlight internal cognitive processes. As a result there is a tendency to reproduce the 'social' as the last layer of an onion where the section on internal psychological processes (the hierarchy of effects and so on) represents the core. One reason for not reproducing this is that existing texts deal with this subject matter in such a consummate and comprehensive manner that there is no point in seeking to reproduce that particular wheel. More importantly, by focusing so heavily on such internal processes, other important issues tend to be sidelined.

WHAT IS CONSUMPTION?

It is usual when describing a topic to turn first to its dictionary definition. The definition of consumption, according to *Collins Concise Plus Dictionary* (1989: 274), derives from the Latin *consumere*, which in English means: '1. To eat or drink 2. To obsess 3. To use up or expend 4. To destroy or be destroyed 5. To waste 6. To waste away'. The various aspects of the definition indicate that there are several points of view about consumption.

Different agencies focus on different aspect of the dictionary definition. The 'common sense' view is reflected in the first aspect. The second aspect of consumption as obsession is close to the position adopted by critics of consumer society such as members of the Frankfurt School, who argue that it produces narcissists who are obsessed with living up to an unrealizable image. Some environmentalists are concerned by the extent to which consumption destroys by using up irreplaceable resources; others are more concerned by its production of waste, arguing that 'consumption is toxic and tragic, not magic', and that consumption which has run out of control provides the greatest single threat to ecology since whatever it was that killed off the dinosaurs. Others liken the environmentalists to po-faced prophets of doom, latter-day Malthusians and pessimists whose cries of 'fire' during the early 1970s came to nought. An entirely different argument suggests that the anti-consumption lobby is selective, in arguing that the Third World should abandon its aspirations to join the feast while those already at the table should be allowed to stay. One might take instead the injunction of the UN Human Development Report, that the principle of human development should be based on 'a world where consumption is such that we all have enough to eat, no child goes without education, no human being is denied health-care and all people can develop their abilities to the fullest extent', to be beyond dispute. Such rhetoric might have gone down well in the 1960s, but in the jaded twenty-first century it is more likely to be seen as an extension of that philosophy of 'public good works' which extends the basics to the poor but which does not recognize that they want access to the good things in life, not just the necessities. Others extend Marx's idea that consumption only really makes sense as the other side of production and that in contemporary society the cycle of production–consumption will accelerate to such a state that it will ultimately outdo not only itself, but all of those who live under its spell. To clarify matters further, some 'postmodernists' argue that consumption is itself a form of production, in that it constitutes consumer identity. If despite the clarity of the above description you are still a little hazy, it may help to know that some people have put a (rough) number on it: $25 trillion at the turn of the millennium. Anthony Giddens provides a useful ready-reckoner which helps reduce numbers from the level of the incomprehensible to more human proportions. If a million dollars were presented in a stack of hundred-dollar bills, that stack would be eight inches high. A billion dollars – or a thousand million – would stand higher than St Paul's cathedral in London. A trillion dollars – a million million – would be over 120 miles high, 20 times higher than Mount Everest (1999: 9/10). The text seeks to cover several important themes, which are discussed briefly below.

THEMES

Community–society (Gemeinschaft–Gesellschaft)

This explores the proposition that traditional bonds of community are progressively destroyed by the shift towards a more abstract and rationalized society, composed of unfulfilled, isolated and lonely individuals. This theme is addressed to some extent or other in every chapter of this book. A range of different arguments are advanced; from those such as Elias (Chapter 1), who holds the emergence of the self-controlled individual to have been co-extensive with the civilizing process, to Pasi Falk (Chapter 7), who raises this in relation to the decline of the primitive eating community. This is discussed in Chapter 4 in relation to gift exchange, where counter-arguments are advanced in the discussion case, featuring Muniz and O'Guinn, among others.

Freedom vs determination

Three interrelated ideas are explored here. First is the extent to which one can be 'free' of power. This is addressed principally in Chapter 3, where liberal, reformist, radical and disciplinary formulations of power are discussed. There are key points of tension between liberal and some radical views of power, which view the subject as unitary. Foucault's approach views liberal freedom as itself a construction which is infused with power. The second formulation relates to the 'nature–nurture' debate with respect to the extent to which the 'self' and consumption practices are produced by biological and cultural forces. Second is the extent to which 'postmodern' consumers are free from social constraint. Within a social perspective, Pierre Bourdieu, following Norbert Elias, argues that changing consumption practices are explicable as the result of differentiation between groups, and that within groups there is remarkably little room for choice. The equivalent psychological view would stress peer pressure – the power of conformity. A different view suggests that the power of social class is slipping, as witnessed by the process of 'informalization' which is spreading across the whole sphere of what counts as 'manners': in clothing, from formal wear to 'casual Fridays'; in food, from formal meals to snack 'as-you-go' and a proliferation of self-imposed taste preferences and restrictions ranging from vegetarians to fruitarians. Thus Zygmunt Bauman argues that in the realm of consumption, people are more free than in any other sphere and are confronted with the problems of living in a risk society where they have the freedom and responsibility to create a self-identity.

Marketing and consumption

There are several thematic elements which link marketing to issues discussed in the text:

- In relation to the previous theme: marketing as the production of goods (through branding) and the minimization of bads; and marketing as the production of bads (via the destruction of community) and the minimization of goods.
- The relations between marketing and the construction of identity through branding. The reciprocal relation formed between marketers, consumers and anti-consumers. How marketers encode meanings into brands which are recirculated by consumers as commodity-identities. How 'aberrant' consumers fashion anti-brand identities which are recycled by marketers into 'anti-hero' or 'rebel' brand identities. Relevant Chapters are 5 (semiotics), 6 (identity) and 9 (brands).

Consumption and identity

Here we discuss relations between identity and consumption/anti-consumption. Relevant Chapters are 5 (semiotics), 6 (identity), 7 (body-image), 8 (eating disorders) and 9 (brand identity).

AIM AND SCOPE OF THIS TEXT

The aim of this text is to enquire into the diverse set of meanings and practices which today constitute consumption, how these are implicated with processes of power and how marketing activities are related to these. The effect of all of this is to 'de-centre' the activities of marketers. The activities of marketing managers are important to this text insofar as they can be said to illuminate issues which are considered to be of central importance to people in relation to their consuming behaviour.

Fortunately for the author, the issues raised above have been the concern of some mainstream marketing interest. Issues relating to commodity and gift exchange, the implications of the growth of consumer society for notions of community, identity and the body, and conceptualizations of power in marketing have been addressed in the top marketing journals. This text represents a modest attempt to put some of these interesting developments in perspective – maybe not as many as the author would have wished for, but nonetheless a start.

OUTLINE OF CHAPTERS

Chapter 1 adopts an historical approach towards developing an explanation of the origins of contemporary consumer societies and of the types of consumer personality which populate these. Chapter 2 develops this historical theme by considering the relation of consumption to the conception of time and space. The chapter compares two different approaches to the ordering of space in modernity: that of Weber via the rationalization of space, and that of Marx via the annihilation of space through time. There then follows a discussion of the possibility that in the postmodern world, time may being eaten by space.

Chapter 3 considers the complex subject of power. This is divided into two principal sections – sovereign power and disciplinary power. As a lot has been written with respect to the concept of sovereign power, this section is divided into three sub-sections dealing with liberal, reformist and radical views. The section on disciplinary power contrasts the views of Norbert Elias, discussed in Chapter 1, with those of Michel Foucault.

Chapter 4 is divided into two related sections featuring the discussion of consuming needs and values. Abraham Maslow's theory of needs is re-evaluated here, following which there is a discussion of the issues surrounding the debate about 'true vs false' needs. The values related to consumption are organized within the framework devised by Maurice Holbrook, after which there is a general discussion of the meaning of value in contemporary consumer society.

Chapter 5 is concerned with exploring a key theme of this text: what do things mean to people? Here different theories and techniques used by those who study the science of signs (known by some as semiology and others as semiotics) are described and illustrated in order to seek to answer this question.

Chapter 6 considers different theories which purport to explain the significance of identity in contemporary consumer societies, seeking answers to questions such as 'why is identity important?' and 'how can processes of identity formation be understood?' A number of theories are compared and contrasted in order to address this last question. In many respects, Chapter 6 is pivotal as Chapters 7 to 9 can all be read from the point of view of identity. While these chapters introduce new material, they can also act to provide a means for illustrating and testing the theories outlined in the first six chapters. Chapter 7 takes consumption and the body as its topic, an important area which has tended to be marginalized in academic discourse until comparatively recently. Chapter 8 considers the more specialized and troubling area of eating disorders in seeking to contrast social, psychoanalytic and biological explanations. Chapter 9 considers the topic of brand identity. Finally, Chapter 10 takes the challenging subject of addiction as its topic.

ANTICIPATING SOME QUESTIONS

Why bother with Freud?

Given that most traditional marketing texts have more or less discarded Freudian theory, why the emphasis on Freud? While recognizing that many of Freud's original ideas have been superseded, here are my reasons for including this:

- Freud's work via adaptations by Lacan and Althusser among others, provides the basis for an ideological critique of marketing and for the development of poststructuralism and postmodern theory.
- Marketing academics continue to draw selectively on neo-Freudian theory, for example through citing the work of Erikson, among others, in seeking to explain the formation of consumer identity.
- Freudian discourse (unconscious, repression etc.) is still commonly used among 'ordinary' people.

Why bother with the Greimas boxes?

These are used (in Chapters 2, 6 and 9) to address aspects of consuming identity. The intention is to provide a template for discussion of this complex topic and also to help sew the text together by addressing the same issue in slightly different ways in the different chapters.

A partial text

An almost inevitable feature of a general text is that it is difficult to do justice to the complexity and variety of an author's work. In constructing the text, some difficult choices had to be made. For example with respect to the work of Lacan, one major omission concerns feminist theories which seek to build upon and/or reject the Lacanian view of the position of women in relation to the symbolic. This partiality holds true for all the authors discussed in this text. The intention is not to provide an exhaustive account and critique of the work of each author, but rather a reading of some of their key ideas as the basis for comparison with others. The obvious danger is that the complexity and subtlety of the original is effaced. Taken to its extreme, such a 'comparative' approach can reach the 'friction-free' status described by Ritzer as a form of theoretical 'McDonaldization'. While this presents an obvious danger, the intention is that the text should open a territory which some, particularly in marketing, may have been loath to explore because they have had few maps. The ultimate intention is that the reader can throw this map away and construct his or her own. In other words, it is hoped that rather than being a device to close meaning down, the text will stimulate readers to engage with original works and to gain some critical insight into the partial position adopted here.

READING GUIDE

In this text, a number of references will be made to periods in European history, such as the Middle Ages, the Renaissance and the Enlightenment, and to a form of periodization which splits European history into premodern, modern and postmodern periods. As such terms are often used interchangeably by authors with few references to dates, the crude scheme below provides some form of guide (see Figure I.1). Generally what is referred to as the 'Middle Ages' relates to the time between the decline of the Roman Empire in Europe, which took place over a period from the third to the eighth century AD, and the Italian Renaissance which took place in the fourteenth century. The European Enlightenment took place during the eighteenth century. Several authors link such developments to a form of

Pre-Industrial	Industrial		Post-Industrial
Premodern	Modern		Postmodern
Middle Ages	Renaissance	Enlightenment	Liquid modernity
AD 200–1300	AD 1300–1500	AD 1700 1900	AD 1970
* * *	* * *	* * * *	
			# #
			$

Figure I.1   Scheme for periods of European History (* = Reuben Fine/Norbert Elias; # = Stuart Ewen; $ = Michel Maffesoli)

periodization which moves from communal to premodern, modern and most recently postmodern societies. What is meant by 'modern'? According to the authors of the *European Values Survey* (Ester, 1994), modernization 'refers to the independent fundamental changes in the economic, technological, socio-cultural and political domain which took place after the (eighteenth century) events of the French Revolution and the Industrial Revolution in England'. Such changes had consequences for the entire organization of European society, involving profound alterations: in the conduct of economic affairs, including those activities involved in production, exchange and consumption and the technologies used to drive these; in the organization of the social sphere, including the irruption of a new mechanism of power based on surveillance; and even, as we shall see in Chapter 2, in the organization of space and of time, with the introduction of new social spaces together with the political space of 'citizenship'. The term 'premodern' loosely corresponds to that period of history prior to the Enlightenment of the eighteenth century, although processes of modernization were underway well before this. The 'modern' period is from the eighteenth century onwards. Authors differ with respect to the beginnings of the postmodern period. In any case, as we shall see, this is a controversial term. David Harvey (1989) reckons the beginning of postmodernism to be at the time of the 1970s.

The legend to Figure I.1 refers to authors who are covered in Chapter 1 and the periods which they have considered.

REFERENCES

Ester, Peter, Halman Loek and Ruud de Moor (eds) (1994) *The Individualizing Society: Value Changes in Europe and North America*, European Values Studies series, Tilburg University Press.

Giddens, Anthony (1999) *Runaway World: How Globalisation is Shaping our Lives*, London: Profile Books.

Harvey, David (1989) *The Condition of Postmodernity*, Oxford: Basil Blackwell.

1 CONSUMING TALES

LEARNING OBJECTIVES

- To address the question of the extent to which current conceptions of consumer society are unprecedented
- To situate discussion of current consumption practices within different historical narratives
- To build an awareness that narratives involving 'real' historical changes do not unfold neatly in linear and orderly sequences
- To introduce the reader to accounts of the rise of consumer societies in Europe and in the USA
- To acquaint the reader with contemporary debates surrounding the state of postmodernism

1.1 INTRODUCTION

This chapter is divided into five parts. Following an introductory section which considers what consumption is and how it has been conceptualized by academics from a variety of disciplines, the aims and rationale of the module are outlined. The second part of the chapter contains brief descriptions of the contents of the module. Part three traces the growing importance of consumption in people's lives, asking questions such as: Did this happen suddenly or has this been the result of a more sudden transition? This question is addressed first by considering two stories of the development of consumer society in Europe and the USA. The first story is fashioned after the argument put forward by Grant McCracken who discusses the rise of a consumer society involving sixteenth-century English nobility and who traces subsequent more inclusive developments in France and Britain in later centuries. The second story is drawn from the work of Stuart Ewen and is based on the emerging consumer society of the USA in the 1920s. This is followed by a brief comparison of the similarities and differences between the two stories. In the fourth part the discussion is expanded to take into account the work of Norbert Elias and of Pasi Falk. Elias's work is important for two reasons: first, because it provides another place from which to view the particular characteristics of the modern self; second, because it forms a benchmark for comparison with other theories. While Norbert Elias focuses on the changing role of manners in the civilization process, Falk explicitly places consumption at the centre of his explanation. The final part of the chapter is devoted to a brief discussion of the ideas of Michel Maffesoli who, along with many others, asserts that Western society has changed fundamentally in recent years and that we are living in a new form of society – in the postmodern age.

1.2 TWO TALES OF CONSUMPTION

Is the phenomenon of consumer society a recent irruption in the lives of billions of people or can this be traced as part of a more continuous development through the ages of human existence? These questions are considered in the following stories which explore the roots of today's global consumer society.

Several authors note that the idea of a consumer society is not new, but that our current consumer society is part of a more or less continuous development which has spanned centuries. For example Mukerji (1983) discusses the emergence of a form of consumer society in sixteenth-century Europe. In order to explore the role of consumption in everyday life, it is useful to consider the historical significance of another term, **narcissism**, which has a similar provenance to that of consumption. For example Reuben Fine (1986) asks of narcissism (self-love) whether this is a new phenomenon to describe the 'me' generation or whether narcissism has developed as a concept through the ages? Fine explores the reasons why the term 'narcissism' is generally used pejoratively as a term of opprobrium in contemporary culture, by exploring its use in its original context, in ancient Greece. His investigations led him to conclude that narcissism could not be tolerated in ancient Greece because it expressed an extreme form of individualism which conflicted with the demands of the State for docile and obedient citizens. From this view any form of self-involvement such as narcissism (or its opposite as expressed in self-hatred) is considered to be inimical with respect to the maintenance of social order. Fine notes that while a succession of rulers from the Roman emperor Nero onwards used the word 'narcissistic' as a means of labelling those who were enemies of the State, they could be and were as narcissistic as they liked in terms of their own lifestyles. However Fine charts a progression of events by which the narcissism of the ruling class has been supplanted by that of the common man. He suggests that this has been so since the nineteenth century.

'Today we call it the sense of identity, or self-image. It resulted from the overthrow of absolutism and the recognition of the significance of the individual.'
[1986: 22]

To my mind there are important links between narcissism and consumption. For example one explanation of narcissism is as a form of consumption of the self by its image. Like narcissism, consumption is often referred to pejoratively through terms such as excess, self-indulgence, hedonism and decadence. The recent rise of consumer society in Europe during the 1950s and 1960s was also regarded pejoratively by many social commentators as a form of decadence which would destroy all civilized values. Modern consumers are narcissists to the extent that consumption is regarded as a frivolous individual activity opposed to the solidarity which is created through 'honest' work. In addition, the typical consumer is thought of as an individual who achieves a form of identity through consumption. Of course narcissism and consumption are equal partners at the feast, as the lavish displays of opulence and self-indulgence from the time of Nero to that of the 'Sun King', Louis XV of France, attest.

1.2.1 Tale 1: Consumption in Europe – from the Middle Ages to the eighteenth century

For many generations it was only those who ruled who could enjoy the fruits of consumption. For example when Grant McCracken (1990) discusses the spectacular 'consumer boom' which took place in sixteenth-century England, this 'boom' included at most a few thousand people. The 'boom' was instigated and perpetuated by Queen Elizabeth I of England as a means of subjugating her nobility and aggrandizing herself. As McCracken observes:

> 'In the last quarter of the sixteenth century, a spectacular consumer boom occurred. The noblemen of Elizabethan England began to spend with a new enthusiasm, on a new scale. In the process they dramatically transformed their world of goods and the nature of Western consumption. They rebuilt their country seats to a new and grander standard, and they began to assume the additional expense of a London residence. They changed their patterns of hospitality as well, vastly accelerating its ceremonial character and costs. Elizabethan noblemen entertained one another, their subordinates, and occasionally their monarch at ruinous expense.'
> [1990: 11]

According to McCracken this ruinous round of expenditure changed the nature of the Elizabethan family and locality. Prior to this, the noble was considered to be the caretaker or curator of the family. As such, he was expected to purchase items corporately with the long-term interests of the family in mind. The prime consideration in buying goods was thus for their **patina**, that quality which indicated that what was purchased would not only last, but would become increasingly valuable in creating honour and respect for succeeding generations. Much of the expenditure of a nobleman was spent locally, to the benefit of the local community. McCracken argues that the pattern of value surrounding this corporate, generational expenditure was destroyed by the fierce social competition of the Elizabethan era. In the face of such competition the value of 'patina' or the worth of goods for succeeding generations was forgotten and replaced by the idea of 'fashion', or the demand for novelty. Second, the local character of expenditure was replaced as the nobles sought to better one another through ostentatious displays in London, to the detriment of local communities. Third, as the result of this explosion of consumption, nobles developed tastes that were quite different from those of their subordinates. McCracken suggests that these changes resulted in a move away from family consumption to individual consumption, from generational value to fashion, and a dissolution of the close social relations between nobles and local communities. He notes that this shift had particular effects:

> 'Noblemen now looked to a pan-European level of consumption, while their subordinates looked on with astonishment at their new tastes and excesses. Sometimes disdainful of superordinate consumption, subordinates nevertheless followed this behaviour with care. Thus were they primed for a round of consumer excess that would begin a century later.' [1990: 16]

The next major wave of consumption which came in the eighteenth century was a product of the explosive growth of markets in both time and space. This consumer revolution was the 'missing half' of the Industrial Revolution. While most commentators focused on the huge changes in production during this period, these changes could not have come about without a commensurate change in tastes and preferences. As McCracken notes, this time the 'subordinate classes, which in the sixteenth century could only watch in horrified fascination as the nobility cultivated a new scale and new tastes in their consumption, could now become participants in this consumption' (1990: 17). It was during this period that enterprising industrialists such as Josiah Wedgwood took advantage of the increasingly **emulative** character of consumption, whereby the subordinate classes seek to imitate the superordinate classes. Wedgwood sought to infiltrate his goods into the lifestyles of the upper classes in the hope that the demand for these would thereby trickle down to the lower classes. This was a time when the world of goods expanded dramatically to include new opportunities for the purchase of furniture, pottery, silver, cutlery, gardens, pets and fabric in addition to the frequency with which goods were bought. By this time the purchase for the self instead of for the family was well established, as was the growth of obsolescence through fashion change. McCracken notes that the intensity of consumption was raised to such a pitch in the eighteenth century, that some observers claimed an 'epidemical madness' had taken hold of England (1990: 17). This was also a time for the development of marketing devices such as fashion plates, fashion magazines and the fashion doll.

McCracken claims that in contrast to the eighteenth century, there was no consumer boom in the nineteenth, but rather that by then the transformation which had begun in the sixteenth century had become a social fact, so that by the nineteenth century consumption and society were inextricably linked in a process of continual change. Developments such as the department store and the emergence of new consumer 'lifestyles' were major features of this period. Turning to discuss the development of consumption in nineteenth-century (postrevolutionary) France, McCracken notes that even 'though the nobles were supposedly banished during the Revolutionary period, their way of life lived on, as it was aspired to by the bourgeoisie'. During this period other lifestyles emerged to challenge this style. One such lifestyle was that of the 'dandy', which was promoted by Beau Brummel, who sought to create a new elite on 'good taste', rather than 'breeding'.

Tale 2: US consumption in the 1920s

In contrast to the previous story, this story is based on developments in the USA during the 1920s. Stuart Ewen studied the role played by modern advertising in the construction of mass consumption in the USA during the 1920s. The name which he gives to the rise of mass consumption is **consumerism**:

> 'Consumerism, the mass participation in the values of the mass-industrial market, thus emerged in the 1920s not as a smooth progression from earlier and less "developed" patterns of consumption, but rather as an aggressive device of corporate survival.'
> [1976: 54]

Ewen does not share in the idea of the smooth development of patterns of consumption described above by McCracken. Instead the creation of a mass consumer culture is explained as being part of an ongoing development of **social control**. This began in the early stages of industrial development, at the beginning of the nineteenth century in the field of production, when labourers became subjected to new disciplines, including the observance of the mechanical 'clock time' of the factory and the machine-like character of the assembly line. This reached its heights in the mass production assembly-line processes developed by the Ford motor company, and the universaliza-tion of such practices in what Ewen calls the 'Fordizing' of American industry. However such controls invited powerful and potentially revolu-tionary forms of worker resistance. As a consequence of this resistance, management introduced new and softer forms of control, including welfare programmes, industrial democracy and community-based initiatives. Such developments also helped forestall a looming crisis of overproduction by creating the means for newly affluent workers to participate as equals in the 'democracy' of the marketplace. The invitation to workers to partake in the 'freedom' of the marketplace removed the potential threat of worker revolu-tion by distracting workers' attention from the stultifying and monotonous conditions of the workplace and onto the anxieties and opportunities offered by the construction of a 'self' in the marketplace. Ewen notes that workers were not passive but actively demanded access to the new world of goods, a demand which was in perfect accord with the requirements of capital.

Ewen argues that some businessmen spotted in the marketplace an oppor-tunity for extending the relatively narrow range of control in the workplace, to control over the entire social realm by becoming **captains of consciousness** through mass advertising. He argues that modern advertising must be seen as a direct response to the needs of mass industrial capitalism. By transforming the notion of (the working) 'class' into (the consuming) 'mass', business hoped to create an 'individual' who could locate his needs and frustrations in terms of the consumption of goods rather than the quality and content of his life (work). Advertising became the means for efficiently creating consumers and as a way of homogeneously controlling the consumption of the product. In creating consumers, the admen welcomed the work of psychologists such as Floyd Henry Allport (see note i). Allport contributed not only the notion of attitude to consumer behaviour, but also theorized consumer identity as the 'social self'. The idea of the **social self** may be summed up in his saying that; 'our consciousness of ourselves is largely a reflection of the consciousness which others have of us . . . My idea of myself is rather my own idea of my neighbour's view of me' (see note ii). According to Ewen, this view of the self as being 'the object of continual and harsh social scrutiny' was to form the basis for much of the advertising from the 1920s onwards. The shift to a focus away from the functional characteristics of the product and onto the anxieties of the 'social' self of the consumer is extremely important in understanding advertising's role in getting people to consume and keeping them consuming. As an antidote to the guilt of the social self, advertising offered up a commodity self which presented a ready-made solution to each of the problem zones identified:

> 'Each portion of the body was to be viewed critically, as a potential bauble in a successful assemblage. Woodbury's soap was offered as a perfect treatment for the "newly important face of Smart Today"; another product promised to keep teeth white: "a flashing smile is worth more than a good sized bank account, It wins friends." After she has used Caro Cocoanut Oil Shampoo, a dashing gentleman informs the lady, "I'm crazy about your hair. *It's* the most beautiful of any here tonight".' [1976: 47].

Ewen describes how advertising was used in the USA as a form of 'civilizing' influence, particularly with respect to immigrant groups. It promoted new values based on the use of consumer goods as a means for expressing a unique 'American' identity, based on the 'facts of the marketplace', while simultaneously discouraging traditional values and lifestyles. For example the advertising agency Louis N. Hammerling played a leading role in selling advertising to the foreign language immigrant press which it also compromised by forcing editors to accept unpaid editorial and news material pushing 'American' values, as well as ads. The traditional homespun practices of immigrant women which used few resources were especially targeted as being 'UnAmerican'.

With the advent of consumer society, Ewen argues that the very idea of the family became modelled according to the demands of business. This involved a shift from a tight-knit, collective and largely self-reliant group, to a 'loosely articulated group' which was more a collection of individuals than a consuming unit. Advertising also affected roles within the family; for example in elevating women to the status of 'purchasing managers' for the household, men's role was divested of all social authority, except insofar as their wages underwrote family consumption. However, in pushing consumer goods into the home, advertisers were aware that the traditional role of women had to be subverted. For example bread-making in the home was seen as the greatest impediment to progress confronted by the biscuit industry. Looking at the 1920s, Ewen argues that the feminist demand for freedom and equality for women was appropriated into the jargon of consumerism. Advertisers cleverly traded off women's aspirations for more freedom by linking this concept with the desire for and use of consumer goods. The public relations genius Edward Bernays devised a cunning campaign which joined commodities to women's liberation by focusing on the rights of women to smoke in public. The campaign itself featured women who took direct action by smoking in public. Campaign publicity indicated that in this context cigarettes were 'torches of freedom' for women who demanded the right to smoke in public. Consumer goods were also promoted as being time-saving devices which would free women from household drudgery. However advertisers were also careful to point out that although women were powerful in buying, they must play a secondary role to men, in the position of quartermaster rather than as general of the mutual organization that was marriage (see note iii). According to Ewen it was clear that the directive power behind this was really industry and that the woman was little more than a factory operative or, as Christine Frederick put it, 'the woman is no longer a cook, she is a can-opener.' Additionally advertising idealized youth. The important productive role of youth, coupled with the pleasure-seeking conception of youth, called for the child as a representative of a desirable reality. Advertising was also targeted directly at children. Where ads were not directly targeted at the young, they often spoke for the young against parental values. Non-consuming parents were chided as not properly looking after their offspring – promotion of the general attitude that 'youth' was a good thing, of 'filiarchy', rule by the young. Ewen reads into this the creation of youth as an industrial ideal, destructive of patriarchal authority. Corporations which demanded youth now sold it through their products; youth became a commodity.

1.2.3 Discussion of the two tales

The above two tales of consumption diverge in certain important respects. Most obviously they site their narratives in different places and periods. A more important distinction is that the first tale describes the rise of consumption as a centuries-old process whereby different groups become gradually incorporated into consumption at each successive stage of development. To begin with, this includes only the richest nobles; two centuries later we can speak of the consummatory emancipation of the 'lower' classes (who were still extremely rich). To this extent we might consider Stuart Ewen's account of the development of consumer society in the USA in the 1920s as another logical phase in the spread of the 'good life', or as Reuben Fine would put it as part of the 'narcissism of the common man', which came later to other countries (for example to the UK in the early 1950s; Ireland in the late 1950s), while others are still waiting at the door. On the other hand in describing the sudden onset of consumerism in the 1920s, Ewen considers this to be a rupture or sharp break with what came before.

Both stories discuss the onset of consumer society as being largely coercive in nature. For example in the first story, McCracken discusses how Elizabeth I found the stimulation of a ruinous competitive consumption among her nobles to be a highly effective means for controlling them. Anyone who did not spend huge amounts in impressing others faced social oblivion. Ewen also talks of the creation of an arena of consumption as a means for one class (capitalists) to control another class (workers) by displacing attention from exploitation at work towards the satisfactions that could be gained in the marketplace. The captains of industry thus became captains of consciousness, to the extent that advertising was employed simultaneously as a device to focus attention on how commodities could help armour the self against social criticism and in derogating any form of traditional practice that militated against the use of commodities in the marketplace. In this sense Ewen places much more power in the hands of marketers, who seem to be able to mould and to influence consumers, than does McCracken.

Both stories differ with respect to their moral content. The first tale regards consumption cautiously but generally as a 'good thing', as something which, by increasing the power of the individual, in parallel with the rise of democracy, liberates the 'common man' from the constricting demands of communities and the arbitrary power of despots. On the other hand the second tale promotes the view that consumerism represents a false system of values, which strips people away from their traditional communities. This is sanctioned in the interests of the powerful and insinuated into the minds of consumers by the consciousness industry, which centres on the endless creation and recreation of the 'social self'; a self, which plagued by uncertainty and self-doubt, turns increasingly to the world of commodities for (never to be reached) solace and fulfilment.

Despite their differences, both stories agree on certain points. One is the growing significance of consumption in the lives of more people over time. Second, both agree that consumption is linked to individualization. For example, in the first tale, we are told that as the result of highly competitive consumption, the Elizabethan noble begins to detach himself from the tight circle of obligations that bound him to his family, where his duty lay in contributing to the 'patina' of the family, and to his community, as the ultimate source of his honour. Ewen talks of the ways in which the family became moulded to the demands of industry, how people came to be addressed as and to think of themselves primarily as individuals.

Both stories illuminate certain aspects of the consumption experience which will become central aspects of this text, involving how terms such as 'community', 'individualism', 'fulfilment' and 'doubt' relate to consumption. However these stories are lacking in several important respects, which are addressed in the next section where more accounts of consumption are told.

Taken together the two stories above describe the development of consumer societies through distinct historical periods in particular societies. In the first story we discussed an early form of consumer society which was restricted to the queen and her nobles in sixteenth-century England; there then followed a new period in the eighteenth century, which involved a greater number of people. However it was not until much later, during the late 1950s and early 1960s, that commentators began to mention that England was becoming a mass consumer society. While the US consumer society originated much later than in England, it developed faster to the extent that the development of mass consumer culture in England was partly brought about as the result of the importation of styled mass-produced products from Italy and the USA.

The important point to note from the above is that the development of the consumer society unfolds within distinct periods of time. The first phase is during the rise of the feudal monarchy; a second takes place in some European countries at the time of the Industrial Revolution; much more recently there is the development of the mass consumer society as a primary mode of economic and social organization around the world. Now it is time to consider the development of consumer society within a broader scheme which covers the unfolding process of civilization itself. The following discussion focuses mainly on the development of European society from the Middle Ages to the Enlightenment.

1.3   NORBERT ELIAS: THE CIVILIZING PROCESS

Norbert Elias sought to explore the origins of the modes of behaviour which are now considered to be typical of modern Western civilization (see note iv). Elias was influenced by the work of Freud to the extent that he uses terms such as 'id', 'ego' and 'superego' in discussing the civilizing process. He was also interested in considering how these features of the human psyche developed and changed as society itself, as bound by the relationships between people, changed. To put this more formally, his investigation required the study of **psychogenetic** processes (involving the structure of personality; how for example the partition between id, ego, and superego is formed over time), within the context of a **sociogenetic** explanation (involving changes to the structure of society over time). For Elias one cannot understand the psychological makeup of the individual independently of the sociogenesis of his or her 'civilization'.

Elias's (1994) research is organized into two major works, *The History of Manners* and *State Formation and Civilization*. In these books, Elias traces developments in European history from the decline of the Roman empire and the resurgence of tribal societies between the third and the eighth

9

DBS Arts Library

centuries, to the very gradual consolidation of society by means of feudal court systems of the sixteenth century and later the court systems of the absolute monarchs of the eighteenth century. While Elias did find a pattern in the development of civilized behaviour, this was uneven, slow and characterized by constant reversals. For example he found that modes of conduct which were characteristic of tenth-century France were still to be found in isolated areas at the time of the French Revolution, which took place early in the nineteenth century. To sum up this change, Elias contends that passions that were impulsively and often violently expressed in earlier times became subject to constraint by being internally contained in later times. The basis for social order changed from the exercise of external violence to that of internal self-discipline conditioned by feelings of shame at one's own conduct and embarrassment at the conduct of others; the nature of conflict itself changed from external conflict with others to conflict within the human psyche. Furthermore, the social perception of the body and the expression of bodily functions changed fundamentally as part of this slow transition.

From the above it is apparent that the system of relations which existed between people in the Middle Ages was quite different from that which operates today. The example of road traffic described below illustrates the central points of the transition from a 'primitive' to a 'civilized' society in Europe (see note v):

'One should think of the country roads of a simple warrior society with a barter economy, uneven, unmetalled, exposed to damage from wind and rain. With few exceptions, there is very little traffic; the main danger here which man represents for other men is an attack by soldiers or thieves. When people look around them, scanning the trees and hills or the road itself, they do so primarily because they must be prepared for armed attack, and only secondarily because they have to avoid collision. Life on the main roads of this society demands a constant readiness to fight, and free play of the emotions in defence of one's life or possessions from physical attack. Traffic on the main roads of a big city in a complex society of our time demands a quite different moulding of the psychological apparatus. Here the danger of physical attack is minimal. Cars are rushing in all directions; pedestrians and cyclists are trying to thread their way through the mêlée of cars; policemen stand at the main crossroads to regulate the traffic with varying success. But this external control is founded on the assumption that every individual is himself regulating his behaviour with the utmost exactitude in accordance with the necessities of this network. The chief danger that people here represent for others results from someone in this bustle losing his self-control. A constant and highly differentiated regulation of one's own behaviour is needed for the individual to steer his way through the traffic. If the strain of such constant self-control becomes too much for an individual, this is enough to put himself and others in mortal danger.'   [1994: 446]

The above quote illustrates the complex set of changes which have taken place in society; they characterize a shift from an orientation towards the external world which is fearful and violent to one which is controlled by the 'self-steering' individual.

1.3.1   Life in the Middle Ages

People living in the tenth century lived with the awareness of constant danger from both human and natural enemies. Aggressiveness was openly prized. War was the normal state of affairs for most of the population which was organized into groups of armed bands; it occurred at many different levels, from large-scale warfare to family feuds and vendettas. Warriors took great pleasure in killing and in torturing others, which was a socially permitted pleasure. As prisoners were regarded as a drain on resources in times when food was scarce, they were either killed or sent back home so mutilated that they could no longer go to war or work. With a few exceptions of those women who chose to emulate men, the role of women was difficult in this warrior society; women were regarded as the property of the warrior class, useful for procreation and enjoyment but little else. In contrast in modern 'civilized' societies, the control of force is centralized in the hands of the State; consequently, the use of physical violence by individual citizens is regarded as being unacceptable. Instead, individuals must control and regulate those emotions which found free expression by people who lived in the tenth century.

By today's standards of conditioning, many of the relationships and practices of medieval times would appear to be embarrassing or at least unattractive to the more modern sensibility. To illustrate this point, Elias quotes from the *Diversoria* (1523) where the scholar Erasmus describes a scene in a typical German inn of the time where some eighty or ninety people from all kinds of social positions are seated together:

'Garlic smells and other bad odours arise. People spit everywhere. Someone is cleaning his boots on the table. Then the meal is brought in. Everyone dips his bread in the general dish, bites the bread, and dips it in again. The place is dirty and the wine is bad. And if one asks for a better wine, the innkeeper replies: I have put up enough nobles and counts. If it does not suit you, look for other quarters.

The stranger to the country has a particularly difficult time. The others stare at him fixedly as if he were a fabulous animal from Africa. Moreover, these people acknowledge as human beings only the nobles of their own country.

The room is overheated; everyone is sweating and steaming and wiping himself. There are doubtless many among them who have some hidden disease.'

[1994: 57/8]

Many diseases were not so hidden. Most people were infested with lice and frequently passed worms, some through the ears and eyes as well as through the more traditional routes. The most appalling disabilities were also openly displayed. During the Middle Ages people lived in and for the present and expressed their emotions spontaneously; everything was out in the open; people publicly practised and spoke of activities such as urinating, farting, defecating or sexual encounters; legitimate and illegitimate children were raised together, with no hint of secrecy or shame. Elias reminds us that in addition to aggression and brutality there was much gaiety and joy during this period which was characterized by an intensity, openness and lack of constraint of human behaviour that most modern 'civilized' people today would find shocking.

1.3.2 The transition

Elias notes that much of what was considered to be normal and to cause pleasure during the period from the tenth to the sixteenth century would cause revulsion today. He seeks to explain why in contrast to this, citizens are nowadays expected to show a very high degree of self-control. The spontaneous outpouring of emotions characteristic of the Middle Ages has been suppressed and as a result a wall has been built between one body and another so that people nowadays avoid contact with the mere approach of something which has been in contact with the mouth or hands of someone else, and are embarrassed at the mere sight of the bodily functions of others or even of their mention and feel shame when our own bodily functions are exposed to the gaze of others. How did this happen?

1.3.3 Development of 'court' society

In his research Elias found that the change in what he calls 'drive-control' (as represented by the control of the id by the ego under the influence of the superego) conduct is very closely related to the growing interweaving and interdependence of people over the ages. During the tenth century the vast majority of the population still lived in localities defined by independent tribal bands, which later shaped themselves into feudal and manorial units. The economy was based largely on barter; money was mistrusted and was solely used as a form of commerce with outsiders, who were generally viewed with suspicion. There was little mixing between different classes; the warrior elite generally held the impoverished peasantry in contempt. However, towards the end of the Middle Ages, during the eleventh and twelfth centuries, new forms of consolidation emerged as some warriors gradually gained predominance over others across a more extended area. The residences or 'courts' of these new rulers became a focus for the concentration of armed forces, for a new band of administrators (the forerunners of the bourgeois class) and also became the homes of musicians and other entertainers who could attest to the prestige of the ruler. The development of the courts, which required a degree of interdependence between different groups of people, led to the demand for greater restraint of emotions and the exercise of foresight in exploring the consequences of actions. Elias says that:

> 'Here, for the first time in secular society, a large number of people, including men, lived together in constant close contact in a hierarchical structure, under the eyes of the central person, the territorial lord. This fact alone enforced a certain restraint on all dependants. An abundance of unwarlike administrative and clerical work

had to be done. All this created a somewhat more peaceful atmosphere. As happens whenever men renounce physical violence, the social importance of women increased.'

[1994: 326]

Within the strictly hierarchical and restricted court circle, and encouraged above all by the presence of the lady, who was the wife of the lord or ruler, more peaceful forms of conduct become obligatory. While knights or troubadors (musicians) could act with brutal violence towards their own wives, or women of lower rank, they were expected to act delicately with respect to those above them in rank, and particularly with respect to the lady of the territorial lord. The demand for stricter control of impulses and emotions was thus first imposed by those of high rank on their social inferiors. To begin with, restraint on the expression of desires was imposed only when in the company of others. For example one author admonishes people not to pare their nails or fall asleep or expose themselves by not being properly attired 'except among people before whom one is not ashamed' (1994: 114). First it becomes a distasteful offence to show oneself exposed before those of higher or equal rank. With inferiors such behaviour could be seen to be a sign of benevolence. Over many centuries as society became more equal, so such behaviour came to be seen to cause general offence.

Elias notes that the development of the court as a centre for the concentration of armed force and as an administrative and commercial centre benefited some rulers more than others and in particular the king. The courts were at the centre of a money economy which grew primarily as the result of taxation but also with respect to the need to buy things which could not be produced locally. This increased the relative power of the king over other nobles as other high lords or chieftains of the time were paid either in barter or in fixed rents while the king's taxes were paid in monetary form. With the increased power of the king or queen, more of the nobility were forced to rely on his or her financial support and so the court of the king grew larger. In this process a very important development took place whereby these nobles were transformed from being a class of knights to being a class of courtiers. Elias sums up the process in the quote below:

'The closer the web of interdependence becomes in which the individual is enmeshed with the advancing division of functions, the larger the social spaces over which this network extends and which become integrated into functional or institutional units – the more threatened is the social existence of the individual who gives way to spontaneous impulses and emotions, the greater is the social advantage of those able to moderate their affects[1], and the more strongly is each individual from an early age to take account of the effects of his own or other people's actions on a whole series of links in the social chain. The moderation of spontaneous emotions, the tempering of affects, the extension of mental space beyond the moment into past and future, the habit of connecting events in terms of chains of cause and effect – all these are different aspects of the same transformation of conduct which necessarily takes place as the result of the

[1] Affect: another word to describe 'emotion'.

13

monopolization of physical violence, and the lengthening of the chains of social action and interdependence. It is a "civilizing" change in behaviour.' [1994: 448]

However Elias suggests that despite this capacity for the self to reflect on action, this was not equivalent to the modern superego or conscience. During the fifteenth and sixteenth centuries the process of differentiation of functions and the increasing interdependence of a larger number of classes accelerated. As the money supply increased more quickly the wealth of the aristocracy declined more sharply. At the same time the aristocracy in France began to be challenged by a new pressure from the new bourgeois class whose members emerged initially to become scribes, counsellors and tax administrators for the king and as merchants in the newly expanding towns. This effectively initiated the class system, with the court nobility representing the 'upper class' who strove to differentiate themselves from usurpation by the bourgeoisie.

1.3.4   Psychologization and rationalization

Elias states that not only within the Western civilizing process, but within every major civilizing process, the transition of warriors to courtiers is one of the most decisive transactions (1994: 467). For those knights who became courtiers during the course of the sixteenth century, the rules of life took on a new meaning and the entire personality gradually changed. The spontaneous resort to physical violence which had been used to resolve disputes in earlier times was not appropriate in the context of the concentrated central power of court society. However competition among the nobles at court for rank and for favour was intense. Individual nobles gained rank by associating themselves with others of higher rank. As the fortunes of these favoured nobles frequently changed, there was a constant vigilance and struggle for favour. Plotting and intrigue came to the fore as did the tendency for people to mask and suppress their true feelings. Vigilant self-control and perpetual observation of others became extremely important for the maintenance of one's social position. Elias argues that in the transition from knights to courtiers the entire personality of the nobility changed as nobles were transformed from being warrior knights to being dependent courtiers.

By the term **psychologization**, Elias refers to the fact that within court society a 'psychological' view developed as a person's social position demanded vigilant self-control and careful observation and analysis of one's own behaviour and of that of others in terms of a complex series of motives and causal connections. Conflict, which could previously have been expressed in terms of direct action, gradually became a matter of internal reflection and calculation. Elias detects this process occurring also in the increased demand for books during this time, as the skills needed to read a book demand a well-defined ability to transform and regulate the emotional drives. The reading of books allows a person to play out in fantasy those tensions which hitherto would have found release in the resort to direct violence.

Rationalization is similar to the concept of calculation. Where a knight might seek to further his ends by resorting to impulsive and violent action, the courtier sought to work primarily through reason to influence those in a powerful position. As opposed to the knight, the courtier had to use foresight in calculating how to achieve his ends. To Elias this 'courtly rationality' played an even more important role than the urban–commercial rationality and foresight instilled by functions in the trade network in the development of the eighteenth-century 'Enlightenment'.

<h2>1.3.5   Shame and embarrassment</h2>

For Elias shame and repugnance (embarrassment) played an equal role to those of psychologization and rationalization in moulding the behaviour of the new class of courtiers. **Shame** is a form of conflict, not with someone outside, such as social opinion, but with something within the person's own personality, a part of himself that represents social opinion. In feeling shame as a conflict within his own personality a person fears the loss of the love or respect of others to which he attaches value. Shame is associated with the breach of social constraints. Elias argues that feelings of shame emerge more clearly with every spurt of the civilizing process and finally predominate over other fears – particularly the physical fear of others. As the shame which a person can experience in monitoring his own actions increases, so does the capacity for **embarrassment** or repugnance at the behaviour of others.

For Elias, the development of a more psychological inner reflection and rationalization in the courtier is linked to the heightened capacity to feel shame and embarrassment. This is because each of these requires more differentiated foresight and the development of a long-term view. These become necessary in court society so that larger groups of people may preserve their social existence in an increasingly differentiated society where the restraint of emotions is called for and where the direct expression of physical violence is no longer an option. Elias also sees in the development of rationalization and the intensification of shame, a growing differentiation between id, ego and superego, whereby the role played by the ego in regulating self control is advanced considerably (1994: 493/4). The same is true of embarrassment, which is defined as 'displeasure or anxiety which arises when another person threatens to breach, or breaches, society's prohibitions represented by one's super-ego.' (1994: 495).

<h2>1.3.6   The development of manners</h2>

The compulsion for self-control increased as courts grew ever larger and chains of dependence between courtiers became more dense with the increasing division of functions. As people became more integrated and the contrasts between noble and bourgeois classes diminished, so the greater was the sensitivity to changes, shades or nuances of conduct and the more finely attuned people became to minute gestures.

1.3.7   Distinction: growth of the class system

Elias notes that one key difference between the knight and the courtier was the contempt with which the latter viewed those of a lower rank, particularly the bourgeoisie. He explains this as the result of a tension between the noble courtiers, who had been progressively impoverished and were dependent upon the king for support, and the rising bourgeoisie, who threatened to take their position. Such tensions were apparent from the beginnings of the emergence of the bourgeois class. Faced with competition from the bourgeoisie, the courtiers could only infrequently resort to physical violence, which resulted in a strong inner tension in the members of the threatened upper class. The fears of the aristocracy instead manifested themselves in a general revulsion of anything which 'smells bourgeois', which was associated with vulgarity. Courtiers modified their speech, gestures, social amusements and manners in a bid to distinguish themselves from this pressure from below. However as courtiers actively sought to distance themselves from the 'vulgar' bourgeoisie, so many of the bourgeoisie sought to emulate the practices of the courtiers to be seen to become the same as them. As one and then another of the 'distinctive' courtier styles was adopted by the bourgeois, so each style progressively failed to perform its function as the basis for distinction between the two groups and so new styles were developed. Again and again as a result of this emulation, styles which were once considered to be 'refined' became regarded as being 'vulgar' as they were taken up by the bourgeoisie.

1.4   DISCUSSION OF ELIAS'S CIVILIZING PROCESS

The contribution of Norbert Elias is summarized here and is linked to the work of other authors.

- *Elias's Influence*: First, the similarity of Elias's work to authors including Michel Foucault, Pierre Bourdieu and Pasi Falk, whose work is discussed in subsequent chapters, should be noted.

- *Relation to McCracken (1990) and Ewen (1976)*: Second, Elias's work illuminates important aspects of the two stories which were described earlier. For example we can locate Grant McCracken's (1990) study of the court society of Queen Elizabeth I of England as an example of developments which took place in an early court society. Developments within Elizabeth's court, involving a greater dependency among the nobles for the Queen's favour and the growing individualization and distinctiveness of the Elizabethan nobility, were not unique, but formed an early highpoint of a progressive pattern towards the establishment of formal court societies across Europe. Elias's work also has implications for what Stuart Ewen claims in relation to the development of the 'social self' and the role of advertising. It is clear that the idea of a 'social self' as evidenced by the ability to experience shame and embarrassment and to monitor closely and in minute detail the behaviour of others in addition to one's own, existed well before the twentieth century. While advertising may have played on the existence of this social self, this form of self had existed for many years beforehand.

- *Significance: Bodily Discipline and Control*: Third, the main themes to which Elias refers are, if true, of the utmost significance for any discussion of developments in contemporary consumer societies. He describes in great detail the curbing of the emotions in favour of rationality and foresight and the trend towards the development of a self which is contained, the individual self. Emotions which had previously been expressed spontaneously and openly were now contained and acted out within the individual psyche. This was facilitated by the increased attention to books, whereby acts could be played out in the imagination of the reader rather than in real life. Elias's discussion of the change whereby the body is no longer disciplined by the application of external force but to a much greater extent by a more powerful self-discipline based on shame and embarrassment is a subject which has been addressed by Foucault (1978) among others. It can be argued that in contemporary society the body is subjected to a much more differentiated range of disciplines than was the case during the period discussed by Elias, including crash diets, slimnastics, gymnastics, aerobics, swingnastics, muscle toning, deep toning, tanning, strip-waxing, various forms of 'cosmetic' plastic surgery including rhinoplasty, breast enlargement and cellulite reduction, to name a few.

- *The Civilizing Process*: Perhaps the most forceful point made by Elias is the manner by which all forms of natural bodily functions and their descriptions, including urinating, defecating, scratching, copulating, passing worms and self-exposure, which were treated as more or less normal parts of everyday life in medieval times, are progressively hidden behind the scenes, first from the gaze of those who are considered inferior in status to the self and then as differences between classes become more refined, virtually completely removed from the social scene. What is striking here is the huge degree of control or self-discipline required to enforce such a rein on the emotions. This is more striking when one considers that the distance in behaviour and in psychical structure between children and adults increases in the course of the civilizing process. Elias thus likens the medieval character to that of a child. In learning how to be competent and self-disciplined adults in today's society, Elias argues they must experience and absorb, in a few short years, the progressive civilizing disciplines of hundreds of years.

- *Uneven Development*: Elias's thesis is that, despite differences in the patterns of development between countries, one can discern a glacial mainstream of movement towards civilization. To draw upon the glacial metaphor, while the ice of civilization sometimes retreats, the mainstream of movement over centuries is in one direction. Within this general movement each country develops structural characteristics of its own which correspond to the different social structures and the specific ways in which the emotions are regulated. For example he argues that in comparison with France, England had a short courtly absolutist phase. The English nobility and bourgeois classes struck a form of alliance much earlier than in France; however the amalgamation of upper- and middle-class behaviour took place over a longer period than in France. In contrast to England and France, Germany was decentralized and relatively poor following the Thirty Years War. Compared to the others, Germany had a long period of absolutism, exercised through a few small courts. Here, too, differences between bourgeoisie and nobility were much more pronounced. Elias argues that the army played a huge role in moulding the German population, as compared say with England where it played a relatively weak role. In the former the bourgeoisie became habituated to a strong external state authority, resulting in a 'command–obedience' relation to self-control, as opposed to the form of 'teamwork' which evolved in England. Elias argues that England's role as a colonial power aided the development of a differentiated form of 'self-steering' or self-control.

In discussing the contribution of Norbert Elias we can see how the modern self-disciplined individual self emerges hesitantly from the court society of the later medieval period. The modern self is primarily a rational individual who is expert in controlling and containing a range of emotions. Or is he or she? In the next section we discuss the rather controversial contribution by Michel Maffesoli, a postmodernist, who claims that this is not at all the case, but that in recent years the entire process has gone into reverse.

1.5 POSTMODERNISM AND THE NEO-TRIBES: RETURN TO COMMUNITY?

The trends described by Elias towards **psychologism**, **rationalism** and an **individualism** which derives from feelings of shame and embarrassment, are cornerstones of what is called **modernism**, a process which has characterized European thought since the days of the Enlightenment and which has spread throughout the world. Modernism celebrates rationalism over the emotions, the mind over the body and science over superstition. For example the French Revolutionaries were fired with enthusiasm to get rid of anything that seemed irrational and re-ordered administrative districts and even the streets of Paris along strictly rational lines. Similarly, scientists have been concerned to dispel myth and illusion and to found a rational basis for the discussion of physical and social phenomena. While modernity has been reflected on by many authors as a fundamentally progressive movement, a growing number of critics became concerned about what they considered to be the insidious power of the modern machine to penetrate every aspect of life and consciousness. Paradoxically in this age which was supposedly the supreme age of the individual, dominated by *homo economicus*, there was an accompanying fear of incorporation, of being swallowed whole by what was outside the self. This was reflected in a number of popular films and books which appeared during the course of the twentieth century, for example Charlie Chaplin's film *Modern Times*, George Orwell's book (and film) *1984* and in the film *The Stepford Wives*.

So is the rational, isolated individual the exemplar of contemporary society? In *The Time of the Tribes* (1996), Michael Maffesoli argues that, at present, another fundamental change in society is underway, a change in which Elias's gradual progress towards civilization goes into reverse and where solitary individuals become assimilated into a huge network of amorphous but interlacing groups: the neo-tribes:

> 'Two centuries of autonomy, separation and frantic individualism have led us to believe that these are natural states of the world, and that if there is any evolution left it is towards an ever-accentuating perfection of these ideals. Therefore, we are particularly struck today by observing the persistent and imperious need to be 'en reliance', to be bound together, which is manifested in the unproductive expenditure and bodily game of consuming together. It is in this sense that I speak of tribalism, which is a way of being that favours fusion, or perhaps even emotional confusion.'
> Maffesoli (1997: 32)

Maffesoli's argument is that people living presently in 'advanced' consumer societies are not the rational, isolated, self-disciplined individuals which Elias's conclusion suggests would be typical of people today. Instead Maffesoli contends that people are joined together by powerful emotional bonds and are 'connected' through a variety of diffuse and fleeting encounters, from those which bind together people who live in city neighbourhoods and ghettos, to those swarms of consumers who populate city-centre high-streets and shopping malls, to the temporary crowds which lie on crowded beaches, or constitute the television audiences for mass media spectacles such as 'Live-Aid', the marriage of Charles and Diana, and Diana's funeral, to the nebulous groups which populate USENET, mobile telephone networks and the virtual communities of the Internet. In this view cities are not spaces where individuals freed from the constraints of community can make rational relationships, but are themselves communities which are constructed out of a multiplicity of small enclaves and interdependencies, where people are bound together by proximity and some form of 'emotional glue' (see note vi). This 'glue' comprises some form of affectual sharing; for example affection may be based upon cultural pursuits, sexual tastes, clothing, habits, religion, intellectual pursuits and politics, to name but a few.

Maffesoli suggests that the current transformation signals much more than the reconnection of one individual to another. He argues that just as individuals are becoming connected to one another, so the connection is not just between people but is also experienced as a form of connection within the person and in particular with respect to the body. During the modern age, the body had been perceived to be separate and distinct from the mind which disciplined and ruled over it. Maffesoli suggests that the current age is associated with a re-integration of body and mind. As a result, he claims that the present concern in consumer societies for appearance and for adorning and working on the body is by no means superficial. He argues that as the individual body is the foundation of the social body, so the frivolity of the new consumer society and its fascination with bodily concerns, such as fashion, design, eating and drinking and anything that expresses the cult of the body, are fundamental to this reconstructed sense of community. He also argues that what is predominant in present society, what ties people together, is aesthetic experience, the ability to feel emotion together, to share the same ambience.

Why has this transformation taken place? In Maffesoli's radical interpretation, the growing individualism, rationalization and abstraction of everyday life in present-day society has reached such a level that these forces have collapsed inwards on themselves. He draws upon the analogy of a 'black hole' to explain this. The political sphere is likened to a black hole, where a star collapses under the pressure of its own mass and thereby gives birth to another space. Likewise the political system has become so abstract and disconnected from the everyday concerns of ordinary people that the existing political universe is collapsing and a new space is being created. Political parties respond by focusing on the message, on image and on stirring the passions rather than reason. Furthermore, high-level politics is overrationalized and exhausted. The citizenry on the other hand are more concerned with concrete street-level issues which they personally care about. The old 'party' politics was too abstract and rational and now its politicians are using marketing tools to seek to regain their constituency. The public space which forms the forum for traditional party politics is dying and as it dies a new space is created for 'community' politics. There are many examples of such communities including the various networks and affinity and interest groups or neighbourhood groups that go to make up what he calls the 'megalopolisses'. Other groups coalesce around the shared sentiment created by issues which to them are of pressing concern, whether this be animal welfare, destruction of the environment or genetically modified foods and organs. Such communities do not require physical proximity for the establishment of a community 'neighbourhood'. Rather, existing technologies such as the mass media, which are also becoming more localized in relation to local television and radio, can unite people through their access to a common experience. It has also been argued that the Internet and in particular the Web, are enabling the creation of such groups. In addition to differentiation and localism in the political sphere, Maffesoli suggests that another response to feelings of detachment from the abstract public sphere is for people to invest their energies in a range of other activities such as physical pleasure, hedonism and the body.

Within the new tribes, solidarity is derived from an emotional commitment or shared sentiment, the aesthetic, a form of fellow feeling, however fleeting this might be. Examples of such shared sentiment include the 'Band-Aid' phenomenon of the late 1980s which mobilized the collective emotions of millions of people across the Western world in support of long-term relief for famine-hit countries such as Ethiopia. Maffesoli attributes an importance to the media in constructing solidarity by circulating images which, he suggests, are the equivalent of icons, in that they enable members of the tribe to identify with the image (for example whether this is Michael Jackson or Coca-Cola) and through it with one another. He suggests that advertising addresses 'target' audiences, which he calls tribes, with such images and that the 'tribes' respond by 'recognizing' themselves in such images by using and wearing the products and services advertized (1996: 138).

According to Maffesoli, the crowds of people who watch such television spectacles and participate in events are bound together by shared sentiment. The metropolitan tribes are bound together by means of local membership, the neighbourhood and mechanisms of solidarity which create the whole. The vitality of these tribes springs from **proxemics**, 'being close' to others through sharing the same space and a common sentiment; for example skate-boarding, a shared love of 'nature', or owning the same car. The linkage of these and the very fact of being introduced and chatting produce a sense of community. Maffesoli notes that traditional communities are tied together by means not only of an intellectual knowledge but also of a **connaissance**, a feeling knowledge, which forms part of the 'palaver'. It is not impossible that with technological developments the growth in urban tribes has encouraged a 'computerized palaver' (see for example the newly emergent 'palaver' used by British youth in 'texting'), a ritual which is similar to those of traditional communities. Rather than the computer disconnecting us from reality, Maffesoli argues that the networked computer is much closer to the concept of oral conversation than is the relatively isolated activity of reading a book and that because of this the computerized society will develop new forms of relationship and community.

Maffesoli further argues that the growth of mass media with its tendency to excavate alternative points of view, has led to the disintegration of universal bourgeois values. This fragmentation of values has helped recreate an oral traditional culture. By presenting images of life, a political event, or the life of a star can take on mythic proportions. The media reaffirm the feeling of belonging to a larger group or getting outside of oneself, of allowing the expression of a common emotion, which causes people to recognize themselves in communion with others. He believes that even buildings which have linked access to cable television will perhaps experience values not far removed from those which guided the clans or tribes of traditional societies.

Thus while some lament the end of all collective values and the withdrawal into the self, Maffesoli's hypothesis is that a new and evolving trend can be found within the growth of small groups and existential networks. This represents a sort of tribalism which is based at the same time on the spirit of religion and on localism, as instanced by proxemics and nature. What has been responsible for such developments? Maffesoli attributes a lot of influence to technology and the mass media such as computer networks and cable television.

What are the implications of what Maffesoli is saying for what has gone

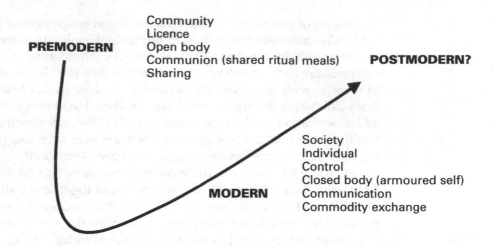

Figure 1.1 A scheme for the movement from premodernity to modernity and postmodernity

before? Unlike Norbert Elias who provided the backing of a detailed empirical study, Maffesoli tends to make generalizations which are not supported by anything other than the argument which he weaves. This does not mean that we should reject Maffesoli's argument, but rather that this should be checked in line with the available data from other sources.

To summarize, Maffesoli disputes the idea that contemporary consumer societies are characterized by the collapse of collective ideals and increasing levels of rationalism, individualism and constraint of the emotions. Instead he argues that such societies are in fact seething with examples of social configurations which go beyond individualism, being composed of crowds of people and showing the rebirth of tribalism through the neo-tribes, which consist of a mass patchwork of small local entities. The glue which holds such tribes together is the aesthetic of emotional 'fellow feeling'. Maffesoli argues that *homo economicus*, the self-contained individual, is dead or at least mortally wounded, as the forces which shape society turn back from a focus on the creation of isolated individuals towards a focus on the aesthetic and the re-birth of community. Maffesoli is thus arguing that contemporary society manifests a return to societal characteristics which are reminiscent of the Middle Ages. This is summed up figuratively in Figure 1.1.

1.6 DISCUSSION OF POSTMODERNISM AND THE NEO-TRIBES

Is there evidence that the general direction of change in consumer societies is towards the reaffirmation of community bonded by the spirit of 'fellow-feeling', as Maffesoli suggests, or does the evidence suggest the contrary? In this discussion we consider the results of some empirical research and some theoretical contributions in order to seek answers to these questions.

Secondly, if it does seem that a change is underway, then what changes in society (sociogenetic factors) might help explain the change in the psychogenetic makeup of individuals?

The European Values Study Group conducted a series of studies which have measured the changes in European and other Western values in 1981 and in 1990 (see note vii). One of the central hypotheses of the study was that as countries advance economically, the values of their populations shift in the direction of individualization. The process of individualization refers to the growing autonomy of individuals in developing their own values and norms, free from the constraint of tradition. From our previous discussion, this is common sense in that one would expect that where community is powerful, community norms will prevail. One would also expect to see an increased liberalization of lifestyles in Western societies, particularly within the domains of religion, morality, sexuality and areas of life such as leisure time, where personal choice is to be expected. At the same time, the authors of the study expected to find that the value orientations of Western societies are converging. Value convergence might be predicted in view of the growing social, economic and political convergence between societies, and trends towards more cosmopolitan ideas and lifestyles through the global influence of modern media should provide signs of the process of global convergence, in short the world as a 'global village'.

With respect to religious values, the researchers found that society in the 1990s was more individualized and secularized than it had been in the 1950s, but that these changes had occurred well before the 1980s. They also found that economic individualism increased in most countries during the 1980s, although only marginally. Cultural individualism (based on the extent to which people expressed respect for authority and a willingness to follow instructions) increased, principally in regard to decreased respect for authority. Also confidence in democratic institutions declined, particularly in the USA. While it was hypothesized that sustained individualism would also imply an increase in tolerance, in contrast tolerance declined during the 1980s. It was hypothesized that with increasing individualism, the level of political interest would rise, as individualism implies self-reliance on the part of citizens which, in turn, might cause an interest in politics as well as political participation to increase. The results of the study supported this hypothesis suggesting that the level of political interest rose as did the proneness to protest by means of direct action, including petitions, boycotts, demonstrations, unofficial strikes and occupations. The authors also hypothesized that they would find a shift in concern from one's own material wellbeing to a concern with issues related to quality of life. They called this term **postmaterialism** to reflect the idea that people nowadays may be moving away from an emphasis on consumer goods as being related to happiness and wellbeing.

The authors of the report found that contrary to their expectations, the hypothesis which suggested a decreasing importance of social class in predicting a person's left–right political orientation was not supported. A summary of some of the key results is shown in Table 1.1. The data in the

Table 1.1   **Development of economic and cultural individualism, confidence in democratic and authoritative institutions, and tolerance towards ethnic groups and deviant behaviour**

Country	Individualism		Confidence		Tolerance	
	Economic	Cultural	Democracy	Authority	Ethnic	Deviance
USA	0.04	0.19	−1.21	−1.00	−0.06	−0.05
Canada	0.04	0.20	−0.21	−0.45	−0.3	−0.4
West Germany	0.15	0.02	−0.13	−0.48	0.14	0.01
France	0.23	−0.11	0.04	−0.35	−0.24	−0.20
Great Britain	0.04	0.10	−0.16	−0.65	0.05	−0.01
Spain	0.11	0.08	−0.40	−0.87	−0.08	−0.04

Source: Adapted from Table 4.1, page 76, of Chapter 4, 'Political Culture: Patterns of Political Orientations and Behaviour' in Ester *et al.* (eds), *The Individualizing Society: Value Change in Europe and North-America*, by Andries van den Broek and Felix Heunks, 1994.

table summarize those differences in mean scores for the two studies in 1990 and 1980. For example this means that in the USA, the mean score for economic individualism increased by 0.04 during the period, while that for confidence in democratic institutions decreased by −1.21.

From the table there are a number of differences between countries. One might also conjecture that the authors would have found some high differences between regions within a country, which they did not test for. The authors felt that, despite such differences, the hypotheses for a 'sustained process of individualization were largely confirmed' (Ester *et al.*, 1994: 95). However, some were clearly refuted; for example there were no signs of increased tolerance nor of political fragmentation. In a further section of the report, the authors found that they could not conclude that modernization is a process by which traditional values are uniformly replaced by individualized values in all domains of behaviour.

What bearing does the above have for the positions of Elias and Maffesoli? It extends some comfort to each explanation. The findings may be interpreted in line with Maffesoli by drawing on the findings that faith in democratic institutions has decreased, but political interest and critique have increased and action based on unconventional politics is increasing. While the authors of the European values survey interpret this to mean a rise in individualism, Maffesoli could quite legitimately claim that the rise in road protests, marches and other such unconventional political activity requires as a first instance a form of group formation and emotional bonding that gives birth to the 'neo-tribes' which organize such activities. The survey also found strong support for environmental issues, with approval ratings of up to 98 per cent. However, the authors comment that while the environment may form the basis for much talk, the membership of environmental organizations can be tiny. For example approval for ecology and nature protection in Portugal was 98 per cent, but active participation was 1 per cent. Membership in some other countries was equally small, but varied considerably and constituted up to 10 per cent in the USA and 23 per cent in the

Netherlands. Such groups require a large degree of 'grass roots' organization and may be interpreted in line with Maffesoli's argument for the existence of 'neo-tribes'. With respect to the above, the rise of individualism and of the 'new tribes' are not necessarily mutually exclusive. As traditional ties of community and tradition give way in some areas to an increased individualism, so new forms of association are found. However, the report also indicates that older formations of group influence have not been lessened, as evidenced by the finding that people are less tolerant and by the continued importance of social class.

How does this fit in with Norbert Elias's account of the 'civilizing process', which was discussed earlier? You may remember that Elias describes the internalization of external controls together with progressive emotional restraint and individualization.

Elias has in fact slightly shifted his explanation about the onward progress of civilization to take into account developments which have taken place in European society since the 1960s. Elias agrees that during this period the tight regulation of emotional controls by individuals began to relax and people in Western countries began to explore aspects of their emotions which had previously been forbidden. He considers such developments, which were associated with the middle class, to be related to a new and more calculating hedonism. This calculation is summarized by describing it as a form of 'controlled de-control' of the emotions. This is evidenced by a whole range of behaviours; the idolization of images of youth expressed in theme parks, the exploration of emotions by means of the growth of a 'therapeutic culture', and the current craze for extreme sports which promise perfectly safe, 'near-death' experiences.

1.7	APPLICABILITY TO OTHER CULTURES

How applicable is all of this to those who were born and raised in cultures other than that of the European which is described here? Undoubtedly much of the material discussed here is specific to the experience of being 'European'. As such it is useful to a specific non-European experience to the extent that it provides a point of contrast to developments which have taken place in that country and within that culture. On the other hand, it might be argued that similar changes are occurring in different countries around the world. So perhaps we can close this section by asking some questions which you may consider with respect to a specific non-European culture. Are traditional communities disappearing? Are there apparently contradictory signs of increasing individualization coupled with new forms of association, similar to those of the 'neo-tribes'. Do people generally exert a high degree of control over their bodily expressions? Are people currently experimenting with forms of bodily expression in that culture? If the answers to most of the above questions is 'yes', then the issues which have been discussed here are of relevance to that culture.

1.8 CHAPTER SUMMARY

This chapter focused on different accounts of the rise of consumer society. The first account detects in the mass consumer society a mass democracy and instances the 'narcissism of the common man' as the end point of a constant progressive movement which has its roots in ancient times. Whereas this narcissism could only be afforded by the ruling few until comparatively recent times, it is now open to the masses.

The second account focused on the development of a mass consumer society in the USA during the 1920s. This account countered the first one to the extent that consumer society was described as a repressive apparatus which planted anxieties in the individual and which created an insidious cycle of work and spend for the majority of the population.

The third account focused on the research carried out by Norbert Elias. This stressed the importance of realizing how different modern individuals are with respect to a whole range of behaviours, including systems of 'manners' and control. Elias's work helps us understand that the exercise of tight self-discipline, of constant vigilance over the behaviour of the self and of others may be traced back several hundreds of years in Europe. Elias's work, while itself not perfect, applies a corrective to the earlier accounts. First, if we are to speak of 'progress' in society, such progress takes hundreds of years to develop itself into a sustained pattern. Second, it introduces the important concepts of rationalization, control and discipline into the explanation of current consuming behaviour.

At first it seems as if the contribution by Maffesoli has overturned Elias's carefully researched conclusions. This is because Maffesoli argues that, in place of a society of disciplined individuals, consumer societies are made up of a myriad of expressive new group formations, whether these be shoppers, television viewers or anti-road protestors. Such groups are held together by aesthetic emotional ties of 'fellow feeling'. However more recent work suggests that there is evidence that Western society is undergoing a period of transition and that forms of experimentation including 'controlled de-control' are signs of this.

END-OF-CHAPTER REVIEW QUESTIONS

1. What is meant by 'patina'? How might patina be distinguished from 'fashion'?
2. What is meant by the following terms: 'Gemeinschaft' and 'Gesellschaft'?
3. Are the terms 'premodern' – 'pre-industrial', 'postmodern' – 'postindustrial' equivalent?
4. What are the distinguishing features of the premodern, modern and postmodern eras?
5. To what extent can we blame advertising for an anxious 'social self' which constantly scrutinizes its own appearance and behaviour and that of others?
6. Summarize Elias's (1994) main conclusions. To what extent are his conclusions borne out by more recent theories and evidence?

REFERENCES AND FURTHER READING

Douglas, Mary and Baron Isherwood (1978) *The World of Goods: Towards an Anthropology of Consumption*, London: Allen Lane.

Elias, Norbert (1994) orig. 1939 *The Civilizing Process: The History of Manners and State Formation and Civilization*, trans. Edmund Jephcott, Oxford: Basil Blackwell.

Ester, Peter, Halman Loek and Ruud de Moor (eds) (1994) *The Individualizing Society: Value Change in Europe and North America*, European Values Studies series, Tilburg University Press.

Ewen, Stuart (1976) *Captains of Consciousnesss: Advertising and the Social Roots of the Consumer Culture*, New York: McGraw-Hill.

Fine, Reuben (1986) *Narcissism, the Self and Society*, New York: Columbia University Press.

Foucault, Michel (1978) orig. 1976 *The History of Sexuality, An Introduction*, London: Penguin.

Fullerton, Ronald, A. (1988) How Modern is Modern Marketing? Marketing's Evolution and the Myth of the 'Production Era', *Journal of Marketing*, vol. 52 (January): 108–25.

Giddens, Anthony (1989) *Sociology*, Oxford: Polity Press.

Harvey, David (1989) *The Condition of Postmodernity*, Oxford: Basil Blackwell.

Hyde, Lewis (1999) *The Gift: Imagination and the Erotic Life of Property*, London: Vintage.

Kotler, Philip (1972) A Generic Concept of Marketing, *Journal of Marketing*, vol. 36 (April): 46–54.

McCracken, Grant (1990) *Culture and Consumption*, Bloomington and Indianapolis: Indiana University Press.

Maffesoli, Michel (1996) *The Time of the Tribes: The Decline of Individualism in Mass Society*, London: Sage.

Maffesoli, Michel (1997) 'The Return of Dionysus', pp. 21–38. In Pekka Sulkenen, John Holmwood, Hilary Radner and Gerhard Schulze (eds), consultant editor, Jo Campling, *Constructing the New Consumer Society*, New York: St. Martin's Press (now Palgrave).

Milgram, Stanley (1967) The Small World Problem *Psychology Today*, 1: 61–7.

Mukerji, Chandra (1983) *From Graven Images: Patterns of Modern Materialism*, New York: Columbia University Press.

Tucker, W.T. (1974) Future Directions in Marketing Theory, *Journal of Marketing*, 38 (April): 33–5.

NOTES

i   It is fascinating to note how many 'objective' social scientists were recruited to work on behalf of the military machine and in industry. For example John B. Watson, founder of modern behavioural psychology, was a proponent of transferring psychological development away from the traditional areas of socialization, such as the family, and for making the 'realities' of commercial life the basis for child-rearing. According to Ewen, Watson 'labelled all but the "gratifications" of the marketplace as perverse and psychologically and socially damaging' (1976: 83).

ii Source: Ewen (1976: 34).

iii Source: Ewen (1976: 171). Quotation attributed to Christine Frederick.

iv This discussion is based largely on the 1994 English translation of *The Civilizing Process*, translated by Edmund Jephcott.

v   Elias is very careful to use the word 'civilization' in a non-judgemental way. Each society represents a patterning of social relations which presents opportunities for the patterning of the psychological apparatus and of social conduct that are different from all other societies.

vi Among other things Maffesoli was fascinated by the study carried out by Milgram (1967) which showed that with the help of five or six relayers, one could establish contact between two people living in opposite corners of the United States. Maffesoli suggests that such communication was rendered possible because each individual formed part of a micro-milieu, which was connected to other milieux. Links included bars, churches and university laboratories, each linked to the others in a complex network.

vii The first study, which included 26 countries, was the largest comparative research project ever carried out. The second wave of the study, which was carried out in 1990, included almost all of the countries in Europe, the USA and Canada.

CONSUMING SPACE AND TIME

LEARNING OBJECTIVES

- To sensitize readers to the importance of time and space, and to the relations between material practices and representations of time and space
- To understand the changes in representations in time and in space that have taken place as the result of processes of modernization
- To seek to explain such changes with respect to two broad theoretical traditions associated with Weber and Marx
- To situate the growth of spaces for consumption within the modernizing process by offering specific examples of 'consuming spaces'
- To discuss classification in contemporary society in terms of access to the goods of consumption

2.1   INTRODUCTION

This chapter is devoted to understanding the relation of time and space to consumption. Following from the assumption that perceptions of time and space are linked to changes in social structure, it aims to discuss different accounts of the reordering of these relations during the phase of modernization. One account is based on the work of Max Weber and explores the extent of the rationalization of space and time. George Ritzer's 'McDonaldization thesis' is then discussed as a form of extension of Weberian thinking. This is followed by a section on globalization. The second major perspective, which is based on the work of Karl Marx, suggests that flux is a more apt term to describe current conditions. David Harvey focuses on the transformative power of capitalism in changing the social relations between time and space, by means of a process which, following Marx, he refers to as the 'annihilation of space through time'. Such views are explored in relation to the perception that time appears to be simultaneously speeding up and slowing down; speeding up, to the extent that the pace of life appears to be getting faster and faster; slowing down, to the extent that images of past and future are giving way to that of an interminable 'present' in contemporary consumer society.

2.2	CONSUMPTION: SPACE AND TIME

Concepts of time and space are not natural phenomena but are constructed by human beings. For example the conventional wisdom current in physics holds that the human perceptions of the flow and passage of time are little more than an illusion. One point of view in social science holds that the 'objective' conceptions of space and time are not natural or given, but are created through material practices. According to this view, time and space are structured according to the ways in which society is structured. This implies that the concepts of time and space change their meaning as society itself changes. In Chapter 1 we discussed the transition from feudalism to capitalism in western Europe during the eighteenth century as being pivotal, involving a range of changes at a number of levels of society. It is not surprising that this period is often cited by authors as being the locus for a major change in material practices which, in turn, resulted in a major reordering of concepts of space and time (McCracken, 1990: 21).

2.3	THE PLACE OF COMMUNITY VERSUS THE SPACE OF SOCIETY

A number of authors contend that a major aspect of this change has been the erosion of the place of community and the emergence of more abstract notions of time and space. As community is the starting point of our discussion of space and time, we must first ask what is meant by the concept of 'community'. This question has already been partially answered in Chapter 1. The sociologist Pierre Bourdieu (1977: 163) argues that social orderings of space and time provide a framework for experience whereby they tend to organize not only how a group perceives the world but the group itself, which orders itself according to these representations. Bourdieu's study of the way in which the Kabyle people ordered space and time showed how this ordering reinforced social integration and a division of labour between the sexes, ages and occupations. Bourdieu's representation of the Kabyle calendar is shown in Figure 2.1. The activities for autumn, winter and spring were divided into times for ploughing, sowing, germination and growth and were associated with the female, whereas spring, summer and autumn were associated with the characteristics of growth, ripening, harvest and stubble which were associated with the male part of the cycle. For the Kabyle, life was ordered according to the rhythms of nature and of gender and was orderly; there was a time and a place for every activity.

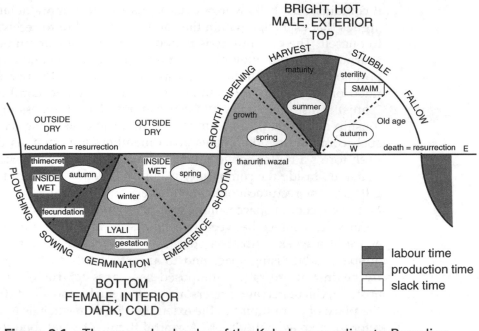

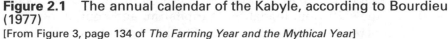

Figure 2.1 The annual calendar of the Kabyle, according to Bourdieu (1977)
[From Figure 3, page 134 of *The Farming Year and the Mythical Year*]

The social and temporal rhythms of the Kabyle world are insinuated into the **place** which they inhabit, a place where everything has its place, including its inhabitants who call it home. The place is organized in terms of the meanings which people give it, with respect to their language and practice, where perhaps every rock and tree has a meaning and plays a role in relation to the history of the community. Many of us too grew up in distinct places, defined by the communities which contained us, although few places would have been as contained as the place of the Kabyle. Places are thus **embedded**, to the extent that the people within them define themselves, their identities and history in terms of that place. Places exist in a curious state in relation to time. To the extent that a 'place' for community remains the same, we can talk of **tradition** (the continuity of the same place through time) rather than **progress** (changing place over time). The idea of the place is contained in the myths or stories which the community narrates to itself, thus recreating the place itself and the community; through the story, the community and the place become one and the same. One should not be overly romantic about the place of community, which can impart feelings of claustrophobia and loss of identity in the modern mind (see note i). The stories which bind together community and place are not amenable to comprehension by **strangers** from outside the community. There is little or no concept of private space within the traditional place of the community. This is because the boundaries of the self spill beyond the contours of the body and into the community which contains it; the community forms a second protective skin around the person

31

it contains. Pasi Falk, whose work is discussed in more detail in Chapter 7, argues that exchange within the community is akin to receiving and giving to oneself. The community is bound together as a community by means of sharing food (communion). The ritual sharing of food and its physical incorporation function simultaneously as an act whereby the partaker is incorporated or 'eaten into' the community; eating together (com) the same bread (panis) transforms eaters into companions. The closeness of such companionship means that the community is thought of as being part of the self. In such communities the bodies of its members are open, as the community itself forms a buffer between what is regarded as being 'inside' and what is 'outside'. Inside the community is bound together through the exchange of gifts and the reciprocal obligation to respond to the gift.

The concept of **space** is more abstract than that of place, in that it refers to an area, a distance between two points or to a temporal expanse ('in the space of a week'). Abstract spaces such as city centres, transport systems, airspace, advertising space and to an extent cyberspace are not places for **living in** but are rather composed as spaces for **travelling through**. The abstract, calculated and impersonal look of such spaces is differentiated from the place of community to the extent that authors such as Marc Augé (1995) refer to them as 'non-places'. A central theme of what follows is that during the shift from feudalism to capitalism and continuing into the present, the **place** of traditional community has been progressively 'emptied out' or **disembedded** by the rational ordering of space. According to some authors this process began as early as the sixteenth century. For example McCracken (1990) notes that during the Elizabethan period (of the first 'consumer boom') England was substantially rebuilt to accommodate new ideas of privacy both within the home and beyond it, a trend which was to expand dramatically during the eighteenth century. Additionally the novel focus on purchase-for-self rather than purchase-for-family during the Elizabethan era opened a gap between the noble and the community which had previously formed his 'second skin'. The consumer boom of the eighteenth century and those which have followed in its wake have opened up the spaces of individuality and identity for progressively more and more people. The effects on perceptions of space–time of the rational organization of space are discussed in more detail below.

2.4 MAX WEBER: MODERNITY AS RATIONAL ORDERING OF SPACE

It is important in understanding Weber's contribution to our current understanding of what constitutes rationality that what we take for granted today as 'rational' is not natural but has developed historically. The period from the decline of feudalism to the beginnings of modernism has proved to be a rich feeding ground for academics who have sought to trace changes in the form of rationality in Western human conduct. David Harvey (1989) describes how the human capacity for rational abstract thought and the expectation that all humans are rational have developed slowly and unevenly throughout the ages. Abstract thought requires the ability to take a **perspective** with respect to one's own conduct and that of others. Harvey shows how this ability developed formally within Europe during Renaissance art, and later through the work of map-makers such as Mercator, who became renowned for his ability to render three-dimensional features in two-dimensional space during the sixteenth century. More recently the development of photography allowed individuals to develop a sense of perspective on their 'selves' through its ability to strip away form from substance. You will remember that Elias discusses this emergent rationality in relation to the development of court societies within Europe. The sociologist Max Weber, whose work is discussed in more detail in this chapter, treats the subject within the complementary context of Reformation religion from whence, he argues, there developed a specific **formal rationality** which was especially suited to the nascent economic system of capitalism. This is not to suggest that there was no space for rationality before this time. What interests Weber is the extent to which a particular form of rationality comes to pervade institutions, social action and people's expectations of one another. This formal organized and rule-based rationality includes the ability to distinguish means from ends and to formally specify these, to be able to calculate and specify in advance the likely benefits and costs of following one means as opposed to another and to devise some form of strategy for the attainment of ends as a result of that evaluation.

2.4.1   Calvinist rationality: the spirit of capitalism

Norbert Elias, whose work was summarized in Chapter 1, argued that the development of court societies involved a transition from medieval Catholic to a Protestant superego formation characterized by the internalization of fear and conflict. Here it is likely that Elias is referring to the work of Max Weber and in particular his book published in 1905, entitled *The Protestant Ethic and the Spirit of Capitalism*. In this work Weber discusses rationality in relation to the development of that 'sober bourgeois capitalism with its rational organization of free labour', characteristic of modern industrial capitalism. Weber's thesis is that the unique mix of factors which led to the development of capitalism in western Europe included first the technical utilization of scientific knowledge; secondly, the development of a rational system of law and administration based upon formal rules; finally and most importantly for Weber, the ability of people to adopt certain types of practical rational conduct. Weber then seeks to forge a link between the demands of modern industrial capitalism and ascetic Protestantism which, he argues, provides the economic spirit or ethos of capitalism.

Weber's text focuses upon Calvinism, a variant of Protestantism based on the fundamental tenet of predestination, the belief that one's ultimate fate (in heaven or in hell) is preordained by God and unchangeable by the efforts of humanity. Weber describes as 'extreme inhumanity' the inner isolation suffered by the Calvinist believer who 'is forced to follow his path alone to meet a destiny which had been decreed for him for eternity'. While other versions of Christianity allowed for some form of atonement or intercession by which the sinner could be redeemed, such 'magic' counted for nought within Calvinism. Calvinist doctrine promoted an impersonal individualism over communal fellow-feeling by warning against reliance upon others and by preaching a form of 'brotherly love' which was 'peculiarly objective and impersonal'. This may only be properly understood within the context of the Calvinist framework. Calvinists regarded themselves as being predestined to eternal glory. The sole role of the believer was to magnify the glory of God. Believers could prove their faith by viewing the objective results of their magnification of the glory of the Lord. In this way 'good works' and success in the material world could be regarded as proof of their belief (that they were indeed the chosen). Weber describes how, compared to most Christians of the time who lived a moral life which was pretty much 'hand to mouth', the Calvinist believer's life became viewed as a **project** involving systematic **self-control**. He contends that as a result, the life of the believer became rationalized; regulated and controlled in a manner which was reminiscent of the rule of the Christian monastic orders such as the Benedictines and Cistercians. The difference was that while these monks adopted a systematic method of ascetic rational control in seeking to free the spirit from worldly preoccupations, Calvinist asceticism was essentially of this world. Calvinists had to prove their worth in worldly activity. Weber argues that the central idea of Puritanism (Calvinism) was active self-control involved in the reining-in of the emotions:

'Contrary to many popular ideas, the end of this asceticism was to be able to lead an alert, intelligent life. The most urgent task was the destruction of spontaneous, impulsive enjoyment, the most important means was to bring order into the conduct of its adherents.'   [1930: 119]

If believers were to prove that they were in fact 'elected' they faced a maze of (self-imposed) sanctions and prohibitions. Anything which did not add to the greater glory of God was to be avoided, including 'idle' talk, over-sleeping, sexual activity not directly associated with procreation, inactive contemplation and the pursuit of sports other than those which provided the recreation necessary for physical efficiency. The glory was magnified only by a life of hard, continuous bodily or mental labour. The acquisition of wealth was regarded as a potential danger only insofar as it might encourage relaxation and idleness; used industriously and wisely, wealth could be counted as an instance of God's blessing. Puritans placed great store on the idea of the 'calling', a duty by which a person was called by God to live an industrious and productive life; to wish to be poor was to be unhealthy. The unequal distribution of goods was interpreted as a sign of the bestowal of God's favour.

Puritans were predominant among the rising classes during the Industrial and Agrarian Revolutions. They were counted among the *petit bourgeois* (as distinct from the administrative bourgeois class featured in Elias's discussion) and farmers. Once established in positions of power, the Puritans fought against the abuses of protectionism and monopoly which had been the lynchpin of the mercantile system. Instead they placed their faith on rational, individual acquisition which was guaranteed by law. Weber notes the resonance of the Puritan view with the ideas promulgated by the economist and social theorist Adam Smith, whose work is discussed in more detail in the next chapter. They shared a belief in what Smith has called the division of labour; the idea that the specialization of occupation leads to a qualitative and quantitative improvement in production, which serves the common good (which is identified with the utilitarian ideal of the greatest good for the greatest number). This culminated in the idea that the notion of the 'self-made man' amounted to the pinnacle of ethical achievement. Weber concludes his tale in describing the irony by which the widespread dissemination of Puritan values and their articulation with capitalist enterprise was coupled with the demise of the religious component. The Puritan rationality peculiar to Calvinism was best suited to the demands of the emergent capitalist system. As capitalism expanded so this form of rationality diffused throughout society and began to dominate its morality. However in the process of diffusion this rationality became stripped of its religious component. Weber illustrates this through his discussion of a Puritan thinker:

> 'In Baxter's view the care for external goods should only lie on the shoulders of the "saint" like a light cloak, which can be thrown aside at any moment. But fate decreed that cloak should be like the shell on a snail's back.'

Within the Puritan ethic, the only interest offered by goods was to magnify the glory of God. Overattachment to the material things of this world was a dangerous thing in that this opened the way to temptations of the flesh, perhaps even idolatory. Yet this seems to be what Weber is arguing for; in modern society the care of goods which in Puritan thought should be worn like a light cloak (because God is central) itself becomes central to human aspirations. The phrase above has been underlined because there is some dispute as to its precise meaning. Ritzer interprets this (following Talcott Parsons who translated the original text from the German) as meaning 'iron-cage'. Zygmunt Bauman (2000) argues that the meaning comes closer to 'steel-cloak'; whereas Barry Smart (1999) suggests that the idea of the shell on a snail's back is more acceptable. Why quibble over the precise meaning of such a short phrase? Because, as we shall see, this makes a lot of difference to how one interprets instrumental rationality: as something which comes from outside and is imposed upon us, or as much part of 'our' makeup (i.e. 'modern' consumers) as the shell on a snail's back (Sayer, 1991 in Smart, 1999).

2.4.1.1 *Homo consumans*: consumption as Puritan duty?

Weber may have established a link between Puritan rationality and the spirit which infused that 'sober' capitalism he was describing, but how could this possibly link with the cornucopia of delights offered by consumption? Jean Baudrillard disputes Weber's argument that this occurred because capitalism no longer needed religious asceticism since it rested on mechanical grounds. Baudrillard's alternative explanation suggests that, contrary to what people might think, the Puritan ethic is alive and well in the spirit of modern consumption which, he argues, has very little to do with pleasure. As we shall see in later chapters, Baudrillard argues that the primary motivation for modern consumption is the feeling of a lack of, or of a hole in, the self which has little to do with pleasure. In any event, he argues, the objective of consumption is not pleasure but duty:

> 'The puritans considered themselves, considered their actual being, to be an enterprise to make profit for the greater glory of God. Their "personal" qualities, and their "character", which they spent their lives producing, were capital to be invested wisely, and managed without speculation or waste. Conversely, yet in the same way, man-as-consumer considers the experience of pleasure an obligation, like an enterprise of pleasure and satisfaction; one is obliged to be happy, to be in love, to be adulating/adulated, seducing/seduced, participating, euphoric and dynamic.'   [Baudrillard, 1988: 48]

Baudrillard argues that the new ethics of consumption is equivalent to the traditional constraint of labour and production. Nowadays consumption is a duty; a person must seek to actualize all of his or her potential for consumption. What appears to be a 'fun' morality involves the complete exploitation of all the possibilities of being thrilled. Credit and debt are the means for disciplining consumers. While credit is presented under the guise of gratification, of freedom from thrift, it is a form of **rationalization** of consumers, a disciplinary process which extorts savings and regulates demand, just as wage-labour was a rational process in the extortion of labour power. Baudrillard argues that the rational and disciplinary ethics which, according to Weber, was at the origin of modern capitalist productivism has come to inhabit a whole domain which had previously escaped it; having socialized the masses into a labour force, the industrial system has had to socialize them (control them) into a force for consumption. To support this view he cites an example first described by J.K. Galbraith, whereby 'carefree Puerto Ricans' were transformed into a modern labour force as the result of being first tied to the consumption of commodities, which had to be paid for. In this view, production and consumption are two sides of the same process. Notions of the 'liberation of needs', of 'individual fulfillment', the themes of expenditure, pleasure and non-calculation, 'buy now pay later' have replaced the Puritan themes of thrift, hard work and parsimony. Baudrillard illustrates his argument in describing the various ways in which the idea of thrift has become regarded as being 'UnAmerican', an argument which you will remember was also advanced by Stuart Ewen, whose work is discussed in Chapter 1, in relation to the 'socialization' of immigrants into the USA. Both authors argue that the efficient industrial system needs people to be consumers for several reasons. One is to mop up constantly expanding production. Secondly, consumption is seen to be a powerful element in social control, by atomizing individual consumers. Yet it also requires the intensification of bureaucratic control over the processes of consumption, which is subsequently heralded as the realm of freedom.

Bureaucracy

For Weber the modern economic order is bound to the technical and economic conditions of machine production. In this view **rationalization**, together with its twin, **bureaucratization**, stand at the heart of the capitalist modernizing process. The rationalization of action 'refers to the substitution for the unthinking acceptance of ancient custom, of deliberate adaptations to situations in terms of self-interest' (Weber, 1947: 123). In a manner which may seem incongruous to us now, Weber was struck by the stability of the market system in the absence of such custom; the more strictly rational economic actors are, the more they tend to react similarly to the same situation. While the bureaucratic form had developed under the aegis of Catholic clerical organization, Weber recognized its compatibility with capitalist enterprise. He believed that the bureaucratic form was technically the most rational type which responded to the capitalist's need for stable, strict, intensive and calculable administration. Bureaucratic control meant fundamentally the exercise of control on the basis of knowledge:

> 'From a purely technical point of view, it is capable of attaining the highest degree of efficiency and the most rational known means of carrying out imperative control, in precision, stability, discipline and reliability. It makes possible a high degree of calculability of results for organization's heads; superior in intensive efficiency and scope of organization, of application to all administrative tasks.'
>
> [Weber, 1947: 337]

For Weber, bureaucracy was the most prominent expression of the institutionalization of formal rationality, a form of organization of rules and regulations which was considered to constitute an optimum means for realizing preordained ends. The large corporations represented for Weber a type of bureaucracy rivalled only by the state bureaucracy in promoting rational efficiency, continuity of operation, speed, precision and calculation of results. Weber likened bureaucratic rationality to the smooth, impartial, inexorable workings of a great machine; with all of the benefits and disadvantages of the machine process. While standardization, constancy of quality, predictability and control are advantages which might lubricate the cogs of the capitalist enterprise (generating 'satisfied' consumers), it did so at the price of expunging what was particularly human from its workings.

2.4.2.1 'Fordism'

Coined by Antonio Gramsci, 'Fordism' relates back to that day in 1914 when Henry Ford introduced his five-dollar, eight-hour day as payment for workers manning the new automated car-assembly plant at Dearborn. Ford's vision of mass production was shaped by his experience of the vast scale of organization in Chicago's slaughterhouses. Ford was acutely aware that it was not enough to manufacture the goods, the demand had to be there too. While being scarcely unique in terms of the adoption of standardized routines involving the mass production of homogeneous products, Ford came to stand out as the icon of or 'ideal-type' of the bureaucratic process, through the specialization associated with its assembly line operation, leading to repetitive and standardized work and the intensification, homogenization and deskilling of labour, under a strong hierarchical organization.

2.4.3   Ritzer's 'McDonaldization' thesis

George Ritzer's book *McDonaldization of Society* represents his interpretation of Weber as the model for a spirited attack on what he perceives to be the progressive rationalization of humanity by systems of modern bureaucratic control. Ritzer outlines familiar 'Weberian' themes related to bureaucracy; that it is the most **efficient** structure for handling the large numbers of tasks; that bureaucracies act in a highly **predictable** manner; that **calculability** or quantification is of extreme importance; that they exercise **control** over people through the replacement of human by non-human technology. Finally he contends that bureaucracy suffers from the **irrationality of rationality**. By this he means the manifold contradictory consequences which often flow from bureaucratic regulation, including the clogging of efficiency by 'red-tape', the production of the bland, the multiplication of the same, and above all these, dehumanization.

Ritzer is not a fan of rationality, especially of the rationalization process, which he believes is colonizing every aspect of modern life, such that now there is no way out. His book is a veritable catalogue of the horrors of 'McDonaldization', which he neatly parcels in terms of its effects of efficiency, calculability and predictability, with a sprinkling of the irrationality of rationality towards the end. Thus in a snapshot:

- For efficiency, examples include drive-in churches and 'McDoctors' who treat the surgery process as an assembly-line.
- For calculability, he offers as the exemplar the McDonald's hamburger which must weigh exactly 1.6 ounces, constitute 19 per cent or less fat, and be no more than 3.875 inches across, with a 3.5 inch bun.
- Predictability, or the effort to enable people to know what to expect at all times and in all places, is evidenced by the overbearing repetition of the same in the consumption. Vast boxlike out-of-town superstores, cars, suburban homes, franchise cafes and TV dinners share one thing in common – they all look the same and are virtually identical in every respect.
- Control is exemplified by the control of the production process, which is increasingly rationalized in the form of industrial processes of production or 'factory farming' applied to the intensive production of chickens, pigs, cattle, fish and an increasing range of livestock.

The irrationality of rational processes is illustrated by the inefficiency, unpredictability, incalculability and loss of control that wash back from the enforcement of such unreasonable and dehumanizing systems. The real experience of driving a car is that of standing on the tightrope of road-rage while snarled in smog; that of visiting a McDonald's, the long queue; the fact that to eat out is often more expensive, and ultimately less rewarding in 'human' terms than home-cooking. Towards the end of the book, Ritzer counsels how to combat the process, arguing that this can be achieved simply by going for the more 'homely', idiosyncratic and less efficient alternative; staying at the 'B&B', not the 'McDonaldized' hotel chain; preferring the local 'greasy spoon' to the franchise; enrolling at the small custom-universities which eschew custom-made majors and working part-time, feature on his list.

Ritzer conceives recreation as one of the few escape routes from the steady rationalization of life (at this point you might wish to look back at the Puritan perception of recreation as a point for comparison). However he believes that the process of rationalization is so insidious that over the years even the 'escape' routes offered by recreation have themselves become rationalized on the model of the fast-food chain:

> 'For those Americans who wish to escape to less rationalized European society, there is the package tour which rationalizes the process. People can efficiently see, in a rigidly controlled manner, many sights, while staying in conveyances, staying in hotels, and eating in fast-food restaurants that are predictably like those they are accustomed to at home. For those who wish to escape to the Caribbean, there are resorts such as Club Med that offer a large number of routinized activities and where one can stay in predictable settings without ever venturing into the unpredictability of native life on a Caribbean island. For those who want to flee back to nature within the United States, there are rationalized campgrounds where one can have little or no contact with the unpredictabilities of nature. One can even remain in one's camper and "enjoy" all of the rationalized forms of recreation available at home – TV, VCR, Nintendo, CD player. The examples are legion, but the point is that the escape routes from rationality have been rationalized.'
>
> [Ritzer, 1993: 23]

While Ritzer's argument is persuasive, it can be critiqued. For example, given that 'McDonaldization' is taken to be an inexorable process, how might it explain the irruption of countercultural forces such as punk rock, rave culture and animal rights activism which sprang from the grey 'McDonaldized' loins of suburbia? Such developments can hardly be accounted for by Ritzer's idea of 'resistance' which Parker (1997) acidly avers is akin to asking people to use a knife and fork rather than to eat with their fingers. The idea of 'McDonaldization' as a Fordist machine which swallows all that it encounters leads logically to the idea of the death of community. However, as we saw in the previous chapter, Maffesoli argues that the idea of 'community' is being reborn in the postmodern era as a new form of proxemics.

It is also difficult to know precisely whether Ritzer locates 'McDonaldization' as something which is purely external to the individual

DBS Arts Library

who resists it or whether this forms part of the person's identity. Through the course of his book he talks of this as if it is an external constraint on the human. This is reinforced through his use of Parson's original translation of the 'iron-cage' of modernity which surrounds the individual. Towards the end of the book Ritzer seems to come closer to the view that 'McDonaldization' is not purely external but is part of the makeup or fibre of modern identity. He suggests that 'McDonaldization' has become regarded as such a desirable process that it is entered into for its own sake, as individuals and members of institutions have come to value efficiency, calculability, predictability and control. However his argument stresses that the primary reason for this is externally motivated through the power of advertising. He suggests that people come to adopt such values simply because McDonald's and other companies spend vast sums of money in persuading us that choosing in favour of their offering is 'really' more rational, convenient and sensible than the alternative. However Ritzer is also aware that consumers are not merely passive dupes of corporate propaganda but may choose to lead 'McDonaldized' lives because of the practical exigencies of their existence. He is thus aware of the pressures imposed by changes in society, such as the demise of the nuclear family, the increase in dual-career households and increased time-pressure, as well as the role played by technology in facilitating McDonald's-style operations. While these massive changes in the context of consumption involving changes in the perceptions of space and time are mentioned by Ritzer, they are back-lit in order not to steal the show from the main act, which is 'McDonaldization'. Let us now quest further to explore the issue of the 'McDonaldization' of global space.

2.4.4 The global machine: rationalization of global space

To what extent could it be argued that we are witnessing the rationalization of global space? The authors of the UN Human Development Report argue (1999: 28) that the world has been changed immeasurably during the past decade through immense political, technological and economic change. They note an ideological shift towards the liberalization of trade, increased reliance upon the market and a diminishing role for the nation-state. Somewhat acerbically they note that, as a result, foreign direct investment poured into China, Vietnam, Poland and the Russian Federation 'as did McDonald's, Hollywood movies and CNN real-time global news' (1999: 28). The growth of global capital was truly unprecedented during the dying years of the last millennium. By then, US multinationals (MNCs) accounted for more than a quarter of US GDP, or $2 trillion. Multinationals are becoming even larger through the proliferation of takeovers and mergers (1999: 31/2). The revenues of giants such as General Motors ($164 billion) and Ford Motor Co. ($147 billion) are greater than the GDP of countries such as Thailand, Norway, Poland and South Africa, to name but a few. It should not be surprising if the process of rationalization described by Ritzer is occurring on a much grander scale.

2.4.4.1 Themed spaces

The rise of themed spaces, such as the mall, the theme park and the themed bar, has been such that several authors have written that this now forms the basis for understanding the society which lies outside these themed environments.

The planned shopping centre had humble beginnings before the Second World War. In 1950 there were fewer than 100 shopping centres in the USA; however forty years later there were nearly 35,000 offering a total of almost 235 km² (2.5 billion ft²) (see note ii). More recently the cultivation of bargain-hunting consumers has seen the progressive rationalization of space through 'boxification' (proliferation of box designs) of out-of-town sites by category killers such as 'Toys 'Я' Us', warehouse clubs such as Costco and deep discounters like Walmart. Through the creation of themed spaces, the mall seeks to go one better than reaching the bargain hunter, in offering to exchange the chore of shopping for the fantasy of fun (at a price). While not quite making it on the Internet, the 'malling' of the physical world has seen airports and railway stations transformed to such an extent that the facilitation of travel seems to have been relegated to an ancillary function. The mall is a nested collection of rationalized spaces. The overall theme and design of each zone has been calculated from the perspective of maximizing its returns. Nothing is accidental.

The themed world is constructed on the basis of the image of the real thing, as for example in the reconstruction of a mythical past, represented in the nostalgic ideal of Disney's 'Main Street'. Some argue that the image is now valued more than the 'real thing'. The worldwide spread of Irish 'theme' bars such as 'O'Neills' contrives an identity based on a stereotype of 'Irishness' suggesting that the pub is the centre of a welcoming Irish identity which blends music, conviviality and Guinness in an enticing mix. While this format is a novel caricature of most real Irish bars, the attraction has grown to the extent that when visiting Dublin some tourists have asked 'Are there any Irish bars here?' – a question which might be regarded as being nonsensical; however what they mean is 'Are there any Irish (theme) bars here?' For them, the deliberately contrived theme bar represents the 'real' Ireland. The implication is that people have come to prefer and even to confuse the theme situation (the hyper-reality) with the real thing (real Irish bars). And who can blame them. 'Real' Irish bars may often seem old, draughty, dingy and unwelcoming as opposed to their themed counterparts.

The model for all themed environments must be the multinational Disney Corporation. From being a successful producer of films, the construction of Disney World and EPCOT have provided models which have been copied around the world. Disney has now branched out from being a provider of entertainment via its film and theme-park businesses to enter the real world by building its new model town of Celebration in Florida. Celebration is a simulation, a town which is constructed on an image or model, in this case the 'wholesome' image of Disney itself. In Celebration there is no town government; Disney makes the rules. The company hands out booklets directing residents how to park their cars politely and specifies particular coloured shrubs for gardens. Behind the scenes, Disney has consolidated a lot of power. Florida's lawmakers have allowed Disney to build its own international airport and nuclear power plant, to run its own utilities, write its own building codes and levy taxes. The issue of themed spaces is developed in more detail in relation to the discussion of semiotics at the end of Chapter 5.

2.4.4.2 Surveillance

While themed spaces are designed specifically to facilitate the pleasurable experience of walking through, browsing and, above all, spending money, the people who walk through them are constantly on view. Remote surveillance is now the rule rather than the exception in the context of consumption. Surveillance now works at a number of levels. On one level video footage may be used for monitoring 'hot' and 'cold' spots within stores in order to try to increase the level of 'footfall' within the store, as well as for surveillance. At another level specialist research organizations offer their expertise to 'profile' a company database according to their internal analysis of consumer characteristics. In the UK these organizations will already have access to individual data which is in the public realm, such as Census data. Through their credit referencing systems they will also have information on Court judgements and can tell whether a person has been in default on a mobile phone or other bill. Add such data to a sophisticated in-house database, like those maintained by the larger retail chains, and it would not be unreasonable to suggest that the company would probably be able to tell you some things about your consumption behaviour that you yourself were unaware of. While this sort of surveillance is an example of the 'few' watching and recording the actions of the 'many', this situation is reversed in other contexts. For example mass media consumer affairs programmes and other 'fly-on-the-wall' documentaries about 'real-life' interaction allow the many to observe the detailed consumption behaviours of a few people. The differentiation of surveillance is a process which is happening simultaneously around the globe and above it, at the level of the satellites which encircle it.

2.4.4.3 Global brands

The most potent visible sign of the growth of global capital is the brand. Reputedly Coca-Cola sells roughly half of all global soft drinks and Gillette retains an even larger share of the global shaving market, while McDonald's has now opened more than 25,000 restaurants worldwide. As Table 2.1 shows, the world's biggest brands engage billions of dollars' worth of advertising space. But how many of these are truly global operations? For many of the companies shown in the table, the USA and/or western Europe constitute the principal focus of activity.

The true extent of the global power of these companies tends to be masked as they use different branding policies. For example Unilever, like many

Table 2.1   **Global brand power**

Company	Rank	1998/9 ad spend	Sample brands
Unilever	1	$3.7 bn ($3.1 bn)	Global brands: Lux, Dove, Organics and Magnum Others: Bertolli, Blue Band, Flora, I Can't Believe It's Not Butter!, Cornetto, Solero, Lipton, Calvé, Ragú, Bird's Eye, Gorton's, PG Tips, Chicken Tonight, Jif, Domestos, Omo, Ala, Snuggle, Persil, Rinso, Sun, Sunlight, Surf, Vim, Wisk, Axe and Lynx, Calvin Klein, Close-Up,
Nestlé	3	$1.9 bn	Nescafé, Crosse & Blackwell, Perrier, Spillers – major interest in L'Oréal
Coca-Cola	4	$1.5 bn ($1.2 bn)	Coke, Cherry Cola, Sprite, iced coffee
Ford Motor Co.	5	$2.4 bn ($1.2 bn)	BMW and Mazda – Jaguar, Aston-Martin, Lincoln, Mercury, Volvo cars
Mars	11	$1.1 bn ($793 m)	
Henkel	13	$700 m ($699 m)	Schwarzkopf & Henkel, Persil, Theramed, Loctite, Clorox, Manco
McDonald's	20	$1.2 bn ($592 m)	25,000 restaurants worldwide
Ferrero	21	$581 m ($559 m)	Mon Cheri and Ferrero Rocher, Nutella, Kinder Surprise chocolate eggs, Tic Tac mints
Benckiser	27	$491 m ($386 m)	Electrasol, Calgon and Finish, Coty (From 1999 Reckitt & Colman brands, Disprin, Lemsip, Harpic, Mr. Sheen, Dettol)
Kellogg's	28	$404 m ($302 m)	
Beiersdorf		$342 m ($324 m)	Nivea, Labello, Atrixo, Hansaplast medical dressings and Tesa adhesive tape
Mattel	38	$516 m ($272 m)	Barbie, Fisher-Price, Matchbox, Cabbage Patch Kids
Disney	40	$1.1 bn ($263 m)	Mickey Mouse etc.
Diageo	42	$917 m ($254 m)	Guinness, Baileys, Malibu, J&B, Burger King, Seagram (with Pernod Ricard)
British American Tobacco	45	$319 m ($235 m)	State Express 555, Dunhill, Rothmans, Benson & Hedges, Lucky Strike, Kent, Peter Stuyvesant, John Player Gold Leaf and Winfield.
Time Warner	47	$1.1 bn ($226 m)	CNN, Time Magazine, Bugs Bunny, Friends, ER
Bacardi	50	$227 m ($203 m)	
Sara Lee	56	$340 m ($183 m)	akery products, Douwe Egberts, Kiwi Shoe Polish, Brylcreem hair gel, Radox bath salts, Playtex, Dim and Wonderbra
American Express Service	95	$382 m ($83 m)	American Express Card & Travel

Source: Derived from Marketing Information Net Directory URL: http://www.mind-advertising.com and from company supplied data. Figures in brackets denote expenditure outside the USA.

other companies, employs an 'individual' brand policy, which effectively masks the relation between the brand and the company which stands behind it. However only a proportion of brands are marketed on a truly global basis. British American Tobacco (BAT) divides brands into three categories: international (Rothmans, Dunhill); regional (Belmont, Embassy); and national (HB, Jockey Club) brands. Unilever has changed its position with respect to global branding. Up until the end of 2000, the company tailored brands to the needs of different regions and countries, in addition to promoting their 'global' brands such as Lux, Dove, Organics and Magnum. At the end of that year however, they announced plans to dispose of 75 per cent of their 'regional' brands to focus on the global 'power' brands. However even where the same standard physical product is offered globally, the actual presentation of the brand offering may vary radically in terms of the target market and the marketing programme which is used to support the brand-position. Finally it remains the case that most trade takes place within countries and regions and that despite their apparently vast scale, particularly their colonization of space through advertising, the global brands still represent a comparatively small proportion of overall global expenditure on goods and services.

2.4.5 The production of consumption-related identities

Is there such a thing as a 'global' consumer? This question may be raised at a number of levels. The first level to be explored below is the extent to which the inclusion, exclusion, longing for and hatred of consumer society can provide resources for identity formation in a range of global contexts. The quite different question which relates to the homogenization of consumer identity is addressed in the next section. Figure 2.2 is based upon the idea of the **semiotic square** devised by Greimas. The idea behind this is that the meaning of a concept such as consumption is largely captured by what it is not. Starting at the top left-hand quadrant, the mainstream identity within consumer society is represented by the integrated consumer; consumers and tourists are included and integrated into consumer society, as they broadly believe that consumption is a good thing. Immediately below consumers are those consumers who feel disaffected from consumer society in some way. Such disaffection may take form in actions such as vegetarianism or road-protesting. To the right of consumers, oppositional groupings include reactionaries such as fundamentalists and revolutionaries. Diagonally opposite consumers, the bottom-right quadrant contains the underclass or 'quarte monde' in 'advanced' consumer societies and peasants in 'developing' societies, who together constitute four-fifths of the world's population which is excluded from the consumer feast and who currently remain largely reconciled to their fate. Finally we discuss three **liminal** identity positions. The word 'liminal' was used by V.W. Turner to describe those identities which are 'in-between', or in a state of transition. As we shall see, such liminal or transitional spaces open up a paradoxical space whereby the bearer is freed from

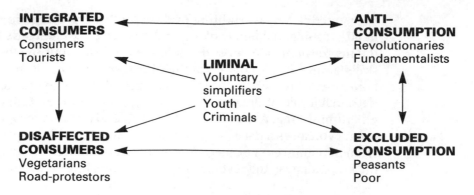

Figure 2.2 Consuming space as a resource for the construction of identity

one set of constraints but is in danger of being fixed by another set. The liminal identity positions discussed here include voluntary simplifiers, youth and criminals.

Note that Figure 2.2 has been designed more to form the basis for discussion rather than being posed as a model. The arrows are intended to illustrate the possibility for mobility between the identities specified.

2.4.5.1   Integrated consumers

The ideal of the integrated consumer is the engine that drives consumer society. The ultimate responsibility of the consumer is to sustain constant economic growth. The stereotypical face of the rationalized consumer which still peers out at us via a host of media, including marketing textbooks, is that of a woman. The story goes that since the division of labour which took place during the eighteenth century, men went to work while women stayed at home (a suburban 'box') where she nurtured her children and serviced the consumption needs of the household. The stereotype then unfolds that production is associated with the world of power and of men; consumption with the world of women; that marketers have traditionally treated the (female) consumer as being passive and stupid. The story then suggests that as gender boundaries have begun to blur in Western societies so consumption has changed its nature. The contemporary consumer is now seen to be active, competent and in control.

Like all stereotypes, there is a kernel of truth in this story. Many women are 'homemakers', live in suburbia and have been patronized for decades by advertisers. Recent research by Colin Campbell (1997) lends support to the view that women tend to enjoy shopping (well at least the less-boring non-supermarket variety), while most men hate it. However the story of the relations between marketers and women is much more complex than this. For example Ewen's (1976) account of the development of consumerism in the 1920s tells the story that, as US women began to enter the workforce, they were enticed to trade in their traditional forms of consumption which demanded heavy expenditure of their productive energy in making clothes, hand-washing, baking, cooking and cleaning, for the ready-made goods of the marketplace. However this story is not just about the loss of productive skills and of the resultant commodification of women. In chapter 5 of his book, Ewen also relates that this occurred at the same time as the traditional patriarchal role of the male, now a wage-slave in the productive apparatus, was diminishing. At this time industry and advertisers recognized the power of the woman as a decision maker in her own right. Ads appealed directly to women, who were not seen to be a mere appendage to her husband. In fact the situation was the reverse of this (see note iii). As Ewen says:

> 'Thus while women were cultivated as general purchasing managers for the household, the basic definition of men in the ads was as bread-winners, wage-earners. Man's role was divested of all social authority, except insofar as his wages underwrote family consumption.' [1976: 153]

It is not difficult to understand why in the USA of the 1920s advertisers cleverly associated the appeal of their modern new products with modern liberated women, for while both may have had quite different reasons, they had a common aim, the defeat of traditional values.

As opposed to many who are poor, consumers have a certain leeway or freedom of expression with respect to identity; consumer society itself offers an extensive palette of commodity identities. Consumers may become activated through a sense of moral concern or through boredom to play with more countercultural identities, perhaps through 'becoming' a part-time road-protestor or part-time anti-capitalist demonstrator. However the consumer lifestyle is anything but comfortable. Consumers are prey for criminals as is testified to by their embrace of loft-living and gated communities. The increasingly frenetic consumer lifestyle (discussed below) has led some to become voluntary simplifiers.

The **tourist** represents that aspect of the consumer when she or he is on the move, whether this is on business or holiday. Decreasing 'real' costs of air travel (which do not cover the real environmental costs) have led to a huge increase in the number of people visiting tourist destinations. According to the UK Office for National Statistics, overseas visits to the UK in the three months to July 1999 numbered 6.4 million, while the number of UK residents' visits abroad came to 13.6 million for the same period.

2.4.5.2 Disaffected consumers

Many consumers are disaffected with some aspect of the society in which they live. This means that they are unhappy with at least one aspect of consumption and as a consequence seek to reduce their own consumption and perhaps that of others, in some way. Some are unhappy with a particular aspect of this society and construct an identity around a particular issue, such as the exploitation of labour or animals; others feel more generally disaffected about the entire system of consumption. Let us consider the creation of issue-based identities first. While all vegetarians abstain from eating meat-products, a minority do so for animal welfare reasons. Because of its moral base, vegetarianism forms a key component of the identity for this latter group. Some vegetarians will confine their disaffection to their own consumption lifestyle – simply by maintaining a 'meat-free' lifestyle. Others may go further in joining a group such as the Vegetarian Society. Some may be drawn by association into related areas concerned with animal welfare, including anti-vivisection groups and the anti-fur lobby. At its most extreme, such disaffection may stray over the line from inclusion to exclusion, for example where a person joins a group such as the UK Animal Liberation Front, which has been proscribed by the government as a terrorist organization. Disaffected consumers may find solace in a range of identity-building activities, ranging from road-protesting to new-age spirituality. Alongside issue-based groups there are others which tend to engage in a more wholehearted rejection of values encapsulated in 'anti-capitalism' demonstrations. That these 'tribal' identities are more transient and fluid is perhaps unsurprising, given that youth constitutes a large proportion of the overall membership. Such groups often engage in forms of direct action, for example in seeking to restrict the development of new spaces for consumption by staging public occupations of sites for proposed new airports, supermarkets and motorways. While such forms of protest may seem to be a relatively new phenomenon, in Great Britain there is a long tradition of such protest (see McKay, 1996).

2.4.5.3 Anti-consumerism

While one could argue that disaffected consumers are to an extent anti-consumerist, there is a tendency which finds its purest form in the groups discussed here. The key defining characteristic from the groups discussed in this section is that those who are disaffected are also able to function 'normally' within consumer society, which they do not ultimately wish to destroy but to improve. The anti-consumerist groups occupy a variety of stances against what they perceive to be the dangers of consumerism (see note iv). Bauman argues that the **fundamentalist** identity is a specifically modern form as it arises as a reaction to the forces of modernism, including the extension of commodity culture. For fundamentalists, consumer society can seem to represent a whole range of insidious values, often based on stereotypical 'US' values: the levelling down of traditional culture, materialism, the spread of rampant individualism and consequent loss of community. While fundamentalists reach for the immutable values of religion, **revolutionaries** are future-oriented in seeking to transcend the capitalist order. The revolutionary identity is thus modern to the extent that its aims are in 'sympathy' with the modernizing process concerned with undoing and transcending the existing order. The Cuban Che Guevara is an exemplar of the classic revolutionary figure who sought to raise the consciousness of South American peasants to further the cause of communism and the overthrow of capitalism. As Manuel Castells (1997) notes, the composition of revolutionary groups is not at all clear cut. The Zapatista revolutionary movement which has had a large amount of success in the Chiapas region of Mexico was composed of at least two groups of people, of radical left-wing intellectuals who saw the revolution as the path to a better society, and of peasants who on the contrary wanted to gain entry to the consumer society.

2.4.5.4 Excluded identities

In the world where the consumer is king, one-fifth of the population is excluded because they are poor. The poor live a life of involuntary simplicity; they have no option but to be poor. The gap between the rich and poor is widening. At the millennium the 'top' fifth of countries controlled 86 per cent of world GNP, 82 per cent of world export markets, 68 per cent of foreign direct investment and 74 per cent of world telephone lines; the 'bottom' fifth of countries controlled just 1 per cent of each (UN Human Development Report, 1999: 3). Perhaps more startling is the knowledge that the world's 225 richest people have a combined wealth of over $1 trillion, which is equal to the annual income of the poorest 47 per cent of the world's poorest people (2.5 billion people) (UN Human Development Report, 1998: 30). Linda Alwitt (1996) notes that in addition to being economically disadvantaged, poor people are treated as outsiders or strangers within consumer societies, thus increasing their separation from the mainstream. For poor people the marketing exchange is usually unbalanced in favour of the marketer. As a result of this imbalance, not only do poor people have restricted access to the world of goods, they must pay more for goods and services in many marketing exchanges.

Poverty is a relative concept. For example in 1996, whereas 19 children per thousand born died before the age of five in Cyprus, the corresponding figure in Sierra Leone was 448 per thousand. In similar vein in 1995, 3 per cent of people in Cyprus and 50 per cent of those born in Sierra Leone could not expect to live to the age of forty. The same stark pattern is repeated across a range of indicators: adult literacy, underweight children, GDP per capita, sanitation, access to safe water and daily calorific supply. Even the poor in developed countries might seem to be well off given these comparisons. However this denies an essential aspect of poverty, which is its association with social exclusion. For example William J. Wilson (1987) was moved to write of a new phenomenon which he detected in US society, the underclass. Wilson described the underclass in terms of six characteristics:

> 'residence in a space isolated from other social classes; long-term joblessness; consequentially, female headed households; absence of training and skills; long spells of poverty and welfare dependency; and a tendency to engage in street crime.'
> [Lash and Urry, 1994: 148]

According to Wilson, the underclass was created as the result of the departure of working-class and middle-class families from urban inner-city areas in the USA. During the course of the 1980s and 1990s poverty progressively shifted to the young as the result of government policy changes and the deterioration of the labour market. Linked to this was a huge rise in female-headed families living in bereft inner-city areas which Lash and Urry (1994) call impacted ghettoes.

Regardless of where they live, the poor tend to have shorter lives than others. The past century has seen a massive increase in life expectancy for men and women born in developed countries. Life expectancy in England and Wales increased from 52 years for men, and 55 years for women in 1910, to 74 years and 79 years respectively in 1994. Over the same period, infant mortality fell from 105 per thousand to 6 per thousand. However this progress masks a considerable variation which is due to social classification. For example inequalities in health in the UK are standardized according to the SMR, or Standard Mortality Ratio. SMRs below 100 indicate lower than average mortality whereas a high SMR, for example 200, would indicate twice as many observed deaths as expected. According to this criterion those in Social Class V (the poorest) have mortality rates well in excess of other social groups for deaths by stroke, ischaemic heart disease, lung cancer, accidental death and suicide, and have the rate of one and a half times the SMR of the nearest class (see note v). In all there is a difference of five years in life expectancy between men in Social Classes I/II and IV/V. While class inequality decreased in the 1920s, it increased again in the 1960s and by the 1970s it was greater than it had been in the early part of the century. The Black research group, which was set up in 1977 to investigate this lack of progress, concluded that social inequalities in health could be blamed in the main on socio-economic factors.

The picture is equally bleak with respect to mental health. For both depressive episodes in men and obsessive–compulsive disorders in women, individuals in Social Class V are much more likely to report symptoms than those in other social classes (see note vi). Those in Social Class V are also prone to higher blood pressure which is a risk factor for several major diseases including coronary heart disease and stroke.

There are also clear indications of social class effects with respect to consumption. According to the National Food Survey (1995) consumption of fats and sugars increases with decreasing income; with income group E1, households without an earner with an income of over £140 per week, consume on average 300 grams of fat per day, nearly twice that consumed by income group A. Fruit consumption decreases with decreasing income. Income group D, households with one or more earners and income of less than £140 per week, consume an average of 65 per cent less fruit than income group A (see note vii). As we shall discuss in Chapter 10, those in lower socio-economic groups are also more likely to smoke cigarettes.

Over the ages the poor have sought to advance their position through forming alliances with disaffected intellectuals and revolutionaries. The irony is that while revolutionaries are motivated by a desire to destroy the 'system' in order to transcend it, the poor simply want to gain admission to it. In the UK, groups such as Telco, Impact and Citizens are connected through a national network to the Community Organising Foundation

(COF), which, according to some reports, has drawn more than 100,000 people into direct action so far (see note viii). Actions include hundreds of group members joining a Building Society to persuade it to give 1 per cent of its pre-tax profits to local homeless people, direct action to persuade large employers to take on local labour, targeting of polluting factories and bad service supermarkets, and a campaign to urge banks to reopen branches in poor and isolated areas.

2.4.5.5   Liminal identities

Liminal identities are in a state of transition 'betwixt and between' other identities. To this extent there is a sense of flow and freedom associated with the identities of youth, voluntary simplifiers and criminals. On the other hand such identities are often transient; youth grows older and becomes more set in its way, simplifiers are often relegated to the ranks of the poor, and criminals are often caught (or so the government tell us).

The **voluntary simplicity** lifestyle, which has been described by a number of authors, most notably by Elgin (1993), adopts goals of moral behaviour, spiritual growth and self-actualization, with emphasis placed on ecological responsibility and self-sufficiency. Voluntary simplifiers often start out as well-positioned 'integrated' consumers whose frenetic lifestyle leads them to re-evaluate their position and ultimately to make the decision to live a frugal life in order to liberate themselves from what Schor calls the 'squirrel-wheel' of work-spend, to free themselves of the clutter of too many possessions and to live a 'frugal' life in order to get close to nature. In comparison with the voluntary simplifier, the life of the consumer is either involuntarily or voluntarily complex, in that he or she actively enjoys or perhaps stoically endures the complexities of managing life in contemporary consumer society. Rudmin and Kilbourne (1996) have written an insightful piece on the paradoxical position of voluntary simplifiers. The risk, and indeed the likelihood for the integrated consumer who seeks to become a voluntary simplifier is that they become 'involuntary simplifiers' and join the ranks of the poor who have no choice but to be poor. The position of voluntary simplicity is thus perched on the edge between the 'haves' and the 'have-nots'. Rudmin and Kilbourne note that consequently the voluntary simplicity lifestyle may appear to have a false or ersatz quality to it; to the poor, these may appear to be rich people who are merely playing at poverty; to their ex-colleagues in business or journalism, they may seem to be foolish, even crazy.

Youth is another group which is 'betwixt and between' categories, caught between the certainties and dependence of childhood and the anxieties and responsibilities of adulthood. Since 'teenagers' came on the scene in the 1930s (Danesi, 1994), youth movements have not simply comprised a target for the creation of commodity identities; emergent youth styles, particularly countercultural styles, have been raided by marketers and recycled into mainstream fashion. Youth is not of course a simple category but is composed of many different streams. Nevertheless one could assert that youth tends to play an ambivalent role in relation to consumer society and consumption. On the one hand it rejects those objects which are seen to represent those aspects of the cultural mainstream against which it differentiates itself. On the other hand youth uses objects as vehicles to craft its own identity. For example working-class youth styles of the 1950s included 'Teddy Boys' whose style involved velvet 'drape' suits with skintight trousers, custom shirts with shoestring ties and 'winkle picker' shoes. The investment which a 'Teddy Boy' made in constructing this style could not be taken lightly; together these could amount to several months' wages. Like the Teds, other youth lifestyle movements have actively embraced commodity identities. For example the ownership of a Piaggio or Lambretta scooter was central to the style of the UK 'mod' scene of the 1960s; but this extended to many other forms of commodity-based consumption. Other groups such as the 'beats' (1950s), 'hippies' (1960s) and 'punk' tended to reject consumerist values. In the early 1990s UK Rave culture started spontaneously with groups such as the *Exodus* collective initiating informal open-air parties. As one member recalls, 150 people turned up on the first night, 1000 on the third night and soon after crowds of over 10,000 would join in an all-night experience (see note ix). Such open-air raves soon moved into huge edge-of-town warehouses, leading to the growth of 'house' parties that incorporated massive 'stacks', a wall of speakers 12 feet high and 30 feet across, free access to water and 'E' (the 'house' drug, of which an estimated one million tablets were consumed per week) (see note x). Early spontaneous raves were organized on the basis of a 'gift' community. They were 'free', organized either by local collectives or by 'travellers' who arranged somewhat arbitrary 'bucket' collections, the proceeds of which were used to buy bigger 'stacks' and for other projects which were regarded as being 'worthwhile'. The folklore of this movement recalls the growing commercialization of raves.

The story of hip-hop band Run-DMC exemplifies the ambivalence of the position of US black youth. In the early 1980s, hip-hop, which had started in the 1970s as the expression of poor and working-class black youth in the South Bronx, relocated to middle-class Queens. Run-DMC was the standard bearer for this second wave of hip-hop, maintaining the music's minimalist 'street' sound but writing its own music (most, though not all, of the first wave's tunes were lifted from popular songs of the day), and raising the standard for complex wordplay in lyrics delivered at high speed, internal rhymes and puns all over the place. 'Raising Hell', which came out in 1986, was a massive crossover hit, the commercial breakthrough which cemented their success. One reviewer of the album said 'There is some real good stuff on here, although the socially-conscious numbers ('Proud To Be Black') are soft-pedalled in favour of harmless humour ('You Be Illin'), corporate endorsements ('My Adidas') and misogyny ('Dumb Girl'). As the result of their 'Adidas' rap, Run-DMC projected the brand into the stratosphere.

Criminals are described as being a liminal group because they potentially stride the barriers which lie 'betwixt and between' several worlds: the world of crime and the straight world which the criminal despises; the world of poverty and that of affluence; the free world 'outside' and that of prison

DBS Arts Library

'inside'. Criminal proceeds account for a huge proportion of global trade. Take illegal drugs. By the millennium, the total value of the illegal drug trade was estimated to be $400 billion, constituting 8 per cent of world trade. It is estimated that there are now 200 million drug users around the world (Human Development Report, 1999: 41). Many crimes, and in particular those connected with consumption, are not committed by hardened criminals. Cecilia Fredriksson describes instances of criminality within the Swedish department store EPA. During the depression of the 1930s, EPA formed a shelter for the unemployed who availed themselves of its warmth and cheap coffee. EPA was the first chain of stores where everyone was allowed to visit and could stroll freely around without being asked if they required assistance. The self-service system avoided this form of control. While it offered a new sense of space and freedom inside the store, it was also easy to disappear into the crowd and to slip something into your bag or pocket.

Shoplifting comprised one-third of goods stolen, with the remainder taken during delivery or by staff. Fredriksson found it difficult to compile accurate data for shoplifting as staff often chose not to report young people and old people. In the early nineteenth century, shoplifting was described as a form of loss of control embodied in 'kleptomania', an urban sickness that afflicted people who were not in control of their senses. The explanation for this behaviour was that the variety of goods on display in the new department stores was too much for some people. The typical kleptomaniac was a middle-class woman. It has since been argued that the medicalization of such theft provided a convenient means for explaining an otherwise illogical and unacceptable threat to moral values: the idea that middle-class women, 'pillars of society', could also be common criminals. Towards the end of the nineteenth century, the explanation for shoplifting changed. Now it was considered that the milieu of the store exposed customers to temptation, creating a new acquisitiveness. Such people could be distinguished from another, arguably more dangerous shoplifter, the 'shop-rat'. Shop-rats used the crowd and clutter of the department store to steal from other customers. However the most common form of shoplifter, but one that was rarely brought to the attention of the police, were young children, and in particular young boys who engaged in this activity as a form of 'dare'.

2.4.6 Globalization of identity

From the above it can be seen that consumption provides resources for the construction of a diverse range of identities. This thus provides some limited support to the contention made by Fukuyama (1992) who argues that in the era of the global triumph of capitalism, consumer goods begin to play a key role in satisfying the human desire for recognition. It is thus fair to say that consumerism is at least a global aspiration and if consumers around the world progressively become more affluent so they will have further means for realizing this. This in turn should provide a rallying point for those who wish to oppose consumption or to reduce its effects. To this extent one might conditionally agree with the contention that identity has been rationalized in the modern age. This gives rise to two other important questions:

- Is the diversity of global values and cultures being levelled down and homogenized by a bland, uniform Western culture?
- Can consumer culture be said to substitute economic individualism for the ties of the local community?

These questions are discussed in the next two sub-sections.

2.4.6.1   Globalization as Coca-colonization

Often referred to as 'Coca-colonization' this argument, which is usually pejorative, insinuates that globalization is in fact 'Americanization'. Put somewhat crudely, this suggests that the USA is an 'advanced' consumer culture which through the massive propagation of its bland, individualist, consumerist values, overwhelms the cultural and communitarian bonds of traditional societies, converting them into mini-versions of itself.

We have already discussed the domination of global markets by 'northern' brands and of global communications by 'northern' media. But does this lead to the homogenization of values? Take the example of Coca-Cola. According to Levitt, a key aspect of Coke identity is that it should look the same and taste the same no matter where you are. One might therefore conclude that Coke is proof for the existence of the global consumer. In discussing this question Joy and Wallendorf argue (1996: 132) that although it is true that Coke is consumed in a number of 'developing' nations, we do not know the myriad of meanings it assumes in these varied contexts. In his study of Trinidadian identity, Daniel Miller found that Trinidadians identify Coke with 'blackness' and its chief competitor, Red Cola (which is produced by Indians), with 'redness'. Thus within Trinidadian culture cola has become a vehicle for signifying identity (who you are) to others. This is not to suggest that black people drink only Coke and Indians drink only Red Cola. Many Indians like to drink Coke in order to identify with the values associated with it, while many blacks drink Red Cola. What are the implications of Miller's study for the understanding of globalization? The globalization argument suggests that global brands carry with them the values of their country of origin. In this case the argument would be that, in drinking Coke, Trinidadians would be literally swallowing US culture. Miller found that this is not the case and that the 'global' brand Coke was incorporated into the construction of Trinidadian identity in a unique way which reflected the customs and signifying practices of those living in the island. So, the same global brand or signifier, 'Coke', is decoded differently and can signify different things, according to the code which is used to decode its meaning, and the point of view of the receiver.

In any case it would be disingenuous to imply that globalization is all one way. Salsa music, Thai cuisine and many other traditions have spread globally, and more nations are becoming multi-ethnic. Having said all of that, the term 'Coca-colonization' was never intended to describe a process of progressive homogenization but rather one of alienation. The term was reputedly coined by Jean Ki-Zerbo, an anthropologist from Upper Volta, in his address on behalf of African developing countries to a conference held at the Sorbonne (Cinquin, 1987). In his address Ki-Zerbo was most critical of the manner by which villagers found themselves swamped by 'implements made of plastic and provided by the dominant economy'. The point made by Ki-Zerbo was that the people could not recognize themselves (their work or value) in things which they had not produced themselves. This point is also made by Daniel Miller who argues that the idea that consumer culture is inherently 'Western'

'is probably as insidious as the relative inequalities in wealth in sundering people from the goods in which they increasingly live.'   [1996: 157]

Miller argues that this representation creates severe difficulties for those peoples who are characterized as peripheral. Furthermore his research in Trinidad revealed that the main difficulty experienced by people with respect to consumer goods was not their inability to purchase them, but their inability to respect either their own local production or local consumption. For example he offers the following explanation for one Trinidadian's obsession with blue jeans – he had 25 pairs in all:

'It became clear that underlying this obsessive purchasing was the sense that although he could buy them, he could never feel a sense of possession. As long as commodities are seen as authentically American, his wearing of them seemed inauthentic.'

2.4.6.2   Individualization: destruction of community?

Another claim is that global commodity culture individualizes culture and destroys bonds of community. This is an important point which forms a key theme in this text. For example Elias's central argument is about the individualization of what he calls 'self-steering' mechanisms, which arose as the consequence of the development towards a 'court-society'. However the development of a commodity culture plays a peripheral role in Elias's explanation. You may also remember that while the European Values Survey confirms that economic individualism increased in most countries in Europe during the 1980s, this individualism did not permeate through all modes of behaviour. As we shall see in Chapter 7, which discusses the consuming body, Pasi Falk (1994) argues that the decline in the ritual family meal and the rise of snacking is a key determinant in loosing the bonds of community. While Daniel Miller argues that capitalism seems to thrive well in collectivist cultures without prejudicing their collective nature, Falk argues that there is in fact an inexorable drift towards individualization. In arguing for the existence of neo-tribes, Maffesoli is also arguing that a quite different, less articulated and differentiated form of community is emerging. At present the issue is still open to debate. Some might argue that the 'one-child' policy in

China has resulted in a form of individualization in a formerly collective culture. This policy resulted in female infanticide to the extent that in 1992 it was estimated there were 20 million fewer women than men. As a result China's 'Little (male) Emperors' stand at the centre of attention for their grandparents and parents. It is estimated that in China in 1996 there were 250 million young men aged between 5 and 14 years old and following from the lack of women in society it is anticipated that these will be lonely young men, with high expectations (see note xi). However the creation of the 'Little Emperors', though complex, can be explained more by recourse to 'culturally pragmatic' responses to shifts in government policy in order to curb future overconsumption, than to the advent of consumerism.

2.4.7　Discussion

This look at modernism through the theoretical lens outlined by Max Weber has emphasized the progressive rationalization of space in modernity. Authors have argued that this has occurred through a focus on efficiency, predictability, calculability and control. Neologisms such as 'McDonaldization' and 'Coca-colonization' were discussed in relation to the rationalization and globalization of consuming spaces. This suggests that through processes of rationalization everything comes to resemble everything else, so that ultimately all that is magical and uniquely expressive of a way of life is lost. As we have seen, it is not difficult to prove that consumer society has had a major effect on the organization of space; from the proliferation of monotonous strip-developments which seem to be inevitably populated by the 'McCompanies' of the world, to the spread of global brands. However the discussion of globalization indicated that just because everything begins to look the same does not necessarily lead to the conclusion that there is a homogenized global culture. This is because the same goods can signify different things to people in different cultures. Martin Parker (1997), among others, is concerned at the apparent cultural elitism of this critique which pours scorn on establishments such as Disney and McDonald's which are taken to be emblematic of the popular. He notes that the critique seems to miss the point that most people value and enjoy the standards and levels of service provided by them and goes on to argue that at base level the critique may seem to boil down to little more than a crude form of anti-Americanism. As we have pointed out here, the traffic in globalization is not all one-way as national foods, dance-cultures and music become transformed into the international arena.

One might argue that as a consequence of rationalization, time and space have themselves become separated from one another. How has this happened? Anthony Giddens argues that in premodern settings, time and space were connected through the situatedness of place. The **separation of time from space** involved the creation of an abstract or empty dimension of time. This was achieved through the invention of the mechanical clock with its neat divisions into hours and minutes. In modern life we take it for granted that the measurement of time by clocks is standardized around the world and that this makes possible the complex international transport and communications systems on which our lives depend. However it was not until a conference convened in Washington in 1884 that agreement was reached on partitioning the world into twenty-four time zones, each one hour apart. Combined with the universal dating system this means that our experience of space and time is quite different from that of those premodern societies where, depending on the place where one lived, the perception of time was related to local custom, which was in turn influenced by the rhythms of the seasons and the available hours of daylight.

For Giddens the global modern map performs a similar role to that of the mechanical clock in that it 'empties out' space. By this he means that it reproduces the place of community, where time and place are sewn together as a place for living in. The global map replaces this with abstract gridlines structured by an abstract 'view from nowhere', which fashions a place which is conducive to those strangers who wish to travel through it (tourists) as opposed to those who live in it (community).

So the world in which we live is rationalized from top to bottom, inside and out. But does that lead us to assume that as a result this is a world where everything is the same, where all is homogenized and subject to rational control, which as a result is more likely to be stable and boring rather than being turbulent? The answer (which is 'no') is discussed in more detail below.

2.5   KARL MARX: MELTING MODERNITY

So far, the modernizing process has been discussed with respect to the process of rationalization. Here we discuss a radically different view which insists that modernity is best characterized by the idea of 'creative destruction', of constant change and flux. The geographer David Harvey says that modernism 'takes as one of its missions the production of new meanings for space and time in a world of ephemerality and fragmentation' (1989: 216). Harvey's position is based on that of Karl Marx, whose work is discussed here.

Against the 'Weberian' notion of 'administered man', Karl Marx argues that the spirit of capitalist modernization is better conceived of as involving struggle, contradiction and change. In this 'McDonaldized' age, characteristic of the 'one-liner', we should not be too surprised to note that, of all his vast output, Marx should become known for the simple phrase 'all that is solid melts into air'. Yet this phrase encapsulates a great deal of the force of Marx's arguments about capitalist modernization. Like Max Weber, Marx was keen to explore the dynamics of modern bourgeois society. The above quote comes at the high-point of a discussion of modern bourgeois society. Marshal Berman provides an admirable summary of Marx's explanation for this:

'First of all, there is the emergence of a world market. As it spreads, it absorbs and destroys whatever local and regional markets it touches. Production and consumption – and human needs – become increasingly international and cosmopolitan. The scope of human desires and demands is enlarged far beyond the capacities of local industries, which subsequently collapse. The scale of communications becomes worldwide, and technologically sophisticated mass media emerge. Capital is concentrated increasingly in a few hands. Independent peasants and artisans cannot compete with capitalist mass production, and they are forced to leave the land and to close their workshops. Production is increasingly centralized and rationalized in highly automated factories. (It is no different in the country where farms become 'factories in the field', and the peasants who do not leave the countryside are transformed into agricultural proletarians.) Vast numbers of the uprooted poor pour into cities, which grow almost magically – and cataclysmically – overnight. In order for these changes to go on with relative smoothness, some legal, fiscal and administrative centralization must take place; and it does take place wherever capitalism goes. National states arise and accumulate great power, although that power is greatly undermined by capital's international scope. Meanwhile industrial workers gradually awaken to some sort of class consciousness and activate themselves against the acute misery and chronic oppression in which they live.'   [1982: 91]

Berman notes how, as we read this, we find ourselves on familiar ground, as these processes are still at work in the world a century after Marx wrote about them. Two factors are at the heart of his concern; first, the **annihilation of space through time**, which relates to the perpetual upheaval and renewal in the entire fabric of personal and social life; secondly, the **fetishism of commodities**, whereby under industrial capitalism the market appears to stand aloof from society like a great god.

2.5.1   Marx and the fetishism of commodities

We have already described how global culture is now, at least in part, a commodity culture. As we shall see in the next chapter which discusses consuming power, liberal discourse argues for the extension of the 'freedom' of the marketplace to all. The identity conferred upon the consumer is similar to that of the citizen with the exception that the consumers' 'votes' are numbered by their relative resources. No matter, every consumer receives equal protection under the law. The central idea behind the fetishism of commodities is that this seemingly egalitarian system which works for the greatest good of the greatest number, masks gross inequalities and inequities, particularly in the area of production.

The ways in which consumer goods are advertised or presented for sale lead to a focus on their present state. Consumers rarely learn, nor usually do they enquire, about the origins of the goods which they have bought, what these goods contain and what will happen to them when they are discarded. Such thoughts are conveniently pushed aside in the advertising or the shopping context. The only other ways in which we might learn about the otherwise hidden spaces of production and disposal are via the fairly predictable format of the television or newspaper exposé featuring the exploitation of some distant workforce or the illegal or dangerous dumping of toxic wastes. A central aspect of Marx's notion of the fetishism of commodities is that when presented in the marketplace, commodities hide the real social relations objectified in them through human labour. Commodities reveal and conceal: they reveal their capacity to be satisfiers and, at the same time, they draw a veil over their origins. Sut Jhally (1990) provides a list of the means by which commodities conceal their origins. Jhally argues that all of the following constituents of the meaning of products are systematically hidden:

- the process of planning and designing products;
- the actual relations of production that operate in particular factories around the world;
- the conditions of work in factories;
- the level of wages and benefits of workers;
- whether labour is unionized or non-unionized;
- quality checks and the level of automation;
- the treatment of 'sensient' inputs to the production process (animals);[1]
- market research on consumers;
- the effect on the environment of producing goods through particular industrial processes;
- the renewable or non-renewable nature of raw materials used;
- the relations of production that prevail in the extraction of raw materials around the world.

While one might think that issues concerned with planning and design are relatively innocuous, the UN argues that tighter control of innovation in the hands of multinational corporations ignores the needs of millions. For example it argues that the needs for cosmetic drugs and slow-ripening tomatoes are regarded by biotechnology companies as constituting more pressing priorities than the development of a vaccine against malaria or drought-resistant crops for marginal lands (UN Human Development Report, 1999: 68). With respect to the production context, media exposés of the exploitation of workers by manufacturers supplying Walmart, Levi's and The Gap are commonplace, as are their attempts to rehabilitate themselves through the development of ethical codes linked to extensive publicity campaigns. Few consumers of chocolate know that slave labour is still widely employed in the harvesting of cocoa beans. Despite current concerns over food-safety and animal welfare, it is difficult if not impossible to gain access to intensive facilities which rear animals for mass slaughter. Since the Second World War the United Kingdom has adopted a policy of providing cheap food to the population, which has generally been successful. However many question the 'McDonaldized' factory farm system which treats sentient animals as if they were nothing more than units of production.

Even though market research data, particularly that which can be used for 'one-to-one' marketing, is the holy grail of the direct marketing industry,

---

[1] This is additional to the list provided by Jhally.

firms are coy when it comes to informing consumers as to the vast amount of information which they hold, not only on every aspect of their purchasing behaviour, but also on other aspects which may be regarded as 'safely' personal and private.

Waste disposal is now a major issue for all consumer societies. For example a difficulty associated with the disposal of non-ferrous metals is that the 'recycling' process itself, although highly profitable, also constitutes a major hazard to the local environment and to health. The recycling of copper from cable requires that the insulation, which contains deadly dioxins, is burnt off. In the past, Western computer companies exported everything from PCBs to asbestos overseas for reprocessing. When overseas governments tried to counter this trade, Western governments insisted that this went ahead as part of 'free trade'. It is not surprising that Western governments are loath to deal with this waste at home. According to Greenpeace, the incineration process itself generates all sorts of new poisons, some of which end up in landfill sites. The largest dump in the USA, which is operated by Waste Management, opened in 1978. At that time it was said that the dump would not leak for one hundred years. It did so in six (see note xii).

2.5.2   The annihilation of space through time

This refers to the requirement of the market system for constant growth, resulting in massive flux and change. This need for constant revolution in material and social affairs eventually reaches such a pitch that capital eventually gathers up all of these forces into a maelstrom where 'all that is solid' – firms, communities and industries, together with all of human worth and value – 'melt into air'. The geographer David Harvey draws upon Marx's observation that one of the most salient features of the capitalist system is that of the **annihilation of space through time**. This refers to the progressive conquest by capital of space, the tearing down of spatial barriers. This occurs as the result of the drive by capital to organize space in such a way as to facilitate the growth of production, the reproduction of labour power and the maximization of profit.

According to Thomas Friedman (1999), free-market capitalism is the driving force behind globalization. Friedman argues that the current wave of globalization is quite different from its predecessors. This is for the following reasons. First it has its own defining technologies (digitalization, satellite communications, fibre optics) which have effectively shrunk space to the level of the 'global village' presaged by Marshall McLuhan in the 1960s. The key defining aspect of such technology is speed. Attached to this new technology is the 'electronic herd', that free-floating group of Internet investors who lurk on the fringes of Wall Street, London, Hong Kong and Frankfurt, who, acting individually but in concert, have the ability to speedily wreak havoc with economies and communities anywhere in the world. Evidence of the growing power of the electronic herd is not hard to find. The gentle rumble of hooves into the Pacific Rim area in the late 1990s was followed by a mad stampede to get out. As a result, massive currency flows hit Thailand, Indonesia, Korea, Malaysia and the Philippines with the force of a financial typhoon resulting in the loss within weeks of $105 billion, or 11 per cent of the GDPs of these countries, with knock-on effects for bankruptcy, rising unemployment and poverty, reduced schooling and public services and increases in suicide, domestic violence and street crime (UN Human Development Report, 1999: 40). More recently, the herd pushed up the value of technology stocks to unrealizable heights. The authors of the UN report note that while social problems are increased, the provision of caring labour, which is not counted as 'productive' labour by capital, is squeezed out.

2.5.3 Globalization of insecurity and risk

Table 2.2 illustrates the range and complexity of linked global insecurities, which range across the spectrum from the economic to the social and personal. Today, 'all that is solid', which once seemed so secure, can vanish in an instant with hardly a trace that it was ever there. Growing ties of trade and interdependence of ties between nations provide disease with a free ticket to ride to every point of the globe. Ulrich Beck argues that this has partially contributed to the global spread of risks and the creation of the risk society, which is illustrated further in Chapter 3 under the discussion of global hazards.

Volatility is experienced at the level of the firm which is driven constantly to outdo itself in bringing new products to market faster and cheaper than the competition. This leads to a constant drive for cheaper and faster means of production (Figure 2.3). The focus on progress is tied to a future orientation, to the idea of becoming rather than on being. Within this perspective, time takes on the character of an arrow, and the individual and the organization alike are oriented primarily towards the future.

Material commodity exchange entails some form of movement between locations. Overcoming these spatial barriers takes time and money. For example a firm based in Scotland which supplies shirts to a retailer in London pays more for transport costs but possibly less in wages than a supplier which is based in London itself, where labour costs more. Overcoming these spatial barriers costs time and money; the firm based in Scotland must pay for the cost of transport of goods to London and the transport takes time to get there. The efficiency of spatial organization and transport systems is therefore an important issue for all firms. Harvey has coined a concept which he calls the **turnover time of capital** to refer to the time of production together with the time of circulation in exchange. The faster that capital which is launched into circulation can be recovered, the greater the profit will be. According to Harvey there is a universal incentive for individual firms to accelerate their turnover time with respect to the average for their industry, an activity which all firms engage in and which promotes a trend towards faster average turnover times. In pursuit of this objective, individual firms make continuous efforts to shorten turnover times.

Table 2.2   **The global economy: growing disparity and flux**

Widening gap between rich and poor	• 'In 1960 the 20% of the world's people in the richest countries had 30 times the income of the poorest 20%; 1997, 74 times as much. This continues a trend of two centuries' • The assets of the world's three richest people are greater than the combined GNP of all the least developed countries • The assets of the 200 richest people are more than the combined income of 41% of the world's people (UN Human Development Report, 1999: 36/8) • Increasing disparity between rich and poor within OECD countries and in eastern Europe and the CIS countries
Economic insecurity Financial volatility	• Asian financial crisis • NASDAQ dive • 'Financial volatility is a permanent feature of today's globally integrated financial markets'
Job and income insecurity	• UK textile industry experiences massive domestic job losses and relocation to Indonesia, Taiwan, Sri Lanka and Bangladesh • Labour 'reforms' in Latin America mean that between 30% and 40% of workers have no contract (UN Human Development Report, 1999: 37) • Corporate restructuring
Health insecurity	• HIV/AIDS • Drug-resistant bacteria
Environmental insecurity	• Fresh water availability and forest coverage are 60% of 1970 levels • Chronic reduction of fish stocks in North Sea • Global warming? Prediction of steady rise in sea temperatures with 17% of land area of Bangladesh, 12% of Egypt and almost all of the Maldives flooded • El Niño disaster estimated at $33 billion. La Niña kills 9000; 1 million homeless
Political insecurity	• Manhattan, September 11, 2001 • Decline of nation-state and rise of superordinate and subordinate powers • Civil wars – of the 61 armed conflicts between 1989 and 1998, only three were between states
Personal insecurity	• 500,000 women are annually traded to western Europe for sexual exploitation • Illegal drug trade estimated at $400 billion (1995) or 8% of global trade • 200 million drug-users worldwide • International crime syndicates gross £1.5 trillion annually

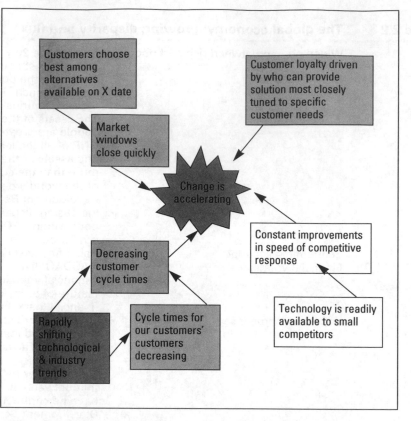

Figure 2.3 Annihilation of space through time: a firm's view

Harvey notes that a peculiar secondary effect of this process is that in the process of tearing down spatial barriers, new spaces are created. Nowadays these **non-places** as Marc Augé calls them – rail, road and air routes and the panoply of spaces that facilitate these – take up progressively more space. Take for example the space of the railway. When railways were first constructed in the USA and in Europe they opened up vast tracts of land which hitherto had been considered inhospitable and inaccessible. However, in opening up these new spaces and in reducing the time taken to reach them, the new space of the railway itself had to be built, including stations, tracks, rolling stock and manufacturing facilities for these. Similarly while the car opened up a new space, it also required spaces (roads, roundabouts, junctions, bypasses, petrol stations, garages, manufacturing facilities) which themselves take up a large amount of space. The breaking down of other spatial barriers has thus entailed the creation of further new spaces, for example in retailing. The hyperspace created by the Internet is an especially interesting phenomenon as it not only creates a virtual 'space' for global villagers to interact with one another simultaneously, but its nodes are progressively invading real spaces in homes, offices and in other media.

Harvey contends that the process of speed-up of production cycles and of transport leads to **time–space compression**. By this he means that the turnover time of production has reduced steadily as distributive and communications technologies have speeded up, to the extent that spatial barriers such as the effect of distance have almost entirely collapsed. There have been parallel developments in the areas of exchange and consumption, such as plastic money and electronic banking. Nowadays the idea of a 'global village' appears to be closer than ever to describing the reality. As a result of these changes, Harvey argues that the world has seemed to fold in upon itself, to collapse inwards and shrink.

Teresa Brennan (1994) shares Harvey's main argument and develops this to suggest that competitive pressures within capitalism are such that consumption constantly outstrips generational time, or the time period over which resources would naturally reproduce themselves. As one natural resource is used up, demand switches to alternatives. Brennan notes that the availability of substitutes and alternatives is such that it will be possible for producers to switch resources for many years to come; but that ultimately this form of consumption is unstable and threatens the entire global ecology. She argues that this logic is partially responsible for the technological drive involving risky experiments with genetic engineering, the demand for animals and plants which grow faster and larger than ever before. As a consequence, turkeys, hens and pigs have now been bred to develop so quickly that their legs cannot sustain their weight. In consuming living resources faster than they can be reproduced, she argues that consumer society constitutes a danger to its own survival as well as that of others.

Brennan maintains that few bother to consider the real (environmental) cost of international and global trade. One research study considered the real cost of strawberry yoghurt (Paxton, 1994 with reference to a study carried out by the German Wuppertal Institute). In order to produce the yoghurt and transport this to a central distribution outlet in South Germany, strawberries were transported from Poland, yoghurt from North Germany, corn and wheatflour from the Netherlands, jam from West Germany and sugarbeet from the east of the country. The aluminium cover for the strawberry jar was manufactured 300 km away from the yoghurt producer. Only the milk and glass were produced locally. This specific case seems to be illustrative of the general trend. Evidence from SAFE is that the distance food is being transported has increased by 50 per cent between 1978 and 1993 (Paxton, 1994: 18/19). Such developments are possible because of a decrease in the 'real' (economic) cost of transportation, which does not take into account the real environmental costs of replacing resources used in transporting the materials nor the environmental effects of pollution occasioned by it.

2.5.4 Post-Fordism

David Harvey argues that the changes wrought by the peculiar dynamics of capitalism have led to the formation of new systems of production which are no longer centred around the mass production of homogeneous products, but are specialized, capable of producing small batches targeted at market segments within heterogeneous and highly differentiated markets. In Harvey's view, the shift to post-Fordism, which he terms flexible accumulation, is essentially linked to the speed-up in the turnover time of capital. One could argue that the entire history of manufacturing has been dedicated to the removal of barriers in pursuit of this goal. This encapsulates the history of technical and organizational innovation including the initial development of the assembly-line process (from cars to battery hens), the reduction of set-up times and the acceleration of physical processes (for example genetic engineering). Harvey argues that increases in the turnover time of production would be of little consequence if the turnover time of consumption were not also reduced. Consequently marketers have increased the rate of product obsolescence, paid much more attention to stimulating the adoption of quick-changing fashions, the extension of credit and to marketing and promotional activities.

Harvey believes that of the many developments in consumption, two stand out as being of particular importance with respect to issues of time, space, distance and speed. First, **fashion** in mass markets has provided a means to accelerate the pace of consumption not only in clothing, but in a variety of lifestyles and recreational activities such as leisure, sport, pop music and games. A second trend has seen a **shift towards the consumption of services**. The huge rise in the production of services includes not only personal, business, educational and health services but also entertainment and the provision of spectacles such as mass pop-concerts; the entire city of Las Vegas, for example, could qualify as a spectacle in its own right. Although it is hard to estimate, the lifetime of such services (for example a movie, rock concert, or a visit to a museum) is much shorter than that of a car or a washing machine. Harvey suggests that the main dynamic for this rise of services has been the limits to growth in the production and consumption of physical goods. While some people buy enormous quantities of physical products (Imelda Marcos reputedly had 6000 pairs of shoes), it is in practice difficult to persuade consumers to own more than one or two variations of a physical product. On the other hand it is much more difficult to place limits to the growth of services, because of their perishability and shorter lifespan. Services are used up faster.

One need not be quite so deterministic about the attempt to stimulate demand. While traditional industries such as automobiles and many sectors of clothing remained relatively low-growth, there has been a massive increase in growth of the 'knowledge' industries which offer a differentiated array of Internet-enabled hardware devices (including PCs, game-machines and palmtops), linked to a vast supporting web of software. Marketing activity has also been greatly enhanced through the compilation of precise geo-demographic customer databases and their use in direct marketing. This technological innovation is what lies behind most of what I call relationchip marketing. Added to this is the increased importance of commodities in consumer lifestyles and identity-formation. As we shall see shortly, it seems a little 'chicken and egg' to determine the extent to which this has been cynical exploitation by firms or merely the opportunistic response to the initiatives of consumers in appropriating commodities to their own ends.

2.5.5 Responses by firms to instability and flux

One can think of two alternatives that firms can follow in such times of flux: 'make the market', or 'go with the flow.

2.5.5.1 Make the market

The idea of making the market is the traditional way of 'doing' marketing. This involves intervening directly in the production of volatility by seeking to influence taste or opinion either through being a fashion leader or by saturating the market with images so as to shape that volatility to your particular ends. Advertising is the traditional marketing approach used to influence taste and opinion. Over the years there has been an increase not only in the production and marketing of advertising images, but in the channels used to advertise. Advertising does much more than sell a product: it triggers the hierarchy of effects, connotes an experience, 'sells' a lifestyle. Otherwise undifferentiated products are imbued with meaning by borrowing meanings from referent systems. For example images of fashion models are often associated with perfumes to lend them an aura of celebrity and chic.

2.5.5.2 Go with the flow

In his book *Future Shock*, written in the 1960s, Alvin Toffler coined the term 'throwaway society' to describe the growing impact of ideas of disposability and obsolescence on Western culture. The idea of a throwaway society did not just refer to the rapid obsolescence of products and services but to a general sense that not just products but also people, institutions (the Church, marriage) and values that people of a previous generation had thought eternal (truth, honesty, love) were also disposable. David Harvey suggests that, in addition to this, the volatility in marketplace fashions has made it difficult for firms to engage in any form of long-term planning. This means that it becomes important for them to be highly adaptable and fast-moving in response to market shifts. Halevi Ganetz (1995) argues that while the fashion industry used to be able to dictate what was 'in' and what was 'out', this is no longer as true as it used to be. She suggests that this is for three reasons. The first is that women, the traditional 'fashion victims', used to be treated as, and to go along with, the idea of the female stereotype – that they were pretty, passive and stupid. Ganetz argues that while the vast majority of women have not participated in the women's movement which has challenged such ideas, they have become more liberated to the extent that they interpret fashion in their own ways. Second, she argues that the authority of the fashion houses has declined in line with the power of tradition and that consequently the young are expected to choose more for themselves. Finally she contends that with the development of mass production and more effi-cient distribution systems, a huge array of fashions that were once only avail-able to a few are now available to almost everyone, thus enabling considerable variations in style. As a result of such changes, she argues that fashion is heavily influenced by subcultures, the street fashions which are increasingly becoming a source of inspiration for the creators of the fashion world, who take over the styles of the subcultures, and who then repackage these for the mass market.

The above can be illustrated through a number of relevant examples. The British sociologist Angela McRobbie discovered that the fashion item 'leggings' emerged initially as a part of punk style. However it is not just clothing which is subject to 'street' fashions. Bernard Cova and his co-researchers have explored the patterns of interaction of some of the 'neo-tribes' discussed by Michel Maffesoli (1996). For Cova the golden rule of 'tribal marketing' is to consider the value of a product in terms of its linking value (to others in the tribe) rather than to its use value. He suggests that it is much more important for the firm to know how its product supports the tribe 'in its very being' than how to deliver the product to the customer. Cova (1999) studied the 'tribe' of inline skaters in France. They found that for members of the inline-skating tribe, having the right 'threads' is an impor-tant prerequisite for belonging to the tribe. This includes a full range of acces-sories, including shoes, key chains, hats, belts, backpacks and sunglasses. The inline-skating tribe provides rich rewards for those marketers that can successfully adapt to their requirements. Companies such as ski-giant Saloman sponsor events and skating stars; others have opened websites dedicated to inline roller skating.

One feature of the contemporary tribal scene is that companies are some-times caught unawares when their brands become coveted tribal icons. During the 1980s punk youth in the UK created a style of their own based on the detritus of consumer culture; towards the end of that decade the US trash group 'The Beastie Boys' popularized the wearing of Volkswagen grille badges as a form of jewellery. This craze became so widespread that these items were stripped out of most of the Volkswagens in the UK. Adidas could scarcely believe their good fortune when top rap band Run-DMC wore their brand and helped them turn the tables on Nike and Reebok. Once they did understand what was happening, some skilful promotion of bands such as the Spice Girls led to a strictly enforced dress-code which demanded that the Adidas uniform be worn by a wide section of youth. The current phase of the commodification of the pop industry is thus reflexively tied to the construction of icons, the reproduction of iconic dress-codes and nodes which link to the assemblage of other accessories. Nor is it enough to have all of the relevant items; the style with which the assemblage is carried and worn determines the extent to which one is 'in' or one is 'out'. One could argue that it is this fear, the fear of exclusion and mimetic rivalry, that forms the basis for the vast unstable edifice upon which global brand power is built. Such power can humble the mightiest of brands. When one brand is 'in', another is 'out'. So when at the beginning of 1998 the word began to circulate that trainers were now 'out' and Timberland shoes were 'in', companies such as Nike and Reebok were caught with massive stocks on their hands.

2.5.6   Responses by people to instability and change

What are the effects of such developments on the lives of people? This issue has been partially addressed in section 2.5.5 which considers the inexorable logic to the creation of consumer identity which clearly marks out the 'haves' from the 'have-nots'. Let us first consider the life of consumers in contemporary society.

2.5.6.1   The 'time-squeezed' consumer lifestyle

Authors make a number of points about the contemporary consumer lifestyle. Elizabeth Schor argues that consumers are economists with respect to time, in that they are keenly aware of the price of time, in terms of the extra income earned with a second job, or overtime. As a result, she suggests, they have forgotten the real worth of time. During the Industrial Revolution workers struggled against the very idea of the attempt to introduce time discipline. Nowadays, she argues, most people treat time as a commodity like any other, which can be bought and sold, and that the workers of today, far from being resistant to time discipline, fight for overtime – the right to sell as much time as they can. Where time is money, she argues, it is hard to protect those such as low-wage workers, children and community organizations, who cannot pay for it. She further contends that those Americans who were fortunate enough to be in work during the late twentieth century were working longer hours than their predecessors ever had. Schor argues that even during the medieval period, which she claims was exceptional in history, work did not entail the continuous toil which is characteristic of modernity. She claims that in previous times there was much more leisure.[2] Schor's main argument is that the key incentive structures of capitalist economies contain biases towards long working hours and that this has resulted in the growth of 'long hour' jobs. While trade union resistance improved this situation for a time, she argues that this has become steadily worse. A second major point which she makes is that these workers, which she estimates to number 40 per cent of the US population (1991: 113), have become entrapped in an insidious cycle of work–spend. Consumerism is central to Schor's bleak account. As consumers become accustomed to the material rewards of prosperity, their desire for leisure time is eroded and instead they increasingly look to consumption to provide satisfaction and meaning in their lives. As a result, in both the

[2] For example Athenians in ancient Greece had fifty to sixty days annually; while in Rome, 109 of the 355 days were designated as political holidays, rising to 175 days by the end of the fourth century.

DBS Arts Library

workplace and the home, progress has translated into the consumption of more goods and services rather than more free time. Schor raises several issues in her wide-ranging discussion, two of which will be argued in more detail below. The first is that people are no happier, despite their rising levels of consumption, and that in fact they are more discontented; secondly, she suggests that people want more 'free' or leisure time in which to develop themselves.

Are consumers working harder?

Schor focused on the USA in her study. The UK interest group *Demos* published a compendium of papers under the title of *'The Time Squeeze'* (1995), to which a number of prominent authors contributed. To what extent do they reflect Schor's concern that those who are in work are working harder and that such workers become trapped in a 'squirrel-wheel' of work–spend? First there was a general consensus among contributors that fundamental changes in time and space are underway. For example Mulgan and Wilkinson (1995) liken the differences between industrial and postindustrial time to that between the mechanical watch and the programmable watch. In postindustrial societies the new root of the social order is 'software', in the form of the knowledge industries which are the new source of value; the 'hardware', comprising smokestack industries, has now largely moved 'offshore' chasing higher productivity and lower wages. Ray Pahl (1995: 15) comments on the new illnesses which have accompanied this transformation, which he names generically 'hurry sickness', triggered by what he terms an exaggerated sense of urgency. One American study quoted by Pahl noted that computer-related distress manifests itself in a form of 'temporal schizophrenia' – that people who move in and out of computer time become less tolerant of interruptions, more impatient and less capable of slow reflection. Writing for the same collection, Carol Samms argues that this has produced a global phenomenon:

> 'In the 90's, there is a sense that people everywhere are faced with increasing time pressures in all facets of their lives and are searching for mechanisms which give them greater control. People are looking for institutions, companies, services, brands and communications which enable them to take greater control of their lives and to allow them more space for themselves.' [1995: 33]

Samms suggests that this is not solely an American and European phenomenon, and that similar trends are appearing in Japan and in China. With respect to the realm of work, several of the contributors to the *Demos* collection have noted that, in developed countries, the number of hours worked has decreased steadily during the course of the twentieth century. However, since 1980 this trend has gone into reverse for some countries such as the USA, Canada, Sweden and the UK (thus confirming Schor's findings). However despite the overall trend of decline, a large group of people are suffering from stress resulting from the rising intensity of work and leisure.

According to Robert E. Lane (1995: 2), 44 per cent of the UK workforce now report coming home exhausted from work. Ray Pahl argues that the changes in the structure of work associated with delayering, flexible employment and the gathering pace of the development of the 'knowledge society' have created a deep unease in the middle class in North America and in Europe. The assumption that a job might exist for life is gone, leading to an increasing fear of redundancy and unemployment.

Are consumers happy people?

Schor draws on the evidence of opinion polls to suggest that despite better material wellbeing, people are no happier than they were (two polls suggested that this peaked in 1957!) and that, in fact, many are more discontented than they have been in the past. The key of Schor's argument is that longer hours of work are not driven by the free choices of individuals but by the demands of capital. To support this she cites two studies: one in 1978 where 84 per cent of respondents indicated that they would trade off some or all of a 10 per cent pay increase for more free time, and a similar survey conducted in 1989 where 80 per cent of respondents indicated that they would sacrifice career development in order to spend more time with their families. The contributors to the *Demos* collection of articles argue that the greatest potential of the changes with respect to time and space are for the world of leisure, or how people spend their free time. Robert E. Lane considers a range of studies of quality of life in advanced economies and concludes that 'the economists' belief that money buys happiness is largely wrong' (1995: 12). He reports that for 80 per cent of the population, there is almost no relation between happiness or life satisfaction and income. He explains that this is not to say that changes in income do not give joy and sorrow, but that people adapt rather quickly to any particular level of income and the new level becomes the standard for assessing their wellbeing. This is similar to the analogy of the 'squirrel-wheel', the cycle of work–spend, discussed by Schor (1991). Gary Cross (1995: 21) suggests that increased consumption has been a more powerful compensation for bureaucratic and mechanized work than has increased free time. This is because the notion of 'free time' has negative connotations of unemployment. The bias towards work and spend – having a house and a car – best exemplify the twin needs for social identity. When one considers the level of satisfaction rendered by consumer goods as measured by their hedonic yield, the conclusion is not much different. Lane cites the results of one study where bought goods and services rank only eleventh in a list of thirty sources of life satisfaction, well below for example 'things you do with your family'. He concludes that, with the exception of the consumption of education and culture, it appears that consuming is the least likely to increase happiness, as compared to work and leisure.

Zygmunt Bauman (1995) suggests that **anxiety** is central to the psychology of the consumer. He links anxiety to freedom – to having too much choice. This is not simply a matter of choice of what to buy; rather it refers to the decline of traditional community and family life, leading to the constant negotiation of roles within households (although the majority of this burden, including childcare, shopping and house maintenance, seems still to fall on women). This is supported by Carol Samms (1995) who reports that consumers, and primarily women, report that they are 'over-choiced', experiencing severe time pressure with little enjoyment of either core shopping or basic household management. This is supported by research from the Henley Centre, which suggested that UK women on average 'work' for 86 hours each week, compared to 71 hours for males. While men may spend more than 5 hours more at work than do women, the latter spend twice as much time on 'essential' shopping (3.1 hours per week), twice as much time on 'essential cooking and cleaning' (15.4 hours) and up to three hours more on personal hygiene! (see note xiii).

Anxiety is further compounded by what Anthony Giddens terms **institutional reflexivity**. While modern institutions such as science aim to produce a secure foundation for knowledge, they are governed by the principle of doubt, which means that no matter how cherished and apparently well-established a given scientific tenet may be, it is always capable of being revised or even discarded, in the light of new findings. The reflexivity of science is existentially troubling to ordinary individuals who must live in a world where whatever passes for 'truth' must always be placed in doubt.

Taking another point made by Giddens, the consumer can be said to be **disembedded** from community, which means that he or she must place increasing faith on distant experts (for example the engineering expertise that produces the food which we eat, which offers us advice about which food is currently dangerous). Unfortunately, expert opinion is often divided. Additionally the credibility of experts has been seriously eroded following a number of major food-scares involving E. coli in eggs, listeria, BSE and foot and mouth disease. The (post)modern consumer is thus faced with the position of having to assume an almost unbearable responsibility for their own consumption.

What do consumers do with leisure time?

Schor (1991) suggests that if people spent less time in working and consuming, they would have more time for self-development. This raises the question of how leisure time is actually spent. Traditional economic theory suggests that people prefer leisure to work. Schor suggests that increasing leisure time is of great potential benefit because it offers the means for greater self-development, in music creativity and the arts. However Lane (1995) disagrees with this view and contends that increased leisure time, when it has been offered, leads to more time sleeping, car travel and watching television, a set of activities which does not exactly match the ideal described by Schor.

2.5.6.2 The time-squeezed and time-rich poor

It scarcely makes sense to ask if the poor are contented. For some, perhaps a budding voluntary simplifier, the idea of belonging to a primitive peasant community may provide a warm glow of nostalgia. However for the vast majority, the idea that people are 'poor but happy' is a dangerous myth. Schor postulates that while it could be argued that everyone has 24 hours in each day, money skews the distribution of time to some extent, in that wealthier people live longer. The sale of time undermines its egalitarianism. Those with money can economize on it by hiring people to wait on them and watch their children. Those whose time is being sold are less economically well situated, as happened earlier in the nineteenth century when growth of the middle classes increased the demand for servants. Establishing a right to free time may sound utopian, but it is not legal to sell oneself into slavery. For the underclass, including those on welfare and illegal immigrants seeking to improve their lot, time may thus be an even more scarce resource than it is for the wealthy. However if a person lives according to the welfare rules and does no additional work, it may be the abundance of time which weighs heavily upon them. While the challenge for the consumer is to have enough time in the day in order to complete all the tasks which they need to do, those on welfare have an abundance of time but nothing to fill it with.

2.5.6.3 Speed-up and changing perceptions of space and time

It has been argued that continued acceleration associated with speed-up has led to changing perceptions of space and time with the proliferation of spaces and an apparent slowing down in the march of time, giving the impression that we are living in an eternal present. For example retailers in search of increased added-value provide products which used to be seasonal on a year-round basis. It used to be that products were available only during the seasons when they naturally germinated and ripened. Strawberries came in the summer months, apples and pears in the autumn, new potatoes in the springtime. Now all of these products are available throughout the year. Furthermore they are often set alongside products from around the world. For example French cheeses, which were unavailable except in a few gourmet stores in the 1970s, are now widely sold throughout the world. In addition to this, people can purchase from a vastly increased range of beers and wines in addition to pak choi flown direct from China, blue crabs and oysters from Baltimore, Maine lobsters, mange tout from Kenya, and Chilean grapes.

One can talk of the recreation of the present with respect to changes in patterns of work and reproduction, for example the blurring between home and workplace as more people work from home, and new commitments towards lifelong learning in place of a fixed period at school or university. Instead of having a fixed period for having and raising children, child-bearing is spread into the late 40s, 50s and even 60s.

Another way in which traditional rhythms of temporal order may be changing is with respect to the development of the '24-hour city', which some authors suggest is a logical response to contemporary lifestyles. Franco Bianchini argues that these trends include the 'new consumerism' of those in relatively high-paid jobs who are working longer hours and who find it difficult to access the services they need during the day. Robert E. Lane suggests that a more powerful logic for this development lies in its ability to offer a clearly visible goal which seems to address a number of problems. This view of the future promises great efficiencies in fields such as tourism or transport by reducing the need for investment at peak loading of summer time or the morning rush hour. It promises genuine full-time operation for manufacturing, distribution and retailing with obvious benefits for productivity. Pressures in this direction are giving rise to the creation of a more 'flexible' workforce.

Temporal order is also disrupted through the constant search for images which can be used as the basis for the establishment of corporate and brand identities. As will be argued further in Chapter 6, images are of central importance in consumer society as they provide resources for the construction of consumer identities. However with the acceleration of change, the shelf-life of images is strictly limited. Images of celebrities such as Michael Jordan, Michael Jackson and the Spice Girls may add millions of sales to companies such as Nike and Pepsi, but they inevitably will have a shelf-life of a few years at most before another image must be crafted and put in their place. As advertisers must constantly be on the lookout for new images and styles, so they raid the stock of images from both the past and the future. For example in one year perhaps the 1980s genre will predominate; the next it is the 1950s and the year after that style may be modelled on some futuristic sci-fi image. Some authors argue that the net effect of such constant recycling not only exacerbates feelings of impermanence and the ephemeral nature of images, it also evokes the feeling that we live in an era which constantly recycles the styles of all the eras that have ever been and some that have yet to be (as in the recycling of styles based on fantasies). In a peculiar way, it seems not only that time is standing still, but that it is being consumed by space, by the spaces of consumption.

2.6   DISCUSSION

The previous section has considered a predominantly 'Marxist' explanation for changing relations between space and time. The idea of the fetishism of commodities focuses our attention upon the inequality and exploitation present in hidden spaces of production far away from the glitz and 'equality' of the marketplace. In this sense the activities of global brands such as McDonald's come into focus not as steamrollers which act to 'level down' culture, but in relation to the exploitation carried out as part of the process of production. This argument appreciates that consumers may want quality products at cheap prices but goes further to insist that this very availability blinds them to the exploitation of people and other inputs into the production process. When you are hungry, want something to eat and have a couple of pounds or dollars in your pocket, the last questions on your mind will be whether the cow had a good life and whether it was reared at the expense of the destruction of virgin rainforest. It is in this sense that one can argue that the overwhelming presence of the marketplace draws a veil over the conditions in which commodities are produced.

On the other hand the idea of the annihilation of space through time, coupled with notions of speed-up and time–space compression create a vertiginous feeling. This comes close to Anthony Giddens' description of postmodern society as a 'runaway world'. The need to constantly outdo the competition in the drive for profit leads to the constant relocation of capital as it chases lower costs, resulting in feelings of insecurity among workers. This also provides the motor for constant changes in fashion, in the recycling of images to promote these and in the creation of new services. Such processes increase the separation of space from time through the constant recycling of fashions and images.

2.7	CONCLUSION

One might argue that both Weberian and Marxist approaches can be useful in illustrating aspects of contemporary life in consumer society. The Weberian focus on rationalization draws our attention to certain aspects of contemporary society – the drive to understand and control the world and make it predictable through being able better to understand it. It allows us to realize the thoroughgoing rationalization of time and space which has occurred during modernity, from the creation of time-zones to overtime, quality time, post-codes and those digitized spaces where much of our 'personal' details are kept on file. While this approach can also make a valuable contribution towards understanding the impact which the rationalization of science has made on daily life, it tends to ignore reflexivity, the principle of doubt which drives science forward. Perhaps most of all Weber was prescient in noting that, once Puritanism was stripped of its religious ethic, what was worn like a 'light cloak' by the pilgrim would become like the 'shell on a snail's back' for the consumer.

On the other hand the Marxist analysis draws our attention to dynamism and flux; a world unmade and in perpetual motion. It calls our attention to the ways in which the marketplace, while purporting to offer freedom and a kind of equality, fosters oppression and exploitation in the circuit of production. It also provides a means for understanding the truly dramatic implications of speed-up for all aspects of our lives.

2.8 CHAPTER SUMMARY

This chapter constructed two rather crude categories linked to 'Weberian' and 'Marxist' views in order to discuss changing relations between space and time in consumer societies. 'Weberian' approaches foreground the trend through modernity for situated places to be converted into rationalized spaces. In this sense one can argue that modernity consists of the construction of a myriad of rationalized spaces, for example the space of 'consumer identity' and 'global' space. Such spaces are amenable to control to the extent that they are predictable and provide opportunities for marketers. Authors suggest that taken to its zenith, the process of rationalization turns back upon itself as the 'irrationality of rationality'. Thus instead of neat orderly rationalized spaces, consumer societies are frequently described as being chaotic and fragmented. While such flux constitutes an outcome of the rationalizing process in 'Weberian' explanations, it is pivotal in 'Marxist' accounts. Central to this is the idea of the 'annihilation of space through time', which relates to the perpetual upheaval and renewal in the entire fabric of personal and social life. Marxist accounts also highlight the process of commodification, which acts to reveal some of the workings of the marketplace (its apparent fairness and freedom of choice) and to highlight other aspects (such as exploitation).

2.9 CASE STUDY: DOWN ON THE OLD FACTORY FARM
(based on Ufkes, 1995; Ikerd, 1999a, b)

It can be argued that for those of us who are affluent and in particular those who have lived their lives untouched by war or famine, the real meaning of words such as 'scarcity' and 'starvation' has been largely lost. Yet it is only some 50 years or so since Europe and much of Asia was ravaged by the Second World War, when scarcity was a byword and starvation was experienced by many. It was during this time of shortage that the seeds of what came to be known as the 'Green Revolution' were sown. Propelled by existing shortages and by the prospect of a vastly increasing global population there was a need for such a revolution, which would ensure that scarcity would become a thing of the past.

The 'Green Revolution', which started in the 1950s, was based on adopting a more rational and scientific approach to food production. The search began for high-yield crops and for those which were most resistant to disease and pestilence. The development and use of pesticides such as DDT and of chemical fertilizers to replenish the soil, allowed the practice of monoculture to take hold. Rather than using traditional farming methods of crop rotation and leaving fields fallow, monoculture depends on fertilizer and pesticides to allow this intensive farming of the same land to continue year after year. Monoculture has a number of important benefits, certainly in the short-term. The crop, being uniform, is easier to manage. Greater densities of planting can be achieved, and there are generally high yields. Monoculture's greatest strength – uniformity – is also its greatest weakness. If a disease or virus should become resistant to the pesticide, it will wreak havoc on the entire crop.

While monocultural practices were initiated over half a century ago, the last decade has seen a marked intensification of farming with more power accruing to fewer, larger, specialized companies, especially in the USA. According to the USDA report by the Commission on Small Farms, '*A Time to Act*', four firms now control over 80 per cent of the beef market. About 94 per cent of US farms are small farms, but they receive only 41 per cent of all farm receipts. The US cattle industry has been dominated by large corporate feedlots for many years. In 1998 it was estimated that the largest 30 cattle producers had pen-space for 2 million head of cattle, just over half the total on feed. In contrast hog production was almost entirely independently owned until the early 1990s. By 2000 the 50 largest operations controlled over half of the total production through contractual arrangements. There was talk in the industry that beef cowherds would be next. Within a decade it is thought that the small independent producer will be a rarity. In March 2000, US agriculture secretary Dan Glickman worried that traditional American farmers were being pushed into a 'feudal-type situation' whereby they became totally dependent on a few huge global agribusiness companies for their livelihood. In the USA the domination of this trend is not only apparent in traditional 'factory' farming, but also in organic production.

The industry view

Ikerd (1999b) suggests that there is a widespread belief that the progressive industrialization of livestock production is not only inevitable, but is also desirable for producers and consumers alike. Proponents of this view contend that the technologies employed in large-scale specialist operations are more efficient than their counterparts. They further argue that through specialization, standardization and centralization of control, they can realize significant economies of scale resulting in a cheaper product which better fits the consistent quality demanded by consumers. In relation to the environment, they suggest that where problems arise, it will be easier and less costly to deal with the problems created from a few large operations, which in any event have the resources to invest in modern waste-handling technology. They suggest that large-scale farming operations will improve the scope for rural employment, providing a net benefit even when the decline of (less cost-efficient) traditional farming employment is taken into account. Complaints about odours surrounding such facilities are met with the riposte that the smells associated with farming have always been pungent to those who are not accustomed to them; although few people would want a hog farm in their 'backyard', they nevertheless have to be somewhere. These producers also argue that the animals themselves benefit from a cleaner, less variable environment, and also that it is against their self-interest to create stress.

Opposing views

While the production costs of large-scale operations may be lower than the average of smaller independent operations, Ikerd argues that the top 20 to 40 per cent of independents are well managed and can actually produce at lower cost. He also disputes the benefits to consumers, citing the example that if one assumed 5 per cent lower production costs for large-scale operations ($2/cwt for live hog and $3.50/cwt for fed cattle), the maximum savings to consumers would amount to 2 cents per dollar spent on beef and pork at retail. In any event he suggests that as farming becomes dominated by fewer, larger producers, prices will eventually be driven up. The variety of food available to the customer will be less, as meat from factory operations will be more uniform because it comes from the same genetic stock and is produced using the same management practices. The illusion of variety is gained by dressing up (cutting up, processing and packaging) the same generic cow, pig or chicken in dozens of different ways. Proponents of industrial farming claim that livestock factories offer more employment and better and safer job opportunities than traditional farming. However such operations tend to substitute capital and technology for labour and management, to make it possible for fewer people to produce more. While the risks are less and the pay is steady, livestock factories do not require skilled labour but technicians who can follow the procedures laid down in the operations manual. A detailed knowledge of hogs, cattle or poultry is no longer required of those whom they are entrusted to. Ikerd argues that big hog operators preferably don't want to hire people who know anything about hogs as 'an experienced hog farmer might start thinking, asking questions and mess up their process' (1999b: 3). Additionally the farmer is reduced to little more than a hired hand; he may own the production facilities but, once he has signed the comprehensive production contract all the key decisions, from delivery of genetically modified and patented stock to the specification of feeding and medication regimes and timing of placement and delivery of the finished product, are decided elsewhere. To provide a flavour of this, consider the following excerpt from the United States Department of Agriculture, National Commission for Small Firms, 'A Time to Act. A Report of the USDA National Commission on Small Farms', January 1998:

'The poultry industry is perhaps the most industrialized subsector of agriculture, with 89 per cent of poultry farms using contracts and about 86 per cent of the total value of poultry production grown under contract. Testimony presented to the Commission included the results of a 1995 survey of poultry contract growers conducted by Louisiana Tech researchers describing the average poultry grower. The average poultry grower is 48 years old, owns 103 acres of land, 3 poultry houses and raises about 240,000 birds under contract annually. The grower has been contract-growing birds for 15 years and owes over half of the value of the farm to the bank. The contract poultry grower's gross annual income is about $66,000 and the grower's profit, before paying themselves for their labor, is about $12,000. Raising poultry on contract may appear to be a way of reducing price and income risk. However, it provides a modest living at best and, under current contract practices, is far from risk-free.'

Claims that large-scale operations are better for the environment are also open to challenge. The intensification of the process requires that animals are concentrated on one location as opposed to being scattered over a number of fields. Ikerd notes that where ten thousand cattle are spread over ten thousand acres, the disposal of waste is not a problem. Where they are concentrated into a five-acre feed lot, the effects can be startlingly different.

Case-study questions

1. Which system of production does that described in the case study conform to most closely?
2. In what specific ways do Fordist systems of production act to 'dehumanize'?
3. How and under what conditions would 'post-Fordist' agriculture be developed?

END-OF-CHAPTER REVIEW QUESTIONS

1. What does it mean to say that social institutions in traditional communities are 'embedded' and that those in modern societies are 'disembedded'?
2. Which theorist argues that the dynamism of modernism disembeds social institutions? How does the process of disembedding take place?
3. What is meant by the increasing turnover time of capital?
4. Describe what David Harvey means when he refers to the 'annihilation of space through time'.
5. What responses can firms adopt to time–space compression?
6. What is meant by a 'liminal space'?
7. What is meant by the following terms: 'underclass', 'impacted ghetto', 'shop-rat', 'voluntary simplifier'?

REFERENCES AND FURTHER READING

Alwitt, Linda (1996) 'Marketing and the Poor', pp. 69–87. In Ronald Paul Hill (ed.), *Marketing and Consumer Research in the Public Interest*, Thousand Oaks, California: Sage.

Augé, Marc (1995) *Non-places: Introduction to an Anthropology of Supermodernity*, trans. John Howe, London: Verso.

Baudrillard, Jean (1988) orig. 1970 'Consumer Society', pp. 29–55. In Mark Poster (ed.), *Jean Baudrillard: Selected Writings*, Cambridge: Polity Press.

Bauman, Zygmunt (1995) *Life in Fragments. Essays in Postmodernity*, Oxford: Basil Blackwell.

Bauman, Zygmunt (2000) *Liquid Modernity*, Oxford: Basil Blackwell.

Belk, Russell R. (1997) 'Been There, Done That, Bought the Souvenirs: Of Journeys and Boundaries', pp. 22–46. In Stephen Brown and Darach Turley (eds), *Consumer Research: Postcards from the Edge*, London: Routledge,

Benzeval, Michaela, Ken Judge and Margaret Whitehead (1995) *Tackling Inequalities in Health*, London: King's Fund Publishing.

Berman, Marshall (1982) *All that is Solid Melts into Air: The Experiences of Modernity*, London: Verso.

Bianchini, Franco (1995) 'The 24-hour City', p. 47. In *The Time Squeeze*, Demos, 5.

Bourdieu, Pierre (1977) *Outline of a Theory of Practice*, Cambridge University Press.

Brennan, Teresa (1994) *History After Lacan*, London: Routledge.

Campbell, Colin (1997) 'Shopping and the Sex War'. In Pasi Falk and Colin Campbell (eds), *The Shopping Experience*, London: Sage.

Castells, Manuel (1997) *The Power of Identity*, Oxford: Basil Blackwell.

Cinquin, Chantal (1987) 'Homo Coca-Colens'. In Jean Umiker-Sebeok (ed.), *Marketing and Semiotics,* Berlin and New York: Mouton de Gruyter.

Cova, Bernard (1997) Community and Consumption: Towards a Definition of the Linking Value of Products and Services, *European Journal of Marketing*, vol. 31, no. 3/4: 297–316.

Cova, Bernard (1999) 'Tribal Marketing: A Latin Deconstruction of a Northern Construction'. Presented to the *First International Conference on Critical Management Studies*, UMIST, Manchester, 14–16 July.

Cross, Gary (1995) 'The All-Consuming Work Ethic', pp. 21–2. In *The Time Squeeze*, Demos, 5.

Csikszentmihalyi, Mihaly (1977) *Beyond Boredom and Anxiety*, 2nd edn, San Francisco: Jossey-Bass.

D'Silva, Joyce (1998) *BST – A Distressing Product: An analysis of the health and welfare problems of dairy cows injected with BST*, Petersfield: Compassion in World Farming.

D'Silva, Joyce and Peter Stevenson (1995) *Modern Breeding Technologies and the Welfare of Farm Animals*, Petersfield: Compassion in World Farming.

Danesi, Marcel (1994) *Cool: The Signs and Meanings of Adolescence*, University of Toronto Press.

Elgin, Duane (1993) orig. 1981 *Voluntary Simplicity: Towards a Way of Life that is Outwardly Simple, Inwardly Rich*, New York: William Morrow & Co/Quill.

Ewen, Stuart (1976) *Captains of Consciousness: Advertising and the Social Roots of the Consumer Culture*, New York: McGraw-Hill.

Falk, Pasi (1994) *The Consuming Body,* London: Sage.

Fine, Reuben (1986) *Narcissism, The Self and Society*, New York: Columbia University Press.

Foxall, Gordon and Paul Hackett (1994) 'Consumers' Perceptions of Micro-Retail Location'. In Mark Jenkins and Simon Knox (eds), *Advances in Consumer Marketing*, London: Kogan Page.

Fredriksson, Cecilia (1997) 'The Making of a Swedish Department Store Culture'. In Pasi Falk and Colin Campbell (eds), *The Shopping Experience*, London: Sage.

Friedman, Thomas (1999) *The Lexus and the Olive Tree*, London: HarperCollins.

Fukuyama, Francis (1992) *The End of History and the Last Man*, London: Penguin.

Ganetz, Halevi (1995) 'The Shop, the Home and Femininity as Masquerade'. In John Formas and Goran Bolin (eds), *Youth Culture in Late Modernity*, Thousand Oaks, California: Sage.

Giddens, Anthony (1991) *Modernity and Identity: Self and Society in the Late Modern Age*, Cambridge: Polity Press.

Giddens, Anthony (1999) *Runaway World: How Globalisation is Shaping our Lives*, London: Profile Books.

Goss, Jon (1992) 'Modernity and Post-Modernity in the Retail Landscape'. In Kay Anderson and Fay Gayle (eds), *Inventing Places: Studies in Cultural Geography*, Cheshire: Longman.

Harvey, David (1989) *The Condition of Postmodernity: An Enquiry into the Origins of Cultural Change*, Oxford: Basil Blackwell.

Holbrook, Maurice B. (1997) 'Walking on the Edge', pp. 46–78. In Stephen Brown and Darach Turley (eds), *Consumer Research: Postcards from the Edge*, London: Routledge.

Ikerd, John (1999a) 'Organic Agriculture Faces the Specialization of Production Systems; Specialized Systems and the Economic Stakes. Presented at *Organic Agriculture Faces the Specialization of Production Systems*, sponsored by Jack Cartier Center, Lyon, 6–9 December 1999.

Ikerd, John (1999b) 'The Real Economics of Factory Livestock'. Presented at the *1999 Big River/Clean Water Week*, sponsored by the Sierra Club, Washington DC, 10–15 June 1999.

Jhally, Sut (1990) orig. 1987 *The Codes of Advertising: Fetishism and the Political Economy of Meaning in the Consumer Society*, New York and London: Routledge.

Joy, Annamma and Melanie Wallendorf (1996) 'The Development of Consumer Culture in the Third World'. In R. Belk, N. Dholakia and A. Venkatesh (eds), *Consumption and Marketing: Macro-Marketing Dimensions*, Ohio: South-Western College Publishing and International Thomson.

Kamenka, Eugene (1969) *Marxism and Ethics*, London: Macmillan (now Palgrave).

Lane, Robert E. (1995) 'Time Preferences, the Economics of Work and Leisure', pp. 12–14. In *The Time Squeeze*, Demos, 5.

Lash, Scott and John Urry (1994) *Economies of Signs and Space*, London: Sage.

Levitt, Theodore (1986) *The Marketing Imagination*, London and New York: Free Press and Macmillan (now Palgrave).

McCracken, Grant (1990) *Culture and Consumption: New Approaches to the Symbolic Character of Consumer Goods and Activities*, Bloomington and Indianapolis: Indiana University Press.

McKay, George (1996) *Senseless Acts of Beauty: Cultures of Resistance since the Sixties*, London: Verso.

Maffesoli, Michel (1996) *The Time of the Tribes: The Decline of Individualism in Mass Society*, London: Sage.

Malyon, Tim (1998) 'Tossed in the Fire and They Never Got Burned: The Exodus Collective', pp. 187–207. In George McKay (ed.), *DiY Culture: Party and Protest in Nineties Britain*, London: Verso.

Marsh, Alan and Stephen McKay (1994) *Poor Smokers*, London: Policy Studies Institute.

Miller, Daniel (1996) 'The Myth of Cultural Erosion'. In R. Belk, N. Dholakia and A. Venkatesh (eds), *Consumption and Marketing: Macro-Marketing Dimensions*, Ohio: South-Western College Publishing and International Thompson.

Miller, Daniel (1998) 'Coca Cola: A Black Sweet Drink from Trinidad', pp. 169–89. In *Material Cultures: Why Some Things Matter*, London: UCC Press.

Mukerji, Chandra (1983) *From Graven Images: Patterns of Modern Materialism*, New York: Columbia University Press.

Mulgan, Geoff and Helen Wilkinson (1995), 'Well Being and Time', pp. 2–11. In *The Time Squeeze*, Demos, 5.

Pahl, Ray (1995) 'Finding Time to Live', pp. 15–16. In *The Time Squeeze*, Demos, 5.

Parker, Martin (1997) 'Nostalgia and Mass Culture: McDonaldization and Cultural Elitism'. In M. Alfino, J. Caputo and R. Wynard (eds), *McDonaldization Revisited: Essays on the Commodification of Culture*, Connecticut: Greenwood.

Paxton, A. (1994) *The Food Miles Report: The Dangers of Long-Distance Transport*, Sustainable Agriculture, Food and the Environment (SAFE) Report, London, September, 59 pp.

Raban, Jonathan (1988) orig. 1974 *Soft City*, London: Collins Harvill.

Rheingold, Howard (1994) *The Virtual Community: Finding Connection in a Computerized World*, London: Secker and Warburg.

Ritzer, George (1993) *The McDonaldization of Society*, Thousand Oaks, California: Pine Forge Press.

Rudmin, F.W. and W.E. Kilbourne (1996) 'The Meaning and Morality of Voluntary Simplicity: History and Hypotheses on Deliberately Denied Materialism'. In R. Belk, N. Dholakia and A. Venkatesh (eds), *Consumption and Marketing: Macro-Marketing Dimensions*, Ohio: South-Western College Publishing, International Thomson.

Samms, Carol (1995) 'Time in the Global Village', pp. 35–6. In *The Time Squeeze*, Demos, 5.

Schama, Simon (1987) *The Embarrassment of Riches*, London: William Collins.

Schor, Elizabeth (1991) *The Overworked American: The Unexpected Decline of Leisure*, New York: Basic Books.

Silverstone, Roger (ed.) (1997) *Visions of Suburbia*, London: Routledge.

Simmel (1978) *The Philosophy of Money*, London: Routledge and Kegan Paul.

Smart, Barry (1999) 'Resisting McDonaldization: Theory, Process and Critique', pp. 1–22. In Barry Smart (ed.), *Resisting McDonaldization*, London: Sage.

Ufkes, Frances M. (1995) Lean and Mean: US Meat-Packing in an Era of Agro-Industrial Restructuring. *Environment and Planning D: Society and Space*, vol. 13: 683–705.

United Nations (1998) *Human Development Report*. http://www.undp.ong\hdr1998\

United Nations (1999) *Human Development Report*. http://www.undp.ong\hdr 1999\

Venkatesh, Alladi (1994) 'Gender Identity in the Indian Context: A Sociohistorical Construction of the Female Consumer', pp. 11–42. In Costa, Janeen (ed.), *Gender Issues and Consumer Behaviour*, London and New York: Sage.

Weber, Max (1930) orig. 1905 *The Protestant Ethic and the Spirit of Capitalism*, trans. Talcott Parsons, London: George Allen & Unwin.

Weber, Max (1947) *The Theory of Economic and Social Organization Being Part I of Wirtschaft and Gesellschaft*, trans. A.R. Henderson and Talcott Parsons, London and Edinburgh: Hodge.

Wright, Mary Anna (1998) 'The Great British Ecstasy Revolution', pp. 228–42. In George McKay (ed.), *DiY Culture: Party and Protest in Nineties Britain*, London: Verso.

NOTES

i   The novels of Nawal El Sadawi, author of *Woman at Point Zero* and *God Dies By the Nile* (1990), should be enough to dispel any romantic fantasies, particularly for women. M. Estelle Smith (1988) discusses how the traditional culture of the Pueblo Indians deals with 'troublemakers', those individualists who challenge their customs or religious-grounded systems of rule. Troublemakers are first made aware that their behaviour is a threat to the entire community's wellbeing. If they persist in their actions they may be considered sick, full of confused thoughts and in need of a cure. The cure consists of gathering green pine which is burned to produce a spiritual smoke. By holding the head of the offender constantly over the smoke, elders suggest that the confusion of the troublemaker is soon cleared.

ii   *Source*: National Research Bureau, 1990.

iii   The power of men to control the management of family finances in Western society was considerable until fairly recently. The management of finances posed a major problem for many women whose husbands predeceased them, as their husbands retained rigid control of the family finances until they died. A major Scottish Bank only recently closed its 'ladies' branch, which was specifically designed to help such women.

iv   For those who would like to visit related websites, try searching the Web using keywords 'Consumer Culture'. Search also for ConsumAsiaN, a research network on consumer culture and consumption in Asia. Disgruntled site which can be found at: http://www.disgruntled.com/ offers a range of services for consumers who are seeking to pursue complaints, in addition to an 'anti-Nike' site.

v   *Source*: Health Inequalities, 1997, Table 8.4, page 100.

vi   *Source*: Health Inequalities, 1997, Table 15.9, page 205.

vii   *Source*: Health Inequalities, 1997, Tables 15.10 and 15.11, page 213.

viii   *Source*: Andrew Marr, 'Direct Action, The New Politics', *The Observer*, 15th November 1998, Politics section, page 22.

ix   *Source*: Malyon (1998), page 188.

x   *Source*: Wright (1998), page 229.

xi   *Source*: The Henley Centre (1998) *Consumer and Leisure Futures*, Issue 5: 28/9.

xii   *Source*: Taiwanese example from UK Channel 4 programme 'Global Dumping Ground'.

xiii   Adapted from Table 2, page 25, Demos, 5: 1995.

CONSUMING POWER

LEARNING OBJECTIVES

- To illustrate the links between morality and power
- To offer two broad levels of analysis of power in relation to consumption based on macro and micro views
- To discuss liberal, reformist and radical accounts of power in relation to the macro level
- To situate the work of Elias and Foucault within the micro level
- To locate mainstream marketing theory within a liberal approach to power

3.1   INTRODUCTION

The chapter is divided into two sections, one dealing with 'sovereign power' reflected in the macro-environment of power, the second with the micro-politics of 'disciplinary power'. The first section, whose organization is indebted to that first devised by Steven Lukes (1974), discusses the 'macro' relations of power with respect to liberal, reformist and radical explanations. Each position is outlined, discussed and critiqued with respect to its implications for the understanding of power, its relation to morality and the role played by marketing and consumerism in creating a good society. The section begins with a description of economic liberalism. Mainstream marketing theory is discussed in this section as it is argued that marketing theory shares a common moral basis and theory of power with economic liberalism. There follows a discussion of liberalism which questions its key assumptions of individualism, rational calculation and free access to information. Next the celebrated reformist critique of liberalism associated with the views of J.K. Galbraith is presented, whereby through concepts such as the revised sequence, he seeks to turn liberal marketing theory on its head. Finally radical theories are discussed in relation to the work of Althusser and Chomsky in respect of the concepts of ideology and the manufacture of consent. There follows a brief evaluation of 'macro' theories. The second section focuses on the operation of power at a quite different level, that of the regulation and discipline of the self and the body. This has already been addressed to an extent in the work of Norbert Elias, who traces the development of self-discipline into the modern period. Elias's work is buttressed through a discussion of the work of social theorist Michel Foucault who made these concerns his life's work.

3.2 SOVEREIGN POWER

In Elias's discussion of the civilizing process discussed in Chapter 1, late medieval European court societies were organized on a hierarchical basis with the king or queen at the apex exercising legitimate power through being sanctified by the Church with the divine right to rule. Within this system the king and his subjects were together regarded as the body politic. This ideal of sovereign power is reflected in Hobbes' portrayal of *Leviathan* (1651). Here the body of the sovereign contains also the social body of those who are ruled and forms the body politic. Apart from the Church which had a certain independence, most social institutions including the mercantile system came under the sway of the monarch's patronage and favour.

Hobbes' *Leviathan* was to be shaken to its foundations by a seismic shift in the topology of power wrought in the period of transition which took place from the closing years of the seventeenth century to the eighteenth century. The concept of the sovereign as absolute ruler, imbued with a 'divine' right of patronage in religion, legal affairs and the mercantile system, was swept aside in a number of cataclysmic revolutions which inaugurated the 'modern' era: in the realm of politics, the American and French Revolutions; in the realm of economy, the Industrial and Agrarian Revolutions. The political sphere resounded to the cry for liberty, freedom and equality under the law; not just freedom from colonization but individual freedom enshrined in individual rights (see note i). While Hobbes had focused on one right – the right of a person to defend themselves if attacked – the idea of rights was further developed by John Locke, and principles guaranteeing individual rights were enshrined in Jefferson's Declaration of Independence and in the Declaration of the Rights of Man produced by the National Assembly of France during the French Revolution (see note ii). While change on the ground came slowly and more often than not as the outcome of violent struggle, these revolutions eventually overthrew Hobbes' *Leviathan* and inserted in its place the concept of the 'modern' democratic nation-state as the new sovereign power (see note iii). It is within this context that the discussion of liberalism is situated.

3.2.1 The liberal tradition

One must be very careful in discussing 'liberalism' as the word has diverse meanings and the way in which it is used here assumes a very specific meaning. Here **liberalism** refers to that tradition which arose in the seventeenth and eighteenth centuries which argued for the principle of individual freedom and self-determination in economic and political life, and which valued the operation of the market as the best guarantor of individual freedom and of the good society. In Chapter 2 we discussed the growing individualism of society. Liberalism arose within the current of change that brought about the Puritan revolution in England, the later revolutions in France and America, and last but not least the Industrial Revolution, which wrought massive change in trade from mercantile to industrial capitalism.

In *The Wealth of Nations*, Adam Smith, known as the 'father' of classical economics, outlined his solution to what he perceived to be the greatest evil of his day, the mercantilist system. The basis of this system was protectionism: the promotion of exports and the limitation of imports, in order to preserve home production. Smith argued that such protectionism acted to distort the market in line with the interests of powerful domestic merchants. The distortion resulted in gross inequities, resulting in the suppression of wages, the neglect of industries which benefited the poor and the wholesale exploitation of consumers. Smith found this latter point particularly galling as consumption:

> 'Is the sole end and purpose of all production; and the interest of the producer ought to be attended to only so far as it may be necessary for promoting that of the consumer.'   [1793: 155]

Instead, Smith argued that within the mercantile system the interest of the consumer was sacrificed to that of the producers and that the system behaved perversely as if production and not consumption was the end object of all commerce. Not content to merely comment on this state of affairs, Smith moved beyond this to suggest a means for dealing with it in his chapter on *The Division of Labour*. Here Smith considers how, of all the different species, mankind is reliant on others for his sustenance. However he should not rely on the benevolence of others for this but rather:

> 'He will be more likely to prevail if he can interest their self-love in his favour, and show them that it is for their own advantage to do for him what he requires of them. Whoever offers to another a bargain of any kind, proposes to do this: Give me that which I want and you shall have this which you want, is the meaning of every such offer; and it is in this manner that we obtain from one another the far greater part of those good offices which we stand in need of. It is not from the benevolence of the butcher, the brewer or the baker that we expect our dinner, but from their regard to their own interest. We address ourselves, not to their humanity but to their self-love, and never talk to them of our own necessities but of their advantages.'   [Smith, 1793: 21/22][1]

Smith is making a fundamentally important point here; although humans rely on others for their sustenance, the key to obtaining satisfaction is not to

---

[1] Spelling altered to reflect modern usage.

rely upon their good nature but to give them something in kind, which they want, in return. Smith's statement is paradoxical because it appears that he is arguing that a better form of society than that which laboured under the mercantile system will emerge as the result of the selfish actions of individuals. Here we must clarify a point about selfishness. Moral philosophers distinguish between **selfishness**, the tendency for people to seek and promote their own benefit over that of others, and **egoism**, which merely holds that the best society is one where one gets what one wants from life, whether this be the assemblage of a personal fortune or in devoting one's life to the care of others. You may well find this point hard to resist; after all, what can possibly be wrong with arguing that people should be able to get what they want from life? By placing self-love and the satisfaction of wants at the core of his proposition, Smith's argument represents a form of egoism, which holds that the good society should be organized on the basis of the fulfilment of individual desire. Smith's thesis supposes that all human actions can ultimately be explained in terms of the desires of the people whose actions they are, which sounds like a common sense type of argument until one thinks carefully about how people actually do act (see note iv). Basically, you can get what you want by giving other people what they want. Smith paradoxically locates the best possibility for societal wellbeing in competition between sovereign actors following their own self-interests in the marketplace. In ethical terms Smith's theory is **consequentialist** in that he argues that the most good will likely come about as the result of the spontaneous collaboration of free economic actors in the marketplace. While people may not know the full consequences of their actions, they are likely to know best what is in their own best interests; in acting in the marketplace they are indifferent to the effects of such actions on others.

The role played by the marketplace may be depicted in different ways depending on which subsequent variant of liberal thought the question is based on. For neo-classical economists, the market is a means for regulating the interests of buyers and sellers via the price mechanism; for utilitarians, market processes create the best prospects for achieving the good society; for those of the Austrian school such as Hayek, the market plays a role in creating knowledge. For Smith, the main promise offered by market liberalism is, to use modern parlance, its 'trust-busting' potential; or its use as a means for curbing the cosy relations, 'mean rapacity' and 'monopolizing spirit' of merchants. Although such practices may never be eradicated, Smith argues that the promotion of competition provides the best hope of tempering them. Protectionism on the other hand encourages monopoly practices.

Almost three centuries later, Smith's argument was vigorously adopted and espoused by neo-classical economists of the New Right, including Friedrich von Hayek and Milton Friedman, who argued furiously against growing State intervention which had increased significantly since the 1960s in Western economies and which continued apace in the following decade. Like Smith in the work cited above, Milton Friedman advances the view that ecological and consumer concerns, among others, are best addressed through economic actors seeking to fulfil their desires in the marketplace (Friedman and Friedman, 1979). Such views were popularized by the Reagan and Thatcher administrations of the 1980s. Hayek considers the market to be a spontaneous form of human order which is beneficial in its communicative function. As absolute knowledge of the multi-dimensional market is impossible, Hayek argues that agents must be free to act in the marketplace according to their own assessment of the market.

Those holding the liberal view see millions of independent individuals, each actively following his or her interests. Each individual is taken to be a relatively free and rational agent. Agents are taken to be rational to the extent that they will tend to choose that action most appropriate to the successful pursuit of their interests. Contemporary taken-for-granted notions of 'consumer' and 'consumer sovereignty' are reflections of the liberal view. Consumers are held to be more or less rational and as being actively engaged in problem-solving activities and the expressions of preferences in the marketplace. The classic pluralist position as exemplified in the work of Hayek and Friedman is that market-based competition should be the supreme arbiter in disputes; those firms which do not fully meet people's needs will tend to be shunned, those which do so will be embraced. Take the following quote from David C. Green (1987):

> 'The new liberals have typically argued, not that selfishness is a good thing, but that selfishness exists whether we like it or not, and they have urged that we must therefore strive towards institutions which prevent selfishness from doing too much harm. Competition is said to be the chief safeguard available, preventing any producer whose principal aim is to make money from doing so except by serving the consumer. It is conceded that competition may have perverse results, and that in these circumstances the government may step in, but if it does so then it should reinforce rather than replace competition. But it is a mistake to regard profit seeking as the only approved motivation. The case for liberty rests only in part on the value of competition in channelling the efforts of possibly selfish individuals into the service of their fellows. It also rests on the belief that there are any number of alternative ways of meeting human wants – some like charity and mutual aid are the very antithesis of profit seeking – and only in a free society can such alternatives flourish.'

Green's summary of the new liberal argument is consistent with much of the argument advanced by Adam Smith: the good society is based on the satisfaction of wants which can be satisfied in any number of ways. While this is not explicitly stated, the argument is closely linked to **hedonism**, the belief that pleasure is the only good worth pursuing. Hedonism is perfectly consistent with charitable giving. For example, a person might be moved to pity at the sight of a beggar on the street and may give to the beggar in order to remove their discomfort caused by the sight. Note the focus on the individual; for liberals it is paramount that individuals have the freedom to transact with one another. Where a person does act selfishly by ruthlessly promoting their own benefit over that of others, liberals argue that competition provides the best curb. The selfish person may deceive another once and get away with it but with active and lively competition, the duped party, having learnt their lesson, can go elsewhere next time.

3.2.1.1 The liberal view of power

The liberal definition of power is conceived as a form of capacity exercised by one individual over another. Dahl frames this in individual terms:

> 'My idea of power then is something like this. A has power over B to the extent that he can get B to do something that B would not otherwise do.'   [1957: 203]

Power is conceived as a relation between sovereign individual actors. Within this conception power has a source or base, such as love, fear or money. Most children will recognize that physical strength is a source which provides some children with the ability to do things which they would not otherwise do. Or again there is a common belief in society that wealthy individuals can effectively 'call the shots' over others who cannot equal their command of resources.

Michman and Sibley (1980) constructed a list of seven bases of power which are drawn upon by firms in constructing their power in the distribution system. Two of these are economic, including the size of the firm and the resources which it has at its disposal. The remaining five bases are related indirectly to these. First is the ability of a firm to reward others; second is its level of unique knowledge or expertise in areas which are crucial to economic success; third is referent power, or the degree to which other firms seek to emulate the firm; fourth is legitimate power, the degree to which the firm is larger and controls more resources which in turn define a superior–subordinate relationship in relation to other firms; finally there is coercive power, as reflected in the ability to punish others. This scheme has been used to analyse relations in the supply chain. For example the power of the massive US retailer Walmart can be analysed in terms of its ability to reward and to punish others (Walmart's $167 billion annual turnover enables it to 'reward' those who will work within its extremely tight cost-control policies and delivery schedules), and its unique knowledge (in the ability to track real-time logistics and transactions data). It is a company whose competence in logistics and cost-control has gained the grudging respect of competitors, which rightly fear its size, and which has the power of life and death over small suppliers, particularly those which trade in the Third World.

3.2.1.2 Liberal pluralism

A clear theme running through the liberal argument is that morality is associated with the rational pursuit of self-interest and that 'enlightened' self-interest is linked to attending to the interests of those others upon which one's own interests are based. How does this individualist conception accommodate the differences between economic and political actors of quite different scales of organization? Surely theorists do not mean to suggest that 'Joe Public' can take on the likes of giants such as the Microsoft Corporation? Liberal pluralists would deploy two arguments here. The first argument is that government should keep a close eye on restrictive practices and attempts by companies to control markets, for example by means of mergers and acquisitions. Within this view a lack of competition is seen to be the bedfellow of practices such as price-fixing, and its proponents argue that the role of government is to ensure that the market is allowed to work free from constraint. A second means is that it is rational for consumers to seek out those who have similar preferences to club together in their own interests to exert pressure on firms and on government. It follows logically, since consumers are assumed to be rational, that the absence of such pressure would signify that the individual's interests are being fully met.

The influence of liberal theories in the field of politics is exemplified by liberal pluralist theory. The **pluralist** perspective on democratic politics comes close to economic liberalism in that it conceives society as made up of a plurality of groups, each composed of like-minded individuals in pursuit of their self-interest. Such groups are associations of rational individual interests. The state is considered to be politically neutral and to be separated from economic power in society; in other words democratic politics and capitalist economics are thought to be quite distinct. The liberal commitment to individual freedom insists that the role of the state should be largely passive, acting to provide a minimal framework for the conduct of economy and society. The role of the state is thus to be responsive to the needs of society. In the first instance liberals would argue that this is achieved through the provision of an electoral mandate by the people to those who govern; during a government's period of office such needs may be channelled through the representations of interest groups. Elections are considered to be forms of competition between two or more political parties, which must compete for the endorsement of the electorate. Within pluralist theory the state is held to be responsive to the expressed needs of the people, as to be re-elected, governments must pursue policies which command sufficient popular support. The electoral system is supplemented by interest-group activity to which the state also responds. It is also assumed that the more intense the feelings of a group of citizens on a particular issue, the more likely they are to have an influence on policy. Interest-group activity therefore provides more information between elections which allows the decision-makers within the state to weight preferences during the formulation of policy.

Interest-group formation: Yannacone, DDT and the EDF

Since the 1960s there has been an explosion in the numbers of groups which purport to represent the interests of one group or another to the state. An early example featured the issue surrounding DDT, the wonder pesticide that many believed would permanently eradicate killer diseases such as malaria. The publication of Rachel Carson's book *Silent Spring* and a one-hour television documentary dampened such enthusiasm and instead provoked widespread concern about the adverse effects that DDT might have on wildlife, particularly upon birds and fish. Soon after this the wife of Long Island resident Victor Yannacone spotted a major fish-kill near her home, which she found had happened subsequent to spraying with DDT. Once informed, Yannacone was incensed by this and established the Environmental Defence Fund which had the aim to ban the use of DDT. The EDF used the emerging discipline of ecology as its main argument, contending that chemicals such as DDT were spreading uncontrollably with potentially disastrous effects for the peregrine falcon, among other birds. In 1968 the EDF found an obscure law in Wisconsin, which stated that a person or group could obtain a legal hearing if a claim was associated with water pollution in the state. The subsequent hearing, which took place in the vast state legislature, quickly became a trial of DDT. Yannacone's group had to prove that one part DDT per million was significant. They did so through the inadvertent assistance of an expert from the pro-DDT lobby. Next day the media ran with the story: 'Noted Scientist Says DDT Destroys Sex (Hormone)'. Another scientist claimed to have discovered DDT in (human) mothers' milk, stating that if babies drink the milk of cows which graze on grass sprayed on DDT, their fat is going to contain DDT, and as fat is in the brain, then brains will be loaded with DDT. This was in all of the Sunday papers. The opposition were furious, claiming that scientific evidence had been sensationalized through media spin. However the case went the EDF's way and fuelled by public concern, DDT was officially banned. Many felt that the outcome was a victory for media 'hype' over scientific fact. Farming groups advertised against the decision, arguing that city people were not aware of the real facts and that this would set aside years of progress. But DDT was not rehabilitated. The media subsequently became preoccupied with the harmful effects of chemicals which they portrayed as malign. When ultimately they sought, reputedly with EDF support, to link DDT to cancer in humans, Yannacone left the EDF. He did not believe the link to be based on fact.

In the above example we see the clear division into two sides: those for and against the use of DDT. Interest groups included the 'EDF', 'farmers' and 'scientists'. The EDF would be classified as a promotional interest group as its members are held together by a shared attitude (with respect to DDT). The EDF differs from sectional groups, for example those which represent farmers, or small business, who exist to represent the interests of their members. It is clear from the case that those for the ban on DDT 'won' – DDT was banned.

3.2.1.3 Consumer power: where does 'direct action' fit in?

According to the liberal pluralist view, issues related to the economy should be regulated through the mediation of the preferences of millions of actors through the marketplace, while those of the polity should be regulated through the system of elections and inter-election representation by pressure groups. The resort to direct action by pressure groups is thus regarded as threatening the stability of pluralism, whose legitimacy is founded on the efficacy of these mediating mechanisms. As a consequence, liberal theorists have little truck with those who engage in forms of 'direct action' (which may equally be viewed as a weakness of their ability to explain current developments).

According to some liberal accounts the dollar or pound in a consumer's pocket is equivalent to a vote. Those offerings that receive the most 'votes' are rewarded for their success in giving the market what it wants. Liberals would then propose a simple solution for the person who doesn't like the product that a company produces, the service it offers, its environmental policies or the way in which it treats its workforce: withdraw your 'vote' and spend your money elsewhere. As a result, if enough people feel like you then competitive offerings that do take your preferences into account will emerge to displace the firm which displeases you. On the other hand, if other people do not see the situation in the way that you do, you may vote with your money but nobody else will follow.

Consumer power: boycotts

One could describe the consumer boycott as one tactic whereby an interest group seeks to change the direction of perceived corporate misbehaviour through organizing the collective voting behaviour of customers. This was used to some effect in placing pressure on the South African government (through the organization of a boycott of South African produce) and in targeting companies which stood as icons of support for the regime. As part of this latter action the End Loans To South Africa (ELTSA) campaign targeted Barclays Bank, which at the time was one the largest UK banks lending money to South Africa. Among other things, ELTSA set up a 'shadow board' which produced an alternative annual report, picketed branches and distributed leaflets. On the face of it the boycott was successful: Barclays ended its relations with the apartheid government in 1986. However the full story is more complex and involved more actors and factors than can adequately be covered here. The same is true for the Nestlé 'baby milk' boycott. As in the Barclays case, Nestle was not the only 'offender' but it was one of the largest.

Consumer power: other forms of direct action

A difficulty arises when those who are concerned about some aspect of corporate misbehaviour with respect to some issue feel that these 'votes' will not make a difference. Thus they may be too poor to have a vote, or they may be disenfranchised to the extent that they cannot marshal enough 'votes' to matter – because the 'general public' are indifferent to the issue of their concern, because the use of their 'vote' has been disqualified or disabled in some way, or because they believe that the pluralist system is a sham. Whatever the reason, the precedent for the use of such action in the corporate context is provided by earlier political movements such as Gandhi's formulation of *ahimsa*, or non-violent direct action in India, which in turn provided the inspiration for the US Civil Rights movement of the 1960s. One example of the attempt to disable the right to 'vote' is provided by GM soybeans. In the late 1990s, despite the expressed concerns of UK interest groups including environmentalists and retailers, US soy producers announced that in future all consignments of soy would contain some genetically modified produce. As soy is an ingredient in hundreds of products, this could have been regarded as a ploy to forestall any protests or boycott of GM soy.

Interest groups are likely to use direct action as a last resort, and particularly if their world view is sufficiently apocalyptic ('We've got to save the planet now, at all costs!'). Research carried out in the early 1970s seemed to suggest that promotional groups such as the EDF would be more likely to resort to direct action because they were perceived to be 'outsiders' with respect to the decision-making process. This could hardly be the case nowadays when groups such as Greenpeace and WWF are considered to be mainstream. These have been replaced by other groups whose very structure makes it difficult if not impossible to integrate them within the liberal consensus. For example the Animal Liberation Front (ALF) is proscribed as a terrorist organization. Many organizations conform more closely to Maffesoli's description of the 'neo-tribes', with a fluid amorphous structure and no clear hierarchy. Such groups include 'New Age travellers' and the UK road protestors, whose history is described by George McKay in his book appropriately entitled *Senseless Acts of Beauty*. The UK fuel protests which took place in 2000 provide another example of direct action; television reporters initially searched in vain for the 'leaders' of this movement. The 'spokespersons' who eventually and somewhat reluctantly came forward insisted that there was no leadership.

Anti-consumption action

It is one thing to seek to stir up outrage at corporate malpractice and to scapegoat a likely target. It is quite another to question the very act of consumption itself. After all consumption is normal. More than that, as Baudrillard notes, it is our duty; if we do not consume regularly and in sufficient quantities we may destroy economic growth and our own wellbeing. Baudrillard also notes that the market system encourages us to think of consumption as a primarily individual and solitary affair, asking:

> 'Can we imagine a coalition of drivers against car registration? Or a collective opposed to television? Even if every one of the million viewers is opposed to television advertising, advertisements will still be shown.'

The dilemma faced by anti-consumerists is how to reduce the power or the hold of consumption in the everyday lives of the citizen. Consider the approach of one anti-consumer group called *Enough*. The challenge identified by *Enough* is how to sell the message about the negative impact of consumption on workers' lives, the environment and on the Third World, without wearing a hair shirt. In other words, if consumption is thought of as being equated with fun for most people, then to be anti-consumption could easily be construed as being 'against fun'. Members of *Enough* are concerned about the exploitative effects of the '24/7' consumer society for those workers who must man the supermarkets and call centres which service its demands. They are also concerned about the aspects of waste and environmental destruction associated with the consumer society. However the group are also keenly aware that consumption is seen generally to be a good thing by many people and that people do not like being preached at. As a result the group have developed a combination of approaches including seminars and spectacular events such as 'No Shop Day', which is usually held in November. The aim of the event is to avoid associating the event with feelings of guilt and to link the idea of anti-consumption with humour.

Politics isn't working: the possibilities for consensus in a fractured society

A key issue concerns the implications for society when, in seeking to push their agenda, the activities of interest groups spill over the boundaries of legality. Such activities may range from NIMBY (Not In My Back Yard) protests against the location of waste incinerators to bomb attacks by the Animal Liberation Front. To make matters more complex the same industry may be attacked by different interest groups at the same time but for different reasons. In recent years the Shell Oil Company has been targeted by Greenpeace among others for attempting to dispose of the Brent Spar platform at sea and for their exploitation of indigenous cultures. Concerned by their attempts to frustrate the Kyoto accord, ecologists have argued for boycott action to encourage oil companies to develop alternatives to the use of the internal combustion engine. On the other hand UK fuel protestors virtually closed the country down in pursuit of their aim to reduce the crippling prices of fuel which were perceived to be wreaking devastation for small road hauliers and the rural community. Given the divergence in aims of different groups and the increasing tendency to resort to boycott and other direct action tactics, there is growing concern among some commentators that this poses a grave threat to the 'liberal consensus' where legitimate action is deemed to be taken through political representation and the courts.

3.2.1.4 Liberal marketing theory

In terms of market transactions, if one agrees that consumers are sovereign, then ultimately it is those firms which provide the most satisfying assortments in terms of matching consumer desire that will survive and prosper over the competition; similarly governments whose policies do not meet the needs of the electorate lose their mandate at the next election. If, according to liberal economic theory, such outcomes are best left to the survival of the fittest in the marketplace, what additional role can be played by marketing? As we shall see this is far from clear.

If one accepts the current rather limited historical record of the development of the academic discipline of marketing, this originated in departments of economics in the United States towards the end of the nineteenth century. The German-educated academics at the rural University of Wisconsin were wary of liberal market theory, contending that the market is subject to distortion and inefficiency. They were consequently interested in investigating among other things the real extent of consumer sovereignty. One project studied whether small farmers and consumers were being exploited by powerful intermediaries in the dairy business (Sheth *et al.*, 1988: 96/7; Jones and Monieson, 1990). While the state-funded academics at Wisconsin viewed the marketing activities of firms and intermediaries from a disinterested and sometimes critical viewpoint, a managerialist strand of marketing developed whereby the academic study of marketing was identified with the interests of the firm. At Harvard University, marketers were concerned to develop a bundle of techniques with which to educate a cadre of marketing managers who could fill the higher echelons of corporate America. The managerialist approach truly came into its own between the 1940s and 1960s with the development of tools such as the 'marketing mix' and market segmentation for use by marketing executives.

It is clear that some marketing management theorists saw their version of marketing as not simply comprising a bundle of techniques but as a means to improve the morality of trade. Marketing chronicler James Bartels argues that the development of marketing management is central to the evolutionary development of trade, away from deception and other 'base' practices, to a new and higher level (Bartels, 1988: 7/8). The moral rationale for marketing management is enshrined in the marketing concept, which Sheth *et al.* (1988) say is 'the most famous axiom developed in marketing history'. This was first outlined in the following quote by J.B. McKitterick:

> 'Turning the issue around, if business enterprises are to compete successfully in the quicksilver of modern markets, something more than sophistication in means of doing marketing work is going to be required. Indeed, to plan at all, and think adequately of what competition might do and its possible effects before committing multi-million dollar resources, requires knowledge of the customer which penetrates to the level of theory. So the principal task of the marketing function in a management concept is not so much to be skilful in making the customer do what suits the interests of the business as to be skilful in conceiving and then making the business do what suits the interest of the customer.' [1957: 78]

The 'concept' as outlined in the last sentence above, asks that marketers do not do what suits the interests of the business but instead make the business do what suits the interest of the customer. There is a paradox here which can be cleared up if one modifies the passage to read 'not so much to be skilful in making the customer do what suits the *short-term* interests of the business as to be skilful in conceiving and then making the business do what suits the interest of the customer *and thereby serving its long-run interest'*. This reading recognizes three important things.

1. *The short-term and the long-term*
This notes a difficulty with liberal economic theory: that in practice, in the short-term, firms may provide customers with poor value. This has engaged some of the best brains in marketing who have sought (and continue to seek) to develop a range of ingenious explanations for firms' perennial failure to deliver customer 'value'.

- *Marketing vs. selling orientation*: In distinguishing the long- from the short-run expectation, marketers are at their most vitriolic in distinguishing marketing from selling. Returning to the discussion of selfishness with respect to liberal economic theory, selling is associated with **selfish** behaviour where an individual acts purely in his or her short-term interest without regard to the interests of others, especially customers. In contrast, marketers seem to believe that marketing is imbued by a species of **enlightened self-interest** in that the interest of the firm is ultimately dependent on serving the desires of its customers (see Levitt, 1962).
- *Marketing myopia*: Theodore Levitt popularized the notion that marketing managers may become blinded to what is in their (real) long-run interests by focusing on (false) short-term cost and production efficiencies. He identifies other forms of myopia in cautioning managers against the seductive belief that success in the marketplace could ever be due to the intrinsic nature of the product which they make, its technology, or the production process by which it is made. The blunt message for those managers who do seduce themselves is that they will ultimately fall on the sword of their own misplaced desire, as sovereign consumers march to their own tune.
- Interestingly, none of the above explanations places the blame on an intrinsic flaw in the market mechanism itself. It becomes clear why this is the case as McKitterick invokes the ultimate power of consumer sovereignty, arguing that while in the short-run a firm may get away with the delivery of poor value, in the long-run, given competition and a rapidly changing marketplace, only those who excel in understanding and responding to customer needs will survive. Of course in a quote attributed to Keynes: 'in the long-run we are all dead'.

2. *The customer as moral object*
The second point to note from this reading is that while consumer sovereignty is placed in a position of key importance in the concept, the 'customer' is not regarded as an end in himself or herself, but rather as the means to an end (as the key to the long-run survival of the firm). Marketing management intrinsically views people not as 'persons', constituting them as individuals of unique moral worth, but as being 'valuable' to the extent that as 'customers' they can contribute to the long-run value (the bottom line) of the firm. In subsequent definitions of the marketing concept, the question of the extent to which consumer sovereignty should be emphasized to the exclusion of profitability has been fudged by combining both

in the idea that the firm should seek to satisfy customer needs at a profit. While this formulation of the concept sits uncomfortably astride the fence between sovereignty and 'self-interest', which ought to be one and the same thing, most marketers leave no doubt about which side of the fence they are ultimately on. For example in the unlikely event that marketers get carried away into loving the customer at the expense of their own self-interest, the 'offensive marketer' Hugh Davidson (1987) abjures against those marketers who become 'consumer worshippers' as being one of the *marketing perverts*.

3. *Externalities*

Finally, factors which are considered as being external to the transaction between marketer and customer, for example the treatment of inputs to production and the environmental costs of outputs and wastes from production and consumption, are not considered as being relevant.

By the early 1960s marketing academics had come to believe that marketing disciplines had truly raised the 'base practices' of trade into a new marketing era. Authors argued that true marketing practice had emerged through a series of phases or 'eras' (from a 'mass-distribution' or 'production era' to 'aggressive selling' and now to a genuine 'marketing orientation'), such that by the 1960s it was considered *unAmerican* for a company not to practise the marketing concept (see for example Stidsen and Schutte, 1972; Lipson and Paling, 1974). The difficulty with this line of thought was that it was totally detached from social reality. The claims made by marketers seemed to fly in the face of developments on the following grounds:

- The growth of a countercultural movement in the USA and in Europe during the 1960s was associated with a growing cynicism towards business and marketing in particular. In one year only 8 per cent of Harvard graduates decided to elect for business careers! (Gartner and Riessman, 1974).
- Marketing malpractice, especially with respect to selling and advertising, was singled out as the most controversial and most criticized single zone of business (Bauer and Greyser, 1967: 2).
- Business, and marketing in particular attracted unprecedented attention from the US government which passed a wave of consumer legislation (see note v).
- This was also a period when a large number of consumer affairs offices were established to advise the public of their rights (see note vi).
- An array of increasingly powerful interest groups were spawned in part as the result of a growing awareness of the growth of industrial power and of its effects on the human and natural environment. Public awareness was raised by the works of authors such as Vance Packard, who highlighted issues concerned with the use of subliminal advertising techniques and of rapid product obsolescence by firms, and Ralph Nader, whose *Unsafe at any Speed* cast doubt on the safety record of automobiles, among other products.

Marketing academics reacted in a number of ways to the paradoxical state of affairs whereby marketing was simultaneously eulogized (by the marketing academics themselves) and denigrated (it seemed, by everyone else):

- Some argued that the massive growth in government regulation was at least in part the result of poor communications between government and marketers and that both sides should move closer to the customer (see Bauer and Greyser, 1967).

- Others responded belligerently to Vance Packard's criticism about product obsolescence, firstly arguing that marketers were innocent and that the blame if any should be attached to production personnel, and secondly that in any case consumers themselves ought to be more responsible for their actions (see Stidsen and Schutte, 1972).

- Marketing guru Peter Drucker (1969: 61) took a different tack, maintaining that the rise of the consumer movement was shameful to marketing, that basically marketers had let their side down, that consumers felt that manufacturers simply could not be bothered to ascertain their needs, and that there was a need to get back down to brass tacks and take the consumers' point of view.

- Philip Kotler (1972a) backed up Levitt, pleading for restraint and understanding among marketers who were hostile to the rise of consumerism, which had come as a shock to all concerned. The nub of his explanation for the rise of consumerism hinged around the marketing concept. In one paper he argued that while the business community had got the hang of the *spirit* of the marketing concept and while it was espoused by senior managers, line managers didn't *practise* it faithfully (see note vii). Kotler argued that marketers had been hard on Ralph Nader and other consumerists, suggesting that in fact consumerism could be viewed as being pro-marketing and beneficial to all parties because it helped balance the power of sellers.

- In a later paper Kotler (1972b) suggests that what went wrong in the 1960s was that firms had equated the fulfilment of consumer desires with consumer satisfaction. However many products which are desired by customers, such as cigarettes and alcohol, are also harmful to them. He argues (1972a) that while such products may be desirable in the short-run they are harmful to the consumer's long-run interests. Companies should thus reformulate such products to make them more socially desirable. Perhaps the chief executive officers of the tobacco companies were out that day and failed to get his message. Kotler argued that the marketing concept should be modified so that in addition to providing customer satisfaction and profitability, firms should act in the long-run interests of customers as the key to attaining long-run profitable volume. He named this reformulation of the marketing concept the **societal marketing concept**.

The shock of the 1960s spawned some critical offshoots of marketing thought, including macromarketing which concerned itself with a review of the systemic impact of marketing practices, and green marketing which concerned itself with exploring their environmental impact. However for most of the next two decades it was 'business as usual' for mainstream marketing, until the moral debate opened once more under the auspices of **relationship marketing**. This time the impetus came from over 'the pond', from the Nordic School of marketing to be specific. Salient among this group, Christian Grönroos and Evert Gummesson deployed moral arguments to suggest that despite all the years of proselytizing by marketing academics, marketing practice was still rife with instances of deception (Gummesson, 1994), and that marketing practice had become manipulative and distant from customer concerns (Grönroos, 1996) and was in need of a new approach. These authors place most blame on the toolkit of techniques known as the marketing mix, which they suggest is programmed and formulaic, requiring the full-time attention of marketing specialists. They argue that the formulaic notion of the mix has encouraged a mechanistic approach to marketing and that its manipulation by specialists distances marketing from those at the 'front-end' of the organization who may have most to do with actual customer interaction. Their solution is to reconnect customers and employees through the cultivation and maintenance of long-term relationships. However recently authors have suggested that rather than mechanistic marketing being humanized by 'relationship' marketing principles, the reverse seems to have happened (Fovenier *et al.*, 1999). Another recent concern within the marketing academy has been to question the relevance of marketing theory for firms. For example Wensley (1994) raises concerns about the quality of academic research in marketing in relation to key concepts such as segmentation, marketing orientation and interfirm networks. Together with Douglas Brownlie and Michael Saren, he convened a special conference in 1996 in order to 'rethink' the relevance of marketing. In one of the most radical bids to 'rethink' the subject, Stephen Brown (1995, 1997) argues that marketing management should abandon its pretension to be a science and restructure itself as an art-form.

3.2.1.5 Discussion

Let us recap on some of the essential features of the liberal argument prior to considering its critique. While liberal economists place their faith in an external object – market forces and the power of competition – to bring about the best possible economic order, marketers emphasize the internalization of the marketing concept as an article of faith. In particular, marketers are inclined to invoke the power of competition in order to hint darkly at what will befall the foolish firm that seeks to deny customer value (and therefore its own long-run interest) by acting selfishly in the pursuit of its own short-term interests.

Liberal economists might wonder at the ambition of marketing management theory which seeks to contain the dynamics of the market mechanism within its own processes. Kotler's reformulation of the marketing concept argues that it is not sufficient for the firm to recognize the power of competition; it should also pay heed to the power of government to legislate, and to the power of the consumer movement, other stakeholder groups and in particular the media, to do harm to its long-term welfare. Some might regard as unrealizable Kotler's suggestion that firms attempt to contain the dynamic forces at work in liberal pluralism within their own decision-making apparatus. For this to be effective decision-makers would be expected to determine the interests of stakeholders and to simulate the changing force relations between them, in order to respond effectively to these. Economic liberals might well consider the societal marketing concept as being morally questionable, unrealizable and unnecessary in its attempt to suborn the interests of others through simulating the workings of the 'invisible hand' of the marketplace. Alongside recent questions about the relevance of contemporary marketing one must ask what it adds beyond the concept of consumer sovereignty on which it rests.

Marketing management theory acts in a dual relation to the consumer who is elevated to the status of supreme arbiter of managerial decisions while being simultaneously rendered as a moral object, the means to the attainment of the organization's goals. The pursuit of this latter object has led to the construction of a formidable set of technologies whose aim is to establish a complete knowledge of every aspect of consumer behaviour. In this context it is easier to understand marketers' overtly hostile reaction to the emergence of real consumer power through the consumerism of the 1960s.

Marketing academics have acted in a dual role as legislators and as apologists for marketing 'practice' since the marketing concept was defined. As legislators they seek to instruct marketing managers of the moral rectitude of implementation of the marketing concept. They inhabit a nether-world in the space between the short-term and the long-term by constantly warning managers about short-term 'myopic' thinking, 'transactional' marketing orientation and other dangers. They thus place themselves in the position of being the moral guardians of business, electing to stand above the fray to legislate what business ought to do. They have also become apologists for corporate malpractice. Given their unquestioned belief in the ultimate power of consumer sovereignty, they cannot blame malpractice on some form of market failure, but must instead resort to other forms of explanation (based for example on some variant of 'myopia', or 'transactional' focus).

Which returns us to the core assumptions of liberal economics: that economic actors enter into such voluntary exchange as individuals; that each economic actor has access to perfect information about alternative customers or producers and so can trade between these in seeking the best deal; and that all economic actors are rational in advancing their own self interest. The basis for critique lies in the extent to which the real world falls short of these ideals. It is not difficult in practice to knock down the 'straw man' which constitutes *homo economicus*. Let us now consider some of the realities of the present global market landscape.

3.2.1.6 Questioning liberal assumptions

To what extent are the claims made by liberals justified in reality? Below we consider some of the key liberal assumptions.

Free competition between individuals?

To what extent is Adam Smith's liberal ideal of the 'free' market a reality? You may remember that he was especially concerned to redress the inequities of mercantilism, involving collusion between producers, particularly with respect to price-fixing in markets. Many believe that collusive or anti-trust (see note viii) activity by firms is as prevalent nowadays as it has ever been. **Anti-trust** offences refer to business practices that limit or block competition and deny consumers access to goods or services at normally competitive rates. Such offences are classified into two categories. Horizontal anti-trust offences involve two or more competitors who meet in order to set the price of a product that each company produces. Vertical anti-trust actions on the other hand involve price-fixing within a supply-chain, between manufacturers, suppliers and distributors.

It is impossible to determine the true extent of price-fixing and bid-rigging in the economy. It may be unwise to use data for cases and convictions as a basis for generalization, as those who are caught may merely be those who take the most chances because of the circumstances which they are in (see note ix). The US Department of Justice site documents hundreds of cases which have been processed since 1994 (see note x). To give some idea of the scale of this, one study (Jamieson, 1994: 40) indicated that one-third of the Fortune 500 had been named in an anti-trust case. The scale of cases can be huge. For example the Florida Attorney General's Office first noticed suspicious-looking bid patterns by milk suppliers and brought this information to the attention of the Antitrust Division's Atlanta field office in 1986. The Division began a grand jury investigation which uncovered a state-wide conspiracy to rig bids to public school districts in Florida and evidence of similar conspiracies in other states. Since 3 May 1988, the Division has filed 134 milk bid-rigging cases, involving 81 corporations and 84 individuals. Criminal fines totalling more than $69.8 million have been imposed on corporations and individuals, and 29 individuals have been sentenced to jail. Cases span a range of industries. Ross (1992) notes that actual cases are the tip of what could be a very large iceberg. He quotes one anti-trust lawyer who has said that if the US Antitrust Division tripled their staff, they would triple their cases. The legislative environment obviously plays a role here. During the Reagan era, the US Justice Department's Antitrust Division challenged few of the corporate mergers that restructured American capitalism. At that time the view of the Division was that they saw no threat, and perhaps heightened economic efficiencies in these consolidations, whereas traditional trustbusters feared an inexorable trend towards monopoly. Ross (1992) regards anti-trust as 'an activity of contagious and stubborn persistence.'

Some scholars insist that anti-trust laws are counterproductive and dysfunctional, in part resulting from government distortion of 'free' markets. Without government intervention, so the argument goes, businesses would operate more efficiently and cost-effectively, enabling the economy to regulate itself naturally. This view holds that oligopolies develop because they are more efficient industries composed of large companies able to maintain low costs, low prices and accordingly consumer loyalty. Those who favour regulation insist that the higher profits of such companies come from charging higher prices.

Rational calculation of interests?

A key assumption of rational economic theory is that people are fundamentally problem-solvers. This functionalist perspective implies that conscious rational problem-solving is a key heuristic, or rule of thumb, used by economic actors to respond to change. This implies that confronted with a change with respect to some situation (perhaps they have run out of milk), they will: set goals as to where they would like to be (to have milk); systematically evaluate alternative strategic options in the light of available information (drive to supermarket, walk to local shop); select the most optimal option (walk to shop); implement the preferred alternative; and finally evaluate the success of the strategy set goals (it rained on the way to the shop, you got soaked and they had no milk, so you will drive next time). Classical economic theory assumes that economic actors act rationally to advance their self-interests. To what extent is this true?

To what extent do organizations act rationally?

- **Organizational decision-making**

The embodiment of rationality in firms would be where organizational decision-making is based on the ideal of strategic decision-making and where the organization structure is based on the model of a bureaucracy involving a formal specialized hierarchy and specification of tasks. The decision-making process itself would be based on the rational evaluation of costs and benefits, which would seek to minimize the former and maximize the latter. One would expect that no individual would have complete control over any aspect of the decision-making process. While the extent of organizational rationality is still the subject of research and is a matter of some dispute, most researchers assume that this is generally the case (see note xi).

But what of the day-to-day rationality exercised by managers? It has long been argued that managers' rationality is bounded, to the extent that they do not evaluate the likely effects of every single course of action open to them. Managers also tend to be influenced by pressure from outside the organization. For example Fineman and Clark (1996) found that managers are usually influenced by only a few stakeholders, particularly environmental campaigners or regulators, as these have the ability to do serious damage to the organization. Do managers make choices based on their own or on organizational principles while at work? Researchers are split on this, with some such as Tony Watson (1998) arguing that managers do actively bring their 'outside' ethics to bear inside the organization. However the majority finding is that generally employees tend to bracket their personal morality while at work and to substitute this with the interest of the organization (see note xii). The available evidence seems to indicate that (a) organizational structures and cultures are moulded in such a way as to optimize the rational self-interest of the organization and (b) employees may or may not substitute this form of rationality for their own set of principles in making judgements.

- **Firms' attempts to control the consumption environment**

One might argue that the claim that firms seek to rationally manipulate the consumption environment scarcely needs to be proved – the evidence is all around us. For example this thread runs through George Ritzer's 'McDonaldization' thesis, discussed in Chapter 2. Thus anything that might resemble a product offering has usually been subjected to the most rigorous rational evaluation from the design of the mall to that of the store, the cues which are present in the specific retail space in which the product is presented, the lighting (warm, yellow for bread; cold, clinical for cosmetics), smells (the smell of leather in a car), taste ('free' nibbles) and touch ('silky' feel). Detailed research on perception and in particular on how consumers respond to sensory cues with respect to colour, taste and smell are routinely built into product offerings. Advertising is only one means, albeit an important one, of seeking to ensure that the good things of life are constantly on display. A tendency nowadays is for the interpenetration of environments whereby these become mutually reinforcing; thus advertising which once constituted its own micro-climate within the television schedules now features in programmes of 'my hundred favourite ads'. Likewise advertising plays with genres usually reserved for soaps operas and movies, while consuming a movie requires the mandatory consumption of the product-placement contexts supplied within them.

Subliminal advertising

What is perhaps more worrying and potentially less legal is control by what cannot be seen. In the mid-1950s authors such as Vance Packard railed against the 'hidden persuaders' of advertising. This criticism related to the use by advertisers of motivation research and the use of subliminal advertising. Subliminal refers to the process whereby advertisements are presented so that they evade conscious detection by passing below (sub) the 'limen', or threshold, of consumer consciousness. This ad-man's dream (and consumerist's nightmare) was that consumers would comprehend advertising projected at 1/60,000th of a second, even though they could not see it. Subliminal advertising was first tried out in the USA in 1957, where audiences were subjected to 'subliminal' images (which stated 'Drink Coca-Cola' and 'Eat Popcorn' on alternate nights) which were projected at regular intervals during a movie showing in Grover's Mill, New Jersey. While the researcher claimed that this was a success and that sales of both Coke and popcorn had increased following the viewing, these results were placed in significant doubt by subsequent research findings.[2] Two intriguing studies carried out by Martha Rogers and her colleagues shed some light on the

---

[2] See Rogers (1992/93) for an easy-to-read description of the original test, and Moore (1982) for a more heavyweight treatment of contemporary issues relating to subliminal advertising.

subject (Rogers and Seiler, 1994). The first study indicated that even in the 1990s most Americans (75 per cent to 85 per cent) believed that advertisers use subliminal advertising. The second study indicated that 65 per cent of advertising professionals thought that it was used, although all but 18 (7 per cent) said that they had never personally used it. Follow-up questions revealed that most of these did not really understand what 'subliminal' meant, confusing its meaning with the use of 'subtle' cues, about status and other persuasive elements which are routinely encoded into ads. The survey revealed only one real occasion of the use of subliminal advertising, where the word 'sex' had been hidden in the background of a bank ad; however this had been an 'inside' joke. The misinterpretation of the word 'subliminal' is reinforced through books such as Bond and Kirshenbaum's (1998) *Under the Radar*. By 'radar' the authors are referring to the use of perception selection by the cynical and jaded consumer, who constructs a 'radar shield' which effectively screens out advertising messages. They then devise ten 'rules' for advertisers who wish to evade this surveillance device, including 'don't look or sound like an ad', alongside stalwarts such as the use of humour and sexual appeals. Their final injunction is to break the rules:

> 'Consumers are like roaches. We spray them with marketing and, for a time, it works. Then, inevitably they develop an immunity, a resistance. And the old formulas stop working. So what we have to do is to keep breaking the rules to stay ahead of the consumer's ever evolving defenses.' [1998: 92]

So the evidence suggests that while many advertisers think that subliminal advertising is used, this is generally because they confuse the technical meaning of 'subliminal' which is a very specific form of advertising with 'subtle' cues which work on the 'subconscious'. The key issue is that advertisers continue to deploy the might of their creative weaponry in seeking to penetrate 'below the radar'.

A relatively innocent example of the manipulation of hidden space is the 'large' pack of cereal which is only half-filled. Less innocent (and legal) is the practice of increasing the value of 'original' prices on the labels of goods which are then offered for 'sale' at their normal retail price. Another ruse reported by Blumberg (1989) is the short-weighting of products. Such duplicity is not required for products which are themselves so confusing that it is almost impossible for the consumer to calculate which alternative represents the best value. **Confusion marketing** is the buzzword used to describe such practices, although the art of sewing confusion in the mind of the customer has been practised for years. In the UK this has been applied to the 'mis-selling' of pensions and to the purchase of mobile telephones. Speaking of the former at a meeting which I attended, a former chairman of the Scottish Institute of Bankers said that he still could not understand the new 'improved' pension products, and he was an actuary. The approach is quite simple really. By virtue of the number of combinations of variables that are introduced into the offering, it is virtually impossible for the consumer to decipher the 'true' value of what is on offer, by comparing 'like' with 'like'.

Another issue is the concealment by producers of information which they believe may be prejudicial to their interests. For example for many years UK consumers had no idea that it was common practice for cattle feed to contain animal by-products, including those from sheep which had been infected with scrapie. Likewise UK farmers have claimed that feed companies refused to divulge ingredients of animal food during the mid-1980s; nor were they made aware that the temperatures used to render meat had been changed. Deliberate deception is perhaps the ultimate form of concealment. Paul Blumberg lists a host of deceptions practised by firms, ranging from the petty to the monstrous. The cigarette and sugar industries have been accused of the systematic deception of the public for almost fifty years.

While hiding information which they would prefer consumers not to know, firms use surveillance routinely in retail contexts not only as a means for preventing crime, but also as a means for analysing the shopping behaviour of customers.[3] Aided by firms that profile their customers, companies have been enabled to compile formidable customer databases.

Consumer rationality

In neoclassical economic theory, consumers are assumed to act rationally in furtherance of their self-interest. The prevailing conventional wisdom is cognitive, following the view that people are rational but do not wish to overburden themselves with information about products. To what extent does actual consumer behaviour conform to this image?

Liberal economic theory assumes that buyers and sellers have knowledge of what they are purchasing and have perfect access to information. Here we discuss this in relation to the growing interdependency and mediation of product-related information – the ability of consumers to understand complex products and attempts to deceive consumers.

Consumers' ability to process information

The idea that the parties to a transaction are informed assumes that they have the requisite literacy and numerate skills required to become so. While to be knowledgeable does not require one to be literate and numerate, nevertheless the growing complexity of products, particularly financial services products, requires high levels of both if one is to detect what is contained in the 'fine print' or to discern precisely what an 'APR' might be. How knowledgeable are consumers? Research in the UK carried out by a study group headed by Sir Claus Moser indicated that 1 in 5 of all UK adults, seven million in all, were functionally illiterate. By this he means that if given the alphabetical index to the *Yellow Pages*, they cannot locate the page reference for plumbers (see note xiii). The figure for poor literacy is roughly in line with those for Ireland and the USA, although it is slightly higher than those

[3] Headline in *Scotsman* newspaper, Thursday, 3 December 1999.

for some other European countries.[4] Problems with numeracy are even more common than with literacy. Some researchers suggest that nearly half of all adults in Britain have numeracy skills below the level expected of an 11-year-old. A quarter are estimated to have 'very low' numeracy skills, which means that they are unlikely to be able to perform even the simplest calculations. The lack of the requisite skills of literacy and numeracy on the part of consumers is borne out by the massive scandal involving the 'mis-selling' of pensions in the UK during the 1980s and 1990s, when millions of people were persuaded to abandon relatively secure and rewarding company schemes for personal pensions.

A study for the UK Food Standards Agency indicates that consumers do not fare much better when it comes to evaluating food labels. Most respondents (60 per cent) claimed to refer to labelling information 'always' or 'usually'. Those who reported never attending to labels tended to be younger and poorer. While only a quarter of respondents said that labels were difficult to read and understand, remarkably few respondents were able to tell whether the stated amount of sugar, salt or fat was 'a lot', or 'a little'. The question put to respondents was whether 10 grammes of sugar, 0.5 gram of salt or 20 grammes of fat, within a food product was 'a little' or 'a lot'. In all cases the correct answer was 'a lot'. However between 14 and 18 per cent simply did not know the answer; two-thirds were correct about sugar and slightly more were correct about fat, while only one-third offered the correct answer with respect to salt. Another question referred to a common practice by advertisers, which is 'informing' consumers about the proportion of their product that is 'fat-free'. In answer to the question '80 per cent fat-free product' contains what amount of fat per 100 grammes?, 12 per cent of respondents thought this was less than 20 per cent, 32 per cent could not answer the question and 55 per cent offered the correct answer. The oldest and poorest respondents were least likely to answer the question correctly.

Mediation of knowledge environment

The mediation of knowledge refers back to Giddens' point about the proliferating media of exchange, discussed in Chapter 2. This relates to the continuing trend for the specialization of knowledge which increases consumers' reliance on experts. While the period from the dawn of the microcomputer in the 1980s to the end of the century was generally known as the information age, the catchphrase for the twenty-first century is that this is the knowledge era. And yet despite this, writers like Zygmunt Bauman (1988) and Paul Blumberg (1989) argue that citizens and consumers find themselves increasingly ignorant about the knowledge-rich world they inhabit. It is now centuries from the age of the polymath, geniuses such as Leonardo who could possibly know and understand all that there was to

---

[4] The percentage of adults with literacy skills at the lowest level is estimated to be: Poland 44 per cent; Ireland 24 per cent; Britain 23 per cent; USA 22 per cent; Switzerland 19 per cent; Belgium, France, New Zealand, Canada 17 per cent; Germany 12 per cent; Netherlands 10 per cent; Sweden 7 per cent.

know of their times. Medicine, the arts and sciences have become increasingly specialized over time. This is also true of trade. In the early days of the automobile, anyone with a scrap of intelligence and will could fix most common problems. Nowadays even trained mechanics must take a backseat to elaborate computer systems used for diagnosis and even rectification of faults.

Bauman notes that as a result of the complexity outlined above, consumers place more reliance upon experts. However, concerns have arisen over the manner by which scientific data are reported by the media. The issue is about the power of media, for example 'glossy' magazines, and the power of specialist interest groups and scientific specialists who have an investment in either spreading scare stories in order to gain research funding, or to protect the fruits of their own research, or to demand forms of 'absolute' verification that something (perhaps a chemical agent or animal feed) is dangerous, such that by the time that it is certified as being dangerous it is too late to do anything about it. Some commentators are becoming concerned that the power of the mass media to frame the agenda and to influence law is something we should be concerned about, claiming that most media documentaries on risks are low on content and high on style and emotion. A number of 'independent' organizations sprang up in the wake of such concerns in order to seek to plug what they perceive to be the 'credibility gap'. One example is STATS (see note xiv), a US-based non-profit organization which cites as its main objective 'the accurate use of scientific and quantitative information in public policy debate', with the intention 'to weed out bad data and research before it enters the media stream'. SIRC, the Social Issue Research Centre (see note xv) is another independent non-profit organization which aims to provide 'a balanced, calm and thoughtful' perspective on social issues promoting 'open and rational debates based on evidence rather than ideology'. A number of celebrated 'scares' or hazards are shown in Table 3.1. Social theorist Ulrich Beck (1995) would probably argue that the activities by groups such as the SIRC are politically naive as the entire arena of global risks has become politicized. As a result of the collapse of consumer belief in the objectivity of science, consumers live in perpetual anxiety. This is compounded by monumental errors in regulation and by the process of institutional reflexivity. With respect to the former the following incident is depressingly familiar. 'How do you inform the public that they're eating shit?' lamented one European Commission official. He meant it literally. In this food scare the French government admitted the run-off from septic tanks and waste water from animal-processing had been found early that year in feed destined for pigs and chickens (see note xvi).

As the principle of doubt is key to institutional reflexivity, scientists are rarely surprised when other scientists dispute and in some instances overturn their findings. However the media reporting of individual papers provides a gloss which makes it look as if the scientific finding is cast in stone. This results in the consumer being confronted with constantly changing guidelines as what is 'safe' to consume.

Table 3.1 **Some modern hazards**

Name of hazard	Date	Location	Description of agent	Description of hazard	Government action
DDT/DDE – organochlorine	1962	Global	Pest control; estimated to have prevented 500 million human deaths	Cancer in humans Thinning of bird shells 'Gender-bender'	Banned USA, 1971
Cyclamates	1969	Global	Sweetener	Cancer	Banned USA, 1970
Saccharin	1977	Global	Sweetener	Cancer	Warnings on labels USA, 1978
4-MMPD	1977	Global	Hair dye	Cancer Genetic mutation	Warning, USA, 1978 Manufacturers remove it from products
Tris	1977	USA	Clothing, fire retardant	Mutagen Cancer	USA Manufacturers withdraw, 1977 USA Exports banned
Love Canal	1976	USA	Chemicals from landfill	Birth defects Chromosome damage Peripheral nerve damage	Permanent relocation of residents
Chernobyl		Soviet Union		Various toxic effects	Evacuation of area Global restrictions on agricultural exports
Three Mile Island	1979	USA	Nuclear plant partial meltdown	Radiation sickness	Evacuation of 60 per cent of residents within 5-mile range
Asbestos	1979		Hair dryers	Cancer	Withdrawal from market
	1993		Schools	Cancer	None
Coffee	1981		Drink	Pancreatic cancer	None
Benzene in Perrier	1990		Hydrocarbon in drinking water	Leukemia at high dose	Withdrawal of 72 million bottles Cessation of production
EDB			Anti-'knock' agent in petrol/fumigant	Carcinogen	Banned, 1983
Alar	1989		Growth regulator for ripening apples	Cancer	Withdrawn, 1989
Amalgam dental fillings	1990		Mercury poisoning	Range of toxic effects	None

Source: Compiled from a range of sources. See Carmichael (1998) and Lieberman and Kwon (1998) for more.

3.2.1.7 Evaluation of the liberal approach to power

The above review supports the contention that many firms actively seek to control prices and many other aspects of the consumption environment. It also suggests that a large number of consumers have not developed the requisite skills in order to live up to the ideal promulgated by economists, and that consequently their sovereignty is, at best, limited. Consumer ignorance is somewhat ameliorated by consumer 'rights' legislation and the proliferation of self-appointed organizations and media watchdog programmes which purport to represent the consumer interest, not to mention those who are canny enough to make the most of their 'consuming rights'. But what of the ability of pluralism to explain the things which matter with respect to power?

There are several advantages to considering power as the means by which A can get B to do something which B would not otherwise do. The first is that it is simple, accords with 'common sense' and can be researched and tested in a range of situations. For instance in researching the 2001 'foot and mouth' crisis which spread through the UK and into part of mainland Europe, one could explore the ways in which different actors drew upon different bases of power in order to seek to realize their own best interests. Likewise, one could use this framework to explore the workings of power at the level of global institutions with respect to the plurality of groups involved in negotiating the TRIPS agreement on global intellectual property rights.

On the downside, critics accuse this conception of power as being overly individualist and of not recognizing the fact that power relations are socially constructed. This would imply that a focus on the 'rational' consumer or the scapegoated company alone would ignore the most important aspects of the operations of power. This argument suggests that singling out Nestlé, GAP, Levi's or some other 'bad apple' to be boycotted, provides the excuse that everything will be alright once these bad individuals are 'reformed', pretends that no other companies are involved in similar practices and, worst of all, provides an alibi which suggests that the system, which created such conditions in the first place, is really working.

Again, as a result of its individualism, the liberal view of power has little to say about the power of conformity. Yet social psychological experimentation has consistently shown that the power of conformity is one of the most potent and frightening aspects of power. One might surmise that while the power of conformity would be especially significant to children and young adults, it would remain as a potent force even among adults.

Some would argue that the A/B formulation does not adequately capture the essentially fluid and dispersed form of power groupings. Consider the idea of having 'mainstream' culture (A) which is opposed to the counterculture (B). Does it make sense to think of such 'hard' categories as a definable 'mainstream' which seeks to exert its power on the 'counterculture' and vice versa? Theodore Roszak (1970) noted the problems with this view in respect to 1960s counterculture when he commented that the 'counterculture' were those people that parents looked at every morning on the other side of the breakfast table – their own children!

The idea of an 'A/B' of power also refers to the power of the state over its citizens who are subject to its laws. However, according to theorists such as Ulrich Beck (1999), the power of the nation-state has been weakened on a number of fronts. Nation-states have been forced to rein back welfare expenditure and corporate taxation in order to make themselves attractive to global capital. Secondly, nation-states have ceded much of their power to regional and international agencies, from the European Union to international trade agreements such as GATT. Third has been the development of what Beck calls 'sub-politics', based on direct action and concerned with global risks and issues which are usually at least partly beyond the control of national governments.

How would liberalism seek to counter such claims? While this is not the place to discuss specific responses, the 'bottom-line' liberal argument is that no-one ever suggested that the liberal system was perfect. Rather the argument goes that the best, or least-worst, form of political and economic organization must be based on some form of recognition of the rights of individuals. In the political sphere this is based on the principle of universal suffrage; in the economic realm it is recognized in the ability to transact with others in the marketplace free from the command or intervention of others, especially the state. However, what liberalism does not explain is the extension of the market and of consumerism into the political realm. The 'rolling-back' of the state since the Reagan–Thatcher era is part of a major process involving the wholesale privatization of spaces which had previously been considered to be public, with private business becoming progressively involved in a range of activities such as the administration of power-generation, health, universities, prisons and even cities. Business is even taking over the role played by legislation; for example Bird's Eye Walls acted in its long-run interest by developing and implementing a code for sustainable fishing practice among its suppliers (see note xvii). Even more significant is the idea that citizenship, with its attendant rights and responsibilities, is being supplanted by consumerism, where hard-won rights of the citizen (for example, to free speech) are no longer guaranteed.

<table>
<tr><td>3.2.2</td><td></td></tr>
</table>

3.2.2   Reformism

While the liberal explanation of power focuses on the ability of A to make B surrender to his or her will, a second model of power recognizes that power is exercised not only in making a decision that goes against B but in the 'non-decision' or 'non-event' that keeps the questions that are in B's interests but not in A's from even arising. This means that conflicts of interest can be covert as well as overt.

Bachrach and Baratz (1962) argue that the pluralist analysis of power does not distinguish between important and unimportant issues. Linked to this is the issue of **'non-decisionmaking'**. This means that A devotes his energies to creating and reinforcing political and institutional practices which limit the scope of politics to issues which are innocuous to A (1962: 948). In this view

A seeks to ensure that the 'rules of the game', or accepted and dominant values, work in his favour and to the detriment of *B*. There are three ways in which this process can work in favour of *A* through non-decisionmaking. First the powerful party, *A*, may not bother to admit, attend to or listen to the demands articulated by *B*. Even if these are admitted they may be tied up by endless requests for clarification or by endless committees or other delaying tactics. For example one can think here of those decades where the issue of the regulation of the tobacco industry was tossed back and forth between government departments, despite knowledge in the early 1950s that tobacco presented a clear danger to the health of smokers. A second possibility is that *B* anticipates *A*'s likely opposition and consequently doesn't even bother to raise the issue, because of the power exercised by *A*. Finally *A* can dominate *B* without *B* being aware of this through the **mobilization of bias**. This refers to the degree of control which *A* has over the political process and over the beliefs and opinions of less powerful groups, so that *A* can effectively determine not only whether certain demands are to be expressed but also whether those demands will even enter people's minds (Saunders, 1979: 30). These ideas will now be illustrated with respect to the work of J.K. Galbraith.

3.2.2.1   J.K. Galbraith's view of power

Bachrach and Baratz's concept of non-decisionmaking can be illustrated in relation to the works of J.K. Galbraith, who attempts to turn the conventional wisdom of liberal economics on its head. In *The Affluent Society* (1958), Galbraith outlines his argument which seeks to explain demand as the outcome of production and not the other way round. He expands on this account in *The New Industrial State* (1967), where he attacks the general consensus regarding the existence of consumer sovereignty, arguing instead that a better explanation for real conduct in the marketplace is based on what he calls the **revised sequence**. By this he means that rather than considering firms as being submissive to the whims of sovereign consumers, it is more realistic to consider that consumers are largely submissive to the desires of firms.

In order to more fully understand Galbraith's views, we must first briefly summarize his explanation of power in relation to economic life. Galbraith first equates the exercise of power as the exercise of one's will on others – the greater the imposition of the will, the greater is the power. Alongside Bachrach and Baratz as quoted above, and in contradistinction to the liberal view of power, he argues that some use of power depends on its being concealed, and that submission to such power is not always evident to those who experience it. Also the instruments for subordinating people and the sources of this ability are changing. Galbraith's scheme has three instruments for wielding power which he labels condign, compensatory and conditioned power. **Condign power** involves alternatives to individual or group preferences being sufficiently unpleasant to lead to abandonment of such alternatives. While condign power is a negative instrument, **compensatory power** is positive, based on the offer of a reward or inducement of some kind.

Conditioned power is exercised by influencing a person's beliefs; persuasion, education and social commitment about what seems to be natural, proper and right causes the individual to submit to the will of others, without necessarily being aware that he or she is doing so. Submission takes place because this seems to be the right and natural thing to do, and the fact of submission is not recognized. The idea of conditioned power is thus similar to that of the 'mobilization of bias' described by Bachrach and Baratz above. Galbraith cites as examples of conditioned power, the role played by formal education in the transmission of 'acceptable codes' through the family, schools and universities. These seek to create submission to group values, such as 'patriotism' or the virtues of 'free enterprise', being taken for granted as the right way to think of one's country and the functioning of the economic system. In particular he singles out the role played by advertising in cultivating beliefs. In this view, advertising plays a key role in bringing the buyer to a belief in the purposes of the seller as a form of submission: 'He or she submits to the will of the purveyor of the beer, cigarettes, detergent or political purpose' (1984: 30).

Galbraith's typology includes three sources of power.; these are personality, property and organization. He notes that whereas in primitive societies **personal power** was linked primarily to the exercise of force (condign power), in contemporary societies it is more often linked to the ability to instil beliefs (conditioned power). If one has sufficient **property**, including income, then one can purchase the submission of others. He believes that the central tool in marketing effectiveness lies in winning the submission of customers. This depends on the effectiveness of **organization** in securing the submission of employees, particularly full-time employees, and most especially the most senior employees, in the pursuance of corporate goals. Thus:

> 'No senior executive would presume to suggest that the cigarettes his company makes cause cancer, that its automobiles are unsafe, that its pharmaceuticals are medically suspect. Or that some political initiative sought by the company – improvement of competition allowances or the reduction of foreign competition, is in conflict with the public interest.'   [1984: 59]

Galbraith's view of power is systemic in that he argues that modern society is in equilibrium between those who exercise power and those who counter it. In this view the usual and most effective response to an unwelcome exercise of power is to build a countervailing power. For example if sellers overcharge then buyers will come together with other buyers to boycott or bargain. In modern societies, he argues, it is the state which acts as arbiter of power. Different groups in society seek the support of the state in winning the submission of others or in resisting the power of others. The state regulates condign power. It also regulates forms of compensatory power such as the use of bribes or kickbacks. In the USA particularly, the state guarantees the use of conditioned power through the exercise of 'freedom of speech'.

Galbraith's account of the exercise of power in high capitalism

In discussing the exercise of power in contemporary society, Galbraith first refers his reader to Adam Smith's *Wealth of Nations*. Galbraith argues that the works of Smith, allied with others such as Malthus, Ricardo and Bentham, have been particularly influential in socially conditioning those who ruled the state to a belief in industrial capitalism. Thus Bentham's argument for utilitarianism representing 'the greatest good for the greatest number' seems best adapted to Smith's policy of 'laissez-faire', which equates the pursuit of all economic self-interest with the public good. Galbraith says that it would be hard to think of any idea so serviceable to industrial power. In this view the actions of industrialists are rendered ultimately virtuous 'by an overriding law to which he, however selfish or sordid his purpose or motivations, was wholly subject' (1984: 113).

Galbraith argues that in today's world Smith's notion of the operation of the 'invisible hand' of the marketplace is a sham. Smith originally proposed this in order that competition might break the power of the great chartered companies. Yet, Galbraith argues, competition is precisely what is lacking in reality today. As a consequence, Smith's rhetoric of competition operates as a powerful tool for large companies which seek to condition others into believing that it still prevails. Why has competition disappeared? Galbraith argues that capitalism grew on the back of powerful personalities (Carnegie, Rockefeller etc.) who came to control massive properties. In time, such property came to be seen less as the extended arm of the boss and to be governed by management specialists. Through compensatory power, industrialists bought legislators and consumers. In the modern age, organization in the form of the **technostructure** has emerged as the source of power in industrial capitalism. The technostructure can best be thought of as a vast managerial bureaucracy which subverts the marketplace in seeking to serve its own interests over those of shareholders and customers.

Galbraith argues that oligopoly is the reality for most markets, which are dominated by a few large sellers. He suggests that there is general agreement among economists that this is the case, that such firms wield considerable control over prices and that price-fixing is endemic in ensuring an 'orderly' marketplace. Furthermore, anti-trust legislation merely serves the purpose of denying market power to those who do not have it or who have difficulty in exercising this, while according immunity to those who already have such power. For example he suggests that while the top three US automobile manufacturers can control prices with little or no interference from regulators, if three or more subcontractors tried to do so, the law would be on them like a tiger (1967: 192). He further asserts that the practical effect of the anti-trust laws is obscurantist; while their stated aim may be to improve the operations of the marketplace, in reality they add to the illusion of marketplace control and consumer sovereignty.

The main aim of the technostructure is to ensure its own survival, which means at bottom that it is free from control by either customer or stockholder (Galbraith, 1967: based on chapters 15–19, 34 and 35). It seeks to ensure that consumers buy what is available at whatever price it determines and that stockholders receive a return which is adequate or enough for them not to wish to rock the boat. The need to manage both aggregate and specific demand is due to the ability through increased technology and operational efficiencies to produce very large volumes. Galbraith deploys the neologism of the **revised sequence** in order to explain this. In this view the 'accepted sequence' encapsulates consumer sovereignty and the marketing concept: that all needs start with consumers, and that the expression of such needs sends signals to producers who respond to this message of the market and the instructions of the consumer. The revised sequence in contrast refers to the reality, whereby producers condition the creation and satisfaction of needs and wants in the interests of the technostructure. Advertising is especially important to the technostructure as there is a need to create a ready market for the goods on offer. In response to the statement that much advertising is informational, Galbraith sardonically replies 'Only a gravely retarded person would need to be told that the American Tobacco Company has cigarettes for sale' (1967: 210). The presumption that the marketplace is dominated by *homo economicus*, that individual rational agent, utility maximizer and originator of his needs, supposes any interference with the expressed preferences of this sovereign individual to be unwarranted. As a result, any public objections to lethal automobile design, disabling drugs, disfiguring beauty aids or high-calorie reducing compounds are interpreted as constituting interference with the individual's design for maximizing his satisfaction and with the resulting economic response. This provides a powerful protection for the technostructure which hides behind the rhetoric of the sovereign individual as a cover for its wholesale manipulation of the marketplace. As a result everything from retail strip developments to industrial farms and air and river pollution is justified on the basis of the rhetoric of 'freedom of individual choice'.

What solutions does Galbraith offer to this abuse of power represented by the technostructure? He argues that this must be broken in order to ensure a safer basis for underwriting technology, the expansion of socially useful services and the emancipation of education. There is no point in looking to the state for this, as there is an 'increasingly artificial and indistinct' line drawn between the technostructure and the state. Rather he sees the intellectual community as the vanguard of this change. This is because he believed at that time (in the 1960s) there was a strong and independent sense of academic freedom of intellectuals in the USA which was not constrained by bureaucracy nor compromised through reliance on the technostructure. One wonders what he would think now.

3.2.2.2 Evaluation of Galbraith

Galbraith's work is unusual in that it exemplifies his theory itself; during the 1960s the idea of the 'technostructure' formed a rallying ground for those countercultural forces which sought to undo the perceived power of capital. How relevant are his ideas now? The power and concentration of industrial capital is much greater now than it was in the 1960s. For 'global' and 'anti-capitalist' protestors such power is encapsulated in the perceived non-accountable actions of the G7/G8, World Bank and other powerful interests. One could argue that the concept of the technostructure has been made flesh through the formation of the Bilderberg group, which represents an elite coalition of government and business interests which meets periodically with the aim of discussing and acting upon important global issues away from the media spotlight (thus justifying its shadowy existence). However while the existence of the Bilderberg group may be a conspiracy theorist's dream, one might conjecture that any attempt to control the global economy in the era of 'post-Fordism' and the 'electronic herd' would be doomed to failure. Additionally authors have taken Galbraith to task with respect to the idea of the 'revised sequence', arguing that this exaggerates the true state of affairs. Others argue that it is accepted in economics that production decisions have to be made in anticipation of consumer demands, and that while consumers may be led to the product, they are not obliged to buy it. For example the Ford Edsel was reckoned to be, in real terms, the most expensively researched product ever developed. Backed by a massive advertising blitz, the Edsel fell flat on its face once launched because in the period between conception and launch the style became unfashionable. Galbraith thus tends to reinforce the collusive operations of industrial power while neglecting the power of consumers to deviate from those intentions. Nevertheless his argument with respect to the organization of industrial power adds some substance to the arguments of those who question the liberal view.

3.2.3 Steven Lukes: a radical view of power

Steven Lukes' radical formulation of power extends the reformist argument of non-decisionmaking one further step. If for instance we assume that 'news management' through the **mobilization of bias** is endemic in pluralist societies, then what if this has reached such a peak that large sections of the population no longer recognize what their true interests are? This idea – that (particularly working class) people live in an imaginary relation to their real conditions of existence – describes the negative view of **ideology**. This is negative in that it describes a person as living a false or inauthentic existence. To say that a person lives in an imaginary relation suggests a form of fantasy. Below we will discuss two negative views of ideology. The first is based on a psychoanalytic view and argues that important critical elements within a person's psyche have been repressed. A second 'narrow' view simply argues that ideology is transmitted through advertising.

3.2.3.1 Herbert Marcuse: ideology as repression

Linked to the idea that ideologies are created and circulated by the ruling class is the idea that a person's personality is shaped by ideology. You will remember from Chapter 2 that Reuben Fine suggests the modern character has become more individualized and narcissistic. Norbert Elias's account of the changing topology of the self also supports such a view, arguing that psychogenetic processes involving the structure of personality are intimately related to and dependent upon changes in social organization (sociogenesis). Elias draws upon Freud's concepts of id, ego and superego to suggest that, because of increased social dependencies, the superego role is enhanced in modern societies; this places pressure on the ego to conform to the demands of society to sublimate the energies of the id in socially acceptable ways. In this view the ego in consumer society acts more forcefully to repress id energies. Herbert Marcuse, a 'guru' of the 1960s, based his theory on ideological repression of erotic desire through a process which he termed 'repressive desublimization' (Marcuse, 1964), which will be explained below. Marcuse bases his explanation on Freud's hydraulic model of human motivation. In this view both physical and psychical growth arise as the result of the constant exchange of energy. The id is presented as a storehouse or cauldron of energy which is invested into the world by the ego in the hope that this will be returned with interest. For example hunger arising in the body provides energy which seeks sustenance and the food received replaces the energy which has been lost and gives back an additional amount. The hydraulic analogy is thus appropriate in that the person is seen as 'growing' and developing physically and psychically through the constant exchange of energy flows. The name which Freud gave to this energetic principle was Eros, which represents the life-force which develops as the infant develops. The infant is thus governed by id forces associated with the pleasure principle, which is innate and leads to the gratification of instinctual demands through wish-fulfilling fantasies, which have no relation to the demands of reality. This is consistent with the state of **primary narcissism** where the young child has yet to define and construct an ego or sense of self. The emerging ego is shaped slowly as the result of parental guidance and discipline. As opposed to the pleasure principle which is driven purely by internal desire, the emerging ego is governed by the reality principle, in that it must take into account the demands of society, as represented by the superego, for civilized behaviour.

Marcuse begins by insisting that 'a comfortable, smooth, reasonable, democratic unfreedom prevails in advanced industrial civilization'. By this he means that the topology of the self has been changed in modern industrial society. Marcuse argues that because modern life is so bland and so comfortable, the critical dimension of self represented by the ego has failed to develop and largely disappeared, leaving the total domination of id forces by the superego, which represents the demands of the industrial system. What used to be liberty is represented as a pseudo 'freedom of choice' in the world of goods. As a result people come to identify themselves purely within the realm of commodities – of automobiles, hi-fis, split-level homes, kitchen equipment and so on. The notion of **repressive desublimization** refers to the loss of the traditional role of the ego in mediating or sublimating id-instincts in socially acceptable ways. Marcuse argues that the traditional role played by sublimation was a painful but important means for facilitating the transfers of energies between the self and the world. But consumer society destroys the ability to sublimate (to increase the flow to the world and back to the self) of this energy. Marcuse illustrates processes of sublimation/repressive desublimization through a number of examples: the wandering poet/the modern tourist, the craftsman/the assembly line worker, factory-produced bread/the home-made loaf and making love in a meadow/making love in a car. The alternatives offered by consumer society (listed to the right) illustrate for Marcuse the de-eroticization of a whole sphere of life, which as a consequence has led to a reduction in the amount of energy produced. In the modern mechanized condition cathexis, or investment of energy, is blocked and this limits the scope for and the need of sublimation. While society purportedly operates under a regime of sexual freedom, this is in fact the age of a **general repression of genuine sexuality**. False needs are those which are superimposed upon the individual in his repression.

Marcuse represents just one strand of opinion within that dissident school of thought known as the Frankfurt School. Erich Fromm (1978), whose work is discussed in more detail in Chapter 10, discusses the anxiety-ridden 'marketing character', who comes to see himself as a form of commodity to be branded and displayed in the marketplace of commodities. Others liken modern consumers to narcissistic infants, who though passive believe that it is they who are active and controlling (see for example Lasch, 1979). You will find that Brennan (1993), whose work is discussed in Chapter 2, takes a similar point of view.

3.2.3.2   Ideology: distortion through transmission of 'ruling ideas'

Compared to the idea that ideology is a form of repression, the narrower formulation of ideology describes it as a form of *inversion which is based on a distortion which is made to seem as if it is natural and inevitable*. Generally this is associated with the 'mystifying' effect of 'ruling ideas' in perpetuating **'false consciousness'**. Let me try to translate this into English. In this formulation, ideology is said to be an inversion because people (the working class) believe that the state of affairs in which they live (contentment) is quite different from their real situation (immiseration by capital). They argue that this state of affairs has arisen as a result of indoctrination through state-sponsored media, which include not only the mass media of television, radio and newspapers but also schools and religious and other forms of education. Through this indoctrination, it is argued, people come to think of things which have been socially created (their position in the world, the nuclear family) as being somehow natural and inevitable. This is similar to the idea of the 'mobilization of bias' developed by Bachrach and Baratz and of conditioned power developed by J.K. Galbraith, which were outlined in previous sections of this chapter. It is also central to Stuart Ewen's explanation which formed the basis for the second 'story' told in Chapter 1 (Ewen, 1976, 1986).

One view about the role played by 'ruling ideas' is that consumer society creates particular types of character, or more specifically that advertising creates false needs or that it 'normalizes' the values of the ruling class. This view corresponds to John B. Thompson's claim that to study ideology is to consider the ways in which meaning serves to sustain relations of domination.[5] Here the topic for research is the advertising system and in particular the ways in which this acts to reinforce the acceptance of 'ruling ideas' by the 'masses'.

One discussion relates to the creation by advertising of false needs, the other to the communication of dominant values. The discussion of false needs has attracted a lot of attention, not least from the work of Raymond Williams (1962: 188/9) and J.K. Galbraith (1958). For Williams the 'magic' effected by advertising is to link products to meanings which have significance for individuals, but which act to mask the social nature of many real needs. This issue is discussed more fully in the next chapter which covers the issues of exchange, needs and values.

Construction of 'woman' through advertising

With respect to the communication of dominant values, Lee and Murray (1995) discuss the process whereby advertising functions as a form of 'super-structural' knowledge which communicates the values, interests, opinions and lifestyles necessary to fuel a materialistic economy based on overproduction and at the same time distorts a clear picture of this society. The authors argue that advertising plays a role in social control. For example they contend that advertising depicts a narrow range of social and occupational roles for women.

According to Lee and Murray (1995), advertising serves the 'need' for low-cost (therefore exploited) labour; if women perceive themselves to be inferior, they might agree to a lower wage for equal work. This argument is representative of what passes for many as 'crude' Marxism – the view that a person's material (class) position determines their real relation to the world, although they suffer from a distorted 'false consciousness' brought about by the dissemination of 'ruling ideas'. To what extent can this be substantiated? Most authors agree that while early advertising targeted women as homemakers, fashion objects or sex objects, studies carried out in the early 1970s suggested that advertising was beginning to recognize women's role in the (non-domestic) workplace. However Erving Goffman was to show that women continued to be presented in subordinate roles, at least until the end of the 1970s. In *Gender Advertisements*, which was to become a classic, Goffman (1979) conducted a detailed analysis of hundreds of print ads. This exquisitely detailed analysis shows how the presentation of gender in advertising is marked by the tiniest differences in relation to posture, the position of the hands, facial expressions and so on. The research indicated that ads work in subtle ways to frame views of the normalcy of the nuclear family and of the role played by men and women within it. In one section entitled

---

[5] This is referred to by Eagleton (1991: 5) as the most widely accepted definition of ideology.

'The Ritualization of Subordination', Goffman describes how contemporary ads depicted women as being systematically portrayed in subordinate positions to men, with their knees often bent, or lying on beds or floors, or positioned behind the man or below the man.

While the presentation of ads may be said to be ideological, how do women relate to the stereotypical occupation roles and the postures contained within them? In seeking to answer this question Wortzel and Frisbie (1974) conducted a study to explore women's perception of advertising which targeted them. Participants were invited to construct their own ads for a range of products, using a 'role-background' where they could choose from a menu of roles – from a 'neutral' role to that of a 'career' woman or 'family' woman, the 'fashionable' woman or the woman as 'sex-object'. Findings suggested that if the results were generalized then women would be likely to adopt different roles depending on the product being advertised. Those who participated in the study preferred the family role-background for food and large appliances, with 'fashion', 'career' and 'neutral' roles emphasized for grooming products (none chose the 'sex-object' role-background). The authors also analysed the data in relation to attitudes towards women's liberation. Interestingly they found that participants who were positive towards women's lib tended if anything to prefer to choose traditional family roles in constructing their ads. In general the authors concluded that their findings could support two quite different explanations with respect to the roles portrayed by advertising. On the one hand the findings could provide support for the traditional view which argues that women are perfectly satisfied with the range of roles on offer. The alternative explanation is that advertising has itself socialized women to expect and to accept traditional role portrayals in ads. Some years later Lyonski and Pollay (1990) reported the results of two long-term studies which investigated changes in attitudes of US women towards role portrayal in advertising from the 1970s to the 1980s. Findings indicated that while women had become even more critical of advertising, they were less prone to boycott goods as a result than they had been ten years before. In a related study, they found that young adults from Denmark, Greece and New Zealand were even more critical than the Americans. De Young and Crane (1992), who explored the perceptions of Canadian women towards advertising in the 1990s also found that a majority of respondents thought that the portrayal of women in advertising was inaccurate and unrealistic, portraying them as homemakers or sex objects rather than representing the role of career woman.

To sum up the above, research indicates that while advertisers do tend to reproduce prevailing social stereotypes in their advertising, women are not happy with the way in which they are portrayed. Research thus partially supports the view that advertising seeks to inculcate a dominant ideology. Against the idea that women passively adopt these views, research evidence suggests that they are aware of these stereotypes and actively oppose them. This suggests that even if it were true, as in Goffman's time, that advertisers continue to embed stereotypical representations of gender into their ads, this would be of little consequence, as women are already aware of these and react critically to them. This accords with Stuart Hall's explanation, which suggests that while advertisers may encode their ads with stereotypical or other cues which they would *prefer* the reader to decode, in actually decoding the message, readers may accept, reject or change this preferred meaning in line with their own experiences and the views which they have constructed through conversations with others. The idea that people use advertising for their own purposes is the keystone for **uses and gratifications** research. This takes a virtually opposite line to the dominant ideology thesis, in suggesting that people are active agents who attend to and respond to ads within their own interpretative experience. This was the approach adopted by Stephanie O'Donohoe (1994) whose research suggests not only that the audience is active, but that it is plural, encompassing different points of view to the same ad content. O'Donohoe's findings are supported by Elliott *et al.* (1993).

Other arguments suggest that advertising normalizes and naturalizes the idea of consumption as a global panacea. Wernick argues that advertising 'typifies what is diverse, filters out what is antagonistic and depressing and naturalizes the role and standpoint of consumption as such' (1991: 42). Similarly Goldman (1992) portrays the role of advertising as a key institution in producing and reproducing the material and ideological supremacy of commodity relations, using everything from shock ads to 'feminine' ads and 'feminist' ads to 'anti-hero' ads and even 'not ads' and 'anti-ads' as vehicles. Goldman develops the device of the mortise and the frame to illustrate how advertisers maximize the chances that the audience will base their reading of the ad on the preferred reading. Given the pervasive nature of advertising and commodity relations in Western society, the observation that advertising orients expectations to those of the marketplace is scarcely novel nor surprising.

3.2.3.3 Neutral definitions of ideology

Judith Williamson's classic *Decoding Advertisements* (1978) renders a quite different articulation of ideology from those described above, which derives from a 'structuralist' reading of de Saussure via Levi-Strauss, Lacan and Althusser. She takes up Althusser's formulation of ideology as a form of **misrecognition**: '*Ideology represents the imaginary relationship of individuals to their real conditions of existence*' (1978: 40). In this account, advertising (among other ideological apparatuses) calls or **interpellates** people to participate in an exchange of meaning whereby they invest in an image in return for the promise of an (illusory) sense of wholeness. In this view people are not deceived by someone else putting over false ideas, but are active in 'freely' creating themselves in structures which have already been created for them. Advertising works as an ideological apparatus which mystifies history, nature and society and objectifies those it incorporates. It creates a dream-world of images which are commonly perceived to be more real than the real world of isolated personal experience. For example if one considers the way in which animals are represented in advertising, then based on a brief non-systematic survey, one genre focuses on a 'humour' appeal which concentrates on comic and fanciful images of dancing cows, happy hens and fluffy contented sheep. This is at once a joke (I know or at least suspect the reality) but which calls me to an imaginary state where I *wish* it were true that such things existed and come to prefer the image to the reality. In this way it can be argued that ideology acts to 'reproduce' capitalist social relations according to the 'requirements' of the 'system'.

This view of ideology is similar to that adopted by Stuart Hall and his colleagues. Hall viewed Althusser's formulation as opening up the door towards a **discursive** formulation of ideology by focusing on the processes by which people actively enter into it. Influenced by the work of Laclau (1983), Hall began to move from a negative conception of ideology as 'distorted ideas' or as 'false consciousness' towards a more neutral approach which is reflected in his definition of ideology as:

> 'the mental frameworks – the languages, the concepts, categories, imagery of thought, and the systems of representation – which different classes and social groups deploy in order to make sense of, define, figure out and render intelligible the way society works.'   [Hall, 1996: 26]

This neutral definition is wider than the negative one in that it can be used to refer to all organized forms of social thinking. It contends that people can recognize the same capitalist relations of production in different ways. For example we have already discussed liberal and reformist perspectives in this chapter. You will remember that the liberal argument insists that the market is the best or least-worst mode for organizing economic relations because it grants equal rights to all individuals to freely engage in transactions. Economic actors are rewarded to the extent that the gains which they make can be held as private personal property. Advocates would argue that the market system is preferable because it is a less centralized and authoritarian means for conducting economic affairs, since it involves the active participation of a myriad of actors each pursuing their self-interest rather than labouring under bureaucratic control from a centralized authority. In line with the neutral view of ideology, Hall does not suggest that those who believe in liberal principles are foolish, misguided or wrong; the market does indeed advocate and to an extent uphold such principles. Rather than blame the people, he locates the problem in the way in which the market itself operates. The market does not exist in isolation but is one moment, the final one, in the **circuit of production**. Other moments which are included in the circuit of production include the conversion of nature into 'raw' materials for production, their transport to centres of production and subsequent conversion into products through the labour process. In this respect liberals who focus purely on the virtues of the marketplace do so at the expense of the other moments of the circuit of production. In this account, one moment of the circuit of production – the marketplace – is made to stand in for the whole circuit. As we shall see in Chapter 5, this is a metonymic substitution of the part (the market) for the whole (the circuit of production). This recalls the discussion of Marx's concept of the **fetishism of commodities** in Chapter 2.[6] You should remember that his argument suggests that capitalism calls us to view the market as being somehow natural and inevitable, standing over those who are subjected to it in the likeness of a great god, an idol worshipped by some and hated by others but perceived by all to be beyond the control of mere mortals. Marx argued that such a view masks the reality that markets are created by human activity. While the rhetoric of the marketplace cites certain principles – the 'freedom' of any individual to transact with any other, the equality of those who wish to take part, the respect for 'private' property and for self-interest – Marx argues that these act to conceal inequality. Those inequalities which are concealed lie in those other 'moments' which are concealed through the metonymic substitution of the market for the circuit of production: of living nature which is converted into raw materials at a rate which is faster than it can naturally reproduce, and of human energy which is converted into labour power and which is exploited by capital. However, because we encounter the marketplace on a daily basis, we take the reality of its principles for granted and do not recognize the exploitation that exists in the other moments of the process. This above analysis is not organized around the differences between the 'real' and the 'false'; ideology is not considered as a trick or illusion, nor is it attributed to false consciousness. What is ideological in the above is the substitution of the marketplace for the circuit of production. In this respect ideology is a very specific form of distortion in reality which plays out in the realm of representation as a specific form of false consciousness: 'The very reality of the market relations creates a world of appearances which dupes people' (Larrain, 1995: 59). In this view ideology is not linked to the realm of the imagination but is integral to the operations of the market which purports to be based on principles of freedom, equality, property and self-interest, and conceals its true exploitative nature. In this more neutral sense of ideology, the conveyance of 'ruling ideas' through advertising and other media which act to represent the interests of the ruling class is not strictly ideological. Rather, advertising as an extension of 'ruling ideas' might better be thought of as enhancing the appearances of the market which are already there. What is ideological is that it is the market itself which appears as if imbued with the properties of freedom, equality, property and self-interest. However, subjects may not necessarily fall victim to the ideology that the market is really free and fair, based on equivalent exchange.

Discussion of radical view of power

This section has considered several aspects concerned with the topic of ideology. Negative views of ideology are coloured by the view that consumer society is undoubtedly a bad thing, in that the 'me' society

---

[6] This reading is based on Larrain (1995).

suffocates critical thought and arrests the potential for forward movement towards a better society, inaugurating a new and more truly 'human' era. Having said that, the type of 'capitalism' which each of these authors is referring to is different in each case. For Erich Fromm it is the aggressive capitalism of the early twentieth century; for Marcuse it is the instrumental rationality related to Fordism that concerned many others who wrote in the 1960s, including J.K. Galbraith's image of the technostructure; while for Brennan, capitalism appears in a voracious guise which one might associate with the Reagan–Thatcher period. While it could be argued that this does not invalidate these arguments, but rather highlights the powerful dynamic element of capitalism, one does begin to wonder whether an 'authentic' liberated character will emerge one day or whether this is all just pie-in-the-sky.

These works have also been criticized as being elitist. While the consumer mass lies dazed by the drug of consumer society, the critics have managed to rise above all of that to see what is 'really' going on. One of the legacies of this mode of thought is the idea that consumer culture is aggressively territorial – that it progressively globalizes and homogenizes, uprooting and destroying pre-existing economic and cultural systems and throwing up new characters such as 'Homo Coca-Colens' and 'Homo Dalensis' (Cinquin, 1987) in its wake. These ideas have already been addressed in the section on globalization in Chapter 2 and are central to the argument put forward here. Attacks on globalization have spilled beyond the academy to the anti-capitalist protests played out in Genoa, Seattle, Prague and a host of other venues where G7/G8 and the World Trade Organization meet to seek to resolve issues with respect to world trade. Against this view a number of authors have pointed out that the fact of the matter is that most of those who are excluded from consumer culture are united by their demand to share in the feast (Roszak, 1970; Castells, 1997: 75/6; Miller, 1998; Rudmin and Kilbourne, 1996). For example the desire to trade the Trabant for a Mercedes society was a major aspiration for those caught behind the 'wall' of East Berlin. Additionally, participants to the WTO and other talks from less 'developed' countries have argued that protestors' attempts to frustrate these have been to the detriment of those who live in poorer countries. Ideology theorists might of course reply to the above that this is clear evidence of more or less complete dominance of the 'ruling ideas' of the marketplace in the world today. However their critics might then attack on a second footing, to suggest that talk of 'protecting' 'traditional' cultures from the ravages of consumerism might alternatively be construed as a kind of smokescreen which merely serves to maintain the status quo with respect to the imbalance between rich and poor; as Miller puts it – 'the castle of consumerism pulling up the drawbridge' (1996: 197). They might also suggest that 'when push comes to shove', remarkably few First World moralists opt for a life of voluntary simplicity; it can be 'cool' for intellectuals to rail against the system that maintains their own prestige and to dream of its ultimate ruin or transformation, however it is very unlikely that they would do so 'for real'.

3.3   DISCIPLINARY POWER

The second major approach to the analysis of power which is discussed here is based on the concept of disciplinary power. There are two different approaches to theorizing this form of power. The first of these, which sees discipline as being a form of repression, is closely linked to the negative view of ideology as repression, discussed in the previous section. The second discursive explanation of disciplinary power is based on the writings of Michel Foucault.

3.3.1   Disciplinary power as repression

Here it is useful to revisit some of the theories which were first discussed in Chapter 1. Norbert Elias's explanation of the development of Western civilization contends that the modern self emerged slowly as communities within society became more interdependent, to the extent that people began to find themselves living and working among strangers. You will recall that growing interdependency between strangers necessitated the rapid growth of an abstract system of value which recognized the right of individuals to trade across community divides. This move towards external exchange presupposes the difference and separatedness of the parties involved. There is a paradox here, as Elias notes, because this growing interdependency was linked to the removal of bodily contact; he describes the change as akin to a wall being placed between one human body and another. Bodily activities and emotions which for centuries had been openly expressed were progressively shifted behind the scenes into the private domain. In this sense it is possible to discern the development of a new topology or configuration of power in society based on the growth of the space of individual self-consciousness as the result of the fear of judgement by others, and the development of self-discipline through the emphasis on shame and embarrassment and the 'view' of the body as an object. Elias uses the id–ego–superego terminology developed by Sigmund Freud to illustrate the change in the topology of the psyche. Thus with the build-up of external constraints for the adoption of more 'appropriate' behaviour, as represented by the superego, the ego takes on more of a role in mediating between the demands of the id for immediate gratification and those of society for civilized conduct. The character of the 'sober' Puritan described by Weber in Chapter 2 fits well with this image of powerful restraint and repression of desire.

This explanation also forms the basis for some ideological critiques such as that formulated by Herbert Marcuse, whose work was discussed in the previous section. This suggests that the bourgeois class imposes its sexual repression onto its workers. The 'proper' use of sexuality is linked to reproduction. The modern nuclear family is thus stripped from its extended context and fitted out for work in capitalist enterprise, in order to meet the demand for a stable, punctual workforce. The consumer society is interpreted in this context as a means of distracting workers from their real authentic interests and perpetuating that 'comfortable smooth' unfreedom which Marcuse talks about. Thus the idea of **self-discipline** is linked to changes in the social scene. In their formative years, children are trained to repress their desires. In Elias's explanation, the inculcation of such discipline helps develop the space for '*homo economicus*', the rational and reasonable 'self-steered' individual. For Marcuse this same individual is rationalized; the critical power of the ego has been reduced to the extent that all desires are subject to social control.

3.3.2   Michel Foucault: a discursive account of discipline

For many years Foucault agreed with the above account of the repression of sexuality. However as the result of his own research, he reasoned that this was an inadequate explanation of historical events. On this basis he began to formulate a new approach to understanding the constitution and the workings of power.

Let us consider the historical state of affairs first. Foucault found that far from being repressed, sexuality became increasingly subject to **discourse**, being talked about (by professionals), written about, medicalized and pathologized during the eighteenth and nineteenth centuries. Related to this, while Marcuse and others argue that sexual repression was foisted onto the working classes, Foucault found that this discourse of 'sexuality' was first applied to the bourgeois class by its own members. Most importantly, Foucault disagrees with the idea that there ever was a period of repression. In order to understand this we must revisit the events of the eighteenth century when the bourgeois class began seriously to compete with the nobility, which was briefly discussed in Chapter 2. At that time, when it came to matters of distinction, the nobility had an ace up its sleeves – 'breeding' or 'blue blood'. How could the bourgeoisie compete against such pedigree? Foucault (1979: 126) argues simply that: 'It converted the blue blood of the nobles into a sound organism and a healthy sexuality'. The bourgeoisie thus became preoccupied with ensuring and increasing the **normality**, health and longevity of their stock. The creation of a 'healthy' sexuality involved the identification and rooting out of all that was 'unhealthy' in the social body of the bourgeois class. This involved the construction of a 'body' of knowledge by medics and other experts (who were of course themselves bourgeois). The mechanism for revealing this knowledge was borrowed from the Church in the form of the confessional. People confessed their diverse problems to the medics and the medics in turn came up with a range of perversions and other 'unnatural' sexual identities. Sexuality thus began to be seen as the object of medical attention, via the understanding of the etiology (cause) of 'nervous disorders', and of psychiatric attention, via the labelling and understanding of 'mental illnesses'. The role of the expert was to identify the 'unnatural' or 'perverted' in the same way that a surgeon might identify a lesion. An entire mechanism of power was thus brought to bear on the body, on identifying what was 'normal'. There was an important difference between the way in which perversions were treated by Christianity and by the new medicine. The focus of Christianity was upon the act or the sin. 'Buggery' was thus a repugnant act for which a person should confess and do penance. Medicine on the other hand located the act as an essential part of the identity of the person. We see here what was scattered (the sin) becoming solidified and essentialized in the construction of an identity for the person. As a result the person becomes identified on the basis of his or her sex – 'homosexual'. As Foucault notes (1979: 43): 'the sodomite had been a temporary aberration, the homosexual was now a species'.

Initially the actions of the medics focused solely on the bourgeoisie, in identifying deviancy and in seeking to prevent this or to cure it. The creation of healthy bodies was seen to be an essential act of self-affirmation on the part of the bourgeois class. However with the growing power of capitalism and also in response to concerns about the spread of diseases such as cholera, the body of the 'healthy' worker began to be explored, regulated and disciplined in like manner. A concern with reform flowed also through the prison system. The ultimate aim of disciplinary techniques was to produce useful individuals and healthy vibrant bodies, through discouraging debauchery and other perversions among the general population and 'reforming' criminals so that they could become useful members of society, acting according to the principle of 'homo economicus'. Prisons became centres which sought to transform the individual through training in work according to a strict timetable and the discipline resulting from isolation in cells (a term borrowed from Christian monasticism). Most importantly the regime developed a knowledge of each individual based on detailed observation during the course of their period of incarceration. Foucault argues that this form of disciplinary apparatus began to become characteristic of institutional life; one which integrated ideas about normalcy and the creation of 'healthy' bodies through constant surveillance, examination and discipline.

Rational disciplinary power was exercised primarily through the organization of space. The pyramid style of **bureaucratic organization** (see Figure 3.1) was taken to be an apt means for controlling the wayward activities of the populations of army camps, factories, schools and hospitals. For example with respect to children, meticulous attention was paid to the organization of dormitories (with or without partitions, or curtains) and the rules for monitoring recreation activities and sleep periods. Control of spaces for storing materials (which could be stolen) and the regulation of the work-rate of people became important issues in factories which were becoming ever larger. The pyramid structure ensured constant supervision and **surveillance** of the spaces of the soldier, student, worker and patient. Within these disciplinary spaces, behaviour was oriented around the need to **measure up to the norm**, where the main motivating factor was the fear of being branded as being abnormal. Those who excelled were awarded rank, while those who failed were subject to a range of micro-penalties. The system was thus a balance of rewards and punishments with the emphasis placed upon rewards.

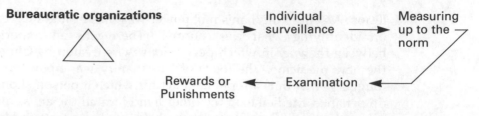

Figure 3.1 System of disciplinary power

The **examination** played a very important role in the system in classifying (mad/sane; normal/abnormal; competent/incompetent), qualifying (pass/ fail), rewarding and punishing those who were subject to its discipline. While usually it is thought that individualization or the recognition of a person as an individual attends only those of high status or rank, this is reversed in disciplinary regimes where those at the bottom of the heap are individualized. Thus what was previously regarded as a mob, or a lumpen mass, became transformed into a codified and disciplined body of individuals comprising soldiers, students, workers and patients.

The idea of the examination privileges the faculty of sight or vision. In the army, school, prison and hospital, the individual is constantly on view. Discipline is exercised through the visual examination, whereby those who do not measure up to the norm may be subjected to ridicule. According to Foucault, the perfect disciplinary apparatus would make it possible for a single **gaze** to see everything constantly. A central point would be both the source of light, which would illuminate everything but would mask who was (or was not) behind it, and also the focus for the convergence of all that was known. This image fits almost exactly with Jeremy Bentham's design for the **Panopticon**, the inspiration for the construction of Strangeways gaol in Manchester, England, among others.

Foucault argues that these disciplinary power mechanisms began to spill beyond institutions such as the prison and school to invade the whole of society. For example as the training of children had been entrusted to teachers in schools, teachers became interested in the quality of the life of the child beyond the school and in the activities of parents and their neighbours. He cites as early examples of more fluid disciplinary mechanisms, those religious groups which visited the poor, checking on their welfare and at the same time ensuring, among other things, the 'stability' of the household and that children were not sleeping in the same bed.

3.3.2.1 Power in consumer society

Foucault's conception of power differs from the idea of A/B power in several ways. He argues that the concept of sovereign power is outdated, that there is no one centre of power (A) which represses another (B). Rather power works through discourse in constructing the identities of As and Bs. Language, or discourse, is not neutral but is shaped by and reflective of power. Thus medical discourse is not neutral but constructs and essentializes the 'normal healthy' body against which to frame those of 'deviants'. Discourse can act in both ways: in transmitting power, but also in undermining and exposing it. For example Foucault argues that the creation of a whole series of discourses which labelled the species of 'homosexuality' enabled not only the creation of a series of social controls but also of a 'reverse discourse' which used the same vocabulary and categories to argue that homosexuality is 'natural'. To sum up his theory of power (based upon Foucault, 1979: 93/4) we should say that:

- Power is not something that is acquired, seized or shared, it cannot be held.
- Power is closely related to knowledge.
- Relations of power are not outside other relations. The identities which comprise *A* and *B* are themselves artefacts of power. Thus while Marcuse could write as if he stood outside the system of power which he was describing, Foucault could not.
- Power comes from below; it is not something which is exerted by *A* who is 'above' *B*.
- Power is intentional and rational to the extent that it has an aim and objective, but it should not be thought of as the creation of an individual agent, nor of a grouping such as the state.
- Where there is power there is resistance, but resistance is not outside power.

Starting from the 'bottom up' in this way, Foucault was able to conclude, in opposition to Elias and many others, that the idea of sexual repression is largely a myth. Rather than repressing sexuality, the bourgeois class in distinguishing itself from the nobility began progressively to open itself up to the scrutiny of a range of experts who would ensure the vigour and good health of this class. The resultant examination of the bourgeois family achieved several results. First it fixed what had previously been scattered and indeterminate (sexuality) into a set of diverse sexual identities. This in turn led to the development of a set of discourses which aimed to improve the social body through the close supervision and maintenance of real bodies.

Briefly, he is arguing that we should abandon the attempt to analyse power from the top down – for example through asking questions such as 'what role did the construction of the consumer play in the maintenance and extension of the power of capital?' Instead we should explore power from the bottom up and seek to understand the ways in which local centres of power–knowledge are created and how these are in turn related to larger strategies of power. By this he means that the focus of research should not be defined in relation to the grandiose sovereign operations of the state, but to the mundane, day-to-day practices, for example the medical or psychiatric examination. Working upwards from these one can discern the construction of the whole apparatus of discourses which thread through the medical establishment.

One could argue that the unravelling of a system of power and resistance may be located by focusing on the mundane, quotidian routines of shoppers; perhaps those groups of young women or men who enjoy shopping with their friends on a Saturday. We could note how the store environment is organized in such a way as to invite some constructions of identity and to foreclose others. We could seek to understand how the store has been constructed as being conducive and inviting to them, including the various cues which construct a discourse of the 'normal' body via images (thin?) and the size range of the goods on display (size 10?); the constant monitoring of activity by staff and by CCTV; the use of lighting and mirrors in changing rooms to enhance the look and shape of the body; and the role of the shop-assistant in reinforcing these other cues. Then there are the possible points of 'resistance', perhaps the attitude of the shop assistant does not conform to that specified in the training manual, or maybe 'resistance' is a function of how the women use the space in ways not intended by the store or perhaps in the 'deviant' ways in which they wear the clothes. Working upwards from such localities one could perhaps trace the multitude of marketing 'practitioner' and 'academic' discourses of the body. What is the objective and strategy behind the exercise of such power? Is this the creation of healthy bodies as it was in the eighteenth and nineteenth centuries?

From modernism to postmodernism: 'healthy' to 'fit' bodies?

Foucault's work which details the discursive construction of the healthy body focuses on the modern period. Is this discourse still at work in postmodernity? Bauman (1995) suggests that while modernity called for the training and regimentation of the 'healthy' body for soldiers and workers, postmodernity calls for that of the 'fit' body. For example he notes that Rowntree, in calculating the materials required for the minimum standard of living for his workers at the dawn of the twentieth century, excluded tea because it had no nutritional value (despite the fact that tea was seen to be an indispensable social drink). Bauman argues that nowadays the opposite is true, that bodies are framed through a multitude of discourses as consuming bodies, and that the measure of their proper condition is the extent to which they can consume what the consumer society has to offer (Bauman, 1995: 116). The fit body is a 'DIY' creation, which creates a strange and untenable position: 'S/he must be in control but s/he must be controlled' (Bauman, 1995: 118).

Sandra Bartky and Hilary Radner have taken different approaches to understanding the development of 'fitness' in women. Bartky (1992) argues that women are disciplined to produce and maintain a 'properly feminine body' which is pleasing to men. They are not forced to do this: as Bartky says, 'no-one is marched off for electrolysis at gun-point'. Nevertheless she argues that the attention which women pour into body maintenance, which is well above that invested by men, has to do with the simple fact that women are subordinate to men and must use their bodies to gain entry to the world of men and to compete with other women in the competition for men and for jobs. Bartky argues that if a woman refuses to go along with social expectations of what constitutes an acceptable appearance, she faces severe sanctions of being scorned, or shamed at being overweight or refused male patronage. On the other hand Bartky argues that body discipline can also have a positive side in that women who diet, exercise and work out can feel empowered from such activities, even though these activities shape women's bodies in the ideal-image of men.

Hilary Radner (1997) thinks that Bartky is making too much of the idea that women are disempowered in contemporary society. She takes the example of Jane Fonda who has produced a number of exercise videos for public consumption by women. Radner says that Fonda's public recognize her as a producer not a product, and as someone who can form a role model for those who seek to take control of their lives. The bodies of the models used by Fonda do not correspond to the pencil thin bodies usually propagated by the media. Radner argues that the body which results from the Jane Fonda workout tapes is a body which is neither erotic nor designed to please men, but one which is suitable for public life and for work. Radner argues that working out is an assertion of control. By assuming control over her own body and by making it into an image that is her own, Fonda rejects a feminine image of helpless passivity. In her books and films she offers a model through which women can reconstruct themselves and which allows them to develop a sense of autonomy. Radner also discusses how Fonda chose to have plastic surgery, arguing that this is a logical extension of the Fonda workout. It is voluntarily engaged in as the woman receives a return in terms of status and even pleasure.

The 'fit' organization

One major implication of Foucault's work is that language is not neutral but works through discourse to establish 'truth' effects. Brownlie and Saren (1997) explored this in relation to the deployment of marketing management discourse.[7] They cite as an example some research where the focus was on a presentation given by one manager to some of his colleagues. The manager had recently attended a marketing course and used the 'Boston Box' to organize the presentation. The authors suggest that one can read his use of the Boston Box in a number of ways. Firstly one can say that this was nothing more than an attempt to use a marketing tool to illustrate a real problem. However the use of formal marketing discourse has a persuasive effect, which highlights some features of the situation (related to cash flow and market share growth) and masks others. The 'proper' use of the Boston Box rests on a number of disciplines as it effectively condenses a huge amount of intelligence. For example one must have defined the market: estimated not only its size but also its growth rate, and plotted relative growth rates of the firm's products against those of competitors. The Boston Box thus acts as a crystal which filters the world in such a way that managers can use this to gain a clear vision in an otherwise chaotic environment. The use of the Box provides a conceptual vocabulary which highlights some issues (growth, cash flow) while masking others (real environmental costs; welfare issues).

[7] Thanks also to Charles Beard.

One can say that the Boston Box is not neutral but forms part of a rhetorical or persuasive strategy by the manager. The manager in this context has the knowledge (of the Box) and can use the Box as a vehicle to frame discussion at the meeting. While he is advantaged through its use, those unfamiliar with its terms will be disadvantaged. Power thus infuses the entire exercise, but with the productive end, of improved performance, leading to a fitter and leaner organization.

The discursive construction of power is particularly relevant given the proliferation of marketing discourse into almost every facet of everyday life. Take for example its effects on the construction of space. As a citizen one is entitled to free speech and the free occupancy of public spaces, so long as one observes the respective responsibility to be peaceful. As public space becomes privatized, such freedoms may no longer be taken for granted. As distinct from the public spaces of the square or park, the shopping mall is constructed as a space where it is safe for consumers to shop. If you wish to voice your anti-consumption sentiments or to 'loiter' in this space you can be quite legally and forcefully excluded. The space which marketing discourse configures is also a space for resistance. Traditionally a hospital 'patient' is subject to medical discourse and is subject to the benefits and constraints exercised within this. With the increasing privatization of health and education in the UK, 'patients' and 'students' come to see themselves as 'customers' who seek to invoke the expectation of consumer 'rights', an idea which would have been greeted with incredulity thirty years ago.

3.3.3   Discussion of disciplinary power

This section discusses two explanations for disciplinary power based on the work of Norbert Elias and Michel Foucault. Foucault's account challenges the basis for what he calls the 'repressive hypothesis' which underpins the thought of Elias among others. Foucault also critiques the traditional binary approach to power which discusses this in terms of 'A over B', arguing that neither A nor B can stand outside power. Rather one should conceive of individual identity (as consumer, worker, 'straight' or 'gay', 'anorexic') as itself being an effect of the exercise of power. Foucault's dismissal of the idea that power is repressive leads him to the conclusion that the exercise of power in modernity has been essentially productive, through the attempt to create useful and healthy bodies. Additionally Foucault tends to play down the extent to which individuals are self-directing or, as Elias would have it, capable of 'self-steering'.

Despite these important differences, there are many points of common ground between Foucault and others. He shares with Elias and Weber a concern to understand the widespread employment of disciplinary practices in modernity. He shares with Marcuse and the other ideology theorists an interest in the operations of power. In fact the work of Stuart Hall, discussed in the section on ideology, has itself been heavily influenced by that of Foucault. Foucault's work can serve as a most useful foil to the construction of a 'neat' and 'packaged' theory and can thus provide a useful counter-weight to several of the main arguments which are advanced in this text.

3.4 CHAPTER SUMMARY

This chapter discussed issues of sovereign and disciplinary power in relation to consumption. The first section considered different approaches to the creation of the 'good society' and in particular the forms of economic, social and political organization which might lead to the best (or least-worst) form of society. This involved the description and discussion of liberal, reformist and radical forms of power. The second section discussed disciplinary approaches to power.

3.5 CASE STUDY: GLOBAL RESISTANCE – TURNING THE HEAT UP[8]

Seattle, Prague, Gothenberg, Genoa – each a milestone signalling heightened levels of confrontation between protestors and state agencies. The following is a statement made before the Genoa summit of G8 leaders, by Precari Nati, an Italian communist group based in Bologna:

'If we are here, it is not as professional activists of anti-globalization, trying to find a position of mediation between the puppets of the economy and its "victims", by acting on behalf of others. We are not interested in representing anyone, and we spit in the face of those who wish to represent us. We do not understand exclusion as exclusion from the centres of economic decision-making but as the loss of our everyday life and activity as proletarians because of the economy.

'If we are here, it is not because we prefer fair trade to free trade, it is not because we believe that globalization weakens the authority of nation-states. We are not here because we think that the state is controlled by non-democratic institutions, nor because we want more control over the market. We are here because all trade is the trade of human misery, because all states are prisons, because democracy conceals the dictatorship of capital.

'If we are here, it is not because we see proletarians as victims, nor because we want to place ourselves as their protectors. We didn't come here to be impressed by spectacular riots but to learn the tactics of everyday class war by the strikers of Ansaldo and the disobedient proletarians in the metal industry. We come here to exchange our own experiences as the dispossessed of the whole world.

'If we are here, we do not come as members of the numerous NGOs, official lobbies, ATTAC or the rest of those who merely wish to be included in the discussions over the modernization of capitalism and who hope that their proposals will

---

[8] *Resistance* is the monthly agitational bulletin of the Anarchist Federation. The following excerpt is taken from Issue 28: http://burn.ucsd.edu/~acf/res/resist28.html

be able to save capitalist social relations, i.e. the same relations which perpetuate our alienation and exploitation.

'If we are here, it is as proletarians who recognize capitalism not in the meetings of the various gangsters but in the daily robbery of our lives in the factories, in the call-centres, as unemployed, for the needs of the economy. We do not speak on behalf of anyone, we start from our own conditions. Capitalism does not exist because of the G8, the G8 exists because of capitalism. Capitalism is nothing but the expropriation of our activity, which turns against us as an alien force. Our festival against capital does not have a beginning or an end, it is not a pre-determined spectacle, it does not have a fixed date. Our future lies beyond all mediations, beyond nation-states, beyond all attempts to reform capitalism. Our future lies in the destruction of the economy. For the total abolition of the state and capital. For the world human community. Proletarians against the machine.'

Case-study questions

1. Which orientation does this perspective fit best with: liberal, reformist, radical or Foucauldian?
2. How might a liberal seek to argue with this perspective?
3. A number of groups associated with the Drop the Debt campaign also attended the summit. Which orientation would their arguments fit best within?

END-OF-CHAPTER REVIEW QUESTIONS

1. What is meant by 'liberal pluralism'?
2. List some factors which work against the ability of consumers to make fully informed choices.
3. Briefly summarize the key arguments advanced by Bachrach and Baratz against the liberal view of power.
4. What does Marcuse mean when he talks of 'repressive desubliminization'?

REFERENCES AND FURTHER READING

Abratt, R. and Sachs D. (1988) The Marketing Challenge: Towards Being Profitable and Socially Responsible, *Journal of Business Ethics*, vol. 7: 497–507.

Althusser, Louis (1971) *Lenin and Philosophy and Other Essays*, trans. Ben Brewster, London: New Left Books.

Bachrach, P. and M.S. Baratz (1962) Two Faces of Power, *American Political Science Review*, vol. 56: 947–52.

Bartels, R. (1988) *The History of Marketing Thought*, Columbus, Ohio: Publishing Horizons.

Bartky, Sandra (1992) 'Foucault, Femininity and the Modernization of Patriarchal Power', pp. 103–18. In Kourany, Janet A., James P. Serba and Rosemarie Tong (eds), *Feminist Philosophies*, New York and London: Harvester Wheatsheaf.

Baudrillard, Jean (1988) orig. 1970 'Consumer Society'. In Mark Poster (ed.), *Jean Baudrillard: Selected Writings*, Cambridge: Polity Press.

Bauer, Raymond A. and Stephen Greyser (1967) The Dialogue that Never Happens, *Harvard Business Review*, November/December: 2–4, 6, 8, 10, 12.

Bauman, Zygmunt (1988) *Freedom. Concepts in Social Thought*, Minneapolis: University of Minnesota Press.

Bauman, Zygmunt (1995) *Life in Fragments*, Oxford: Basil Blackwell.

Beck, Ulrich (1995) *Ecological Politics in an Age of Risk*, Cambridge: Polity Press.

Beck, Ulrich (1999) *World Risk Society*, Cambridge: Polity Press.

Birsch, Douglas (1994) 'Whistle Blowing, Ethical Obligation, and the Ford Pinto Case', pp. 199–219. In Douglas Birsch and John H. Fielder (eds), *The Ford Pinto Case: A Study in Applied Ethics, Business and Technology*, State University of New York Press.

Blumberg, Paul (1989) *The Predatory Society: Deception in the American Marketplace*, New York and Oxford: Oxford University Press.

Bond, Jonathon and Richard Kirshenbaum (1998) *Under the Radar: Talking to Today's Cynical and Jaded Consumers*, New York: Adweek.

Brennan, Teresa (1993) *History After Lacan*, London: Routledge.

Brown, Stephen (1995) *Postmodern Marketing*, London: Routledge.

Brown, Stephen (1997) *Postmodern Marketing 2: Telling Tales*, London: International Thomson.

Brownlie, Douglas and Michael Saren (1997) Beyond the One-Dimensional Marketing Manager: The Discourse of Theory, Practice and Relevance, *International Journal of Research in Marketing*, vol. 14: 147–161.

Carmichael, Helen (1998) Sex Offenders, *Chemistry in Britain*, October: 25–8.

Carson, Rachel (1994) orig. 1962 *Silent Spring*, New York: Houghton-Mifflin.

Castells, Manuel (1997) *The Power of Identity*, Oxford: Basil Blackwell.

Cinquin, Chantal (1987) 'Homo Coca-Colens'. In Jean Umiker-Sebeok (ed.), *Marketing and Semiotics*, Berlin and New York: Mouton de Gruyter.

Communication and Food Standards Agency (2001) *Consumer Attitudes To Food Standards: Final Report*, prepared for COI Communications and Food Standards Agency, UK, ref. 4695: January.

Crane, A. (1997) The Dynamics of Marketing Ethical Products: A Cultural Perspective, *Journal of Marketing Management*, vol. 13 no. 6: 561–77.

Dahl, Robert A. (1957) The Concept of Power, *Behavioural Science*, vol. 2: 2–15.

Davidson, Hugh (1987) *Offensive Marketing: How To Make Your Competitors Followers*, London: Penguin.

De Young, Susan and F.G. Crane (1992) Females' Attitudes Toward the Portrayal of Women in Advertising, *International Journal of Advertising*, vol. 11, no. 3: 249–56.

Dowie, Mark (1994) 'Pinto Madness'. In Douglas Birsch amd John H. Fielder (eds), *The Ford Pinto Case: A Study in Applied Ethics, Business and Technology*, State University of New York Press.

Drucker, Peter (1969) The Shame of Marketing, *Marketing Communications*, August: 60–4.

Eagleton, Terry (1991) *Ideology*, Harlow, Essex: Longman Critical Readers.

Elias, Norbert (1994) orig. 1939 *The Civilizing Process: The History of Manners and State Formation and Civilization*, trans. Edmund Jephcott, Oxford: Basil Blackwell.

Elliott, Richard, Susan Eccles and Michelle Hodgson (1993) Re-coding Gender Representations: Women's Cleaning Products and Advertising's 'New Man', *International Journal of Research in Marketing*, vol. 10: 311–24.

Ewen, Stuart (1976) *Captains of Consciousness: Advertising and the Social Roots of the Consumer Culture*, New York: McGraw-Hill.

Ewen, Stuart (1986) *All Consuming Images: The Politics of Style in Contemporary Culture*, New York: Basic Books.

Fine, Reuben (1986) *Narcissism, the Self and Society*, New York: Columbia University Press.

Fineman, S. (1998) 'The Natural Environment, Organizations and Ethics'. In Martin Parker (ed.), *Ethics and Organizations*, London: Sage.

Fineman, S. and K. Clarke (1996) Green Stakeholders: Industry Interpretations and Response, *Journal of Management Studies*, vol. 33, no. 6: 715–30.

Foucault, Michel (1977) *Discipline and Punish: The Birth of the Prison*, London: Penguin.

Foucault, Michel (1979) *The History of Sexuality*, trans. Robert Hurley, London: Penguin.

Fovenier, Susan, Susan Dobson and David Glen Mick (1999) Preventing the Premature Death of Relationship Marketing, *Harvard Business Review*, Jan–Feb: 42–51.

Friedman, Milton and Rose Friedman (1979) *Free to Choose*, London: Penguin.

Fromm, Erich (1978) *To Have or to Be?*, London: Abacus.

Galbraith, John Kenneth (1958) *The Affluent Society*, London: Penguin.

Galbraith, John Kenneth (1967) *The New Industrial State*, London: Penguin.

Galbraith, J.K. (1984) *The Anatomy of Power*, London: Hamish Hamilton.

Galbraith, J.K. (1992) *The Culture of Contentment*, London: Penguin.

Gartner, Alan and Frank Riessman (1974) *The Service Society and the Consumer Vanguard*, New York: Harper & Row.

Gioia, Dennis A. (1994) 'Pinto Fires and Personal Ethics', pp. 97–116. In Douglas Birsch, and John H. Fielder (eds), *The Ford Pinto Case: A Study in Applied Ethics, Business and Technology*, State University of New York Press.

Goffman, Erving (1979) *Gender Advertisements*, New York: Harper Torchbooks.

Goldman, Robert (1992) *The Mortise and the Frame: Reading Ads Socially*, London: Routledge.

Graham, Gordon (1990) *Living the Good Life: An Introduction to Moral Philosophy*, New York: Paragon Issues in Philosophy.

Green, David (1987) *The New Right: The Counterrevolution in Political Economic and Social Thought*, London: Wheatsheaf.

Grönroos, Christian (1996) From Marketing Mix to Relationship Marketing: Towards a Paradigm Shift in Marketing, Keynote paper, MCB University Press: http:www.mcb.co.uk

Gummesson, Evert (1994) 'Relationship Marketing: Its Role in the Marketing Economy', script prepared for the Conference on *Understanding Service Management: Integrating Marketing, Organisational Behaviour and Human Resource Management*, University College Dublin, 30–31 May.

Hall, Stuart (1980) 'Encoding, Decoding in the Television Discourse'. In S. Jall, D. Hobson and P. Lowe (eds), *Culture, Media, Language*, London: Hutchinson.

Hall, Stuart (1996) orig. 1983 'The Problem of Ideology: Marxism Without Guarantees', pp. 25–47. In David Morley and Kuan-Hsing Chen (eds), *Critical Dialogues in Cultural Studies*, London: Routledge.

Jackall, R. (1988) *Moral Mazes: The World of Corporate Managers*, New York: Oxford University Press.

Jamieson, Katherine M. (1994) *The Organization of Corporate Crime: Dynamics of Antitrust Violation*, SCLJ 11, Thousand Oaks, California: Sage.

Jones, D.G. Brian and David D. Monieson (1990) Early Developments in the Philosophy of Marketing Thought, *Journal of Marketing*, vol. 54 (January): 102–13.

Kotler, Philip (1972a) What Consumerism Means for Marketers, *Harvard Business Review*, May–June: 48–57.

Kotler, Philip (1972b) A Generic Concept of Marketing, *Journal of Marketing*, vol. 36 (April): 46–54.

Laclau, E. (1983) 'Socialism', 'The People', 'Democracy', The Transformation of Hegerionic Logic, *Social Text*, vol. 7: 115–19.

Larrain, Jorge (1995) 'Stuart Hall and the Marxist Conception of Ideology', pp. 47–71. In David Morley and Kuan-Hsing Chen (eds), *Critical Dialogues in Cultural Studies*, London: Routledge.

Lasch, Christopher (1979) *Culture of Narcissism: American Life in an Age of Diminishing Expectations*, New York: W.W. Norton.

Lee, Renée G. and Jeff Murray (1995) A Framework for Critiquing the Dysfunctions of Advertising: The Base–Superstructure Model, *ACR*, vol. 22: 139–43.

Levitt, Theodore (1960) Marketing Myopia, *Harvard Business Review*, July–August: 45–57.

Levitt, Theodore (1962) *Innovation in Marketing, New Perspectives for Profit and Growth*, New York: McGraw-Hill.

Lieberman, Adam J. and Simona C. Kwon (1998) *Facts vs Fears: A Review of the Greatest Unfounded Health Scares of Recent Times*, 3rd edn, New York: American Council on Science and Health.

Lipson, H.A. and J.R. Paling (1974) *Marketing Fundamentals: Texts and Cases*, New York: John Wiley.

Lukes, Steven (1974) *Power: A Radical View*, London: Macmillan (now Palgrave).

Lyonski, Steven and Richard Pollay (1990) Advertising Sexism is Forgiven but not Forgotten: Historical, Cross-cultural and Individual Differences in Criticism and Purchase Boycott Intentions, *International Journal of Advertising*, vol. 19/4: 317–30.

McKay, George (1996) *Senseless Acts of Beauty: Cultures of Resistance since the Sixties*, London: Verso.

McKitterick, J.B. (1957) 'What is the Marketing Concept?' In F. Bass (ed.), *The Frontiers of Marketing Thought in Action*, Chicago: American Marketing Association.

Marcuse, Herbert (1964) *One Dimensional Man*, London: Routledge.

Moore, Timothy E. (1982) Subliminal Advertising: What You See is What You Get, *Journal of Marketing*, Spring: 38–47.

Michman, Ronald D. and Stanley D. Sibley (1980) *Marketing Channels and Strategies*, Columbus, Ohio: Grid Publishing.

Miller, Daniel (1998) 'Coca Cola: A Black Sweet Drink from Trinidad', pp. 169–89. In *Material Cultures: Why Some Things Matter*, London: UCC Press.

O'Donohoe, Stephanie (1994) Advertising Uses and Gratifications, *European Journal of Marketing*, vol. 28, no. 10: 52–75.

Packard, Vance (1961) *The Waste Makers*, London, Pelican.

Pollay, R.W. (1986) The Distorted Mirror: Reflections on the Unintended Consequences of Advertising, *Journal of Marketing*, vol. 50 (April): 18–36.

Radner, Hilary (1997) 'Producing the Feminine: Jane Fonda and the New Feminine', pp. 108–33. In Pekka Sulkunen, John Holmwood, Hilary Radner and Gerhard Schultze (eds), *Constructing the New Consumer Society*, London: Macmillan (now Palgrave).

Robin, Donald P. and Eric Reidenbach (1987) Social Responsibility, Ethics, and Marketing Strategy: Closing the Gap Between Concept and Application, *Journal of Marketing*, vol. 51 (January): 44–58.

Rogers, Stuart (1992/93) How a Publicity Blitz Created the Myth of Subliminal Advertising, *Public Relations Quarterly*, Winter: 12–17.

Rogers, Martha and Christine Seiler (1994) The Answer is No: A National Survey of Advertising Industry Practitioners and their Clients About Whether they Use Subliminal Advertising, *Journal of Advertising Research*, March–April: 36–45.

Rogers, Martha and Kirk H. Smith (1993) Public Perceptions of Subliminal Advertising: Why Practitioners Shouldn't Ignore the Issue, *Journal of Advertising Research*, March/April: 10–18.

Ross, Irwin (1992) *Shady Business*: Confronting Corporate Corruption, New York: Twentieth Century Fund Press.

Roszak, Theodore (1970) *The Making of a Counter Culture: Reflections on the Technocratic Society and its Youthful Opposition*, London: Faber.

Rudmin, F.W. and W.E Kilbourne (1996) 'The Meaning and Morality of Voluntary Simplicity: History and Hypotheses on Deliberately Denied Materialism'. In R. Belk, N. Dholakia and A. Venkatesh (eds), *Consumption and Marketing: Macro-Marketing Dimensions*, Ohio: South-Western College Publishing and International Thomson.

Saunders, P. (1979) *Urban Politics*, London: Penguin.

Sheth, Jagdish N., David M. Gardner and Dennis E. Garrett (1988) *Marketing Theory: Evolution and Evaluation*. New York: John Wiley.

Smith, Adam (1793) *An Inquiry into the Nature and Causes of the Wealth of Nations*, vol. 1, 7th edn., London: A Sraten and T. Cadell.

Stidsen, Bert and Thomas F. Schutte (1972) Marketing as a Communication System: The Marketing Concept Revisited, *Journal of Marketing*, vol. 36 (October).

Watson, Tony (1998) 'Ethical Codes and Moral Communities'. In Martin Parker (ed.), *Ethics and Organizations*, London: Sage.

Wensley, Robin (1994) 'A Critical Review of Research in Marketing', presented to the *British Academy of Management Conference*, Lancaster, 13 September.

Wernick, Andrew (1991) *Promotional Culture: Advertising, Ideology and Symbolic Expression*, London: Sage.

West's California Review (1994) 'The Pinto Fuel System'. In Douglas Birsch and John H. Fielder (eds), *The Ford Pinto Case: A Study in Applied Ethics, Business and Technology*, State University of New York Press.

Williams, Raymond (1962) 'Advertising: The Magic System'. In *Problems in Materialism and Culture*, London: New Left Books.

Williamson, Judith (1978) *Decoding Advertisements*, New York: Marion Boyars.

Wortzel, Lawrence H. and John M. Frisbie (1974) Women's Role Portrayal Preferences in Advertisements: An Empirical Study, *Journal of Marketing*, vol. 38 (October): 41–6.

NOTES

i   Source: John Locke (1690) *Second Treatise of Government*. American Declaration of Independence, 2 July 1776; Declaration of the Rights of Man, 26 August 1789.

ii   From the Declaration of Independence: 'We hold these Truths to be self-evident, that all Men are created equal, that they are endowed by their Creator with certain unalienable Rights, that among these are Life, Liberty, and the Pursuit of Happiness – That to secure these Rights, Governments are instituted among Men, deriving their just Powers from the Consent of the Governed, that whenever any Form of Government becomes destructive of these ends, it is the Right of the People to alter or to abolish it, and to institute new Government, laying its Foundation on such Principles, and organizing its Powers in such Form, as to them shall seem most likely to effect their Safety and Happiness.' From the Declaration of the Rights of Man, Article 2: 'The aim of all political association is the preservation of the natural and imprescriptable rights of man. These are liberty, property, security and resistance to oppression.'

iii   'The principle of all sovereignty resides essentially in the nation. No body nor individual may exercise any authority which does not proceed directly from the nation.' – Article 3 of the Declaration of the Rights of Man; approved by the National Assembly of France, 1789.

iv   It is not difficult to find examples of people who do not actively choose that which is most pleasing to them. For example someone may find it pleasing to smoke tobacco, but forego consumption of cigarettes because they know that it is in their long-term interests to do so. Another person may enjoy eating fish but may reduce their consumption of fish in order to conserve fish stocks. A third may avoid purchasing products which they believe to be fabricated by exploited labour as they may believe that it would not be in the long-term interests of society to do so. From an ethical point of view the focus on interests represents a form of ethical egoism (as opposed to psychological egoism which concerns itself with the satisfaction of desires or wants). For many writers on ethics, ethical egoism is regarded as a 'strong' position to argue from in that it is based on the recognition that the individual acts in his or her best interests (not desires) and seems to employ the idea of objective value.
[Graham, 1990: 26]

v   Bauer and Greyser (1967) refer also to President Kennedy's attempt in 1963 to establish the rights of consumers – to be informed, to choose, to have safe products, to be heard (Office of the President, 1963). Consumer 'rights' referred to include the true interest cost of a loan, the true cost per standard unit of competing brands (unit pricing), the basic ingredients in a product (ingredient labelling), the nutritional quality of foods (nutritional labelling), the freshness of products (open-dating) and the prices of gasoline (sign posting rather than pump posting). President Johnson also made a 'consumer message' in 1966 which raised interest in these affairs. Major legislation in the late 1960s included important laws relating to consumer protection in the USA: Labeling Act (1966); Child Protection Action (1966, amended 1969); Traffic Safety Act (1966); Flammable Fabrics Act (1967); Wholesale Meat Act (1968); Consumer Credit Protection Act (1968); Wholesale Poultry Products Act (1968); and Radiation Control for Health and Safety Act (1968).

vi In 1960, in the USA, no State had a consumer affairs office; by 1970, 33 did and, by 1973, all 50 did. In 1970 the ten most common complaints received were in respect of automobiles, advertising, appliances, credit, non-delivery of merchandise, home improvements, franchise dealers, warranties, guarantees and sales tactics. *Source*: Office for Consumer Affairs, State Consumer Action, Summary 71 (Washington DC, US Government Printing Office).

vii The formalization of the marketing concept may be traced to McKitterick (1957). The principal task of the marketing function is not so much to be skilful in making customers do what best suits the business 'as to be skilful in conceiving and then making the business do what suits the interests of the customer.' Kotler (1972a: 54) says 'the marketing concept calls for a customer orientation backed by integrated marketing aimed at generating long-run customer satisfaction as the key to attaining long-run profitable volume'.

viii In the USA the Sherman Act, Clayton Act and other federal and state legislation prohibit activities such as collusion by firms to fix prices, divide markets and territories or to engage in bid-rigging.

ix Jamieson (1994) for example has found that large, poorly performing companies in profitable industries, with fewer managers, tend to engage most in anti-trust activities. More serious cases occurred where the industry was also performing poorly. Jamieson notes that these latter cases 'may require riskier means of acquiring elusive resources that ultimately result in detection' (1994: 94).

x See those listed at http://www.usdoj.gov/atr/cases.html

xi For example Jamieson (1994), in her study of anti-trust activity, assumes that managers are rational actors who determine costs and benefits of courses of action and that the decision to use illegal means will depend on their evaluation of the costs and benefits involved. In general, marketing academics assume that managers follow rational–instrumental decision processes. Revisiting the earlier discussion of the marketing concept then, McKitterick (1957), Kotler (1972a, b) and Grönroos (1996) all share the view that managers act rationally in furtherance of the firm's interests.

xii For example Jackall (1988) holds that managerial life in major corporations such as Ford is shaped by bureaucracy, suggesting that employees within such organizations tend to substitute the corporate moral system for their own personal morality while at work. Dowie (1994) argues that such principles were embodied by Ford managers who purportedly used cost–benefit analysis to assess whether or not to modify the gas tank of the Ford Pinto, which they knew could rupture in low-impact rear-end collisions with a high probability of risk to life and limb of passengers. Dowie says that managers sought to justify their decision on the basis of rational self-interest, in that the costs of the modification would outweigh the benefits in dollar terms. In commenting on the case of the Ford Pinto, the explanation given by Robin and Reidenbach (1987) is that profits and efficiency dominated Ford's value system. Management preached these values and rewards were driven by them. However there is no clear evidence that Ford actually used cost–benefit analysis in this context. Crane (1997) and Fineman (1998), in their separate studies of managerial decision-making with respect to 'sustainability' and 'green' issues, found the decision process to be framed within a rational 'self-interested' (from the perspective of the firm) context. The managers in Fineman's study described themselves as being 'light green', 'but their beliefs (whether moderate or radical) and their moral agency were suspended when they slipped into their work roles' (1998: 243).

xiii From chapter 1 of *Improving Literacy and Numeracy, A Fresh Start* by Sir Claus Moser. http://www.lifelonglearning.co.uk/mosergroup/rep01.htm

xiv http://www.stats.org/about/index.html

xv http://www.sirc.org/index.html

xvi *Source: The Economist* (US) (1999) 'Food Scares: Fear and Loathing', 21 August 1999 vol. 352 i8133, page 42.

xvii The organization is the Marine Stewardship Council: http://www.msc.org/

4 CONSUMING NEEDS AND VALUES

LEARNING OBJECTIVES

- To understand the key differences between gift exchange and commodity exchange
- To understand the relations between needs and values in commodity exchange
- To understand the role of needs within commodity exchange
- To be able to follow the various arguments in the debate surrounding the existence of 'true' and 'false' needs
- To understand the relationships between Maslow's (1954) theory of needs (Maslow, 1970a) and Holbrook's (1994) typology of consuming values
- To be able to discuss the different values which consumers may derive from consumption, including efficiency, excellence, status, esteem, ethics and spirituality

4.1 INTRODUCTION

This chapter discusses several issues which are of great significance with respect to developing an understanding of how people relate to consumption through different media of exchange. The chapter begins by outlining and then comparing two different systems of exchange: **gift exchange**, which together with **barter** was predominant in premodern times and still forms a large component of exchange today, and **commodity exchange**, which is a primary aspect of current consumer societies. The focus then shifts to considering the role played by consumer needs and values in commodity exchange. Economic, psychological and sociological perspectives on human needs are discussed first, then there is a further discussion which considers the debate about true and false needs. The final section introduces the concept of **consumer values**.

4.2 FORMS OF EXCHANGE

In this section, systems of gift exchange and commodity exchange are compared and contrasted.

4.2.1 Gift exchange

No doubt you will have exchanged gifts with others, perhaps by exchanging presents with loved ones to mark important occasions such as birthdays or religious festivals. Anthropologists have studied gift systems around the world in order to try to explain the functions played by gifts in different societies. Their research findings indicated that gift institutions are universal among tribal peoples. The following stories illustrate some of the qualities of gift exchange. Those native tribes such as the Kwakiutl and Tlingit, which once occupied a large section of the Pacific coast of north-west America, were dependent on the ocean and particularly on the abundance of the salmon for their survival and livelihood. As part of their rich mythology they developed a story according to which the salmon live in a great lodge beneath the sea; during their time in the lodge, they go about in human form, but once a year they change into fish bodies, dress themselves in robes of salmon skin, swim into the mouths of the rivers and voluntarily sacrifice themselves so that their land brothers can have food for the winter. The tribal peoples held the salmon in great respect, treating the first salmon to arrive each year as a visiting chief, then cooking and eating it in a ritual meal, before returning its bones intact to the sea. This was done because they believed that when placed into water, the bones of the salmon would reassemble and the fish would swim back to its lodge and revert to its human form. Thus, according to the myth, all the bones of all the salmon had to be returned in order that they might thrive.

This story illustrates several aspects of gift exchange. The **gift** is a means of giving thanks for what has been received. There are two gifts in the story. The first gift is that which the people from under the sea make of themselves to their brothers who are on land. This gift which comes from the bounty of the sea calls for a counter-gift. The second gift is the return of the bones of the salmon so that they may reconstitute themselves, return to their lodge and increase. Thus the transactions between the salmon and the tribe are **reciprocal**, to the extent that the gift moves continually from one to the other. The gift is also in continual motion and this motion is associated with an increase; by placing the bones back, the salmon remain plentiful. Finally the constant exchange of gifts and the rituals which surround the giving of these establishes bonds of obligation and respect. This establishes a gift relationship with nature, a form of give and take that acknowledges the tribe's participation in, and dependence upon, natural increase.

The story illustrates some universal aspects of gift exchange. There is the gift itself, which sets up a form of obligation that the gift is returned; gifts are thus in perpetual motion. Secondly, the mutual obligations between giver and receiver, if fulfilled, create further ties of respect and of community, those with whom we exchange gifts are part of 'us'. Finally, the increase in worth and respect are dependent on how much is given away. These universals are illustrated with respect to another example of gift exchange, the Kula.

4.2.2 The Kula

One well-documented system of gift exchange is the Kula, the ceremonial exchange of the Massim peoples who occupy the South Sea islands near the eastern tip of New Guinea. The anthropologist Bronislaw Malinowski spent several years living on the Trobriand islands, the most north-western group of these islands, in the early twentieth century.[1] Two ceremonial gifts are at the centre of Kula exchange – armshells and necklaces. Armshells are large shells which have been fashioned into rings and polished, while necklaces are made with small flat disks of a red shell strung into long chains. Both armshells and necklaces circulate throughout the islands, passing from household to household. The presence of one of these gifts allows the custodian to talk of its history, how it passed to him and who he plans to give it to next, and is a favourite source of tribal conversation and gossip. The social use and value of Kula gifts far exceed their practical use. Malinowski found that a distinct pattern pertains to the circulation of Kula armshells and necklaces. Each moves in a circle by being transported by canoe over distances of hundreds of miles, around a wide ring of islands in the Massim archipelago; the red shell necklaces, which are considered to be 'male' and which are worn by women, move clockwise, and the armshells, which are considered to be 'female' and are worn by men, move counter-clockwise. The Kula armshells and necklaces move continually around a wide ring of islands.

What can be said about the Kula? Malinowski noted that the gifts are in constant motion, and no-one ever keeps the gifts for any length of time. Thus the idea of property which is associated with Kula exchange is quite different from that of Europeans. Within Massim society a person who owns a thing is regarded as being its trustee and is expected to share it. Secondly, while it is expected that the Kula gift is exchanged for something that is of equivalent value, there is never any discussion or bargaining about this. A person may wonder about what may come in return for his or her gift, but he or she is never supposed to comment or raise this issue. There is therefore an important distinction between Kula gift exchange and economic trade. Whereas barter and trade are concerned with seeking to make the best deal, and defaulters are sanctioned, in Kula a gift is a gift and there is no sanction.

4.2.3 Gift communities

The Kula exchange requires that each person must have at least two gift partners. The gift moves in a circle; no-one ever receives a gift from the same

---

[1] It should be noted that while Malinowski's methods have been recently critiqued, the central aspects of Kula exchange have been recently verified by other authors.

person he gives it to. In this sense one might say that the gift dissolves the boundaries of the individual ego and ties this up with the community. The community is equated with the self; tribal peoples such as the Australian aborigines often refer to their own clan as 'my body'. The Kula gifts move through the community and by means of this passage they create a bond between people who are scattered across an archipelago stretching for hundreds of miles.

How many people are required to effect a gift transfer? Lewis Hyde (1999) suggests that the answer is 'one'. As individuals who can treat ourselves as if 'we' were an object outside the self, it is quite possible to engage in self-gratification, via the provision of **self-gifts**. This is the narrowest form which the gift can take and has been explored by Mick and Demos (1990) in relation to gift-giving behaviour in the USA. The idea of the 'self-gift' is linked to the Puritan ideology discussed in Chapter 2. For Puritans the idea of delayed gratification is important as the primary role for a person is the glorification of God and not personal indulgence. Stripped of its religious dimension such delayed gratification plays a role in self-motivation (play hard now, reward yourself later), which advertisers are all too aware of. A second form of gift community appears in the first example, which featured a **reciprocal** exchange between the people of the sea (the salmon) and those on land (the tribe). When this exchange takes place on a grand scale, most of us are familiar with such reciprocal exchanges. For example at Christmas in Ireland it is usual for people to buy gifts for family and friends and sometimes small gifts for close neighbours. Generally people do not ask for a gift. However if they receive one from someone unexpectedly and have no return gift at hand, this may cause a deal of embarrassment. It is also an expected, though unstated assumption that the gifts should be equivalent to one another. In the relatively fluid social structure which is characteristic of modern social organization it may often be difficult to determine what is appropriate as a gift. Sherry (1983) notes the difficulties in establishing reciprocity or balance in the social relationship where donors and recipients risk imputations of ostentation or meanness in their behaviour. Imagine my uncle's consternation when his brand-new neighbour, recently arrived from overseas, presented him with a colour television set at Christmas (this was in the late 1970s when such sets were still quite rare). His choice of gift for the neighbour had been a box of chocolates but this seemed to be totally inadequate once he had been presented with the television set. He explained to the neighbour that the gift of the television was beyond expectations and returned it. They rarely spoke again. This severance of the relationship is one of the outcomes discussed in a fascinating paper by Ruth *et al.* (1999). When the dominant system of exchange involves the exchange of gifts between three or more people we may talk of **communal gift exchange**. Russell Belk (1979) discusses the role played by gifts in establishing, defining and maintaining interpersonal relationships. In this respect gifts can be said to play a role in socializing children with respect to the formation of important values regarding materialism, giving and receiving. From the above, gift exchanges may involve just one person or an entire community, such as the Kula exchange. Lewis Hyde describes it thus:

'The gift can circulate at every level of the ego. In the ego-of-one we speak of self-gratification, and whether it's forced or chosen, a virtue or a vice, the mark of self-gratification is its isolation. Reciprocal giving, the ego-of-two, is a little more social. We think mostly of lovers. Each of these circles is exhilarating as it expands, and the little gifts that pass between lovers touch us because each is stepping into a larger circuit. But again, if the exchange goes on and on to the exclusion of others, it soon goes stale. D.H. Lawrence spoke of the *égoisme à deux* of so many married couples, people who get so far in the expansion of the self and then close down for a lifetime, opening up for neither children nor the group, nor the gods. A folk tale from Kashmir tells of two Brahmin women who tried to dispense with their alms-giving duties by simply giving alms back and forth to each other. They didn't quite have the spirit of the thing. When they died, they returned to earth as two wells so poisoned that no-one could take water from them. No-one else can drink from an ego-of-two. It has its moment in our maturation, but it is an infant form of the gift circle.' [1999: 18]

In the above, Hyde submits that the gifts mark the boundaries of community. Inside the community, gift exchange prevails and outside the community the prevalent system is commodity exchange.

4.2.4 Barter

As opposed to the gift, barter is a form of exchange whereby some forms of equivalent are exchanged for one another; to use the old economist's example, I may trade so many guns to you in return for so much of your butter. Barter is different from gift exchange in that people are keenly aware of what is being traded in advance of the transaction; the parties to the transaction may seek assurances as to the trustworthiness of each other, and they will also bargain to get the best deal possible. Generally barter, like gift exchange, was prevalent in premodern times in Europe. Since the rise of the money system it has faded into the background, although in the form of counter-trade it still comprises an important aspect of international trade.

4.2.5 Commodity exchange

Commodity exchange or money exchange is the system which has facilitated the development of present-day world trade. The system of money facilitates exchange by individual strangers, whether these are persons or corporations. The development of equivalence between different systems of money through the money markets means that money may be used to purchase goods and services anywhere in the world, at any time. Because of its abstract nature, money may also be used to buy future money, via a chain of derivative products, so that the money system itself forms a large part of the total system of commodity exchange. There are some interesting differences between the system of gift exchange and that of money or commodity exchange, and these are considered below.

DBS Arts Library

141

Comparing gift exchange to commodity exchange

Commodity exchange, involving market exchange and economic exchange processes, are all linked to the money economy and the principles espoused by *homo economicus*. Several authors suggest that the rationale of commodity exchange is markedly different from that of the gift system, although their logics are frequently intertwined in contemporary society. Such differences may be summarized in terms of how status is achieved: the alienability of objects, the establishment of qualitative versus quantitative relations, differences between worth and value, and finally differences with regard to the respective decision processes of both modes of exchange.

4.2.6.1 Acquiring status: through giving away vs through accumulation

First, within the spirit of gift exchange a person increases in status by giving something of themselves away (the gift). This may be illustrated with reference to the example below. Here *A* gives *B* a canoe, which is ranked higher than yams, and in return receives three yams for it. The arrows indicate increase and decrease in status.

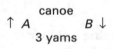

As the result of the gift of the canoe, *A* increases in status, to the extent that with respect to the reciprocal 'return gift' *A* owes *B* three yams and *B* owes *A* a canoe. Within the commodity exchange market, *B* would have been considered to have made a good deal; however in terms of gift exchange *B* has been lessened as he is now in debt to *A*. Commodity exchange is fuelled by the reverse idea that self-fulfilment comes from accumulation, from filling the self up. In societies where commodity exchange is dominant, the person who accumulates most is often deemed to have the highest status (see note i).

This indicates that there is something quite different between a society where gift exchange is predominant and one which is dominated by commodity exchange. The function of the gift within the social body of the gift community is equivalent to that of oxygen in the human body. Within the gift community, the individual is protected (and constrained) by the second skin of community which is woven around him or her. On the other hand, market exchange requires the existence of autonomous individuals. In modern societies the cocoon provided by the second skin of the community has largely disappeared and this has left a hole in the self of the individual, who is dominated by the desire for self-fulfilment. In place of the comfort and security of community which was sustained by communal feasts and the gift, the individual seeks to fill this hole by filling the self up with commodities.

4.2.6.2 Alienable vs inalienable objects

Secondly, gifts are inalienable objects while commodities are alienable. For example consider once more the exchange between yams and the canoe:

$$A \xleftarrow{\text{3 yams}} \xrightarrow{\text{canoe}} B$$

With respect to the gift exchange, this simply means that when the return gift is called for, *A* owes *B* 3 yams and *B* owes *A* one canoe. Commodity exchange however seeks to establish an equivalence and common standard between the two terms in the exchange. In commodity exchange terms 1 canoe = 3 yams, or to put this another way, 1 yam = $\frac{1}{3}$rd of a canoe. The system of commodity exchange is thus more abstract than that of gift exchange in that it seeks to render everything equivalent to everything else.

4.2.6.3 Qualitative vs quantitative relations

This raises the third distinction, which is that the gift establishes a **qualitative** bond and obligation between both parties. On the other hand if this were a commodity exchange, then the relation would be expressed quantitatively, as one canoe = 3 yams.

4.2.6.4 Dependence vs independence

Fourth, because gift exchange establishes a qualitative relation between people which ties them together in bonds of mutual obligation, it creates dependence. Commodity exchange, in contrast, requires separate independent parties to the exchange. Hyde (1999) notes that the principal difference between the gift and the commodity is that the gift moves between different parties in order to make connections between them, whereas the relation between those who participate in commodity exchange is essentially disinterested. The implication is that while gifts are exchanged between members of a **community**, commodities are exchanged primarily between **strangers**. The relation between gift and commodity frequently, but not always, parallels that between community and 'others'; gifts demarcate who 'we' are and commodity exchange, including the charging of usury or interest, extends to all strangers who are considered to be beyond the boundaries of the community. Thus gifts are associated with belonging and with being obliged to others, and commodities are associated with alienation and freedom. At times, people may feel that the bonds and obligations imposed by the gift community constrain their identity and limit their freedom of movement. For example Hyde offers the example of the adolescent who wants to create his or her 'own' identity and decides not to participate in the usual exchange of presents with others at Christmas. To those bound up in a gift community, the lure of commodities lies in their offer of a range of individual identities:

'The excitement of commodities is the excitement of possibility, of floating away from the particular to taste the range of available life. There are times when we want to be aliens and strangers, to feel how the shape of our lives is not the only shape, to drift before a catalogue of possible lives, staring at the glass arcades of shoes that are sensible and shoes for taking a chance, buses leaving town and the grey steam railway depot where men and women hurry by with their bags.'

[1999: 69]

4.2.6.5 Does commodity exchange destroy community?

Some go so far as to suggest that commodity exchange destroys the idea of community. For example Hyde discusses how, when the Vietnamese refugees settled in Southern California, they found its culture to be toxic to something they had always taken for granted – their family life. Elizabeth Hoyt (1921) describes the American tribal society of the Yurok, who held shell-money in great esteem as an example of extreme individualism, with virtually none of the usual trappings of community. The Yurok calculated the precise price of everything and almost all forms of exchange, including the establishment of bride prices and blood money. The Yurok did not recognize such a thing as society, but instead saw an aggregation of individuals, where those of low wealth clustered around those who had it.

The example of the Yurok calls to mind the more recent quote attributed to the former British Prime Minister Margaret Thatcher, a champion of the 'free market', who is reported to have said 'There is no such thing as society'. The freedom of the 'free' world thus offers the prospect of liberating us from the ties of giving and receiving which bind together communities. It seeks to replace these bonds of obligation with the 'friction-free' realm of commodity exchange which fulfils the requirements of strangers for freedom and anonymity; the freedom to transact with whoever they want without fear of sanctions, apart from those which pertain to the exchange contract itself. This in turn raises serious ethical and legal questions concerned with externalities. For example, what if A sells arms to B which are used to kill C (for example where Britain and the USA sell weapons to Iraq or Indonesia, which are in turn used to kill Kurds and the East Timorese?). Do the victims have any rights? However, the relations between gift exchange are complex and frequently interwoven. Gregory (1983) notes that Kula exchange is still flourishing in the Trobriand islands alongside commodity exchange (see note ii).

In present-day society, commodity exchange and gift exchange link together in many ways, some of which seem to be clearly inappropriate. The border between the two is enhanced through the telling of stories and jokes. Gifts are traditionally associated with marking points of transformation and change, such as birthdays, graduations and weddings. Woody Allen told a joke at the end of his stand-up routine, in which he would take a watch from his pocket, check the time and then say 'It's an old family heirloom. [pause] My grandfather sold it to me on his deathbed'. The joke works because market exchange seems inappropriate at this point of transformation on the threshold between life and death. Lewis Hyde tells of the story of a woman who participated in a Minnesota study of organ donation who was to receive a kidney from her daughter. The daughter said that she would donate the kidney only if her mother bought her an expensive coat! This is what the mother said about the daughter's behaviour:

> 'She's a very selfish girl and not very mature in many ways . . . She's not used to doing things for people. She didn't think her life should be constricted in any way . . . She wanted a fur coat. It really shook me up. It was unnerving. She was reluctant and unenthusiastic . . . She's very calculating.'   [Hyde, 1999: 70]

There is thus some irony in the fact that in contemporary consumer society most of our gifts are bought in the commodity marketplace. In fact a huge proportion of what is commercially bought and sold ultimately becomes a gift of one kind or another. The case study at the end of this chapter explores this idea further.

4.2.6.6 Commodities and gifts: value and worth

Value can only exist by comparing something with something else. A thing has no market value in itself except when it is in the marketplace. What cannot be exchanged has no exchange value. In comparison, the worth of a gift cannot be expressed adequately in value terms. For example Robert Grafton-Small (1992) discusses the worth of his grandfather's bow-tie, a gift which was passed down to him. In economic exchange terms the tie was virtually valueless, which was in contradiction to the worth which the bow-tie held for Grafton-Small. For him the act of wearing the bow-tie re-creates the place of family, by binding together the generations:

> 'When my grandfather died and the time came to divide up his estate, we found two bow-ties amongst his personal effects. One, worn every day until his final illness, was in tatters and ripe just for throwing away, but the other was still in its original wrapper, the colours unfaded and the fabric intact. For all sorts of reasons, some spoken, some felt, the rest not clear even now, it seemed fitting that I should take the brand-new bow-tie and likewise dispose of the tatters though I'd never owned such a strip of silk and could not manage the knots.

> 'Since then, however, I have made a point of learning and whilst this red and blue ribbon is bound to be my first, it is no longer my only bow-tie, for nowadays I buy them on my own account. I think of my grandfather, all the same, whenever his choice is around my neck and I must look into the mirror to make good the knot.'
> [1992: 1]

The 'gift' of the bow-tie is implicit. It 'seemed fitting' to Grafton-Small that he should take both ties, discard the old one (which his grandfather had worn onto death) and take up the baton of the 'new' (unworn) tie as his own and in so doing, symbolically tie the generations – his grandfather's tie around his own throat, recognizing his grandfather's face in his own, each time he looks in the mirror to tie its knots. While the tie is of immense symbolic value to Grafton-Small, in commercial terms it is 'second-hand' and virtually valueless.

On the other hand, consumer researchers such as John Sherry (1983) and Russell Belk (1993) seem to disagree with the point which Grafton-Small is making (about the worth of the gift versus the value of the commodity), when they argue that there is an important economic dimension to modern-day gift-giving behaviour. In Sherry's terms this means that when giving a gift, the donor, who knows its value, will tend to calculate what is appropriate to receive in return. Belk found that respondents who were dating each other looked upon the gifts which they exchanged as being commodities with utilitarian value, and felt that an unfair disparity had occurred if their gift was not adequately reciprocated. However there is not necessarily a disagreement here. In both of the instances cited by Belk and Sherry, the economic value of the gift plays a secondary role to issues related to reciprocity and fairness, and acts as a kind of measure for what might be deemed to be appropriate.

Another important point raised by Sherry (1983) is that in the modern world gift-giving behaviour connotes some sense of personal value or self-worth to others. In this respect the gift functions as a kind of judgement of the character of the sender, a sense of what is appropriate and tasteful. Belk (1979) notes that through the gift the donor may seek to signify a perceived self-trait (I am artistic, I am tasteful) to the receiver through their choice of gift. At the very least they will seek some form of validation which is hopefully gained by the recipient's approval of the gift.

4.2.6.7 Gift exchange and commodity exchange decision processes

Commodity exchange involves rational calculation of costs and benefits – thus for example one classic way of evaluating the production, sale or purchase of a commodity is **cost–benefit analysis**. The person lines up his choices, assigns prices to them, weighs them up against each other, chooses his course of action and then acts. Gift exchange is usually marked by a different process. For example a kidney donation calls for the exchange of a very important gift. The greatest problem with transplants is that the recipient's immune system reacts to the transplanted organ as if it were a disease and attacks and destroys the new kidney. The closer the match between the blood types of the donor and of the recipient, then the less likely it is that the kidney will be regarded as being foreign and rejected. Kidney transplants are therefore likely to be successful when the donor is a close relative. In 90 per cent of cases transplants from a twin are likely to be viable after two years. With other related donors the success rate is 70 per cent. Kidneys from non-relatives are usually accepted half of the time. The decision to donate a kidney is not a trivial one. There is some risk as about 1 in every 1500 donors dies as a result of his or her gift. The operation is major, calling for several days of hospitalization and a month or so of convalescence. It involves considerable pain and leaves a scar which goes halfway around the abdomen.

So how do people choose whether to make kidney transplants? Some do

Table 4.1   Summary of principal differences between gift exchange and commodity exchange

Gift exchange	Commodity exchange
Status increases as one gives things away	Status increases as one accumulates
Objects are inalienable	Objects are alienable
Establishes a qualitative relation between parties, builds community	Establishes a quantitative relation between strangers
The exchange is backed by the need to reciprocate	The exchange is backed by law
The exchange creates dependence	The exchange maintains independence
The exchange creates worth	The exchange creates values
The decision process is based on the demands of community and reciprocity	The process is rational, calculative and linear

this in classic economic fashion, seeking detailed information first and then weighing up the costs and benefits. From such a point of view, what is surprising is that the majority of kidney donors volunteer to give as soon as they hear of the need. The choice is instantaneous, there is no delay or period of deliberation. As an expression of social emotion, gifts make one body out of many, almost literally in this case. Emotional connection tends to preclude economic quantitative evaluation.

4.2.7   Summary

Table 4.1 summarizes some of the main differences between the systems of gift exchange and of commodity exchange.

While to an extent this division ignores the fact that both gift exchange and commodity exchange processes co-exist with each other and that there are a range of intermediate positions in any contemporary consumer society, nonetheless this should sensitize us to the idea that many of the decisions which we make with respect to consumption can be located within different concepts and systems of exchange. We now examine the concept of 'needs' within the context of the system of commodity exchange by considering economic, psychological and social explanations, prior to discussing the question of whether or not one may differentiate needs into 'true' needs and 'false' needs.

4.3   THE ISSUE OF NEEDS IN COMMODITY EXCHANGE

In marketing textbooks, needs are usually defined within a functionalist perspective, whereby needs are generated when an organism experiences an imbalance or shift which moves it into disequilibrium. The concept of 'need' is thus tied up with that of 'lack'; a need implies that something is missing, which must be replaced for equilibrium to be restored. We first describe an economic view of human needs followed by brief descriptions of psychological and sociological theories. We then use the claim that advertisers create 'false' needs as a device to explore the nuances of each approach and the differences between them.

4.3.1 Economic approaches to needs

'There is a fable. There was once a man who lived in Scarcity. After many adventures and a long voyage in the Science of Economics, he encountered the Society of Affluence. They were married and had many needs.'   [Baudrillard, 1988b: 35]

In this section we consider two economic approaches to the question of needs; that adopted by the 'conventional wisdom' in economics, which is compared with that advocated by John Kenneth Galbraith. The conventional wisdom in economics associates needs with **homo economicus**, who is rational to the extent that he will pursue his own happiness without any hesitation and who prefers objects which provide him with the maximum satisfaction. John Kenneth Galbraith (1958) notes that the economic theory of consumer demand, which informs the conventional wisdom, is based on two broad propositions: first, that the urgency of wants does not diminish appreciably as more of them are satisfied; secondly, that wants originate in the personality of the consumer. As we shall see, Galbraith relates both of these together in constructing his own explanation which is based on the idea that we should recognize that there are limits to needs, and that wants, or the expression of needs, are the creations of the industrial system. In other words he is suggesting that the economist's presupposition that consumers are sovereign and free is nothing more than a sham.

Let us consider the idea that the urgency of wants does not diminish appreciably as more of them are satisfied. Economists stipulate a difference between **physiological** and **psychological** needs. Those goods which are referred to as physiological are catered for by necessities (where the price elasticity of demand is inelastic), such as basic foodstuffs, whereas psychological needs are catered for by luxuries (where the price elasticity of demand is elastic). According to classical economic theory, when a person has satisfied his physical needs, then psychologically grounded desires take over, and such desires can never be satisfied.

Galbraith notes that the economic explanation of consumer behaviour has its ancestry in the oldest problem of economics, that of the determination of exchange values or prices. Basically this problem revolves around the fact that some of the most useful things have little or no **exchange value**, whilst some of those items with most exchange value appear to have little **use value**. This problem is similar in nature to our previous discussion of the difference between 'worth' and 'value' in relation to gift exchange and commodity exchange. Adam Smith, founder of the modern discipline of economics, described the difficulty in the following manner:

'Nothing is so useful than water; but it will purchase scarce anything; scarce anything can be had in exchange for it. A diamond on the contrary, has scarce any value in use: but a very great quantity of other goods may frequently be had in exchange for it.'   [Galbraith: 1958: 142]

A potential solution to this dilemma was not reached until the end of the nineteenth century, when the doctrine of **marginal utility** was devised virtually simultaneously by three different economists. According to this, the urgency of desire is a function of the quantity of goods which the individual has available to satisfy that desire. The larger the stock, then the smaller the satisfaction from an increment, and consequently the less the willingness to pay for an increment. Since the supply of diamonds is comparatively small, the satisfaction gained from an additional diamond is great and likewise the price that one is willing to pay for it is high. On the other hand, the reverse is true with respect to water (and here we must remember that these economists are discussing the situation in Europe where water supplies have been plentiful).

Galbraith notes that the doctrine of diminishing marginal utility suggests that as *affluence* rises, production becomes *less* important. With rising personal incomes, people can satisfy additional wants, which are of a *lower order of urgency*. He argues that this being so, the production which supplies these wants must also be of smaller importance. Thus he reasons that the effect of increasing affluence ought to be to minimize the importance of economic goals and that, as a result, production and productivity become less important. However Galbraith contends that this is denied by mainstream economics which came to a quite different account of marginal utility whereby the decrease in the urgency of wants was not admitted. Instead economists are trained not to enquire about the urgency of needs; for example with respect to the equivalence between the desire for more food and the desire for another car, the economist must take each as 'given' (1958: 144). Secondly, Galbraith argues that mainstream economists take the view that in consumer societies an almost infinite variety of goods is available for consumption. They also suggest that while the marginal utility of the *individual* good declines in accordance with the law of diminishing marginal utility, the utility or satisfaction gained from a new and different good is *not* lower than from the initial units of those which precede it. In other words, so long as the individual seeks variety, rather than quantity, he or she can, like a museum, accumulate without diminishing the urgency of his or her wants. This introduction to classical economic theory, and the challenge by Galbraith, sets the background to our further discussion of 'true' and 'false' needs in section 4.3.4. Next we explore a psychological theory of the genesis of human needs.

4.3.2   Maslow: a psychological approach to human needs

In his book *Motivation and Personality*, originally published in 1954, Maslow (1970a) argues forcefully for the development of a permissive society which, through the cultivation of higher-order needs, will not only lead to a more caring and tolerant society, but will allow its members to reach their full potential. Maslow's argument is radical in that he reverses Freud's idea that civilization must tame the beast within us by insisting that all human needs, and even those which we would normally consider to be social, such as needs for respect, esteem, beauty and belonging, are to an extent innate. In Maslow's view such innate needs, which are fragile, must be protected from powerful social forces, which may destroy them. Maslow denies that there is a distinction between animal needs (for food, sex etc.) and those higher impulses (for truth, love and beauty) which are produced by culture. Instead he argues that both higher and lower needs are instinctual and animal in character, that the need for truth is as animal as the need for food.

According to Maslow the fragility of human needs is related to the way in which the system of needs is structured. According to this system, some needs are pre-potent and must be satisfied before other, higher-order needs may be cultivated. Like the economists, Maslow also stipulates a difference between **physiological** and **psychological** needs. A person who is lacking food, safety, love and esteem would probably hunger for food more strongly than anything else. Maslow's view would be readily supported by many others with respect to this claim. For example Mahatma Gandhi once noted that the only way in which God can appear to the hungry is as food. This has been supported by data from the Minnesota starvation study (Keys *et al.*, 1950), which showed that healthy males who were deprived of their full ration of food for several months became fixated by it, to the extent that images of food came to dominate their subsequent life-choices. When Maslow talks of hunger, he is referring to that quality of hunger as life or death hunger, not mere appetite, which very few, perhaps none of us, has experienced. Such hunger pushes all other needs into the background. The quality of this hunger is such that 'freedom, love, community, respect, philosophy, may all be waived aside as fripperies that are useless since they fail to fill the stomach. Such a man may fairly to be said to live by bread alone' (1970a: 83). This quality of hunger is described very well by Alexander Sol and by Primo Levi in describing the death camps in Nazi Germany. Maslow argues that those who have to live with such hunger pay a terrible price. The hunger itself is only part of this price. What is equally, if not more, important is that the natural process which moves towards the development of higher-order needs has been arrested and they may become fixated by this one need with the result that higher-order needs may either never be sufficiently developed, or, as in the case of a persistent famine, higher-order needs may disappear entirely.

Once lower-order needs have been satisfied, they then exist only in a potential fashion in the sense that they may emerge again if they are thwarted (1970a: 84). While the lower-order needs may demand satisfaction first, Maslow argues that it is the higher-order needs which are of most value to us and to society:

'It is the general clinical finding that the organism, when fed safety, love and respect works harder, perceives more efficiently, uses intelligence more fully, thinks to correct conclusions more often, digests food more efficiently, is less subject to various diseases etc.'   [1970a: 42]

Maslow suggests that if people have their lower-order needs satisfied they are then in a position to cultivate higher-order needs. Once they have learned the value of love, belongingness or respect, they may come to value this to the extent that they may even prefer death to losing its value (consider for example those who use hunger-strikes as a form of moral or political protest). For Maslow the system of needs is fragile and may become atrophied as the result of powerful social forces. Thus higher-order needs for love and respect may entirely disappear as the result of 'training' or unemployment (1970a: 131).

Maslow's theory has clear policy implications. Need gratification must be encouraged; governments and other agencies should aim for development – to feed, clothe and house people, to make them feel secure in order that they might be able to develop higher-order needs. If this is achieved then society itself should be more balanced. When it comes to child-rearing, Maslow suggests that parents and others recognize the 'healthy animality' in children. In an attack on Freudian ideas he argues that tender and fragile needs can be pushed down and crushed by a sick culture. For example he suggests that when children press adults for attention, the tendency to rebuff him or her with 'she's just looking for attention' is to stifle the development of the need for love, a demand which in Maslow's view is as legitimate a need as the need to satisfy hunger and thirst, cold and pain, which should be gratified rather than frustrated.

Maslow also believed that there is a basic aesthetic need, that some people become sick through ugliness and are cured by beautiful surroundings; they crave actively and their cravings can be satisfied only by beauty. He notes this for example in the impulsive tendency for people to straighten the crookedly hung picture on a wall.

4.3.3 Sociological and anthropological approaches to human needs

While economists and psychologists such as Maslow tend to assume that the individual consumer acts as if his or her decision to spend were made in isolation from all other consumers, sociologists and anthropologists view consumption as being socially determined. The importance of the social context is also recognized by advertisers and market researchers who take into account social factors such as age, class and gender issues in developing new products and campaigns. Sociologists look to society, social difference and distinction as the basis for their explanation of needs. One question asked by sociologists with respect to consumer societies is how one can tell the status or rank of the bearer of the commodity. Traditionally goods are used as a form of **material culture**, in that they depict the rank of important personages, and it is thus possible to 'read' the rank of a person by what they are wearing or the goods on display. This is more difficult to do in consumer societies where a person of low rank (for example a bricklayer) may have access to goods (known as **marker goods**) which have traditional associations with class status. Within social explanations, most needs are by-products of the social group which one belongs to. Such explanations also *deny* the separate existence of physiological and psychological needs, arguing instead that all needs share a cultural component.

At the heart of the sociological view is the role played by goods in marking the distinction between groups and in reinforcing identity within a group, or subculture, by means of conformity to group norms, or values. For example you may recall our discussion of the work of Norbert Elias (1994) in Chapter 1, where the court nobility developed an elaborate system of manners as a means to distinguish 'themselves' as a group from the upward pressure of the class of bourgeoisie. The system of manners created a means for preserving the social distance between the two groups. Within each group, however, conformity is expected of those who share the same code (with respect to language, manners and dress).

This idea also forms the basis of the sociological theory of Duesenberry (1949), an economist whose theory held that emulation, fuelled by envy and competitive display, is the driving force behind consumption. According to this theory, a subculture exerts pressure to consume upon its members. This pressure changes according to the standing which a person has within the subculture. Those who are relatively poor would be expected to spend a very high proportion of their income in order to satisfy the consumption requirements that have been socially imposed upon them, whilst those who are better off would be expected to save more, as they would already have met the social requirement (see note iii). While Duesenberry's theory has been supplanted by more recent developments, it forms the basis for a sociological approach which emphasizes the ways in which goods make visible and stable the categories and distinctions of culture. As Douglas and Isherwood say:

> 'Forget that commodities are good for eating, clothing and shelter; forget their usefulness and try instead the idea that commodities are good for thinking; treat them as a verbal medium for human creative faculty.'   [1978: 62]

Several authors have considered the ways in which particular groups within society use the construct of 'taste' as a means of classifying and using goods. For example Douglas and Isherwood (1978) examined the ways in which goods are used to mark social differences in society. The French sociologist Pierre Bourdieu (Bourdieu, 1984; Bourdieu and Passeron, 1990) sought to understand how consumers classify the goods which they use according to their 'taste' and how the exercise of this 'taste' in turn indicates the class position of the consumer. For example Bourdieu (1984), from his study of distinction in French society, notes that working-class people in France when confronted with a work of art featuring a rough drawing of a pair of hands, tend to speculate on the life led by the person whose hands they were, while middle-class people tend to focus more on the formal aesthetic nature of the painting, the colours used, perspective etc. Bourdieu found that social groups were marked by many more types of distinctions in terms of the goods they used and how they used them. For example he noted how men would noisily and copiously evacuate their noses into an enormous hand-kerchief, whereas 'ladies' were expected to daintily use paper tissues; that steak is the choice of the working-class man for a special meal, and is eaten with gusto, while fish is the food of choice for the woman, who tends to pick at it and leave some. Such examples relate the **expression of needs** to the **distinction between groups**.

Some authors who write about postmodernity, for example Mike Featherstone, suggest that the meaning and status of 'marker' goods, those goods which mark the distinction between different groups in society, is becoming blurred as more and more goods become produced:

> 'The constant supply of new, fashionably desirable goods, or the usurpation of existing marker goods by lower groups, produces a paperchase effect in which those above will have to invest in new (informational) goods in order to establish the original social distance.'
>
> [Featherstone, 1991: 18/19]

Featherstone suggests that as more and more goods are created, so marker goods may come to lose their stability. If this happens then the logic of cultural differences within society could become disordered and chaotic.

4.3.4 The vexed question of needs: of chickens, hamburgers and new gowns

In Douglas Coupland's book *Generation X* (1991) Claire is telling Andy and Dag about her date:

> 'My date had a low point, too. Out on highway 111 in Cathedral City there's a store that sells chickens that have been taxidermied. We were driving by and I just about fainted from wanting to have one, they were so cute, but Dan (that was his name) says, "Now Claire, you don't need a chicken", to which I said, "that's not the point Dan. The point is that I *want* a chicken." He thereupon commenced giving me this fantastically boring lecture about how the only reason I want a stuffed chicken is because they look so good in a shop window, and that the moment I received one I'd start dreaming up ways to ditch it. True enough. But then I tried to tell him that stuffed chickens are what life and new relationships are all about, but my analogy collapsed somewhere – the analogy became too mangled – and there was that awful woe-to-the-human race silence you get from pedants who are talking to half-wits. I wanted to throttle him.'
>
> [Coupland, 1991: 7]

Just where did Claire's need for the chicken come from? A classical econo-mist would probably suggest that this is an example of a whole series of potentially unfulfillable needs. J.K. Galbraith would probably take a quite different view, in arguing that her want was stimulated by a false need. In his books *The Affluent Society* (1958) and *The New Industrial State* (1967), Galbraith contests the prevailing conventional wisdom in economics which insists on the homogeneity and insatiability of wants. In his latter book, Galbraith points to the seemingly absurd position within conventional economic theory that:

> 'There is no proof that an expensive woman obtains the same satisfaction from yet another gown as does a hungry man from a hamburger. But there is no proof that she does not. Since it cannot be proven that she does not, her desire, it is held, must be accorded equal standing with that of a poor man for meat.'
>
> [1967: 272/3]

The questions to be addressed in this section therefore relate to the precise status of Claire's need for the stuffed chicken, the hungry man's for the hamburger and the woman's need for the new gown. Unsurprisingly Galbraith criticizes the state of affairs that the economist would treat all three needs as being equivalent. Surely common sense would insist that the hungry man's need is greater than those of both women? By the sound of it the woman already has several gowns, and the stuffed chicken will be discarded soon after it has been acquired, while the man's stomach is empty. One could further argue that the needs for the chicken and another gown are 'psychological' (and potentially insatiable as there is no knowing how many stuffed chickens or gowns may ultimately satisfy these people), whereas his need is 'physiological' (in that it is suggested that he will be satiated by the hamburger). However, as we shall see below, it is a quite different matter to establish such affairs with any degree of certainty. In order to understand why this is so, it is necessary to examine the implications of the story.

First, how are we to establish that the hunger of the poor man is more important than the need of the women for the chicken and the gown? Galbraith is arguing that classical economists avoid the question of which need is paramount by assuming that the needs are equivalent. The implication of Galbraith's story is that **physiological needs** (those related to hunger, sleep etc.) are more important than **psychological** or **cultural needs** but that classical economics does not regard them as such. Because of this, the need of the women for the chicken and a new gown and the man for the hamburger are rendered equivalent within conventional economic explanations.

Galbraith then goes further to suggest that naturally, humankind would seek to satisfy its physiological 'true' needs. However he argues that in consumer societies, the entire industrial machine, driven by the growth imperative, actively exploits the fact that psychological needs are potentially insatiable, by pouring vast resources into persuading people that they need products which, in the ordinary course of events, they would not otherwise need. The charge is clear: if the capitalist industrial system is driven by a growth imperative, in order to maintain growth, then existing consumers must learn to want more and more people must become consumers:

'Hunger and other physical pain have an objective and compelling quality. No one whose stomach is totally empty can be persuaded that his need is not for food but for entertainment. A man who is very cold will have a preference for what makes him warm. But psychic reactions have no such internal anchor; since they exist in the mind they are subject to what influences the mind. Though a hungry man cannot be persuaded as between bread or a circus, a well nourished man can. And he can be persuaded between different circuses and different foods. The further a man is removed from physical need the more he is open to persuasion – or management – as to what he buys. This is, perhaps, the most important consequence of increasing affluence.' [1967: 207]

As we saw in Chapter 3, Galbraith describes the means by which needs are created by the industrial system as the **revised sequence**. This is because the usual accepted explanation offered by economists is that rational and sovereign consumers exercise their freedom in choosing between the variety of goods on offer, including industrial goods, to satisfy their needs. Galbraith argues that this is a sham and that the reality is that the industrial system manufactures both the products and the needs for the products. This is achieved through marketing processes, including mass advertising and the entire propaganda machine of the industrial system. Galbraith goes on to argue that there is a terrible price to pay for this; that while the 'private' sector of 'consumer satisfaction' may flourish as the result of this false stimulus, real needs such as those for health, education and welfare which become the responsibility of public services are starved of resources.

Let us now consider the issues raised by Galbraith: first that of physiological and psychological needs, and secondly that of the creation of false needs by marketing.

4.3.4.1 Physiological and psychological needs

A psychological view

Galbraith's distinction between physiological and psychological needs has been widely shared by economists. What would a psychologist, anthropologist or sociologist make of this distinction? Taking psychology first, what would Abraham Maslow's view be of the example featuring the starving man and the woman who desires another gown? Like many economists, Maslow makes a distinction between physiological and psychological needs. You should remember that he argues that physiological needs such as the starving man's hunger are prepotent. If the man's motivation is physiological in that he is actually starving, then his entire psychological state will be preoccupied with the acquisition of food. If this need is not fulfilled quickly and starvation or semi-starvation is maintained over a matter of months (something which Galbraith does not discuss), then food may even come to shape the man's subsequent life choices, for example he may seek employment in the food industry. To Maslow, another even more depressing consequence of this need remaining unfulfilled is that the man may entirely lose the capacity to experience and seek to fulfil 'higher-order' needs such as those for esteem, respect and self-fulfilment, with potentially disastrous social consequences. It would thus seem that Maslow would argue that the hungry man's need is the more pressing of the two.

However Maslow argues that physiological needs are only *relatively* independent of psychological needs and that these latter needs, for example the need for love or esteem, may be expressed through physiological channels. While a person may express a need for 'hunger' through the desire for a hamburger, this may not be the expression of a physiological need but may rather be the expression of a higher-order 'hunger for love' or 'hunger for esteem'. Maslow points out that those who have experienced such higher-order needs may prefer to die rather than have these needs denied. For example Maslow himself suggests that a desire for ice-cream may actually be an indirect expression of a desire for love, and that if this is the case such a desire is much more important than if the desire was merely to cool the mouth (1970b: 104). Let us say that the man's need for the hamburger is an example of compensatory consumption, in other words it is the expression of a higher-order need for love or respect, or fulfilment. In this case one hamburger will not assuage his 'hunger' because it is no longer concerned with a lack of food but with a lack of love. Let us also say that the need of the woman for the gown is also motivated by the desire for love and for respect. In Claire's story, she wants the chicken because that's 'what life and new relationships are all about'. In her view if Dan buys her the stuffed chicken he is proving his regard for her, and the stuffed chicken is thus a token of his love. From this point of view the needs of all three people are equivalent and we cannot say that one need is in fact more pressing than the other.

Sociological/anthropological views

How would an anthropologist or sociologist view the question which Galbraith raises about the starving man and the woman who desires the gown? In the first instance they would entirely dismiss the suggestion that one can actually separate physiological from psychological needs and their satisfaction. They would also point out that Galbraith's question focuses too much on the individual and not enough on the group.

Taking the first point, about the separation of physiological and psychological needs, then one could argue that the man is not really starving at all, because his need is expressed in the desire for a hamburger. There is something remarkably *cultural* about a hamburger; one can picture it, the piece of meat, sizzling hot, topped perhaps with onion, pickle, red sauce and garnish, and tucked between the lightly toasted halves of a sesame seed sprinkled bap. Dare one say that he in fact desires no less than a 'Big Mac'? (McDonald's did not exist when Galbraith wrote his book.) A man who was starving might well desire a hamburger, but surely if his need was purely physiological, he could extract adequate nutrition by eating grubs, worms, plants and the like? While this may appear to be ludicrous, we must remind ourselves that this is indeed how other cultures, for example Australian aborigines, used to routinely survive in the bush and that such sustenance should be adequate for anyone anywhere. Let us consider this issue from a slightly different angle. William Leiss (1978: 62) draws an example from Zamytin's book *We* to illustrate his point that it is impossible to separate 'physiological' from 'psychological' needs. Everyone in the novel, which is situated at some point in the future, is assured the necessary nutrients and shelter to maintain life. However the sole nutrient is a bland petroleum derivative and the shelter is a small glass-walled cubicle furnished identically for all. The result is that everyone has their 'physiological' needs satisfied but that they simultaneously feel suicidal.

Leiss argues that the separation of needs into categories which imply that 'physiological' needs can be quantified and served independently from 'psychological' needs, which are qualitative, has been implemented in public-policy programmes around the world with the most unfortunate consequences. As implemented by government policy, needs which are identified as being purely 'physiological' can be entirely satisfied quantitatively. Thus a person who is hungry requires food, a person who is homeless requires shelter. The official thinking then suggests that as these needs are 'physiological', they have no 'cultural', 'aesthetic' or 'psychological' component. Following from this line of reasoning, to offer the starving person food which provides for more then their basic sustenance, or to offer housing to someone which is not strictly functional, could and often does invite the charge that the government was squandering 'public' funds. The tendency to separate 'physiological' from 'psychological' needs thus associates the former with quantity and uniformity. Anything which is aesthetically pleasing must be avoided from the calculation. This is evidenced by endless rows of uniformly dreary public housing projects, schools and medical facilities, to be found in towns and cities around the world.

Douglas and Isherwood (1978) support the view that one should not seek to separate 'physiological' from 'psychological' needs as all needs are culturally defined. They also draw our attention to the social context in which such a need might be expressed. Within a traditional society the idea that a solitary person might be without food would be unthinkable, as the body of the individual would be thought of as being an integral part of the body of the wider community. For example even in the fiercely competitive, money-based and individualized economy of the Yurok, no-one was allowed to starve; if there was scarcity, all starved (1978: 73). Douglas and Isherwood would possibly suggest that in posing his question about the man and the hamburger and the woman and the gown, Galbraith was focusing on the issue of poverty and how to address this. If this is indeed the case, they suggest that the alleviation of poverty must be concerned with much more than the provision of food. Indeed they argue that one of the problems suffered by the poor is that they must spend so much of their time and resources in seeking adequate supplies of food. Douglas and Isherwood argue that the primary difficulty experienced by the poor is one of exclusion. Society is composed of different classes of people. Those at the bottom must spend most of their time getting food and preparing it. At the next level is the class of household which has all of the requisite labour-saving devices but which is weak at the third level where inter-household transactions over long distances keep in play a continuous exchange of marking services. Such services include the putting out of laundry, cleaners, expenditure on education etc. These latter services are served primarily by the poor. Douglas and Isherwood further suggest that in all societies, commodities play an important role in marking the distinction between the different categories of people. They then argue that the poor who are excluded from this system are maintained in their poverty by those who frame their problem as being purely 'physiological'. If the plight of the poor is to be addressed, then they argue, policy-makers must devise ways for the poor to be able to find routes out of the isolation of poverty, by enabling them to enter into mainstream social networks and consumption.

In recent years Galbraith's argument, which was raised initially in the name of humanity, has been taken up by ecologists, who suggest that the world faces ecological disaster unless limits are placed on the seemingly relentless growth of consumer society. The so-called 'developing' countries of the 'Third World' smell a rat when they detect in such arguments the plea that they should forego their consumption, but that those in the Western world should continue to enjoy the fruits of consumerism.

4.3.4.2   Does marketing create false needs?

Through the concept of the 'revised sequence' Galbraith argues that the entire edifice of marketing, which purports to uncover, reveal and satisfy the expressed needs of consumers, is nothing more than a sham to enable producers to dispose of their excess productivity. For Galbraith the management of demand involves constructing products around strong selling points, associated with product design features, packaging, performance and sales strategy in addition to advertising. The specific strategy used is that of recruiting a loyal band of customers by building brand recognition and brand loyalty. Consumers are not sovereign:

> 'Persuasion on the scale just outlined requires that there be comprehensive, repetitive and compelling communication by the managers of demand with the managed.'
>
> [1967: 212]

The consequence is that while goods are becoming more and more abundant they do not seem to be less important. According to this argument, the system indoctrinates people to become consumers who constantly want more. Without this persuasion there would be less of a propensity to consume, which would create problems for the industrial system which relies on the expenditure of a constant proportion of income on commodities.

In *The System of Objects* (1988a), Jean Baudrillard agrees with much of what Galbraith has to say with respect to the idea of the revised sequence – that 'freedom of choice' is imposed on the consumer and that firms actively seek to dispose of their surplus by managing demand and by seeking to route the expression of all desire through commodities. However he fundamentally disagrees with Galbraith's reasoning with respect to the example which features the hungry man and the hamburger and the woman and the gown, arguing instead that the pleasure obtained from a second gown, for example, can be experienced as a 'real' freedom. Secondly, Baudrillard is suspicious of the surprisingly easy way in which consumers are manipulated within Galbraith's explanation, where the individual consumer becomes a completely passive victim of the system. Following from this, Galbraith reasons that needs are created by production. Baudrillard suggests that there is a serious psychological problem here, because following from this, it would seem that needs are fixed as they are specified in advance for each object. By this he means that Galbraith focuses on the want for the product, for the hamburger and the gown, but not on the source of the motivation which produces these wants in the first place. Baudrillard argues that once we enquire into this source we find not a rational and orderly system of needs, but a blind and rootless desire. To Baudrillard the products themselves are not at all important. On the contrary he suggests that 'consumers play with needs on a keyboard of objects' (1988b: 42), that advertising is not omnipotent and sometimes produces opposite reactions to what the advertiser intended and that finally in reference to the creation of a single need, objects can be substituted for one another.

Baudrillard advances his own theory, which is heavily based on that of Jacques Lacan. In his view, production does not create individual needs, but rather the *system of needs is created by the system of production*. The entire system of consumption is thus an extension of that of production. He argues that the rationalist theory of needs is as naive and disabled as is traditional medicine when confronted with psychosomatic or hysterical symptoms. Just as for the psychosomatic or hysterical patient, the same underlying cause may provoke a wide range of symptoms; so for the consumer, one underlying cause produces those symptoms of which needs are the expression. The underlying cause which fuels the expression of human needs is *desire*, a desire which is motivated by feelings of lack and of difference. Put simply, individuals living in a market society are motivated by the loss of one-ness; the one-ness which existed while they were in the womb, that tribal peoples feel within the second skin of community. This lack, which is at the centre of their being, gives birth to an endless consuming desire to fill the hole which is perceived to lie at the centre of their being, to replace the lack.

In order to fully understand what Baudrillard is saying, we need to understand the nature of commodities themselves. Commodities do not exist in isolation from one another, but form a vast system of objects. Within the field of their objective function, objects are not exchangeable or substitutable for one another. For example a washing machine cannot be substituted by a refrigerator. But a commodity such as a washing machine or a refrigerator signifies more than this denotation; it also has connotations, perhaps of comfort or prestige. Objects are thus not only material goods, but also function as signs which both denote and connote meaning. While commodities may not be substitutable at the level of denotation (in terms of their use, such as washing), at the level of connotation, many different objects may fill the desire for 'comfort'. This is why Baudrillard likens the system of needs to that of hysteria or psychosomatic illness. In an organic illness, there is a necessary relation between the symptom and the organ (in the same way that there is a relation between a washing machine and the function of washing). However in the hysterical or psychosomatic case, the symptom is relatively arbitrary, in that it may manifest itself as migraine, colitis, lumbago, angina or general fatigue, all of which are interchangeable with one another. With respect to Galbraith's example of the hamburger and the gown, Baudrillard suggests that the desire for the gown or the hamburger could equally be replaced by a desire for a car, chocolate or any other object which momentarily helps to fill the overwhelming desire which is at the heart of all human needing.

Baudrillard suggests that needs are just like hysterical symptoms as they are the surface manifestation of a desire which is insatiable because it is founded on a lack; and this desire, which can never be satisfied, signifies itself locally in a succession of objects and needs. Within a consumer society, all of the means of satisfaction are oriented towards the realm of commodities. Consumer society offers one solution only for the satisfaction of needs; its individualizing tendencies help to loosen social bonds only to re-create them again in terms of consumption communities, a pale shadow of the community which has been replaced. Consumer society says to the person: be all you can be – a consumer. If you are thirsty, drink Coke; if you want to feel safe, drink Coke; if you want to be somebody, drink Coke; if you want to belong, drink Coke.

How might we evaluate Baudrillard's claim? Recall our earlier discussion of commodity exchange and gift exchange, where it was suggested that both forms of exchange co-exist in consumer societies. As gift exchange both nurtures and sustains notions of community, if it is alive and well in many consumer societies, then we could argue that Baudrillard is exaggerating; that in fact many sources of communal need gain satisfaction from the gift economy which works to provide need satisfaction.

4.3.4.3 Summary

This section has raised what I have called the 'vexed' question of human needs. Why is this question vexing? Because it deals with the fundamental processes which drive the tendency for those in consumer societies to acquire possessions and to keep on acquiring them, with no potential limit in sight. J.K. Galbraith hoped to impose some limits to such growth through his argument which related 'physiological' needs to 'true' needs and 'psychological' needs to 'false' needs, and which further suggested that marketing created such 'false' needs. However following a discussion of alternative points of view, the distinction into 'physiological' and 'psychological' needs, which has shaped many policy decisions with respect to the consumption of public goods, is itself found to be deeply problematic and even unsustainable. On the other hand sociologists and anthropologists argue that all needs are intrinsically cultural and that products are used as a form of material culture from which one group establishes boundaries between itself and other groups in society. Baudrillard argues from a different point of view to suggest that the underlying motive behind most consumption in consumer societies is a profound lack which is experienced by those individuals who live in them, and which represents a deep yearning for the community. However Baudrillard's argument may be modified in the light of our knowledge that many aspects of such forms of community still survive and even thrive in consumer societies. We now turn to discuss the values which people derive from commodity exchange in consumer societies.

4.4   CONSUMING VALUES

The issue of value is of considerable importance in understanding consumption. As we saw in a previous section in relation to Grafton-Small's grandfather's bow-tie, the common yardstick of economic value often falls short of the worth which consumers ascribe to objects which have high personal worth but are considered to be economically valueless. One can utilize Abraham Maslow's typology of human needs as a basis for the discussion of the values which people derive from consumption (see note iv). Below are listed some values which might correspond to Maslow's famous hierarchy of needs.

Need	Value	Section
Self-actualization	Spiritual	4.4.5
Identity	Status	4.4.4
Belonging	Esteem	4.4.3
Safety	Quality and reliability	4.4.2
Sustenance	Efficiency and convenience	4.4.1

4.4.1   Efficiency and convenience

It is taken for granted that as consumers, we value efficiency. We value transport systems which are clean, safe and efficient, where cars, trains, buses and planes arrive and depart on time. The grim reality which often results from gridlock on the roads, trains and buses which are often late, overheated in summer and freezing in winter, huge queues at airport terminals and flight delays, makes us realize how much more efficient life could be.

Efficiency is central to marketing theory. The marketer's emphasis on getting the right product to the right person, in the right place and at the right time, cannot be overestimated. In practice the management of time has attracted huge amounts of investment particularly in the manufacturing industry, where the early emphasis on time-and-motion studies has developed via a focus on scheduling work in progress through techniques such as Just In Time (JIT), the development of 'lean production' and efficient customer response systems (Stalk and Hout, 1990).

But why are consumers so taken with efficiency? One version of Freudian theory suggests that because of the huge focus on consumption in contemporary society, many adults have regressed to an infantile oral stage of development. According to this theory, although consumers are passive and utterly dependent upon other people who produce the goods and services on which they depend, they (foolishly) like to think that it is they who are in control and not those who serve them. Theorists argue that this is similar to the behaviour of very young infants who believe that, while they are passive, they are in control of their mother. A second feature of such infantile behaviour is the desire for instant gratification. Young infants who experience a need or lack demand immediate gratification of that need. If this is not satisfied they will yell, shout and scream until it is. Freudian theorists argue that it is only when these infants acquire the ability to symbolize that which they desire that they can begin to defer their gratification. Theorists suggest that adults who have regressed to this oral stage (known in the jargon as secondary narcissism) also demand immediate gratification of their needs. If their needs are not met immediately, they become furiously angry.

4.4.1.1 Consumer goods and convenience

While convenience is of major interest to practising marketers, this topic has attracted the interest of only a few academics. For example Brown and McEnally (1992) asked consumers to talk about what convenience meant to them. The authors were subsequently able to isolate two major dimensions of convenience – time and energy. For example patronizing a fast-food restaurant reduces the mental energy (effort) necessary to obtain a meal, in that the consumer has no need to plan ahead in order to have the necessary ingredients for the meal. To further enhance fast-food convenience, the authors suggest that one could reduce the physical energy (effort) required by ordering this food at the drive-in window. Brown and McEnally suggest that these dimensions of convenience will vary across the consumption phases of acquisition, use and disposal. Clever marketers have sought to make fast food even more convenient by focusing on acquisition – through choosing convenient locations, providing drive-in windows, locating more than one type of fast food store in the same building, and accepting credit cards.

Darian and Cohen (1995) followed up Brown and McEnally's study by questioning the commonly held assumption that the desire for convenience stems from increasing time pressure and the growing numbers of women in employment. They focused on working women who purchased fast food. Their hypothesis was that employed wives would feel more time pressure and would therefore be more likely to buy fast food. They found that time shortage did *not* significantly affect respondents' perceptions of the benefits of fast foods. However they also found that those women who had most time pressure placed a premium on saving mental energy (not having to plan). In a later study McEnally and Brown (1997) extended Darian and Cohen's study by means of a nation-wide mail study in the USA. This investigated a broader spectrum of products (including answering machines, cellular phones, stereo remote controls and microwave ovens), and explored the importance of energy and time with respect to the three phases of the consumption process (acquisition, use and disposal). The authors found that researchers cannot assume that increased employment leads to perceptions of increasing time pressure. However both age and income were significantly related to time pressure, with those in the 25–45 group and those with higher incomes reporting that they had too little non-work time. The study found that income was the major variable associated with a convenience orientation, and that as income increases generally the respondent indicates a higher orientation to convenience. However the research indicated the rather surprising finding that there appeared to be no relation between perceived time pressure and ownership and attitudes towards convenience products. The authors concluded that the relationship between time pressure and convenience is much more complex than had originally been thought.

4.4.1.2 Consumer goods, saving labour?

Do consumer goods actually save time? Such devices are more often referred to as labour-saving rather than being time-saving. Juliet Schor (1991) notes that while some devices are labour saving with respect to some tasks, they create new ones. She cites the example of the refrigerator which, while it eliminated the need for daily shopping and storing ice at home, helped drive out the door-to-door vendor and thereby contributed to the rise of the supermarket with its self-service and greater travel time. Schor also argues that laundry provides the best example of how technology has failed to reduce labour time. Automatic washing machines and dryers were introduced into the USA from 1925 onwards. The new machines did cut the time needed to wash and dry a load of clothes. Yet laundry time rose. The reason for this was that housewives were doing more loads and that laundry which had previously been sent out began to stay at home. At the same time standards of cleanliness also rose sharply. Schor notes that at the time of the British colonial period in the USA, washing would be once a month at most and that most people wore dirty clothes nearly all of the time. By 1925 when the electric washer was introduced, many Americans had a clean set of clothes every Saturday night. By the 1950s and 1960s it became common to wash after one wearing. Standards increased for almost all household tasks over the years. Contemporary standards of cleaning are a modern invention. This issue was raised in Chapter 1 where we discussed this in relation to the theories developed by Norbert Elias. In the period from the tenth to the eighteenth centuries, noses would be blown with the fingers or into clothing, menstrual blood just dripped onto the floor, a crust of dirt was thought to foster a good complexion and faeces were often left lying around the house. It should be noted that in other countries higher standards of hygiene prevailed, and that European travellers to Asia were considered to be extremely uncouth.

Safety

Maslow pointed out that the need to feel safe is a fundamental human requirement. If we do not feel safe then we will tend to react negatively to the world and treat it with suspicion and distrust. This in turn may mean that we turn inwards upon ourselves and shy away from contact with others. Not only does this mean that we fail to develop lasting and rewarding relationships with others, it also means that our self-esteem is wounded. What sorts of values related to safety are related to consumer goods and services? Here we deal with two aspects. People can only feel safe in a society to the extent that they are treated both as moral subjects and as moral agents. Also safety is created to the extent that goods and services are reliable, they do what they are supposed to do and are of dependable quality. First let us consider moral values.

4.4.2.1   Morality

A fundamental value for all people is that they are treated as moral subjects and as moral agents. What is meant by this statement? People desire to be treated as **moral subjects** to the extent that those who are dealing with them treat them fairly and honourably. They often also desire to be accepted as **moral agents** to the extent that they recognize their own consumption behaviour and that of others to be intrinsically moral. A person's sense of safety is threatened when either of these is put into question. For example if I feel that someone is constantly seeking to deceive me, then I may become distrustful and calculating with respect to them. Similarly if I feel that I cannot act morally to make the world into a better place, my sense of security is compromised.

Moral subjects

A fundamental human value is that we are treated fairly and are not cheated. To what extent is this true of modern-day marketing? As I have discussed elsewhere (Desmond, 1998), one of the principal goals of marketing was to transform trade by ridding it of 'base practices', including a whole range of deceptions such as product adulteration, price-fixing and not giving good weight. This was to be achieved through the introduction of a more scientific approach and through the **marketing concept**, which stresses that only those firms which act in the customers' interests will survive into the long-term. The idea of establishing a more just system of trade was not merely the concern of marketing academics. Fairness was a primary motive for the establishment of the first consumer co-operative by the Rochdale Pioneers in England in 1840. Their idea was to provide good weight at fair prices, not to allow adulteration by placing sand in oatmeal and chalk in flour, and to provide good value for money.

Despite the aspirations of marketing academics, in the opinion of a number of authors, the marketing concept has not really had much of an effect on the extent to which marketers try to deceive the public. For example Paul Blumberg's book *Deception in the Marketplace* (1989) delivers a scathing indictment of the types of deception which are routinely engaged in by marketers. According to Blumberg, practices of adulteration and short-weighting of products are still common, as are 'phony' sales, the exploitation of those who are technically uninformed, price-fixing and a host of other deceptions.

Moral agency

Is it true to say that every purchase decision has a moral component to it? The answer is a qualified 'yes'. It is possible to cite many examples of people acting morally with respect to consumption behaviour. Moral actions may be considered negative or affirmative, but are in reality a mixture of both. For example one might consider negative actions to include those where people avoid or actively reject some aspect of consumption because they believe that this is wrong. While the behaviour of these people is negative, it should be noted that this is usually motivated by some positive motive (for example 'to save the environment'). Some people actively reject the entire consumer lifestyle. For example in Chapter 2 we discussed the lifestyle associated with **voluntary simplicity**. You may remember that voluntary simplifiers actively seek to reduce their consumption because they believe that consumerism is intrinsically bad. On the other hand most people do not reject the entire consumer lifestyle, but are concerned about one or more aspects of its operation. Many people believe that it is wrong to apply techniques of industrial production, known collectively as 'factory farming', to the rearing of animals. Some are vegetarian because they subscribe to the utilitarian argument that it is wrong to cause unnecessary pain and suffering to animals where substitutes are available. In fact a range of moral actions are open to consumers at virtually every point in the decision process. For example the decision to buy 'free range' as opposed to 'battery' eggs is a moral decision which people make on a daily basis.

4.4.2.2 Reliability and quality

Reliability is also a value which is cherished by consumers. Reliability is linked to the idea of moral subjectivity in that consumers expect the goods which they purchase to work and to work consistently. Huge strides have been made over the decades with respect to the reliability of a range of consumer goods, to the extent that their reliability is nowadays taken for granted. This is particularly so for electronic goods. For example while television repair centres were common in the UK in the 1970s, there is virtually no need for them now. However there is much more to reliability than this. One argument is that in a world which is constantly changing, where cherished institutions that have lasted for centuries are crumbling, and where images seem to be valued more than substance, people search for reassurance and certainty. They find such certainty in the day-to-day things that they use. For many people their brand of coffee or tea is not so much regarded as a commodity but rather as an old friend, as one of the few things in life that one can rely upon not to change. Companies such as Volkswagen have capitalized on such feelings in their recent advertising which exclaims 'If only everything (love, marriage) could be as reliable as a Volkswagen'.

The 'New Coke' fiasco

During the 1980s American soft-drinks giant Coca-Cola paid a huge price for misunderstanding the importance consumers attached to safety and the perceived reliability of their product. It all started when rivals PepsiCo discovered in blind taste tests that most people preferred Pepsi. However the power of the Coke brand was such that when consumers knew the identity of the brands tasted, most preferred Coke. Pepsi began to capitalize on the fact that in blind tests their brand tasted better by launching a travelling road-show in the USA called the 'Pepsi-Challenge'. The Pepsi-Challenge invited consumers to participate in blind taste tests to see whether they could tell the difference between brands of cola and, if so, to see which cola they preferred. Of course on the basis of their previous research, Pepsi already knew that most people would prefer their brand in such tests. The Pepsi-Challenge seriously worried Coca-Cola executives. Up until the Pepsi-Challenge, the Coca-Cola Corporation had been immensely proud of its formula which was so unique and powerful that no one individual was entrusted with the entire recipe. The Pepsi-Challenge threatened to under-mine the power of Coke itself. In response to this, Coca-Cola researched and tested new flavours until in 1982 it came up with one which was consistently superior to Coke, and more importantly to Pepsi in blind taste tests. It was decided after much deliberation that this 'new formula' Coke should be substituted for the traditional blend. When they launched new formula Coke in a blaze of publicity, using television star Bill Cosby as the vehicle to announce the change, the company was stunned at the hostile reaction of the American public. The public demanded their old and trusted Coke back. The Coca-Cola Corporation was swamped by letters and sales of New Coke failed to take off. In a press conference, Coca-Cola's chairman apologized to the American people. The original Coca-Cola returned under the name Coca-Cola Classic. New Coke disappeared so fast that it never even made it to other countries.

Reconsider what happened here. What did Coca-Cola do wrong? Coca-Cola felt threatened by a rival whose product tasted better than theirs. In response they changed the taste of their product in order to make it smoother and sweeter to match the preferred tastes of consumers. Rather than lauding this development, consumers shunned the new product to the extent that the company had to bring back the original. The Coca-Cola Corporation did nothing wrong in classical marketing terms. They identified a threat and responded to this threat. What Coca-Cola executives did not appreciate was that Coke did not really belong to the Coca-Cola Corporation. Millions of ordinary Americans had been reared on the stuff. While technically it might not taste as good as Pepsi, the taste of Coke was secondary to the fact that Coke had always been there. Coke was an institution – and consumers decided it was one institution that they could stop from crumbling (see note v).

Another aspect of safety is that consumers like to think that they are receiving good value for the money which they spend. The idea of a 'fair exchange' fits with Zeithaml's (1988) finding that consumers value (1) low price, (2) getting what is wanted, (3) quality compared to price and (4) what is received for what is sacrificed. The demand of value for money with respect to low prices is driven by a suspicion that firms are not treating consumers as moral subjects but tend to fix prices. However there is a fine balance here as in the relentless pursuit of lower prices companies squeeze their suppliers to reduce costs further. Ultimately this can result in the mass exploitation of workers.

4.4.3 Aesthetics

The idea of aesthetics is that things should not simply possess the attribute of functional quality, in that they are fit for the purpose for which they are intended, but that they also look good. Abraham Maslow believed that the need for beauty was possibly as fundamental to the human being as any physiological need. He summed up this idea in suggesting the almost universal human desire for good form, as exhibited for example when a person straightens a crooked picture on a wall. An object is valued therefore not only for its function, or the manner by which it conveys status, but also for its aesthetic value, whether it is perceived to be ugly or beautiful, or whether it is in 'good' or 'bad' taste.

While Maslow suggests that the desire for beauty is innate, a product of human genetic makeup, sociologists describe the role of 'taste' in marking social differences. For example recall once more Elias's (1994) description of the way in which the French court nobility used 'taste' as defined in an elaborate system of 'manners' to differentiate between their social position and that of the bourgeoisie. One often hears aesthetic questions (questions about taste, and beauty) with respect to works of art or music. Within this context questions of aesthetics and taste have been the focus of a battleground between traditional cultures and the consumer culture. Frequently the consumer culture is portrayed as being ersatz (false), inauthentic, as something which will level down the authentic values of true culture. In turn this question of levelling down is often associated with the Americanization of culture.

For example Dick Hebdige (1988) describes how between the 1930s and the 1960s, the British cultural elite mounted a fierce attack on American popular culture, which to them seemed to be destroying the very fabric of authentic British culture. During the war, the American GIs brought with them the tokens of US culture – jazz music, cigarettes, chocolate, gum and of course, Coke. Wherever the GIs travelled during the course of the war and its aftermath in Europe, the Pacific or elsewhere, these products went with them. For those who had been defeated the GIs were conquerors. Hebdige relates how:

'There he stands in his bulging clothes . . . lonely, a bit wistful, seeing little, understanding less – the Conqueror with a chocolate bar in one pocket and a packet of cigarettes in the other . . . The chocolate bar and the cigarettes are about all that he, the Conqueror has to give the conquered.' [Hebdige, 1988: 53]

Around the world, wherever the GIs went, products became symbols of the US way of life, objects of desire, signifying status to many. However they were not uniformly perceived in this way. Some saw them as a threat to their cultural traditions and way of life. The rapid increase in the prestige of the USA during the post-war period was paralleled by an equally rapid decline in that of the UK. However during the same period the UK became progressively opened to a flood of US imports including music, such as jazz and rock 'n' roll together with the clothes and venues associated with these forms of music, and Hollywood films and a growing profusion of consumer commodities. These imports were enthusiastically received by youth in particular. To the British cultural elite, they represented the worst aspects of a mass machine-made culture, providing a potent threat to the uniqueness of British 'high-culture'. The new mass 'popular' culture was described by the cultural elite as being inauthentic and ersatz. For example jazz and rock 'n' roll were described as being tasteless, moronic, inauthentic and incoherent (as opposed to more 'natural' forms such as folk and traditional music). Resistance to new 'pop' culture became even more fierce as new streamlined products became available. The idea that products should be 'streamlined' and designed with some aspect of style in mind was regarded by some as being a further signal that life was becoming progressively mechanized and more uniform.

While those authors and musicians who formed the British cultural elite frowned on the growing availability of US cultural imports, these were seized on eagerly by sections of British youth, for example the 'Teddy Boys', 'Mods' and 'Rockers' who used style to construct a sense of identity for themselves. Within such styles great attention was devoted to clothes, what to wear and how to wear them, to hairstyles and the requisite products which reinforced the 'look'.

We have discussed two points of view with respect to aesthetics. On the one hand style is seen to be something which is innate to the human condition. According to this view some people 'naturally' have more style than others. There is also a sense in which one might say that some forms of stylistic representation are more 'natural' than others. However an alternative view portrays aesthetics as being also intrinsically social, shaped by the desire within society for groups to mark their own identity and to distinguish this from others, in terms of 'taste'.

4.4.4 Reputation – esteem

Consumer commodities can play a role in esteem to the extent that they improve one's standing or status in a group using material objects. Esteem is linked to status; to be esteemed usually confers high status on a person. It is linked to a person's reputation, which is what is generally said and believed to be true about a person. Those who feel status most keenly are the 'have-nots', those who are low in self-esteem, and who, if we are using Maslow's typology, express strong affiliation needs. One way in which people with low self-esteem may seek to create status is by using signifiers of style which signal to others that they have 'made it' (although what is implicit in this form of behaviour is the assumption that if you have got real power in society you don't have to resort to such tactics). For example Cab Calloway represented the essence of glamour for young black males in the USA when he wore a 'zoot suit' in the 1941 film *Stormy Weather*. Worn with two-tone shoes and a fedora hat, the zoot suit was a positive exaggeration; there was too much cloth, certainly much more than was needed during war-time rationing when cloth was being restricted. The zoot suit provided a means for black self-expression, a means for the poor to show success.

Since the 1940s black music and black style have played a major role in shaping the identities of young whites. For example the 'hipsters' of the 1950s sought to emulate different styles, wearing zoot suits, biker gear and beat style. During the 1980s and into the 1990s 'hip-hop' outfits like Run DMC, with their huge crossover hit 'Ghetto Life', became icons of style for young whites. The band's aim was to dress down, to get rid of the costume, to bring the beat or beef from the street onto the stage. Central to this style were trainers, tracksuits and baseball caps – but only selected brands. One member of the band noted recently that to begin with, kids would come up and ask why are you wearing Adidas, not Nike or Reebok? Pretty soon Adidas became established as the ultimate in 'cool' street culture. Some whites identified their style with that of rap to such an extent that they became known as 'wiggers' (white niggers) by blacks, a form of reversal of the original term, which was used to signify a group which had lost confidence in itself.

DBS Arts Library

4.4.5   Status

Status reflects the standing which a person has in a particular group or community of peers, within which a person has a particular rank. The idea of status is not restricted to human society. The best-known example is the submission–dominance hierarchy known as the **pecking order**, within which each hen has a position in which she is submissive to all of the hens above her and dominates all of those below her.

Status within society is also distributed in relation to some form of classification, of which **social class** is perhaps the best-known form. For example in Chapter 1 we outlined Norbert Elias's discussion of how the court nobility in France sought to distance themselves from the bourgeois class which had threatened to usurp their position. They did this by means of the development of an ever more intricate system of manners which the bourgeoisie tried hard to imitate. However as the bourgeoisie succeeded in imitating one gesture, the courtly nobles changed the code by dropping this gesture from what constituted 'civilized' behaviour and substituted another. This led to a game of 'catch-up' with the poor bourgeoisie always lagging one step behind. The idea of status thus divides groups into those who have it, and those who don't (the status-seekers). Status thrived in the court society of France because of the perceived competition between the classes which bred intense levels of surveillance and social comparison. This formed the basis for the subsequent development of the 'other-directed' character, the prototype for the contemporary individual who constantly subjects himself or herself to scrutiny.

While status can be said to be a property of the code by which any group is organized, the concept of social class, which is usually measured in terms of occupational status, is often described as the means by which the 'haves' are distinguished from the 'have-nots' in society. In his classic study of classification in French culture, Pierre Bourdieu (1984) analysed the ways in which status and class groups differentiated themselves from one another by means of patterns of consumption which distinguished one group's way of life from another's. A major distinction which Bourdieu made was between social groups with two different types of capital. On the one hand he found that those with a great deal of **economic capital** (associated with business management and finance) tended to adopt lifestyles featuring aspects of conspicuous consumption. On the other hand those with high levels of **cultural capital** adopted a more 'refined' approach.

Status is an interesting concept for several reasons. First, it is an effect of impression management but is presented as being natural. One key aspect of the status display is that this should *appear* to be natural and not contrived. So for example the owner of a sports car may say to her (hopefully envious) neighbour 'I need a fast car to get from A to B', thus implying that what is a luxury for others is a necessity for her. Secondly, status is a phenomenon which always applies to someone else. For example I might sneer at the manner by which an executive seeks to command respect by dressing expensively and driving a Mercedes, while he or she might point out that I seem to be incessantly checking on other people's references to my work in the Social Sciences Citation Index. Status markers, which form the basis for comparison of success and rank, thus vary according to the social group one is in at a particular time.

For materialism to be an important status marker, one would expect that the value of material culture, as evidenced by a high level of attachment to worldly possessions, would be placed as a pre-eminent value in the group. Within the group, commodities may play a role to the extent that they act as signals which signify our prestige to others. This does not work particularly well if we live in a small community where everyone knows everyone else's personal history. However for those of us who live in urban environments, it is possible for people to seek to realize their dreams by managing the way in which they present themselves. For example it might be imagined that the possession of a powerful sports car conveys feelings of power and status onto the driver. From this perspective the car is not so much valued for its functional characteristics, nor for its exchange value, but for what it signifies to other people. Thorstein Veblen pointed out the importance of conspicuous consumption, of achieving social status within a community, as a motivation for the consumption of a unique assembly of 'status goods'. While many people consider status in relation to individuals, status displays can involve groups of people and entire constellations of goods, such as those which might be provided at a lavish party or wedding feast.

Jean Baudrillard notes the irony that while commodities seduce us by telling us that in buying and displaying them we will be different, at the same time most of the goods on offer are mass produced, so everyone ends up looking more or less like everyone else:

> 'Advertising tells us, at the same time "Buy this, for it is like nothing else!" (the meat of the elite, the cigarette of the *happy few*! etc.); but also, "Buy this because everyone else is using it!" And this is in no way contradictory. We can imagine that each individual feels unique while resembling everyone else.'   [1988b: 11]

Here Baudrillard captures an important element of status. People want to look different, but not too different; going too far can invite not envy but ridicule. For example the choice of what clothing to wear has been particularly difficult for female executives. Should they wear a suit (and appear as being too like the men they are competing with) or the dress with the large shoulder pads (and perhaps be considered as being a seductress)? Thus **conformity**, or adherence to group norms, can play an extremely powerful role in shaping how we dress and how we wear what we buy.

4.4.6　Spirituality

In what way can it be said that consumers value spirituality? This concept is linked firmly to that of 'self-actualization' which is the pinnacle of achievement of Abraham Maslow's famous hierarchy of needs. In his less known work entitled *Religions, Values and Peak Experiences*, Maslow focuses on those ecstasies, transcendental or what he calls 'peak experiences', which to him constitute the core of every known religion. Maslow reports that his own investigations yielded up two groups of people with respect to such experiences: a group of those who reported that they had achieved 'peak' experiences, labelled 'peakers'; and a group which he labelled 'non-peakers' who were afraid of peak experiences, who suppressed and denied them. This latter group included compulsive–obsessive types, those dominated by a materialist–mechanistic philosophy of life and of extremely other-directed people 'who scarcely know what is going on inside of themselves' (1970b: 23). According to Maslow, organized religions are made up of peakers or mystics, and non-peakers or religious-organization people. He then argues that while the peaker prizes the mystical, transcendent experience itself, the organization man or non-peaker places more value on the paraphernalia of organized religion – buildings, dogmas, rituals and the like. Maslow also contends that those non-peakers within organized religion are then given the job of translating peak experiences for the laity, resulting in 'the more or less vain efforts' to communicate peak experiences to non-peakers.

As you may imagine from the above, Maslow is no fan of organized religion.

He believes that 'religionizing', or the segregation of religious experience to organized religion, acts to confine what is 'religious' to particular 'religious' stimuli which occur on one day of the week. For Maslow, 'religionizing' one day of the week secularizes the rest of it; it also denies the possibility for non-theists to put the label 'religious experience' on their own peak experiences. Rather, for Maslow, all fully functioning, well and healthy individuals should be capable of transcendental experience. The 'non-peak' experience is a lower and lesser state which indicates that we are not fully functioning. Maslow's message is thus simple: people have no need of organized religion for genuinely religious experience; and, secondly, everyone can be a 'peaker'.

4.4.6.1 Selling peak experiences

Looking at contemporary consumer society then at least on first glance, it looks as if Maslow's wish has come true. A huge and varied industry has sprung up based on the creation and satisfaction of peak experiences, including scary new funfair rides, a range of extreme sports (from sky-diving to hot-dogging), the terrors and pleasures of 'experiential' holiday activities (such as bungee jumping, white-water rafting and swimming with sharks) and television programmes where we can see 'perfectly ordinary people' engaging in activities such as leaping canyons on motorcycles, driving across wires strung across ravines, being wrapped with poisonous snakes and buried underground for days – but with the warning 'don't do this at home'. Not all of these experiences are so physical. For example one can also think of the quasi-religious experiences offered by theme parks such as Niketown, not to mention those offered by different cocktail mixes of dance, drugs and music.

4.4.6.2 Are peak experiences religious experiences?

And so it would seem that the whole peak experience of revelation, ecstasy and the transcendence of the boundaries of the self, which were once the privilege of a selected aristocracy of culture (saints, hermits, ascetics, monks), may be obtained, indeed purchased, by anyone. The sociologist Zygmunt Bauman has pondered over the nature of these peak experiences, asking the question – are these religious experiences? Bauman distinguishes the peak experience from the religious experience in the following simple manner: the religious experience celebrates human insufficiency and weakness (which can only be filled by placing oneself in the hands of God or fate), while the idea of the peak experience appeals to the full development of psychological and bodily resources, and presumes infinite human potency. According to Bauman, the driving force of premodern Christianity was to live the 'pious life', according to which, to the extent that a person mortified themselves and denied the pleasures and temptations of the present world, they would gain in the next world, in heaven. Bauman suggests that those following the pious life pushed this idea so far that they became preoccupied with images of suffering and death to the extent that the continuation of life itself became virtually impossible. With the onset of modernity, rationalists rebuffed the obsession with an 'afterlife', focusing instead on the 'here and now'. However the purveyors of peak experiences have uncoupled the dream of the peak experience from religious-inspired practices of self-denial and withdrawal from worldly attractions, and have harnessed this to the desire for worldly goods:

> 'If the religious version of the peak experience used to reconcile the faithful to a life of misery and hardship, the postmodern version reconciles its followers to life organized around the duty of an avid, perpetual, though never definitely gratifying, consumption.'
> [1998: 70]

Bauman argues that the promise of 'new, overwhelming, spine-chilling but always exhilarating' experience has become the selling point for everything from colas to cars; each offers the potential 'peaker' the prospect of living through sensations never experienced before. 'Each new sensation must be "greater" in that it is more overpowering and exciting than the one before, with the vertigo of "total" peak experience always on the horizon' (1998: 71). Bauman notes that the assumption is that the quantitative accretion of sensual experience will provide a qualitative breakthrough.

The 'peaker' is helped by the 'meta-experiential' industry, which provides the goods and services which are aimed at the enhancement of sensation. Nowadays people (and their bodies) must be trained in the art of experience – the idea that a fit body, served by a well-trained mind, is capable of repeated, even continuous intensity of experience. This is the 'meta-experiential' function fulfilled by 'self-improvement' movements, where the experiential needs of the body are developed through exercise, contemplation and self-concentration. Experience becomes above all a technical problem, a matter of mastering the appropriate technique. These movements are themselves part of the 'counselling boom' and are aimed at producing perfect consumers, 'at developing to the full the capacities which the experience-seeking and sensation-gathering life of the consumer–chooser demand' (1998: 71).

4.4.6.3 Bitter experience and fundamentalism

Bauman thus rejects the idea that the satisfaction of 'peak' experience is a form of postmodern religion. In contrast he argues that this spot is taken up by religious fundamentalism. Fundamentalism appeals most of all to the poor who are 'flawed consumers', who have not got tickets to the consumer party. For them, fundamentalism provides an alternative to the modernist desire for goods. However Bauman also notes that the certainty of fundamentalism also speaks to the bitter experience of postmodern consumers. The bitter experience is the necessity imposed by the constant demand that the consumer exercise 'freedom of choice' in the marketplace. Such freedom is a frightening thing, particularly at a time when long-established institutions are crumbling and when those experts who could once be considered to be reliable guides seem divided against themselves.

4.4.7   Discussion

This section considered a number of the values which people may derive from the consumption of goods. As consumers we value efficiency, in that we often expect to be served in a timely manner, and we value convenience as a form of efficiency. Are consumers interested in efficiency and convenience because they are essentially lazy, self-interested narcissists? The discussion concluded that while there is some evidence to support this interpretation of consumer behaviour, such behaviour is also influenced by the rules defined within different social contexts. The values of status and esteem conferred by the ownership of commodities were found to be important, particularly with respect to youth and other marginal groups. Many consumers also place a high degree of value on moral issues and will even go so far as to boycott products or firms which they believe are engaging in immoral activities. Finally, in consumer societies there is a growing tendency for people to seek spiritual values from the world of goods.

But having said all of that. What is it that consumers value most in life? Time after time research has indicated that the things which people value most tend also to have the least economic value. Like Grafton-Small's (1992) bow-tie, people value those items which, though economically worthless, tie them into the bonds of a wider community. The most precious items are the small things which tie us to memorable events – photographs, wedding rings, holiday souvenirs or trophies won in school sports – or objects whose value is not commercial (Richins, 1994). This brings us back to the discussion at the start of this chapter. Commodity exchange can never really place a value on the worth which some things hold for us.

4.5   CHAPTER SUMMARY

This chapter has involved a discussion about exchange, needs and values. How might these be related to one another? Take the concept of need. On the one hand economists do not traditionally enquire about where needs come from, but assume that their origin lies in the perception of a lack, or desire. Economists distinguish between physiological and psychological, or true and false needs. Physiological needs are those basic needs – hunger, thirst and safety – which must be met to ensure survival of the organism. However psychological needs are potentially insatiable. It is on this basis that J.K. Galbraith argues for the 'revised sequence', in suggesting that the industrial system creates false needs by manipulating psychological needs.

On exploring the views of other academics with respect to this issue, it was noted that Abraham Maslow's psychological theory, while admitting to the existence of physiological and psychological needs, also insists that these are related to one another. Anthropologists and sociologists go further to argue that the division between physiological and psychological needs cannot be sustained, and that all needs are to an extent cultural.

Where does that leave the argument? Jean Baudrillard offers a social semiological argument in suggesting that J.K. Galbraith is both right and wrong. He suggests that Galbraith is wrong in seeking to differentiate between psychological and physiological needs, because such a distinction cannot be substantiated. Classical economists are thus perfectly correct in arguing that demand is potentially insatiable and that one cannot question the equivalence of needs. However Baudrillard agrees with Galbraith to the extent that the system of products moulds the system of needs. For Baudrillard, as for the traditional economist, need is a negative value, it is based on a lack, something which is missing. Baudrillard postulates that all needs are in fact the product of an overwhelming desire for reintegration with the mother, with community. As such, each individual need, whether this is expressed as want for a hamburger, or for a new gown, is nothing more than a symptom of this underlying lack.

If the pattern of needs in a consumer society is driven primarily by lack or desire, then what does this say about the sorts of values which people might gain from consumption? Typical values include efficiency, convenience, excellence, esteem, status, morality, play and actualization. One might imagine that the ultimate value springing from these others would be satisfaction. However in light of our previous discussion concerning true and false needs, it is likely that 'satisfaction' can never be achieved by consuming commodities. We will explore this issue in more detail in Chapter 6, which focuses on the subject of consumer identity.

4.6   CASE STUDY: WHAT'S IN A COMMUNITY?

Is community dead? And if so, is the 'smoking gun' in the hand of consumer society? This seems to catch the general drift of arguments made by Pasi Falk (1994), among others. Decline of the eating community has been accompanied by the rise of the isolated individual, desperately seeking to fill the gap, the hole left by the demise of community. On the other hand Maffesoli (1996) argues that this rationalization of human life has reached its limits and has gone into reverse. Now, he claims, we live in the time of the neo-tribes. Just what is the concept of community about? Some hark back to images of traditional villages and other arrangements, while others eulogize about new communities based upon brand ownership and the Internet. Are these people talking the same language?

As indicated in Chapter 2, discussion of a term like 'community' is difficult. Some authors are highly critical of the ideas of 'Gemeinschaft' and

'Gesellschaft' (Community and Society), arguing that these are highly ideal-ized concepts which were never really true in practice. In any case they suggest that nowadays communities have spilled well beyond the fixity of being located in a particular place. For example Wellman and Gulia (1999) consider the 'virtual communities' of cyberspace whereas Muniz and O'Guinn (1999) offer the example of communities which are constructed around the ownership of brands. The idea of community offered in this text refers to those who share the food which they eat, who are bound in recip-rocal ties of gift exchange and who consequently have little cause to worry about the idea of 'identity'. Let us now consider the other views.

Muniz and O'Guinn (1999) associate community with a different array of concepts in discussing brand communities organized around ownership of Saab cars and Apple Macs. For them, community has three aspects:

- first, consciousness of kind, which refers to a shared consciousness and a similarity in ways of doing things, a knowing of belonging;
- secondly, there are shared rituals and traditions;
- finally, a sense of moral responsibility or duty to the community as a whole.

They found that there was evidence of a consciousness of kind in the form of a 'we-ness'. They suggest that members of Saab clubs or Apple Mac 'communities' feel strong attachment to the brand but an even stronger attachment to each other. Owners refer to themselves as 'Saabers' or 'Mac' people. Evidence that such 'we-ness' transcends geographical boundaries was offered by way of a letter which was received by one Saab club in the USA from a German teenager, which became 'big news' at a meeting and was shown to all present. The authors also found evidence that these brand users sought to differentiate 'legitimate' members of the community from others. For example many Saab owners were sceptical of 'new' drivers such as 'Yuppies' who bought Saabs because they were rich but who weren't really committed to them. A sense of community was also sustained through oppositional brand loyalty; thus Saab owners defined themselves as not-Volvo owners (which they associated with tractors), while Mac users were definitely not 'PC' users. The authors conclude that in terms of consciousness of kind, these communities share many features with other communities. However there were some particularities in that they seemed to transcend political boundaries – all that mattered was that a person appre-ciated the brand and its history. The authors also found evidence of the exer-cise of rituals and traditions in the groups which they studied, including Saab drivers flashing their lights and waving at other Saab drivers. While the authors argue that such rituals may at first glance seem to be insignificant, these function to create consciousness of kind. It was also considered impor-tant to know the history of the brand, which often distinguished the 'true believer' from the acolyte, and to circulate stories or myths. Finally they argued that these groups were infused by a sense of moral responsibility to the community as a whole. The obverse of this was indicated for example when a Mac user who switched to using PCs was regarded as being 'morally reprehensible', a 'Mac turncoat'. Owners helped each other by providing assistance and advice on how to use the brand. The authors suggest that the existence of such communities indicates that, far from destroying community, the principle of community is alive and well in consumer culture. They suggest that such communities are neither more nor less real than any other type of community, but are an adaptive response to a postindustrial age.

Wellman and Gulia (1999) argue that the debate round and about the issue of community is sterile. On the one hand there are those who argue that consumer society or the Internet will create wonderful new forms of community; on the other are those who argue equally forcefully that these will destroy community. They argue that social-network analysts have had to educate traditional place-oriented community sociologists to convince them that community can spill well beyond the neighbourhood. The authors consider four questions in relation to the existence of 'net community':

• What is the extent to which online relationships are supportive?
• In what ways are 'net' ties useful?
• To what extent is there evidence for reciprocity on the 'net'?
• Are strong intimate ties possible online?

They argue that there is evidence for supportive relationships as information is only one of the many social resources which are exchanged; for example women worried about the effects of the menopause found online support in discovering that others were going through the same process. Additionally they found evidence that people value a sense of companionship online. The many 'weak ties' provided by the net, for example the lack of situational and status cues, played a role in linking people together from different social and political backgrounds. The authors suggest that there is a problem with respect to reciprocity in a virtual community, as many of the people involved have not met face-to-face, have only weak ties and are not knit into densely bound structures that enforce norms of reciprocity. Despite this, they found substantial evidence of reciprocity on the net. There were two explanations for this. The first was that where technical expertise formed a strong part of a person's self-identity; secondly, reciprocity is found among those who are strongly attached to the group. They also found that strong online ties have many of the characteristics of those formed offline; they tend to encourage frequent, companionable contact that is voluntary, reciprocal and supportive. Some theorists suggest that the online environment does not give sufficient cues to provide any form of intimacy, that it lacks the emotional investment which it takes to form close friendships.

Case-study questions

1. What criteria are cited (a) in this text, (b) by Muniz and O'Guinn (1999) and (c) by Wellman and Gulia (1999) in judging what a community is? How do these match your interpretations of the nature of community?
2. Do the different ways in which these authors describe 'community' lead to essentially different views or definitions of community?

3. To what extent do you think that Saab owners groups, Mac users groups and people communicating online represent 'real' communities?

END-OF-CHAPTER REVIEW QUESTIONS

1. Read the case study through again and then explain how a classical economist, J.K. Galbraith, a psychologist like Maslow and a sociologist would explain the existence of the need for perfectly white teeth.
2. Why is it that so many publicly funded facilities such as housing projects, hospitals etc. appear to be drab, uniform and austere by comparison with their privately funded counterparts?
3. To what extent do you think people are aware of and will describe affiliation and status needs? What are the implications for marketing research?

REFERENCES AND FURTHER READING

Baudrillard, Jean (1988a) orig. 1968 'The System of Objects', pp. 10–28. In Mark Poster (ed.), *Jean Baudrillard: Selected Writings*, Cambridge: Polity Press.

Baudrillard, Jean (1988b) orig. 1970 'Consumer Society', pp. 29–57. In Mark Poster (ed.), *Jean Baudrillard: Selected Writings*, Cambridge: Polity Press.

Bauman, Zygmunt (1998) 'Postmodern Religion?', pp. 55–78. In Paul Heelas (ed.) with David Martin and Paul Morris, *Religion, Modernity and Postmodernity*, Oxford: Basil Blackwell.

Baumgardner, Ann (1990) To Know Oneself Is to Like Oneself: Self-Certainty and Self-Affect, *Journal of Personality and Social Psychology*, vol. 58 (June): 1062–72.

Baumgardner, Ann, Cynthia M. Kaufman and Paul E. Levy (1989) Regulating Affect Interpersonally: When Low Esteem Leads to Greater Enhancement, *Journal of Personality and Social Psychology*, vol. 56 (June): 907–21.

Belk, Russell (1979) Gift-Giving Behaviour, *Research In Marketing*, vol. 2: 95–126, JAI Press.

Belk, Russell (1988) Possessions and the Extended Self, *Journal of Consumer Research*, vol. 15 (September): 139–68.

Belk, Russell (1993) Gift Giving as Agapic Love: An Alternative to the Exchange Paradigm Based on Dating Experiences, *Journal of Consumer Research*, vol. 20, no. 3: 393–418.

Blumberg, Paul (1989) *Deception in the Marketplace*, Oxford University Press.

Bourdieu, Pierre (1984) orig. 1979 *Distinction: A Social Critique of the Judgement of Taste*, trans. Richard Nice, London: Routledge.

Bourdieu, Pierre and J.C. Passeron (1990) orig. 1970 *Reproduction in Education, Society and Culture*, London: Sage.

Brown, Martha R. and Lew G. McEnally (1992) Convenience: Definition, Structure and Application, *Journal of Marketing Management*, vol. 6: 13–19.

Coupland, Douglas (1991) *Generation X: Tales for an Accelerated Culture*, London: Abacus.

Darian, J. and J. Cohen (1995) Segmenting by Consumer Time Shortage, *Journal of Consumer Marketing*, vol. 12, no. 1: 32–44.

Desmond, John (1998) 'Marketing and Moral Indifference'. In Martin Parker (ed.), *Ethics and Organizations*, London: Sage.

Dittmar, Helga (1992) *The Social Psychology of Material Possessions: To Have Is To Be*, New York: St. Martin's Press (now Palgrave).

Douglas, Mary and Baron Isherwood (1978) *The World of Goods: Towards an Anthropology of Consumption*, London: Allen Lane.

Dube-Rioux, Laurette, Bernd Schmitt and France Leclerc (1989) 'Consumer Reactions to Waiting: When Delays Affect the Perception of Service Quality'. In Thomas S. Srull (ed.), *Advances in Consumer Research*, vol. 15, Ann Arbor, Missouri: Association for Consumer Research.

Duesenberry, J.S. (1949) *Income, Savings and the Theory of Consumer Behaviour*, Cambridge, Massachusetts: Harvard University Press.

Elias, Norbert (1994) orig. 1939 *The Civilizing Process: The History of Manners and State Formation and Civilization*, trans. Edmund Jephcott, Oxford: Basil Blackwell.

Falk, Pasi (1994) *The Consuming Body*, London: Sage.

Featherstone, Mike (1991) *Consumer Culture and Postmodernism*, London: Sage.

Galbraith, John Kenneth (1958) *The Affluent Society*, London: Pelican.

Galbraith, John Kenneth (1967) *The New Industrial State*, 2nd edn, London: Pelican.

Grafton-Small, Robert (1992) 'Consumption and Significance: Everyday Life in a Brand-New, Second-Hand Bow-Tie'. Submitted to the Association for Consumer Research European Conference, Amsterdam.

Gregory, Chris (1983) 'Gift Exchange and Commodity Exchange: A Comparison', pp. 103–21. In Jerry W. Leach and Edmund Leach (eds), *The Kula, New Perspectives*, Cambridge University Press.

Hebdige, Dick (1988) *Hiding in the Light: On Images and Things*, London and New York: Comedia.

Holbrook, Maurice B. (1994) 'The Nature of Customer Value: An Axiology of Services in the Consumption of Experience', pp. 21–71. In Roland T. Rust and Richard L. Oliver (eds), *Service Quality: New Directions in Theory and Practice*, Thousand Oaks, California: Sage.

Hoyt, Elizabeth (1921) *The Consumption of Wealth*, London: Macmillan.

Hyde, Lewis (1999) *The Gift: Imagination and the Erotic Life of Property*, London: Vintage.

Kahneman, Daniel and Amos Tversky (1979) Prospect Theory: An Analysis of Decision Under Risk, *Econometrica*, vol. 47 (March): 263–91.

Keys, A., J. Brozek and A. Henschel (1950) *The Biology of Human Starvation*, University of Minneapolis Press.

Leiss, William (1978) *Limits to Satisfaction*, University of Toronto Press.

McEnally, Martha R. and Lew G. Brown (1997) 'Do Perceived Time Pressure, Life Cycle Stage and Demographic Characteristics Affect the Demand for Convenience?', pp. 155–62. In Basil C. Englis and Anna Olofsson (eds), *European Advances in Consumer Research*, vol. 3, Stockholm: Association for Consumer Research.

Maffesoli, Michel (1996) *The Time of the Tribes: The Decline of Individualism in Mass Society*, London: Sage.

Malinowski, Bronislaw (1961) *Argonauts of the Western Pacific: An Account of Native Enterprise and Adventures in the Massim Archipelago*, New York: Dutton.

Maslow, Abraham Harold (1970a) orig. 1954 *Motivation and Personality*, New York: Harper & Row.

Maslow, Abraham Harold (1970b) *Religions, Values and Peak Experiences*, New York: Viking Press.

Mick, David Glenn and M. Demos (1990) Self-Gifts: Phenomenological Insights from Four Contexts, *Journal of Consumer Research*, vol. 17: 322–32.

Milgram, Stanley, James Liberty, Robert Raymond Toledo and Joyce Wackenhut (1986) Response to Intrusions into Waiting Lines, *Journal of Personality and Social Psychology*, vol. 51: 683–9.

Muniz Jr., Albert and Thomas O'Guinn (1999) 'Brand Community'. Unpublished paper presented as part of the Marketing Roadshow series, Edinburgh University, March 2000.

Richins, M. (1994) Special Possession and the Expression of Material Values, *Journal of Consumer Research*, vol. 21: 522–33.

Riesman, David (with Nathan Glazer and Reuel Denny) (1961) *The Lonely Crowd: A Study of the Changing American Character*, New York: Yale University Press.

Ruth, Julie, Cele C. Otnes and Fréderic Brunel (1999) Gift Receipt and the Reformulation of Interpersonal Relationships, *Journal of Consumer Research*, vol. 25 (March): 385–402.

Schau, Hope J. and Mary C. Gilly (1997) 'Drive-Thru Service Encounters: An Example of Social Conventions', pp. 170–5. In Basil C. Englis and Anna Olofsson (eds), *European Advances in Consumer Research*, vol. 3, Stockholm: Association for Consumer Research.

Schmitt, Bernd, Laurette Dubé and France Leclerc (1992) Intrusions into Waiting Lines: Does the Queue Constitute a Social System? *Journal of Personality and Social Psychology*, vol. 63, no. 5: 806–15.

Schor, Juliet (1991) *The Overworked American: The Unexpected Decline of Leisure*, New York: Basic Books.

Sherry Jr., John F. (1983) Gift-Giving in Anthropological Perspective, *Journal of Consumer Research*, 10/2: 157–68.

Stalk Jr., George and Thomas M. Hout (1990) *Competing Against Time: How Time-Based Competition is Reshaping Global Markets*, London: Macmillan (now Palgrave) and Free Press.

Veblen, Thorstein (1925) *The Theory of the Leisure Class*, London: Allen & Unwin.

Wellman, Barry and Milena Gulia (1999) 'Virtual Communities as Communities: Virtual Surfers Don't Ride Alone', pp. 167–95. In Marc A. Smith and Peter Kollock (eds), *Communities in Cyberspace*, London and New York: Routledge.

Zeithaml, Valerie A. (1988) Consumer Perceptions of Price, Quality and Value: A Means–End Model and Synthesis of Evidence, *Journal of Marketing*, vol. 52 (July): 2–22.

NOTES

i   Although as we shall see later, Bourdieu (1984) found at least two status hierarchies in his study of French society, one based on the possession of 'economic' capital, the other associated with the possession of 'cultural' capital.

ii   However Gregory postulates that Kula exchange has been modified by commodity exchange, as a new term has been created called 'Kitoum' which indicates that while a necklace or bracelet may have been passed from *A* to *B* and thence to *C*, that *A* retains the property rights, or 'kitoum' in the bracelet.

iii   In order to demonstrate this theory, Duesenberry looked at two subcultures in the USA. The study involved a comparison of the savings of blacks and whites at the same income levels. As the black population was poorer than the white population, Duesenberry would have expected that blacks at the same level of income as whites would be able to save a greater proportion of their income, as they are relatively better off. The findings of the research supported this conclusion.

iv   Marketers have developed several variations of this. See for example Holbrook (1994).

v   The debate about Coke continues to this day. The following is taken from a quotation by Bob Rosenberg who is convinced that traditional Coke was never reintroduced into the USA: 'As a consequence, Coke vowed to re-release the original Coke as Coke Classic. They never did. What they did do was bring back the original recipe, but with (significantly cheaper) corn syrup instead of sugar.

'Everyone would have noticed if they had just made the switch directly. Coke would have been forced to return to the original, more expensive, product. But since Classic Coke tasted passably similar to old Coke, people just assumed it was the same, since no one had had any in so long.

'So now you can only get original Coke in the US on Passover (look for Kosher for Passover Coke from about mid March, it will either say KP, or just look for Hebrew letters). Since corn is not kosher for Passover, they release the true original formula with sugar. In Europe, Coke is still made with real sugar.'

Source: http://www.cs.ucl.ac.uk/staff/b.rosenberg/stuff/coke.html

SEMIOTICS: CONSUMING MEANING

LEARNING OBJECTIVES

- To provide a robust introduction to semiotics, covering all the main areas of the topic
- To introduce students to the Saussurian and Peircean traditions of semiology/semiotics and to enable them to distinguish adequately between these
- To enable students to appreciate the usefulness and limitations of semiotics, understanding the manufacture of meaning for people, commodities and advertisements
- To enable students to consider whether it might be possible to think of consumables such as food, clothing and other consumer products as if they were a form of language
- To provide an understanding and a critique of structuralism
- To enable students to use semiotic techniques in seeking to explore the meaning embedded in commodities

5.1 INTRODUCTION

This chapter begins where Chapter 4 left off. The value of things in contemporary consumer societies is related not so much to their **use value**, as embodied in what they do, although a minimum quality is usually demanded, nor even so much to their **exchange value**, but to their **sign value**, to what they signify to us, about us, or to others. In other words what is primarily important about products and increasingly the environments in which these products are situated, is their meaning. This raises several interesting questions. What role do mass-produced consumer goods play in our lives and how do they come to signify particular meanings for us? What are the mechanisms of the signification process, and how does it work? How do firms try to use what they know about how we construct meaning in order to lure us with advertising or with other images? Before going into detail to answer these later questions, let us give a flavour of what is to come by providing an example relating to the first question: 'What role do mass-produced consumer goods play in our lives and how do they come to signify particular meanings for us?'. Think for a moment about whether you associate certain scents or smells with particular people. Do you sometimes encounter the smell of something which troubles you because it seems familiar but cannot be recalled? Think about this for a moment and try to capture this sense if you can. Then read on:

> 'I raised my glass, and – solid, pungent, like the soot-encrusted brickwork
> Of the Ulster Brewery – a smell of yeast and hops and malt swam up:
> *I sniff and sniff again, and try to think of what it is I am remembering*:
> I think that's how it goes, like Andy Warhol's calendar of perfumes,
> Dribs and drabs left over to remind him of that season's smell.
> Very personal, of course, as *Blue Grass* is for me the texture of a fur
> Worn by this certain girl I haven't seen in years. Every time that Blue Grass
> Hits me, it is 1968. I am walking with her through the smoggy early dusk
> Of West Belfast: coal-smoke, hops, fur, the smell of stout and whiskey
> Breathing out from somewhere. So it all comes back, or nearly all,
> A long-forgotten kiss.'
>
> [Excerpt from *Calvin Klein's Obsession*, by Ciarán Carson (1988)]

Carson's poem is intensely personal, whereupon raising his glass, the smell of yeast and hops and malt recalls the scent of the Blue Grass perfume which clung to the coat of a girlfriend. Every time the smell of the Blue Grass hits him, he is drawn back to a particular time (1968) and place (West Belfast). Yet he shares this act of remembering with us and in so doing perhaps strikes a chord, so that we too recall old memories associated with a scent; perhaps the security of a smell which you associate with a grandparent or parent, or like Carson, a smell which recalls young love, or maybe even a smell which you find repellent. Some of you who have not been to Belfast, or even to Europe, will not understand several of the assumptions, nuances and points of connection which the poet makes. This is not surprising, as, because you have not lived in Belfast, you do not have access to some of the local codes which one must have access to in order to decode the meaning of the poem. So for example while you share one very important code with the poet, the English language, without which the entire poem would be incomprehensible, it is doubtful that you will make some connections which rely on local shared knowledge. For example the 'smoggy early dusk' suggests an early autumn or winter evening, clouded by the haze produced by thousands of coal fires. Nor will many of you note the connection that because this young couple were walking in West Belfast, a person from Belfast could tell you what their probable religion was, because the city has been divided on religious grounds. They might also have been incredulous that a couple should be strolling in such a carefree fashion, until the year, 1968, is mentioned. This was the year before the serious 'troubles' started, after which such a walk could never have been so carefree.

For the poet the smell of the product Blue Grass, which features in the poem, triggers a host of associations: with the texture (fur) of a smooth warm feeling (on a damp cold day); with the smells of Belfast, which at the time was a 'hard' but fairly prosperous industrial town; and with the smells of hops and malt, redolent of the 'dribs and drabs' of autumn, which signify nostalgia for youth, the carefree days of summer and of young love. The product Blue Grass, a fairly cheap, mass-produced perfume, has thus achieved a degree of importance in the poet's imagination because of the associations which it conveys.

Semiology or semiotics is the study of everything that can be used to explore such meaning for all forms of communication, including smells like that of Blue Grass, together with textures, words, images, traffic signs and flowers, in fact anything which can signify something to someone about something else, together with the rules governing their use. In marketing it is thus the study of how marketing environments, products and advertisements seek to continually re-create meaning by playing on people's sensual awareness of tastes, sounds, smells, images and words. Such 'things' mean much more to us than the economists' term 'utility' might suggest. In fact it would not stretch the point to say that as humans we are 'meaning machines' in that humans imbue everything that we sense with meaning. We exist to 'mean'. When life is 'meaningless' we want to die. We abhor a meaning vacuum and feel it essential to close meaning down. While we may be very good at generating and construing meaning, our understanding of how meaning is created lags far behind. For example consider the question 'Do advertisements work?' Many people would suggest that ads work if they generate X amount of sales. But if we press them and ask them 'how does the process work by which ads make sense to people to the extent that they are persuaded by the ad to go and buy X?', they often find it difficult to provide an explanation. Those who are interested in the study of meaning in marketing have indeed asked questions as diverse as 'How do ads work?' or 'What do the goods that we buy mean to us?', to much simpler questions like 'What kind of signage system works best in aircraft?' As such they are not so much interested in the advertisement and the consumer good *per se*, but in their role as signs, or communicators of differences – for example the different status conferred on the wearer by the consumption of a Cartier watch as opposed to a Timex, which brackets the purchasers of each into different social groupings. Goods and services are not only consumed as objects, they are consumed as **signs of difference**, which in turn are linked to signs of status and identity.

This chapter is about the meaning that things can have for us. Put another way we are interested in exploring how things signify particular meanings for us. You may well reply that this is surely a simple matter; things mean what they *are*, and nothing more or less than this. The aim of this chapter is to persuade you that this is not the case and that the truth is not only different but much more interesting. What things mean depends to a very large extent on how we view them and this in turn depends very much upon how they interpenetrate with our experience and on the available linguistic codes within which we classify them.

The chapter is structured around the approaches developed by two

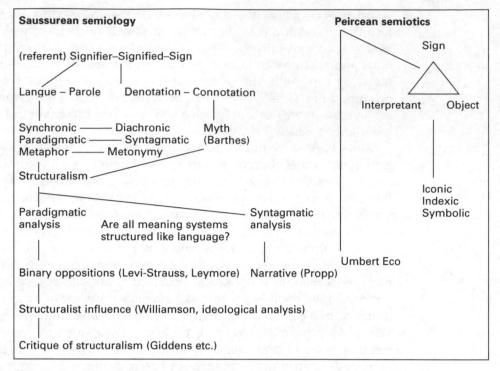

Figure 5.1 Map of relations between concepts and theorists

famous authors, the American pragmatic philosopher Charles Saunders Peirce (pronounced 'Purse'), founder of the study of **semiotics** (the science of signs), and the European linguist Ferdinand de Saussure, the founder of **semiology** (also the science of signs) (see note i). Before discussing these, Figure 5.1 shows a rough pictorial guide of the relations between concepts and theorists mentioned in this chapter.

5.2 THE SEMIOLOGICAL TRADITION OF FERDINAND DE SAUSSURE (1857–1913)

As a linguist, de Saussure was primarily concerned to study how the linguistic terms or words, in language, come to have a unique meaning. In order to do this he considered questions such as 'Is the meaning of a word natural or arbitrary?' and 'What is it that gives a word its unique meaning within a language?'

5.2.1 The arbitrary nature of signs

With reference to the first question above, 'Is the meaning of a word natural or arbitrary?', consider the idea that the meaning of every word is natural. You will probably agree that this is a difficult idea to sustain. For example if we take the word spelled by the letters 'd', 'o' and 'g', then this would imply that 'dog' is naturally linked to the living, breathing, barking animal. However it is clear that this is not the case; the word 'dog' is no more naturally linked to the actual animal (known in semiological terms as the referent) than are the words 'chien' or 'Hund', or the words used in any other languages. In fact it is quite possible that there is a language where the word for dog also uses the letters 'd', 'o' and 'g' to signify the living, breathing animal, but in a different order, as 'god', which could raise some problems if dog/god owners from these linguistic communities ever met.

If you agree with the idea that the word 'dog' is arbitrary, then you would probably also agree that the word which signifies the sound which a dog makes, its 'bark', is not natural either. Some of you might object and say that while it is true that 'bark' is no more natural than any other term, the case of onomatopoeia is an exception in that such sounds really are natural. So while 'bark' is an arbitrary label, the onomatopoeia is natural as it mimics the real natural noise a dog makes when it barks. In fact this is not true. Researchers have found that within different language systems there is a lot of variation even with respect to 'naturally sounding' expressions of onomatopoeia (see note ii).

De Saussure differentiates between three terms: the **signifier** 'canus', as written in the letters 'c', 'a', 'n', 'u' and 's', or the sound which these make when pronounced in the Latin language; the **signified**, which is the concept that appears, to the English speaker who understands the system of signs which comprise the Latinal language, when the word 'canus' is pronounced (Figure 5.2); and the **referent**, which is the real thing, which bites you. According to some semiologists it is not the real thing (the dog) that matters, but how our culture comes to code the real thing.

De Saussure concluded that the relationship between signifier and signified was unnatural and arbitrary, that there was no natural connection between them, a point that makes finding meaning in texts interesting and difficult. How do signifiers generate meaning? How is it that we know these meanings? If the relationship between signifier and signified is arbitrary, the relationship between these must be learned somehow, which implies that there are certain structured associations or **codes** which we learn that help us interpret signs. This issue will be further elaborated upon later in this chapter. However we

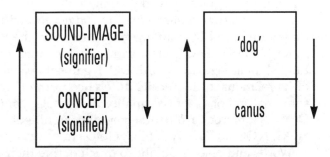

Figure 5.2 Relations between signifier and signified

Figure 5.3 Beware of the dog!

should note at this juncture that de Saussure did make one exception with respect to the idea that the relationship between signifiers and signifieds is arbitrary. This was with respect to symbols, which he suggested are never totally arbitrary. For example consider Figure 5.3. While the symbol shown in the figure was fashioned over one thousand years ago for a resident of the city of Pompeii, we scarcely require the words *'Cave Canem'* or 'Beware of the dog' to gain the sense that is portrayed.

5.2.2 Meaning as difference within a system: langue and parole

Given that the relation between signifier and signified is arbitrary, in other words there is no natural relation between words and what they signify, then what is it that gives a word its unique meaning within language? The meaning of each term is determined by convention within the system of language (**la langue**) used by a language community (the English, the Northern Irish, roller-bladers). Each term gains its meaning by convention. Within the English language, the word 'DOG' gains its particular meaning as the result of its relationship to and its difference from other signs. It is not because of some natural or essential quality that 'DOG' gains its meaning but because DOG is different from other similar signifiers such as LOG, BOG, FOG, HOG, NOG, LUG, LAG, LEG, GOD etc.

Words and objects do not so much derive their meaning from their intrinsic being as from the *differences* that exist between them and other words or objects within langue, the system of language. To illustrate this point Jonathon Culler asks us to imagine that a Martian has just come to our door and asked us to explain the meaning of the word 'brown'. What would you do? One strategy might be to pull out all the 'brown' objects in the house – your 'brown' raincoat, a 'brown' bag, some 'brown' socks, perhaps a 'brown' television set. You should not be surprised if the Martian is still puzzled and asks to see some more. You then decide to amass a collection of one hundred brown objects and point out that they are all brown. Then you take the Martian out of the room and ask it to return and name all the brown objects. It may set about the task but then seems to have difficulty in knowing which objects to select. A more successful approach would be to show brown objects and to contrast these with objects that are of different colours such as red, blue and green. The crucial point to grasp here is that the Martian will never grasp the meaning of the word 'brown' until we have taught it to distinguish between brown and the other colours. The reason for this is that brown is not an independent concept which is defined by some essential properties, but one term in a system of colour terms defined by its relations to the other terms which delimit it. This of course assumes that the Martian will perceive brown in the way that we do. The central point is that meaning is acquired within the context of a set of relationships of differences within a system of language, differences which are arbitrarily set by convention. We shall see shortly that some theorists known as **structuralists** argue that differences in language are not haphazard but are orderly, based on **binary oppositions** between terms. Thus 'rich' does not mean anything unless there is 'poor', or 'happy' unless there is 'sad'. Within such a pattern of oppositions there is always a dimension which they refer to but which is not often dealt with. For example with respect to rich/poor the dimension referred to is 'wealth'; in relation to happy/sad, this is 'mental state'. While la langue refers to the system of differences which structure language, **parole** refers to the ways in which a competent speaker draws from these conventions in constructing speech. De Saussure was more interested in studying the language system than the variations in parole.

5.2.3   The synchronic and the diachronic

De Saussure and his followers explored the relations of meaning within the language system. He drew a distinction between two forms of analysis: the **synchronic**, which involves the investigation of a system of differences (rose, pose, nose) at one point in time, and the **diachronic**, which explores the ways in which meanings shift over time. For example the word 'cattle' at one point in time meant property in general (including women); it then became restricted to four-footed property only and was then further restricted to bovine four-footed property. As de Saussure's main emphasis was on how individual concepts and objects gain their meaning through the position which they occupy within a network of signs, he advocated the synchronic approach.

Syntagmatic relations   *Paradigmatic relations*

The	ship	cut	across	the rocky road
A	plane	danced	through	the rocky waves
	car	hurtled	over	the rocky ridge
		ploughed		

Figure 5.4 Syntagmatic and paradigmatic relations

5.2.3.1 Syntagmatic and paradigmatic relations

Syntagmatic and paradigmatic relations follow from the distinction which de Saussure makes between synchronic and diachronic perspectives. Although these reflect different levels of combination, both interact with each other in the production of meaning. **Paradigmatic** relations explore the words at one point in a sentence, whereas **syntagmatic** relations consider the way in which different words in a sentence construct meaning. Take the example shown in Figure 5.4. The vertical relations, 'ship', 'plane' and 'car', represent paradigmatic alternatives, only one of which may be 'legally' chosen to complete a sentence. The syntagmatic relation is expressed as the number of permissible ways in which words may be combined to form a sentence. The rules which determine this are syntactic rules.

Only some combinations would be acceptable. 'The ship hurtled through the rocky road' does not sound feasible. The meaning of the sentence (the syntagmatic relation) changes considerably depending on the paradigmatic alternatives which are chosen.

5.2.3.2 Metaphor and metonymy

The concepts of metaphor and metonymy are closely linked to the syntagmatic and paradigmatic functions of language. **Metaphor** is linked to the paradigmatic relation. In the example illustrated in Figure 5.4, metaphors include 'cutting', 'dancing', 'hurtling' and 'ploughing'. Can you think of alternative metaphors to replace the 'rocky' waves? Alternative metaphors might include the 'mountainous', 'rough', 'stormy' or perhaps 'tempestuous' waves. Each metaphor provides a different meaning on which to base our interpretation. We cannot refer to two metaphors at the same time as only one can occupy space in the paradigmatic slot that is available.

Metonymy on the other hand is concerned with syntagmatic or contiguous relations, the ways in which meaning is created as words are strung together in sentences. In general, metonymy occurs when something can be said to 'stand for' something else. A particular example of metonymy is **synecdoche**. This is where the part stands for the whole. For example the term 'White House' stands for the presidency of the USA. Between them, metaphor and metonymy constitute powerful means for the analysis of meaning and in particular for the analysis of advertisements, as we shall see shortly.

5.3   ARE OTHER SIGN SYSTEMS LIKE LANGUAGE?

De Saussure's theory may be fine when it comes to studying the way in which language comes to have meaning, through functioning as a system of signs (the langue, or language), which people draw from in constructing everyday speech (parole). But what has this got to do with other systems of signification, for example the system of products that comprises consumer goods, or within this the clothing system, the food system or even the car system? It is important to answer this question because if clothing and food can be likened to forms of language then one can legitimately apply literary tools of textual analysis to these systems. In other words we can explore the ways in which the system of products acts as a code, the syntactic and paradigmatic combinations used within each code of goods, and the ways in which metaphor and metonymy are employed. Roland Barthes strongly advanced this argument in *Elements of Semiology* (1964). While de Saussure had considered linguistics to be part of the general science of signs, Barthes argued that 'it is semiology which is part of linguistics', and that linguistic tools should be capable of application to a wide variety of systems of signification (1964: 11).

5.3.1   Is the system of products structured like a language?

In advancing this argument, Barthes opened up the way for examining collections of objects such as clothes and food, even cars. In so doing Barthes divides clothes into the equivalent of langue and parole; on the one hand there is langue, the language system comprised of patterns of difference which forms the basis for parole, the 'speech' of the individual, as reflected in the unique combination of clothes that each individual wears and of the ways in which they wear them. For example in discussing clothes, Barthes distinguishes clothes as *written about*, as *photographed* and as they are *worn*. He argues that the first two categories, clothes as written about and as photographed, are devoid of speech as these meanings are formed by a group of elite designers and photographers. However he suggests that the language of clothing is made when one considers the ways in which clothes are worn:

- by the oppositions of pieces and types of garment and details, the variation of which entails a change of meaning – for example when one considers the head, then appropriate clothing for the head includes a bowler hat, a beret etc.;
- by rules which govern the variation of the pieces among themselves.

For Barthes, the equivalent of speech in the garment system comprises all of the individual ways in which a garment can come in different sizes, the manner in which it can be worn, and the total combination of pieces.

Or again one can intuitively think of the food system as a kind of language consisting of a range of courses, with variations within each course.

DBS Arts Library

Grant McCracken (1990) criticizes the idea that one can treat clothing like a language. Although he concedes that for some time it was useful to do this, he argues that this is now a dead metaphor which now conceals more than it reveals. Drawing upon an empirical study which he conducted between 1982 and 1983, McCracken outlines how in his view people in real life actually 'decode' or interpret the meaning of clothing, which he claims is quite different from the idea of a language. First, McCracken claims that people do not 'read' a clothing outfit in a linear way, as if it is a sentence, for example by looking at the hat, the blouse, skirt and shoes separately, but rather simultaneously, taking the whole as an ensemble. Second, the meaning of outfits was always rendered in terms of a limited vocabulary of adjectives and nouns which were usually framed in terms of a 'look'. Respondents did not read each item of clothing in its syntagmatic relation to other items of clothing. Rather than seeming to decode a sentence, McCracken felt that they were trying to solve a puzzle. However on the other hand Verba and Camden (1984) conducted empirical research into Maidenform and Vanity-Fair ads to see if they could use Barthes's scheme. They found that the advertisements made use of a set of pre-existing coded conventions which Barthes had outlined in his book *The Fashion System* (1985), which also constituted a readily appropriate *lingua franca* for the receiver to use.

In an article appropriately entitled 'The System of Objects', Jean Baudrillard (1988a, orig. 1968) addresses the question of whether the object/advertising system forms a new language. He considers first that if this were indeed a language, then it would involve a two-way process. Objects would instruct needs and needs would influence the structure of the object world. The buying situation concerns an interaction between a person and a product. The relation between these is the same as any human relation. Baudrillard argues that whereas one part of the interaction, human needs, are fluid and contingent, the system of objects is coherent. The coherent system of objects acquires the capacity to structure the system of needs. The system of objects is a set of expressions, but it is not a language, because it has no syntax. Here we have the 'Tower of Babel'. Needs disappear into products which have a greater degree of coherence. Baudrillard appears to be saying that because the basis of need is a rootless desire, the character of needs is fluid and subject to conditioning by whatever social institutions might prevail. In mass consumer societies the system of products performs this role. Thus in consumer societies people tend to classify themselves and others primarily on the basis of what products they own, those 'marker' goods such as cars, Rolex watches and the like. However while the system of products is a form of classification, it represents a particularly impoverished language. The 'language' which speaks to people in their role as consumers is the language of brands. However while brand advertisements work through metaphor (the paradigmatic relation – thus cigarettes are associated with 'springtime', cars with 'a rugged environment' or 'a beautiful woman'), there is no syntagmatic relation; they have no syntax and as a result the whole system lacks coherence.

For Baudrillard, objects now define what our social standing is.

Traditionally, social standing was 'naturally' 'given' by 'breeding', the quality of distinctiveness between class or caste which correlates with the distribution of power in society. Those with such 'breeding' could afford the very best, for example the ubiquitous Rolex watch. Baudrillard argues that since traditional measures of social standing such as class and caste have waned, all that is left is the code of 'objects', leaving the Rolex itself as the only way in which social standing may be inferred. Nowadays, he argues, the code of objects constitutes a universal system of signs. This is paid for by the price of impoverishment. We are reduced to objects. So Baudrillard argues that consumption is not a passive process but an active one constituting the network of signs on which our whole cultural system is founded. The primary role of consumption is no longer that of consuming the object itself; rather what matters is what the object means in relation to its status associations. Material goods thus are not the objects of consumption. Throughout history people have 'purchased', 'possessed', 'enjoyed' and 'spent', and yet not consumed. For Baudrillard, consumption refers to how all of this is organized as a coherent system in our society. Consumption is when objects lose their focus in use as things and become nodes in a network of difference:

> 'Today every desire, plan, need, every passion and relation is abstracted (or materialized) as sign and object to be purchased and consumed.' [Baudrillard, 1988a]

5.3.2 Use of metaphor and metonymy in advertising

Consider the combinations shown in Figure 5.5, which could be used as the basis for constructing different advertising messages.

It was noted above (in section 5.2.3.2) that metaphor is related to the paradigmatic level of analysis and metonymy to the syntagmatic level. Consider for a moment that you are the advertiser. What is it important to know with respect to these relations? First, the advertiser is interested in which of the metaphors will communicate most effectively with the target audience. This would involve carrying out research into the meaning attributed by this audience to words such as 'maximum choice', 'flexibility', 'freedom' and 'convenience' with respect to the credit-card. Let us consider 'maximum choice' as an example. Let us say that the target group is composed of small

Syntagmatic relations   *Paradigmatic relations*

Our	current	credit-card	promises	maximum choice
Their	new	turbo-car	delivers	flexibility
	future	surf-board	guarantees	freedom
				convenience

Figure 5.5 Syntagmatic and paradigmatic relations for potential advertising copy

farmers. The word 'choice' is viewed by farmers (see note iii) in quite a negative way:

> 'I do not have a whole lot of *choice*.'
> 'When it is dry, you do not have a lot of *choice*, you take a chance.'
> 'Going to spray behind the planter, that is almost your only *choice*.'

The research indicates that the signifier 'choice' signifies negative connotations for the farmers who use it only when they are forced to choose between alternatives. Choice represents the time when farmers 'do not have a whole lot of choice' or when something is their 'only choice'.

As we shall see later, neither the advertiser nor the semiologist can take the meaning of a term for granted. Rather this must be explored with reference to the codes used by the group of people to whom the communication is directed. Before exploring ads, it is useful to consider the mindset of the advertising creatives, the art-workers and copywriters who construct them. In advertising, the author's voice is understood to be that of the company, and the personality to be conveyed is the company's and not the copywriter's. You may rightly point out that a company does not have a 'personality' in the accepted sense, because only an individual can have a 'personality', and a company is not an individual but rather represents a collection of individuals. Often the personality of companies is moulded on that of the company founder or chief executive – for example Bill Gates, Richard Branson or Lee Iaccoca. According to Barbara Stern (1988), where there is no real personality on which to model the company, a **persona** is crafted, which is based on company or brand values which are then communicated to the creative team. The **tone of voice** of an ad persona is very important. Tone is conveyed in all forms of communication. It is constructed by combining a mix of words and images to create the appropriate persona, for example 'forceful', 'caring' or 'natural'. Metaphor is the guiding vehicle for creating overall 'tone', while the metonymic structure of the advertisement paints in the detail which reinforces the overarching metaphoric scheme. Stern analyses two bank ads, one for Merrill Lynch, the other for Fidelity Brokerage Services, neither of which can be reproduced here because of corporate censorship. Her analysis shows how, in each ad, text and images are skilfully interwoven to craft a unique persona. The dominant metaphor which guides the Fidelity Brokerage Services tone of voice is warfare. This is highlighted in the headline and reinforced by the metonymic structure of the text, where phrases such as 'survival of the fittest', 'an entire arsenal of financial instruments', 'sophisticated technology', 'a meticulously-designed system', 'the struggle for wealth' and 'armed and dangerous' link to the metaphor. Stern notes that what emerges here is a 'bellicose persona, barking out martial commands.' (1988: 6). The ad 'works' to the extent that it transfers the idea of war to that of financial services, to the extent that we are expected to believe that the financial services 'arena' *is* warfare. The idea which is conveyed is that one needs weapons in a world which is naturally hostile, where only the fittest survive. In contrast, Stern's analysis of the

Figure 5.6 AutoTrader advertisement

Merrill Lynch ad shows that text and images combine to form a persona which is structured around the metaphor of time. What is the persona that is created for AutoTrader in Figure 5.6? When I first saw this image I thought that someone had scribbled a crude 'heart' shape over the ad. On closer inspection I saw that the 'heart' was produced at the confluence where the two main brushes (which are bright red in the original) of a car-wash come together. Other cues reinforced this interpretation, which collectively produce the functional schema for 'car-wash': the presence of what must be a car behind the 'heart', although we can only see parts of the headlights, chassis and tyres; two brushes for cleaning the tyre rims which hang symmetrically at the side; yellow (in the original) guide-rails; what appears to be a feeder hose at top right; and on closer inspection what appears to be spray on the bottom of the picture. Is the 'heart' shape accidental? Far from it. Everything makes sense when one joins the text '*AutoTrader: Find your perfect partner*' to the image. Your car is the love of your life and AutoTrader will help you find it. In this case the persona that has been created for AutoTrader is that of a matchmaker.

There are different options for portraying the same metaphor, particularly metaphors such as 'flexibility' and 'freedom', where the metonymic linkages are diverse. A particular challenge is to come up with visual signifiers for metonymic images which can be encoded into ads. Think of some words to describe the concept of 'freedom'. For me, 'freedom' is linked to a form of expression, as in 'free speech', and to lack of constraint, openness and space. Try to visualize the ways in which you might picture 'freedom'. Try to be creative. Now look at the set of images in Figure 5.7. First, compare the images which you thought about with those in the figure. Now look at each image in turn and consider how they individually add a different 'spin' for the same term.

A number of metaphors are employed in financial services. For example Desmond (1991) found that UK banks used metaphors associated with

Figure 5.7 Collage Board for 'freedom' [reproduced with kind permission of John Nolan and the Collage Board Shop]

(removing) nightmares, teams (we're all in this together) and empathy (we can put ourselves in your place) in advertising financial services to small businesses. Advertising to other groups of customers made extensive use of metaphor. A small sample is shown below:

> 'How to go brown this summer without going red'
> 'I don't need a savings account for a rainy day . . . I need one for a continuous drizzle'
> 'Are the kids of today beyond saving?'
> 'Me save, what with, same again please love.'

On the other hand when advertising savings products, banks tended to draw upon metonyms which recall the metaphor of nature (Desmond, 1991: 123–8). This is interesting given our discussion of the fetishism of commodities in Chapter 3, where Marx argues that capital seeks to make itself appear as a natural part of life. In reality, as many people can readily testify, making money is sometimes anything but plucking apples off trees:

> 'Making your money grow'
> 'I like to see my money grow and my Nationwide passbook shows me clearly where I stand'
> 'As each month goes out, your income comes in'

The text is reinforced with images. For example one ad portrays a man reaching down from the branch of a tree as if to pluck the 'fruit' (apples, with interest rates written onto them).

5.4   HOW DO PRODUCTS COME TO GENERATE MEANING?

In the real world, companies and brands naturally seem to have a meaning. What are the mechanics of the process by which this takes place? To begin with they have no meaning and so meaning must be borrowed from somewhere else. Judith Williamson (1978) discusses the process by which products move from a position of dependence of being the signified, where they must rely on others for their meaning, to constituting signifiers in their own right; then finally blazing out as active generators of meaning which act as a form of currency for the creation of a person's identity. What does this mean and how does the process unfold?

Product as signified

This is the start point. The product or service initially has no 'meaning' in its own right. Consider cigarettes. When we look at the physical product, then each cigarette looks very much like every other cigarette; it consists of a white tube, filled with tobacco, which often has a filter attached to it. As people are notoriously unreliable at distinguishing the taste of like products from one another, it is unlikely that they will be able to detect much difference between brands on the basis of taste alone. So where is the meaning, the sign value of the cigarettes to come from? Initially this must be borrowed from somewhere else, preferably from a system of meaning with which target customers are already familiar. At this stage something about the product is being signified and the correlating thing or person is the signifier.

Often the creator or founder of the product is the easiest source of meaning that can be drawn upon in creating a product persona. Many famous and lasting brands such as Chanel, Cadbury, Rowntree, Marks & Spencer and more recently the Body Shop and Virgin connoted the values associated with their owners. For example Branson connotes a multi-faceted set of images: the ruthless businessman and smart operator (for example as portrayed by Mike Oldfield); anti-establishment (through associations with the Sex Pistols); an adventurer and brilliant self-publicist (ballooning); and an innovator (Virgin One account) who believes that the values which underpin his brand property can stretch to any field of business. Things are fine while the founder is still alive. But what does one do when they have moved on to the great emporium in the sky? The challenge for those who remain is to re-invent the image of the brand for subsequent generations, for whom the founder has no real significance.

For many years Chanel has borrowed images from the celebrity system, which includes actresses and super-models, from which it draws upon the image of one model as a signifier for its perfume. Judith Williamson picked up the important point here, which is that the most significant thing in attaching meaning to a brand consists in its effective differentiaton from other brands. While it is important for Chanel to have an image, this image

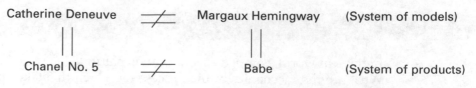

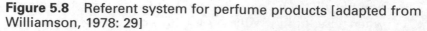

Figure 5.8 Referent system for perfume products [adapted from Williamson, 1978: 29]

must signify a clear set of meanings to its audience (the users). In order to do this, Williamson argued that advertising raids stable cultural stores of meaning for signifiers which are then associated with brands. She uses the example of two perfumes, 'Babe' and 'Chanel No. 5'. While the problem for Chanel was how to re-invent the perfume for another generation of users by communicating the 'brand value' of sophistication, Babe was a new perfume and its marketers wished to convey the meaning that it was youthful, impetuous, a 'tomboy' personality. The way in which this was achieved was to refer to a system that the target audience (women) knew something about – models. At that time Margaux Hemingway, the daughter of the author Ernest Hemingway, was well known in her own right both as a model and a bit of a tomboy. By contrast Catherine Deneuve, actress and model, was (and is) regarded as being chic, the pinnacle of sophistication. Marketers used images of Margaux Hemingway and Catherine Deneuve to provide different images for Babe and Chanel No. 5. This transfer of meaning is reflected in Figure 5.8.

Within the system of models it was known that Catherine Deneuve and Margaux Hemingway were different from one another. By association, the characteristics of the woman ('tomboy'/'sophisticated') were transferred to the product (Babe/Chanel). As Williamson (1978: 210) says:

'The system of signs from which the product draws its image is a referent system in that the sign lifted out of it and placed in the ad (in this case Catherine Deneuve's face) refers back to it. It is not enough simply to know who Catherine Deneuve is: this will not help you to understand the ad. Someone from another culture who knows that Catherine Deneuve was a model and film star would still not understand the significance of her image here, because they would not have access to the referent system as a whole. And it is only by referring back to this system as a system of differences that the sign can function.'

Referent systems are thus used to convey meaning across the entire spectrum of products. Cigarette advertising draws heavily upon the system of nature, where products are situated in landscapes incorporating forested mountains and cascading waterfalls, to convey the image of freshness.

Product as generator of meaning

Once the correlate becomes fused with the product so that it appears that the link between them is natural, the product can then become a generator of meaning in its own right. In this case, if we were to see a person with the product, the transfer might be from the product onto the person. For example the owner of a Mercedes car becomes recognized as being sophisticated, because the signified 'sophistication' has transferred from the car to the person. In this case the person becomes sophisticated as the result of consumption of the car. Here the product purports to become the actual referent for the sign. For example ads tell us that they can create the feelings which they represent (if we buy the Mercedes, we will be sophisticated). Williamson describes this effect when she says that a product can be connected to an emotional referent in two different ways:

> 'you can go out and buy a box of chocolates because you feel happy; or you can feel happy because you have bought a box of chocolates; and these are not the same thing. In the first case the chocolates do not pretend to be "more" than a sign; they mean something, but in terms of a feeling you had anyway. They are a sign for a feeling which is the referent. But if the product creates the feeling, it has become more than a sign: it enters the space of the referent, and becomes active in reality.' [Williamson, 1978: 36/7]

Williamson suggests that products having been associated with a particular feeling for a long time, become linked to the feeling to the extent that they come to 'be' the feeling. For example Lucozade was for many years associated with images of health and energy, and came to be identified with these to such an extent that people who were raised on a diet of Lucozade advertising began to think that only it (or its counterpart Ribena) could create the appropriate healthy feeling. Williamson suggests that this 'Pavlov dog syndrome' is dangerous as the product begins to mould the need or the feeling. This is similar to the point which Baudrillard was making when he suggested that the system of products is more coherent than the system of needs. By means of constant association, products and their meanings, which are related to 'real' feelings, begin to mould the reality of how we experience the world. The result is not only speaking, but also feeling in clichés: 'Happiness is a cigar called Hamlet'.

Products as currency

Products become a currency to the extent that 'happiness means Hamlet' and 'Hamlet means happiness'. In this case, Hamlet acts as a form of currency because Hamlet is presented as a form of currency that will buy happiness. Williamson notes that these products form a kind of intermediate currency between money and emotions; 'money can't buy me love' but shampoos, skin lotions and whitened teeth can. To this extent products are set up to acquire things you cannot buy – esteem, respect, attention and love. A man wants to apologize to his wife. He buys her Milk Tray. Why? Because Milk Tray shows 'he cares'. The man, his wife, Milk Tray, love and care are bound together; the chocolates inject some meaning into their marriage.

5.5   STRUCTURALISM[1]

Semiology became arguably much more interesting and exciting when theorists such as Barthes turned round de Saussure's aim which was to study how language functioned as a system of signification, by taking linguistics as a model and applying this model to other phenomena – texts – and not just to language itself. Authors working within the **structuralist** tradition applied de Saussure's ideas to a great number of areas, including the study of structural linguistics, developed by Noam Chomsky, and structural anthropology, developed by Claude Levi-Strauss. The central theme of structuralism is well summed up in the following quote:

> 'When man perceives the world, he perceives without realizing it, the superimposed shape of his own mind. This turns out to be a two-way relationship of some complexity. For not only does man create societies and institutions in his own mind's image, but these in the end create him.'   [Hawkes, 1977: 13]

Structuralists were motivated by the following interlinked notions:

- things and concepts are not characterized by some essential property, rather it is **difference** which constitutes them;
- reality is not directly accessible but is influenced by the **unconscious mental structures** which we place upon it;
- differences are not haphazard but are regular, structured according to regular **binary relations**;
- the primary task is to **identify** and **describe** these **systematic structures** and to find out the laws which govern them. The difficulty is how to do this, given that these are subconscious.

Finding such laws is not easy. For example it is not sufficient to look at speech to find laws of language (as in the structural linguistics of Chomsky[2]), nor at the superficial aspects of kinship relations to explain kinship (as in the structural anthropology of Levi-Strauss[3]). Structural explanations look to deep underlying structures which often utilize theories of the organization of the unconscious as part of their explanation.

Claude Levi-Strauss shared the notion that culture and history are not given but are made by people. Following from the work of Whorf (1956) and others, he placed the study of language at the centre of his enquiry. To Levi-Strauss, language constituted culture and all of social life. In believing that the inmost nature of such social practices was constituted in the same way as language, he opened the door for the analysis of culture as language. In his

[1] For a more detailed account of the ways in which structuralism and semiotics are related see Hawkes (1977), although you should be aware that his account has been substantively critiqued.

[2] This is because on the surface speech is ambiguous. Take the sentence 'Flying planes can be dangerous'. This sentence is ambiguous and can be read in two ways: 'Flying planes (activity) is dangerous' or 'Flying planes (objects) are dangerous'. To account for the ambiguity we must refer to the 'deep' structure of the sentence, or the relationships between nouns, verbs and complements.

[3] See for example 'Tristes Tropiques' (1989) (1973 orig. trans.).

studies, Levi-Strauss explored the phonetic structuring of what might seem to have been a disparate mass of observations on items such as kinship systems, food, marriage and politics as a gigantic language:

> 'Each system, that is, kinship, food, political ideology, marriage ritual, cooking etc. constitutes a partial experience of the total culture, conceived ultimately as a single, gigantic language.'
> [Hawkes, 1977: 34]

5.5.1 Denotation and connotation

During the 1950s Roland Barthes was perplexed at the way in which newspapers and the other media 'dressed up reality' to make it appear natural and not contrived. This prompted him to write a series of essays which were subsequently published under the title *Mythologies* (1972). In these essays Barthes' goal was to show how significations which are presented to be natural are in fact artificially constructed. How did he investigate this? We have already discussed how de Saussure suggested that signifiers and signifieds are connected together through the process of signification. Barthes suggested that the process does not necessarily end at this point as a sign can take part in a further level of signification where it becomes the signifier for a new signified. The most basic level of signification which Barthes refers to is **denotation**. The further level of signification is known as the **connotation**.

Let us return to Williamson's example of the actress Catherine Deneuve and Chanel No. 5 (Figure 5.9). The signifier (SR) for the first level of signification is the image or photograph of Catherine Deneuve. The signified (SD) is 'this is Catherine Deneuve, the actress', which denotes the first level of signification. The signified 'this is Catherine Deneuve, the actress' then becomes the signifier in the second level of signification. The signified here is 'Catherine Deneuve is chic'. Here Catherine Deneuve turns into a sign connoting her 'chicness'.

For advertisers the denotation 'this is Catherine Deneuve' is uninteresting. It is the connotation 'Catherine Deneuve is chic' which enables her to have a special slot in the celebrity system, and it is thus the association of this

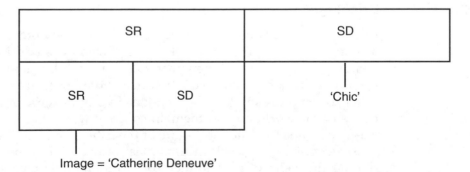

Figure 5.9 Denotation and connotation [adapted from Williamson, 1978: 100]

connotation with the product Chanel No. 5 that is important to them. Deneuve appears to be 'naturally' chic, but this masks the selectivity of the way in which her career was planned, how she was groomed to be an actress and a model. In other words she was not born 'chic', she was groomed to be 'chic'. Now turn back to the *AutoTrader* ad in Figure 5.6 and consider this in terms of denotation and connotation.

5.5.2 Myth

At one point in his career, Roland Barthes produced a number of newspaper articles on the topic of myth. Barthes attaches a slightly narrower meaning to the word 'myth' than its common-sense meaning, which is a form of fantastic story. Like Judith Williamson, he is keen to explore how products fuse with the signifiers borrowed or stolen from referent systems so that they subsequently become 'naturally' and 'authentically' conferred with that meaning. For example in one article he discusses the role played by 'totem' drinks – wine in France, tea in England. As a national drink, wine is a great leveller; it brings down to earth those who prefer 'fancier' assortments such as cocktails. Knowing one's wine and how to drink it is a sign of 'Frenchness'; it is thus an integrating sign. However the myth that naturalizes wine as a key component of French culture, masks the fact that much of this 'natural' French wine is grown on Algerian soil, on the land of the dispossessed. The same can be said for tea. Up until recently, tea was the 'totem' drink of the UK population. During mid-morning and mid-afternoon, the 'tea-break' offered a mandatory rest period for a large number of people. In many people's eyes nothing could be more naturally 'British' than tea. Yet the reverse is true. 'British' tea is produced in India and Nepal where workers are paid a pittance; it is specially blended to the British taste and then often combined with sugar, another product of the British colonies, and milk, before it is drunk. Even in his most seemingly innocent explorations into the meanings of products, Barthes ends with a twist to demonstrate aspects of the 'coercive' nature of consumer society.

5.5.3 Bricolage

Bricolage is a term used by Claude Levi-Strauss, a word which derives its meaning from the work of the 'bricoleur' who does odd-jobs making and mending things, not with new materials but with bits and pieces left over from previous jobs and constructions (see note iv). Levi-Strauss noted how tribal societies constructed their understanding of the world from bits and pieces of the world around them, in concrete ways. The ordering of nature was superimposed onto the culture of the tribe. For example different tribes constructed totems by which tribe X is 'Bear', while tribe Y is 'Eagle'. By sharing the code (of totems) they could differentiate themselves using the material objects around them. Similarly members could identify with their tribe and differentiate themselves from other tribes in terms of the food which they ate; for example food X is 'us', Y is 'not us' and therefore foreign (not the binary distinction into 'us' and 'not-us'). In contemporary societies one can see elements of totemism in the 'Springboks', 'Kiwis', Wallabies' and 'Lions', which indicate oppositional elements of national temperaments in rugby football. Or drawing on the work of Muniz and O'Guinn discussed in Chapter 4, 'Saabers' distinguish themselves from 'Volvo' drivers (whom they disparage as 'tractor' drivers); Apple Mac 'Warriors' distinguish themselves from PC users. Williamson (1978: 101) suggests that advertising agencies act as bricoleurs as they borrow bits and pieces from existing referent systems, in order to create the meaning for products.

5.5.4   Structuralist analyses of advertising

5.5.4.1   Paradigmatic analysis: advertising as myth

In *Hidden Myth*, Varda Langholz Leymore (1975) followed in the classic structuralist tradition of Claude Levi-Strauss in seeking to provide a structuralist account of the advertising system. Like all structuralists, Leymore builds a model to find out how the advertising system works. She views advertising as a form of transformation process which involves the ways in which signs and symbols are transformed into real-life action, the communication process by which advertising (the use of symbols) comes to influence the exchange of values (money and goods).

Following Levi-Strauss, Leymore reasoned that the aim of structuralism is to build a model of how the human mind works. At its simplest, the mind receives a message and then deciphers it to reveal its message. As all such activities are generated by the unconscious which has only one structure, then it follows that this is a universal process where human perception and thought processes follow the same lines everywhere. The simplest and at the same time most abstract manifestations of human thought are to be found in binary oppositions, the organizing templates which constitute the 'invariant universal expressions of the human mind' (1975: 12).

Leymore's task then was clear. As de Saussure and Levi-Strauss suggest, her analysis was paradigmatic. In seeking to freeze the advertising system at (more or less) one point in time, she would be in a position to piece together the entire structure of the advertising system. She had to devise a means of cutting through the layers of ambiguity which inhere in the superficial presentation of advertising, to reveal the binary oppositions which underpin its deep structure. How did she do this? The following is a greatly abbreviated account of how she applied structuralist analysis to what she refers to as 'static' advertising.

Leymore's method

The following has the consistency of a recipe, where the researcher is continually sifting out unwanted elements in order to reduce the ingredients to their purest form.

1. Leymore first argued that one must define the set or the system which one is to research. She argues that for static or print advertising, this should constitute all of the advertisements (irrespective of the existence of competitive brands) which form a product group (such as butter, margarine or baby foods). As an example, a 'permissible' system would be all advertisements for air travel. Advertising for British Airways would not in itself be sufficient to reveal the binary codes which underpin the system. Also brand campaigns do not form lawful subsystems within the advertising subsystem (1975: 25/128).
2. Secondly, if one is to fully analyse the system one must try to obtain as many versions of the advertisements as possible. The more versions collected then the easier it becomes to identify constituent units and the relations between them.
3. Having collected as many versions as possible, the attributes of the advertisements are then listed (such as 'comfort' or 'strength'). All redundant elements (that is where there is repetition) are eliminated until the list is reduced to a non-competitive set of constituent units.
4. The set is then partitioned so that each unit is paired with its binary opposite.
5. The set is further reduced to establish the existence of the Exhaustive Common Denominator (ECD). This is the underlying and unconscious structure which governs the advertising system.

Leymore's study of butter and margarine advertising

Leymore's analysis was based on the advertisements contained in one hundred copies of two women's magazines which appeared in 1970/71. While a period of one year can scarcely be called one point in time, it is probably the most acceptable minimum time period within which to extract a reasonable sample of ads.

First, Leymore sought a relevant theory which would help her predict *a priori* the prevailing tone of voice of butter and margarine advertising. As a structuralist she was inclined to explore previous work carried out in this tradition. Fortunately for her the renowned anthropologist Claude Levi-Strauss had developed a typology of food consisting of a limited number of dimensions. According to this typology, butter and margarine can be distinguished on only one dimension, the level of transformation of the product. This difference in transformation between butter and margarine refers to how close each of them is to the natural situation. Thus one can say that butter is transformed less than margarine as it comes from milk which comes from cows; whereas margarine which is produced from vegetables is subject to a much higher level of processing or transformation. From this Leymore concluded that Levi-Strauss's typology would predict *a priori* that the transformation process involving the naturalness of butter would be the principal point of differentiation used by advertisers of butter and margarine; that butter ads would focus more on how natural the product was, while margarine would focus more on positive aspects of the transformation process.

Leymore's investigation of butter ads supported this hypothesis. Butter ads portrayed butter as being associated with nature, cows, soil, land, green pastures and countryside. In butter ads, margarine was associated with change, science and vegetable oils. Leymore notes that it is 'scarcely surprising' (1975: 41) that most of the advertising appeal for butter lies in conveying images of 'naturalness' and 'basic goodness', and that they would seek to distinguish butter from margarine by portraying margarine as being more artificial. On the other hand margarine ads emphasized the idea that margarine was modern, scientific, and good for health and wellbeing. Once more Leymore found that the position adopted by margarine ads supported that which might be expected from Levi-Strauss's typology. Margarine which is positioned closer to the 'maximal' end of the transformation is perceived to be further from nature than butter. Consequently it must resort to a more 'scientific' approach to promote images of healthier eating, despite its distance from the source.

In analysing the ads, Leymore finds a high degree of **redundancy**, or repetition, in the messages. Ads tended to draw on the same themes time after time. As Leymore is interested in uncovering the deep structure revealed by binary oppositions in the advertising, she ultimately reduces the key components to those shown below. For example the system of butter advertising suggests that butter is:

> *concord* for the *young*
> *content* for the *old*
> *care* for the *father*
> *love* for the *children*

Thus the ideas of concord, content, care and love appeared continuously in butter ads, as did the young, the old, the father and the children. Leymore then considers the left- and right-hand sides of the above phrases separately. She is interested in uncovering the binary oppositions which structure the advertising system and also to reveal the missing term. Along the left-hand side we have the set *'concord, content, care* and *love'*. She notes that very little information will be added to these words by adding new elements of the same type such as *'satisfaction'* or *'happiness'*. In this respect the information contained in the left-hand side is already sufficient and any addition would be redundant. Such redundancy, she claims, is usual in any communication system. Next she turns to the right-hand side, *'young, old, father, children'*. What is important here is that one crucial element is missing, and this omission seems deliberate rather than accidental. Because it is the advertiser's subtle intention to include her as a participant, to draw her into the role of the missing person, the *housewife and mother*, who is the target of the ad, is excluded. Leymore now turns to the elements of the left-hand side, this time to explore the implications of what butter is not (that is, what margarine is). This is not stated but is *implicit* in the advertisements and yields up the binary oppositions which lie at the heart of the structure of the system – which is why in the following the heading 'margarine' is encased in brackets.

	Butter		(Margarine)
Thus butter is to margarine as	*expensive*	is to	*cheap* as
	concord	is to	*protest* as
	content	is to	*discontent* as
	care	is to	*negligence* as
	love	is to	*hate*
ECD	*peace*		*war*

Finally the Exhaustive Common Denominator (ECD) is derived by removing further redundancy from the set. All of the elements on the left-hand side belong to one type, as do all the elements on the right-hand side. The list can thus be further reduced to its most basic level:

ECD = peace is to war like butter is to margarine

At the end of the process, Leymore is arguing that underpinning all butter advertising is the simple and unconscious theme that butter is to peace as margarine is to war, and that housewives and mothers will prefer peace to war. Advertisers themselves are unaware of what they are doing at this level. Unknowingly and collectively they reproduce the same underlying message, and the woman who buys the butter feels better for it:

> 'Advertisers even if they thought about it could never utilize it because of moral and psychological considerations. And yet unknowingly to themselves they somehow together, all of them collectively "put" into the advertisements this vitally important promise, indeed the only promise worth making. Simultaneously, the mother receives the message on a level of which she has no conscious cognition, and is reassured.' [1975: 50]

The implications of Leymore's study are important and potentially worrying. This is because from her argument and analysis it appears that advertising bypasses rational consciousness and appeals at a subconscious level to persuade people of the benefits of one product over another. Thus from the above, if the women who were the target of the ads did not buy butter, the implication is that they are supporting war. If this were true, then the implications would be far-reaching, as women when confronted by such advertising might subconsciously bear a weight of guilt that they had made the wrong decision. In an even more extreme example, Leymore shows that the exhaustive common denominator for the system of baby-food ads that she studied implied that if women bought baby foods their children would live, but if they did not then they would die.

Critique of Leymore

While one must admire Leymore's faultless logic and the rigour of her method, there are some difficulties with the approach which she adopted that must be noted here. For example the meaning of text or pictures is taken to be stable, uniform and invariant. Leymore feels no need to ask those women who consume the advertising what sense they make of different ads. She would probably respond that she is not interested in exploring one or two ads that particular women might have seen, and that it would be impracticable to ask them to look at all of those that she sampled. In any event, she would argue, following de Saussure, the meaning of a term is given by its relative position within the system of differences in which it is situated. She also takes the role of 'disinterested' observer who can stand outside the system and diagnose its effects. In this view the meaning of a word is independent of the observer and is given in language itself. These are important issues which will be discussed later in a critique of structuralist analysis.

5.5.4.2 Syntagmatic analyses

The form of **paradigmatic** analysis takes as its project the system of similarities and differences which constitute an entire system of meaning, such as Leymore's analysis of the system of advertisements for butter and margarine, illustrated above. The emphasis is on studying the system at one point in time, so as to be able to reveal the structure of the system. While this was the mode of analysis favoured by de Saussure, other semiologists were interested in investigating linguistic structure using a **syntagmatic** approach. This involves taking into account the time dimension, as in documenting the changes which take place in language over time, or the composition of folk-tales and other stories that have a beginning, a middle and an end.

In *The Morphology of the Folktale*, first published in 1928, Vladimir Propp studied a group of Russian fairy tales. During the course of his studies he began to find a quite astonishing similarity of form between tales. Not only were similar characters found in different tales, but the plots of the folk-tales were also very similar. In analysing these tales Propp concluded that although different tales may feature different characters, these characters fall into seven types. Moreover despite the surface differences, the actions of these personae served identical purposes in terms of helping the story along. Propp compiled a list of thirty-one functions occurring in his tales. Propp found that typical characters in folk-tales included: the **hero** of the tale; the **false-hero**, who claims to be the hero but is unmasked; the **villain**, who fights with the hero; the **princess**, with whom the hero falls in love, and **her father** who demands seemingly impossible tasks of the hero; and a **magical helper** who comes to the aid of the hero.

Propp found that the story-lines or plots of folk-tales shared a similar underlying structure. Typical functions include: **trickery**, where the villain seeks to trick the victim ('Red Riding Hood'); **struggle**, where the hero and the villain are joined in combat; and **the wedding**, where the hero is married to the princess and ascends the throne. In all, Propp found thirty-five such functions which, he argued, could be used to analyse any folk-tale.

According to Propp, we come to recognize folk-tales because they share a particular structure. They thus collectively form a **genre**, or shared set of conventions. What role does a genre play in the communication of meaning? Greimas, who followed in the tradition of Propp, noted that the meaning of a text is never contained within the text itself, but rather relies on knowledge that is outside the text, to which the text refers. This idea enables one to understand how it is that a person needs only to read one or two lines for a series of possible characters and plots to come to the mind of the listener or reader. It is necessary only for someone to draw from one instance of a genre for us to immediately summon the entire set of conventions according to which it is organized. For example if someone begins, 'Once upon a time . . .', children will immediately recognize that the genre of folk-tales is being drawn from. This immediately summons the knowledge that there will be heroes, villains, false-heroes and magical agents involved, and so on.

It is not surprising to note that advertisers draw extensively on genre conventions in their construction of ads. If it is a television ad, they may have at most 30 seconds in which to convey the message and so must rely to a great extent on the implicit knowledge that the audience hold with respect to different genres. For instance, some examples of the use of the folk-tale genre in advertising are shown below.

> Customer Y has dry, chapped hands from washing dishes. Madge, the manicurist, suggests Palmolive washing-up liquid. Customer Y returns to the beauty parlour with restored hands.

In this case it is Madge, the manicurist, who is the donor that provides the magical charm, Palmolive washing liquid, which transforms the heroine. The following ad is for Flash floor cleaner:

> 'Oh Mrs T,' says the distraught housewife, 'It's nearly 3.00 pm and the floor is in a mess. Whatever can I do.' 'You can trust Flash,' says Mrs T. And sure enough, in no time at all the floor is gleaming clean. 'Whatever would I do without you,' beams the housewife.

In each of the above stories the heroine has suffered a lack or misfortune which is noticed. She comes into contact with a donor who suggests the use of the magical agent. The initial misfortune or lack is liquidated. Often the heroine is then thanked and praised by family members. There are many other such examples which can currently be seen in ads in the UK. One depicts a desperate son whose friends have trashed his parent's house after a party. The magical agent in this case is the *Yellow Pages* telephone directory which helps him locate the appropriate help to repair the damage.

When we come to think of it, there are many different types of genre; for example the American detective-featuring books by Elmore Leonard, among others, whose *Get Shorty* has been made into a movie. Quentin Tarantino's film *Pulp Fiction* relied on the audience knowledge of this genre in order to 'send it up', using irony. On a related theme, the semiotician Umberto Eco has explored the genre conventions embedded in James Bond films. Other oft-used genres include the gangster movie, horror books or films, the soap-opera, the romantic novel and the 'whodunnit' (as in the works of Agatha Christie). Each genre carries with it a particular cultural code. For example in gangster movies a basic opposition is between honour and dishonour. Why don't you try to think of some more now?

5.5.5 Critique of structuralist approaches

As has already been outlined, the structuralist mode of analysis which has just been described, is based on de Saussure's theory of signification in language. Ferdinand de Saussure employed a number of metaphors to illustrate his view of how meaning is conveyed through language. In one illustration, the functioning of language is likened to a train, the Geneva-to-Paris train, to be precise. Thus one can say that the 'same' Geneva-to-Paris train leaves every day at 8.25 pm, even though it is composed of a different engine, coaches and personnel. De Saussure argues that what gives the train its identity are the ways in which this train might be differentiated from other trains which go at different times and by different routes to different destinations.

Similarly, de Saussure argues, the identity of linguistic units such as words or sounds depends upon the differences or oppositions which separate them from one another, not their linguistic content. Just as the train is identified by its route and destination from other trains, so the meaning of a word or sound is already given in language, because of its differences from other words and sounds. This means that it is the differences embodied in the language system (la langue) which are important; these form the basis from which people pick and choose the components of their day-to-day conversation (parole).

Anthony Giddens (1979: 11–18) is one of a number of critics of de Saussure's 'train' metaphor. Giddens argues that de Saussure does not take into account the crucial role played by **context** in defining the identity of the train (and hence of the language system itself). Like many brilliant insights, Giddens's is stunningly simple. When de Saussure suggests that the identity of the train is given by its differences with respect to the time it leaves and its destination, he implicitly assumes the **point of view** of the traveller or the time-tabling official. However the identity of the train would be quite different if one were a train spotter or a railway repair engineer. By association, Giddens argues that the meaning of a term in language cannot simply be taken for granted as issuing from differences within the language system, but must be interpreted according to the point of view of the person who uses the term (who encodes it) or who listens to or reads the term (who decodes it) (see note v).

Because of this criticism, the idea that language exists as a pre-given and fixed structure prior to its realization in speech or in writing has been questioned by a number of theorists and researchers. In a study of advertising, O'Dononoe (1994) describes the uses and gratifications derived from advertising by those who consume it. O'Donohoe focused on 18 to 24-year-old people in order to research their experience of advertising in their everyday lives. Respondents were encouraged to describe those ads which they liked and which they were interested in, using their own language. A typical set of ads included those for alcohol, coffee, soft-drinks, confectionery and jeans. O'Donohoe found that ads served a variety of uses for respondents, one of which consisted in serving as repositories for 'cool' images which could then be integrated into a person's self-concept or identity, by buying and using the product. For example there were several mentions of Rutger Hauer, who had been featured in ads for Guinness and how some drank Guinness in order to be cool like him. Ads were used as posters, or as ways for both men and women to check on what the celebrities who appeared in the ads were using. Ads were valued for all sorts of reasons, from mild sexual stimulation (women said they liked watching ads with 'nice' men in them, like the Levi's ad), peer bonding, entertainment, escapism, play and signalling quality.

While O'Donohoe found that people derive many different uses and gratifications from ads, Sandikci (1997) explored the issue of **polysemy**, or the idea that the same ad may give rise to quite different, even conflicting interpretations, depending on the point of view of the audience. Sandikci was by no means the first to notice this. Many years earlier, Umberto Eco (1986: 141) remarked that an ad for a refrigerator might be interpreted as an invitation to buy one by those who live in the prosperous region of northern Italy; on the other hand for those poor peasants who live in the south of the country, who could not possibly afford such an item, the same ad might be interpreted as a call to revolution. Similarly, Sandikci was concerned by the ways in which advertising researchers traditionally assume that advertising is a one-way communication system and that audiences accept these messages uniformly and uncritically. In particular Sandikci was interested in exploring 'sexist' ads, as she felt that previous investigators had adopted a rather naïve approach to the topic by associating it with nudity and suggestiveness. Sandikci chose four advertisements from women's magazines which she showed to members of two focus groups. Each focus group consisted of six females aged between 20 and 22. The groups differed according to the amount of cultural capital of the group. One group consisted of those who were undergraduate students from middle-income families; the second consisted of eight females whose ages ranged from 18 to 34 who were studying at a local two-year proprietary school. She asked people in the groups to answer questions such as: 'what story is the ad telling'? and 'is this a sexist ad'? She found that when asked to describe what was going on in the ad, the groups came up with more than one story. For example in response to an ad for *Longing*, one group described the woman portrayed in the ad as aristocratic, elite and who has quality, whereas those in the second group thought of her as a desperate, trashy looking tramp who is really insecure and has nothing better to do than lie around waiting for some man to come back to her. Sandikci also found that attributions of sexism in the ads varied. For example with respect to the tag-line 'You've come a long way baby' which had been featured in Virginia Slims (cigarette) advertising for some time, one group thought the slogan to be sexist in that respondents did not agree that women had 'come a long way', and that the epithet 'baby' was patronizing. However the second group (G2) did not view the tag-line as sexist at all and interpreted this in different ways. Some interpreted it as a positive comment that women have the freedom and ability to do whatever they want to do. Another interpretation went like this:

G2: They've come a long way.
Q: What do they mean by that?
G2: That now women if you smoke Virginia Slims that you're going to have more confidence, that before we were like, little, we had to listen to men and do what they say and you know clean the house.
G2: Like now you can get some class or something.
G2: Now you can be your own self. If you want to ride a motorcycle you can ride a motorcycle. If you want to smoke a cigarette you can smoke a cigarette.
Q   Who's telling that 'You've come a long way, baby'?
G2: A woman telling another woman. Be confident, be yourself.

[Sandikci, 1997: 79]

What are the implications of this critique? The most significant implication is that one should not take it for granted in any formal decoding of a message, such as an ad, that one has decoded it in the same way that other people will. This shifts the research focus from the ads themselves (and indeed from any abstract system of meaning) to that of the language-user, the person who actively decodes the meaning of the message or the ad. However researchers still use rhetorical analysis to study the means adopted by advertisers and other marketing communicators in seeking to persuade members of different target groups (as an example, see Berger, 1991).

5.6   THE SEMIOTICS OF C.S. PEIRCE (1839–1914)

Now we turn to the second of the two major traditions of the science of meaning, that of the pragmatic philosopher Charles Saunders Peirce (pronounced 'purse'). Peirce was influenced by the writings of John Locke on logic. Consequently he held the view that logic is at the root of all signification and that therefore logic should form the basis of the science of signs, or semiotics as he preferred to call it. David Glen Mick (1986) conducts an admirable résumé of the 'Peircean' tradition. The focus here is on presenting the basics. Peirce's fundamentals of semiotics are more complex than de Saussure's semiology, as this is based on a threefold scheme. For Peirce, the process of **semiosis** is the process of communication by any type of **sign**, a sign being anything that stands for something (its **object**), to someone (its **interpretant**) in some respect (its **context**). The relations between these terms are shown in Figure 5.10.

First try to make sense of this figure in marketing terms. We wish to enquire what an ad means. The **sign** or advertisement stands for the meaning of the product (**object**) to someone (the **interpretant**). It follows that we

209

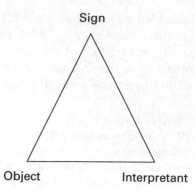

Figure 5.10   Peirce's trichotomy of signification

can explore three different types of relationship: how well the advertisement represents the product; how well the advertisement communicates to the person; finally whether or not the person actually buys the product.

Strictly speaking, the **interpretant** is not a person, but reflects the notion that no sign comes to us whole, something must be added from outside if it is to be effectively decoded. For example I may see an advertisement in which a beautiful woman is pictured next to a new fragrance. I know that the advertisement stands for the fragrance. However in order to fully understand who the ad is aimed at and how it does its work, I might have to bring in knowledge from outside the ad itself – that the actress is Cindy Crawford, for example. The knowledge that the actress is Cindy Crawford acts effectively as a new sign which helps me interpret the advertisement. By asking 'Who is Cindy Crawford?', yet another sign or set of signs may appear in a complex chain or web of meaning. The interpretant enables complex chains of signification to emanate from the sign. In Peircian terms this process is referred to as *semiosis* (see note vi).

5.6.1   Object–sign relations: icon, index, symbol

Much of Peirce's theorizing was based on object–sign relations. In advertising terms this is concerned with how the advertisement represents the object which is portrayed in it. Peirce theorized that such relations are accounted for by three types of sign; iconic, indexic and symbolic. Take the rather innocuous example of a dog. How can signs of dogs be communicated? An **iconic** sign of a dog is based on some form of resemblance or imitation. If we see a photograph of a dog we know immediately 'that is a dog'. An **indexic** sign indicates a form of correspondence or a causal relation. For example if, on a walk, we see some fresh dog-droppings, we might conjecture the proximate existence of the beast itself. Finally we might see some **symbol** of a dog. This could be for example like the representation of the dog found in Pompeii which was shown at the beginning of this chapter. Alternatively it could represent some modern representational system, perhaps modern

French. So, on reading the word C–H–I–E–N, we might conjure up the thought 'Dog'. This latter symbolic representation differs from iconic and indexic forms in that it is arbitrary and conventional. The successful decoding of the sign depends on the decoder's knowledge of an arbitrary cultural code. We might have as much difficulty in recognizing the 'dog' of the cave-dwellers as the cave-dweller might experience in trying to decode modern French. The symbolic relation is the only truly arbitrary relation within Peirce's system, a point which refines de Saussure's contention that all signs are arbitrary. Also the three forms of object–sign relationships are not mutually exclusive but can be found together.

While they do not credit Peirce in their analysis, Zakia and Nadin (1987) employed a form of Peircian analysis in seeking to interpret the meanings which were encoded in an ad for Fidji perfume. Here we will use the *AutoTrader* ad represented in Figure 5.6 to illustrate this form of analysis. Before you read on, look again at this advertisement and consider what icons you can see there. What sorts of images has the advertiser inserted into the ad which she or he hopes will become attached to the image of *AutoTrader*? Note these down and then consider what indexic meanings might be apparent. Indexic signs point to the existence of something else – they pull the reader into thinking about wider schemes of signification. Finally, can you spot any symbolic meanings in the ad? You may wish to take into account the denotations and connotations of some of the images in order to consider this aspect.

One can explore the iconic, symbolic and indexic aspects which combine to produce a persona for *AutoTrader*. The **iconic** images offer a clash of colours (in the original); the flaming red of the confluence of the 'brushes' make the 'heart' shape appear to stand out from the otherwise spartan and functional layout of the car-wash. The classic **symbol** connoted is that of the 'heart' shape = 'love'. This is obviously not a real heart but one which recalls the conventional sign that we see carved into trees and written on walls coupled with the initials of those whom it ties together, which is also reproduced in endless variants of the 'I love New York' sign. This heart is not a broken heart but has been made whole through the merging of the brushes. The size of the 'heart' in relation to the car signifies a super-abundance of love – this is the love of your life. In this context the links between *AutoTrader* and 'finding your perfect partner' now begin to make sense. **Indexically** we assume that those 'bits' of car which we see behind the 'heart' are joined up into a whole vehicle. We are also expected to follow the chain: brushes = 'heart' = 'love' = 'find perfect partner' = *AutoTrader* = matchmaker. There are other indexic signs which may be read into the ad. We know that as this is a 'car-wash', the unity of the brushes is momentary. Some might suggest that the joining together of two parts which had been broken recalls the symbol of the 'broken-token' which has a rich genealogy in folklore. But that might be going too far!

This form of analysis is an example of a **rhetorical analysis** of the ad. This means that the researchers have sought to understand the ways in which the advertising creatives have encoded the ad with a particular array of signs. An analysis of how the ad was decoded by the target audience, or any other audience, would be based on sign–interpretant relations which would require a quite different approach, similar to those used by O'Donohoe (1994) and Sandikci (1997) described above. Such an analysis may yield a host of different connotations. For example one person to whom I showed the *AutoTrader* ad said that she didn't care for it because it was erotic. When asked why she felt like this, she likened the way in which the brushes formed the 'heart' shape to that whereby a stripper teases her audience by artfully using a fan to conceal and then 'flash' her body to heighten the erotic effect of her performance. We now turn to consider some general factors that relate together signification and consumption.

5.7   SIGNS: IDENTITY AND DIFFERENCE

Commodities play an important role in marking out our status in society by signifying to others who we are. From the semiotic arguments which have been followed in this chapter, one would expect the expression of difference from others to be an equally important aspect of the construction and maintenance of identity. Dick Hebdige (1988) in his book *Subculture: The Meaning of Style* (originally published in 1979) considered the role of **anti-style** in the construction of youth identity. Hebdige noted that commodities are used as markers to differentiate different subcultural groups from the more orthodox cultural formations. The creation of anti-style was not just a question of 'lifting' commodities from the dominant culture; instead it involved subverting and transforming those things from their given meaning and use to other meanings and uses, a form of re-signification. For example during the 1980s, 'punks' used what others would have regarded as the 'throwaway' items of the dominant culture – binliners, safety pins, etc. – as a means of self expression. Hebdige draws upon Claude Levi-Strauss's term **bricolage** to suggest that, just like the native peoples studied by Levi-Strauss, 'modern' people also actively construct their identities from the raw materials which are at hand; in this case the marketplace provides a rich source of raw materials which a subculture then uses to construct its own improvisational meanings.

The novel ways in which youth and others adapt and change commodities through the adoption of what has come to be known as 'street' style, has long been recognized by marketers with an eye to the main chance. While punks, new-age travellers and others may raid the pantry of the consumer society in order to construct their identities, marketers in turn scrutinize the dress-codes and behaviour of such groups in order to transform them into fashion accessories for the mass market. This is precisely what happened to the 'punk' style.

The idea of the expression of difference as an important aspect of identity has been taken even further by Mary Douglas (1997), who suggests that consumption behaviour is not only about consumers establishing differences between one another, but is inspired by active hostility. Following from this, she argues that there is a need to get away from thinking of consumption as a manifestation of individual choices:

'Culture itself is the result of myriads of individual choices, not primarily between commodities but between kinds of relationships. The basic choice that a rational individual has to make is the choice about what kind of society to live in. According to that choice the rest follows. Artefacts are selected to demonstrate the choice. Food is eaten, clothes are worn, cinema, books, music, holidays, all the rest are choices that conform with the initial choice for a form of society. Commodities are chosen because they are not neutral: they are chosen because they would not be tolerated in the rejected forms of society and are therefore permissible in the preferred form. Hostility is implicit in their selection.'

[Falk and Campbell, 1997: 18]

Douglas makes the point that people choose goods which they like (which are liked by the people they like) and which make them different from others (who are not like them). She emphasizes the essential part played by hostility in shopping, evoked by phrases such as:

' "I wouldn't be seen dead in it," says a shopper, rejecting a garment that someone else would choose for the very reason that she dislikes it. The hated garment, like the hairstyle and the shoes, like the cosmetics, the soap and toothpaste and the colours signals cultural affiliation. Because some would choose, others must reject.'

[Falk and Campbell, 1997: 18]

According to Douglas, while people are unclear about what it is they want, they are very clear about what they do *not* want.

How do hates become standardized? Douglas considers four distinctive ways of organizing hates according to different forms of lifestyle – individualist, hierarchical, enclavist and isolate – each of which rejects the others. The individualist lifestyle is competitive, wide, open, risky and feels free to change commitments. By contrast the hierarchical lifestyle is more formal and adheres to established traditions and institutions. The enclavist lifestyle is against formality, pomp and artifice and prefers simplicity. Finally, the isolate seeks to escape interactions with others and is uncompetitive. Douglas argues that these are stable forms of social organization which are distinct because they rest on incompatible organizational principles. They do not get along with each other and hostility keeps them going.

5.8	SIGNS CAN TELL THE TRUTH AND . . . SIGNS CAN LIE

Umberto Eco (1976) makes the point that because there is nothing natural about signs, they can tell the truth or they can lie. This means no more or less than that. Thinking for example of the 'starving man' whom we considered in relation to true and false needs in Chapter 4, if he exhibited all of the signs of a 'starving man', being nothing but 'skin and bone', his eyes bulging, stomach distended, unnatural skin-tone, then in the absence of information to the contrary we would probably believe that the signs indicate that this is the truth, he actually is starving. On the other hand we are not to know that he is in fact a skilful actor who has perfected the art of duping others into aiding his plight, which is the alibi that many use for not helping. Signs may be used to lie in all sorts of ways. For example it is reputed that ancient Chinese traders could alter the size of the pupils in their eyes at will, in order to mislead buyers into thinking that they were more, or less interested in a transaction than they really were (enlarged pupils usually signify that we are aroused and interested, while the closer they get to a pin-point, the less interested we appear). Many companies thrive on the deception business. For example the entire cosmetics industry excels in selling the ability to deceive others by manipulating signs; from fake tans, skin lighteners, hair dyes, wigs, hair thickeners, hair curlers, hair straighteners, potions to remove wrinkles, anti-ageing creams, anti-cellulite treatments, to cosmetic surgery, collectively constituting a veritable feast of deception. There is the problem that those who sell deception are also deceiving the deceivers. For example there are ongoing debates about the efficacy of various skin 'toning' and 'weight loss' treatments, and even whether there is such a thing as cellulite.

Signs can tell the truth and . . .

'Here was the marketing world's dream. The endorsements flooded in, the entourage grew . . . Nike signed Agassi early, designing an annual change of wardrobe around their client – hot lime, volcano pink, ecclesiastical purple. Frequently Agassi painted the nail of his little finger a matching colour. The fronts of his shorts were deliberately cut short to reveal his lower chest hair. There were religious earrings, gold necklaces, bandanas, caps, headscarves, a scene from *Treasure Island*. Nike even marketed an Agassi T-Shirt bearing the disturbing message 'Irreverence Justified'.

'Just occasionally, the salesmen over-reached themselves. There was, for instance The Strange Case of Andre's Racket. Since childhood Agassi had used the oversize Prince Racket, an enormously popular brand. On the first of January 1989, his agents signed Andre to a £4 million four-year contract with Donnay, then a Belgian company anxious to recover the share of the market it had once enjoyed under the endorsement of Bjorn Borg. The only drawback to this estimable plan was that Agassi could not get used to the new racket. "Hey Nick," he called out to Bolletieri at the Philadelphia indoor event a month later, "I can't serve with this thing." Desperate compromise followed. At the outdoor Grand Champions Cup in Indian Wells, California, in contravention of the contract but with the approval of Donnay, Agassi used his old Prince racket with a huge D stenciled on the strings. His agent Shelton insisted that the racket was a new prototype but in fact it was a rival product bearing Donnay's logo, an act of mind-boggling foolhardiness in a nation as litigation-minded as the United States. But they got away with it. Agassi became skilled with the new racket and Donnay's sales soared. People, usually very young people, wanted anything – be it clothes, shoes or equipment – bearing Andre's name.

Source: Observer Review, 12.7.92, p. 49, Col. 6. 'Agassi: At the Court of the Coca-Cola King'.

5.8.1   Marketing hyper-reality: the simulacrum

The idea of 'hyper-reality' is the construction of environments which seem to be more real than real, while that of the simulacrum invokes images of falsity, fakes and disguise. How are these related? These ideas have been explored principally by Jean Baudrillard and by Umberto Eco, among others. In his book entitled *Travels in Hyper-reality* (1986), in which he recounts his travels around the USA, Eco identifies the experience with two terms, 'The Real Thing' and 'More'. In his travels around the country, Eco was struck by how often he was promised 'real' or 'authentic' environments and experiences, in surroundings which were artificially fabricated. As a result he began to believe that in this society a strange process was going on whereby the completely real was becoming identified with the completely fake, and that people are actually coming to prefer the latter. For example he discusses how the replicas of the Oval Office and Hearst's castle must be absolutely identical to the 'real thing':

> 'Constructing a full-scale model of the Oval Office (using the same materials, the same colours, but with everything obviously more polished, shinier, protected against deterioration) means that for historical information to be absorbed, it has to assume the aspect of a reincarnation. To speak of things that one wants to connote as real, they must seem real. The "completely real" becomes identified with the "completely fake". Absolute unreality is offered as real presence. The aim of the reconstructed Oval Office is to create a "sign" that will instantly be forgotten as such: the sign aims to be the thing, to abolish the distinction of the reference, the mechanism of replacement. Not the image of the thing, but its plaster cast. Its double in other words.'   [1986: 4/5]

The reconstructed Oval Office appears even more 'real' or authentic than the real Oval Office. It is more polished, shinier and better preserved. The real Oval Office may well look quite drab in contrast to the fake one. Eco was interested to study those instances whereby 'the American imagination demands the real thing and, to attain it, must fabricate the absolute fake; where the boundaries of game and illusion are blurred'. Eco found examples of such simulacra in new museums, Randolph Hearst's castle, hotels and theme parks. For example museums and theme parks often reproduce historical scenes which render the events in images that look much more impressive than the real thing, which seems tawdry in comparison. In marine theme parks, killer whales and sharks, which are ruthlessly hunted in the real world, are humanized and portrayed as 'cuddly'. To Eco, what is disturbing about such environments is that the dark promise of the apocalyptic film (and book) '1984' has been realized through the creation of such environments. By this he means that while the animals are effectively denatured and humanized in the theme-park environment, this is possibly the only environment in which their continued existence can be guaranteed; to survive, the hippopotamuses and the crocodiles must submit to the falsification industry. This leaves us upset, and without alternatives (1986: 52/3).

I have repeatedly been struck while on holiday by how some people seem to value the video-recording of the experience more than they value the actual experience itself. It is almost as if the real experience is negated in the act of constructing the video – which of course can be shown later to family and friends as proof of what a wonderful time they had. This may seem a relatively cynical, even cruel point. Nevertheless the notion that we value the fake more than the real and that we not only confuse fake with real but actually **prefer** the fake to the real was brought home to me recently in the following excerpt (see note vii):

'We are used to seeing war on the television – exciting war, in full colour, wounds and all. The real thing is much less interesting, which makes it seem less real.'

5.8.1.1 Baudrillard: simulacra and simulations

Jean Baudrillard (1988b) discusses the idea of simulation in a number of books, most notably in *Simulcra and Simulation* (originally published in 1981). It has to be said from the outset that Baudrillard's work is neither accessible nor concise. However it is insightful. My interpretation of Baudrillard is that he remains generally true to Lacan's theory of the (negative) role played by images in identity formation (discussed in the next chapter). In this formulation the consumer is cast into an imaginary world where images seem to be more substantial than reality. In *Simulacra and Simulation* he takes this one stage further. Baudrillard argues that in contemporary consumer societies all meaning is suspect, as distinctions between the thing and the idea are no longer valid. In their place Baudrillard fathoms a strange new world constructed out of models or simulacra which have no referent or grounding in any 'reality' except their own. Baudrillard argues that a simulation is different from a fiction or lie in that it not only presents an absence as a presence, the imaginary as the real, but it also undermines any contrast to the real, absorbing the real within itself. Instead of a 'real' world of commodities which is somehow bypassed by an 'unreal' myriad of advertising images, Baudrillard now discerns only a hyper-reality, a world of self-referential signs. Television ads are related to the commodities which they purport to advertise. However Baudrillard argues that the television newscast creates the news in order to be able to narrate it, and that soap-operas have become the reality for many viewers (Baudrillard, 1988b: 6).

What can it mean to say that the 'reality' of the 'news' is false or hyperreal? Most news organizations are owned by publicly quoted companies which must show an increase in returns to their shareholders year on year. The main source of revenue for broadcasters is that which comes from advertising, the returns from which are based on the number of people viewing a programme. The larger the audience, the higher the revenue. As a result, television news companies and programmes carry out audience research in order to judge the kinds of news format and content which lead to higher audience figures. This in turn partially shapes the editorial decision of what to show and when to show it. For example Greg Philo reports such considerations influenced the reporting of the Ethiopian famine of 1984–85. He suggests that one good reason for the BBC covering this story was because they were worried that a competitor might cover it first. Philo notes that competition between television channels can mean that they will all suddenly pursue a story if it is considered important (with respect to viewing figures) and that some will reject a story if they decide that it has already been covered by competitors:

> 'Television is so competitive that even bulletins on the same channel compete with each other over the treatment of specific stories. Michael Buerk told us how this had affected the treatment of his second report from Ethiopia. The Six o'Clock News on the BBC had led with the story as a six-minute piece, giving it a maximum impact. By contrast the Nine o'Clock News had downgraded the story to fourth position and led with a story on the continuing British miners' strike, which was then in its seventh month.'   [Philo, 1993: 113/4]

In any event the decision to use Buerk's and Amin's footage of the Ethiopian famine was based on the fact that it was a slack news day. As Philo's paper shows, the story itself would have got nowhere had it not been for the compelling nature of Amin's images.

When Baudrillard and others refer to the creation of 'hyper-realities' by news media, they have this process in mind. They are also concerned with what Daniel Boorstin (1992) first described as 'news management'. This involves picking an otherwise unremarkable event and 'spinning' this or turning it to best effect. Boorstin notes that nowadays successful reporters are those who can find a story even if there is no earthquake, or civil war, or anything of worth to report: 'If he cannot find a story then he must make one' (1992: 8). This is achieved by means of his persistent questioning of public figures which may trip them up and result in some new revelation, or alternatively may result from the **human interest** which he derives from the story. Boorstin describes such events as **pseudo-events** or 'false' events. In politics this takes the form of what is known as 'astroturf politics' where an otherwise commonplace event is seized upon for political gain. For example during the Bush versus Dukakis fight for the US Presidential election, a research director of the Bush campaign spotted one such item which could be used against Dukakis. Dukakis as Governor of Massachusetts had supported a furlough policy for his state, whereby prisoners were released early on promise of good conduct. Bush's research director noticed that Willie Horton, a black prisoner, had committed rape while on leave from a Massachusetts prison. The Bush campaign team decided that by focusing on Horton's case, they could inflict a major blow on Dukakis. The team conducted focus group research with 'swing' voters, people who were nominally Democrats, who had voted for Reagan but who were leaning towards Dukakis. The issue of Willie Horton played so well (in that it worked against Dukakis) that it became one of the central themes of Bush's national media campaign. The theme was so effective that a post-election poll by the Gallup organization showed that this theme was one of the two 'hot buttons' of the entire Bush campaign (Gallup, 1989: 226–30). The UK Conservative Party used a scare theme as part of a party political broadcast during their 2001 election campaign, which many commentators felt was based on the Horton campaign, but to no avail.

Boorstin refers to the **celebrity system** as the human equivalent of the 'pseudo-event'. He argues that in the past, those who were regarded as being heroes, became heroes through their own genuine distinction, the expression of some inner quality or strength. On the other hand he argues that nowadays one can hire a public relations company that can tailor an image which, with the accompanying hype (hyperbole), creates the 'celebrity' virtually out of thin air:

> 'For the subjects are themselves mere figments of the media. If their lives are empty of drama or achievement, it is only as one might have expected, for they are not known for their drama or achievement. They are celebrities. Their chief claim to fame is fame itself.'
>
> [1992: 60]

By comparison to the heroes of old, who were noted for their achievements, Boorstin argues that celebrities are noteworthy only for the images that they display.

5.9	THE SCOPE OF SEMIOTIC RESEARCH IN MARKETING

From what has been discussed above, one could be forgiven for believing that semiotics focuses purely on the visual register and principally in analysing the efficacy or otherwise of advertising. This impression is quite misleading, but there is a possible reason for this impression. It is misleading because sight is only one of the senses.

In real life, people are continuously processing messages from all five senses. You may wish to turn back to the start of this chapter and re-read the fragment from *Calvin Klein's Obsession* by Ciarán Carson to remind you of the complex ways in which images are tied up with smells and sounds. Touch is very important to people, particularly the 'feel' of a piece of cloth. In fact it is only when we are confronted with signs which say 'do not touch' that we become aware of just how important this is. Hearing conjures up a range of influences from the timbre of a person's voice to the 'mood music' used to influence people at the point of sale. Smell is particularly important in that we associate certain smells with particular people, times and locations. Why is vision so privileged over all these other senses? Norbert Elias (1994) suggests that in the shift from premodern community to the modern individualized society, so those senses which are most proximate and which are concerned with community (smell, taste, touch and hearing) have given way to that sense which is most distant and which enables us to reflect on ourselves, to observe our own behaviour as if it were someone else and also to monitor that of others.

A number of marketing academics have argued that corporate marketers should pay attention to all of the five senses in designing retail environments. For example Patrick Hetzel (1995) argues that retailers should focus more on the creation of a holistic consumption experience. He makes two further points. First, he suggests that corporate marketers should realize that the identity of a particular retail format depends solely on its difference from others. Second, different environmental elements converge to create a global impression which is conveyed to the customer. Consequently he argues that those who design such environments should focus on all of the five senses simultaneously to create what he terms the 'synesthesic' impression. For example in discussing the organization of a Ralph Lauren store, Hetzel notes how the **sight** of the inside of the store leads to the impression that it is like a person's home: the **smells** are all 'natural' smells, of wax, the perfume of flowers, wood and leather; **hearing** is marked by its absence, as sound is muffled by deep pile carpets or by the echo of footsteps on floorboards; touch is based on smooth fabrics; **taste** is addressed by the tea and coffee and whisky which are available.

5.10   CHAPTER SUMMARY

This chapter focused on two different approaches to the study of how people create meaning: the semiology of Ferdinand de Saussure and the semiotics of Charles Saunders Peirce. In discussing the Saussurian legacy it is important to bear in mind de Saussure's division of language into *langue*, the system of conventional signs where meaning is marked by difference, and *parole*. The discussion of whether one may consider other systems of signification to be structured like language was illustrated with reference to the use of linguistic terms such as metaphor and metonymy to advertising. Structuralism was discussed next and was illustrated primarily with reference to Varda Leymore's paradigmatic study of advertising, together with some examples of syntagmatic analysis including the use of stories. This was subsequently critiqued on the basis that it ignores the role played by competent language speakers. The approach of Charles Saunders Peirce was introduced and illustrated with reference to the analysis of sign–object relations, using iconic, indexic and symbolic signs. Following the brief discussion of Peircean semiotics, a consideration of questions of identity and difference, simulation and hyper-reality, and finally the scope of semiotics with respect to the study of consumption and marketing brought the chapter to a close.

DBS Arts Library

5.11   CASE STUDY: WAYS TO GET LAID

What different linguistic codes can be used to decode the meaning of the ad in Figure 5.11? How do the text and images work together to create a persona for the brand? Who is the brand aimed at?

Figure 5.11 Ways to get laid

5.12	CASE STUDY: MARKETING THE PAST – NORKUNAS'S STUDY OF TOURIST SITES IN MONTEREY

It is possible to use semiotic analysis in a range of contexts. One example is the work of Martha Norkunas (1993), who compared the stories about places which are told in tourist promotional literature with those of the inhabitants of the area. Norkunas chose three different tourist sites in Monterey, California as the basis for her research study. The sites which she studied were: The Path of History, a series of historic homes that winds through 'old' Monterey; Cannery Row, the subject of John Steinbeck's novel of the same name, where Monterey's sardine cannery was located; and Fisherman's Wharf, the former fishing pier now occupied by restaurants and shops. Norkunas was interested in how each site was used as a vehicle to convey particular messages about its past and identity.

Norkunas noted how Monterey seeks to carve out a specific identity for itself as distinct from other tourist sites on the Monterey Peninsula, such as Carmel and Pacific Grove. However she also noted that despite the marketing claims for Monterey's uniqueness, such claims were belied by the many ways in which it looked just the same as anywhere else. The main part of Norkunas's research consisted of a review of actual historical and cultural events in Monterey; these were then compared with the depiction of events shown in marketing the locations themselves. Norkunas found that the public history texts constructed by the Monterey State Historic Park and the Monterey History and Art Association tended to flatten and smooth out historical conflicts into a generalized image which reinforced ideas of development and progress. For example Norkunas found that the 'touristic' history outlined on a large wayside display next to Fisherman's Wharf made no mention of the first residents of the area, the Costanoans who lived there some 3000 years ago. Nor was there any mention of some of the more recent immigrants from China, Italy, Portugal, Japan and Mexico or African-Americans. She found that all signs of the industrial working-class culture of Cannery Row had been excised and that it had been remodelled as a nostalgic caricature of John Steinbeck's novel. While the novel itself had been dedicated to the poor and the downtrodden of the Monterey Peninsula and had been criticized by the Monterey Chamber of Commerce, the tourist developers have caricatured the novel, combining the real and the pseudo-real by associating high-priced shopping developments with Steinbeck's name and those of the characters in the novel. The referents to Cannery Row are no longer the actual canneries or cannery workers, but Steinbeck and his fictional characters. Norkunas concludes that instead of striving to interpret the past industrial landscape accurately, Monterey developers were present-oriented and blurred history, fiction and reality.

A major theme of Norkunas's book is the conversion of the real to the hyper-real or simulacrum. She argues that each of the three tourist sites has become transformed from a real living working space into a staged rendition. Nowhere is this more true than with Fisherman's Wharf. Once this was an authentic commercial fishing wharf which was 'saved' from destruction by reconstructing it as a tourist attraction. While it stands right beside the new, authentic fishing wharf, the pseudo-reality has assumed prominence over the reality. The main theme of her work is the Disney-fying and domination of nature, the smoothing out of history and conflict through a portrayal of a linear progression from pre-history to the present day.

Case-study questions

1. Look back over the case study and try to identify the method which Norkunas is using. Does this share any similarities with any particular approach that has been discussed in this chapter?
2. Following from this, how might we seek to critique the method used by Norkunas?
3. Can you suggest any improvements to Norkunas's method?
4. How credible is Norkunas's claim that these tourist sites create pseudo or hyper-realities which become more 'real' than the real thing?
5. If the claims about the construction of hyper-realities are true, what are the implications?

END-OF-CHAPTER REVIEW QUESTIONS

1. What does de Saussure mean when he says that the relations between signifier and signified are arbitrary or conventional?
2. What is the relation between signifier, signified and referent in de Saussure's scheme?
3. What is meant by the term 'code'?
4. In Glasgow it is thought by many people that bringing red and white flowers as a gift to a friend or relative who is staying in hospital is a bad idea. Do you know why? If not, why not?
5. To what extent can we say that food is like a language? Think of some examples.
6. Outline the manner by which structuralists explore the structure of meaning.
7. What critique can be made of structuralist approaches to understanding meaning?
8. What are the key similarities and differences between Saussurean semiotics and Peircean semiology?
9. What did Umberto Eco mean when he said 'signs can tell the truth, and signs can lie'?

REFERENCES AND FURTHER READING

Anderson, Roger (1988) *The Power and the Word*, London: Paladin.

Barthes, R. (1964) *Elements of Semiology*, New York: Hill and Wang.

Barthes, R. (1972) *Mythologies*, London: Paladin.

Barthes, R. (1985) *The Fashion System*, London: Cape.

Baudrillard, Jean (1988a) orig. 1968 'The System of Objects', pp. 10–28. In Mark Poster (ed.), *Jean Baudrillard: Selected Writings*, Cambridge: Polity Press.

Baudrillard, Jean (1988b) orig. 1981 'Simulacra and Simulation'. In Mark Poster (ed.), *Jean Baudrillard: Selected Writings*, Cambridge: Polity Press.

Berger, Arthur Asa (1991) *Media Research Techniques*, London: Sage.

Boorstin, Daniel (1992) orig. 1961 *The Image: A Guide to Pseudo-Events in America*, 25th Anniversary Edition, New York: Vintage Books.

Carson, Ciarán (1988) *The Irish For No*, Newcastle: Bloodaxe Books.

Chomsky, Noam (1965) *Language and Mind*, London: Harcourt Brace & Woned.

Culler, Jonathon (1976) *Saussure*, ed. Frank Kermode, London: Fontana Modern Masters.

De Saussure, F. (1974) *Course in General Linguistics*, London: Fontana.

Desmond, John (1991) 'The Image of Banks and Other Financial Institutions'. Unpublished PhD thesis. University of Manchester, England.

Douglas, Mary (1997) 'In Defence of Shopping'. In Pasi Falk and Colin Campbell (eds), *The Shopping Experience*, London: Sage.

Eco, Umberto (1976) orig. 1967 *A Theory of Semiotics*, Bloomington: Indiana University Press.

Eco, Umberto (1986) 'Towards a Semiological Guerrilla Warfare'. In *Travels in Hyper-Reality*, London: Picador.

Elias, Norbert (1994) orig. 1939 *The Civilizing Process: The History of Manners and State Formation and Civilization*, trans. Edmund Jephcott, Oxford: Basil Blackwell.

Falk, Pasi and Colin Campbell (eds) (1997) *The Shopping Experience*, London: Sage.

Fine, Elizabeth C. (1996) Review Article: The Semiotics of Marginality, *Semiotica*, vol. 111, no. 1/2: 142–52.

Gallup Jr., George (1989) *The Gallup Poll: Public Opinion 1989*, Wilmington, Delaware: Scholarly Resources Inc.

Giddens, Anthony (1979) *Central Problems in Social Theory*, London: Macmillan (now Palgrave).

Hall, Stuart (1996) orig. 1983 'The Problem of Ideology: Marxism Without Guarantees', pp. 25–47. In David Morley and Kuan-Hsing Chen (eds), *Critical Dialogues in Cultural Studies*, London: Routledge.

Hawkes, Terence (1977) *Structuralism and Semiotics*, London: Routledge.

Hebdige, Dick (1988) orig. 1979 *Subculture: The Meaning of Style*, London: Routledge.

Hetzel, Patrick (1995) 'Systemising the Awareness of the Consumer's Five Senses at the Point of Sale: An Essential Challenge for Marketing Theory and Practice'. *Proceedings of the 24th European Marketing Academy (EMAC) Conference, France*, 16–19 May, pp. 471–82.

Levi-Strauss, Claude (1964) *Totemism* (trans. R. Needham), London: Merlin Press.

Levi-Strauss, Claude (1972) orig. 1962 *The Savage Mind*, London: Weidenfeld & Nicolson.

Levi-Strauss, Claude (1989) *Tristes Tropiques* (trans. John and Doreen Weightman), London: Pan.

Leymore, Varda L. (1975) *Hidden Myth*, London: Heinemann.

McCracken, Grant (1990) *Culture and Personality*, Bloomington: Indiana University Press.

Mick, David Glen (1986) Consumer Research and Semiotics: Exploring the Morphology of Signs, Symbols and Significance, *Journal of Consumer Research*, vol. 13 (September): 196–214.

Norkunas, Martha K. (1993) *The Politics of Public Memory: Tourism, History and Ethnicity in Monterey, California*, Albany: State University of New York Press.

O'Donohoe, Stephanie (1994) Advertising Uses and Gratifications, *European Journal of Marketing*, vol. 28, no. 8/9: 52–75.

Philo, Greg (1993) 'From Buerk to Band-Aid', pp. 73–104. In John Eldridge (ed.), *Getting the Message, News, Truth and Power*, Glasgow University Media Group, London: Routledge.

Propp, V.I. (1968) orig. 1928 *Morphology of the Folktale*, Austin: University of Texas Press.

Sandikci, Ozlem (1997) 'Images of Women in Advertising: A Critical–Cultural Perspective', pp. 76–81. In Basil C. Englis and Anna Olofsson (eds), *European Advances in Consumer Research*, vol. 3, Stockholm: Association for Consumer Research.

Stern, Barbara B. (1988) How Does an Ad Mean? *Journal of Advertising*, vol. 17, no. 2: 3–14.

Verba, Stephen M. and Carl Camden (1984) 'Barthes: The Fashion System: An Exploration at the Recipient Level', pp. 471–91. In John Deely (ed.), *Semiotics 1984, Proceedings of the Ninth Meeting of the Semiotic Society of America*, 11–14 October, Bloomington: University Press of America.

Weber, S. (1992) *Return to Freud: Jack Laconis Dislocation of Psychoanalysis*, trans. M. Levine, Cambridge University Press.

Williamson, Judith (1978) *Decoding Advertisements: Ideology and Meaning in Advertising*, London and New York: Marion Boyars.

Whorf, Benjamin Lee (1956) *Language, Thought and Reality* (ed. John B. Carroll), Cambridge, Massachusetts: MIT.

Zakia, Richard D. and Mihai Nadin (1987) Semiotics, Advertising and Marketing, *Journal of Consumer Marketing*, vol. 4, no. 2 (Spring): 5–12.

NOTES

i   This division is for reasons of explication only, and is not intended to infer that the study of meaning is split into European and American schools of thought. For example

Umberto Eco, who is a well-known Italian semiotician, casts his work in the tradition of Peirce.

ii For example *onomatopoeia* refers to human attempts to mimic the real sound that an animal makes; for example in English 'bow-wow' or 'woof-woof' is usually used to indicate the bark of a dog. However even onomatopoeia changes from culture to culture. For example in English the sound of a rooster crowing is depicted as 'cock-a-doodle-do'; whereas in other cultures it can be represented in different ways, 'kie-riki-ri', for instance.

iii *Source*: Adapted from Charles E. Cleveland, 'Semiotics: Determining What the Advertising Message Means to the Audience', chapter 14 in L. Percy and A.G. Woodside (eds), *Advertising and Consumer Psychology*, Lexington, Massachusetts: Lexington Books.

iv *Source*: Levi-Strauss, *The Savage Mind* (1962) and *Totemism* (1962).

v De Saussure also likened the language system to a game of chess. For example Weber (1992: 125) suggests how:

'For Saussure there are many similarities between language and a chess game: the value of particular elements depends upon their given position within the system; the system is only momentary and changes from one moment to the next. However the values depend upon an agreement, through which the rules of the game are set; these exist before the game starts and continue to exist before each move.'

[1992: 35]

Critics have taken a second look at the metaphors of the Geneva-to-Paris train and the unconscious chess player to advance the views that, firstly, language is not pre-given and stable, but is dependent upon context; secondly, that a diachronic understanding of the production of signs is essential if they are to be understood.

vi Peirce developed a complex taxonomy of signs which eventually yielded 10 trichotomies and 66 types.

vii *Source*: William Leith in *The Independent*, The Sunday Review, 3rd February 1991, p. 3.

6 CONSUMPTION AND IDENTITY

LEARNING OBJECTIVES

- To provide a clear account of processes of identity formation, which nevertheless elucidates the complexity of the subject
- To introduce readers to biological, sociological and psychoanalytic theories of identity formation and to enable them to compare and contrast these with one another
- To focus especially on the role played by consumption and marketing processes in the construction of identity
- To introduce aspects of contemporary debates on the subject of identity

6.1   INTRODUCTION

In today's world the subject of 'identity' appears to be on everyone's lips as the key social and political question of the times. Ethnic groups around the world cry that their identities are in danger of being destroyed either as the result of an action by a more powerful group or as the result of being homogenized or 'Coca-colonized' by what is identified as the spreading cancer of consumer society. In what are increasingly called the 'postindustrial' societies of the First World, identities are described as being in a state of crisis and flux as those who previously found meaning and a stable identity in the world of work, must now look elsewhere. This has provided a valuable source of material for authors and film-makers who have capitalized on this flux through films like *The Full Monty*, where a group of men who had been made redundant from their jobs in heavy industry, remade themselves as exotic dancers, and a growing number of television programmes and books on a range of topics from how to be a better parent to how to dress better.

What is identity? Put simply the subject of identity is 'us'; 'identity' is about who 'we' are, whether this 'we' is an individual or a group. In order

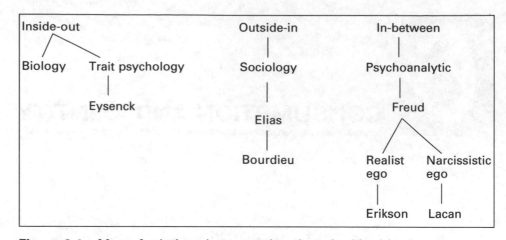

Figure 6.1 Map of relations between theorists cited in this chapter

to focus on the primary objective of constructing a basic understanding of identity, there is much of interest which is not covered here. However this is also a key chapter as it introduces themes and issues which form the basis for discussion in the following chapters. For example to what extent is identity an individual rather than a communal property, or an independent entity rather than one bound by obligations? Finally, how does the concept of identity tie in with the concept of control over the 'self' and of the body?

This chapter is structured according to rather crude distinctions indicated in Figure 6.1. The first division is between what I call 'inside-out' approaches, summed up in the phrase 'I am my genes', which seek to explain human identity as a set of common characteristics which are passed down to us via our genetic inheritance. The second main approach focuses on 'outside-in' approaches which emphasize the role of society in shaping identity. Finally, I discuss several 'in-between' explanations, including those based on Freudian theory which argue that human identity emerges through the ego's attempts to mediate between the demands of biology (the id) and society (the superego).

The subject of identity is introduced first by considering this from the 'inside-out' by means of a biological explanation which considers the extent to which identity is contained within the brain and the role played by genetic factors in conveying aspects of identity including consumption behaviour. Next 'outside-in' approaches to identity are discussed which view the subject from a sociological point of view. Here we revisit the work of Elias (1994) which has already been discussed in Chapter 1. However we build on this by considering the work of Pierre Bourdieu and of George Herbert Mead. Third different psychoanalytic approaches are discussed, which correspond to those centred around the 'realist' and 'narcissistic' egos first outlined by Freud. With respect to the 'realist' ego, I discuss the work of Erik Erikson; the narcissistic view is illustrated by drawing on the work of

Jacques Lacan. The entire discussion is focused in relation to issues of consumption and marketing, how our biological inheritance acts to structure consumption and how social factors including marketing practices seek to structure identity in complex ways. Finally, I consider the eclectic approach of Csikszentmihalyi (pronounced *Chick-sent-mihai*) and Rochberg-Halton (1995, orig. 1981) in relation to the construction of consumer identity. Their approach is eclectic, drawing on the work of Sigmund Freud, Mead (1936) and Erikson (1968).

6.2   INSIDE-OUT APPROACHES TO IDENTITY

The idea that who we are is shaped from the inside-out suggests that who we are is largely shaped by our **biology** and specifically our genetic makeup. Biological approaches focus on the role played by genes in shaping **personalities** which are relatively stable and enduring over time.

6.2.1   Anatomy of the brain

Does the brain contain any clues about how identity, or the sense of a unified self, can emerge from its structure? Perhaps the most striking thing about the brain is its division into two halves, known as the 'right' brain and the 'left' brain (see Figure 6.2).

The way in which brain and nerve pathways are organized is such that information from the left side of the body is communicated mainly to the right side of the brain, and information from the right side of the body transmitted predominantly to the left side of the brain. The **corpus callosum**, which consists of a huge bundle of fibres, connects the two sides of the brain together. In spite of this profound division in the brain, people normally feel themselves to be 'one' and to formulate unitary plans of action. Why is this? One reason may be that the brain seems to act in a holistic and compensatory manner. For example if one brain centre is damaged, the brain functions of other centres will adjust in order to seek to make up for the deficit.

There are two main subdivisions to the nervous system – the voluntary and the involuntary, or autonomic, systems. The **autonomic nervous system** is not under our conscious control and it controls the movement of many internal organs like the heart, blood vessels and gut. At the base of the brain are two structures that release hormones, the hypothalamus and the pituitary gland, both of which lie just above the roof of the mouth. The **hypothalamus** plays a major role in regulating temperature, sexual function, appetite and body-weight, fluid balance and blood pressure among other things. Through the **pituitary gland**, which is situated at the base of the skull, the hypothalamus produces a wide variety of hormones, and thereby influences the activity of the thyroid gland, parathyroids, the sex glands and the adrenals which are attached to the kidneys. The pituitary also produces the growth hormone by which growth in childhood and adolescence is regulated. On either side of

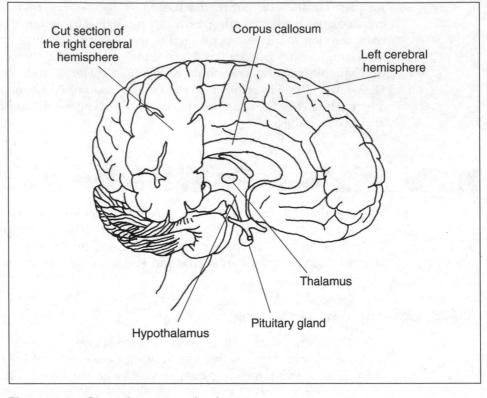

Figure 6.2   Some important brain centres

the pituitary gland lie the two structures of the **amygdala**, an organ shaped like a walnut and of a similar size, which plays a crucial role in emotion. Close to the amygdala is the **hippocampus**, which is involved in the making of memories. These regions have complex connections and interactions with other parts of the brain.

The brain is made up of billions of nerve cells known as **neurons**. Through sensory neurons the nervous system receives information from the external and the internal environment of the body. The brain is a massively complex system, with billions of neurons, each of which interacts with between 100 and 1000 other neurons. The circuits of such interactions determine how we think and behave, because the connections between the neurons determine how the brain functions.

Figure 6.3 illustrates some of the details of a neuron within an array of neurons. The neuron has three parts: a cell body, a long fibre called an axon and many short fibres known as dendrites. At its end, the axon splits into a number of terminal buttons which are located adjacent to the dendrites of another neuron in the chain. The junction between the terminal button and the dendrite is called the **synapse**. The number of synapses in the human brain is around 10 to the power of 15 (one thousand million million). Nerve cells transmit electrical signals from the cell body along the axon. The

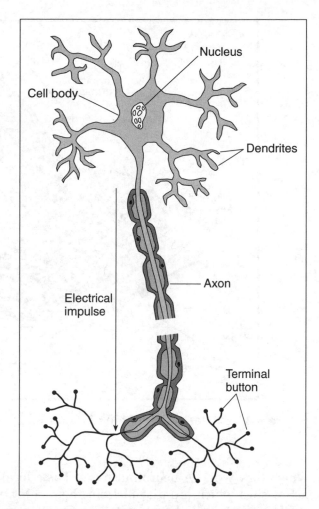

Figure 6.3 Details of a neuron within an array of neurons

impulse, which is also known as the action potential, travels along the axon causing the release of energy from the mitochondria located in the terminal button and of neurotransmitters from storage vesicles. Only these neurotransmitters which have the right 'key' to fit the 'lock' of the receptor in the receiving cell will be able to activate the action potential of the next neuron. Some neurotransmitters have the effect of exciting the cell, others inhibit it. At any given moment a neuron receives thousands of these messages and integrates this input to bring about only one of two possible outcomes – the neuron stays in a resting state or it generates an action potential to communicate with another neuron. Figure 6.4 shows the excitation/inhibition of a neuron by the arrival of a neurotransmitter. Important neurotransmitters include serotonin and dopamine.

A **hormone** is a chemical messenger that is released at one site, carried around the bloodstream and then acts at a distant site. The distinction between hormones and neurotransmitters is with respect to the ways in

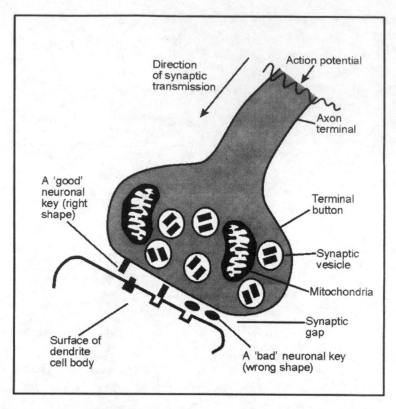

Figure 6.4   Excitation/inhibition of a neuron by a neurotransmitter

which they work. A neurotransmitter has a local action whereas hormones act at sites which are distant from their point of release. Hormones have diverse effects including facilitating digestion or in regulating the speed of the heart. For example in times of acute stress, hormones such as cortisol and adrenaline will be released, triggering a rise in pulse level and blood pressure, with the increased blood flow pumping through the muscles.

Recently, researchers have begun to formulate theories which suggest that moodstates and behaviours such as depression, obsessive–compulsive disorder (OCD), addiction and eating disorder, may be linked to a lack of regulation and possibly to faults in the regulation of complex brain systems. Such explanations link the activities of neurotransmitters such as norpinephrine and serotonin to hormonal reactions which release adrenalin and noradrenalin from the adrenal gland together with cortisol. Some researchers contend that this may help explain why some people exhibit obsessive–compulsive tendencies. The basic argument is that overstimulation or understimulation by relevant neurotransmitters and hormones causes people who are prone to this disorder to constantly experience high levels of acute anxiety. Because of this internal flux and disorder, the issue of control becomes extremely important to them. They tend to be perfectionists, who construct their lives around rigid routines, and attempt to gain a high degree of control over their weight, clothes and body shape, to lead an 'orderly' life and to seek to have an immaculate home with 'everything in its place'. Because they experience very high internal levels of anxiety and chaos, they have extremely low resistance to anything in the environment which appears to add to this. Such behaviour can reach apparently bizarre proportions. However it is not considered further in this chapter, but is elaborated through the discussion on eating disorders in Chapter 8.

6.2.2　The genetic inheritance

Darwin's theory of evolution was a comprehensive attempt to explain the origins of bodily structures and the behaviour of all species. The concept of **adaptation** is important to Darwin's theory. Members of a species thrive best when they display those characteristics which are best fitted to the environment and which grant them an advantage when environmental conditions change. For example there is heavy competition among ruminants for grass and other vegetation. Some animals, such as giraffes, have evolved a distinctively long neck which enables them to specialize in gathering vegetation that is beyond the reach of others. Within the giraffe species, those with longer necks have an advantage over others, as they are able to reach leaves which are further from the ground. However this carries a price, as the longer neck will weigh more and consequently those animals with longer necks will need to eat more. So long as the benefits (the nutrition provided by the leaves on higher branches) outweigh the costs (the need to eat proportionately more than others), there is a net benefit. Our current understanding is that such characteristics are inherited from one generation to the next.

How is the process of inheritance mediated? **Genes** are structures that code for the proteins that make up the body. The actual structure of the body, including the **nervous system**, will be determined by a complex interaction between genes and the environment. In acquiring genes from the parents, sometimes a slight **mutation** occurs in a gene such that what is acquired is slightly different from the genes possessed by the parent. Small mutations in the genetic material can be advantageous, disadvantageous or neutral. For example a gene coding for a slightly longer neck might place its possessor at an advantage and such necks would tend to become more common in subsequent generations. The gene will become more common because of its success. A similar logic applies to nervous systems. Nervous systems acting in combination with the environment determine behaviour. Slight differences in nervous systems can mean the production of slightly different behaviour. Nervous systems are themselves the product of genes and so the behaviours that result from one type of nervous system may be more adaptive and therefore more frequent in the population of a given species. With respect to consumption, we can study how different individuals may be predisposed to consume in similar or in different ways as the result of their genetic inheritance.

6.2.2.1 Twin studies

One way in which scientists have studied the effects of inheritance on identity and behaviour is by studying twins. Identical twins are more formally referred to as **monozygotic**, meaning that both came from one egg. As a result their genes are identical and they are always of the same sex. Fraternal twins are called **dizygotic**, or two egg. They share approximately 25 per cent of their genes, as do any two brothers or sisters. One-half of fraternal twin pairs are boy–girl, one-quarter are boy–boy, and one-quarter are girl–girl.

Social scientists are especially keen to study monozygotic twins who have been separated from birth. As such twins are genetically identical, one would expect that any differences in behaviour would be due to the environment. By studying separated twins, scientists can remove the influence of a common upbringing in a family in studying the effects of inheritance and environment with respect to personality formation. Thomas Bouchard (see for example Bouchard, 1997a and b), of the University of Minnesota, has studied a large number of reunited monozygotic twins who were separated at birth. Bouchard's research study began with the brothers who have come to be known as the 'Jim Twins'.

The 'Jim Twins' (see note i)

Jim Lewis and Jim Springer first met on 9 February 1979 after they had been separated for thirty-nine years. Both had been adopted from birth by separate families in Ohio and had grown up within forty-five miles of each other. Each had been married twice, first to women named Linda and second to women named Betty. Both had children, including sons named James Alan. Both had at one time owned dogs named Toy.

Bourchard conducted a series of tests with the two twins. In one test which measured personality variables, such as tolerance, conformity and flexibility, the scores of the twins were so close that they approximated the average of the totals of one person taking the same test twice. Brain-wave tests in turn, were virtually identical. Their medical histories were also uncannily similar. The twins also shared a number of vocational and consumption preferences. Both had served as Sheriff's deputies in nearby Ohio counties. They each drove Chevrolet cars, chain-smoked, had a preference for beer and had wood-working shops in their garages. They each lived in the only house on their block and both had vacationed on the same beach on the Florida Gulf Coast.

6.2.2.2 Discussion

The story of the 'Jim Twins' seems to indicate that inherited characteristics play a key role in determining identity and consumption behaviour. However one must be cautious in interpreting such findings. For example just as the fact that both boys were called 'Jim' is not an effect of heredity, so it is not at all unusual for middle-aged men from the USA to drive Chevrolets and to drink beer. That the men each married twice, and each time married women with the same name, that they called their dogs by the same names, are fascinating facts; however they do not link in any conclusive fashion to any contemporary theory of inheritance, but rather raise some tantalizing questions. In other studies twins have adopted quite different behaviours. For example one twin in the Minnesota study grew up to be a proficient pianist in a non-musical family while her sister, who was adopted by a piano teacher, did not take to the instrument. However the studies have indicated that twins do seem to share a range of characteristics, from speech defects to proneness to some forms of disease and fear of heights. Another famous pair of twins, Oskar Stohr and Jack Yufe, were separated at birth and raised in very different cultural surroundings. Yufe was brought up by his Jewish father in Trinidad and Stohr was raised in German-occupied Czechoslovakia during the Second World War, where he attended a Nazi-run school. While their attitudes were quite different, they displayed many physical similarities. Both wore short clipped moustaches, stored rubber bands around their wrists and read magazines back to front. Both also shared the habit of sneezing loudly in public in order to attract attention.

While from the above there seems to be little doubt that our biological inheritance plays an important role in determining who we are, much more research needs to be conducted into the relations between biology and environment.

6.2.3 Introversion and extroversion

There is a long tradition within Western medicine which links differences in personality to different 'humours' or bodily fluids, notably phlegm, blood and bile. It was commonly thought that the character of a person could be read from the fluid which was dominant in their body; as a result, some people were considered to by 'phlegmatic', others to be 'sanguine'.

The psychoanalyst Carl Gustav Jung noted two distinct types of personality – the introvert and the extrovert. The **introvert** character appears quiet, placid and unruffled with respect to events in the external world. By contrast **extroverts** appear to be in need of constant stimulation from the outside world. Some years later Hans Eysenck (Eysenck, 1970; Eysenck and Eysenck, 1975) developed a classification of different personality types based on the degree of extroversion/introversion and on the level of personal stability (see note ii):

'The typical extrovert is sociable, likes parties, has many friends, needs to have people to talk to and does not like reading or studying by himself. He craves excitement, takes chances, often sticks his neck out, acts on the spur of the moment and is generally an impulsive individual. He is fond of practical jokes, always has a ready answer and generally likes change; he is carefree and optimistic and likes to "laugh and be merry". He prefers to keep moving and doing things, tends to be aggressive and loses his temper quickly. Altogether his feelings are not kept under tight control, and he is not always a reliable person.

The typical introvert is a quiet retiring sort of person who is introspective and fond of books rather than people. He is reserved and distant except with intimate friends. He tends to plan ahead, "looks before he leaps" and distrusts the impulse of the moment. He does not like excitement, takes matters of everyday life with proper seriousness and likes a well-ordered mode of life. He keeps his feelings under close control, seldom behaves in an aggressive manner and does not lose his temper easily. He is reliable, somewhat pessimistic and places great value on ethical standards.'   [Eysenck and Eysenck, 1975: 59/60]

It should be immediately noted that these are extreme types and that many people occupy the ground between these extremes. Eysenck believed that his dimensions were rooted in the physiology of the brain, with introversion and extroversion being related to the level of arousal of the reticular activating system,[1] and neuroticism reflecting activation of the limbic system, known as the emotional brain. Some individuals (extroverts) have low levels of arousal and seek stimulation from the external environment. Other have high levels of internal arousal (introverts) and so avoid stimulation from the external environment. Eysenck believed that because of their outward orientation, extroverts would be more difficult to condition, would have a greater tolerance towards pain but less tolerance for sensory deprivation, would be more satiated than introverts and would have lower sedation thresholds. Eysenck believed that individual differences in introversion and extroversion were passed on by genetic inheritance. Martin and Jardine (1986) carried out a massive study of 3810 sets of monozygotic and dizygotic twins to test Eysenck's hypothesis that introversion and extroversion would be inherited. The authors concluded this hypothesis was 'vindicated in the strongest possible way'. In fact they reported that their most interesting and surprising finding was that they could find no evidence that family or culture played any role whatsoever in the formation of these traits.

Eysenck's (1980) ideas about smoking behaviour may be used to illustrate his central theory. According to this, one must first distinguish between taking up smoking and subsequent maintenance of the habit. Eysenck (1980) suggested that takeup of smoking is mainly due to the influence of environmental factors, primarily the peer group, with low genetic influence. He developed a model to account for the habit which emphasizes genetic predispositions (diathesis) related to personality factors. His idea is that people with different personalities will react to stress in different ways and that this in turn will relate strongly to the observed pattern of their smoking behaviour which will also be differently expressed. The two motivational causes attributed to smoking are boredom and emotional strain. According to Eysenck, extroverts have less arousal in their cerebral cortex, as mediated by the ascending reticular formation, than introverts and are therefore more susceptible to boredom. Neurotic, anxious persons have labile autonomic nervous systems and are therefore more genetically disposed to react in a

[1] According to Davison and Neale (1986: 601) the reticular activating system is in the core of the brainstem and plays a role in arousal and alertness. The system comprises a vast array of cells (reticular means 'array' or 'network'). The pons and the medula send in fibres which connect with this network which in turn is connected by fibres to the cortex, the basal ganglia, the hypothalamus, the septal area and the cerebellum.

more intensely emotional way to environmental stress. As a result, extroverts and neurotics are more prone to be smokers. However they smoke more for different reasons.

In recent developments, Eysenck postulates a positive relation between smoking behaviour and individual differences in 'tough-mindedness' or psychoticism. This refers to rebellious and aggressive behaviour. He argues that there is a strong genetic component in psychoticism which predisposes those people to smoke more in expressing their non-conformist tendencies. Eysenck also argues that nicotine has a complex relation with cortical arousal in which small amounts provide stimulation that relieves boredom, while large amounts reduce anxiety through a reduction in autonomic nervous system activity. According to Eysenck, males and extroverts who are frequently exposed to boredom-producing situations are more likely to continue to smoke because the stimulation reinforces this behaviour. For those who are high in psychoticism, smoking reinforces their non-conforming behaviour. According to Spielberger (1986) there is reasonable evidence to support this view.

6.2.4   Is there a gene for smoking?

Nowadays one constantly hears about the search for the 'gay' gene or other genes which determine important aspects of human identity. From the above one might be tempted to infer that one day scientists will discover a gene that regulates smoking behaviour. This raises a fundamentally important issue. To what extent is a given behaviour, such as sexual orientation or smoking, biologically (physiologically) determined, and to what extent is it socially determined? The distinction between physiology and biology should alert you to the discussion of human needs in Chapter 4. This concluded with the assertion that it is impossible to separate physiological from psychological needs, because all needs can be thought of as, to an extent, psychological. We can also reverse this statement by stating that equally all behaviour and the feelings associated with this are associated in some way with the brain and hence have a biological basis, and that therefore genes are inextricably entwined with all behaviour. This argument does not lead to the conclusion that differences in either sexual orientation or smoking behaviour can be explained by genetic differences but that rather these result from a complex interaction which includes genes, environment and a person's consciousness. We must be attentive to reactions between the brain and the internal environment, which constitutes the body we inhabit and the external social environment. Since Eysenck developed his initial ideas about the links between biology and behaviour, huge advances have been made in expanding understanding of those complex relations which exist between genetic predispositions and a range of behaviours, including obsessive–compulsive disorder (OCD), addictive behaviour, hyperactivity and eating disorders. However while such advances offer tantalizing glimpses of the kinds of processes that might be at work in activating and maintaining such behaviours, the complexity of the brain itself is such that a coherent explanation of the physiology of such conditions is a long way off. However it is clear that genetic factors play a role in determining who 'we' are.

6.3 OUTSIDE-IN APPROACHES TO IDENTITY

The above discussion briefly introduced how biology can affect who we are, in terms of our possession of a more or less stable set of personality characteristics. In contrast to this, 'outside-in' approaches focus on the ways in which identity is moulded by social and cultural factors. This returns us to the discussion of Elias (1994) in Chapter 1, in particular his description of the complex nature of social change, whereby changes in the social field are related to those in social structures and rules for the behaviour of individual conduct. You should recall the following key points from this:

- The change from warrior societies to court societies has had profound significance for the formation of new classes which come to be pitted in competition with one another.
- With growing interdependence, the open, violent and communal nature of society shifts to a more closed, polite and individual outlook.
- Emotional expression is reined in as people become more self-conscious of their own behaviour (shame) and of feelings of embarrassment in witnessing the misconduct of others.
- The self becomes preoccupied with surveillance of its own conduct and that of others. Control, which at first is observed only in the presence of others, comes to be internalized, exerted by the individual on his or her own behaviour whether others are present or not. The implications for child-rearing are immense. Children who are raised today must be educated in the ways of society, to internalize, in a few short years, social rules which took many hundreds of years to develop.

There are several issues which arise from the above that have significance for the discussion of identity. First, the question of individual identity arises with the decline of community and a growing self-consciousness. Secondly, the emergence of this individual identity is articulated by an internalized control over the emotions. These two issues will form the basis of the following discussion. A third issue, which challenges Elias's explanation in the light of recent social changes, will be discussed at the end of this chapter.

6.3.1 Identifying strangers

The first use of the term 'identity' in Europe was as a legal and political requirement which referred to the copying of a charter in a Chancellory. The Chancellor was responsible for the copy that remained *iden*, that is, the same as, identical to, the original. In this sense, the notion of identification predates the emergence of the modern self. Soon after, the word also became associated with the need to identify strangers:

> 'As early as 1248 Goliards in Burgundy were obliged to carry written credentials: the first step towards the "identification" of a person as an individual.'
>
> [Illich and Saunders, 1990]

Recall, from Chapter 1, Elias's description of how during the medieval period, strangers were scarcely regarded as being human but rather akin to a breed of fabulous animal. Mutual fear and suspicion followed the stranger wherever he went, and it was for this reason that some form of identity or written credentials were considered important. It is this aspect which unites the concepts of identity and branding. Branding, which is discussed further in Chapter 9, was used for many reasons in ancient times, including the brands made upon prisoners and slaves to denote the fact that they constituted the property of another.

6.3.1.1 Bourdieu and the concept of distinction

The very idea of 'community' implies that there must be some form of consensus between its members with respect to the way in which the world is ordered or classified. In Chapter 2 we discussed how different groups of people develop systems of **symbolic classification** which enable communication, the division of roles and the maintenance of social order within communities. Recall sociologist Pierre Bourdieu's (1977) example of the Kabyle calendar which is reproduced in Figure 2.1. The Kabyle organized their lives around the seasons which were divided into 'male' and 'female' seasons: the female time was the period of autumn through to spring and associated with ploughing, sowing, germination and emergence; whereas the 'male' period was associated with growth, harvest, stubble and harrowing. Bourdieu maintains that within communities such as the Kabyle, submission to the collective rhythms of community is rigorously enforced, as these forms of classification structure not only the group's classification of the world but the group itself.

Bourdieu's work follows a similar line of enquiry to that of Elias, as both hold that it is only through mapping the entire social field that one may come to a sufficient understanding of the ways in which different groups mark their identities from others. In his classic work *Distinction* (1996, orig. 1979), which is based on research carried out during the late 1960s and the 1970s, Bourdieu extended the scope of his study to explore the ways in which goods are used to mark the identities of different groups in contemporary French society. He coined the term **habitus** to describe the classification of activities and lifestyles of the social space which comprises society. According to Bourdieu, different conditions of existence produce different forms of habitus. The social conditions which influenced the habitus of the Kabyle are quite different from those which held sway in the medieval French society described by Elias (1994) and these in turn are different from those which shaped the development of French court society during the seventeenth and eighteenth centuries. The habitus is thus stable at any given point in time, and dynamic in that it changes through time.

Consider for example the opposition between the 'working-class' and the 'bourgeoisie' in France. The main opposition which distinguishes these different classes is between those practices which are designated as being 'rare' and 'distinguished' from those which are considered to be 'vulgar' or 'common'. This is very similar to Elias's (1994) discussion of the ways in which the court nobility sought to distinguish themselves from the bourgeoisie in eighteenth-century France, by devising an ever more intricate system of manners. Two centuries later, Bourdieu found that a person's taste was heavily influenced by the amount of economic capital or cultural capital which they owned. **Economic capital** refers to the material resources or wealth which a person has accumulated. **Cultural capital** refers to their perceived level of education, which includes not just what they learned but perhaps, more importantly, where they learned it. The complex pattern of distinctions deriving from these is illustrated below with reference to the consumption of food.

Bourdieu found that the working classes in his study tended to develop a taste for foods which are considered both filling and economical. This is not surprising as Elias (1994) noted that in medieval society only the upper classes could afford meat, while peasants had to make do with legumes and during times of scarcity had to do without food. The bourgeoisie sought to distinguish themselves from the working classes by spending proportionately less on food, particularly 'earthy' forms of food, while the members of the professions, in turn, distinguished themselves from the bourgeoisie by the high proportion of their spending devoted to the consumption of expensive products, especially expensive meats, fresh fruit and vegetables, shellfish and aperitifs (1996: 180). Bourdieu found that a narrow interpretation of social class which omitted consideration of gender and ethnicity provided only a partial explanation of the range of distinctions within French society. Gender provided another key structuring principle for the consumption of food within the French habitus:

'For example, in the working classes, fish tends to be an unsuitable food for men, not only because it is a light food, insufficiently "filling", which would only be cooked for health reasons, i.e. for invalids and children, but also because, like fruit (except bananas) it is one of the "fiddly" things which a man's hands cannot cope with and which make him childlike; . . . but above all it is because fish has to be eaten in a way which totally contradicts the masculine way of eating, that is, with restraint, in small mouthfuls, chewed gently, with the front of the mouth, on the tips of the teeth (because of the bones). The whole masculine identity – what is called virility – is involved in these two ways of eating, nibbling and picking, as befits a woman, or with whole-hearted male gulps and mouthfuls.'

[1996: 190/1]

Bourdieu notes that the masculine body, construed as powerful, big and strong and with brutal needs, is taken as a principle for the division of foods between the sexes. Working-class men are expected to eat and drink more and to demonstrate potency by drinking stronger things. They eat the 'strong' foods, the meats and cheeses, while women tend towards the crudités (raw vegetables) and salads:

> 'Meat, the nourishing food par excellence, strong and strong-making, giving vigour, blood, and health, is the dish for the men, who take a second helping, whereas the women are satisfied with a small portion. It is not that they are stinting themselves, they really don't want what others might need, especially the men, the natural meat-eaters, and they derive a sort of authority from what they do not see as a privation. Besides they don't have a taste for men's food which is reputed to be harmful when eaten to excess (for example a surfeit of meat can "turn the blood", over-excite, bring you out in spots etc.) and may even arouse a sort of disgust.' [1996: 192]

Thus from a person's position in the habitus, as represented by the amount of economic or cultural capital one has, in addition to one's ethnicity and gender orientation, one can infer a great deal about that person's consumption and 'taste', or consumption style. The point about cultural capital is central. The nouveau riche may have 'made it' economically by landing that well-paid job which provides the Mercedes, the house, the maid and the wine-cellar – all of the accoutrements of 'class' – but demonstrating to others of their economic class that they are culturally up to the mark is another matter. It is not enough to have bought expensive wines or to entertain lavishly. Such behaviour may indeed have the reverse effect, being labelled as vulgar by members of the aspirational group. Status is thus not simply conditional merely upon what one has but on one's accomplishment – in the words of a 1980's pop song, 'It's not what you do but the way that you do it' that ultimately gets results.

Holt's replication of Bourdieu

Recently Douglas Holt (1998) conducted a qualitative study which sought to determine the extent to which the pattern of distinction in the USA might be similar to that observed by Bourdieu in relation to French culture. Those who participated in Holt's study included ten people who were drawn from the upper quintile of the population (labelled as HCC – Higher Cultural Capital) and ten people drawn from the lower quintile (labelled as LCC – Lower Cultural Capital). Bourdieu found that those with low cultural capital tended to evaluate items from material culture in ways that were linked to their practical function, while those with higher levels of cultural capital tended to evaluate these aesthetically. Holt found a similar pattern in the USA. Of particular interest are the differing ways in which the HCC and LCC groups use the signifier 'functional' in relation to their consumption.

The meaning of 'functional'

Holt found that while HCCs tended to use objects as vehicles for self-expression, some of them expressed the desire for 'functional' clothing.

However 'functional' had a very different meaning for them than it did for the LCCs. For these high-achievers, 'functional' represented a particular aesthetic value based on parsimonious design and utilitarian construction similar to the functionalism of 'high' modern architecture and design. In contrast, 'functional' for LCCs referred to a pragmatic solution to their everyday needs. LCCs preferred clothes which were durable, comfortable, reasonably priced, well-fitting and which conformed to the norms of colleagues at work.

> *Interviewer*: 'What kind of clothes do you like?'
> *Heather (LCC)*: 'Stuff that will last. I don't really like to go with what's fashionable, necessarily, just for the sake of being fashionable. I like to be comfortable.'

Heather liked to be 'comfortable', was happy shopping at stores such as KMart and WalMart, and found it difficult to spend $30 on a shirt or $60 on a skirt when she could buy the material and make it up herself. On the other hand, consider John's (HCC) answer to the same question.

> *John (HCC)*: 'Today I'm buying practical clothes. That is to say they're mostly cotton. They're all washable. Mostly they don't require ironing because I get tired of ironing . . . I look for – now when I'm buying clothing – I really don't care about the current style anymore. You know it has good design. It will always be in style. And I tend to look for things which probably are more expensive but which I know will be more durable.'
> *Interviewer*: 'Are there any particular clothing styles that you like?'
> *John*: 'Yeah. I guess the best way to say it would be styles that are functional and designed to be worn by human bodies as they are; as opposed to designed and worn only standing up at cocktail parties or the races or, you know, as soon as you sit down you know it was a mistake.'
> [Holt, 1998: 9]

Holt found several other forms of correspondence with Bourdieu:

- **Consumption of cultural texts** (such as films or works of art): Here HCCs engage with texts as being entertaining or potentially edifying but which do not reflect the 'real' world. On the other hand LCCs tend to interpret works of art, films and music from a referential perspective as being more or less realistic depictions of the world that are potentially relevant to their own lives. As a result they tend to be more attracted to programmes and movies that are 'real' and music that speaks directly to their life situation.
- **Materialism-idealism:** Because LCCs are brought up with a shortage of material possessions they often cast the 'good life' in terms of having an abundance of things and having luxurious things which they cannot presently afford. In contrast, HCCs tend to emphasize the metaphysical side of life, in terms of a 'creative, contemplative, aestheticized, abstract engagement with the world rather than brute encounters with an empirical reality (Holt, 1998: 11). Where HCCs and LCCs have equivalent economic capital, HCCs tend to place less value on house size and to have

smaller yards (gardens) than LCCs. Overall, HCCs were more frugal and never stated the extravagance of restaurants as a quality influencing their favourite places to dine.

- **Work and taste**: HCCs tend to work in areas which are highly symbolic such as information management, while LCCs tend to engage in highly routine jobs in the local labour market. In this respect HCCs tend to share a more 'cosmopolitan' rather than a 'local' milieu.
- **Consumer subjectivity as individuals vs local identity:** Holt found that LCCs tended to engage in passionate consumption of particular collective activities. They engaged in hobbies which were autotelic (provided intrinsic enjoyment). In contrast, HCCs tended to focus their consumption behaviour on the acquisition of a unique style; they went for goods considered to be more 'authentic', as being artisanal rather than mass-produced. In contrast to the social orientation of LCCs, their hobbies tended to relate more to individual self-actualization, for example in joining groups such as the 'Daughters of the American Revolution'.

6.3.2 Measuring social classification

While Bourdieu, in the work cited above, explored an entire and diverse system of classification, national governments and market researchers have been interested in measuring social classification more narrowly for their own reasons. In the UK, social classification was until recently measured in terms of the skills of the highest wage-earner in the household. Thus if the highest wage-earner was a senior manager or judge, he or she would be accorded the status of A at the top of the scale. On the other hand, if he or she worked in a car-assembly plant then he or she might be accorded the status C2 (skilled manual worker) or D (unskilled manual worker). Market researchers have been interested in compiling and sorting data on this narrow variable of social classification because they feel that this variable has many associations with consumption patterns. The stated aims of government are different from those of market researchers, and recently the UK government has introduced an 8-point classification which they wish to use in monitoring differences in health and the uptake of social welfare between classes.

Why has social classification been regarded to be so important? The argument is really quite simple and is summed up by the well-known quotation 'birds of a feather flock together'. The assumption is that people in similar occupational groupings will tend to live in similar types of neighbourhood, share similar school, work and leisure environments and activities, and develop similar attitudes towards moral and political issues. In the UK this was true up to a point in time. Since the Second World War ended in 1945 and up until comparatively recently, the two 'serious' English political parties, representing those which habitually swap the reins of power, are the Labour Party, traditionally the party of choice for the working classes, and the Conservative Party, the party for the upper classes. Those from different social classes have worked in different occupations (professional services versus skilled or manual labour), lived in different neighbourhoods, favoured different varieties of religion (as represented by 'high' and 'low' churches) and preferred different holiday destinations (Brighton, Blackpool or Bournemouth for working classes; somewhere overseas for the upper classes). Class differences extended into consumption activities, including education – for example whether or not it was thought appropriate to go to university – and more mundane activities such as whether one drank beer or wine, or for that matter whether one went into the 'public bar' (for the 'local' working-class men) or the 'lounge' (for the middle classes and 'ladies'). Like all powerful systems of classification, the power of social classification was exclusive as well as being inclusive. Bob Tyrell, who was head of the Henley Centre, sums this up in the saying 'People like us don't . . .'. Thus for members of the working class (C2s, D's and E's according to the JICNARS classification), it was usual that 'People like us don't take holidays overseas, don't like "cultural", "arty" things, don't play rugby, don't go to university to get educated, don't drink wine, etc.', because such activities were thought to be indications that one was a 'snob' or that one had 'sold out' of one's class position. Similarly, middle-class people defined their identity in terms of what they were not, which were working-class characteristics.

However while there is no doubt that there are still large differences in income between different social classes, there is evidence of a blurring of distinctions between classes, and greater variety within such classes, especially with respect to consumption practices. Some argue that lifestyle and not social class is now the major factor in constructing social identity.

6.3.3   Individuals: identity and lifestyle

In *The Lonely Crowd* (1961), Riesman traces changes in the development of society in Europe and the USA from patterns based on tradition, to inner-directedness and then to what he calls the 'other-directed' character. Like Norbert Elias, Riesman holds that the relation between the person and society has changed fundamentally over time. The **tradition-dominated person** is very much part of the community to which he or she belongs. In fact such a person scarcely thinks of himself/herself as an individual. Still less do such people believe that they can shape their destiny in terms of lifelong goals. However Riesman notes that the global shift towards rationality and science has led to the development of the idea of the autonomous individual. He maintains that this tendency has been reinforced in societies where the population is in overall decline, where fewer people work in traditional forms of employment on the land or extractive industries, and where hours are short and there is increased leisure and material abundance. According to Riesman, such developments reinforce the development of autonomous individuals because traditional forms of agricultural and industrial work (in shipyards, foundries and mines) create forms of community, while the maintenance of material abundance demands increased time in consuming the products of this activity, and consumption is a more solitary activity.

Riesman argues that the society which the **inner-directed character** inhabits is typical of the European society that emerged with the Renaissance and the Reformation, and that is only now vanishing. During this period, which shows high rates of urban growth, those who lived in rural communities were forced by circumstance to move to the cities where more often than not they found themselves interacting with **strangers**. Unlike those who had spent their lives in the circle of community, the inner-directed character became aware of the existence of different competing traditions. Cut away from the traditional life of community and forced to live with the knowledge of competing traditions, the inner-directed character turned to the world of work for a sense of meaning and identity. In European society this was traditionally more true for men than for women, as it was generally thought that only men should follow a career and that women should be largely concerned with providing for the family. Consumption was thus associated more with the woman's role.

Riesman suggests that the enduring nature and enterprise of the inner-directed character became less necessary in Europe and the USA during the twentieth century. The need switched from a requirement for workers to those who could spend. Riesman notes that at first **'other-directedness'** seemed to be emerging at first in the larger cities. He discusses travellers' accounts of Americans which state the authors' feeling that the 'typical' American seems to be shallower, more profligate with his money, friendlier, more uncertain of himself and his values, and more demanding of approval than the European. The 'new' character seemed to arise within the new middle classes who worked in the service industries. As the result of the relaxation of discipline and moves towards permissiveness, the peer group became more important to the child, while parents made children feel guilty not so much about the violation of inner standards but about failure to be popular or to manage their relations with other children. These pressures are reinforced by the mass media. Under these conditions types of character emerge which are other-directed:

> 'What is common to all the other-directed people is that their contemporaries are the source of direction for the individual – either those who know him or those with whom he is indirectly acquainted, through friends and through the mass media. The source is of course "internalized" in the sense that dependence on it for guidance in life is implanted early. The goals towards which the other-directed person strives shift with that guidance; it is only in the process of striving itself and the process of paying close attention to the signals from others that remain unaltered through life.'   [1961: 21]

A central feature of the other-directed character is the need for approval. While the inner-directed person is inspired by a need to maintain a good reputation and to keep up with the Jones (to have as high a lifestyle as your neighbours), and to conform in terms of external features such as clothes with the 'best people' in one's milieu, the other-directed person seeks to keep up with the Jones more in terms of the quality of his inner experience. He is so much more sensitive to others that he has developed more levels than simply the externals of appearance.

6.3.3.1   Lifestyle and VALS: implications for social classification

The implication of Riesman's theory for social class is that the inner-directed character, the identity which formed the bulwark of the social-class system, has given way to the other-directed character. This shift has entailed a movement away from the defining features of work (social class) towards external features, including aesthetics and style in the construction of social identity. This shift in identity formation seems to be supported by the Values and Lifestyle Study (VALS) which was developed by the Stanford Research Institute (SRI) in 1978. SRI conducted a survey of 2500 people annually. In its first format, VALS identified three broad consumer identities: inner-directed, other-directed and needs-driven. The latter group included those who spent most of their resources on necessities and who thus were of little importance to many marketing firms. In line with Riesman's findings, the VALS researchers found that 'inner-directed' characters, who constituted 21 per cent of the US population, purchased goods to meet their own internal wants and used consumption as a vehicle for self-expression. By comparison outer-directed characters, who constituted 68 per cent of the US population, were heavily influenced by appearances and by what others thought of them. In 1988 SRI introduced a new measure of values called VALS 2, because the segments identified in VALS 1 were thought to be too general. For example as two out of three Americans were identified as being other-directed consumers, this category was found to be too large to be a meaningful differentiator. Instead a new set of groupings was formulated which bears a strong relation to Maslow's (1970) hierarchy, in creating new categories based on esteem and actualization (see Mitchell, 1981).

VALS data suggest that Actualizers tend to own more of everything. For example on a base of 100 they are more likely than average to own a small car (133) and a bicycle (154). However they are much more likely to own a foreign luxury car (363) or sports car (330), but less likely to own a pickup truck (72). On the other hand the Strugglers' ownership of these items is well below that of the Actualizer – bicycle (43), foreign luxury car (3), small car and sports car (5). The only transport items which Strugglers seem to own in any numbers include small to medium cars (54) and pickup trucks (52).[2]

6.3.3.2   Other-directedness and reference group influence

If we take it that Riesman's 'other-directed' character now constitutes the typical character, at least of Western consumer societies, then how does this person orient himself or herself to the social world? He or she is confronted with a diverse range of lifestyles for sale. Every day of the week, television

---

[2] Based on Weinstein (1998): Exhibit 8.3, page 139.

programmes vie for attention ranging from 'fly on the wall' documentaries to serials and 'soaps' such as *Frasier* and *Neighbours*, not to mention specialist 'lifestyle' programmes on aspects of grooming for self, pets, home and car. In addition to this, a vast number of sites has sprung up on the Internet and most obviously on the Web, which seek to cater to the unique requirements of 'lifestyle' groups. One key aspect of identities based on lifestyle is that they are founded on an ideal of consumption and not production. In order to explore this point, let us consider Dick Hebdige's discussion of the emergence of the 'Mods' in the UK.

The 'Mods' and the 'Rockers'

In 1946 and 1947, just after the end of the Second World War, two Italian scooters were marketed which eclipsed all previous models in terms of sales and which fixed the design concept of the contemporary scooter, the Vespa (Wasp) and the Lambretta. The scooters were aggressively marketed and both companies engaged in extensive advertising campaigns, staged exhibitions to promote awareness of the models, then published their own magazines in three European languages, and formed their own scooter clubs with large national and international memberships in order to consolidate support. Part of the marketing appeal of the new scooters lay in the design. As Hebdige notes, 'the scooter buying public voted overwhelmingly for convenience, looks, an enclosed engine' (1988: 96). Scooters were regarded with a degree of scorn by the motorcycle industry in the UK for precisely the reasons cited by the scooter buying public for wanting one. Scooters were regarded as being frivolous by 'serious' motorcyclists, as being underpowered, overdesigned, 'refined', 'streamlined' and 'effete'; in other words quite contrary to the manly image of the grimy, powerful, speedy, 'warts and all', 'natural' image of the traditional motorcycle.

During the 1960s the scooters became associated with the image of the battles between the 'Mods' and the 'Rockers'. Mods were predominantly lower middle-class or upper working-class and worked in skilled or semi-skilled trades, were male dominated and centred on an obsessive clothes' consciousness which involved a fascination with American and Continental European styles. Hebdige notes that while they were English by birth, they were Italian by choice. During one encounter at Margate between Mods and Rockers, it was found that most Mods were from London, whilst the Rockers were more likely to do manual jobs and to live locally. Mods considered Rockers to be 'dirty' and 'ignorant', whilst the Rockers referred to the Mods as 'pansy' and 'soft'. Mods expressed their identity with reference to a furious consumption programme:

'clothes, clubs, records, hair styles, petrol and drinamyl pills – has been described as "a grotesque parody of the aspirations of their parents" – the people who lived in the new towns or on the new housing estates, the post-war working and middle class. . . . The Mods converted themselves into objects. They "chose" in order to make themselves into Mods, attempting to impose systematic control over the narrow domain which was "theirs", and within which they saw their "real" selves invested – the domain of leisure and appearance, dress and posture.'

[1988: 111]

Scooters were combined with a particular musical style and clothing to construct what Hebdige calls a 'unity of taste', an image which signalled to others that Mods were different, that they had a sense of refinement and distance from others. Hebdige argues that Mod had a huge significance and influence. Mod inaugurated the boutique, the discotheque and there was even a Mod television programme called *Ready Steady Go*. There was a thriving teenage fashion industry in London based in Carnaby Street and the King's Road. Mod lifestyle also included bowling alleys, burger bars and six weekly magazines aimed at the Mod market.

6.3.3.3   Reference group influence: aspirational and avoidance groups

To sum the above, Mod was 'about', and Mods found their identity in, a 'look' which was based not on traditional community or in the world of the workplace, but in the 'other-directed' zone of style and image. Mods constituted one of the first lifestyle groups which based its sense of identity in relation to aesthetics and consumption style. In seeking to determine their identity, Mods were clear about who they were in terms of those **aspirational groups** that they aspired to be like (the different pop bands that they followed) and those **avoidance groups** that they sought to differentiate themselves from (the Rockers).

Englis and Solomon (1995) carried out a limited study of consumers' relations to reference groups in the USA, which involved consumers in judging the kinds of products purchased by aspirational and avoidance groups in addition to the group that they occupied. The authors hypothesized that consumers would be able to accurately reflect the actual consumption patterns of aspirational groups. This is because they felt that the aspirational group would be a focus for study and emulation. On the other hand the authors hypothesized that consumers would tend to be less accurate with respect to those products purchased by avoidance groups as they would tend to stereotype these groups.

Unsurprisingly the population chosen for the study was American college students. Two samples were drawn; the first, of 49 students, was chosen to construct profiles of reference groups. Respondents were asked to sort through a commercial lifestyle database called PRIZM and to assign each of the PRIZM lifestyle clusters to one of the following four reference group categories; aspirational, avoidance, occupied and irrelevant groups. Following this exercise the four reference group clusters were developed. The aspirational group was called 'Money and Brains', the avoidance group 'Small Downtown', the irrelevant group 'Middle America' and finally the occupied group 'Young Suburbia'. These four reference groups were presented to subjects who were told to form a mental representation of the

aspirational: ambitious
avoidance:

CONSUMPTION AND IDENTITY

group and to write down all of the products which they associated with that
group.

The results of the study supported the main hypothesis, that consumers
would tend to more accurately describe the actual products used by aspirational groups than by avoidance groups. Respondents described the products owned by the aspirational group, the 'Money and Brains' cluster, as
being likely to drive BMWs, Mercedes, Cadillacs, Volvos, Porsches, Acuras
and Jaguars, which compared well with the top cars actually purchased by
the group. They were also accurate in naming magazines and alcoholic
beverages purchased by this group. The latter included expensive wines,
Scotch, Champagne, Beck's and Heineken. There was general agreement
between respondents with respect to their description of the products they
thought were consumed by the avoidance group, 'Smalltown Downtown'.
As anticipated, this was highly stereotyped and inaccurate, including
pickup trucks and a range of magazines and alcoholic beverages which did
not actually figure in this group's consumption. Englis and Solomon
suggested that the association of a constellation of products with a negative
reference group could effectively stigmatize whole ranges of products. For
these students such potentially stigmatized products included Chevy, Ford,
Budweiser, Miller, Jack Daniels, Brut, Old Spice and Mennen Speed Stick
Deodorant.

6.3.4 How are individual identities created?

Given that the social context plays such an important role in the construction
of identity, then how do people become individuals? A number of sociologists have sought to explain how children become **socialized**, so that they
come to accept and to internalize the rules of society. You may remember
Norbert Elias's (1994) comment that nowadays children are, in a few short
years, expected to conform to a system of manners which has taken
hundreds of years to develop. One early sociologist, Charles Cooley, used the
term the 'Looking-Glass Self' as a metaphor to describe the importance of the
social context in socializing the child such that he or she gains a sense of self
and conforms to the rules of the wider society. The idea which informs the
'Looking-Glass Self' is that in order to think of who 'I' am, I must be able to
reflect on myself as if I were someone else. In this way one can think of the
individual self as a form of social self. Cooley says that:

> 'a social self of this sort might be called the reflected or looking-glass self:
> Each to each a looking glass
> Reflects the other that doth pass.'

> 'As we see our face, our figure and dress in the glass, and are interested in them
> because they are ours, and pleased or otherwise with them according as they do,
> or do not answer to what we should like them to be; so in imagination we perceive
> in another's mind some thought of our appearance, manners, aims, deeds, char-
> acter, friends, and so on, and are variously affected by it.'   [Cooley, 1902: 183–4]

247

This suggests that part of the process of becoming a person consists of the **internalized other**. This means that interaction in a relationship involves putting yourself in someone else's shoes; internalizing involves learning to take the role of the other – we form images of ourselves based on our images of how significant others (parents, friends and the like) think of us.

Cooley's ideas were further developed by the sociologist George Herbert Mead (1936). Mead's theories were influential in the development of the sociological school of thought known as **symbolic interactionism**. This means that a person's self or identity is constructed on the basis of the interactions that the individual has with others and includes the ability of the child to take on the role of another. According to Mead, human individuals develop self-consciousness by learning to see themselves as others see them. He theorized that this process has its beginning when infants and young children start to imitate the actions of those around them. Imitation primarily takes place through play which ranges from simple imitation of the behaviour of adults, among others, to more complex games where the child takes on an adult role.

The ability of the child to take the role of others, by acting as if he or she were perhaps a 'parent', a 'teacher' or a 'nurse', allows the child to reflect on his or her own behaviour from someone else's point of view. This enables he or she to reflect on his or her own behaviour, which can be split into two components, the 'I' and the 'me'. It is this ability which, according to Mead, signals the beginnings of self-awareness in the child. The 'I' refers to the infant whose behaviour is mainly regulated by the demands of biology and consists of the spontaneous expression of wants. By contrast to this, the 'me' is the **social self**. The 'me' is that part of the self which is slowly built up by being able to take the 'I' as if it were someone else. For Mead (as for Freud), the child begins to see himself or herself as an autonomous agent capable of shared understanding and able to operate outside the immediate context of the family at around five years old. During the play stage, toys play a useful role in identity formation, from the kinetic mobiles which parents hang over the crib to the toys which older children use to take the role of the other. While children's imaginations require very little support for whatever role they wish to play, commodities such as pretend uniforms (nurses, doctors, firefighters), Barbie and Ken dolls, toy guns and cars and a wealth of other toys can act as props for such play. Mead theorized that following the play stage, the child then begins to learn more formal games. The difference between child's play and games such as tennis, cricket, baseball and soccer is that the latter are organized according to definite systems of rules which are more systematic than 'play'. Mead argues that it is not until children have passed through this **game stage** that they come to understand overall values and morality and to attain the concept of the **generalized other**. Objects are also important in contributing to the game stage of development. Consider for example the role played by the humble ball in a variety of 'ball' games. The ball is at once the simplest of things, which, within the context of the ball game, takes unique skill and perseverance to master, and those who are masters of these games become **role models** for the children who idolize them.

6.4 PSYCHOANALYTIC THEORY: IN-BETWEEN APPROACHES TO IDENTITY

Several theoretical approaches share the idea that both biology and the social context are important in shaping identity. First we consider the work of Sigmund Freud, another of those twentieth-century intellectual giants whose insight was to influence many of the theorists discussed in this book, not least the work of Norbert Elias whose work was discussed in Chapter 1.

6.4.1 Freud and psychoanalysis

Sigmund Freud's chosen topic was the human condition – how we come to 'be' someone – a subject of immense scope and one which provides formidable obstacles to our understanding. During the twentieth century his theories had a major impact on the study of psychology, linguistics and social theory. Like all great theorists, Freud has come in for his share of criticism; however his arguments still have a great deal of force, as his explanation accounts not only for the pervasive role played by biological instincts, but also for how we internalize the values of society and seek to manage the conflicts brought about between the demands of biology and society through attending to external reality. Freud's main contribution towards knowledge of self is thus to insist on its complexity: what we call the 'self' is the result of the resolution of a complex set of instinctual and social forces. Finally, Freud's theory illuminates the power of the unconscious in directing human thought and action.

6.4.1.1 Concepts of the self: id–ego–superego

Freud's theory is hydraulic in that energy plays a vitally important part in his explanation and provides a key role in understanding motivation. Energy is created by powerful instinctual forces which are produced within the **id**, which Freud likens to a huge reservoir of psychic energy, subject to the observance of the pleasure principle. According to Freud, biological instincts drive the production of energy according to two main principles over the life of the human subject: the life drive, **Eros**, and the death drive, **Thanatos**. Eros 'naturally' should prevail over the birth and growth phases of life, to be replaced as a person grows older by the equally pervasive power of Thanatos. During the period of the predominance of Eros, the instinctual drives push all behaviour in the direction of immediate gratification of biological life-giving needs, the instinctual drives of hunger and sex.

The powerful demand of the id for immediate satisfaction is progressively countered by an equally powerful force which only becomes internalized following the resolution of the Oedipus complex at adolescence. This internalized image of society is known as the **superego** which in the early years consists of parental control. Parents thus pass on their language, customs and cultural values to their children and these are subsequently internalized by the child following a period of struggle in adolescence. The third important aspect of the self is the **ego** which stands between the id and the super-ego. The ego has a fragile existence as it plays the role of arbitrator and mediator between the demands of biology and society by seeking to bring the influence of the external world to bear on the id. The ego thus aims to substitute the reality principle for the pleasure principle which governs the id.

How does the above relate to consumption behaviour? By providing an explanation of the dynamics underlying self-hood, psychoanalytic theory can help explain the role played by goods and services in the makeup of our selves. Put simply, Freud's theory offers an explanation which focuses on the investment of psychic energy (motive force) into consumer goods. Why do we invest such energy into consumer goods? In order to understand this question we need to explore the contradictory nature of the demands of biology and society and how these are partly resolved by means of consumption. Psychoanalytic theory suggests that often, in fact generally, we are unaware of the motives which govern our decisions, as these are largely unconscious. This in turn means that we must explore the importance of the unconscious in directing our thoughts and behaviour.

6.4.1.2   The preconscious and the unconscious

In *The Ego and the Id* (1961, orig. 1901), Freud made the distinction between the **preconscious** ideas which an individual can bring to consciousness almost at will, and **unconscious** thought which because of its disturbing nature is not easily made conscious although it still may indirectly influence behaviour. Freud posited that people may consciously censor and repress, displace or project such threatening ideas. **Repression** is a form of ego defence whereby images which are thought of as being disturbing are shut out of consciousness. As an instance of *repression*, Freud offers the case history of 'Anna O'. Despite the summer heat, Anna refused to drink water. She often raised the glass to her lips only to repel it with an air of disgust. No-one, including Anna herself, knew of the source of this sudden malady. It was only several days later when under hypnosis that Anna revealed that she had gone into someone else's room and had seen a dog drinking out of a glass and how she had felt revulsion and disgust at the sight. Once she had described this, Anna felt better and was soon able to drink. Freud's explanation of Anna's predicament was that this image had so revolted Anna's sensibilities that she had unconsciously repressed all knowledge of the scene and had converted this repressed disgust into a phobia concerning drinking. By contrast to repression, **displacement** occurs when an unconscious impulse is redirected towards a more acceptable target. Displacement can take many forms, but that which is of most interest from a consumer behaviour point of view is called **sublimation**. Sublimation involves the displacement of sexual energy, known as **libido**, to non-sexual ends in a manner which not only avoids conflict but which actively promotes a person's adjustment to his or her social context. Oriented towards the **reality principle**, the ego plays a key role in sublimating id demands by channelling id energy away from the pure investment in immediate gratification demanded by the **pleasure principle** (associated with id impulses) towards a more socially acceptable response. The ego thus plays a key role in sublimating (channelling) desire towards socially acceptable means of expression. A 'Freudian' explanation would thus suggest that within western European culture, consumer goods play an ever increasing role in sublimating those desires expressed by Eros. It is important to note that Freud's idea of 'sexuality' is different from that used generally. For Freud, libido is essentially a drive whose object is the stimulation of various bodily areas or **erotogenic zones**. In order to understand this we need to discuss briefly what Freud means by sexual energy and the developmental process by which this is attained.

6.4.1.3 Sexuality and development

Freud theorized that Eros is composed of ego and sexual instincts. While survival depends on fairly immediate gratification of ego instincts, **libido** or sexual energy is infinitely more malleable. Freud's theory is developmental to the extent that he seeks to explain how the needs of children change as they grown older. According to this theory, children pass through a number of stages of development on their passage towards adulthood and at each stage a different **erotogenic zone** becomes the focus for sexual energy. Either excessive gratification or frustration of this desire will have major consequences for the individual in later life. This will help to determine not only the style of the child's sexual satisfaction in later life but also his or her personality and emotional character. If the child receives too much or too little gratification during a particular stage, this creates anxiety which may result in a fixation on this zone; in adulthood such a person may even regress to this stage of development as the result of some trauma.

Oral stage

In the first year of life, the mouth of the child is the zone of interest and the breast of the mother (or its substitute) is the object of interest. The child obtains most gratification from sucking and when teeth develop, pleasure comes from biting. If the mother responds by either over or under gratifying the demands of the child, then the child may develop great tension and anxiety about feeding. This anxiety may reach intolerable levels, at which stage the ego may act to repress the impulses which are responsible for this tension. Because the ego must expend large amounts of energy in repressing this anxiety, it may eventually develop as a fragile and weak entity. When the child develops into an adult it is likely that the oral zone will be a source of fascination and of anxiety. In focusing on the mouth the adult may experience pleasure and guilt in engaging in oral activities such as smoking, drinking or perhaps a preoccupation with the preparation and consumption of food. However a severe trauma such as the death of a relative may so stretch the resources of the ego that it can no longer contain the repressed anxieties of childhood which return in full force. This can result in a neurotic disorder where the adult regresses back to the oral stage and may exhibit a range of disorders associated with eating.

Anal stage

The next phase which lasts from around one year old to the age of three is the anal phase. By this time the child's sphincter control has reached the point where he or she can take pleasure in holding onto or letting go of bodily wastes. Freud's theory suggests that adults who are fixated at the anal stage may well develop as adults the character traits which reflect his or her difficulties in resolving this stage. Such adults may develop an obsessive regard for order and cleanliness, value hoarding and saving, and have a stubborn nature.

Phallic stage

The phallic stage, which lasts between three and five years of age, culminates in the emotional crisis known as the **Oedipus complex**. Prior to the Oedipus complex (named after the famous Greek myth), both boys and girls identify with their mother. Boys see their father as a rival for the mother's affections but come to fear the power of the father. Their terror of the father becomes so great that eventually the boy splits his affections away from the mother and identifies himself with the father. It is by means of such an identification that the boy child achieves a male identity. In identifying with the father and **introjecting**, or internalizing, the father's values, the boy develops a new structure, the **superego**, or conscience, which replaces the external control that his parents exercised over him. The transition for girls is not so simple. Girls seek to identify with the father and come to see the mother as a rival for his affections; however the girl's physical resemblance to the mother means that she cannot physically identify with the father or with his power. As a result Freud thought that the development of the female superego was a more difficult process. Those who become fixated at the phallic stage become obsessed with power and those things which symbolize power. For example this may be expressed through the purchase of products which are recognized as signifying prestige and power – anything from powerful sports cars to expensive watches or the latest technological toys. In recent years, women executives who mimic male dress codes in businesses (for example by wearing suits which have jackets with wide shoulders) and sometimes even shirts and ties have acquired the label 'power dressers'.

Following the phallic stage there is a period of quiescence known as **latency** which may last between five years of age and puberty. The beginnings of adult sexuality are observed in the **genital period** when the individual's self-love, or **narcissism**, becomes channelled into the love of others.

What can we learn from Freud in terms of the role which goods play in people's lives? Firstly the id is the source of all true needs, providing the energy and motive force for the demand for need satisfaction. The id demands satisfaction in line with the requirements of Eros, the life drive. We are motivated to satisfy directly those needs for hunger and thirst and safety which are directly linked to survival. The sex drive is another major motive force which demands satisfaction. However within Freud's explanation this comes into conflict with the restraining force of the superego which, in its capacity as a proxy for 'civilized' society, reins in the desire for direct sexual satisfaction and replaces such actions with others which are more socially acceptable. In a consumer society, one outlet for the sublimation of sexual desire is through the purchase of consumer goods and services.

During the course of his life, Freud oscillated between two different theories of the ego: the realist and the narcissistic views. Each view has gathered to itself a range of followers. The **realist** view of the ego has generally influenced the US psychoanalytic tradition, while the **narcissistic** view has had a great deal of influence in France. The next two sections introduce and discuss those theories which are most closely related to each of the foregoing views of the ego. First, the realist view of the ego is illustrated with reference to the work of Erik Erikson, who was the first to speak of the concept of identity. Erikson's work is further illustrated with reference to his concept of 'identity crisis' and the life-cycle. The work of a number of different authors is discussed with respect to the view of the narcissistic ego. Most famous among these theorists is Jacques Lacan, whose work is still most influential in this field. The discussion of Lacan is accompanied by reference to the work of Csikszentmihalyi and Rochberg-Halton (1995, orig. 1981), who discussed the meaning of domestic symbols to people, among others.

6.4.2 The realist ego

In this view the **ego** is portrayed as an agency which mediates in the conflict between the endogenous demands of biology, the powerful life-force of Eros which is expressed through the **id**, and the exogenous demands of social reality which are represented by the **superego**. Thus one can picture the ego as being bound by both forces which seek to pull it in different directions. In describing the relation of the ego to the id, Freud likened this to the rider of a powerful horse who must skilfully guide it if he is not to be thrown.

The realist ego faces two ways at the same time as it seeks to effect a rational compromise between the demands of two masters – the 'unreasonable' demands of the id for immediate gratification on the one hand, and the demands of society for restraint on the other hand. With respect to the internal id functions, the ego is a moderating force which seeks to represent the demands of social reality. With respect to the social reality, its aim is to rationalize and justify many of the id's demands.

In this view, the ego is a more or less stable agency which can be equated with the 'self'. It acts to moderate the demands of the pleasure-seeking id and at the same time to influence the id in accordance with the dictates of the reality principle. This view of the ego has become associated with 'orthodox' psychoanalysis which aims to create an ego that is strong enough to cope with the demands of these two powerful masters.

6.4.2.1 Realist views of the ego: Erik Erikson

To a large extent we are subjected to identity; we are born as a male or female, into a family, a community, perhaps a religion, and a nationality. At the same time we tend to identify with the identities on offer. Erik Erikson, who was the first to begin to write about this subject, describes identity as all pervasive yet difficult to grasp because it is a process 'located in the *core of the individual* yet also in the *core of the communal culture*' (Erikson, 1968: 22). He became interested in identity while working with soldiers who had lost a sense of personal and sometimes historical continuity as the result of war, where he became convinced that a sense of **ego-identity**, or sense of self, was not something which was immutable or given to someone at birth, but malleable, an entity which could be changed or even lost. These feelings were reinforced when he then explored what he was later to call **the identity crisis** in the young. By contrast to the soldiers whose identity confusion had an external cause, Erikson felt that the identity confusion in the young was due rather to 'a war within themselves, and in confused rebels and delinquents who war upon society' (Erikson, 1968: 17). You should note the resonance between this explanation and that put forward by Elias (1994) – that conflict which had at one time been freely and openly expressed, comes to be progressively contained within the self (1968: 17).

Erikson's theory of identity is based on Freud's later writings which focus on the **realist ego**. Erikson describes this approach poetically as: 'The mob without, the id within, The fearful ego in between'. Within this explanation the superego refers to the internalization of all of the restrictions to which the child must bow. As the child grows older, so he or she moves away from narcissism (naive self-love) and looks for role models by which to measure himself/herself, seeking happiness in trying to resemble these role models.

As we shall see later, Erikson follows in the Freudian tradition in believing that there is nothing given or essential about the nature of identity; in other words, biology has little to do with it. For example if we were to take gender identity, while we might agree that men and women may be generally differentiated on the basis of biological characteristics which define 'male' and 'female' (see note iii), 'masculine' and 'feminine' gender identities are to a large extent socially constructed. Gender identities are marked out according to cultural conventions or codes, for example dress codes, a codified division of labour and codes relating to the 'appropriate' consumption of food, to name a few. Erikson's theory of identity is non-essentialist, as he reasons that different forms of **cultural consolidation** call for the construction of different identities:

'To put it in terms of what must be studied concertedly: in every technology and at every historical period there are types of individuals who ("properly" brought up) can combine the dominant techniques with their identity development and become what they do. Independently of minor superiorities or inferiorities they can settle on that cultural consolidation which secures them what joint verification and what transitory salvation lies in doing things together and in doing them "right", a righteousness proven by the bountiful response of "nature" whether in the form of prey bagged, the food harvested, the good produced, the money made, or the technology problems solved.'   [1968: 32]

The cultural consolidation thus refers to the collective culture by which human society works to attune itself to the rhythms of nature and to transform it. This work involves a myriad of daily tasks and ritualized transactions (sowing, planting, harvesting, exchange, cooking) which together offer the co-ordinates for a range of identity formations. However a key aspect of identity is **difference**; we are identical (the same as) those who are of 'us' and this makes us different from those who are 'other' to 'us' – 'them'. Humankind is divided into a number of groupings on the basis of tribe, religion or class. Each group believes that it alone is *the* human species and that all others are strange or even freakish. These strangers are regarded as the negative identities which provide the counterpoint to positive identity.

Erikson's definition of **ego identity** stresses the relation between the social and the individual:

'What I have called Ego identity then, in its subjective aspect, is the awareness of the fact that there is a self-sameness and continuity to the ego's synthesising methods, the style of one's individuality and that this style coincides with the sameness and continuity of one's meaning for significant others in the community.'   [1968: 50]

Identity is thus an expression of feeling the same as, at one with or at home with, some people who recognize us as being the same as them with respect to one or more characteristics and with whom we identify on the basis of those characteristics. This common identification differentiates us from others who share and who identify with other characteristics. Thus identity has two faces: one which moves from the outside-in, by which society provides us with the bases for identity formation and also seeks to verify this; the other which is inside-out, the process by which we actively seek to identify with others. He was concerned to chart the dynamic way in which the ego evolves in confronting and resolving a number of crises (eight in all), as the person gets older. Erikson theorized that the ego confronts eight different crises as the person ages through the life-cyle. While the different factors which make up each of the crises are present all of the time, Erikson argued that particular crises confront the ego at different times. The eight crises which take place between infancy and maturity are shown in Figure 6.5.

Stage 1: Infancy (trust vs mistrust). Erikson argued that the earliest crisis involves the infant learning to trust his or her caregivers as well as developing a fundamental sense of his or her own trustworthiness. Like Freud, Erikson theorized that young infants are primarily driven by **oral** and incorporative tendencies. The body of the child is receptive, in all sorts of ways:

Infancy	Early childhood	Play age	School age	Adolescence	Young adult	Adult	Mature age

Integrity vs Despair

Generativity vs Stagnation

Intimacy vs Isolation

Identity vs Identity confusion

Industry vs Inferiority

Initiative vs Guilt

Autonomy vs Shame

Trust vs Mistrust

Figure 6.5   Erikson's stages in the development of personality [adapted from Erikson, 1968: 94]

being picked up if it cries, being fed if it is hungry. Trust builds as the result of the development of harmony and mutual recognition between caregiver and child. The period of weaning may be particularly difficult as this loss of the mother's breast may be interpreted as rejection, the loss of mother love. Erikson notes that even where weaning is relatively trouble free, the child comes to feel that he or she is divided or split, and develops a form of nostalgia for a lost paradise (1968: 101).

Stage 2: Early childhood (autonomy vs shame). Erikson's next stage is linked to Freud's **anal** stage, which occurs when the dependent child begins to experience free-will. Freud had initially thought that the idea of autonomy was strongly linked to the child's developing ability to control sphincter operations, by 'holding onto' and 'letting go' of faeces. Erikson argues that once more culture plays a role as some cultures insist that the child must be trained, while others are less prescriptive. The successful resolution of this stage is very important for the development of a sense of autonomy, which Erikson argues is dependent on the development of a sense of self-control without the loss of self-esteem. If the parent focuses overmuch on training and control, this may result in a loss of self-control by the child and a lasting propensity for doubt and shame. Shame supposes that one is completely exposed and conscious of being looked at. If this stage is not satisfactorily resolved, this may result in compulsive behaviour, resulting in a personality type who is stingy, retentive, meticulous in matters of money and affection as well as in the management of his or her bowels.

Stage 3: Play age (initiative vs guilt). This stage, which begins towards the end of the third year, involves the child finding out about what sort of person he or she might become. This is equivalent to the **phallic stage**, discussed by Freud, where the child fixes on a particular gender identity. The child builds on the developing sense of autonomy which he or she discovered during the second stage, and begins to learn about himself/herself as a person by acting out the roles of authority figures such as parents. This is similar to George Herbert Mead's game stage, which we discussed earlier. The crisis which the child must resolve at this stage is that of initiative versus guilt. He or she uses initiative in taking up various different roles; however this also leads to feelings of guilt that the role is not really his/hers to take.

Stage 4: School age (industry vs inferiority). While at school, the child learns to be industrious and participates in full-time education. However this is where he or she becomes aware that others may be better at formal school activities and in formal games and so may come to feel a sense of inferiority, that he or she will never be any good. During this period Erikson felt that the influence of parents and home lessened and the child began to be shaped more fully by the wider culture and in particular by the peer group. The child's success or failure in resolving this crisis has very important consequences for what happens during adolescence.

Stage 5: Adolescence (identity vs identity confirm). From the play age the child has developed an unlimited imagination of what he or she might become. According to Erikson, identity itself finds its point of crisis during adolescence. During this period the self becomes independent of the family. If the earlier stages are not resolved sufficiently then the seeds for **identity confusion** are sown. The adolescent may become extremely self-conscious, dwelling on the difference between his or her self-esteem and the way in which he or she is perceived by others. Erikson feels that this is a form of reliving the doubt of early childhood. Alternatively, an adolescent who has not successfully resolved the crisis of the play age, by being able to master different roles, may fix on a self-defeating role by dropping out, and become fixed at adolescence within a self-defeating role such as an indolent student, addict or delinquent. This is an attempt to create a negative identity by seeking to become everything that the young person has learned ought to be avoided. Identity confusion is experienced by virtually all adolescents who feel unsure of who they are: 'to keep themselves together they temporarily overidentify with the heroes of cliques and crowds to the point of an apparently complete loss of individuality'.

> 'On the other hand clarification can be sought by destructive means. Young people may become remarkably clannish, intolerant and cruel in their exclusion of others who are "different" in skin colour or cultural background, in tastes and gifts, and often in entirely petty aspects of dress and gesture arbitrarily selected as the signs of an in-grouper or an out-grouper.' [1968: 132]

Such intolerance is a form of defence against identity loss. Adolescence is a period of intense physiological change involving heightened hormonal activity and rapid change in the size and proportions of the body. Erikson believed that by forming cliques and viewing the world in stereotypical ways, adolescents were able to create structures which helped them through this difficult period and which also allowed them to test each others' loyalties in the midst of conflicts of values.

Stage 6: Young adult (intimacy vs isolation). The next major crisis is that of intimacy. Erikson contends that true intimacy is possible only when identity formation is well underway. When a young adult who is not sure of his or her identity shies away from interpersonal intimacy, this may result in a deep sense of isolation; he or she will never really feel himself or herself, although everyone reminds him or her that he or she is a somebody. Intimacy is the ability to fuse with another, to expand the self. The counterpoint of intimacy is distantiation – the readiness to repudiate and if necessary destroy those whose essence seems to be dangerous to one's own.

Stage 7: Adult (generativity vs stagnation). According to Erikson, the adult needs to be needed. Generativity is primarily a concern to establish and to guide the next generation. 'The ability to lose oneself in the meeting of bodies and minds leads to a general expansion of ego-interests and to a libidinal investment in this which is being generated!' (1968: 138). Where this fails, there is regression to a form of pseudo intimacy accompanied by a sense of stagnation and boredom. People treat each others as if they were their own or one another's child.

Stage 8: Mature age (integrity vs despair). The ageing person who has taken care of things and people and who has adapted himself/herself to the triumphs and disappointments of being, the originator of other people and the generator of things and ideas – only in him or her does the fruit of the seven stages ripen into integrity, the ego's assurance of order and meaning: a person who can defend the dignity of his or her lifestyle against others. The lack of this integrity is disgust or despair, a feeling that life cannot be lived over again, of a wasted life.

The identity crisis

Erikson charts the points of crises which occur in a person's identity formation as they negotiate the life-cycle from infancy to maturity. Within this view, life is portrayed as a project, identity as a means of development from one stage to another until at maturity the adult is content and truly integrated. The identity crisis takes place in adolescence. Drawing on Elias (1994) it is not difficult to understand why this might be a time of identity confusion. The child becomes an adult physiologically. However in consumer societies this transition to adulthood is not marked by culture to the extent that it is in more traditional societies. In traditional societies, boys and girls often pass through what are known as **rites of passage**, where the transition to adulthood is marked by formal and often brutal ceremonies in which the insignia of adulthood are often tattooed onto the skin. While a birthday party at age eighteen or twenty marks the transition, these are pale imitations of the traditional rites.

Marketing and the life-cycle

Marketers have been aware of the life-cycle for many years and this has been incorporated by many organizations into their arsenal of segmentation devices. Financial institutions aim to capture their customers early and to maintain their loyalty to the grave. The marketing offers changes through the life-cycle from the early years, when savings are encouraged, to the lean years of student-life (overdrafts and loans); from the demands of the 'full nest' (mortgages, life-insurance, pensions) to investment and remortgage products which are targeted towards 'empty-nesters', whose children have left home. Tesco, one of the UK's leading supermarkets, produces different versions of its magazine for different lifestage groups. The life-cycle data are used in conjunction with affluence, frequency of visits, the value placed on premium lines and brand purchase. Additionally, many organizations focus on just one segment of the life-cycle.[3]

One of the most intensive areas of research and product development for firms has been the start of the life-cycle, where increasing attention is being paid to issues such as brand recognition and advertising effectiveness among infants and young children. This is not entirely concerned with influencing the 'pester power' of the child to influence parental decision-making. Children are important purchasers in their own right of products such as toys, stationery, comics and magazines, computer games, videos, sports equipment and clothes. It has been claimed that in the UK, children as young as two and three years of age are targets of brand marketers, most notoriously those who market cigarettes and alcohol. One reason given for targeting young children is because the young mind is especially retentive of information and any information, including that pertaining to brand identity, and symbolism will be retained for life if the associations are learned young enough. Critics suggest that while young children may know what an ad is, they will not know much about the purpose of advertising until they are much older. This is the approach taken in the Nordic countries where advertising towards children under the age of twelve is banned by law (see note iv). However, as some commentators point out, a ban on advertising may not be particularly effective in preventing brand messages being seen by children, who can plainly make brand associations for alcohol and cigarettes via the clothing of football heroes and Formula One aces. On the other hand some claim that children as young as seven and eight are nowadays as sophisticated as teenagers of old, leading to the creation of a new and monstrous 'tweenie' category, which is relentlessly targeted by marketers.

Erikson's portrayal of the life-cycle promotes a traditional view of the ageing process in that a person increases in integrity, knowledge and respect as he or she becomes older. This has generally been accepted in traditional cultures. In the UK, until comparatively recently 'Victorian' values prevailed – children were to be 'seen and not heard' and were expected to show respect to 'their elders and betters'. This is still the case in many mainland European countries and in Asia and Africa. But is this necessarily true in a consumer society? In Chapter 1 we outlined Stuart Ewen's (1976) argument that

DBS Arts Library

---

[3] Bounty provides samples of baby products together with product information to mothers. Mothercare has segmented the child market into six segments towards which it targets different product offerings. Products for mothers of new-born children are soft and pastel-coloured, in contrast to the more robust and rich colours offered to mothers of two-year-olds. At the other end of the continuum, Saga offers a range of travel and financial services to the 'grey' market.

consumer culture idealizes images of youth, fitness and beauty lifestyles and not of venerable old-age. As a result, 'old' loses its value and anything which is perceived to be old becomes stigmatized.

6.4.3 The narcissistic ego

The image which the realist ego calls most readily to mind is that of an arbitrator which is stable, solid and separate from the two warring parties, the id and the superego. To appreciate fully the idea of the narcissistic ego, we must entirely discard this typology and distinction, for the narcissistic ego is based on a quite different set of premises. The most appropriate metaphor to describe the **narcissistic ego** is a river which has been dammed to form a large lake, and which contains a fixed amount of water. Freud conceived of the narcissistic ego as a storehouse of a fixed amount of **libido**, or psychic energy. Libidinal tributaries flow out of this reservoir as psychic energy is invested into external objects, including its own body. Similarly, energy is absorbed back from those objects from which energy has been withdrawn.

The dependence of the ego's libidinal investment of energy into external objects may be illustrated with respect to two examples – love and mourning. When a person falls in love, the ego invests libido into the love-object (teddy bear, pet, man, woman, car) and the level in the reservoir of ego–libido falls. The process of falling in love risks the safety of the ego (the reservoir has been lowered). However if the love is reciprocated, the ego is replenished with energy proceeding from the beloved (in most accounts, one speaks of the ego investing energy and of this being reinvested). A happy balance between projection and introjection occurs. However when the beloved does not return the love, the unrequited love for the other severely lowers feelings of self-regard or self-worth. At its most extreme, for example in the case of the death or loss of the beloved, the ego goes through an intense process of mourning. In this account, mourning is the gradual process of disinvesting, of gradually reclaiming back all the energy that a person has invested in the lost teddy bear, the dead animal, the lover who scorns us, the wrecked car or the dead spouse. The process of disinvestment and reinvestment back into the self is painful, arduous and often very slow.

There are several differences between the realist ego and the narcissistic ego. While the definition of the realist ego is clear-cut to the extent that it stands between the two combatants (id and superego), the narcissistic ego cannot be separated from its own internal processes, nor from any other object. The realist ego is taken to be self-contained, but the narcissistic ego is dependent upon a person's relations with others. In fact some authors suggest that our very sense of identity, of self, is not at all innate but is conditioned by the ways in which others have treated us as if we have a coherent self. Perhaps the most important distinction lies in that between the mediation role played by the realist ego and the investment role played by the narcissistic ego. The former invites us to think of the ego as if it were rational, reasonable and self-contained. On the other hand the idea that the ego invests energy into a series of people and other objects, including its own body, paints a quite different picture.

6.4.3.1   The narcissistic ego: Jacques Lacan

In order to understand the Lacanian position, one must first accept Freud's contention that the individual's sense of self is not given but is constituted by the interaction between a complex set of forces. Lacan substantially reworked Freud's theory of the constitution of the human subject, placing semiotics and language at the centre of his theory.

Lacan belonged to a movement of artists and intellectuals (known as Dada) who were troubled by the destructive power played by images in society. One must remember that this was just after the First World War which had resulted in the slaughter of millions. Lacan's group felt that those who died had been lured by an image (of national glorification) which had led to profound misery and destruction. Roger Caillois, who belonged to this group, argued that biology supported such a view. His work focused on the **mimetic** or imitative strategy of the preying mantis, which seeks to adapt itself perfectly to the image of its environment. Caillois further argued that the mantis's strategy is maladaptive and destructive; sometimes the insect is mistakenly eaten by one of its own kind or alternatively it cannot be recognized by members of its own kind during the mating season. Caillois argued that the mimicry of the mantis amounts to a kind of insectoid psychosis. Like Caillois, Lacan became convinced that the tendency among humans to model their identities upon images is fundamentally destructive.

Lacan's doctoral thesis included a study of Aimée, a railway clerk who 'inexplicably' attacked one of the best known actresses in Paris and wounded her with a knife. Aimée, who had never personally met the actress, had literary ambitions but these had constantly been thwarted. According to Lacan, Aimée attacked an **ideal-image** of the other woman whom, in Aimée's mind, led a life of freedom and power which Aimée could never enjoy.

Lacan placed the destructive power of the image at the heart of his theory of identity. Like Freud, he theorized that the child is not born with an identity but that this is acquired as the result of an interaction between the child and his or her environment. Lacan also thought that the identity of the child develops through a succession of stages. However these stages are in many respects quite different from those described by Freud.

6.4.3.2   Lacan's theory of development

Lacan's theory of development concerns the relations between three orders, which we may think of as stages: the order of the **real** lasts from birth up to 6 months; the **imaginary**, from 6 months to 18 months; while the **symbolic**, which is the period of the acquisition of language, proceeds from the imaginary stage. Lacan refers to these as orders and not stages, because in his theory adults oscillate between the imaginary and the symbolic throughout their lives.

Figure 6.6   The infant in 'bits and pieces' in the order of the real

The order of the **real,** which is illustrated in Figure 6.6, is the state in which infants exist from the moment of birth to around 18 months. It is difficult for us to imagine but, at birth, infants have very little control over their limbs and may confuse parts of their mother, such as the breast, with their own limbs. Lacan ironically refers to the very young infant as an (h)omellete, to suggest that at this stage the infant spills out in all directions. The reference to this as the 'real' phase indicates that the infant is immersed in nature and has not emerged into the cultural order. At this point in time the child has no capacity for any form of symbolism or language, and has developed no 'ego', but exists purely in the realm of the id. In this sense, Lacan argued that it is only within the realm of the real that it is possible to say that a child has true needs. Later, once the child acquires the ability for representation and language, all needs become mediated through the medium of culture and so can no longer be considered to be real or innate.

The **imaginary** stage represents a profound change for infants. While they lack motor co-ordination and feel that they are in bits and pieces, those adults who care for them treat them as if they were whole, coherent, in control, in other words as if they were individuals. Through time, either as the result of this treatment or perhaps even literally as the result of looking into a mirror and thinking 'that's me!', the infant comes to identify with this masterful image. This moment of recognition is shown in Figure 6.7. It may be that the child really does all at once look into a mirror and think 'that's me!' which is the kind of dramatic moment shown in Figure 6.7. Alternatively, and more likely, is the case that this happens over a period of time. For Lacan, this identification with an image has implications which are as deadly for the human being as they are for the mantis studied by Caillois.

Figure 6.7 Identification with image in the mirror stage: jubilation and emptiness

In fact Lacan refers to this as a moment of **misrecognition**. This is because the image appears to be powerful, whole, complete, and with a sense of control that is almost entirely lacking in his or her bodily co-ordination and movement. The child believes that the image which is whole, complete and in control really is 'me'. However, in a profound way the image is *not* 'me' as the child experiences inside none of the mastery and control displayed in the image. The child wants to believe that the image is 'me' for another reason – inside something seems to be missing. There is a sense of emptiness and loss. Why is this destructive? We need to think back to Caillois. Like the mantis, the child has identified with an image which is external to himself or herself. The image seems to be whole, unified and in control. However inside the child still feels that he or she is in bits and pieces, is split, and is not in control. Simultaneously, with the joy of self-discovery comes an overwhelming sense of loss, the loss of something fundamental that was always there (the mother) but which is now missing. The new ego which has formed is ambivalent, with feelings of mastery and control on the one hand which are associated with the new sense of self based on the mirror image, and of simultaneous incompleteness as the result of loss of the mother. From now on the child's self-concept will never match up to his or her sense of being.

As we shall see shortly, Lacan believes that the identification of the child with the mirror image is very important with respect to the construction of human identity, and that it is also destructive. It is an important moment because it signifies not just the beginning of the establishment of identity, but also represents the origin of language in the child. Lacan theorizes that the idea 'that's me' is evidence of conceptual development. In order to think 'that's me', the child must have a concept 'that is me'. For Lacan, this evidence of conceptual development is the first sign that the child has the ability to gain access to the set of symbols that constitute language.

The **symbolic** refers to the cultural tradition that the child is born into, where an identity is to a large extent already mapped out for him or for her. For example if the child is biologically a girl then in the UK people will have bought pink clothes, which will later be replaced by dolls and other toys which seek to build a feminine-gender identity. If the child is a boy, gifts are likely to be coloured blue and will be consistent with the development of a masculine identity. Parents and caregivers participate in this socialization of the child into 'appropriate' roles. Lacan argues that following the mirror stage, the child is torn between feelings of lack and emptiness (as the connection in the real with the mother has been lost forever), and attempts to counter this by snatching at images which bolster the ego or sense of self, in a bid to regain those feelings of power and control when he or she first gazed into the mirror. The child and the developing adult are thus haunted by an emptiness, a hole which seems to be at the very centre of their being. This emptiness becomes the basis of a powerful demand for the hole to be filled up, a desire for the reconnection to the real, and to the undivided love and attention of the mother. This desire can never be fulfilled. The child and later the developing adult are thus motivated by feelings of emptiness and powerlessness, snatching at images to regain a fleeting glimpse of mastery and control.

6.4.3.3 Lacan: consumption and identity

How does Lacan's theory help us to understand relations between consumption marketing and identity? In the first place, Lacan believes that the self is formed partially as the result of the investment of energy into an ideal-image, an image which suggests that the subject is coherent, autonomous and in control. For most of the time we live in a world where we are divided by culture into a set of diverse identities that reinforce feelings of being split – of ethnicity, of gender, and of many other types that reinforce feelings of loss. But what is the source of this coherent sense of self. The self is formed through energy which is produced as the result of lack or desire – but where does this energy come from? It comes from lack, from a desire for unity, for reintegration with the mother. The self is empty – it is filled up with things. But this desire can never be satisfied.

Many authors have used Lacan's theory as a basis to construct their critique of consumer society and in particular the media and advertising industries. The basis of the argument is that the media bombard consumers with idealized and unattainable images of control, mastery, beauty, perfection and youth, which are snatched at eagerly by those who consume them and who use them to shore up their fragile and battered 'egos'. However the ultimate aim of the entire enterprise, to almost literally climb back into the womb of the mother, is impossible. The quest for wholeness and identity is thus revealed to be illusory and a sham, with modern-day 'Don Quixotes' armouring themselves with brand-names such as Ralph Lauren, Paco Rabanne, Chanel, Matanique, Lacoste, Ferrari, Adidas, Martini, Rolex and Calvin Klein in a futile bid to be 'themselves'.

Judith Williamson (1978) draws upon Lacan to argue that advertising is ideological as ads **interpellate** individuals through the promise of false wholeness. Lacan's theory also informs that of Pasi Falk (1994), which is discussed in more detail in Chapter 9. Teresa Brennan (1993) goes further in arguing that in the quest for an image of authenticity, mastery and control through the consumption of goods, the modern consumer ego seeks to convert all living nature into its own image. She maintains that the consumers' voracious consumption is dangerous not only to living nature which is being consumed at an unsustainable rate, but ultimately threatens the survival of humanity. The search for authenticity, the 'real thing', recalls the moment of misrecognition in the mirror stage. The constant preoccupation with the 'real thing', which sometimes stretches into an obsession, is evidenced at every level of consumer society. You will recall that in Chapter 5 (section 5.8.1) we discussed Umberto Eco's (1986) view of this. One might add to this the observation made by Holt (1998), discussed earlier in this chapter, that the search for uniqueness and authenticity is an important aspect of the HCC consumption lifestyle. Additionally Belk and Costa's fascinating study of the 'mountain-man' myth as a compelling consuming fantasy in the USA mentions the quest for authenticity as an important motivator for those consumers who seek to relive the 'mountain-man' lifestyle (1998: 234).

6.5   THE EXTENSION OF SELF

Other authors have explored the ways in which people construct a sense of self or identity by investing in images and in objects. In their book entitled *The Meaning of Things*, Mihaly Csikszentmihalyi and Eugene Rochberg-Halton (1995, orig. 1981) sought to understand how individuals in the USA relate to things in their immediate environment and in particular to explore the role played by objects in a person's self-definition. In pursuing this goal they adopted Freud's idea of the investment of psychic energy as being central to their explanation. Their theory is eclectic in integrating the work of others which has been reshaped into their own contribution towards the understanding of identity.

In considering what a 'person' might be they focused on the self as something which is **cultivated** in the service of **goals**. The idea of cultivation resists the idea that the self is intrinsic and unchanging, as exemplified in the idea of the 'real me'. Instead of this fixed view, the authors put forward a conception of the self which is malleable, shaped by social forces and by the **investments** people make. Thus in the process of cultivating or making the self, energy is invested into other people, animals or things:

'Cultivation is a psychic activity that is only possible because humans are able to focus their attention selectively in the pursuit of goals. Because attention is the medium through which intentional acts can be accomplished, it is convenient to think of it as "psychic energy".' [1995, orig. 1981: 4]

Attention is a precious resource as at any given moment we are incapable of focusing on more than a few bits of information at a time. It takes effort to concentrate, as you can probably recall from your own experience. Think of how often your attention 'drifts' or 'wanders' when you are reading a newspaper or listening to a friend telling you a story. Like Lacan, Csikszentmihalyi and Rochberg-Halton theorized that a person's 'self' could be determined by the manner in which attention, this limited psychic energy, is invested. They felt that some of the ways in which a person might invest attention would vary in relation to chance factors, for instance inherited characteristics and the circumstances of birth. Nevertheless people pay attention to what they want to within a social context. The social system is also important within Csikszentmihalyi and Rochberg-Halton's scheme, as attention is directed towards others within social systems which may be considered to be shared structures of attention. Social systems survive by structuring the attention of individuals in particular ways. The structuring of attention is achieved by means of a process called **socialization**, which is the means by which individual goals are reordered in line with those of society. Thus the key aspect of the theory is that by the cultivation of goals through the investment of limited attention, within a social system, individuals become persons.

6.5.1 Extending the self into objects

One very important aspect of the theory is that when psychic energy is invested in an object, the object itself becomes fuelled with this energy:

'When someone invests psychic energy in an object – a thing, another person, or an idea – that object becomes "charged" with the energy of the agent. For example if a person works at a task, a certain amount of his or her attention is invested in that task, thus that invested energy is "lost" because the agent was unable to use that attention for other purposes.' [1995, orig. 1981: 4]

Within this view, the energy which is extended into other people and things literally infuses those people and those things with a part of 'us'. When we invest psychic energy into a person or an object we invest a part of our life into it. As a result, who 'we' are also changes. The process of childhood into adolescence represents a process of separation from the family and the creation of an individual identity. Csikszentmihalyi and Rochberg-Halton found that different kinds of objects meant different things to those from different generations:

'One of the few sibling pairs we interviewed consisted of a 12-year-old girl and her 15-year-old brother. Both children independently mentioned the refrigerator as being special, but for quite different reasons. The young girl said that when she felt unhappy all she had to do was go into the kitchen, open the refrigerator and she would already feel better at the thought of being able to fix herself a snack. The boy, on the other hand, said that the refrigerator gave him a good feeling because when his friends came over to visit he could open it and treat them to food and drink.'   [1995, orig. 1981: 98]

The authors offer the above as an example of the young girl being primarily self-oriented, in viewing the refrigerator as a means of satisfying her own individual needs. In contrast her older brother expands the self outwards in considering how the refrigerator can create social bonds. However, as adolescents mature so the relation with commodities changes. Youth tends to value objects which are associated with action and experience, for example musical instruments, sports equipment, pets and vehicles. Stereos are considered as being important not for their intrinsic value, but as a means to the end of listening to music. The boundaries of the self extend or expand outwards as energy is invested in friendships and partnerships such as marriage, so that others (husband, wife, children) become assimilated into the self-concept (1995, orig. 1981: 101). Whereas children tended to focus very much on experiencing objects in relation to their individual self, older people cherish objects which link them to others and which recall memories. Objects such as paintings and photographs are particularly valued as vehicles for contemplation. The authors castigate those government agencies on which caregivers are advised to house older people in 'uncluttered rooms with the bare minimum of objects and furniture'. They argue that such advice is fundamentally wrongheaded as it ignores the importance of such objects for maintaining a sense of personal continuity and meaning in an otherwise impersonal environment.

If possessions can be regarded as part of the self, then an unintentional loss of possessions should be regarded as a loss or lessening of self. Goffman (1961) discusses how institutions such as mental hospitals, homes for the aged and prisons seek to strip away a person's identity by systematically depriving them of all personal possessions such as clothing and money. If one considers Csikszentmihalyi and Rochberg-Halton's view that our 'selves' are constructed in proportion to the amount of psychic energy which we invest, then we should mourn for treasured objects which are taken away from us in a similar manner to the way that we mourn for our loved ones who die. The theory is that we are 'mourning' our own loss of self, that bit of us which we have invested so much energy into and which has now been taken away from us. Belk (1988: 142) reports that in a small-scale test where he talked to burglary victims, they felt not only anger, but also reported feelings of invasion and violation. One might imagine that in contemporary society which is becoming progressively individualized, where possessions take the role of people and vice versa, the investment of psychic energy into things is greater than ever before.

6.5.2   Goods as symbolic and diabolic devices

Csikszentmihalyi and Rochberg-Halton suggest that societies differ to the extent that they emphasize **integration** versus **differentiation**, and that commodities and other things play quite a different role within these different contexts. They further argue that whereas in traditional societies the emphasis is on integration, in contemporary consumer society the focus is on differentiation. Considerations of integration and differentiation have long preoccupied sociologists who seek to understand how modern society holds together. For example it is not so difficult to comprehend that the 'glue' which holds traditional communities and societies together includes shared religion, rituals and customs. The authors discuss how gifts are among the most potent means for creating bonds between people:

> 'Embedded in the context of exchange, objects become containers for the being of the donor, who freely gives up part of him or herself to another. If the gift is reciprocated, a definite tie is established between the partners in the exchange. Again this is not a metaphorical tie, for what has been exchanged is real energy. A small part of my being has been given to another for a small part of his or hers.'
>
> [1995, orig. 1981: 37]

In modern societies the nation state has provided a focus for integration. This is why particular reverence is placed on national symbols, for example the national flag, and in the performance of national sports teams.

All signs of social integration can also act as symbols of differentiation – for example the cross unites and distinguishes Christians from others; the American flag distinguishes those who swear their allegiance to it from those who do not. The cross and the flag are examples of potent symbols. Csikszentmihalyi and Rochberg-Halton describe the meaning of 'symbol' as deriving from 'sym-ballein', meaning 'to throw together', or 'to join'. The phrase came to designate a coin that two friends break in half, each with the hope of reuniting. When the two friends meet once more, the joining together of the two pieces signified the relationship of the two persons, so the token is a sign of unity. The opposite of this is 'dia-ballein', to throw apart or separate, which in our parlance is the root for our word 'diabolic', the essence of evil. Evil is what separates the self of a person into conflicting forces, what divides one person from others, what sets people up against the cosmos. It is chaos, the force of entropy that destroys the order on which life depends.

Csikszentmihalyi and Rochberg-Halton worry that the consumer society which has bred a focus on the pursuit of differentiation, through the pursuit of individual identity, ultimately threatens the order of society itself. They suggest that objects which used to play the role of expressing similarities between the owner and others, in terms of shared descent, religion or some other characteristic, are progressively being used as differentiators, or vehicles of self-expression, which separate the individual from the social context. In the final section we explore the role played by fashion in creating this diabolic state of affairs.

6.6   CONSTRAINT OR FREEDOM? IDENTITY AND FASHION

You may recall that back in Chapter 1, we discussed McCracken's (1991) description of how nobles in sixteenth-century England began to succumb to the demands of novelty and fashion with respect to their purchase of objects. That novelty and fashion are linked to the differentiation of the individual from the social context is not surprising. The search for novelty can be thought of as a quest for self-expression, for those things which offer adventure and escape, freedom from routine, a change of scene, for something that will break the monotony and routine of work, life at home and community. To balance this, people also value a sense of stability and continuity. The desire for novelty offers up the tantalizing prospect of being able to play with identity; however this same desire threatens to fragment a stable sense of identity, of who 'we' are. The acquisition of identity requires considerable investment of self and so continual offering of new values and new identities threatens the stability of the self. As a result one might say that in present-day consumer societies, people are forever involved in a double operation of destructuration (or breaking down their 'old' selves) and restructuration (building up 'new' selves).

The dilemma facing individuals in the twenty-first century is presented in Figure 6.8 (see note v). The square is ordered by two dimensions; those which characterize the relations between community and society, and those which characterize the relations between modernity and post-modernity.

In the figure, the first distinction is between community, where a person has a stable sense of identity but can feel captive, or at least unfree within its bounds. On the other hand there is the image of current society, character-ized by frequent intercourse with strangers. Here we are no longer captive or subject to the demands of community; we do not have to conform to the norms and expectations of the family, the school and the workplace, which

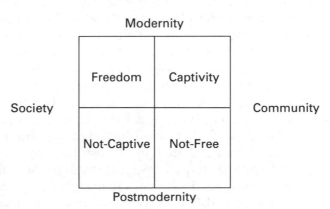

Figure 6.8   Modernity: freedom and identity

form the boundaries of our community. We are enabled to pursue the goal of freedom. However such freedom brings with it the nightmare of choice. For example, particularly among youth, there is a felt desire to cast off the chains which seem to imprison them within the captivity of the daily routines of the family, school and home-work. The desire for freedom can thus be expressed as a means of escape from community and identity, from the ways in which we are defined in these daily situations. The family and school may be communities within which we feel safe and which ascribe us with a (fixed) identity. However the liberal ethos which permeates most high-consumption societies tends to promulgate a quite different ideal, that of individual freedom. The roots of this ethos are complex and may be found in the economic and political liberalism advocated by Adam Smith and his successors, and also to 1960's counterculture. The search for freedom leads to a paradox: the desire for freedom, to escape the chains of identity, leads to a focus on those images which can free us. In the cry 'I want to be free, I want to be me' is the expression of someone who desperately wants to be who he or she really is. However, as we have seen, according to theorists such as Lacan there can be no possibility of finding the 'real' me – the 'real' me is nobody. Erich Fromm tells us that individuals are captivated by freedom, which offers us escape from the certainties of life but at the same time threatens to dissolve our identity. This is what the fashion system plays around with. Fashion is a means of expressing one's individuality. It also allows us to 'play' with different images of ourselves, and provides a means for us to exist through our own aesthetic values.

On the one hand, the desire for images of novelty and fashion springs directly from the desire of consumers. On the other hand, those firms which collectively make up the fashion system actively promote the ideal of *fashionability*. This involves the ability to trade in one identity or lifestyle for another which has more novelty, or seems more appealing to the person who 'wears it'. How is fashionability created? A major task for the fashion industry is to free people from the chains of community and tradition, in order to entice them to explore the range of alternative identities available in the marketplace. Patrick Hetzel (1993) illustrates that this is not a simple matter of converting people from ideas of 'community' to 'society'. First people must come to accept the legitimacy of alternative lifestyles from their own. In this case a person may say, 'I may not be a (punk rocker/new-ager/inline rollerblader) but it is OK with me if you are'. This non-rejection of alternative lifestyles signals a shift from traditional societies where non-adoption is a sign of rejection (this is other to me, I will not wear it, eat it etc.), to a form of non-adoption which says, 'That dress or that food is not my thing, but it's OK with me if you like it'. Hetzel suggests that the transformation involved in the freeing up of lifestyles has largely been the result of the activities of the fashion system, which progressively seeks to marginalize rejection by emphasizing the co-existence of different styles and insisting on non-rejection. It is thus easier to get new objects adopted as soon as there is acceptance of the non-rejection alternative (Figure 6.9).

So can we say that fashion values are imposed? Not really; the two systems, of modern consumers chasing images and of the fashion system seeking to 'free up' the idea of 'non-rejection' of different lifestyles, go hand in hand.

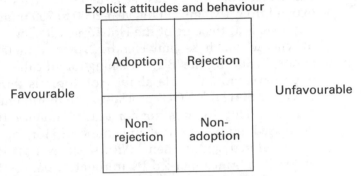

Figure 6.9 Fashion: adoption and rejection [based on Hetzel, 1993: Figure 6]

6.7 CHAPTER SUMMARY

This chapter was the most interesting and challenging to write. After some prevarication it was decided to split the chapter into three sections, comprising 'inside-out', 'outside-in' and 'in-between' theories. One must note a word of caution that these should not be taken literally (which would largely defeat their purpose, because ultimately to progress to a richer understanding they must be destroyed), but rather as rough guides to organizing a broad and complex range of theory. The discussion of 'inside-out' approaches includes a brief account of genetics and of trait theory. 'Outside-in' approaches span a range of theories including those developed by G.H. Mead and Pierre Bourdieu among others. Those 'in-between' approaches relate to Freudian and post-Freudian theory, particularly the work of Lacan. Despite this, there are a number of prominent authors who have not received the attention due to them. Most prominent among these is Erving Goffman, particularly with respect to his work on presentation of self and loss of self. Because of space considerations, the accounts of each theory may come across as being rather dry and anodyne; the reader is encouraged to try to make each theory come to life. One way of trying to do this is to think of each theory as a pair of spectacles. Wearing your 'Bourdieu' spectacles, for example, you should become acutely aware of how people constantly act to classify the world through their language and their behaviour, down to the minutest and routine aspects of speech and behaviour, for example blowing one's nose.

In 1986 Orv Madden opened the first mall-branch of Hot Topic in California. Since then the mall-based group, which is aimed at the teen-lifestyle market, has become one of the fastest growing retailers in the USA, with plans to expand from 193 units in the year 2000 to 700 units by 2010.

Music is at the core of the Hot Topic offering, which consists of a range of 'classic' (such as Jimi Hendrix), heavy metal, punk and 'hard core' bands, including the 'Bible-trashing' band called 'Marilyn Manson'. What is perhaps most notable about Hot Topic is its attitude. 'I DRESS THIS WAY TO BOTHER YOU' proclaims the motto emblazoned on the chest of a T-shirt. Hot Topic is not for adults, nor for the faint-hearted. This is expressed in the look, feel and sound of Hot Topic stores and the product range offered within them. With black walls and ceilings and a Gothic-inspired entrance marked by iron gates, pedestals and even gargoyles at some locations, the stores can look particularly forbidding from the outside. Once inside the atmosphere is lighter and has been compared to a 'really fashionable dungeon'. A high-tech sound system drowns all conversation and features bands like 'Nine Inch Nails' and 'Rage Against the Machine'.

Orv Madden himself has been described as 'a teenager going on 49'. He drives a Dodge Viper sports car, rides a Harley-Davidson and sports a couple of tattoos on his legs. He says that:

'Our target consumers are kids 12-to-22-years old. . . . We want these kids to be totally overwhelmed with our merchandise mix when they first walk in the door.'

One report describes Jacqui Badeau from Mesa, Arizona, as a typical client. Jacqui has two earrings in each earlobe and a clip attached to the top of her right ear. If her mother would let her, she would have a lot more Hot Topic paraphernalia. She says: 'I want to get my belly button pierced and my tongue done and a third hole in each ear and another in the top of my left ear. But my mom won't let me until I move out'.

Hot Topic stores average about 1500 square feet and are stocked with a mix of club- and street-culture fashions, music CDs, logo merchandise and lifestyle regalia. The product mix is varied. Hot Topic carries the latest in club styles, which currently means vinyl, microfibre pants with toggles or jeans with glow sticks in the pockets, and gothic styles, in addition to their own Morbid Threads – blue and black lipstick – and Morbid Metals – the company's line of body jewellery which is reputedly one of its more success-ful offerings. The range also includes licensed band T-shirts, stickers, posters etc. All stores offer ear piercing.

One of the biggest challenges for Hot Topic is how to gauge what teenagers want, to find out what they think is cool. Orv Madden thinks that 'They can be very fickle and in and out of trends in no time'. To address this issue, he uses his reserve army of 2500 store associates to glean market intel-ligence. A passion for music, a love of street culture and the club scene are top criteria for staff recruitment. He encourages his sales associates to e-mail him personally or contact any of Hot Topic's buyers to pass on tips on teen trends, even going so far as paying for rock concert tickets for staff who are willing to write a fashion-report the next day. Every week he receives around 250 ideas which are passed to merchandisers who are required to respond to each suggestion. Recently one sales associate went to a rave and the next day called him to suggest stocking denims with an added pocket to hold glow sticks which ravers wave while dancing. This is now an exclusive item at Hot Topic.

Media such as *Rolling Stone* have acknowledged the 'street cred' of Hot Topic (see note vii):

'Last fall, Limp Bizkit lead singer Fred Durst appeared in the band's *Faith* video wearing a pair of red Dickies. Within months the same trousers were in all 162 Hot Topic stores. That quick reaction time has helped Hot Topic become one of the country's most popular mall-based teen retailers.'

Case-study questions

1. In terms of Erikson's life stages, what kinds of crises would the target market for Hot Topic be going through?
2. Do Hot Topic customers comprise a lifestyle group? Give reasons for your answer.
3. To what extent do Hot Topic customers share the characteristics of a community?

END-OF-CHAPTER REVIEW QUESTIONS

1. Describe the function of the following: hypothalamus, neuron, neurotransmitter and hormone.
2. What is meant by the following terms: 'introvert', 'extrovert'? How might such types respond differently in terms of their consumption behaviour?
3. To what extent can we say that there is a gene for smoking or obesity?
4. What does Bourdieu mean when he refers to the 'habitus'?
5. To what extent does social class determine consumption behaviour?
6. Why would an 'other-directed' character be more amenable to influence by reference groups than an 'inner-directed' character?
7. What is meant by the idea of the 'social self' and how does this develop?
8. Summarize the key differences between Freud's views of the realist and narcissistic egos.
9. Which life stage is most significant with respect to Erikson's theory of identity, and why?

10. How should you pronounce 'Csikszentmihalyi'?
11. According to Csikszentmihalyi and Rochberg-Halton (1995), what roles do goods play as symbolic devices?
12. What role does fashion play with respect to identity?
13. Have a look at the typology for consumer identities which was developed in Figure 2.2 of Chapter 2. Which general approach to identity does this best fit within?

REFERENCES AND FURTHER READING

Belk, Russell W. (1988) Possessions and the Extended Self, *Journal of Consumer Research*, vol. 15 (September): 139–68.

Belk, Russell W. and Janeen Costa (1998) The Mountain Man Myth: A Contemporary Consuming Fantasy, *Journal of Consumer Research*, vol. 25, no. 3: 218–47.

Bouchard Jr., T.J. (1997a). 'The Genetics of Personality'. In K. Blum & E.P. Noble (eds), *Handbook of Psychiatric Genetics*, Boca Raton, Florida: CRC Press.

Bouchard Jr., T.J. (1997b). 'IQ Similarity in Twins Reared Apart: Findings and Responses to Critics'. In R.J. Sternberg and E.L. Grigorenko (eds), *Intelligence: Heredity and Environment*, New York: Cambridge University Press.

Bourdieu, Pierre (1977) *Outline of a Theory of Practice*, Cambridge University Press.

Bourdieu, Pierre (1996) orig. 1979 *Distinction: A Social Critique of the Judgement of Taste*, London: Routledge.

Brennan, Teresa (1993) *History After Lacan*, London: Routledge.

Cooley, C.H. (1902) *Human Nature and the Social Order*, New Brunswick, New Jersey: Transaction Books.

Csikszentmihalyi, Mihaly and Eugene Rochberg-Halton (1995) orig. 1981 *The Meaning of Things: Domestic Symbols and the Self*, Cambridge University Press.

Davison, Gerald C. and John M. Neale (1986) *Abnormal Psychology*, London: John Wiley.

Eco, Umberto (1986) 'Towards a Semiological Guerrilla Warfare'. In *Travels in Hyper-Reality*, London: Picador.

Elias, Norbert (1994) orig. 1939 *The Civilizing Process: The History of Manners and State Formation and Civilization*, trans. Edmund Jephcott, Oxford: Basil Blackwell.

Englis, Basil G. and Michael Solomon (1995) To Be and Not to Be: Lifestyle Imagery, Reference Groups, and the Clustering of America, *Journal of Advertising*, vol. 24 (Spring): 13–29.

Erikson, Erik H. (1968) *Identity, Youth and Crisis*, London: Faber & Faber.

Ewen, Stuart (1976) *Captains of Consciousness: Advertising and the Social Roots of Consumer Culture*, New York: McGraw-Hill.

Eysenck, Hans (1970) (ed.) *Readings in Extroversion–Introversion, vol. 1: Theoretical and Methodological Issues*, London: Staples Press.

Eysenck, Hans (1980) orig. 1965 *Smoking, Health and Personality*, London: Weidenfeld & Nicolson.

Eysenck, H.J. and S.B.G. Eysenck (1975) *Manual of the Eysenck Personality Questionnaire*, London: Hodder & Stoughton.

Falk, Pasi (1994) *The Consuming Body*, London: Sage.

Freud, Sigmund (1953a) orig. 1901 'The Psychopathology of Everyday Life'. In J. Strachey (ed.), *Standard Edition*, vol. 6, London: Hogarth Press.

Freud, Sigmund (1953b) 'Three Essays on the Theory of Sexuality'. In J. Strachey (ed.), *Standard Edition*, vol. 6, London: Hogarth Press.

Freud, Sigmund (1961) orig. 1901 'The Ego and the Id'. In J. Strachey (ed.), *Standard Edition*, vol. 19, London: Hogarth Press.

Goffman, Erving (1961) *Asylums*, New York: Doubleday.

Greimas, A.J. (1985) 'The Love-Life of the Hippopotamus: A Seminar with A.J. Greimas'. In Marshall Blonsky (ed.), *On Signs*, Baltimore, Maryland: The Johns Hopkins University Press.

Hebdige, Dick (1988) *Hiding in the Light: On Images and Things*, London: Comedia.

Hetzel, Patrick (1993) *The Role of Fashion and Design in a Postmodern Society*, IAE de Lyon, Recherche URA CNRS 1257, No. 24.

Holt, Douglas B. (1998) Does Cultural Capital Structure American Consumption?, *Journal of Consumer Research*, vol. 25, no. 1: 1–26.

Illich, Ivan and Barry Saunders (1990) *The Alphabetization of the Human Mind: The History and Impact of Literacy from Homer to Huxley and from UNIVAC to Uniquack*, London: Penguin.

Lacan, Jacques (1977) *Ecrits: A Selection*, London: Tavistock.

McClelland, David (1951) *Personality*, New York: Holt Rinehart & Winston.

McCracken, Grant (1991) *Culture and Consumption*, Bloomington and Indianapolis: Indiana University Press.

Martin, Nicolas and Rosemary Jardine (1986) 'Eysenck's Contributions to Behaviour Genetics', pp. 13–47. In Sohan and Celia Modgill (eds), *Hans Eysenck: Consensus & Controversy*, Philadelphia and London: Farmer Press.

Maslow, A. (1970) orig. 1954 *Motivation and Personality*, New York: Harper & Row.

Mead, George Herbert (1936) *Mind, Self and Society*, Chicago: University of Chicago Press.

Mitchell, Arnold (1981) *Changing Values and Lifestyles*, Menlo Park, California: SRI International.

Oswald, Laura (1999) Culture Swapping: Consumption and Ethnogenesis of Middle-Class Haitian Immigrants, *Journal of Consumer Research*, vol. 25, no. 1 (March): 303–24.

Riesman, David (1961) orig. 1950 *The Lonely Crowd: A Study of the Changing American Character*, Yale University Press.

Schouten, John W. (1991) Selves in Transition: Symbolic Consumption in Personal Rites of Passage and Identity Reconstruction, *Journal of Consumer Research*, vol. 17 (March): 412–25.

Spielberger, Charles D. (1986) 'Smoking, Personality and Health', pp. 305–17. In Sohan and Celia Modgill (eds), *Hans Eysenck: Consensus and Controversy*, Philadelphia and London: Farmer Press.

Weigert, Andrew J. and J. Smith Teige (1986) *Society and Identity: Towards a Sociological Psychology*, Cambridge University Press.

Weinstein, Art (1998) *Market Segmentation: Using Demographics, Psychographics and Other Niche Marketing Techniques to Predict and Model Consumer Behaviour*, New York: McGraw-Hill.

Williamson, Judith (1978) *Decoding Advertisements*, New York: Marion Boyars.

NOTES

i   Based on articles from the *Smithsonian*, 1980, *Newsweek*, 8th November, 1993 and *New Yorker*, 7th August 1995 as discussed on http:ww.twinspace.com/twinstudy.htm

ii   Eysenck was a very prolific writer. The 1970 volume contains a collection of some of the most important papers relating to the dimensions of Neuroticism, and Introversion–Extroversion, including Gray's suggested modification to these.

iii There is more diversity in sexual difference than is implied here.

iv   Nordic countries: Chapter 7, Section 4 of the Swedish Radio and Television Act (1996: 884), which prescribes that commercial advertisements (commercials) in a television broadcast must not have the purpose of attracting the attention of children under the age of 12. By a reference to Section 4 of the Swedish Marketing Act (1995: 450), such commercials are considered to be unfair.

v   This is based on the use of the semiotic square as described by Greimas (1985). I am grateful to Patrick Hetzel who uses this square in his own exposition.

vi   http://www.hottopic.com/default.asp

vii *Rolling Stone*, 27 May 1999.

THE CONSUMING BODY

LEARNING OBJECTIVES

- To be in a position to appreciate different theoretical approaches to the body
- To understand how different theories approach the issue of bodily control in contemporary consumer societies
- To be able to discuss the relations between marketing, the body and consumption

7.1 INTRODUCTION

In Western academic circles the body is now a hot topic for discussion, debate and publication. Academics insist that this is because the body itself is becoming recognized as being more important within society. So far in this text we have discussed two academic perspectives for understanding the body – those of Norbert Elias and of Michel Foucault.

7.1.1 Explaining the importance of the body

The changing relation to the body forms a considerable part of Norbert Elias's thesis concerning the civilization process which was discussed in Chapter 1. You may remember that Elias suggests that a new way of viewing the body becomes conditioned by the cultivation of shame and embarrassment in emerging court societies. In Elias's account, the maintenance of distinction between social groups through the creation of systems of manners plays a formative role in the creation of this new view. The role played by new systems of 'manners' in the management of the body is exemplified by Shaw's play *Pygmalion*, subsequently adapted for the big screen as *My Fair Lady*. In the play, every gesture and nuance of bodily conduct comes under scrutiny in determining one's 'class' or 'breeding'. Elias's account seeks to relate changes in the topology of the self (psychogenesis) to changes in the relations between groups in society (sociogenesis).

The discursive approach adopted by Michel Foucault is briefly outlined in Chapter 3. Historically Foucault shows how, during the eighteenth century, a new form of power comes into being which assumes that individuals possess a mindful intelligence and which seeks to discipline that intelligence through surveillance as part of a general strategy of creating healthy bodies. He contends that this strategy becomes the central preoccupation of a number of agencies associated with (but not reducable to) the sovereign power of the state – medics, psychiatrists, schools, social workers and so on. In this view the creation of healthy bodies is invariably bound up with that of 'normalizing' bodies, with the isolation of aberrant types such as the perverted adult, hysterical woman, and masturbating child, as measured against the 'normal' married couple. Foucault argues that as a result of this, the state and its agencies, including the medical establishment and others such as church groups, gained a considerable amount of knowledge of (and therefore power over) the bodies of individuals, against which their 'normality' could be measured.

While neither Elias nor Foucault place capitalism at the centre of their explanations, Turner (1991) provides a multifaceted account where commercial considerations do play a role. Turner seems to come close to Elias's argument about the internalization of control in arguing that attention to the body has emerged as the result of a relative decline in the operation of organized religion as a force for moral restraint in Western countries. He further asserts that this decline, when coupled with an increase in the prosperity of most workers, has led to the development of a hedonist consumer society. Within consumer society the body has become commercialized and used as a vehicle for advertising. Second, Turner suggests that feminists have, through their focus on the demand for women to 'reclaim their bodies', brought issues related to the body to centre stage. Third, he notes the demographic transition in many countries towards the greying of the population, with its focus on medical provision and the body.

Like Turner, the work of Pasi Falk (1994), which is used as a vehicle to discuss the body in this chapter, owes more to Elias than to Foucault, in that his account seeks to relate psychogenetic processes involving changes in the topology of the self to social changes. Elias's views are used to illustrate those aspects of Falk's argument which discuss the transition from communal to individual identity. This is bolstered by drawing on the work of Stephen Mennell, which extends the 'civilizing process' in relation to the consumption of food. The main discussion involves Falk's account of the decline of the eating community, the separation of the individual from community, the creation of the empty self, and attempts to armour the self through the incorporation of images. While Foucault's perspective has not been incorporated into the central explanation in this chapter, it is referred to occasionally to illustrate potential points of difference.

7.2   FALK: IDENTITY AND THE BODY

Falk (1994) describes his approach as **topological**, as he is interested in how the concept of identity relates to conceptions of what is perceived to be 'inside' and 'outside' the 'self'. Nowadays we take it for granted that our bodies define who 'we' are (by which we mean our individual selves). 'Our' selves are defined by the contours of 'our' bodies. The use of inverted commas around some words is to indicate that there is nothing natural about this co-incidence between the boundaries of the self and the body. Pasi Falk argues that the idea of the 'I' of identity as being a self-contained individual which is within the shell of the body, is a modern development.

These issues can be clarified by going further into Falk's explanation whereby he invites us to consider that the relations between the 'inside' and 'outside' of identity in the primitive eating community are defined quite differently from the way in which they are defined in modern consumer societies.[1] Identity in the primitive eating community is expressed in Figure 7.1. Figure 7.1(a) depicts the manner by which the individual is contained by the group-self of the community. The inverted 'C' shape represents the person who is held within the community, in the same way that the young child might be thought to be held in the embrace of its mother nowadays. The community forms a powerful group-self which incorporates the person. Falk contends that rituals surrounding food are extremely important as they simultaneously create the group-self (the collectivity which emerges as the meal is shared) and the individual self (the person who eats the food is a member of the community). Figure 7.1(b) illustrates the shared meal or communion by means of which the community re-creates itself, forming a bond between its members. The wide band in Figure 7.1(c) illustrates the barrier between the community, which protects its members within from others who are outside the community.

In order to illustrate this, let us briefly revisit the work of Norbert Elias (1994), which was originally discussed in Chapter 1, in the light of what Falk is suggesting. You should remember that Elias argues that the person living in medieval Europe had a sense of self which was quite different from that of the modern isolated individual. In particular the former did not ever develop an internalized critical awareness of his or her own conduct and that of others, to the same extent as moderns have done. This is because the person living in medieval Europe (which constitutes a variant of the primitive eating community) simply had no *need* to contain or bottle up his or her emotions inside the 'self', as he or she could spontaneously and openly vent such feelings.

---

[1] In a similar fashion to Elias (1994), who does not mean 'civilization' to signify 'better', Falk does not intend 'primitive' to signify 'worse'.

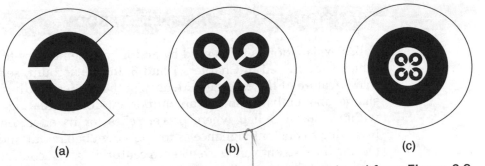

(a)   (b)   (c)

Figure 7.1   The primitive eating community [Reproduced from Figure 2.3, page 22, of Falk (1994)]

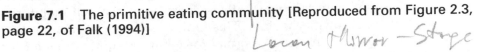

To the medieval person, the body was not taken to be an object which is seen to be separate from the self. To be seen as an object requires that the body is distinguished from, or reflected off, something else. The idea of taking something as an object is equivalent to saying that one is viewing it from a distance. In turn the idea of viewing something invokes the faculty of sight or vision. However the person in the primitive eating community did not attach any special privilege to the faculty of sight or vision over the other senses, but rather apprehended the world using all five senses – hearing, sight, touch, smell and taste – more or less equally. It is only the modern isolated individual, largely removed from the community context, who tends to privilege those senses that work at a distance, such as sight and hearing. Thus the idea of *viewing* the body as an object, as a shell which contains the self and as something that is distant and capable of being reflected critically upon, would have been quite foreign to those living during the medieval period. It is only in the transition to modernity that one has evidence of an increasing restriction and containment of emotions 'inside' the self and of the emergence of critical self-control. How did such changes come about?

Elias argues that these changes in topology came about as communities within society became more interdependent to the extent that people began to find themselves living and working with strangers. Growing interdependency between strangers necessitated the rapid growth of an abstract system of value which recognized the right of individuals to trade across community divides. In the transition from the eating community to modern society there is no doubt that there is a movement towards 'external' exchange which presupposes the difference and separatedness of the parties involved. And so one may say that for Elias, as for Falk, there is a great deal of difference between the identity of the people who lived in primitive communities and those who live in contemporary consumer societies, a difference where the containment of bodily expressions and control are of key importance. Let us consider some of the more mundane ways in which this process occurred.

| 7.3 | **TRANSITION TO THE DISCIPLINED BODY** |

Falk's explanation is influenced by and is complementary to Elias's account which is discussed in Chapters 1 and 3. In this account, self-discipline is a major feature of the emerging identity of the modern individual. Individual shame and embarrassment are important for regulating social conduct within a social milieu where power relies for its effect on self-discipline involving a constant vigilance as to one's own behaviour and that of others. During the sixteenth and seventeenth centuries, social control by brutal force gradually gave way to the exercise of internal self-monitoring and control of one's own behaviour. This form of self-control was not taught through the arbitrary exercise of brutal force but in a quite different form, through the enforcement of a system of 'manners' based on politeness. Elias provides an instance of this turning point in behaviour in recounting how the Bishop of Verona sought to change the behaviour of a certain Duke Richard who had come to dine with him. While the Bishop considered Duke Richard to be a 'well mannered man', he noted that the Duke exhibited a single but deadly fault – at dinner he smacked his lips too loudly when eating. Following the dinner the Bishop sent an emissary, who was known to have particularly good manners acquired at the courts of the great, to visit the Duke. During the course of a conversation with the Duke, the emissary gently pointed out his bad habit (of loudly smacking his lips) as a 'favour' to the Duke. Elias feels that:

> [This] 'polite, extremely gentle and comparatively considerate way of correcting is, particularly when exercised by a social superior much more compelling as a means of social control, much more effective in inculcating lasting habits, than insults, mockery, or any threat of outward physical violence.'   [1994: 65]

During this time of transition, people might still openly break wind or speak of it (which they would later become embarrassed by). However, in eighteenth-century France, the demand grew that all natural functions such as urinating, defecating and sex be removed from the view of others. Strict control of bodily impulses and emotions was first enforced by those of high rank on their social inferiors. However this gradually trickled down through the various levels and layers of society. Eventually the task of training young children to conform to these social expectations became the primary function of the family. Elias documents the growth in such controls through the number of manuals which became available for the regulation of 'civilized behaviour'. For example with respect to nose blowing:

fifteenth century (see note i):

> 'It is unseemly to blow your nose into the tablecloth.'
> 'Do not blow your nose with the same hand that you use to hold the meat.'

The handkerchief first originated in Italy during the Renaissance and diffused according to its snob value.

sixteenth century:
Erasmus notes that handkerchiefs are not used much. That a person should use two fingers for this act and that if anything falls out of the nose, then they should tread upon it.

eighteenth century:
Use of the handkerchief is widespread but use of the hands and fingers is still common. A prohibition arises on looking into the handkerchief after evacuating the nose into it.

By the mid-twentieth century, the use of a handkerchief is taken very much for granted; what is notable is what kind of handkerchief is used and how it is used. In his discussion of systems of classification in French society of the 1960s, Bourdieu (1984) brings Elias's story more or less up to date in recounting below the differences in which a woman is supposed to use a Kleenex and a man a large cotton handkerchief in twentieth-century France:

> 'It would be easy to show, for example, that Kleenex tissues, which have to be used delicately, with a little sniff from the tip of the nose, are to the big cotton handkerchief which is blown into sharply and loudly, with the eyes closed and the nose held tightly, as repressed laughter is to a belly laugh, with wrinkled nose, wide-open mouth and deep breathing ("doubled up with laughter"), as if to amplify to the utmost an experience which will not suffer containment, not least because it has to be shared, and therefore clearly manifested to the benefit of others.'
> [1984: 192]

There are two lessons to be learned from the above. The first is that even the most mundane and apparently trivial physiological function may be used to mark complex social differences. Second, such markers change over time and are related to control over bodily expressions. From the passage above, the degree of bodily control expected of women with respect to the use of the handkerchief is more rigid than that for men. One might suggest that this observation can be generalized across the range of bodily expressions for men and for women and that it is not limited to Western societies. Within society, gender is thus an important factor in determining the degree of self-control that is to be expected of a person in a given situation. Elias argues that the control and repression of bodily expressions can have severe consequences for many women and for society itself.

7.3.1   Diet: the disciplining of appetite

Stephen Mennell (1991) demonstrates that the civilization of appetite runs parallel to those changes described by Elias. Appetite is not equivalent to hunger, but represents the idea that all hunger is to an extent not only physiological but also psychological. Mennell notes that the period of the Middle Ages was characterized by lavish banquets among the nobility. For example he quotes the menu for the feast for the enthronement of Archbishop Nevill at York in 1465, where one thousand sheep, two thousand pigs, one thousand geese, four thousand rabbits, fish and game by the hundreds, numerous kinds of bird, and twelve porpoises and seals were eaten. However such great banquets are highly misleading as a guide to medieval patterns of appetite, which were often relatively frugal and were largely dependent on the rhythms of what the seasons had to offer. Often people had to fast and to do without. Mennell notes that the oscillation between feasting and fasting runs parallel to the extreme emotional volatility of medieval people noted by Elias (1994). This oscillation reflects the general precariousness of life during a period when few were entirely sure of where their next meal was coming from. By today's standards, life was very insecure. Mortality rates were high, brought on by epidemics of disease, by fire or as the result of crop failures resulting in famine.

As a result of those factors discussed above, the exercise of **self-control** over the appetite was not a major problem for the vast majority of people in the transition from the medieval period to modernity. Rather **external control** was exercised on the appetite. Mennell argues that during the Middle Ages there were three external constraints on the exercise of appetite in Europe. The first of these was the Catholic Church which insisted that members fast for three days every week. However as time passed the strict requirement of fasting diminished. The Protestant reformers disapproved of fasting and so this aspect of the control of diet lost its force for a large number of people. Second, states passed sumptuary laws to control the social display of gluttony. However these were not effective and were rarely enforced. Finally, medical opinion in Europe had favoured moderation in eating in the treatment of numerous illnesses. Doctors were aware of the medical dangers of obesity, although they tended to interpret this as the result of laziness rather than of overeating. However, as one might imagine, the views of the medical profession had considerably more impact on those who were ill than upon those who were healthy.

Mennell argues that none of the influences discussed above were sufficient to lead to the modern emphasis on the governance of the appetite. He suggests that one potent factor rests in the way in which food is used as a **social marker**. When food was scarce, the rich distinguished themselves from their inferiors by the variety and sheer quantity of the food that they ate. However by the mid-eighteenth century extreme gluttony among the wealthy became the exception. Mennell explains this change as the result of the increasing security, reliability and variety of food supplies. As more food became generally available, so the elite sought to distinguish their appetite in other ways from those who were their social inferiors. In parallel to the development of the system of manners described by Elias (1994), the focus with respect to food shifted for the nobility from quantity to matters of individual **taste**, and to the ability of chefs to invent an elaborate variety of ever more refined dishes. This enabled the elite to maintain their social distance but also gave rise to a powerful desire to emulate or copy this behaviour by those in the classes below. Mennell recounts how the mid-eighteenth century was a time of gastronomic controversy, in which those who defended the old style of cooking (based on quantity) argued against what they considered to be the pretentiousness of *nouvelle cuisine* (1991: 144). By this time, larger segments of the bourgeoisie were seeking to copy the courtly models of refined and delicate eating, which probably provided an impetus towards the development of even more refined dishes. Those who wrote on culinary matters tended to emphasize the need for a discriminating palate and scorned any notion of a quantitative display of food for the middle classes. The idea of moderation was also promulgated and was increasingly associated with health. Mennell notes that although dieting for health and slimness became a prominent concern in mass circulation publications like women's magazines only after the Second World War, the ideal of the slim body-image had begun to appear in elite social circles considerably earlier.

Thus Mennell attributes increasing self-control in the governance of appetite and in the cultivation of a slim body-image to the emergence of, and changing relations between, social classes. The middle classes came progressively to define themselves and their bodies in relation to a model which moderated its eating and which maintained a slim and healthy body, in contrast to the working classes who focused on quantity in eating and who regarded the body as being a means to an end and not an end in itself.

| 7.4 | MODERN IDENTITY |

Elias (1994) noted that the changes in human identity and conduct which have evolved over many centuries, must be learned by the human infant during the course of a few years. Falk seeks to illustrate this through his portrayal of the emergence of human identity, which is shown below in Figure 7.2. This may be used to consider the ways in which relations between 'inside' and 'outside' change as the child is born and the infant ages. It may also be used to illustrate the differences in the relations between 'inside' and 'outside' in the eating community and in modern consumer society. Figure 7.2(a) portrays the child (the inverted 'C' shape) as being contained by and inside the mother. This condition persists into the early post-natal period when the child's being is similar to that described by Lacan (whose work we described in Chapter 6); at this stage the child is merged into mother nature and exists as a jumble of bits and pieces, undifferentiated from the ground of which it is a part.

Figure 7.2(b) depicts that intermediate state when the child becomes partially aware of separatedness, of the presence and absence of the mother. You will notice that this is very similar in topography to Figure 7.1(a) which describes the identity of the person in the tribal eating community. This corresponds loosely to Freud's anal stage, Erikson's stage of autonomy/shame and also to the first stirrings of Lacan's 'mirror stage'. This is where the child begins to achieve a sense of autonomy which is separate from the mother.

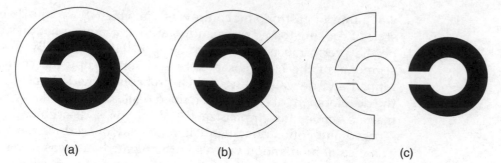

(a)   (b)   (c)

Figure 7.2   The emergence of the modern self [Reproduced from Figure 2.2, page 17, of Falk (1994). Original title 'The constitution of inside/outside and subject–object']

Falk argues that while members of primitive eating communities were undoubtedly individuals, to the extent that they developed a sense of autonomy, they did not achieve a sense of identity, as this is known today. Figure 7.2(c) illustrates the development of a separate identity whereby the child separates from the mother (and those other close networks of family and community). What is characteristic of modern identity (and is lacking in traditional communities) is the hole which appears at the centre of the separated individual. This void or gnawing emptiness at the heart of the self represents the lack of the mother and the withdrawal of the second skin of community. This lack can result in a rootless and futile desire to be rejoined with that which has been lost. In this view, which is very close to that described by Lacan, the identity of the modern individual is based on something which is 'inside', but something which is missing. Thus if the concept of identity refers to a sense of wholeness, completeness or continuity of the self then, according to this view, the quest for identity (for wholeness and completeness) is doomed, as once a person has separated from the mother and from community he or she cannot be rejoined to them. This separation results in freedom, the freedom to be 'yourself', to be whoever 'you' want to be, unconstrained by the ties of community. But this freedom is paid for by the price of separation. As a result the modern person is forever haunted by the idea of being empty and by a desire for wholeness or identity. It is this emptiness at the centre of the self which provides the motive force for the individual's illusory search for wholeness and identity.

The difference between the member of the primitive eating community and the modern individual is topological to the extent that the former is largely contained inside the second skin of the community, while the latter feels empty inside. Food plays a key role in Falk's explanation. The sense of community which envelops the identity of the member of the primitive eating community is based on the ritual shared meal (communion) as an integrating mechanism. The ritual sharing of food, and its physical incorporation, functions in traditional societies simultaneously as an act whereby the partaker is incorporated or 'eaten into' the community; eating together (com) the same bread (panis) transforms eaters into companions. The closeness of such companionship means that the community is thought of as being part of the self. In such communities the bodies of its members are open, as the community itself forms a buffer between what is regarded as being 'inside' and what is 'outside'. The transition to modern society shows a decline in the eating community which is reflected in the decreasing importance of the ritual meal.

> 'Shared meals as such do not disappear: the family meal still prevails to some extent (usually at weekends) and people dine out (or in) with their friends. However, the role of the meal as a collective community-constituting ritual has been marginalized – even in the case of the nuclear family. On the other hand the integrative function of a modern meal resides primarily in the other oral dimension, that of speech and communication (in distinction to communion), aptly exemplified by a "dining out" situation in which every individual partaker makes his or her individual choice of course in the menu.'   [1994: 25]

Falk contends that the observation of silence was important with respect to the sharing of traditional ritual meals. He cites by way of example the ritual meals of the Kwakiutl where especially talking about food while eating was rigorously forbidden (1994: 36). In contrast, the primary characteristic of the modern meal is not so much the food itself, but rather the conversation. Those who partake in a modern meal are no longer 'dissolved' into a unity by means of shared and incorporated food but are rather linked together by means of conversation. The shift from eating community to modern meal is thus expressed as one from the passive incorporation of food, which simultaneously 'eats one' into the community, to the modern situation of 'dining out' where each makes his or her choice from the menu while contributing to the conviviality of the event. Falk argues that the event is still shared, but the link between the partakers is now primarily constituted by the words that are exchanged rather than the food which is silently incorporated. This reflects a change whereby the tight bond which unites the members of the eating community is replaced by a much looser connection, in sharing a common system of representation, through the conversations by which people reciprocally respect the individual autonomy of others. Falk places great store by this shift from proximate communal passive incorporation to distant, individual and active acts of self-expression.

7.5 BODILY STRATEGIES: SELF-PROTECTION – SELF-FULFILMENT – SELF-EXPRESSION

- To summarize my interpretation of what Falk (1994) is saying about the changes in the body: nowadays we participate much less often in communal rituals where the food which is consumed has been lovingly prepared by us (or takes the form of sharing and gifts from others), where the food is silently and reverentially incorporated and where the ritual binds the members of the community together. Instead many consumers tend to snack, 'graze', wolf down their fast-food on the hoof, or purchase frozen or ready-made meals which are taken into the home, microwaved and eaten individually.

- As the silent community-building food ritual has declined, so there has been an increase in conversations around and about food and images of food. These changes are linked to changes in the transition from a group-self to an individual identity, to a person who actively cultivates his or her individual identity through self-fulfilment and self-expression. Whereas in the eating community the community itself formed the outer-wall or barrier between the group-self and other different communities, the modern individual who is free of the ties of community must construct his or her own defences. The body becomes regarded as something which must be armoured or defended.

The rest of this chapter discusses how in present-day consumer societies the body plays an active role in armouring the self, in self-fulfilment and in self-expression.

7.5.1   Self-protection: armouring the self

You should not think it particularly surprising to agree with the statement that in present-day consumer society, the body is constantly on view. Developments such as Closed Circuit Television (CCTV) cameras which are posted in city centres and increasingly in workplaces and the huge number of 'fly on the wall' television documentaries lead to the belief that we are constantly being watched and are permanently on show. Earlier we offered a partial explanation of the development of individual self-control and surveillance. Control became internalized into the self, as a form of self-discipline as the result of the growing interdependency of people within society. It became unacceptable for people to express emotions; instead it became the expectation that these should be contained.

7.5.1.1   Importance of images

The idea that we are on view is related to the **internalization of control**. The shift from an intimate communal setting to the more distant society, precipitated a move from a reliance on the close contact senses (smell, taste and touch) to those senses which operate by distance (the ear and the eye). As more people moved from the country and into the cities, so they began to consider how people looked and to reflect on how they themselves compared with others. In the large city, where one must constantly evaluate strangers, outward appearance is taken as an important cue for interpreting what is inside. The body and the body's body (the clothes) come to act as expressions of social and personal identity. As such, the body comes to be viewed as an instrumental object. Mike Featherstone (1991: 173) notes how shopping came to encourage voyeuristic consumption. The creation of department stores during the nineteenth century meant that shopping ceased to consist of a quick visit to a local store, but instead became an organized expedition into the centre of town, where certain standards of dress and appearance were thought to be appropriate. The invention of the camera and the photograph added to the idea that images were important. The birth of the motion picture industry and of the Hollywood 'star' system drew attention to images and in particular images of the body. Hollywood projected images of the glamorous celebrity lifestyle to a global audience. Featherstone (1991: 179) notes that to ensure that the images of Hollywood stars would look perfect on the big screen, new kinds of makeup, hair care techniques, electrolysis, cosmetic surgery and toupees were invented to mask imperfections. As we shall see next, magazine commentary and advertising images played an important role in the creation of anxiety which fuelled the self-critical view of the self.

7.5.1.2 The role of marketing images in armouring the body

The question of the extent to which marketing practices and images play a persuasive role in the construction of the armoured body is the focus of much debate. On the one hand there are those authors such as McLuhan (1967a, b) and Ewen (1976, 1988) who argue that marketing images present the body as a machine-like object, composed of perfectable parts, and that advertisers create shame and embarrassment in target customers in order to persuade them to buy. Other authors focus not on the message but on the way in which such messages are interpreted by the audience in suggesting that such images are often dismissed as fanciful or outlandish by sophisticated consumers. These views were discussed in Chapter 3 in the section on ideology.

7.5.1.3 The ideal woman: subordinate and thin?

To recap briefly on these views, you will remember that Goffman (1979) demonstrated that during the 1970s women were framed in US advertising as being subordinate to men. In their study of magazine ads in the USA, Japan, Mexico and Australia, Notorantonio and Quigley (1992) found subordination of women to be universal, although the USA was most likely to portray them in professional or executive positions and less likely to show them as sex objects. Leupnitz argues that the representation of womanly shape upheld by fashion models, beauty queens and film stars is of a childlike, slender woman, small, firm breasted with slim thighs and buttocks and a flat belly. The ideal for a man is less widespread, less oppressive and more easily ignored by adolescent males than females (Leupnitz, 1988: 224). Sarah Grogan (1999) notes that there is also general agreement that social pressures on women to be a particular shape and size are more pronounced than pressures upon men, and that advertising plays a major role in promoting these.

Advertising has generally focused on the 'attractive' female body as being a thin body. Recent studies suggest that this is particularly the case with respect to younger women. An investigation of *Seventeen* magazine (whose main audience is composed of a much younger age-group), between 1970 and 1990 by Guillen and Barr (1994), concluded that the images portrayed in the magazine reinforced the social ideal of thinness for women. In May 1996, Omega, the Swiss watch manufacturer, withdrew all advertising from *Vogue* magazine as it felt that the fashion models portrayed in it were so thin as to appear anorexic. It has been estimated that women's magazines are read by up to half of the female population of the UK. For example a single issue of *Vogue* is thought to be read by sixteen women.

However the discourse is not all one-way. When seen against 'normal' people, supermodels look out-of-place. One commentator who had attended the wedding of Scottish supermodel Kirsty Hume on Loch Lomondside said of the event (see note ii):

'On the cat-walk, in glossy magazines, mannequins appear so beautiful, so elegant. Yet in the flesh, stalking through the kirkyard at Luss, Kirsty's guests looked like aliens from another planet. Head and shoulders above the small crowd of villagers who had gathered to gawk, Stella Tennant, Helena Christiansen and Amber Valleta looked painfully thin. The mask-like skin, too tightly drawn across prominent cheekbones, reminded me of Holocaust victims in concentration camps. I was taken aback by the grotesqueness of the fashion industry in presenting such sad specimens as the ideal.'

The commentator then reflects on the commercial stupidity of using such models as a platform for selling products, suggesting that for every one shopper who buys a product in the deluded hope of looking like Naomi Campbell, many more don't buy the product because their shape in the changing-room wall doesn't match up to Naomi's.

7.5.1.4 Heroin chic

Another controversial link has been made between fashion and drug-use. In the fashion business the link between slimness and smoking and the use of harder drugs like heroin and cocaine is well-known. Referring to a well-publicized anti-heroin campaign run in the UK during the mid-1990s entitled 'Heroin Screws You Up', commentator Lowri Turner says (see note iii):

'Heroin may screw a girl up, but at least it doesn't make her put on weight.'

Associations between fashion and drug-use reached a peak during the 1990s with 'heroin chic', the depiction of drained, sallow, skinny, moody models to sell fashionable items. This reached such proportions that it prompted President Clinton to speak out about the practice, thus encouraging a much greater publicity burst for it.

7.5.1.5 Machine bodies: hard bodies

Marshall McLuhan, the twentieth-century communications 'guru', was among the first to become concerned about the portrayal of the female body in the media. McLuhan criticized advertisers for portraying the body as if it were a form of machine composed of replaceable body-parts, with different ads highlighting different parts, and making claims that these could be perfected through buying products. He strongly objected to this approach as he felt that it has led to people viewing their own bodies as if they were machines. In his essay *Love-Goddess Assembly Line*, McLuhan argues that the Hollywood film industry and advertising industry act as production lines which turn out female 'stars' to a machine-like formula of an abstract 'ideal' shape for women as bust 36", waist 19", hips 34", ankle 7" (1967a: 96). As a result of a seemingly endless parade of such 'perfection', he argues that people are encouraged to think less of a woman as a person and more of her as a machine-like object:

> 'Telephone numbers of girls who are good numbers, smooth numbers, hot numbers, slick numbers, Maxfactorized, streamlined, synthetic blondes – these are at once abstract and exciting. Girls become intoxicating "dates" when they are recognizable parts of a vast machine. To be seen in public with these numbers is a sure sign that you are clicking on all cylinders.' [1967a: 96]

In his essay *The Mechanical Bride* (1967b), McLuhan discusses the process by which in turn legs and then noses and other body-parts are singled out for attention by advertisers. He argues that such ads ultimately result in boredom and jaded weariness on the part of their audience. What survives is the view of the human body as a mechanical love machine, capable of specific thrills. McLuhan's argument is that advertising, by presenting women's bodies and body-parts as objects, results in an objectification of the female body and of femininity itself. The body comes to be seen as instrumental, as a means for obtaining certain ends.

While McLuhan focuses on the machine-like character of advertising, Stuart Ewen (1976) seeks to unravel the processes by which women in the USA were made to feel unsure and insecure with respect to their own bodies. The primary role of advertising was to create a dynamic of dissatisfaction. Ewen focuses on the ways in which fear appeals were used extensively in early ads in order to create anxiety. A good example of a fear appeal is shown in Chapter 9 on consuming brands.

In contrast with women, images of men tend to be associated with a hard muscular frame. Several researchers have noted that since the 1980s the male body has become more 'visible' in the popular media in both the UK and the USA. Such images place men under increased pressure to look slender and muscular. Some suggest that the pressures of society to conform to this image may be producing more body dissatisfaction and low self-esteem in men. For example Frank Mort (1988) and Joan McAlpine (1993) have noted this trend in the UK. McAlpine, who interviewed male body-builders, found that there seemed to be evidence to support the view that men are coming under increased pressure to attain this shape. New magazines such as *Men's Health*, which stress the importance of maintaining a fit body, proclaim 'Bigger Chest, Better Sex' on the cover and have recorded sales of 1.3 million copies per month in the USA. Advertising also employs powerful images of the male body to sell a range of products from clothing to deodorant and sports competitions (see note iv). A more detailed discussion of academic studies of the impact of images on body-perception is discussed in the next chapter.

7.5.1.6 Fighting back

While it would be easy to paint a picture of the consumer as nothing more than a passive effect of the propagation of such images, this is belied by the evidence. In Chapter 3 we discussed how O'Donohoe, among others, has demonstrated that most consumers are highly advertising literate. Secondly, one might argue that some images (for example of successful athletes) form effective role models which lead to a positive discipline of the body. Third, the discourse in magazines and other mass-media is not all one-way. Although rare, some advertising (unsurprisingly for beer) parodies images of the 'fit' muscular body. There is a lively debate on television, in newspaper columns and in magazine editorials about the use of unrealizable (for most) 'size 10' models. In 2000 the British Government organized a special event as a forum for the fashion industry, media representatives and others

---

'Sponsor Starving Models
by Buying our Clothes'
advertising campaign.

Ms. Pat Malone, CEO
Gucci America Inc.
50 Hartz Way
Secaucus, NJ07094

According to the American Medical Association (1998), eating disorders rank as the third most common illness among adolescent females in the US, with an estimated prevalence of 4%. The National Eating Disorder Awareness and Prevention Program (EDAP) estimates that 5–10% of girls and women in the US struggle with eating disorders (that means 5–10 million girls and women).

Figure 7.3 About-Face commentary on Gucci ad[2]

[2] http://www.about-face.org/

to meet to discuss this issue. In Foucault's terms, the 'discursive field' is thus made up of a number of competing discourses.

The Internet has provided a useful space for those who seek to counter the dominant discourse which features the thin or 'anorexic' body. About-Face is a California-based group which regularly features the names and addresses of their latest 'top 10 advertising offenders' on the website (see note v). As I have been advised by my publisher that the Gucci ad I wanted to include could result in a lawsuit against me, I have reluctantly had to withdraw this. However if you want to view similar ads for world-famous brands which feature starved women then go to the About-Face website. The tactic used by About-Face is to provide a critical commentary in addition to a visual of the ad, followed by the name of the CEO and the address of the 'offending' company. Figure 7.3 shows what About-Face had to say about the Gucci ad which I could not include.

7.5.1.7   Closing the body

Falk's (1994) account portrays the person as playing an active role in the construction of the body. As we have already noted, his explanation is based on the decline of community and the rise of the autonomous, vulnerable individual. He contends that, with the decline in the eating community, the bidirectional nature of eating, whereby this is simultaneously a means of incorporating food and of being eaten into the community, is lost. Identity retreats from the group-self to be contained within the contours of the individual's body. As the second skin of the community peels away, the isolated individual is motivated by a powerful desire to rid the self of a terrifying feeling of emptiness. The modern individual self eats (consumes) both material and symbolic signs which are associated with self-protection, with incorporating the good things of life so that he or she may become whole once more. The individual thus proactively reaches out and grasps at images which offer the illusion of wholeness. In a consumer society, many of the images which are consumed are commodities that hold out the promise of filling up and protecting the self. However the satisfaction offered by them is transient and the modern self is doomed to continue on a course of grasping and incorporating images which are absorbed into the self and which, given time, are discarded in favour of new ones. A vast range of products signify the promise of protecting, caring for and insulating the self. Consider as an example of this the short list of descriptions which have been placed on the labels of a number of common personal care items, which are shown in Figure 7.4.

The messages on the product labels are simple, powerful and to the point: 'Use me, consume me and you will be OK. Use me in the morning before you go to work and I will protect you; use me at night when you want to ensure that no unsightly stains or odours may escape from my betraying body, use me and allow me to go to work'.

Shampoos
'Clairol Daily Defense'
Alberto Balsam 'Pro-Vitamin Strengthening System: Nourishing Shampoo'
Clairol 'Herbal Essences: Extra Body for Fine Hair'
Protects Coloured/Permed/Dry Hair
Pantene 'Hair Repair Treatment'
Aussie '3 Minute Reconstruction'

Mouthwash
Colgate Fluorogated? Prevents cavities
Listermint: strengthens teeth, fights plaque, freshens breath
Macleans Mouth Patrol stops fillings, strengthens teeth and cleans up after brushing
Macleans Mouth Guard strengthens teeth and freshens breath

Figure 7.4   Marketing images as body-armour

7.6   SELF-FULFILMENT

Within Falk's (1994) analysis, both self-fulfilment and self-expression play a major role in the construction of the body. Self-fulfilment means exactly what it says; filling the self up with food and with images which help to armour the self. The closing of the body creates an empty inside, both in physical and in mental terms which is to be filled up with all of the good things that it lacks. The person seeks to build up his or her ego using images. In order to do this they must first be in a position to relate to their body as if it were an object.

The dominant image of the role played by the body has changed over the years in the Western world. Christianity shaped the idea of a distinction between body and soul, the idea being that the body was of this earth and provided a source of temptation for the everlasting soul. The body thus had to be disciplined, purified and mortified so that it could make a fitting place for the Spirit to reside in. The Enlightenment rationalists maintained this duality but changed its emphasis from a spiritual to a more material basis in differentiating between the mind and the body, or culture and nature. The argument put forward was that both internal and external nature should be tamed or subjected to the discipline of the mind. The duality between mind and body facilitates the way in which the body can be viewed as an object, so that the 'brute' body and 'brute' nature must be contained, disciplined and controlled. In consumer culture the armoured, hard machine–body is an object par excellence (see note vi):

> 'Like cars and other consumer goods, bodies require servicing, regular care and attention to preserve maximum efficiency.'

The urge to tame nature and to control the body lies deep in the psyche. Thompson and Hirschman (1995) suggest that the duality between an enduringly youthful inner self who must inhabit an ageing body underlies a consumption ideology in which the use of products and services offered by the cosmetic, beauty, medical and fitness industries is portrayed as a decision to take control of one's life. They offer as an example the vast multi-billion dollar industry which has grown up to obscure signs of ageing, from the consumption of hair-colouring products to hair-loss remedies, skin-care products and cosmetic surgery. Once the body is put on display as an object, it can then be used to express the aesthetic desires of its owner. It can be shaped to represent ideal images of youth and beauty.

7.7 SELF-EXPRESSION

In Chapter 2 where we discussed the 'style' of rap band Run-DMC, the importance of external appearances or style was highlighted for those whose identity is placed in question. Style or external appearance was self-consciously adopted as a means of building the self up using images. Grogan (1999) picks this point up nicely; if you were an immigrant in the USA, what mattered was how you looked; if you dressed like an American, then you looked like an American, therefore you were an American. Style allowed people to put up a front in a hostile environment – a front to protect one's inner self:

> 'As a kind of armor for city life, style taught people that they could gain comfort from self-estrangement from erecting a visible line of defense for a subjectivity that often experienced a sense of jeopardy.' [1999: 79]

According to Ewen (1988), fashion creates 'neo-mania' or to put it literally, a craze for whatever is 'in' or new, RIGHT NOW. For a person who lives part of his or her life in thrall to an ideal image, the body itself must be changed to conform with prevailing images. Ewen suggests that the style of the moment is for a 'hard body', a body which is well toned, slick and lubricated like a machine.

7.7.1 'Health' and 'fitness'

In Chapter 3 we discussed Bauman's (1995) distinction between health and fitness, arguing that a discourse of fitness is replacing that of the healthy body. The two terms are quite different and people associate them with different places – the clinic and the gym. The clinic is where you go if you feel unwell, the gym is where you go if you want to become fit. Many people who visit clinics do so because they have placed their systems under untoward strain since the fitness programme they have been pursuing has placed too much strain on muscle, bone or on their cardiovascular system.

While the healthy body comes in a diverse array of shapes and sizes, the fit body is determined by 'the look' as defined by the fashion images of currently popular athletes, supermodels and rock-stars. More and more the 'fit' body is becoming shaped like a machine. Before beginning classes in many centres this body-machine is checked over for suitability. The checklist includes BMI (Body Mass Index) and cardiovascular checks, and a fitness 'programme' is then designed for the novice to follow. Once inside the gym, the novice is shown around the array of machines which comprise the Nautilus suite or its equivalent. The Nautilus has twelve 'stations' in all. As one moves from one machine to the next so different muscle-groups are worked on – hips, buttocks, thighs, calves, back, shoulders, chest, upper arms, forearms, abs, neck, body. The person who regularly uses such devices is encouraged to think of his or her body as a work of art. In the gym there is nothing to do but to glance sideways at the small television (if one is included), and perhaps at the same time to listen to a CD on one's personal stereo. However, above all else, the larger than full-size mirrors encourage one to gaze and to reflect upon one's body.

7.7.2   Body-building

Rom Harré (1989) suggests that body management, coupled with a large element of self-presentation, is involved in most of the reasons people have for 'working out'. Body management is usually carried out to improve one's general health (fitness) or to 'get in shape' for some other bodily activity, for example, football. On the other hand, the ideal of body-builders is to transform the bodily form itself. In this view the body is taken to be a work of art, as a form of raw material to be transformed into body sculpture. The body itself is thus regarded as a psychologically detached art object, already partially but imperfectly formed. It needs to be worked on. For Harré, this artwork on the male body is an example of the Exaggeration Principle, the idea that, 'if this big is good, huge is better'. He offers some other examples of the Exaggeration Principle, for example that 'if low salt is good then no salt is better' and 'some bran is good so a great quantity of bran is better'. In this respect the body-builder regards his body very much like specialist breeders regard their dogs or custom car builders their cars. For example with body-builders the musculature of the body is divided into muscle groups and each group becomes the focus of effort. The Exaggeration Principle is applied to improving the size and definition of muscle groups by using Nautilus machines or perhaps free weights. The same technique of isolation of parts and the development of individual parts is evident in the custom car cult. For example, exhaust manifolds and tyres are isolated conceptually and then grossly exaggerated. This differential emphasis gains its effect by leaving the rest of the machine essentially unchanged. Harré argues that a latent symbolism of power underlines both the body-builder and the custom car enthusiasts. It is not the engine itself that is displayed but the implicit marks of its potency – the exhausts through which the sound of the power comes and the tyres through which it is transformed into acceleration.

7.7.3 The sculpted body

While exercise ultimately results in creating a hard, muscled body, there are some aims which exercise on its own will not achieve. One perceived block to the acquisition of the 'perfect' physique (machine-body) for men and for women is body-hair. Bikini waxing has now become standard practice for a number of fashion models and film-stars and increasingly with 'ordinary' women, while that of waxing chest-hair is reported to be catching on quickly with some segments of the male market (see note vii).

Surgeons have now perfected a number of short-cuts for those who would prefer to do without the exercise of going to a gym. Cosmetic surgery (see note viii) is of course much more versatile than this, offering a whole range of solutions to those who would like to enhance aspects of their bodies or de-enhance others. Body dissatisfaction may be such that a person wishes permanently to alter a particular feature. Traditionally affordable only by the rich and famous, cosmetic surgery is now within the reach of the average consumer. For example in 1997 the going rate for liposuction and liposculpture was reputedly £2400 in the UK, with a breast implant at £3300 and ear correction £1600 (see note ix). While eyelid surgery, rhinoplasty (nose jobs) and breast implants have all been popular in the USA, liposuction, or the removal of fat from the thighs, is reported to be the most common procedure (see note x). New technology is playing an increasing role in shaping the body. For example liposuction is now being replaced by liposhaving, a procedure which minimizes bleeding, swelling and bruising (see note xi). Lasers are being used in an ever-expanding array of applications from removing birth-marks to removing tattoos and hair. Having your face 'laser-resurfaced' involves the partial or complete removal of the skin's outer epidermal layers to make way for smoother, less lined, less acne-scarred or less sun-damaged new growth (see note xii):

> 'It's fabulous. I've had 10 mad, bad years in which I lived in the Far East and Spain, smoking, sunbathing and drinking too much, and I came back to the UK looking raddled and much older than my 59 years. Now I look a great 59. Everyone says I look wonderful. It's the tone and texture of my skin: it looks fresh and glows.'

Cosmetic surgery has its down-side. It was reported that in 1994 there were nearly as many breast implant removals as breast implantations. Some media reports of the effects of plastic surgery pull no punches. For example Joanna Briscoe, researching a novel whose focus was to be on narcissism and the power of beauty, found herself becoming almost obsessed with the way in which the perceived physical limitations of the body seem to be melting away and how the body is increasingly being taken as an aesthetic, perfectable object. However she was shocked by the violence of the operation itself: 'the surgeon's hand right inside the woman's face, punching and tearing her separated skin only anchored at the nose and mouth' and wondered whether such mutilation is a more extreme example of how women cope with the frustration and stress of everyday life in the modern world (see note xiii).

7.7.3.1 Why do it?

But why would anyone want to put themselves through such discipline? One view is that this is a means to change one's identity through the creation of a 'rite of passage'. An explanation which is similar but is based on Foucault's concept of power suggests that this constitutes a paradoxical act of self-affirmation.

A rite of passage?

John Schouten (1991) chose to look at the role played by the consumption of aesthetic cosmetic surgery in relation to the reconstruction of identity. Schouten based his research on Erich Fromm's description of the 'marketing character', what Riesman *et al.* would later call the 'other-directed' character. In particular Schouten wanted to research two objectives: (1) to examine several *a priori* themes in the context of plastic surgery consumption and (2) to identify and analyse emergent themes in the hope of expanding under-standing of the self-concept in consumer behaviour. Because the self-concept is complex and is sensitive to social and situational contexts, Schouten chose an ethnographic method to explore this area. He chose nine key informants, all of whom had undergone plastic surgery, and supplemented the data received from these people with further information which was supplied by their friends. Schouten's analysis supported the *a priori* themes which had been generated from previous research findings. The following themes were identified:

Theme 1: Motives were associated with dissatisfaction with a particular body part.

Theme 2: Informants were keenly aware of impression management.

Theme 3: Major changes in roles led to feelings of inadequacy and thence to change.

Theme 4: Informants formulated both positive and negative possible selves in assessing the change.

The first two themes indicate that the respondents belonged to that category which Riesman *et al.* refer to as 'other-directed'. The informants reported that their self-esteem had improved significantly as a result of surgery, leading to feelings of self-confidence and increased attractiveness. Their negative body images tended to emerge during adolescence. Some even remembered that their parents had criticized their bodies when they were children. Theme 3 relates to the changing character of ego identity over time. Six of the nine informants underwent plastic surgery at a time when their lives were in flux or transition, following or anticipating life events including childbirth, career choices, divorce or even death of a close relative. Within this context, plastic surgery was viewed as being either a means of regaining control of the self by reintegrating the self concept, or as a catalyst for further self-change. With respect to the former, surgery played an important part in reintegrating the self concept by erasing the previous dissatisfaction which the person had experienced with the body. For example one woman reported feelings of dissatisfaction with her breasts from the age of 12, following which she had begun to avoid 'feminine' pastimes and dress. She even sought out a 'male' occupation in oil exploration. However when she and her husband settled down and she became pregnant and then had a child, her small breasts made her feel incomplete as a woman. Augmentation mammoplasty allowed her to make a complete transition to womanhood. Other people used the surgery as a means for precipitating further self-change. For example one woman who had a rhinoplasty and a chin implant felt that her increased self-esteem enabled her to escape from an unhappy marriage and to build a new life.

Paradox of self-affirmation

On the other hand an explanation based on the work of Foucault would suggest that body modification is engaged in as a paradoxical response to the operations of discourses in society. In this explanation, those in Schouten's study are all responding to a societal ideal of health and fitness. While the act of working on the body or having it sculpted may bring them a sense of completion, power and control, it also effectively reproduces the system of power which led them to have the operation in the first place. For example Hilary Radner discusses Jane Fonda's decision to have plastic surgery as part of what she labels the 'paradox of the feminine culture of the body'. In this view, women purposefully enter into exercise programmes such as the 'Jane Fonda Workout' and may decide to have plastic surgery in order to gain the feeling of control over their bodies. In engaging themselves in this process, through getting 'fit' they are fitting themselves out for the world of work and in society at large where the tanned, slim, smooth body is valued. The paradox is, that while this may increase the feelings of worth and power of the person who develops a 'fit' and 'sculpted' body, it also reproduces the values of fitness. Placed at a remove from itself, the whole process is shocking. Fonda relates her shock when told that a Vietnamese prostitute felt she could raise her prices if she 'Americanized' her face and body through cosmetic surgery:

> 'I was shocked into the realization that I myself had played an unwitting role as a movie star and sex symbol in perpetuating the stereotypes that affected women all over the world.'
> [Fonda, in Radner, 1997: 128]

What is perhaps more shocking is that Fonda herself subsequently opted for the same course of action. French performance artist Orlan takes plastic surgery to its shocking extremes in seeking to literally remake her face as a work of art. Orlan has attempted to have her face remodelled in line with a composite digital image based on mythic images of feminine beauty, incorporating the Mona Lisa's forehead, the chin of Bottichelli's *Venus* and the eyes of Gerome's *Psyche*, among others. More recently she had horn-like implants inserted into her forehead. Orlan's self-professed aim is to present herself as a living reflection of what modernity is doing to the body, to be revolting and revolutionary (see note xiv).

Finally a word about men. Although only one in every ten cosmetic surgery operations is performed on men, there are reports that this number is increasing. According to one report, while traditionally men have dominated the market for hair transplants, they now engage in different techniques such as pectoral implants, liposuction and penile enhancements (see note xv).

7.7.4 Future bodies – obsolete bodies/no-bodies: body-hatred?

One of the most distinctive features of humankind is in its capacity as *homo faber*, the maker of things. Early on in its development, humanity spotted the usefulness of tools in achieving its ends. Nowadays we take for granted those tools which have been developed and refined over thousands of years, including shoes, clothing, tools for working with materials, hammers, chisels, knives and forks, chopsticks, pens, paper, guns, *Stealth* fighters, cars, spacecraft, personal stereos, mobile phones, palmtop computers and implants. We tend to regard many of these tools not as extensions or even prosthetics, but as essential parts of ourselves. What would we be without shoes, cars or networked computers? Such tools are quite literally extensions of the self. The idea that the human body changes and adapts differently to its environment through the development of new prosthetic devices is not original. It forms the basis for example of many of the speculations by media 'guru' Marshall McLuhan. What some would regard as an extension of a Christian desire to negate the body and others would argue is entirely new, is the desire to be rid of the body itself.

In the late 1980s and early 1990s new-wave science fiction writers such as William Gibson, in his classic book *Neuromancer*, and features in digital-age magazines such as *Wired*, began to label the body as 'meat'. In the 'wired' universe, the argument goes, humanity will no longer require the 'meat' of the body. The body is vulnerable, slow and constitutes a drag on the power of the mind. This is the vision shared by Stelarc, a performance artist who desires to take the body to its limits, to push it to the state where it is no longer a body as we recognize it (see note xvi):

'It is time to question whether a bipedal, breathing body with binocular vision and a 1400cc brain is an adequate biological form. It cannot cope with the quantity, complexity and quality of information it has accumulated; it is intimidated by the precision, speed and power of technology and it is biologically ill-equipped to cope with its new extraterrestrial environment.

'The body is neither a very efficient nor very durable structure. It malfunctions often and fatigues quickly; its performance is determined by its age. It is susceptible to disease and is doomed to a certain and early death. Its survival parameters are very slim – it can survive only weeks without food, days without water and minutes without oxygen.

'The body's LACK OF MODULAR DESIGN and its overactive immunological system make it difficult to replace malfunctioning organs. It might be the height of technological folly to consider the body obsolete in form and function, yet it might be the height of human realizations. For it is only when the body becomes aware of its present position that it can map its post-evolutionary strategies.

It is no longer a matter of perpetuating the human species by REPRODUC-TION, but of enhancing male–female intercourse by human–machine interface. THE BODY IS OBSOLETE. We are at the end of philosophy and human physiology. Human thought recedes into the human past.'

Like many others who share his vision of a transhuman or posthuman condition, Stelarc wants to transform the body fundamentally so that humans can survive in interstellar space:

'Off the Earth, the body's complexity, softness and wetness would be difficult to sustain. The strategy should be to HOLLOW, HARDEN and DEHYDRATE the body to make it more durable and less vulnerable.'

In seeking to live out his theory, Stelarc has allowed his own body to become colonized by, and to become a container for, technology. Stelarc has had a 'sculpture' inserted into his stomach, as he explains it, not as a prosthetic device but as an aesthetic device. Stelarc shares his vision of the future with other groups, for example the Extropians whose president Max More includes the following statement as part of the Extropian Principles (see note xvii):

'We challenge the inevitability of ageing and death, and we seek continuing enhancements to our intellectual abilities, our physical capacities, and our emotional development. We see humanity as a transitory stage in the evolutionary development of intelligence. We advocate using science to accelerate our move from human to a transhuman or posthuman condition.'

While the sentiments expressed by Stelarc and the Extropians might seem to be rather extreme, even mainstream medics now suggest a 'new dawn' for the body. Over the past twenty years, developments in medical technology have effectively decoupled sex from reproduction. Some suggest that as a result of developments in biotechnology, the ageing process will be radically reduced enabling (some) people to live for double their lifespan or perhaps for even longer. Such hopes are pinned on the current ability to clone new body-parts, to replace those which have been worn out or to enhance those which appear to be unsatisfactory. Some academics are already expressing disquiet about the extent to which expectations are being created via relatively modest innovations such as Viagra and the 'orgasm' pill for women, so that seventy-year-olds are beginning to believe that they should be like and perform like twenty-year-olds (see note xviii).

Debates about the future of the body seem to be peripheral to the everyday lives of people. Some will question the sanity of those who seek to justify the massive expenditures on bodily-improvements during an era when the increase in global population is such that humanity is beginning to threaten global ecology. Others fear that the two developments are linked, that the dream for some is ultimately escape from an overpopulated, polluted, lawless planet, to live forever in seeking their destiny among the stars. A related explanation is that the sentiments of Stelarc, the Extropians, and increasingly 'mainstream' corporations and medics, are premised on a Western mind–body dualism taken to its very extremes. To this extent they reflect on the fact that at the beginning of the twenty-first century, for some people at least, even the 'armoured body' is no longer sufficient.

7.8   CHAPTER SUMMARY

In this chapter, which takes the human body as its concern, the topological approach of Pasi Falk (1994) was adopted to explain differences in traditional and modern perceptions of the body and also to illustrate the linkage between the identity, body, food and images. In discussing the transition to the disciplined body, the work of Norbert Elias (1994) is recalled and extended to discuss the disciplining of appetite. The modern body is described as being one which is subject to critical self-monitoring and control. The history of mind–body dualism in Western society is discussed in the sections on fitness, body-building and cosmetic surgery. These are used as examples which illustrate how the body in contemporary consumer society is constructed as an object, to be disciplined by the mind; as a thing which is malleable and which must be hardened to protect its 'occupant'. The final section on the future of the body suggests that at its extreme, such divisions result in body-hatred.

7.9   CASE STUDY: JUST HOW BEAUTIFUL IS BIG?

In 1998 the fashion models Sophie Dahl, Sara Morrison and Lorna Emme hit it big in the UK and the USA. Emme, four inches taller, ten years older and six stone heavier (14 stones) than Kate Moss, was chosen as the new face of giant cosmetics firm Revlon, whose main model is Cindy Crawford. In the UK, Morrison caused a similar storm when she appeared in *Vogue* magazine. Sophie Dahl modelled nude for *i-D* magazine, photographed by Nick Knight who decided to computer-enhance her size 14 image to add extra volume. Given that around 47 per cent of women in the UK are size 16 and over, comparative giants when compared with Kate Moss and Jodie Kidd, the notorious 'stick insect' models who stalk the cat-walks of the fashion highway, many people welcomed these events as signs that perhaps times are changing.

Others are not so sure. Emme, Dahl and Morrison appear to be the exception rather than the rule. According to one report, *Vogue* had not used another model over size 10 since. Some commentators suggest that the only reason why photographers and firms use larger models (whose image they digitally enhance to make them even larger), is to create a freak-show stereotype to titillate the palates of fashion and magazine audiences jaded by a constant diet of skinny freaks, which they counterbalance (see note xix). Of course another reason why such models are used is to sell product. The famous withdrawal of Omega watchmakers from advertising in *Vogue* magazine because of its use of matchstick models was countered by a series of ads from rival company Accurist, which featured a victim of malnutrition wearing one of their 'chunky' watches, with the ad bearing the strapline 'Put some weight on'. According to Tamsin Blanchard, no watchmaker has put his or her money where his or her mouth is by actually using a larger model.

Sadly it appears that the employment of larger women in the pages of top-notch women's fashion magazines may be no more than a fad. When another larger-than-usual model made it into *Vogue*, the picture was used not in the fashion section but in a feature on diet pills.

Case-study question

1. How might you begin to change the situation described in the case study?

END-OF-CHAPTER REVIEW QUESTIONS

1. How important is food in defining national identity? Consider the national cuisine of your own country and that of your near neighbours, and think of how they differ.
2. According to Elias (1994) and Falk (1994), what were the principal vehicles for the disciplining of the body?
3. According to Mennell (1991), what were the most important factors in the disciplining of appetite?
4. To what extent do marketing images lead to the desire by consumers to armour the self?

REFERENCES AND FURTHER READING

Bauman, Zygmunt (1995) *Life in Fragments*, Oxford: Basil Blackwell.
Bourdieu, Pierre (1984) orig. 1979 *Distinction: A Social Critique of the Judgement of Taste*, trans. Richard Nice, London: Routledge.
De Young, Susan and F.G. Crane (1992) Females' Attitudes Toward the Portrayal of Women in Advertising: A Canadian Study, *International Journal of Advertising*, vol. 11: 249–55.

Elias, Norbert (1994) orig. 1939 *The Civilizing Process: The History of Manners and State Formation and Civilization*, trans. Edmund Jephcott, Oxford: Basil Blackwell.

Ewen, Stuart (1976) *Captains of Consciousness: Advertising and the Social Roots of the Consumer Culture*, New York: McGraw-Hill.

Ewen, Stuart (1988) *All Consuming Images: the Politics of Style in Contemporary Culture*, New York: Basic Books.

Falk, Pasi (1994) *The Consuming Body*, London: Sage.

Featherstone, Mike (1991) 'The Body in Consumer Culture', pp. 170–97. In Mike Featherstone, Mike Hepworth and Bryan S. Turner (eds), *The Body: Social Process and Cultural Theory*, London: Sage.

Gardner, R.M. and Y.R. Tockerman (1993) Body Dissatisfaction as a Predictor of Body Size Distortion: A Multi-Dimensional Study of Body Image, *Genetic, Social and General Psychology Monographs*, vol. 119: 125–45.

Gibson, William (1995) *Neuromancer*, New York: Ace Books.

Goffman, Erving (1979) *Gender Advertisements*, New York: Harper Torchbooks.

Grogan, Sarah (1999) *Body Image: Understanding Body Dissatisfaction in Men and Women*, London: Routledge.

Guillen, E. and S. Barr (1994) Nutrition, Diet and Fitness Messages in a Magazine for Adolescent Woman 1970–1990, *Journal of Adolescent Health*, vol. 15: 464–72.

Harré, Rom (1989) Cults of the Body and Their Aesthetic Underpinnings, *International Journal of Moral and Social Philosophy*, vol. 17 (March): 119–25.

Leupnitz, D.A. (1988) *The Family Interpreted: Psychoanalysis, Feminism and Family Therapy*, New York: Basic Books.

McAlpine, Joan (1993) 'Mr. Muscle Cleans Up', *The Scotsman*, 13th August, p. 4.

McCauley, M., L. Mintz and A.A. Glenn (1988) Body Image, Self-esteem and Depression-Proneness: Closing the Gender Gap, *Sex Roles*, vol. 18: 381–91.

McLuhan, Marshall (1967a) orig. 1951 'Love-Goddess Assembly Line', pp. 93–8. In *The Mechanical Bride: Folklore of Industrial Man*, London: Routledge & Kegan Paul.

McLuhan, Marshall (1967b) orig. 1951 'The Mechanical Bride', pp. 98–102. In *The Mechanical Bride: Folklore of Industrial Man*, London: Routledge & Kegan Paul.

Mennell, Stephen (1991) 'On the Civilizing of Appetite', pp. 126–55. In Mike Featherstone, Mike Hepworth and Bryan S. Turner (eds), *The Body: Social Process and Cultural Theory*, London: Sage.

Monteath, Sheryl A. and Marita P. McCabe (1997) The Influence of Societal Body Factors on Female Body Image, *Journal of Social Psychology*, vol. 137, no. 6: 707–28.

Mort, Frank (1988) 'Boy's Own? Masculinity, Style and Popular Culture'. In R. Chapman and J. Rutherford (eds), *Male Order: Unwrapping Masculinity*, London: Lawrence & Wishart.

Notorantonio, W. and R. Quigley (1992) Reported in *Adweek*, Eastern Edition, 27th April, vol. 17: 10.

Radner, Hilary (1997) 'Producing the Feminine: Jane Fonda and the New Feminine', pp. 108–33. In Pekka Sulkunen, John Holmwood, Hilary Radner and Gerhard Schultze (eds), *Constructing the New Consumer Society*, Basingstoke: Macmillan (now Palgrave).

Schouten, John (1991) Selves in Transition: Symbolic Consumption in Personal Rites of Passage and Identity Reconstruction, *Journal of Consumer Research*, vol. 17 (March): 412–25.

Stephens, Debra Lynn, Ronald Paul Hill and Cynthia Hanson (1994) The Beauty Myth and Female Consumers: The Controversial Role of Advertising, *Journal of Consumer Affairs*, Summer: 137–53.

Thompson, Craig J. and Elizabeth C. Hirschman (1995) Understanding the Socialized Body: A Poststructuralist Analysis of Consumers' Self-Conceptions, Body-Images and Self-Care Practices, *Journal of Consumer Research*, vol. 22, September: 139–53.

Turner, Brian (1991) 'The Discourse of Diet', pp. 157–70. In Mike Featherstone, Mike Hepworth and Bryan S. Turner (eds), *The Body: Social Process and Cultural Theory*, London: Sage.

NOTES

i   *Source*: Based on Elias (1994: 121–3).
ii *Source*: Margaret Morrison, 'Women's image in bad shape', *Scotland on Sunday*, 11th October 1998, p. 15.
iii *Source*: *Sunday Mirror*, 1st January 1995, p. 11.
iv For images of Joel West, Antonio Sabato Jr. and Marky Mark – see http://www. geocities.com/WestHollywood/Village/2550/
v   http://www.about-face.org/gallery/newten/eight.html
vi *Source*: Grogan (1999).
vii *Source*: *Cosmopolitan*, August 1998: 107–8.
viii Cosmetic surgery is usually associated with aesthetic improvements to the body. There is often no medical reason and the decision usually relates to personal choices and preferences. In contrast, plastic surgery usually refers to surgery which is carried out for medical or acute psychological reasons, for example as the result of damage caused by cancer, congenital abnormalities and accidents.
ix *Source*: *Keynote* (1997: 15) – see note xiii for full reference.
x   *Source*: *Industry Week*, 5th February 1996, vol. 245, no. 3: 19.
xi *Source*: *Industry Week*, 6th May 1996, vol. 245, no. 9: 15.
xii *Source*: *Weekend FT*, Issue 22, February 1998, p. 30.
xiii *Source*: Joanna Briscoe (1997) 'The Skull Beneath the Skin', *Guardian*, Tuesday, 19th February 1997, pp. 2/3.
xiv *Source*: *Observer*, Life, 17th April 1994, pp. 38–40.
xv *Source*: Richard Cains (ed.), *Keynote* (1997) Cosmetic Surgery 1997 Market Report.
xvi http://www.stelarc.va.com.au/
xvii http://www.extropy.com/
xviii Clark, Ginny (1998) 'Making Healthy Profits Out of Sex and Drugs', *The Scotsman*, Wednesday, p. 14.
xix *Source*: *Independent*, 10th July 1998.

CONSUMING 'DISORDERS'

LEARNING OBJECTIVES

- To investigate in more detail explanations relating to the crisis of control in consumer societies
- To enable the reader to understand the complex nature of eating disorders
- To provide an understanding of different theoretical accounts of eating disorders
- To elaborate on theories discussed in previous chapters in order to illustrate the nature of eating disorders and to integrate knowledge of these theories

8.1   INTRODUCTION

This chapter discusses different theoretical explanations of what the medical literature refers to as 'extreme consumption disorders', first the starvation disorders anorexia nervosa and bulimia nervosa (see note i), and second obesity, a disorder which has long been associated with overeating. Over the past twenty years there have been many claims in the media, particularly in Western countries, that such disorders have reached 'epidemic' proportions. For example it is claimed that 58 million Americans are sufficiently overweight to warrant concern about their health, and that this number has risen from one-quarter of the population in 1980 to over one-third today. At the other extreme, some sources have claimed that eleven million women and one million men in the USA suffer from starvation disorders – either as the result of self-induced semistarvation (anorexia nervosa) or a cycle of bingeing and purging with laxatives, self-induced vomiting or excessive exercise (bulimia nervosa). Starvation disorders are often linked with the constant bombardment through advertising and other media of feminine body-image ideals which are physiologically impossible for real women to achieve. Obesity is often blamed on the growth of snacking and a 'cafeteria culture' within consumer societies and of the greed of those who succumb to its lure.

While the central explanation for such disorders concerns aspects of control, different theoretical explanations situate control in quite different ways. For example a social explanation might consider the way in which a person is controlled by conforming to peer expectations and to advertising and other pressures which are circulated in the media. A quite different aspect of control is highlighted if the focus is on the role played by neurotransmitters in the autonomic nervous system. This in turn differs markedly from a psychoanalytic view which considers the importance of developing appropriate mechanisms of control and autonomy in the growing child during the life-cycle. In evaluating such theories it is all too easy to forget that these effect real people. It must be stated clearly at this stage that this chapter forms a basic, partial and oversimplified account of such disorders which should on no account be used as a basis for counselling others. Different theoretical perspectives of the starvation disorders anorexia nervosa and bulimia nervosa are discussed in the first section and obesity is covered in the second section of this chapter.

8.2	STARVATION DISORDERS: ANOREXIA NERVOSA AND BULIMIA NERVOSA

'I believed that my power – it was a general sort of idea – would be incrementally increased with each pound lost. There is plenty of research to show that I was not alone in that belief. Studies of girls show that they associate thinness with both academic and social success. I saw it more as a prerequisite to success of any sort. I saw it as the ticket out of my suffocating suburban life, out of the torrent of untoward thoughts in my head, out of the self that was simply not good enough.

'The anorexic body seems to say: I do not need. It says: Power over the self. And our culture in such a startlingly brief period of time has come to take literally the idea that power over the body has a ripple effect: Power over the body, over the life, over the people around you, power over a world gone berserk.'

[Hornbacher, 1998: 85]

Marya Hornbacher is lucky to be alive. For many years she has suffered from anorexia nervosa and her book is an account of how she has survived with this for many years. One can see from this fragment of her account that the issue of control is extremely important to her; she believes that the more weight is lost, the more control she will have. What is it that must be controlled? For her, these factors include the 'suffocation' of suburban life, which reveals the desire for autonomy or some form of identity; a head which is buzzing with a 'torrent' of thoughts; finally esteem, the belief that she simply is not good enough. The social ideal of thinness buttresses her own bid to take control over her body in a 'world gone berserk'. In this section we consider theoretical accounts of anorexia which highlight different aspects of Hornbacher's explanation.

8.2.1   Description and prevalence of starvation disorders

Anorexia nervosa (AN) has the highest death rate of any psychiatric illness. According to Halmi (1998), anorexics share four features which are:

- first, they weigh below 85 per cent of the normal weight for their age and height;
- second, they share an intense fear of gaining weight;
- third, they share a disturbance in body image, which is greatly distorted so that they appear to themselves as overweight even when malnourished;
- fourth, they suffer from amenorrhea (loss of menstruation).

Differences between anorexia nervosa and bulimia nervosa (BN) are twofold: first there are thought to be more BN than AN sufferers; second, while BN sufferers also starve themselves, they cannot resist the biological drive to eat and so engage in periodic 'binges', where they will stuff themselves with a huge variety of foods, which they will purge themselves of by means of self-induced vomiting, misuse of laxatives, diuretics and enemas. There is a complication in that some anorexics also binge and purge themselves. These are differentiated from bulimics as the latter tend to weigh within 85 per cent of their bodyweight and do not suffer from amenorrhea.

Although much epidemiological work has focused on this area, obtaining reliable data is difficult as large discrepancies exist in estimates for the prevalence of both AN and BN. Because AN is so rare, it poses major problems as very large populations are required to provide reliable estimates. An added difficulty is the reluctance of subjects with AN to participate in population studies. Despite these difficulties it is emerging that prevalence of AN, while still rare, is increasing in all the countries where reliable longitudinal studies have been completed.

Studies of BN have found that self-report questionnaire surveys tend to provide inflated estimates of bulimic symptoms. However there appears to be some agreement among researchers that 3–5 per cent of young Western women suffer with significant symptoms of eating disorder. Drawing upon US data, Russell (1995) contends that the incidence of BN is rising.

8.3   EXPLANATIONS OF ANOREXIA NERVOSA AND BULIMIA NERVOSA

In this section, social, psychoanalytic and biological explanations of eating disorders are described, compared and contrasted.

8.3.1   Social explanations of eating disorders

8.3.1.1   The fear of fatness

Stephen Mennell (1991) notes that it would be interesting to find out whether or not fatness was common in medieval and early modern Europe. He suggests that the ideal of the slender female form may be traced back to the court circles of the early Middle Ages. However it is also possible to find literary evidence that being fat or plump was considered to be attractive during that period and even may have been a mark of prestige. The fear of being overweight seems to have started from the top of the social scale and to have progressed steadily downwards. The change of the bodily ideal from an ample frame to one which is slim came about at the time of the Romantic Movement when the standard of beauty for both men and women among the upper class was for paleness, slenderness and frailty. While there are very little data with respect to the actual weight of people and how this may have declined, there is a lot of evidence which suggests that obesity was regarded as being a worry among the upper strata of European society in the nineteenth and early twentieth centuries. Nowadays while there is a general concern with obesity, those who are poorest are most likely to be overweight. Mennell notes that it is hardly surprising that the poor, who have had to live with the fear of not having enough to eat for centuries, did not immediately develop self-control when confronted with plentiful supplies of food. In fact clinical evidence suggests that psychological pressures to overeat are often rooted in past hunger, perhaps in a previous generation.

Mennell argues that, conversely, cases of anorexia nervosa (AN for short) arise disproportionately among the well-to-do strata, and in particular among women. There is some evidence to suggest that AN was present from the sixteenth century onwards, but the condition did not attract much attention or interest until the latter half of the nineteenth century when doctors noticed its prevalence in middle-class girls. He notes that nowadays AN is a very familiar illness in Europe and in North America. He draws what he considers to be a 'clear connection' between the onset of diseases such as AN and the plentiful supply of food, in that AN is not reported from countries where there is widespread starvation or famine, nor among blacks and other underprivileged groups in the USA. Mennell argues that AN and obesity can be seen as two sides of the same coin; as similar but opposite disturbances of the usual patterns of self-control over appetite now normally expected and necessary in prosperous Western societies. He contends that weight-watching and slimming have gradually become more widespread in all ranks of society, and links this with the constant portrayal of an ideal of slimness, particularly with respect to females. British and American studies of Afro-Caribbean, Asian and Hispanic women support the view that they report higher desired bodyweights, larger desirable body shapes and fewer weight concerns than white women (see note ii).

8.3.1.2 Link between images and eating disorders

Sociocultural explanations of AN and BN tend to look beyond the individual and towards society in seeking to develop explanations. Some views suggest that capitalist economic and social relations are not merely incidental to the development and expression of eating disorders but are to an extent constitutive of them. The focus is on the competitive and highly individualistic

Figure 8.1   The media and body-image

nature of contemporary consumer society where individuals are the subject of a number of competing claims from the food industry, the diet industry and the mass media which together bombard them, and particularly women, with a range of images (Figure 8.1). Television advertising on the one hand gives permission for women to consume fattening foods such as chocolate and cream which the slogan proclaims are 'naughty but nice' and on the other hand features ads for slimming and other dietary products. The typical women's magazine is a patchwork of editorial, advertising and advertorials (half advertising and half editorial) where any message can usually be placed so long as the advertiser has the money to pay for it. Features and editorial sections which warn of the dangers of attending to matchstick images jostle for the viewers' attention against the images themselves; as if overcome by a fit of amnesia, authors and editors are apparently unaware that the self-same images are promoted in their own publications (see note iii).

While there is little doubt that the 'ideal' images which are portrayed in the media are unrealizable for the vast majority of women and men, do people take such images seriously, or are they merely regarded as fantasy, or a form of entertainment? In a longitudinal study of eating habits in Fiji, Anne Becker of the Eating Disorders Center at Harvard Medical School noted a dramatic increase in disordered eating among teenage girls which she believes is linked to the recent introduction of television, and which appears to be changing the way in which Fijian girls view themselves and their bodies.[1] Most studies of the effects of images on bodily perception tend to be

[1] *Source*: News release from the Harvard Medical School on 17 May 1999.

situated in Western societies and laboratory based. In the section on ideology described in Chapter 3, it was maintained that, far from being 'taken in' by such advertising, most women find such images to be offensive – that advertising does not portray women as they really are. Grogan (1999) found that many of the women in her study were highly critical of the fact that 'skinny' models and actresses were represented as 'normal' body shapes in magazines and on film. However while women may be highly critical of advertising which features such images, they may still have an effect on their body-perception. In order to test this proposition, Myers and Biocca (1992) split their sample of seventy-six female students aged between eighteen and twenty-four into two groups: one group watched television images related to body-image; the other watched neutral programming. Respondents were then asked to evaluate mood and estimated body size. The findings indicated that watching a thirty-minute tape of body-image oriented advertisements had a significant effect on body-size orientation and mood levels, with increased reports of body dissatisfaction among respondents. Grogan (1996) investigated the effects on forty-nine men and forty-five women of viewing same-gender, slim, conventionally attractive models in relation to their evaluation of body esteem. Body-esteem scales were completed before and after viewing pictures of same-gender photographic models (experimental group) or landscapes (control group). According to Grogan, women scored significantly lower on the self-esteem scale, irrespective of which group they were in, which indicated that they were generally less satisfied with their bodies than the men. Grogan noticed several interesting differences between the experimental and control groups. Body-esteem scores decreased significantly, and to a similar degree, for both men and women who viewed the same-gender photographic models; whereas men and women in the control group who viewed landscapes showed no change. Grogan concluded that this suggested that 'at least in the short term' these men and women felt significantly less satisfied with their bodies as the result of seeing well-toned, slender and attractive same-gender models. This effect could have been achieved as the result of upward comparison with the models' bodies, or a shift in the 'ideal body shape' towards a more slender (for women) or muscular (for men) ideal.

From the above, one might then expect that, as the result of viewing such images, there may be some long-term distortion in the way in which women relate to their body images. Gardner and Tockerman (1993) found that on average, women tend to underestimate their body sizes. These results differ from McCaulay et al. (1988) who found that 55 per cent of female undergraduates perceived themselves to be overweight, whereas only 6 per cent fell within that weight category. Monteath and McCabe (1997) theorized that these differences could be explained as the result of the employment of different methods. For example McCaulay et al. (1988) focused on the perception of body weight, while others have focused on body shape. Monteath and McCabe (1997) themselves used a video recorder to measure women's perceptions of body shape. Each respondent was placed in front of a television screen on which her shape was projected. She was then given a control knob and asked to adjust the image on the screen until it represented how she thought her body looked. She was then asked to adjust the image on the screen until this represented how she would like her body to look. The final set of instructions asked her to adjust the screen to represent how society expected her to look. The results indicated that 56 per cent of the women underestimated their body sizes, 25 per cent correctly estimated their body sizes and 15 per cent overestimated their body sizes. Whereas 94 per cent expressed a strong desire to be smaller than their current size, 5 per cent were content and 1 per cent wanted to be larger. With respect to the societal ideal, 96 per cent of the women perceived themselves to be larger than the societal ideal. Overall the data supported the prediction that perceptual distortions occur across all weight and age categories. So in conclusion while there seems to be some dispute about methodology, current evidence supports the view that the mass media do tend to have an effect in distorting body-image for some women.

Irving (1990) sought specifically to investigate the role played by images on women with BN symptoms. She investigated the impact on self-esteem of thin, average and oversized models and concluded that exposure to the thin models resulted in lowered self-esteem. In another study by Heinberg and Thompson (1995), the investigators explored relations between television images and body satisfaction. Pre-test and post-test measures of body dissatisfaction were applied to gauge respondents' levels of body-image disturbance and awareness towards thinness. Findings indicated that those who scored high on 'body-image disturbance' were significantly less satisfied with their bodies after viewing the appearance-related images. As a result, the authors concluded that those who are vulnerable to body-image disturbance are especially prone to influence by images which relate to appearance.

The available evidence thus suggests that there is a link between body dissatisfaction, eating disorders and images of attractive models. However one cannot say from the evidence that body dissatisfaction leads to eating disorders. Those who suffer from eating disorders do not simply feel dissatisfaction with their bodies; they also have deeply problematic relationships with food and family, many of which seem to revolve around the issue of control. For example Grogan (1999) notes that while AN women overestimate the size of their bodies, they do this only to the same extent as do 'normal' women (see note iv).

8.3.1.3 Diet and eating disorders

AN and BN are overwhelmingly disorders of young women which reach a peak age of onset in mid to late adolescence, the period of the identity crisis. Dieting has been identified as the common factor which is necessary for the development of anorexia nervosa. Halmi (1998: 6) attributes the increase in anorexia nervosa to the fact that over the past two decades many more women have been 'seriously and strenuously' dieting compared with earlier decades. Linked to this she suggests that the societal influence on dieting has occurred because of Western values which equate slimness with sexual attractiveness. Also certain occupations, including actors, models, dancers and athletes, are at risk from AN because they emphasize body shape and bodyweight for professional competences (see note v). Garner *et al.* (1980) obtained the recorded weights of contestants for the Miss America Pageant from 1959 to 1978 and found that in comparison with national norms, the mean percentage of average weight was 87.6 per cent for the period 1959–70 and 84.6 per cent for the period 1970–78, indicating that 'beauty' contestants averaged weights well below the national norm. The authors concluded that there had been a clear shift towards a thinner ideal body shape for women in Western culture over the twenty-year period.

There is considerable evidence to support the view that dieting, or restrained eating, is common among girls and women in Western consumer societies and also that many of them are troubled by issues of food, eating and body shape. Some authors have noted the steep increase in diet-related articles in women's magazines and in the popular press since the 1960s (Garner *et al.*, 1980). Other studies have shown that models in women's magazines have become slimmer (Silverstein *et al.*, 1986). Further research indicates that in Western culture the view that 'fat = bad' is generally shared, as are idealizations of thinness (Harris *et al.*, 1991). A number of authors share the view that there must be some relation between cultural prescriptions regarding the body, particularly the female body, and recent increases both in dieting and in eating disorders.

That the typical sufferer of AN is a white, 'middle-class' woman also tends to support Mennell's (1991) view that culture plays a part in this disorder. Recent evidence that the incidence of eating disorders is spread across all social classes and ethnic groups within Western culture lends support to his 'trickle-down' theory. The data with respect to non-Western countries are generally anecdotal, but suggest that the incidence of AN and BN is rare; where they are found, they occur in Westernized segments of the population (Szmukler and Patton, 1995: 186). Some authors such as Edwards-Hewitt and Gray (1993) attribute this to the dissemination of Western cultural ideals of female beauty, thinness and dieting to such sectors. For example, the prevalence of anorexia nervosa in Greek and Turkish girls living in Germany who were exposed to Western ideals of thinness was twice that of Greek girls who remained in Greece or Turkish girls who remained in Turkey and were not exposed to Western values of body-image (see note vi). Cases of BN and AN have also been reported in black and Asian groups living in the West. A study by Pumariega (1986) found that 'eating attitudes' among young Hispanic American women were correlated with 'acculturation' to American cultural values.

8.3.1.4   Critique of social explanation

There is a growing body of evidence, from the above and from other studies, which suggests a link between the sociocultural environment and eating disorders. However there is a danger in adopting an overly determinist view for culture by suggesting that eating disorders are only affected by cultural factors. It might be tempting to infer that AN and BN are no longer solely associated within relatively affluent white, middle-class women but have been spread to all social and ethnic groups with the spread of the consumer society. An alternative explanation could be that these disorders have always been present in all groups but have not been diagnosed. Second, the idea that BN and AN sufferers simply 'internalize' the images of a competitive media ideal could be thought to be a gross oversimplification which ignores the role of wider political and cultural factors, the family and biology, and the fact that people are not passive recipients of images but actively accept, reject or negotiate such images. Notwithstanding this, from the above discussion, it would be scarcely surprising if young impressionable women developed a distinctly problematic orientation to food in relation to their body image.

One difficulty with social explanations is that some recent research suggests that one may find instances of AN in societies where being 'fat' is not considered to be socially unacceptable. If this is indeed the case then one would be forced to conclude that at least some proportion of the prevalence of AN is genetic in origin. One study carried out by Dr Hans Hoek of the Hague Psychiatric Institute focused on the territory of Curacao, an area which is considered to be generally free of Western influence, where fat has positive and not negative connotations. Hoek's study of over 144,000 medical records over a three-year period yielded up 8 cases of AN, which he felt was in broad proportion to the incidence of AN to be expected in Europe (see note vii). Another hint that genetic factors may play a role in the incidence of eating disorders is that AN and BN tend to run in families: this suggests that genetic factors do play a role. Treasure and Holland (1995) note that the most significant difference between anorexics and others is that anorexics tend to be perfectionists and to suffer from obsessive–compulsive disorder. Researchers also found that mothers of patients with AN are likely to have obsessive–compulsive disorder. As the result of these and other studies, the focus of research into eating disorders has begun to shift from culture to the quest for a more detailed understanding of the neurobiological factors in the aetiology (causation) of eating disorders.

8.3.2 The biology of eating disorders

Bulimia nervosa and anorexia nervosa present a very complex challenge to researchers. Those who base their findings on the self-reports of sufferers must confront a baffling range of potential cause–effect relations. For example some sufferers associate the beginning of their problem with anxiety over body image, how they felt 'dumpy' at school, how they were bullied by other girls who were 'slim' and 'delicate'; how eventually they began to diet to become more like those slim and delicate girls; how they started to slim but couldn't stop. Or perhaps the problem would be associated with a 'dysfunctional' family, where the sufferer claimed to be a buffer between warring parents. On the other hand there are those who claim that they were happy at school, had loving parents and a good family relationship but that AN had always somehow been there.

8.3.2.1 Starvation models

Despite the wide variations in self-reports cited above, researchers detected one or two common features across cases, for example the relation of AN and BN to obsessive–compulsive disorder (OCD). It is well known among sufferers and their families that both BN and AN sufferers tend to be obsessed by food. However obsession with food is not solely linked to these conditions. The Minnesota Starvation Study carried out during the Second World War had the aim of working out the most efficient means for refeeding starving Europeans. The subjects for the study consisted of US conscientious objectors who were fed half their normal intake of food and who lost over one-quarter of their bodyweight in six months. Researchers noted that images of food began to dominate the lives of those subjects who participated in the study, to the extent that images of food even shaped subsequent career choices. Those who were involved in the treatment of AN drew on these conclusions to assume (mistakenly) that, as AN sufferers also obsessed about food, this was simply due to their starvation and that if they could regain their normal weight the symptoms would stop. This belief that the root cause of AN lay with the starvation itself led to the initiation of force-feeding programmes which were initially successful in leading to increases in bodyweight but which in most cases led to relapse. Clearly the causes of BN and AN were to be more complex than this.

However several researchers have noted a link between obsessive–compulsive disorder (OCD) and eating disorders (Rastam and Gillberg, 1991; Treasure and Holland, 1995). Eating-disorder sufferers are not only obsessive in relation to food, but to a whole range of behaviours such as washing, cleanliness and tidiness. They also demonstrate a number of other symptoms such as an inability to sleep.

8.3.2.2 Biological explanations: the hypothalamus and the serotonin system

Studies of monozygotic twins provide support for the view that there is a genetic component in the development of AN and BN. The evidence for AN is strongest with concordance rates at around 50 per cent, indicating high heritability (Meyer *et al.*, 1998: 301). However there is considerable uncertainty about how genetic and environmental factors combine to produce these conditions. According to Steiger *et al.* (1996), one part of the explanation is that children come to adopt their parents' concerns with eating, but this is not sufficient for the development of AN or BN as it applies to all children. They suggest that genetics may play a role in heightening vulnerability to these disorders (see note viii).

In exploring the neurophysiology of eating disorders, researchers began to investigate the role played by the hypothalamus, that area of the brain which governs appetite and mood and in particular the role played by neurotransmitters and hormones in relaying signals within this centre. First we discuss the possible role played by the serotonin system.

The serotonin system

In Chapter 6 we described how, inside the hypothalamus, brain cells communicate with each other by means of neurotransmitters or chemical messengers, one of which is serotonin. The hypothesized link between serotonin and food is that starches and sugars are converted into insulin and this in turn is converted into the amino acid tryptophan. Tryptophan is then converted into serotonin (5-hydroxytryptamine), which is often referred to as 5-HT. It has been suggested that of all the neurotransmitters, serotonin is perhaps the most implicated in the aetiology (causation) and treatment of disorders including depression, obsessive–compulsive disorder, schizophrenia, stroke, obesity, bulimia, anorexia, pain, hypertension, vascular disorders, attention-deficit disorder (ATHD) and nausea. As a result, the serotonin system has attracted intense interest from pharmaceutical and biotech corporations which are pouring billions of dollars into research in seeking to unravel the complex set of interactions within the serotonin system, and between this system and others within the brain and body. This system is a target for many of the major legal and illegal drugs, including cocaine, MDMA, ecstasy, LSD, fenfluramine (marketed as Redux and recently withdrawn), fluoxetene (marketed as Prozac), sumatriptan (targeted at migraine-sufferers) and ritalin (which addresses ATHD).

How does this system work? The following discussion is illustrated in Figure 8.2. Serotonin was first isolated from blood by Page and his co-workers in 1948 and was later identified in the central nervous system. Page commented that no physiological substance known possesses such diverse actions in the body as does 5-HT. However, to simplify its neuronal function, one can say that it produces its effects as a consequence of interactions with appropriate receptors. Like other chemical neurotransmitters, serotonin is synthesized in brain neurons and stored in vesicles. Activated by an electrical impulse, it is released into the synaptic cleft where it interacts and binds with post-synaptic receptors. The actions of serotonin are terminated by three major mechanisms: by being diffused, metabolized or transported back into the pre-synaptic receptor for storage.

The actions of 5-HT can be theoretically modulated by: agents that stimulate or inhibit its synthesis (step 1); agents that block its storage (step 2); agents that stimulate or inhibit its release (step 3); agents that mimic or inhibit its actions at its various post-synaptic receptors (step 4); agents that inhibit its uptake back into the nerve terminal (step 5); and agents that affect its metabolism (step 6).

Serotonin is relevant to eating disorders in two ways. First it is thought to modulate feeding by producing fullness or satiety. Anorexic patients often complain of being very full after eating a small amount. Serotonin antagonists that decrease serotonergic neurotransmission or block receptor

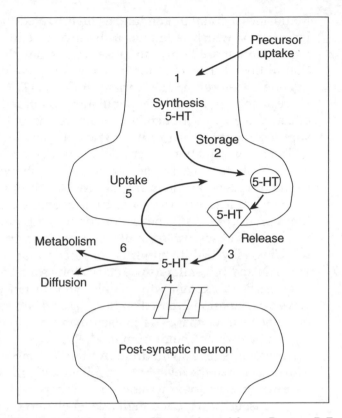

Figure 8.2 The serotonin system [Reproduced from Borne, R.F. (1994) Serotonin: The Neurotransmitter for the 1990s, *Drug Topics*, Oct 10th: 108]

activation increase food consumption and promote weight gain. Conversely serotonin agonists decrease food intake; however a second effect of serotonin pathways is with respect to the modulation of mood, impulse regulation and obsessionality. AN patients are especially rigid, inhibited, ritualistic and perfectionistic, which are characteristics often present in obsessive–compulsive disorder. Feelings of fullness or satiety have been addressed by drugs that are serotonin antagonists, such as cyproheptadine, which reduce such feelings and increase food intake. On the other hand serotonin agonists reduce obsessive thinking and compulsive behaviour. A number of drugs have been developed which seek to affect aspects of this system and in particular step 5. For example tricyclic antidepressants block the uptake of norepinephrine and also, to varying degrees, 5-HT. However these are known to have major side-effects. During the clinical trials of Prozac (fluoxetene), which is an SSRI (Selective Serotinin Re-uptake Inhibitor), it was shown that the drug had considerable success in the treatment of depression (see note ix). Fluoxetene has been useful in preventing relapse in BN patients, who have been restored to 80 per cent of a normal weight range (see note x).

The serotonin system is further complicated by the fact that different categories of 5-HT receptors are involved. A research team based at the

Maudsley Hospital in London has investigated the influence of one particular receptor which is known to be involved in regulating feeding. Drugs which block it are known to cause weight gain. Research has found a variation in the 5-HT2A receptor in many AN patients, leading to the overproduction of serotonin. This variant of the 5-HT2A receptor was found to be twice as common in the AN population compared with a control group. The effect of the overproduction of serotonin is not only a powerful appetite suppressant but is also known to raise anxiety levels.

The overproduction of serotonin may also account for the high observed levels of stress, anxiety and obsessionality shown by those suffering from eating disorders. Furthermore, external levels of stress raise serotonin levels even higher, leading to a vicious circle of ever-escalating stress–anxiety–serotonin production. One means for coping with anxiety is to exert control by resorting to obsessive–compulsive behaviour. However Dr Walter Kaye of the University of Pittsburgh is convinced that there is a biological reason why AN and BN sufferers use starvation as a means to escape from anxiety. The task is to explain why people who do not eat feel better as a result. Kaye's explanation is based on the relations between serotonin and food. We explained earlier that 5-HT is itself made up from an amino acid known as tryptophan which comes from food. If no tryptophan is taken into the body then serotonin levels will drop. By starving oneself of food, the AN sufferer is driving down the level of tryptophan going into the brain and this may be a way of driving down serotonegetic activity. So it may be that sufferers from eating disorders have too high a level of serotonin, which makes them feel very anxious and uncomfortable, and by starving themselves they feel better.

However one must still explain the difference between AN and BN. While BN sufferers are still 'normal' to the extent that they cannot ignore the fundamental biological drive to eat – even if subsequently they vomit what they have eaten, AN sufferers have suppressed the drive to eat entirely. This is of major significance as most 'normal' people will eat the most unimaginable foods in order to stay alive under conditions of starvation. Researchers at the Maudsley Hospital in London have explored anorexics' apparent fear of food and have conjectured that in AN patients some aspect of the appetite system is not functioning properly. In examining this, the researchers explored the biology of stress (see note xi). The body's response to stress begins as a cascade of hormones originating in the hypothalamus and ending in the production of cortisol and adrenaline, stress hormones which are pumped around the body, propelling the instinctual 'flight' response as the pulse races and muscles fill with blood. As well as filling muscles with blood and increasing heart rate, cortisol and adrenaline also act to suppress appetite. Try to think back to when you have had a particularly stressful experience. No doubt the last things on your mind at the time were having a good meal or going to sleep! In 'normal' people, once the stress has died down the hypothalamus releases another hormone, AVP, which reduces the effects of the stress hormones and turns appetite back on. If stress becomes persistent then AVP should become more dominant, moderating the stress response by allowing some appetite to return. But if that does not happen, as seems to be the case with AN, then sufferers are locked into a situation of chronic stress. The basis for this explanation is thus that the AVP switch seems to be faulty in AN sufferers. Because of the high levels of stress generated by this chronic condition, further sources of environmental stress may make life feel truly unbearable for such sufferers. This chronic overproduction of cortisol and adrenaline are also thought to shrink the hippocampus.

The treatment of eating disorders has been complicated in part because AN sufferers in particular have a marked preoccupation with control and autonomy, and so are resistant to taking medication of any kind (see note xii). A second major factor consists of the complex causal linkages between eating disorders and other symptoms such as depression. Antidepressants are the most commonly prescribed drugs for eating disorders. However a difficulty has been recognized in that starvation brought on by the eating disorder can itself cause the depression rather than the other way round. While a few uncontrolled studies in the 1970s reported success from tricyclic antidepressants in producing short-term weight gain, other controlled experiments showed no effect and the conclusion is generally that depressants have a very limited role to play in AN. In fact it has been shown that some depressants can precipitate weight gain and a craving for carbohydrates, which may induce panic and fear in the patient.

8.3.2.3 Critique of biological explanation

Some argue that the relatively recent discovery of leptin, which is discussed in more detail in the next section, provides a boost for the biological explanation of eating disorders. Connan and Treasure (1998: 220) suggest that this discovery supports the hypothesis that weight is held constant by means of a signal from the fat stores which is relayed to the brain and which controls appetite and food intake. The gene for leptin is expressed in fat tissue and is dysfunctional in the 'ob' (obese) mouse which is phenotypically fat, infertile and inactive. If leptin is given to ob mice their appetite decreases, metabolism increases, activity increases, weight falls and they become fertile. A primary role for leptin may be to provide a signal to the hypothalamus that fat stores are sufficient for reproduction. However leptin is by no means the only factor to take into account in explaining the incidence of eating disorders. While huge strides have been made in understanding the neurobiology of the regulation of appetite, researchers have also learned more about the true complexity of the functioning of such systems. Some of the more interesting findings reinforce the view that a satisfactory explanation will involve the complex relations between biology and environment (see note xiii).

8.3.3 Psychoanalytic views of eating disorders

Psychoanalysts have been interested for some time in the aetiology of eating disorders. The classic psychoanalytic explanation related AN to difficulties during the oral and anal phases of development. The preoccupation with food was interpreted as demonstrating that the mind of the anorexic was under the influence of the earliest oral sexual energies. The personality characteristics of perfectionism, rigidity and defiance were linked to anal sexual drives. In Chapter 6 we discussed how Erik Erikson considered the crises during these early phases of development to centre on trust and mistrust and autonomy and shame. Dare and Crowther (1995: 129) argue that the problem of control of impulses is great and of general importance for eating disorder patients, and that this can be expressed in relation to struggles between sufferers and parents over feeding and wider issues of autonomy for the developing person. They also suggest that the loss of control that occurs in bingeing needs examination in understanding bulimic sufferers and that the psychodynamic approach is useful in exploring such issues.

8.3.3.1 Eating disorders as hunger-strikes

There is a long tradition within the psychoanalytic view of treating eating disorders as if they were forms of protest as embodied in hunger-strikes. Alfred Adler (1924) explained eating disorders as a fear of eating, a form of neurotic hunger-strike, an attempt by means of exaggerated abstinence to retard the development of the female form. Adler theorized that eating disorders arose as the result of the conscious or unconscious realization of the loss of power resulting from the fixing of a female gender identity on the girl child. To such children the value of an eating disorder was as a form of 'hunger-strike', a means of gaining power which had probably been tested by the child at an earlier age. By doing this, everything revolves around her and her will dominates. This explanation once more places control at the centre of the argument. The anorexic adolescent is aware that she lacks power in the family and in society because she lacks a penis. She reacts in horror to the physiological changes which take place within her body at the onset of puberty and attempts to 'perfect' herself physically by destroying the unacceptable (feminine) appearance. In this instance the starvation represents the young woman's rejection of her femininity and her subservience to the fantasy that she could reach another ideal state or image. Adler regarded this form of hunger-strike as an artifice of the weak, a form of infantile inferiority, of 'to and fro', of frittering time – the 'hesitating attitude' when faced with the demands of life.

More recent psychoanalytic explanations of eating disorders have moved away from an explanation which centres on some form of 'penis envy'. Instead the explanation relates to fundamental processes of differentiating the self from other people and finding that separatedness to be bearable. The developing child may come to fear the consequences of separateness from the other, and in addition may come to be angry and fearful that others can be a source of support and comfort for the loved one, the mother. This gives the (m)other power over the self. The second aspect is concerned with the extent to which people and the self are seen as containing admixtures of good and bad; anorexics tend to see others and themselves as being either perfectly good or absolutely bad:

'The anorectic symptom is at least twofold in its meaning. On the one hand the intense concern over food intake expresses a message: "This is an area in which I am in control, which makes me feel I am being myself, by which I can defy the demands of others." On the other hand, and at the same time, the symptom appears to say: "I am only a little child, I cannot live by myself, I have to be looked after; I am not going to take up much space; I do not want to make demands on resources".'
[Dare and Crowther, 1995: 135]

While retaining the notion of a 'hunger-strike', Susie Orbach's (1993, orig. 1986) explanation is much closer to this view than that advocated by Adler, as cited above.

8.3.3.2 Susie Orbach: the hunger-strike revisited

In her book which is pertinently entitled *Hunger Strike* (1993, originally published in 1986), Susie Orbach describes anorexia nervosa as a rising epidemic which is a central metaphor for our times, as perhaps the most dramatic outcome of Western consumer culture's obsession with body size. In this view, AN is 'the excruciating spectacle of women actually transforming their bodies in their attempts to deal with the contradictory requirements of their role in late twentieth-century America and England' (1993: 4). Orbach disagrees with the argument that AN represents a denial of femininity and is a refusal to be an adult. She argues that those who do see AN in this way are enmeshed in a paradox – while on the one hand they view the anorexic as weak and childish, she is also depicted as a strong, crafty and unyielding opponent. As a result, she argues that those medics who seek to control eating disorders end up involved in what can only be described as being a struggle for power over who is to control the individual woman's body. To Orbach, the procedures such as force-feeding, enforced bed rests and constant supervision used to control AN are so intrusive, brutal and invasive that they represent a form of rape of the female body.

Orbach argues that in spite of the rhetoric of women's equality in Western countries, they must conform in the main to masculine values and accept entry to society on that basis. To put it crudely, while women have been offered career opportunities in the 'masculine' world of work, they are also still expected to be the primary caregiver in the family. As a result, women are culturally and psychologically prepared for a life in which they continue to service the needs of others, while at the same time they are teased with the possibility of living a life for themselves. Thus, Orbach argues, women end up being pushed and pulled in opposite directions.

Orbach's central views are thus that first the female form is an object of desire for men and that consequently in their passage towards femininity all girls experience the desire to be attractive, to make their bodies conform to the designated ideal of the day, which in contemporary Western societies is to be slender, tall, curvaceous, slim-hipped or pointed-breasted. The second imperative is the paradoxical relationship between women and feeding. The woman must feed others but must restrain her own desires for that very same food through dieting.

She links eating disorders directly to the rise of consumer society. In Western consumer societies, people come to see their bodies less as contributors to production, most of which has been moved 'offshore', and more as vehicles for consumption activity. Commodities are no longer valued for their usefulness or the quality of labour that was invested into their manufacture but rather for the values which they signify for the consumer. Women's bodies are used in a host of marketing contexts from advertising to fashion shows, to give meaning to a vast range of products from cars to Coke. Orbach argues that as a result such products come to be seen as vehicles for shaping a person's own sexual identity. The body itself has become a commodity in the marketplace, a kind of object with which people negotiate the world. Women are encouraged to see their bodies from a 'third eye', which is outside; they look upon themselves as if they were commodities. The woman's experience of her own body stems from two sources – how she has learned to relate to her body in early life and how she believes her body compares to the images of women portrayed in films, television programmes, magazines, advertising and other mass media. Orbach considers that if a woman has grown up with a reasonably good feeling about her body shape and female body functions then she may just about be able to survive the tyranny of the diet and 'beauty' industry's 'daily assault' upon women' (1993: 16). The use of women's bodies in the promotion of products leads to all sorts of body-image problems for women in creating a distortion in their evaluation of their bodies and in creating a dysjuncture from their bodies.

Figure 8.3 shows a remarkably honest self-portrait of photographer Jo Spence which she entitled 'I recreate my journey into emotional eating, a rebellion against parental disapproval'. In her book *Cultural Sniping* (1995), Spence talks of how she took her initial (working-class) identity from her parents which she subsequently rejected. Why is it that so many women in particular come to develop an extremely problematic relation to food? Orbach's explanation follows that of Erikson (1968) which was outlined in Chapter 6. In one sense AN can be seen as an extreme response to anxieties about parenting, in that it symbolizes a search for order and certainty in the face of tumult. Orbach describes the period from the Second World War until the present day as being especially fraught from the point of view of parenting, as social expectations have shifted considerably with respect to the role of women. In turn, the shifting sense of self of women and the possibilities which they have envisioned for their children can be very confusing for the child. Orbach argues that the ways in which mothers socialize their children is fundamentally gendered. To illustrate this point she quotes a study which shows that during the **oral phase** (in the USA), fewer girls were breast-fed and the time allotted to feeding activities was considerably less for girls than for boys, thus setting the pattern for later life. Major problems may also occur during the course of the next stage of development from the age of six months to two years when the child confronts the crisis of autonomy. Boys' curiosity and initiatives are encouraged, while girls' sense of exploration and

Figure 8.3   Jo Spence/Dr Tim Sheard (1989): Greedy [Reproduced with kind permission of Terry Dennett and the Jo Spence Archive]

curiosity is reined in by the mothers who are aware that their daughters will be required to defer to males in later life. Girls are thus encouraged to display a range of dependent and deferential behaviour, and are guided to convert their own wish to be cared for into the care of others. As a result, Orbach argues, there is a problem of individuation for girls, many of whom do not perceive that they have developed an identity which is autonomous of the mother. The little girl may become overly 'clingy' as the result of her dependency being encouraged by the mother, who may often react negatively to this, resulting in the girl becoming uneasy and confused in expressing her needs.

As girls enter **adolescence**, the unresolved issues from the earlier developmental phase where autonomy is developed are reconstituted in a new and dramatic form. Adolescence is a time of detachment from the family and of realignment with peers. The girl may desire separation at one level;

however the wish to stay close and protected within the family is in conflict with the desire for separation and autonomy. Orbach cites evidence which suggests that, at this stage, parents of anorexic children interfere with the child's attempt to establish normal peer relations which are important in the construction of pre-adult identity. The insecurity experienced by the girl, resulting from feelings of being simultaneously pulled in opposite directions, is heightened as her body itself begins to change in ways which seem to be beyond her control. She may well respond to this growing anxiety by developing an overwhelming desire to conform. Orbach argues that as a girl's relations with her mother are often tension-filled, the daughter may seek confirmation outside her family through her girl-friends and the magazines which are written explicitly for teenage girls:

> 'One thing that adolescent magazines uniformly preach as the solution to the crises of adolescence is dieting and weight control. Young women read that dieting is both the passport to teenage life and the answer to a whole host of named and unnamed problems. The psychic insecurity is now addressed by the modern panacea – diet and control. The girls are initiated into the adult relationship they are to have with their bodies. Be vigilant, control your desires for food (and incidentally for sex), be frightened of your own body, it is always waiting to let you down.'
> [1993: 27]

In this way Orbach argues, the adolescent girl learns to make a split between her body and herself. Her body is rapidly being presented to her and being perceived by her as an artefact. The body thus becomes a source of anxiety.

8.3.3.3 Critique of psychoanalytic explanation

Psychoanalytic explanations are complex, including interactions between person, environment and parenting. The supposed interactions between mothers and daughters are also interesting as they add a generational element to the quality of explanation. The difficulties in psychoanalytic explanations are that they are based on the assumption of the existence of stages of development and of internal conflicts which cannot really be proven. Secondly, the focus on the mother–child relationship assumes that anorexia is contained within the parameters of this relationship or of the family which contains it. There is thus a tendency to lay a lot of emphasis on parenting in such explanations, which again requires more proof. While psychoanalytically inspired approaches, such as that developed by Orbach, acknowledge the power of the peer group it is possible that this is underestimated in such explanations. The psychoanalytic explanations also tend to play down the power of general cultural factors. Finally, Orbach's explanation ignores and even discounts an explanation of the incidence of male AN. It may well be that Orbach has identified the basis for a sound explanation of AN in females; however this cannot form the basis for the incidence of AN in males.

8.4   A DISCURSIVE 'FOUCAULDIAN' INTERPRETATION OF ANOREXIA

In *The Thin Woman* (1998), Helen Malson seeks to understand anorexia through the lens developed by Michel Foucault, whose approach was partly outlined in Chapter 3. Malson's aim is to understand how anorexia has been constructed and defined in the modern era as a medical condition presided over by experts. In this view, anorexia is not natural but is constructed through **discourse**, and a key aim of research is to document and analyse those discourses which constitute it. The focus of research is thus not the person, or 'patient' who 'suffers' from anorexia, but the discourses in which this has emerged as an 'abnormal' disorder. Like Foucault, Malson is interested to provide a **genealogy** or history of the present, in other words, to seek to understand how present medical understandings of anorexia have come about. She is also interested to explore the relations between power and identity, how the 'anorexic' identity is produced by discourse and the ways in which those diagnosed with anorexia appropriate and resist the effects of such discourse. Finally her aim is to provide a gendered description to account for why AN is overwhelmingly suffered by women. Malson's method involved a review of documents, coupled with a detailed analysis of the talk of 23 women who were diagnosed with anorexia.

8.4.1   Early religious descriptions of starvation in Europe

In conducting a genealogy of AN, Malson notes that the earliest written descriptions of starving women relate them to a religious context. References from the thirteenth to seventeenth centuries in Europe mention starving women such as St Catherine of Sienna and 'Joan the Meatless' within a context of Christian holiness, whereby they are considered to have an extraordinary link with the divine. While noting that there are similarities between medieval descriptions of fasting women and twentieth-century descriptions of AN in terms of the physical effects of starvation, Malson is suspicious of modern-day researchers who consider these 'starving women' to be early examples of what is now labelled as AN. This is because medieval meanings of food and fasting are very different from what they are today. Fasting was regarded as being useful as a means of atoning for sin and drawing closer to God, while the Eucharist was food for the soul and many fasting women abstained from all food but that in expressing their spirituality. As a result, she feels that any argument of equivalence between the two is meaningless.

8.4.2   From religious to early medical discourse

Malson notes that with the Protestant Reformation, traditional Catholic practices such as harsh asceticism, including fasting, were disavowed. As a result, female fasters came under greater scrutiny and suspicion. While accounts of 'fasting girls' were recorded during the post-Reformation period within a religious framework, they became increasingly described in medical terms. Physicians and magistrates began to be considered as suitable investigators of claims of miraculous fasting. With the ascendancy of the medical profession by the end of the eighteenth century, a new medical technology emerged which became openly critical of the religious interpretation of 'fasting girls'. Early medical accounts tended to explain AN as associated with the 'humours' or a function of the 'nervousness' of women. Throughout the eighteenth and nineteenth centuries, medics linked 'wasting' or 'fasting' to disturbance in the gastric nerves or to a form of 'hypochondriacal delirium'. The term 'hypochondria', which was first defined at the turn of the eighteenth century, was initially defined as a somatic abdominal disorder accompanied by multiple symptoms moving around the body. However, during this period, ideas of sensibility to suffering and of 'exquisite feeling' and 'nervousness' came to be linked together and associated with those of superior caste. Hypochondria became associated with the idea of 'nervous delicacy', which was thought to be present more in women than in men. As it began to be thought that any illness could be caused by the imagination, the meaning of hypochondria changed to represent an imaginary complaint. The idea of 'nervousness' became increasingly feminized so that women came to be thought of as fragile, delicate and 'sickly', prone to neurasthenia and invalidism. The increasingly prominent notion of feminine nervousness came to be epitomized through the concept of **hysteria**, which was considered to be a fundamentally gendered disorder. Initially ascribed as a disease of the womb, hysteria came to be associated with a nervous disorder and increasingly came to be described by medics as a consequence of medical weakness or suppressed feelings. The late nineteenth century was thus labelled the 'golden age' of hysteria.

Malson (1998) considers the emergence during the twentieth century of 'anorexia', which has come to be explained in a number of ways, to be the result of a natural disease – a genetic predisposition and a psychodynamic disturbance. She maintains that all these discourses are necessarily partial and are problematic in the ways in which they seek to explain anorexia.

8.4.3 Anorexia and the discursive production of gender: the meaning of the thin body

Malson argues that the body is subject to a range of discourses which collectively tangle together in ways which produce a multiplicity of meaning. It is within this entanglement, and in the slipping of signification from one discourse to another, that alternative and often contradictory meanings of what a 'woman' is and what 'her' body is, are constructed. Below we consider some of these entanglements. Her own research focuses on the meaning of the thin body, which, she suggests, can be viewed as a site of struggle over the multiplicity of its meanings. Malson found that on the one hand it could be taken to symbolize a 'perfect' femininity; on the other it could be read as being a 'non-body', through being symbolized as being boyish or androgynous.

8.4.3.1 'Perfect' femininity

In common with many women, Malson's interviewees consider fatness to be unattractive and shameful, linked to introversion and low self-esteem. The ideal of 'femininity' is linked by them to size, to not being bigger than a 'size 8 or a size 10'. Linked to this is the desire for a childlike body, to look like a 12-year-old and to be able to wear children's clothes, which was seen as an indication of success. Malson suggests that in this respect, thinness 'signifies a delicate, meek, childlike femininity' which is also 'perilously disempowered' (1998: 108). This can be taken to reinforce the predominant position of male power (known as patriarchy) in society. Malson maintains that this is unsurprising as the dissemination of disempowering images of women is widespread, citing examples from the media where 'anorexic' women are described as being 'childishly petulant', an image which parallels nineteenth-century descriptions of the 'hysterical' woman. She asks how can we justify describing 'anorexics' as being immature when the fashion industry regularly churns out waif-like images of Madonna, Courtney Love and Naomi Campbell? She contends that these media images emphasize one of the many profound contradictions in the category of 'woman'. While 'womanhood' is an ostensibly adult status, it is frequently portrayed as being childlike, dependent and passive. In this respect, femininity is small and small is inferior.

On the other hand, not all discourse reinforces such patriarchal imagery. Malson notes that one discourse to be found in women's magazines, which she labels the 'Be More Beautiful' discourse, is not constructed around the notion of getting a man, but of being so for herself, for her own 'salvation'. However for the 'anorexic', the idea of dependency is consolidated through the idea that she is ill with the 'slimmers' disease'; which again has similarities with the 'fragile' and 'delicate' 'woman' of romantic discourse.

The thin body may also be understood as comprising a 'boyish non-femininity' which constitutes resistance to the patriarchal construction of the perfect female body. In this respect amenorrhea may be construed positively as a form of resistance towards or rejection of an 'imposed' femininity.

8.4.4   Discourse of 'Cartesian' dualism

One of the main points which Malson seeks to make is with respect to 'Cartesian' dualism. While she identifies this as an important element of the talk of the women whom she interviewed, this concern springs directly from her reading of Foucault. 'Cartesian' dualism is traced to Descartes famous quote *'cogito ergo sum'*, which effectively creates a distinction

Figure 8.4   Can only the male body be positively portrayed as being fat?

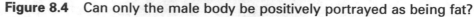

between the mind and the body, where the mind is equated with the 'self' which controls the body. Malson argues that this discourse of control is pervasive in liberal discourse. Think for one moment of 'who' 'you' are. Do you define your body as part of your 'self' or as a separate entity which is controlled by 'your' mind? According to Foucault, this 'self' which feels that it is autonomous and 'self'-directing is in fact a fiction. This is because the 'self' is constructed through those often conflicting discourses which operate within language.

The discourse of 'Cartesian' dualism shares similarities with the structuralist position which was outlined in Chapter 5, as meaning seems to be structured according to stable binary oppositions, where one side is privileged over the other. For example Malson's analysis of anorexic discourse indicates the following set of oppositions (derived from Malson, 1998):

Non-self		*Ideal-self*
Fat body	vs	Thin body
Letting yourself go	vs	Self-control
Body	vs	Mind
Eating food	vs	Starvation
Fat	vs	Absence of fat
Evil	vs	Good
A blob	vs	Defined-self
Low esteem	vs	Confidence
Superficial	vs	Deep

The desire to control the body so that it is thin in order to be some-body which gives a woman confidence is not only perceived as a good thing by anorexics, but by most women in Western culture. Malson argues that the idea that the mind and body are split, so that the body is no longer perceived to be 'me', informs a variety of cultural practices such as dieting and exercising as well as self-starvation and purging. In this respect, anorexia is an extreme expression of the way that most women come to construct themselves in relation to their bodies.

The anorexic body is a **controlled body** while that of the fat body is considered to be beyond control. Weight control, self-control and control over one's life are articulated together. Being thin comes close to the ideal of being in control. In this respect, the thin body is valued as being an outcome of self-control. However, food and body weight are construed narrowly as the *only* means by which self-control can be realized. Thus the thin/anorexic body may signify the quasi-feminine ideal of being in control of her life, but that control is restricted to the traditional female areas of food and the body. Here the controlled body becomes a metonym for a controlled life, so that not eating and staying thin specify a total control. The body is thus construed within 'Cartesian' dualism as an alien, the mind as being superior. Again, the anorexic view is an extreme version of 'normal' activities:

'One of the most dramatic aspects of this form of this dualistic fiction of subjectivity and embodiment is the fantasy of dictating one's own body shape, a fantasy that manifests itself not only in anorexia and in dieting but also in normal/obsessive exercise and body-building, in the fantasies of halting the aging process and dictating body shape that pervade numerous advertisements for cosmetics and cosmetic surgery.' [1998, 124]

'Cartesian' dualist discourse constructs the body as an alien to the mind/self. **Eating** is an example. Eating is construed as a bodily desire which is entirely alien to the mind/self. Malson quotes from one interviewee, Emma, to illustrate this point:

'In a way it feels like it's not me. It feels it takes over. It's not me saying: oh you know do it. It's something completely (. . .) something completely dissociated from me that just kicks in and says: yeah do it you know. But I'm not thinking about it at all. I have to clear up the mess once I've done it and sort out what you know what's been going on because I haven't been there all the time that's all been happening.' [1998: 125]

Malson explains this as an example which illustrates that the bodily experience of eating becomes dissociated from the experience of self. Within this discourse food becomes construed as something which is desirable and yet also a profoundly dangerous temptation. One interviewee described food as being 'dirty and disgusting'; another said that while she used to talk about food with other people, she came to see it as a form of poison. Layla, another interviewee, says 'I loved food. I loved food. But that meant fat legs, fat bottom, ugliness, unaesthetic, dangerous' (1998: 126). The relation with food is thus construed as being both necessary and dangerous; it is simultaneously nice and horrible.

Fat is construed as being both negative and completely alien; losing fat appears to be an aim in itself. As Emma says:

'I just hate it. It just . . . doesn't feel like it should be part of me, you know. It feels all wrong. And I feel that something I did a few years ago has forced it to be there and now I've got to force it to go away again you know.' [1998: 129]

For some of the women, fat is seen to be akin to **evil** in that it is morally bad. Jane, another interviewee, recalls that when someone asked her to confront her emaciated mirror-image, all that she could think of was the need to lose another stone. She explains that she hated herself and saw herself as an evil person, 'and I thought that the more fat I lost the more evil I could get rid of'.

8.4.4.1 'Renunciation of the flesh'

Rather than see her interviewees as pathologized individuals, Malson argues that this discourse relates to the **cultural context** and in particular to the Christian ascetic ideal of the 'renunciation of the flesh'. And these traces of Christian asceticism are also evidenced in the discursive construction of 'control' itself as a form of denial of the body rather than as conscious or deliberate self-determination. Controlling one's food is about resisting temptation, denying the body and its desires. She draws on Orbach who argues that food for millions of women has become a combat zone, a source of incredible tension. For many women, getting fat is their greatest fear. Self-control versus 'letting-yourself-go' is the greatest value held up by columnists in beauty magazines. Likewise the diet industry reinforces the idea of 'burning' calories. Malson argues that the same moral theme occurs in all accounts – fat is morally bad. Ultimately this 'renunciation of the flesh' has its zenith in the desire to disappear altogether, to become a 'non-body'.

8.4.5 Anorexia, identity and power

The women interviewed by Malson experienced starvation as being **empowering**, something which made them feel good. In this respect she argues that this discourse is informed not by Christianity (which emphasizes self-denial) but Stoicism (which is linked to affirmation). Being thin provides identities which are self-productive and self-destructive. Interviewees reported how the diagnosis of being AN made them feel good; that they had a sense of control over their eating and their lives. Control is strongly linked to a sense of identity or self, doing what *I* want: 'Anorexia is produced discursively as something that's her own, *her* control and *her* property that marks *her* identity' (1998: 146). The idea that AN is 'owned' by the anorexic who views it as a way of life contrasts sharply with its medical definition as a pathology or disease. In this respect the doctor–patient relationship may be construed as a contest for control of the anorexia. While anorexia provides the resources for identity construction, it also highlights a 'self' which is otherwise lacking an identity. For example Nikki says:

> 'It's like it was a way to have an identity. And I didn't care if people saw it as bad cos it was how I was. And if it, if I didn't have it, if I wasn't thin then I wouldn't have an identity. I'd just be this big bad blob. It was my thing. Before I'd felt just like nothing. Now I had something to focus on and something to be.'
>
> [1998: 148]

While the fat body signals an absence of identity, the anorexic body provides it. To be fat represents a lack of definition for the self, 'this big bad blob', whereas to be anorexic provides a defined identity.

Malson's interviewees seek to base their identity as something which is 'deep' as opposed to the 'superficial' identity which is based upon an image. This construction of identity as being 'deep' is oriented against the 'superficial' notion that a feminine identity is based on physical appearance. In this respect, anorexia constitutes a rejection of femininity; fear of fatness is coupled with the desire not to be like a 'normal' woman. This is because 'normal' women are fatter, their identities subordinated to those of men. Becoming a 'normal' woman is thus construed as a loss of identity, becoming a generic 'blob'. This in turn consolidates the desire to be thin, to achieve ever firmer body boundaries.

8.4.5.1 Discourse of 'individualism'

Malson argues that interviewees' expressions of being autonomous, empowered and 'in-control', of 'being your own woman', are indicative of a liberal discourse of individualism. In common with Foucault, she sees the self as being constructed or positioned through discourse. Thus she disputes any idea of the existence of a 'core' personality, which she argues is linked to a discourse which argues that the individual is a being who can largely live and act autonomously of society (which she believes to be nonsensical). Malson found that interviewees construed themselves as acting autonomously, free from social pressures. Although admitting to media and other pressures, they believed that to 'give in' to these was to abnegate one's 'inner' self. They accounted for their desire to be thin as being 'natural' and for reasons of 'health'. Yet while her interviewees argue that this desire arises naturally, Malson notes that this idea of being 'naturally healthy' is promulgated by the fashion and diet industries, where health and beauty are conflated. In her interpretation, the idea that their 'condition' is 'natural' allows women in general to depoliticize the experience. She argues that this same dilemma applies to anorexics. Several of her interviewees specifically disassociated their anorexia from media images of slim women. Even though most had been diagnosed with anorexia, the majority discounted this as a 'slimmers' disease', but rather as being implicated with their sense of identity.

8.4.6   Negative constructions of the self

While being labelled as 'anorexic' can be affirming, on the other hand it may be construed as a means of avoiding the responsibilities of adulthood. One might be 'in control' of the body and of food but not in other areas. The 'self' is viewed negatively as being 'undeserving' of food. This mortification of the flesh extends to other forms of harm such as 'cutting' the body, exposing it to cold, engaging in extreme forms of exercise and purging.

8.4.7   The disciplined self

From a Foucauldian perspective, modern individuality is produced precisely through the exact observation and detailed examination of the body and the self. The anorexic can be read as an exemplar of such discipline. As we saw in Chapter 3, observation, surveillance and the examination are key to this. Malson argues that as the body becomes progressively smaller, it becomes less visible and AN may thus be read as an attempt to evade the disciplinary gaze that controls and individualizes. Anorexia may thus be construed as an exemplar of discipline and as resistance to the individuality that discipline produces.

8.4.8   Critique of discursive view

Malson charts how discourses about 'anorexia' have changed substantially since the late nineteenth century; how they constitute anorexia in different and often conflicting ways so that we now have a multiplicity of truths about anorexia. Through positioning women in particular ways (as a medical patient, as an analysand, as a member of a 'problem' family), she argues, the power of such discourses has real effects on the lives of real women.

The view of the anorexic described by Malson is complex and riddled with paradox. The anorexic believes herself to be a self-determining individual but the 'self' which she constructs is built within the frame of existing and contradictory discourses. Her anorexia may be taken as an attempt to grasp the image of an idealized waif-like femininity. On the other hand it may signify the desire to resist inclusion in male-dominated society through being reduced to a 'female' blob. Whether accommodating to power or resistant to it, the actions of the anorexic are always contained within the bounds of discourse.

Malson's work is descriptive and offers no remedy. She argues that clinicians might usefully work within a framework that questions the medical model of 'anorexia', that acknowledges its socio-historical context and that acknowledges the discursively constituted nature of women's experiences. Her contention that there really *is* no remedy for anorexia, as the causes of this form of subjectivity are at work in the discourses which work through us, provides cold comfort to the friends and relations of those classified as being anorexic.

A second critique comes from biology where some researchers claim that anorexia exists in all cultures, even those where 'fatness' is considered to be a positive value. Malson would possibly retort that such instances of starvation should not be considered to be equivalent to Western medical models of anorexia but that the discursive context which constructs such positions within these countries should be explored further.

A third critique relates to the manner by which Malson makes connections between what women say in interviews and 'macro' discourses such as 'Cartesian dualism', Christianity and Stoicism. Some might argue that the interpretative leap she makes is too great. It is clear that when interviewing her subjects, Malson was already aware of, and primed by, the theory of Foucault. One might suggest that this itself acts just like any discourse, in that Malson attends to those features which are considered important within the discourse and omits others. Malson would probably agree that this is an inevitable outcome.

Fourth, while purporting to provide a 'gendered' explanation, Malson restricted her study to women. This would seem strange to a 'natural' scientist who would think that one should include both male and female subjects if one was to construct an explanation based on gender. On the other hand Malson's detailed and time-consuming methods in seeking to engage with the real lives of women offer a unique insight.

8.5	**SUMMARY ON EATING DISORDERS**

Social explanations

Social explanations highlight a range of factors which are thought to be important in precipitating and maintaining eating disorders:

- *Dieting*: Several researchers believe that increases in eating disorders are primarily due to dieting linked to body dissatisfaction, which is in turn linked to image.
- *Image*: The focus on conformance to an image or body ideal of slimness developed during the Romantic period and has been greatly inflated by the image-making machinery of consumer society. Currently available evidence lends support to the view that people tend to express body

dissatisfaction on comparing their bodies with ideal images. Evidence suggests that the expression of eating disorders spreads with the dissemination of Western ideals of fitness.

- *But*: AN existed well before the advent of the consumer society in Europe. Recent evidence suggests that it also exists even in cultures where fatness is valued.

Biological explanations

- The suggestion of a genetic vulnerability, particularly to AN.
- Additional focus on the role played by serotonin and other hormones and neurotransmitters.
- One suggested causal factor for AN lies with the overproduction of serotonin, which, it is thought, may lead to high levels of anxiety. By starving themselves and thereby reducing levels of tryptophan, and 5-HT, those who suffer from eating disorders seek to control this anxiety. This would also explain obsessive–compulsive behaviour.
- For anorexics it is thought that the AVP switch may be faulty.
- *But*: Research suffers from major problems. It is extremely difficult to isolate causes from effects of eating disorders. There are high levels of conjecture built into these explanations. Neurobiologists recognize that new explanations will involved complex interactions between different systems in the brain. Many neurobiologists agree that eating disorders are framed culturally.

Psychoanalytic explanations

Psychoanalytic explanations focus on the idea of the hunger-strike:

- The earliest explanation suggests that young girls who do not wish to be made passive by playing a female role, fight against this using the only weapon they have.
- More recent explanations focus on parenting and the individuation of the female child. Those who have difficulty in achieving a sense of autonomy at an early age may not be able to cope with the flood of media-images of the body during adolescence and may begin to diet.
- *But*: Psychoanalytic explanations such as Orbach's do not offer any explanation for the onset of male anorexia.

Discursive explanations

These are similar to social explanations but are based on the power of discourses which work through language rather than the transmission of images. The argument is that anorexia is constructed through an entanglement of discourses. As a result:

- The subjectivity of the anorexic is positioned in ways which are often contradictory.

- Such positioning allows for containment within and resistance to discourse. For example while on the one hand it may be argued that anorexia is contained within a patriarchal discourse which idealizes diminutive, waif-like features and links these to notions of childish passivity, the assumption of 'boyish' features may be deemed to be a form of resistance towards traditional views of femininity.

From the above, it can be clearly seen that all four explanations focus on the concept of control:

- In the social explanation, the person is *controlled* by a media-generated ideal-image, the diet industry and by being a member of a specific social class.
- In putative biological explanations, the individual starves herself in order to *control* anxiety, which is internal, but is fuelled by external stress.
- Psychoanalytic explanations focus on the achievement of autonomy and *control* in the developing child, and on the power and control of societal expectations of children coupled with the power of the media.
- The discursive explanation posits that the person believes herself to be in control, although her 'identity' or sense of self is in fact determined by pre-existing discourses which exist independently of the individual (beauty, the thin-body, fear of fatness, mind–body dualism etc.).

8.6   OBESITY

Paul Barker contends that the greatest social divide in the USA is not between rich and poor, or even between black and white, but between thin people and obese people (see note xiv). The British and American people seem to be indifferent to the exhortations of public health campaigns to eat properly and exercise (see note xv). On the other hand the 'fat-free' industry is booming with variants of everything, including fat itself coming in 'diet' form. In this section we explore some possible reasons why obesity is regarded as being such a problem, considering social, psychoanalytic and biological explanations.

Obesity is the excess accumulation of body fat. One can be overweight without being obese: a body-builder who has a lot of muscle, for example. However, for practical purposes, most people who are overweight are also obese. Doctors and scientists generally agree that men with more than 25 per cent body fat and women with more than 30 per cent body fat are obese. However, it is difficult to measure body fat precisely. The most accepted method has been to weigh a person underwater. But underwater weighing is a procedure limited to laboratories with special equipment. Two simpler methods for measuring body fat are skinfold thickness measurements and bioelectrical impedance analysis (BIA). Skinfold thicknesses are measures of the thickness of skin and subcutaneous (lying under the skin) fat at targeted sites of a person's body such as the triceps (the back of the upper arm). Measurements of skinfold thickness depend on the skill of the examiner, and may vary widely when measured by different examiners. In addition to skin-fold thickness measures and BIA, doctors also use weight-for-height tables and body mass index measures (BMI) to determine if a person is at a desirable body weight. Doctors and obesity researchers prefer BMI to other measurements. Body mass index is found by dividing a person's weight in kilograms by height in metres, squared. When a man's BMI is over 27.8, or a woman's exceeds 27.3, that person is considered overweight. The degree of obesity associated with a particular BMI ranges from mild obesity at a BMI near 27, moderate obesity at 30, severe obesity at 35, to very severe obesity at 40 or greater. An estimated 41 per cent of the population has a BMI greater than 25. Like weight-for-height tables, BMI does not measure body fat. While limited, these measures nevertheless help doctors, patients and the public assess a person's desirable body. In the UK, statistics suggest 54 per cent of men and 45 per cent of women are overweight, and that about 13 per cent of men and 15 per cent of women are obese. This is a significant increase from the 6 per cent of men and 8 per cent of women recorded in 1980 (see note xvi).

Michaels (1994) suggests that the American habit of 'dressing down' has less to do with egalitarianism than with being overweight: 'There's a connection between loose and baggy fashions and the bagginess of ageing American males'. As Americans have got fatter, so smart clothing companies have started to make clothes which are 'comfortable' rather than form-filling. The concern with weight in contemporary society is staggering. One estimate suggests that as long ago as 1991, US companies sold goods worth $8.4 billion to dieters. Weight Watchers International claims that since September 1997, more than 3.7 million Americans participated in its new programme where they collectively lost 34.6 million pounds (see note xvii).

8.6.1 Social explanations of obesity

Social explanations of the prevalence of obesity relate this to the social context and issues of class distinction. Linked to the argument advanced by Mennell earlier in this chapter, one would expect the incidence of obesity to be greatest, the lower the social class. The trend towards obesity is of considerable importance given the links between obesity and increased morbidity and mortality. Obesity is measured by the Body Mass Index (BMI) which is calculated by relating weight (kg) and height. The data shown in Table 8.1 relate to obesity in the UK.

The data indicate that while there is not much evidence of a social-class effect for men, this is especially pronounced for women. There are many possible explanations offered for this, for example consumption of 'fatty' foods as a response to the belief that the social acceptability of 'plumpness' differs across social-class boundaries. It is true that being overweight is viewed differently in different social contexts. For example while being regarded as 'plump' is viewed negatively in many Western countries, this is a comparatively recent phenomenon. Research in Latin America, Puerto Rico, India, China and the Philippines supports the view that an increased

Table 8.1 **Age-standardized prevalence (percentage) of raised BMI by social class – men and women aged 16+**

Social class	BMI over 25		BMI over 30	
	Men	Women	Men	Women
I	55.3	43.3	9.6	11.7
II	57.5	44.7	12.9	13.0
IIIN	58.2	45.2	13.6	14.5
IIIM	58.9	50.1	14.1	19.1
IV	52.4	53.1	14.6	21.8
V	53.2	54.9	13.2	21.1
All	56.8	54.9	13.3	16.9

Source: *Health Inequalities*, Table 15.15, page 218. Dresser and Whitehead (1977).

standard of living is linked with increased bodyweight and that this is linked in turn with wealth and with health (Rothblum, 1990).

The above supports the position of Bourdieu (1984) and Mennell (1991) who suggest that the volume and quality of what we eat is strongly influenced by our social position. During the early medieval period, feasting and gluttony could be indulged in by the warrior class and the nobility, but most infrequently by the poor. Several hundred years later, the court nobles sought to maintain their social distance from the bourgeoisie by developing finesse in table manners and restraint in eating, and more recently still the middle classes in France have sought to maintain their social distance from the working class through their consumption of *nouvelle cuisine*. In addition to this, Bourdieu (1984) argues that different classes in his French study adopted different attitudes towards the body. The working classes tend to develop an instrumental and functional, rather than an aesthetic relation to the body. The body comes to be seen as a means to an end (training to be able to be a better footballer, for example) rather than in making it more healthy or more aesthetically pleasing.

The social context may help explain why levels of obesity are rising. For example US statistics indicate that consumption of fats, oils and sweeteners increased by 16.5 per cent from 1989 to 1995, to a total of 58.8 billion pounds. This increase has been attributed to a number of factors such as:

- Consumers' limited discretionary time for preparing meals, which has led to the consumption of more manufacturer-prepared foods and more eating-out. While such offerings often claim to be 'reduced fat', they frequently contain large 'hidden' amounts of fats and sugars, to improve taste.
- Claims that the food industry has deliberately suppressed the publication of relevant scientific data.
- The development of a more sedentary lifestyle; with more time spent at the wheel of a car or before a computer screen or television set.
- A corresponding drop in exercise levels, which is particularly notable among children, who are ferried to school by parents and who more often forego exercise to watch television or play video games.
- An increase in snacking and a decline in the family meal.

There is a paradox here. On the one hand the modern consumer never seems to have enough time, and is constantly rushing from here to there. On the other hand the consumer lifestyle is sedentary. The paradox is explained by the fact that when we are 'rushing' here and there, it is often not 'us' who is doing the rushing, but a car. To compensate, an adult may go to the gym to 'exercise' twice a week – possibly spending half an hour in traffic either side of this. What they will not do is walk. Peculiarly for those who are fixated by 'exercise', walking is not seen as a means to get 'fit'.

Susan Bordo (1993) argues that corpulence went out of fashion for the middle classes at the beginning of the twentieth century, when a slender ideal became associated with success and will-power, and corpulence with a lack of control. This kind of 'trickle down' theory may partially explain the prevalence of obesity in working-class women, described earlier in this chapter. This might be explained by a plentiful supply of cheap food, enabling the woman in her role as mother to purchase products which are cheap, filling and which often contain a large 'hidden' element of fat and sugar. Additionally Bordo (1993) notes that the 'ideal-images represented by the media of working-class women often portray them as being over-weight'. One could arguably suggest that working-class women will also be taunted by svelte images of supermodels. They will also be the target of advertising and marketing programmes which encourage people to reward themselves with sweets which are 'naughty but nice', effectively giving them 'permission' to consume high-fat foods. This has been hugely compli-cated by the recent arrival of 'fat-free' fats, the advertising for which invites people to indulge to their fill in items which were previously regarded as being saturated in fat. The decline in the family meal and the increase in snacking or 'grazing' have also exacerbated this situation. Research indi-cates that people who are overweight tend to underestimate what they eat by up to eight hundred calories per day, and grazing is thought to add to this problem.

8.6.2   Psychoanalytic explanations of obesity

The most pertinent psychoanalytic explanation of obesity is to link this form of behaviour to the oral drive. Here Falk's (1994) explanation, which was discussed in Chapter 7, suggests that the modern individual feels empty inside, alone and unfulfilled. A simple explanation would thus be to suggest that in a world where the second skin of community has been removed, the individual responds to this loss (and to memories of the loss of the mother) by attempting to fill the gap inside the self, by means of the consumption of food. This will be aggravated in people who are poor, who would be likely to suffer from increased stress and whose access is restricted to 'comfort' foods which are often high in 'hidden' fats and sugar. Such consumption will lead to brief periods of satiation, quickly followed by guilt at having 'broken' the diet, thereby inaugurating a 'vicious circle' of anxiety–consumption–guilt, which is continually replayed.

8.6.3   Physiological explanations of obesity

In September 1995 an Oakland, California jury awarded John Rossi one million dollars in compensation for being fired from his job for being too fat. According to Rossi's lawyer, the case hung on expert evidence that 80 per cent of the cause of obesity is genetic and 20 per cent environmental (see note xviii). In Maryland and New York in the USA there have been calls for legislation which bans discrimination against overweight people. Just as with AN and BN, a growing number of medics argue that obesity is a disease which like any disease can be moderated by taking some form of prescription drug. Supporting such a view, there is increasing evidence that genetic factors account for a proportion of what is termed 'the obesity crisis' which is occurring in the USA and other Western countries.

The theory goes that many people are genetically misprogrammed for an era of abundance and consequently that they lack the internal signals by which body and mind tell each other that the danger of starvation is long past. In 1995 a research group led by Jeffrey Friedman at Rockefeller University discovered in experiments on mice what has come to be known as the obesity or 'ob' gene (see note xix). This discovery has led to the discovery of a hormone called leptin which signals to the brain how much fat is stored in the body. The discovery of leptin has boosted the age-old view that the body has a built-in thermostat which regulates the degree to which calories are 'burned off' and that this is largely determined by genes. Studies of leptin show high correlation with the level of BMI, with those of a higher body mass tending to have more leptin. They have also indicated that women have significantly more leptin than men, which reflects that they have higher body fat content than men (see note xx). According to Connan and Treasure, it is thought that obese people might be particularly resistant to leptin, having very high levels of leptin in their system. This may be because the hypothalamus receives a reduced leptin signal which underestimates the amount of fat stored and which, therefore, fails to trigger weight control systems to generate weight loss (1998: 227).

Following from this discovery, the US Institute of Medicine declared obesity to be a chronic disease, noting among other things that genes may account for one-third of the variation of weight across the population. Because they regard obesity as a form of illness, some authorities maintain that dieting is a virtual waste of time, money and energy. This is obviously a threatening prospect for the dieting industry which has been valued in the USA at $2 billion per year, but makes an attractive proposition for pharmaceutical companies which stand to gain large rewards from investments into drugs which may be prescribed over the period of a person's lifetime. Up until recently, obesity has been treated with serotonin boosters such as fenfluramine and phenteramine (known in the trade as 'fen–phen'). Together these medicines suppress appetite and speed the burning of calories. Fenfluramine, which is akin to the 'recreational' drug of abuse MDMA, acts upon serotonin synthesis and metabolism by releasing 5-HT from pre-synaptic vesicles, producing a profound decrease in brain levels of serotonin. One source quotes 'fen–phen' as being the 'heavy artillery in the battle of the bulge' (see note xxi). There are however concerns about the use of such drugs. A few decades ago amphetamines were heavily prescribed to control weight. These worked to a limited extent; however they had serious side-effects on the nerves of those who had to take them. While amphetamines were prescribed over the short-term, these new drugs may well require to be prescribed over the entire lifespan. Both 'fen–phen' drugs have side-effects: phenteramine heightens alertness while persuading the body to burn more calories; while fenfluramine, which cuts the craving for the sugars and starches that ultimately end as 5-HT, can induce drowsiness and a racing heartbeat. In 1997 a medical research study indicated that 'fen–phen' was implicated in valvular heart disease and revealed fenfluramine to be the likely culprit (see note xxii). Dexfenfluramine (brand name REDUX), an appetite-suppressing drug used for years in Europe for treatment of obesity, was approved on 29 April 1996 by the FDA for use in the USA. However, because of fears about its effects with respect to valvular heart disease, dexfenfluramine and fenfluramine have since been withdrawn from sale in the USA (see note xxiii).

During clinical trials of Prozac (the brand name for fluoxetene), one side-effect which was noted was weight loss. The team at MIT who developed Prozac theorized that this occurs because dietary starch is converted to sugar, which stimulates the pancreas to produce insulin. Insulin raises the levels of the amino acid tryptophan, and tryptophan is a precursor of serotonin (5-HT). Through this set of neural pathways, serotonin elevates mood and produces a sense of wellbeing. This suggests that obese people tend to load up on carbohydrates in order to elevate mood. It was thus thought that fluoxetene produces a similar effect by reducing serotonin re-uptake into the pre-synaptic neuron. Eli-Lilly were among the first to spot the potential for fluoxetene, which was reformulated with a higher dose and a new name – Lovan.

8.6.4 Discussion: eat fat?

Obesity is a chronic condition with worrying links to a host of illnesses. However, as the saying goes, one person's misfortune is another man's gain, and obesity is good news to a number of companies. Stories of obesity have aided the growth of the diet industry which thrives on such tales in gaining 'problem recognition'. Secondly, stories about the failure of diets are good news to pharmaceutical companies, which are aggressively competing to produce the 'magic bullet' that will sort the problem out (and provide access to a reputed $18 billion market). Nor will they do any damage to the fashion industry, which continues to pump out unrealizable models of thinness. However it surely strains credibility to think that obesity might do the food industry any good. After all, if people consume less food then that means reduced sales, less profit, fewer employees and so on. This line of reasoning is based on a misconception about value. Foods which are 'fat-free', or at least 'diet' foods, are priced at a premium and contribute added-value to the bottom line. Even more remarkable has been the creation of 'fat-free' fats, which are the food industry's contribution to the issue.

So there we have it. 'Obesity' constitutes a market worth billions, which is being aggressively targeted by some of the most powerful industries in the world. This, more or less, is the text of Richard Klein's (1997) book which is entitled *Eat Fat*. The simple message in this simply written book is that in consumer societies, eat and fat are virtually substitutable for one another (as indeed the actual words are). Klein's book is motivated by a sense of rage:

> 'the rage I feel towards the word obesity. This ugly noun, with all its pejorative implications, this term for unhealthy corpulence, has been mobilized by the medical–health–beauty industry, and wielded by food packagers, in order to stigmatize people who don't conform to an absurdly restrictive concept of ideal weight.'
> [1997: 92]

8.6.4.1   The 'magic bullet'?

Klein does not deny that a faulty genetic 'switch' may provide an explanation for obesity in a tiny proportion of the population. However he points out that, first, the mechanisms by which leptin overproduction result in high levels of weight in those with very high BMIs are by no means clear:

> 'When scientists discovered that genetically obese rats got thin when they gave them leptin, they hoped that fat people were similarly deprived. No such luck. On the contrary, fat people have more leptin and more insulin than thin people; they just don't use it efficiently, or something. It's as if they were leptin resistant; even vast amounts of it don't seem to make any difference. The paradox, then, would be something like this: Your body contains a substance that keeps you thin, as long as you are thin. If you are fat, you have the same substance in much larger quantities, but it doesn't work to affect your fat. So therefore it follows, leptin given to thin people would work brilliantly to make them thinner, but wouldn't do anything at all for people who are fat.'
> [1997: 105]

Added to this is the controversy over 'fen–phen', which had been thought by many to be a 'magic bullet' that would control obesity at one stroke, but which was approved by the US Food and Drugs Administration amid considerable controversy. The subsequent withdrawal of both dexfenfluramine and fenfluramine amid claims that they cause valve damage and also lead serotonin axons to tangle, has not done the industry's image much good. Nevertheless the search for a 'magic bullet' continues. This is scarcely surprising when one learns that 85,000 prescriptions for dexfenfluramine were written each week and that estimated sales of dexfenfluramine alone were in excess of $20 million per month in the USA (see note xxiv).

8.6.4.2   Health

Klein contests the idea that obesity is a disease. He argues that fat is unhealthy *and* it isn't – some people are unhealthy and fat, other people are healthy and fat. He suggests that those who are not morbidly obese are fat for lots of reasons. These include because they eat to deal with stress, or because their whole family is fat, or because they can't find time to exercise. He asks:

> 'would it be a good thing if these people who are clinically obese, twenty pounds or more above their ideal weight, but otherwise perfectly healthy, were put on drugs that drastically change metabolisms and alter mental states, in order to get the benefits of being thin?'

In addition to this, Klein argues that many of the academics who work in this area are not as neutral and impartial as one might expect. Those who seek to medicalize the condition of obesity often have vested interests in that their research units and research projects are subsidized by drug companies. They may also work as consultants for them (see note xxv). Klein quotes some contrary research which suggests that being thinner than 'normal' entails a greater statistical risk of dying early. In fact, most research seems to support the association between lower mortality and increased weight as one grows older.

8.6.4.3   Diet

While diet companies seek to convince us that their programmes are the road to salvation by telling us how many millions of pounds have been lost by ex-fatties, drug companies state bluntly that diets don't work. Klein recalls how his mother, whom he has always thought of as being 'beautiful and fat' but who is 'obese' by the doctor's rule, has struggled to conform herself to the ideal of beauty that told her she must be thin:

> 'And she did get thin, many times, at vast expense. She lost thousands of pounds of fat, and the more she lost the more she gained, and fat she is to the end.'
>
> [1997: 104]

Klein argues that Americans are not obese because of the fat that they eat. The French, who load their tables with butter, cheese, steak and fried potatoes, are much less obese than Americans. Instead he argues that Americans have bad eating habits – they have no discipline of eating. The French have by and large, maintained the discipline of the meal. The general rule is non-eating between meals. In France, pleasure is not immediate, the desire for food must be postponed. He suggests that to diminish obesity in the USA requires a change of habits and not of diet:

> 'And to do that would represent an intolerable intrusion of government into our already overregulated lives. And furthermore it is not even imaginable, politically, that any institution in this country would take on the industries that have

made vast fortunes exploiting and encouraging those habits. How would you get people to stop snacking in front of the television – if you wanted to? You could make television interactively able to watch you each time your hand goes to that bowl of peanuts. Big brother lies at the end of the dreams of some of those who want us, at all cost, to be healthy, slim and beautiful.'   [1997: 108]

So ultimately Klein associates obesity with an increasingly frenetic lifestyle which paradoxically is leading to increasingly heavier people. The issue of control is once again paramount.

8.7   SUMMARY ON OBESITY

Control plays a key role in the explanation of obesity, just as it does within that of the starvation disorders which we discussed earlier.

Social explanations, which focus on changes in lifestyle, highlight issues which we discussed in Chapter 2 with respect to time and to space. In contemporary consumer society, time seems to speed up so that there is never enough time to do anything properly: no time to devote the appropriate care and attention to the preparation of a meal (which is frequently 'just for you'); no time to walk to work, or go for a stroll each day. Instead daily life is chopped up into segments where people rush from one station to the next, but paradoxically with little exercise. As we discussed in more detail in Chapter 2, leisure time is spent 'chilling out' in front of the television or computer-game.

Biological explanations of obesity have identified a genetic abnormality in the control system of the hypothalamus, which explains a proportion of what is known as 'morbid obesity' in those who have a BMI of 30 or above. However there is a strong belief by some that modern humans are genetically misprogrammed for an age of abundance, and that consequently the only solution to this difficulty will be some form of drug or 'magic bullet'.

Psychoanalytic explanations of obesity focus on the desire to fill the 'empty' self with the good things in life. The prevalence in snacking behaviour is not merely a conditioned response to advertising but reflects a reversion to an early oral stage of behaviour.

8.8   CASE STUDY: NOW EAT THIS! OLESTRA, THE FAT-FREE FAT (see note xxvi)

Olestra, the 'fat-free fat', was launched in 1996. The product, which took thirty years and reputedly $200 million to develop, was the outcome of a joint venture between Frito-Lay Inc. and Procter and Gamble (P&G). Years earlier, executives in both companies had spotted the potential offered by a fat-substitute which could be included in traditionally high-fat snacks, which form a key part of the notorious 'grazing' diet which seems to stack pounds onto already overweight consumers. P&G plans currently to market olestra – a synthetic made from sugar and vegetable oil – under the brand name Olean in its savoury snacks, and to sell Olean to other snackmakers.

For many years, food manufacturers have been aware that while government campaigns urge consumers to incorporate less fat into their diet, consumers respond by opting for taste and convenience. Such consumer habits have led to the public's appetite for and approval of manufactured sugar substitutes, such as aspartame, but low-fat alternatives have not fared so well. Food-industry sources reckoned that the reason for this was that consumers could not bear to trade off taste for less fat. While olestra has gained the American FDA seal of approval, the product has not escaped entirely unscathed. The FDA is insisting that all products containing olestra carry an informational label which reads:

> 'This product contains olestra. Olestra may cause abdominal cramping and loose stools. Olestra inhibits the absorption of some vitamins and other nutrients. Vitamins A, D, E, and K have been added.'

The FDA has also insisted that fat-soluble vitamins A, D, E and K be added to olestra-containing products. Also P&G will have to monitor long-term consumption to ascertain how the fat substitute affects the absorption of carotenoids, the presence of which is associated with cancer risk. P&G has attracted controversy with another product 'Sunny Delight', which also contains added vitamins but has been referred to by a number of critics as being little more than sugar and water. In the UK, the Food Commission launched a campaign in April 1996 against official approval for olestra. A spokesperson said (see note xxvii):

> 'We believe the product to be anti-nutritional – depleting the body of essential health-promoting vitamins and carotenoids – and we do not believe it will encourage healthier diet.'

The spokesperson also maintained that there had also been complaints that the product ' "leaks", leading to stained underwear, and that it makes the toilet oily'.

Olean is made with sucrose and soyabean or cottonseed oil. It is then processed, creating an oil that looks, cooks and tastes like ordinary fat, but isn't broken down by the body. As a result, Olean adds no fat or calories to foods. A one-ounce serving of potato crisps fried with Olean contains only 75 calories and 0 grams of fat – compared with 150 calories and 10 grams of fat in regular chips. That constitutes one-half of the calories and none of the fat in regular potato chips. Tortilla chips fried with Olean contain one gram of fat per serving because, unlike potatoes, corn itself contains fat.

Frito-Lay reported that it sold 80 million packs of 'WOW', its fat-free crisps, in the first two months. In 1996, P&G test-marketed Olean Pringles in Colombus, Ohio and reportedly sold 1.7 million packs between September and 22 October 1996. In February 1998, the company announced that the production plant for manufacturing Olean was up and running, and that 28 million servings of Pringles had been sold in test markets. Advertising for Olean commenced during the Winter Olympics in 1999.

Despite continuing worries about its effects on health, Olean received clearance from the Food and Drug Administration in June 1996, following 30 months of tests. A more recent study found that olestra-eaters in the top 10 per cent of chip consumption had somewhat more frequent bowel movements than other volunteers, while those in the top 10 per cent of regular chip consumption had somewhat fewer than average, and that overall olestra did not create gastro-intestinal problems. P&G's hopes for olestra go well beyond the development of 'fat-free' savoury snacks. P&G's kitchen experiments with Olean include fried chicken, pastries and mayonnaise – providing a taste of what could come beyond the snack bar.

Case-study questions

1. Who do you think is most likely to benefit from olestra and why?
2. What potential problems and difficulties might olestra create? For whom?
3. Would you try olestra if it was available to you?
4. What alternative means might have been used to alter the nation's diet?

END-OF-CHAPTER REVIEW QUESTIONS

1. Compare and contrast the similarities and differences between social explanations for AN and BN and for obesity.
2. What type of explanation do the following terms relate to and what do they mean: 'aetiology', 'SSRI', 'tryptophan', '5-HT re-uptake inhibitor'?
3. What does BMI refer to and how is this measured?
4. How is it thought that tryptophan might be related to AN, BN and obesity?
5. Compare and contrast the two psychoanalytic explanations for AN.

REFERENCES AND FURTHER READING

Adler, Alfred (1924) *The Practice and Theory of Individual Psychology*, trans. P. Radin, London: Kegan, Paul, Tranch, Trubner.

Anonymous (1995) Too Many Torts, *Forbes*, 9 October, vol. 156, no. 8: 18.

Averett, Susan and Sanders Korenman (1995) The Economic Reality of the Beauty Myth, *Journal of Human Resources*, vol. XXXI, no. 2: 304–30.

Bordo, Susan (1993) *Unbearable Weight: Feminism, Western Culture and the Body*, Berkeley, California: University of California Press.

Bourdieu, Pierre (1984) orig. 1979 *Distinction: A Social Critique of the Judgement of Taste*, trans. Richard Nice, London: Routledge.

Connan, F. and J.L. Treasure (1998) 'Stress, Eating and Neurobiology', pp. 211–37. In Wijbrand Hoek, Janet L. Treasure and Melanie A. Katzman (eds), *Neurobiology in the Treatment of Eating Disorders*, Clinical and Neurobiological Advances in Psychiatry, Chichester: John Wiley.

Dare, Christopher and Catherine Crowther (1995) 'Psychodynamic Models of Eating Disorders', pp. 125–41. In George Szmukler, Chris Dare and Janet Treasure (eds), *Handbook of Eating Disorders: Theory, Treatment and Research*, Chichester: John Wiley.

Department of Health (1993) *The Health of the Nation*, London: HMSO.

Dresser, Francis and Margaret Whitehead (eds) (1977) *Health Inequalities*, DS no. 15, London: HMSO.

Edwards-Hewitt, T. and J.J. Gray (1993) The Prevalence of Disordered Eating Habits and Behaviour in Black American and White American College Women: Ethnic, Regional, Class and Media Differences, *Eating Disorders Review*, vol. 1, no. 1: 41–54.

Erikson, Erik H. (1968) *Identity, Youth and Crisis*, London: Faber & Faber.

Falk, Pasi (1994) *The Consuming Body*, London: Sage.

Fichter, M.M., M. Elton, L. Sordi *et al.* (1988) Anorexia Nervosa in Greek and Turkish Adolescents, *Eur. Arch. Psychiatry Neurol. Sci.*, vol. 237: 200–8.

Gardner, R.M. and Y. Tockerman (1993) Body Dissatisfaction as a Predictor of Body Size Distortions: A Multidimensional Analysis of Body Image, *Genetic, Social and General Psychology Monographs*, 199/1: 127–45.

Garner, D.M., P.E. Garfinkel, D. Schwartz and M. Thompson (1980) Cultural Expectations of Thinness in Women, *Psychological Reports*, vol. 47: 483–91.

Grogan, Sarah (1999) *Body Image: Understanding Body Dissatisfaction in Men and Women*, London: Routledge.

Halmi, Katherine A. (1998) A 24-Year-Old Woman with Anorexia Nervosa. *JAMA, Journal of the American Medical Association*, vol. 279 (24 June): 1992–8.

Harris, S. (1994) Racial Differences in Predictions of Women's Body-Image Attitudes, *Women and Health*, vol. 21: 89–104.

Harris, M.B., L.C. Walters and S. Waschull (1991) Gender and Ethnic Differences in Obesity-Related Behaviours and Attitudes in a College Sample, *Journal of Applied Social Psychology*, vol. 21: 1545–66.

Heinberg, L. and J.K. Thompson (1995) Body Image and Televised Images of Thinness and Attractiveness: A Controlled Laboratory Investigation, *Journal of Social and Clinical Psychology*, vol. 14: 325–38.

Hornbacher, Marya (1998) *Wasted: A Memoir of Anorexia and Bulimia*, London: Flamingo.

Irving, L. (1990) Mirror Images: Effects of the Standard of Beauty on the Self- and Body-Esteem of Women Exhibiting Varying Levels of Bulimic Symptoms, *Journal of Social and Clinical Psychology*, vol. 9: 230–42.

Kaye, Walter H., T.E. Weltzin and L.K.G. Hsu (1991) An Open Trial of Fluoxetene in Patients with Anorexia Nervosa, *Journal of Clinical Psychiatry*, vol. 52: 464–71.

Klein, Richard (1997) *Eat Fat*, London: Picador.

Lilenfeld, L.R. and W.H. Kaye (1998) 'Genetic Studies of Anorexia and Bulimia Nervosa', pp. 169–94. In Wijbrand Hoek, Janet L. Treasure and Melanie A. Katzman (eds), *Neurobiology in the Treatment of Eating Disorders*, Clinical and Neurobiological Advances in Psychiatry, Chichester: John Wiley.

McCauley, M., L. Mintz and A.A. Glenn (1988) Body Image, Self-esteem and Depression-Proneness: Closing the Gender Gap, *Sex Roles*, vol. 18: 381–91.

Malson, Helen (1998) *The Thin Woman: Feminism, Post-Structuralism and The Social Psychology of Anorexia Nervosa*, London: Routledge.

Mennell, Stephen (1991) 'On the Civilizing of Appetite', pp. 126–55. In Mike Featherstone, Mike Hepworth and Bryan S. Turner (eds), *The Body: Social Process and Cultural Theory*, London: Sage.

Meyer, C., G. Waller and A. Waters (1998) 'Emotional States and Bulimic Psychopathology', pp. 271–88. In George Szmukler, Chris Dase and Janet Treasure (eds), *Handbook of Eating Disorders: Theory, Treatment and Research*, Chichester: John Wiley.

Michaels, James W. (1994) Fuelling the Fantasies of the Unfit and Fiftyish, *Forbes*, vol. 54, no. 13 (5 December): 10.

Monteath, Sheryl A. and Marita P. McCabe (1997) The Influence of Societal Body Factors on Female Body Image, *Journal of Social Psychology*, vol. 137, no. 6: 707–28.

Mort, Frank (1988) 'Boy's Own? Masculinity, Style and Popular Culture'. In R. Chapman and J. Rutherford (eds), *Male Order. Unwrapping Masculinity*, London: Lawrence & Wishart.

Myers, P. and F. Biocca (1992) The Elastic Body: The Effects of Television Advertising and Programming on Body-Image Distortions in Young Women, *Journal of Communications*, vol. 42: 108–33.

Orbach, Susie (1993) orig. 1986, *Hunger Strike: The Anorectic's Struggle as a Metaphor for Our Age*, London: Penguin.

Pumariega, A.J. (1986) Acculturation and Eating Disorders in Adolescent Girls: A Comparative and Correlational Study, *Journal of the Academy of Child Psychiatry*, vol. 25, no. 2: 276–9.

Rastam, M. and C. Gillberg. (1991) The Family Background in Anorexia Nervosa: A Population Based Study, *J. Am. Acad. Child Adolesc. Psychiat.*, vol. 30, no. 2: 283–9.

Rastam, M., C. Gillberg and M. Garton (1989) Anorexia Nervosa in a Swedish Urban Region: A Population Based Study, *British Journal of Psychiatry*, vol. 155: 642–6.

Rothblum, E. (1990) Women and Weight: Fad and Fiction, *Journal of Psychology*, vol. 124: 5–24.

Russell, Gerald F.M. (1995) 'Anorexia Nervosa Through Time', pp. 5–19. In George Szmukler, Chris Dare and Janet Treasure (eds), *Handbook of Eating Disorders: Theory, Treatment and Research*, Chichester: John Wiley.

Silverstein, B., B. Patterson and L. Perdue (1986) Some Correlates of the Thin Standard of Bodily Attractiveness for Women, *International Journal of Eating Disorders*, vol. 5, 895–905.

Sobal, J. and A. Stunchard (1989) Socio-Economic Status and Obesity: A Review of the Literature, *Psychological Bulletin*, vol. 105: 260–75.

Spence, Jo (1995) *Cultural Sniping: The Art of Transgression*, London: Routledge.

Steiger, H., S. Stotland, J. Trottier and A.M. Ghandrian (1996) Familial Eating Concerns and Psychopathology Traits: Causal Implications of Transgenerational Effects, *International Journal of Eating Disorders*, vol. 19: 147–57.

Stephens, Debra Lynn, Ronald P. Hill and Cynthia Hanson (1994) The Beauty Myth and Female Consumers: The Controversial Role of Advertising, *Journal of Consumer Affairs*, vol. 28, no. 1: 137–53.

Stipp, David (1995) New Weapons in the War on Fat, *Fortune*, December 11, 132/12: 164–71.

Szmukler, G.I. and G. Patton (1995) 'Sociocultural Models of Eating Disorders'. In George Szmukler, Chris Dare and Janet Treasure (eds), *Handbook of Eating Disorders: Theory, Treatment and Research*, Chichester: John Wiley.

Treasure, Janet and Anthony Holland (1995) 'Genetic Factors in Eating Disorders', pp. 65–81. In George Szmukler, Chris Dare and Janet Treasure (eds), *Handbook of Eating Disorders: Theory, Treatment and Research*, Chichester: John Wiley.

Vaisman, N., H. Voet, A. Akivis and I. Sive-Ner (1996) Weight Perception of Adolescent Dancing School Students, *Arch. Pediatr. Adolesc. Med.*, vol. 150: 187–90.

Wakeling, David (1995) 'Physical Treatments', pp. 351–62. In George Szmukler, Chris Dase and Janet Treasure (eds), *Handbook of Eating Disorders: Theory, Treatment and Research*, Chichester: John Wiley.

NOTES

i Stephens *et al.* (1994: 137).
ii See Harris (1994) for example.
iii For example, article on p. 14 of *Scotland on Sunday* entitled 'US males pose anorexia

risk', July 5th 1994. See also 'Women's Image in Bad Shape', *Scotland on Sunday*, Analysis section, 11 October 1998.

iv   Grogan (1999: 41).

v   It should be recognized, however, that there is some controversy about this claim, with some medics suggesting that although they share similar diets and similar thoughts about body configuration, ballerinas are very different from anorexic individuals. The basis for this argument is that to develop AN, one must be physiologically vulnerable and that it is therefore not possible to 'catch' it. See for example Vaisman *et al.* (1996).

vi   *Source*: Fichter *et al.* (1988).

vii   *Source*: While Hoek's article has not been accessed, the data came from two sources: one a television programme featuring Hoek's research; the other a report in Policy.com http://www.policy.com/issuewk/98/0504/050498o.htm entitled 'Women's Issues, Women's Lives', 4 May 1998, which cites a recent study by Hoek in the *New England Medical Journal*.

viii   See also Lilenfeld and Kaye (1998).

ix   According to some sources, more than 38 million people have been prescribed Prozac to date.

x   *Source*: Kaye *et al.* (1991).

xi   For example, see Connan and Treasure (1998).

xii   The main source used for this section was Wakeling (1995), especially pp. 354–60.

xiii   For example, Connan and Treasure (1998) point out that mice bred to have no 5-HT2C receptors are overweight and have an increased appetite. There is evidence from studies of mice (mice with no 5-HT2C receptors which are overweight, paired with a 'wild' mouse) – the offspring do not become obese) that 5-HT2C receptor effects are behavioural and not metabolic.

xiv   Barker, Paul, 'America's Greatest Social Divide is not Between Rich and Poor, or even Black and White', *New Statesman*, vol. 125, no. 4299 (6 September 1966), p. 54.

xv   Taninecz, George, 'Fat Chance', *Industry Week*, 18 March 1996, vol. 245, no. 6, pp. 69–71.

xvi   *Source*: *The Economist* (US), vol. 339, no. 7965 (11 May 1996), p. 54.

xvii   *Source*: http:www.weightwatchers.com/news/

xviii   *Source*: Anon (1995).

xix   For those of you who may be interested, a really excellent full-content website providing a great deal of information on leptin may be found at http://www.loop.com/~bkrentzman/obesity/leptin.html

xx   *Source*: http://www.rockefeller.edu/pubinfo/leptinlevel.nr.html

xxi   *Source*: Stipp (1995: 2).

xxii   *Source*: http://www.weight.com/heart.html

xxiii   http://www.fda.gov/cder/news/feninfo.htm

xxiv   *Source*: *Horizon* (1999) Transcript, 'Fat Cats, Thin Mice', p. 15: http//www2.bbc.co.uk/horizon/fatcattran.htm

xxv   *Source*: Klein (1997: 151–3). See also previous footnote which also contains references to such compromises.

xxvi   *Sources used*: Company http://www.olean.com/

xxvii   *Source*: http://www.gurney.co.uk/foodcomm/

CONSUMING BRANDS

LEARNING OBJECTIVES

- To aid understanding of what brands are and of their symbolic importance to people
- To build an understanding of managerial discourses of brands
- To evaluate the usefulness of the notion of the brand personality
- To build an awareness of the relationship between products and brands
- To evaluate the extent to which people use brands as resources for the construction of identity

9.1 INTRODUCTION

Some time ago, one of my neighbours returned from church incensed that a young woman had stood up in the pulpit and told her to stop drinking 'her' brand of coffee. It transpired that the local minister had been approached by an activist who wished to speak to his congregation about ethical consumption, and in particular what practical steps they could take to bring this about. Inspired by her experiences of the marketing of baby milk substitutes in Africa, the activist had drawn her audience's attention to the anti-Nestlé campaign and had asked them to consider boycotting Nestlé products, including Nescafé. In searching for the source of my neighbour's palpable anger it was difficult to distinguish her attachment to her favourite brand of coffee, which had formed a routine part of her daily consumption for years, and her umbrage at the audacity of this 'young' woman who had dared to stand up and tell her (a senior member of the church) what to do. I cannot recall the exact words she used but they went along the lines of: 'How dare she ... it's perfectly good coffee'. In her explanation, attributions about people are combined with those about things (the brand). She does not however personalize the brand, but simply refers to its functional attributes ('it's perfectly good coffee'). As we shall see, this is important as the issue of personalization marks a distinction between authors who argue that brands provide important symbolic resources for the construction of personal identity and others who suggest that they play a more routine role.

Branding is an important and interesting concept in that it links together what are taken to be quite different entities: personal and corporate identity. Branding has a long history in relation to personal identity as it has been used for centuries to classify and to identify the property of another. More recently, brands have been developed by firms which have linked this concept to the creation of added value. There have been further developments which link the personal and the corporate together. One development which has been noted in Western countries is the recent trend whereby individuals brand themselves through being tattooed or having their body pierced, which has led to the growth of a small but thriving retail sector. Another development is with respect to individuals who model their own identities on those of commercial brands.

The earliest instances of the use of branding was in the branding of slaves and criminals for purposes of identification. Thus branding has always been associated with property in its widest sense. Although a slave is undoubtedly a person, in ancient times slaves were treated as if they were socially dead. To mark this event, slave owners habitually renamed their slaves with contemptuous titles such as 'irritation'. Within this context, branding is associated with power and control, a sign of ownership indicated through marking a brand physically on the body and property. Recent branding has taken on a more positive aspect through the development of commodity brands which offer to protect and heal the self. Individuals now mark themselves with brands as a means of self-affirmation rather than negation. In this chapter we consider how discourses around brands offer resources for the construction of identity to firms and to people.

The relations between companies and brands are discussed first. The discussion suggests that companies build brands because these offer value, as represented in 'bottom-line' value and in connoting and consistently delivering value to customers. The construction of the brand persona is then briefly outlined. The relations between people and brands are discussed next. The role played by brands in identity formation is considered using a template which is based on Figures 2.2 and 6.9. This suggests that brands offer resources for the creation of a range of identities.

9.2   BRAND VALUES

Nowadays it is virtually taken for granted that successful branding lies at the heart of marketing and business strategy. This is because the establishment of a strong successful brand image in the mind of the customer can lead him or her to prefer the brand over alternatives and to pay more for it. The notion of brand value is literally true in two senses: first, the customer perceives the brand to be of value in relation to alternatives; secondly, brands add value to the 'bottom line' of the business. This second aspect of value is known as 'brand equity'.

9.2.1   Brand equity: value to the 'bottom line'

If a consumer can come to rely upon a brand and to consistently demand it, the brand may command a price premium over those which purport to service the same core need. Second, the brand may capture a higher market share than alternatives, resulting in experience curve benefits and higher profitability. Third, brands generate loyalty which maintains stability over time. Brands are not built quickly. Often they represent the accumulation of many years of advertising and promotion, coupled with customer experience. Strong established brands have value; in some instances, as in the case of Microsoft, they can be of immense value. This has even prompted some companies to list brands on the asset side of the balance sheet which is a controversial move. This is understandable when one considers that Nestlé paid £2.5 billion for Rowntree – six times the value of net assets.[1] When a company buys a brand it is buying market share. PIMS data (see below) suggest that there is a strong positive relationship between high market share and profitability. More importantly, brands offer the promise to the purchaser of consistent profitability.

9.2.1.1   Bottom-line value: market share and profits

Successful brands will generate a high market share – despite the price premium that many brands command, they also generate customer loyalty. One source of information about the relative performance of brands is to be found in the PIMS database (Buzzell and Gale, 1987). This contains financial and strategic information collected by the Strategic Planning Institute (SPI) on 2600 strategic business units which form part of 450 institutions in the USA. Subsequent analyses of this database have revealed the six 'PIMS principles'. The first and most important of these principles relates to perceived quality, that in the long run the most important single factor affecting a business unit's performance is the quality of its products and services relative to competitors. By building in higher perceived quality, it is argued that units can charge a higher price and reflect this on the 'bottom line' or on R&D and new product development. There is also a strong positive relationship between perceived quality and profitability, which occurs as the result of customer loyalty, more repeat purchases and less vulnerability to price wars.

PIMS findings indicate that, on average, brands with a market share of 40 per cent generate three times the return on investment of those with a market share of 10 per cent. In supporting this view, Doyle (1997) argues that strong brands generate exceptional levels of profit through **a triple-leverage effect**. The most obvious effect is through the higher volume which provides 'experience curve' effects, involving higher asset utilization and scale economies. The second source of advantage is through the

---

[1] Consider this against the average valuation of a UK company at around twice the net balance sheet assets.

higher price that the brand commands. Sometimes this price premium holds at the final consumer level, although it is usually at the retailer or distributor level that it is most apparent. Because they build such loyalty, successful brands are able to generate superior earnings. A premium brand can earn 20 per cent higher returns than discounted products. Since they can take advantage of experience effects, brand leaders also have lower unit costs. This may occur primarily in development, production or marketing, depending on the industry's value chain. The bigger the brand, the more is spent on the total marketing effort; and the bigger the brand, the less is spent in unit cost terms on marketing. The end result is that the brand leader's market-share advantage is substantially magnified at the profit level. Here a brand advantage of 3:1 results through leverage in a profit contribution of nearly 6:1.

9.2.1.2 Brand failure

You may well be asking if there is a price to pay somewhere for this added value. There is. When a brand fails, the market (and the media) can be unforgiving. For all of the brands which have established themselves, there are many more which have now sunk without trace. Consider 'Vector' and 'Orchard', the financial services brand packages that Midland Bank spent millions in creating. Where are they now? For that matter where is Midland Bank now?

9.2.2 Brands connote values

On most occasions, consumers do not decide to purchase a product purely on the basis of its technical performance. Few products are simple enough to warrant direct comparison, and the time which one might spend in comparing the various features of more complex products is enormous. Considering the volume of transactions which most people enter into in one day – and the often confusing array of different features attached to different product offerings – people tend to systematize their behaviour, and branding is one form of 'short-cut' for the consumer to take.

We discussed in Chapter 5 how brands such as Chanel connote a range of values to their target market. The transmission of such values is only partly in the control of the firm which sells the brand. The power of a reference group to decide which brands are 'in' and which brands are 'out' can play a decisive role in whether or not a brand is perceived to be a 'dud' or a 'must have'.

What kinds of meanings can brands connote? Branding is a sign of ownership. This is indicative of an early use of the brand mark that is illustrated in Figure 9.1.

The steer which has been sizzled with this brand, clearly belongs to the 'Lazy S' ranch. In semiotic terms this is not just a positive mark, but is also defined negatively:

Figure 9.1   The 'Lazy S' brand mark

- The brand acts as a sign of **differentiation**, literally a mark of distinction – 'Lazy S' cattle are not the same as other cattle because they are branded differently. As the whole purpose of a brand is to differentiate something, the 'Lazy S' brand mark is different from the brand marks used by other ranches.
- This also connotes the idea 'don't copy me'; the brand mark is a **legal sign** in that someone who takes a 'Lazy S' steer could be legally charged with theft. As Naomi Klein (2000) notes, 'stealing' the mark itself is punishable by prosecution. This has reached such an extent that Klein argues it has become a powerful new form of censorship, as global brands dominate huge swathes of social and cultural space.
- The brand mark is also a **shorthand device** in that it readily identifies what belongs to one person, what that person has a right to that is different from what belongs to other people. The brand mark needs to be distinctive and easily recognizable if it is to fulfil its function.

However, should a brand mark have a direct relation to that which it seeks to represent? Consider the two brand marks shown in Figure 9.2. Both marks have been associated with international oil companies. The 'Shell'[2]

Figure 9.2   Two well-known petroleum brands

[2] The word 'Shell' and the Shell emblem are trademarks; the copyright in the Shell emblem is vested in Shell International Petroleum Company Limited.

mark originated from the shells which the company transported in its ships; ESSO, by contrast, was a clever means of effectively communicating the initials of the original company Standard Oil by building in redundancy (via 'ES', which are strictly superfluous but which reinforce the meaning). Thus while these brand marks have a tenuous relation to the activities of the organizations which bear them, this is indeed a very slim link. The key to branding is thus not that the brand mark bears some form of natural relation to that which it signifies, but rather that an association is built up between the brand mark and what it is supposed to signify in the mind of the customer. The role of advertising is to build and to maintain this association.

In my interpretation, if these two marks could talk (and they frequently do through advertisements), this is what they would say:

> 'Use me, I am reliable, I am an old friend, I have been around since before you were born, the subject of countless advertisements ("Boom boom boom boom . . ./ Put a tiger in your tank"); every time you use one of my petrol stations you will know exactly what to do and what to expect – consistent quality right across the world'.

9.2.3   Brands offer value: filling the self up with good(s)

Falk (1997) suggests that early commodity brands offered to do more than provide positive connotations or good feelings about the brand. The extra ingredient is that they present the possibility of **armouring the self** of the 'individuated' person by offering to fill this fragile self up with good things. In this view, brands are important as they offer the possibility of an instant restorative ('the Gap to fill the gap') to 'empty' consumers. Falk emphasizes how the brand need is anything but physiological – it signifies the emptiness of a continual gnawing desire:

> 'If hunger was just plain hunger and bread just plain bread, then the whole problem of anonymity wouldn't even exist. The naturalist theory of needs has a name for both the deficit (hunger) and for whatever it is that fills the stomach (bread). However a fundamental thesis of modern advertising is that "bread is not only bread", which necessarily means that this applies to the other side of the equation: "hunger is not only hunger".'   [Falk, 1997: 87–8]

In this semiotic explanation, the role of marketers is to name the 'nameless' the (non-material) **deficit**, which the brand seeks to address. This notion may be traced to Levitt's advice to marketers when seeking to define consumers' needs: that it is better to start with the deficit, as for example the market for 'six-inch holes', than the benefit as expressed in the market for drills. A hospital may produce surgery, however customers seek 'relief of pain'. Purchasers of perfume may be purchasing 'dreams', those of cosmetics 'confidence'. According to Levitt (1975), the core brand should reflect the specific quality which makes the brand different from others.

This is known as the 'brand property'. Once this aspect of the 'core' brand has been identified, the marketer has a basis to define the need and the plenitude or wholeness that consumption of the brand will bring. The brand itself is thus a positive creation which offers the promise of negating the evil of the need.

Is all the above fanciful nonsense? There is considerable historical evidence to support the contention that from their earliest incarnations, commodity brands sought to bring good and to eliminate evil. Falk quotes Kitson, who talks of how religion was 'sold' in the 1920s:

> 'the seller may profitably study the methods used by a professional evangelist in "selling" religion. He begins by showing the prospective convert (buyer) how great a lack there is in his life.'   [Kitson, 1921: 180]

Falk has identified an interesting property shared by many early brands. For instance, several brands were initially developed as patent medicines (Coca-Cola and Heinz Ketchup), as part of a controlled 'healthy' diet (Kellogg's Cornflakes), as an aid to the creation of a more 'hygenic' domestic environment through banishing 'invisible' germs and dirt (Sunlight Soap) and in focusing on the development of 'personal hygiene' (Zambuck, Lifebuoy Carbolic Soap, Odorono). Early brand advertising clearly identified the deficit and also the benefit in the shape of the product that could cure it. Emerging through the course of the eighteenth and nineteenth centuries, one cannot but notice the parallels with Foucault's discussion of the emergence at that same time of a range of discourses surrounding the creation of 'healthy' bodies, discussed in Chapter 3. The combination of elements in advertising reflecting the deficit or evil and the cure represented by the brand is captured well by the advertisement shown in Figure 9.3, which plays on the constant and potent fear of 'dirt'.

9.2.3.1 Transition from negative to positive appeals

Falk suggests that at a certain historical point in brand development, the communication of values flipped over from the negative to the positive register. For example, over the period of many years, Coca-Cola was redefined from being a brain tonic to being the Coke we know today:

- 1890s – remedy for headache and a brain tonic;
- 1906 – 'a toast to health and happiness';
- 1916 – 'fun to be thirsty';
- 1982 – 'Coke is it!' (America, youth, beauty, partying, beaches, partying people) – anything GOOD that can be imagined.

The task of advertising thus became transformed to represent the product, to name the opposite of the lack which the brand purports to address (for example a 'non-headache').

Only a blister . . .

a tiny trace of (dirt) . . .

a festering poisoned foot
– the grim fear of
losing a leg!

Why risk it?

**Your surest protection
against dirt-bred germs is to use
Family Health Soap daily**

You never know when dirt-bred germs are
going to strike. A tiny cut or scratch,
a blister, so small you may not even
notice it, may yet be a wide-open
gate for dirt infection. That is
why it pays to make simple
precautions part of your
daily life. Do as doctors
and nurses advise. Always
keep a tablet of Family
Health Soap by the wash-
basin, and see that it is
used. Make every wash
a protection!

Figure 9.3 The evil and the cure [*Woman*, 1 July 1939]

9.3   MANAGERIAL DISCOURSES OF BRANDS

Some academic discourses eulogize brands, arguing that a strong brand
appeal fosters brand loyalty with all of its attendant values. A minority
discourse insists that brand loyalty is characteristic of a limited number of
brands and that consumers buy most brands out of a sense of habit. The
former view is linked to the concept of consumer 'involvement': brands are
purchased by consumers who are 'highly involved' in the purchase because
it is economically important or socially risky, and/or because it is considered
important to the peer group and hence the consumer's self-identity. In this
view, repeat purchase of brands is indicative of the loyalty bred of continuous

satisfaction with the brand. This is disputed by those authors who constitute the minority, who argue on the basis of empirical evidence that most brands are purchased through inertia, merely because they are the least-worst alternative available. The following section rests firmly on the dominant view of the importance of brands to the 'high involvement' consumption context.

9.3.1 Core, tangible and augmented brands

In this view, brands have an irreducible **core**, which is constituted by the need which the brand seeks to fill. The relation between the brand and the physical product, known as the tangible brand, is tenuous. The conventional wisdom has it that it is important for brand 'values' to be stable; components of the 'substance' of the brand may be adjusted as new developments come on-stream, so long as the change lies within the parameters defined by the threshold of the 'just-noticeable-difference' recognized by consumers. Firms may view this change in the physical characteristics of the product in a positive light and communicate it to the audience: for example 'New and Improved' Daz or Ariel or Persil is a familiar clarion call in the detergents' market. This strategy has been known to rebound, for example when 'new formula' Persil was first launched, there were strong protests against the new biological formulation which was said to cause itching and rashes, leading to the formulation being withdrawn. Coke also fared badly when, as a response to Pepsi, they launched 'New Coke' which tasted better in blind tests than traditional Coke. Systems went into rapid reverse following a deluge of complaints from an enraged public. Analysts have subsequently come to the view that, irrespective of the taste, Coke had achieved the status of an American institution that should not be tampered with.

Managerial discourse tends to separate out the brand substance from the **brand image**, which is then attached to it. Despite pressures for standardization, it is often regarded as essential that a brand is clothed with an image which is suitable within the space–time context in which it is to be marketed. A brand which fails to keep up with the times will capture a progressively smaller share of the market. Consequently the brand image is subjected to constant rejuvenation. In 1983 Guinness were still selling 7 million pints a day in 140 countries, but sales had been falling for a decade and the long-term outlook was not good. The brewery mounted a campaign to reverse the image of the drink as something drunk by old ladies in stale smelling pubs, to one which was fit for macho young men. This led to the 'Guinnless' advertising campaign which managed to 'reposition' the product and halt the decline in sales. Product development reinforced the advertising appeal. A new 'cold' Guinness variety was developed which enabled the product to emulate some of the characteristics of lager, a favourite drink of the young male. More recent advertising has sought imaginatively to 'educate' the young consumer that it is good to wait for the 'perfect' pint of Guinness. Older afficionados of Guinness, such as myself, have been less impressed by other less publicized moves which have effectively removed much of the variety and true natural character of the product.

Coupled to the idea that firms should offer consumers a clear benefit is the notion that the brand should 'delight' the customer by offering something *more* than this. This idea runs against another discourse which suggests that the brand should merely match the customers' expectation. This means of **augmenting** the brand is to be found in a huge variety of brand contexts, including larger portions than expected, not only service with a smile but instant change and a refund if dissatisfied, and 'more' 'free' coffee or mints.

9.3.2   Constructing the brand persona

In Chapter 5 we described Barbara Stern's analysis of the different persona's crafted by Fidelity Brokerage Services (warfare) and Merrill Lynch Bank (time). Companies are presented with a range of alternatives with respect to creating a persona. If they offer more than one brand then they may craft an individual persona for each individual brand. For example you may well have heard of Guinness but had you heard of Diageo? As was mentioned in Chapter 2, this is a useful ploy for companies in that it makes it look as if there is more competition than really is the case. Additionally, if there is a problem with one brand, this is less likely to rub off on others. Other approaches include clustering brands by 'families' or 'lines' under the same persona and in offering 'endorsed' brands, where the company and the brand are paired together. How are managers advised to construct this persona? The following 'generic' process has been culled from a range of sources.

1. Identify the brand position

Given that the essential nature of the brand is the range of values which it connotes in the mind of the customer, a key feature of any successful branding policy will be continuous monitoring of customer preferences. The effectiveness of a brand is characterized more by what makes it different from other brands than from any essential quality of the brand itself. It is therefore important to measure the image of brands in relation to other brands which are competing within the same broad marketplace. Another reason for continuous monitoring is the risk of the 'goalposts' moving. What may be a successful brand formula at one point in time may not be so successful at another point. Tastes change and it is necessary for brands to follow such changes. Changing tastes may also provide room for opportunities for brand development.

2. Gap analysis

Investigate whether the exercise carried out under stage 1 above yields up any opportunities and/or threats. For example are there any opportunities for brand extensions or brand stretches?

3. Develop the brand property

The brand property is that element that is 'unique, memorable and indissolubly linked to that brand and no other'.[3] The brand property does not lie in the intrinsic nature of the product – a sweet fizzy drink, a sweet fizzy drink made with apples, a mint-flavoured chocolate, a medium alcohol aperitif – rather it has to be found in the rich tapestry of available referent systems[4] which the advertisers plunder in their search for the creation of the new, the dazzling, the exclusive, the necessity. Through such a process the fizzy drink becomes 'The Real Thing' – Coke; Babycham turns girls into Cinderella or Daley Thompson, depending on which persona you may recall for this gender-bender brand; After Eights are exclusive; while the Martini 'generation' live idyllic lives in tropical bliss (unless this is being ironized).

4. Test alternative propositions

Once developed, brand propositions may be tested with small groups of customers from the target segment, their reactions noted and changes suggested and implemented.

5. Make the 'go'/'no-go' decision

At this stage, decision-makers must decide whether or not to go through with the development of the new brand/changes to the old brand, given the nature of current information. This is vitally important if a long period of time has elapsed between stage 1 and stage 4. As a rule, the time of moving from stage 1 to stage 5 should be as rapid as possible.

6. Construct the implementation plan

This involves a consideration of the four 'P's in relation to the brand. All of these decisions will defer to the notion of 'brand property' and the target market segment which has been identified for the brand (At this time, it might be useful to have a photograph of a representative of this segment pasted to your wall to remind you of precisely who you are dealing with.)

7. Execute the plan

8. Monitor the plan

Go back to stage 1.

---

[3] *Source*: Barry Day, vice chairman McCann Erickson, quoted in Eric Clark's *The Want Makers* (1989).

[4] See the description of Judith Williamson's work in the discussion of semiotics in Chapter 5.

9.3.2.1 'Growing' brands

Key to the entire enterprise is the idea that successful brands adapt by incorporating developments in consumer preferences and lifestyle, and in technology and packaging. The new 'Johnson's Babies' are full-grown males who seem to have a preference for sterile Baby Powder! While the easiest way in which to grow a brand is to extend its geographical range, the brand persona may be developed as an umbrella for a variety of products which are aimed at the same broad market. The practice of developing similar products under the same brand name to appeal to a broadly similar market is known as **brand extension**. Brand stretching is where the development is towards a quite different marketplace, as for example with Porsche sunglasses and Yamaha musical instruments. Examples of brand extensions have been Bells 'Islander' whisky, Mars Ice-Cream and Kellogg's 'Tosta Poppas'.

9.3.2.2 To what extent do brands have personalities?

While the above puts forward a mechanistic plan for the 'creation' of a brand, it tells us little about how the brand persona is created. It is also paradoxical to the extent that it suggests that brands should maintain some 'core' values but at the same time these values can be formulaic and subject to change depending on the changing tastes of the consumer. Some academics argue that the use of words such as 'personality' and 'identity' to describe brands is misleading and at best a form of anthropomorphism, at worst a totally misleading view of processes which would better be discussed in alternative ways. In discussing the related concept of 'corporate personality' in relation to 'corporate identity', Cornelissen and Harris (2001) argue that this is a theoretically naïve and empirically false view. They argue that the use of signifiers such as 'identity' or 'personality', which are usually ascribed to human behaviour, as analogies for explaining corporate behaviour is misplaced, as the inferences do not stretch across the chasm between the two. The authors suggest that the use of such terms leads to the false belief that corporate identity is an expression of an essence of corporate personality or some form of real 'organizational self', which they suggest is 'impotent as explanation of actual corporate behaviour and communication' (2001: 63).

In order to understand what Cornelissen and Harris are saying it is necessary to take a step backwards. They seem to be arguing that it is wrong to suggest that companies or brands have real personalities that provide the basis for the values which in turn provide the basis for the development of corporate and brand identity. By implication they seem to be saying that real people *do* have such immutable personalities. However, as we have seen in Chapter 6, there are a range of theories which put forward markedly different accounts of the formation and role played by identity in personal development. From the discussion in Chapter 6 we might conclude that, while each person is unique, the idea that the self is somehow real or immutable is a minority argument which comes close to a form of biological determinism. In any event, many of those who write about brand personality are careful to discount any idea that there is an intrinsic personality. For example Allen and Olson define personality as:

> 'the set of meanings constructed by an observer to describe the "inner" characteristics of another person.'   [1995: 392]

You should pay particular note to the scare quotes around the word "inner"; it is quite obvious that Allen and Olson mean this to suggest that there are no real inner characteristics, but that such characteristics are attributions made by the observer. If the notion of some form of inner essence is insufficient to characterize the brand personality, then how might this be constructed? Here we may usefully turn to the discussion of semiotics in Chapter 5. In this explanation, personality is constructed through language. You may remember Barbara Stern (1988) likens the brand persona to a metaphor which is crafted through the myriad of linkages which are made in advertising texts. Virginia Valentine (see Valentine and Evans, 1993: 129) takes a similar approach, which explicitly links the construction of such metaphors to metonymic relations. Likewise Judith Williamson (1978) discusses the role played by referent systems in providing meaning for products which are often associated with the meanings of real people.

Attributions and the brand personality

If, contrary to what Cornelissen and Harris (2001) suggest in the discussion above, it is possible to think of brands as being personalities, then what are the mechanisms by which people treat brands *as if* they really are personalities? Allen and Olsen (1995) argue that people make **attributions** about brands in the same way that they do about each others' behaviour. For example if an observer sees another person kicking a dog, they may well think of that person as being 'cruel'. In this view, attributions about personality traits are based largely on experience, observations of behaviour which are supposedly caused by the unobserved personality trait (for example 'the guy kicked the dog because he was cruel'). They suggest that one can use the same logic to conceptualize brand personality. To do so, the brand must seem to perform intentional behaviours – it must seem somehow to be 'alive'. Based on these observed characteristics, consumers make attributions about the brand personality – its 'inner' nature. For example Aaker considers that the personality of Levi's 501 jeans is: 'American, western, ordinary, common, blue-collar, hard working and traditional' (1995: 394). As a result, Allen and Olson urge brand-builders to stress the 'alive-ness' and action potential of the brand which they are advertising.

Brand 'relationships'

Fournier pushes the idea of the 'personality' to its limits in arguing that a brand can be seen to be an 'active contributing partner in the dyadic **relationship** that exists between the person and the brand' (1995: 393). In this view, all marketing mix activities and brand management activities, for example advertising and direct marketing campaigns, are construed as being 'behaviours' that are enacted on behalf of the brand 'personality', which trigger attitudinal and other responses on the part of the customer. According to Fournier, this allows the audience to elevate the status of the brand from that of a passive object to that of being a 'relationship partner'. A possible example to illustrate what Fournier may be getting at is the decision by Nestlé in the summer of 2001 to repackage the famous 'KitKat' brand by removing the aluminium foil and substituting this with a paper wrapper. This received considerable exposure in the mass media where pundits pondered whether this move might damage consumers' relations with the brand. A key feature of using the brand was the sensual feeling of running one's nail along the foil in order to better snap off the tasty fingers of chocolate inside, and it was argued that the substitution of a paper wrapper would provide a quite different feel.

But can we seriously say that the 'relations' between the buyer and KitKat constitute a *relationship*? The word 'relationship' was initially popularized by 'humanistic' psychologists such as Carl Rogers (1981) to describe 'meaningful' interpersonal relationships. Even within its 'proper' psychological context, some people find the word to be clichéed, hackneyed and saccharin-sweet. One could suggest that describing the 'relationship' between a person and his or her brands as being akin to human relations ultimately devalues the latter. In this sense Cornelissen and Harris (2001) may be making an important point. Transferring meaning from what usually defines relations between *people* (identity, personality, relationships) to those relations between people and *things*, may do more than 'humanize' what are otherwise 'impersonal' transactions. It may have the reverse effect in devaluing human 'relations' by rendering these as being thing-like (see O'Malley and Tynan, 1999). Rather than trying to stretch the meaning of relationship to cover 'relations' between people and brands, it might be better to coin one or two neologisms. For example 'relationchip' could be used to characterize the instrumental and ethically suspect buildup of databases by firms to 'capture' consumer behaviour so as to form 'relations' between brands and people. On the other hand 'relationshoppers' are those who are progressively drawn to seek fulfilment in their 'relations' with commodities.

Who controls the relationship?

If we retain the idea of a 'relationship' between the person and the brand then who is in control? Put another way; if consumers think of brands as having 'personalities' which are the result of the concatenation of ad appeals and other brand 'behaviours', this raises the interesting question of the extent to which brand managers are actually in control of this personality. While managers control extensive advertising and publicity budgets, the mass media also provide a strong input which is capable of reversing the attributes intended by the designers of the persona. This happened to the Midland Bank some time ago when it boldly proclaimed that it was the

'Listening Bank'. The press quickly seized on this message, reversing it to create the opposite meaning to that intended:

- 'Listening Bank disciplines managers'.
- 'Listening Bank imposes charges' (see note i).
- 'Is the Listening Bank listening?' (see note ii).
- 'Midland Bank which calls itself the "Listening Bank" has incurred the wrath of a charity after suddenly imposing charges after years of free banking' (see note iii).
- 'Midland Bank is bravely continuing with its "Listening Bank" theme in spite of the way in which it backfired in the headlines and cartoons last summer after a spot of hassle with a woman customer' (see note iv).

| 9.4 | **POPULAR BRAND DISCOURSES** |

Above we described a fairly typical managerial discourse of brands. The aim in this section is to consider the extent to which this discourse travels beyond the firm and into the wider reaches of society, and how this is implicated in the constitution of other discourses concerned with anti-branding, stigmatized brands and 'no-logo' identities.[5] These are represented in Figure 9.4, which bears a strong relation to Figures 2.2 and 6.9.

The figure considers how the concept of a 'brand' offers resources for the construction of a range of identities based on positive and negative evaluations of the managerial discourse of branding. When a brand acts as a **stigma**, it constitutes a sign which marks a person as 'other' to the norm. While this has a long pedigree, brands continue to function in their role as

	Pro-Consumption	**Anti-Consumption**
Positive aspect of brand	Brand as 'Good' (Brand as negation)	Anti-brand as 'Good' (Negation of brand)
Negative aspect of brand	'No-Logo' (The non-brand)	Brand as Exclusion (Brand as stigma)

Figure 9.4 A crude typology of brand-related discourses

[5] The idea of a 'no-logo' identity cited here refers more or less specifically to the group known as voluntary simplifiers and is thus different from the more generic identity referred to by Naomi Klein.

stigmata in contemporary consumer society. Hebdige (1988) describes how skinheads who had themselves tattooed with swastikas during the late 1970s and early 1980s as a bold expression of their counter-cultural identity, endured considerable pain and expense, not to mention scarring, when they eventually had these removed so as to be able to procure a job. The poor are branded through being stigmatized (by association with the brands which they can afford) or criminalized (through organized 'shoplifting' of desirable brands). An undergraduate student project by Heriot-Watt students found that the child who wore (cheaper) 'hi-tech' training shoes to school was likely to be picked upon by others who flaunted their Nike, Reebok or Adidas shoes.[6] Stigmatization means brands which are 'cool' in one context may be stigmatized in another: lilly posted this message (see note v) to a web newsgroup (original spelling has been retained):

> So to cut a long story short I went to O'Reillys, Tara Street on Friday night to meet up with a work party of about 25 people. We got as far as the door and the lovely bloke in a suit said he didn't know my face and that I coulnd't go in. I have been there several times, we were very presantably dressed so as far as I can work out we didn't get in because my boyfriend is black. This is unacceptable in this day and age and I'd like to hear from other people who have this kind of bullshit shoved into their face. Other friends weren't let in because they were wearing Trainers – the famous "trainers = scum bag" equation. Now where did that come from?? ... Mr Bouncer if you are reading this – get a life and a few customer service skills.

It is interesting that 'lilly' equates discrimination according to the trainers or clothes one wears with racial discrimination; people were excluded because of their 'colour' and because of the trainers they wore. This form of determination is commonplace in many cities. In Edinburgh, 'well-dressed' tourists wearing trainers, unaware of the policy operated by some local establishments, are bemused and angry by being turned away from some seedy establishment for the same reason.

Elliott and Wattanasuwan (1998) argue that consumers use brands as symbolic resources for the construction of identity. In this respect the brand is perceived to be **good** as it 'negates the negation', providing a perhaps temporary means for the individual to compensate for feelings of inadequacy and incompleteness through promising to fill the self up with good things.

Consumers may become **disaffected** with brands in two senses of the word. In the first sense this relates to Mary Douglas's (1997) assertion that brand preference is often made on the basis of hostility: 'I wouldn't be seen dead in that'. In particular one might imagine that this comment would be directed at the kinds of brands habitually displayed, worn or used (and therefore stigmatized) by those perceived to be one rung below the purchaser on the ladder of distinction. This view is supported by the Englis and Solomon (1995) study, discussed in Chapter 6, which demonstrated that

[6] Competition has now shifted to mobile phones.

students sought to orientate themselves towards the products owned by aspirational groups and away from those owned by the 'Smalltown Downtown' avoidance group. The idea of avoidance or of the 'undesired self' has been further developed by Hogg and Bannister (2001) who explored this in relation to clothing brands. They found that affiliation and conformity were considered to be very important for their (mixed) focus group members whose expectations of dress codes were acutely oriented towards the 'normative'; breaking from the 'norm' was seen to be potentially risky. Alongside the attachment to the affiliation and aspirational groups was a strong sense of dissociation from perceived avoidance groups. For example one respondent, 'Katie', says:

> 'Well I don't want people thinking I'm a slapper . . . white short skirt and white stillettos . . . somebody might aspire to that . . . whereas we just look and go "Oh my God! Sad" . . . some people might look and think she looks great . . . it depends . . .'
>
> [2001: 90]

While women tended to articulate their negative stereotypes in terms of typical occupations and age, men tended to distance themselves from other men in terms of how 'scruffy' or 'snobbish' they looked. Respondents reported avoidance behaviour associated with retail outlets, for example one man avoided an outlet which he felt sold 'ridiculously scruffy clothes'. While the authors did not report much in terms of brand avoidance, some members noted avoiding Kickers and sports brands.

One may speak of disaffection in a different sense from that described above to refer to those consumers who are becoming increasingly disaffected from the system of brand culture and who seek to flee from it or get away from it in some way. This form of disaffection, described by Naomi Klein as a 'no-logo' brand identity which seeks to rid the self from the (artificial) brand identity in order to build a more authentic sense of self, is ironically appealed to in brand formats.[7] Thus the person who is smart enough to decode the brand system can always buy Sprite if he wants to 'obey' his thirst and not the image dangled before him by cynical marketers (in which case we wonder about how smart he really is). Alternatively the smoker who is tired of the machinations of the tobacco industry may fall for the 'honesty' of DEATH™ cigarettes. Such disaffection may be with particular brands, for particular reasons (smoking kills) and may often be partial (Nestlé/ McDonald's are 'bad', Boots/Burger King/IKEA are good). Alternatively the voluntary simplicity lifestyle actively seeks to escape from the entire brand system.

Rather than seeking to withdraw from brand culture, a person may decide that the only alternative is to destroy it. **Anti-consumers**, who share a variety of ideological positions, are united in their condemnation of what they perceive to be a wasteful and destructive society.

---

[7] Klein (2000). The 'no-logo' brand identity described by Klein comes closer in many respects to anti-consumerism than to a voluntary simplicity lifestyle.

Figure 9.5 Flaunting authority through brand use

While the above presents four different orientations to brands, we now consider the extent to which it might be possible to talk of brand subcultures.

9.4.1 Brand subcultures?

When Hebdige writes about the emergence of 'Mod' and 'Rocker' subcultures in Britain in the late 1950s and 1960s, the brand, the motorcycle or scooter, though central comprises one aspect of an entire subculture of consumption. The 'subculture' is marked off from the mainstream through key elements in style, or the way in which a person comports himself or herself in actually riding the machine (thus distinguishing oneself from 'inauthentic' riders), appropriate clothing combinations and hairstyles, the spaces one frequents, recreational drugs of choice and music. A more recent study by Schouten and McAlexander (1995), which focuses on the Harley-Davidson user, illustrates how the organization of this subculture is layered like an onion, with the 'Easy-Rider' or 'Electra-Glide in Blue' aesthete forming the centre, and daytrippers acting as outriders to the culture. In this view the brand positively plays a role in establishing and maintaining a sense of separation, cohesiveness and solidarity necessary for the formation of the subculture, in addition to providing resources for the identity-work of members.

One might just as easily identify subcultures in groupings of anti-consumers. For Hebdige (1988), the subcultural milieu is 'constructed underneath the authorized discourses, in the face of the multiple disciplines of the family, the school and the workplace' (1988: 35). Subculture forms in the 'space between surveillance and the evasion of surveillance', translating the scrutiny of parents, teachers and bosses into the 'pleasure of being watched. It is hiding in the light'. In this way Hebdige seeks to explain the rebellion of youth via the creation of a profusion of outrageous dress-codes from the teenager of the 1950s to the 'anti-style' effected by the 1980's punk refusal of commodity identity. Similarly it could be argued that the anti-consumerist 'crusties' who formed the 1990's 'hippie convoys', smoking 'skunk' and engaging in impromptu 'raves', comprise a subculture. In the same sense one can think of the 'anti-brand' embodied in the 'Ecstasy' and 'Acid House' subcultures (see note vi).

Interpreted in this 'strong' way then the poor are literally 'sub' or below 'culture' as represented by the dominant consumer elite. The idea of brand subcultures facilitates a comparison of the transactions between these relatively discrete entities. Thus one can consider the manner by which punk appropriates and translates commodity images into its own argot, or alternatively how 'mainstream' culture 'raids' anti-brand street-culture for images to recycle through the mainstream.

9.4.2 The weak view: brand community

On the other hand it may be more appropriate to describe such groupings as tribes, constituting the loose forms of community described by Muniz and O'Guinn (1999) in Chapter 4. This weaker view describes an assortment of brand communities in the stead of relatively homogeneous subcultures. In this view, brand communities such as 'Saabers' and 'MacWarriors' share the minimum resources necessary to constitute a form of 'community'; however this is not a 'subculture' in the manner in which Hebdige or Schouten and McAlexander might describe it. This notion comes close to the concept of the 'neo-tribes' advanced by Maffesoli (1997), whereby members are connected by loose bonds of 'common affect'. The idea of tribal identities accords with the romantic vision which many anti-consumers have of themselves, as guerrillas who hollow out 'temporary autonomous zones' or crevices in the monolithic space of commodity consumption, which become the sites of a never-ending guerrilla war. George McKay's work (1998) provides an excellent summary. One might also argue that it makes more sense to view those excluded from consumption as constituting a number of different marginalized groupings; the aged-poor, immigrants and vagrants rather than a homogenized lumpen subculture. Even the poor have their cherished brands. In the UK, brands such as the *Daily Mirror* and HP sauce were aimed specifically at the 'respectable' working classes and had to be cheap enough for them to afford. In this sense the same brand can operate as an icon to be cherished by one group and simultaneously as a stigma to another.

9.4.3 The individual in brand discourse

The idea of subculture suggests that a person's identity is formed in relation to a 'mainstream' consumer culture. That of a brand community suggests that such connections are more loosely articulated; nevertheless the bonds of community pull people into such clusters and constellations. How do individuals relate to brands? This question can easily be explored using an ideographic method, which focuses on the detailed exploration of one person's constructs of consumption (Bannister and Fransella, 1980). The following is compiled by information supplied by an anonymous informant whom we shall call M.J. Deene. Deene is relatively 'comfortably' off, a mortgaged professional, perched in the 35–45 age group. The research procedure followed a semi-structured approach, loosely based on Kelly (1955), whereby Deene listed elements of his favourite, hated, loved to hate, wouldn't be seen dead in, loved anti-brands, hated anti-brands and no-brands. Finally he was asked briefly to suggest some reasons for his choice of elements. Deene's answers are summarized in Table 9.1.

From the above, Deene articulates or conjoins a range of brand identities to those aspects of his own identity that he loves to love, loves to hate and hates. One can say that Deene's 'love' of football and rugby brands and his 'hate' of Nestlé and Murdoch are not unique to him but are artefacts of the culture in which he was raised. His abandonment of Nike and Adidas brands indicates the desire for distinction (perhaps from youth? or the poor?). Deene seems to relate to brands which he 'loves to hate' in a complex way which seems to indicate an ambivalence towards the behaviour associated with the brand. In 1960's terms he is a 'pseud' as he regularly uses brands which are not those which he admires in addition to using some occasionally that he 'loves to hate'. While admiring the romantic side of anti-brands, he does not want to be preached at.

Does Deene have a stable identity with respect to brands? Despite the range of brand 'identities' adopted, he appears to be one of the fortunate who has a full-time job and therefore is provided with a season ticket into consumer society. As a result he is able to play with identity to an extent. It is clear that many of Deene's preferences and hates do not originate with him but in discourses which, one might say, 'flow' through him from the social world.

9.5 DISCOURSE AND BRAND IDENTITY

In Chapter 3 we outlined Foucault's approach which suggests that we start from the concrete and work up. In this case the task would be to work outwards from Deene's account to the range of discourses which operate in the discursive field to construct this paradoxical brand identity. Some of these discourses (those surrounding HP sauce, Heinz, Sony) link into the 'mainstream' managerial discourse of brands; others (Nestlé, McDonald's, 'Posh and Becks') feed into an 'anti-brand' discourse. In drawing upon 'brand' and 'anti-brand' discourses, Deene crafts a sense of identity for himself while simultaneously reproducing the power of these discourses. Having said all of that, there is a large part of Deene's 'identity' which he

Table 9.1 **Brand affiliations – M.J. Deene**

	Elements	Reasons
My favourite brands	City (soccer team) Nationality (rugby team) Sochony (running shoes) VW (car) Sony music centre/CD player Apple HP/Heinz/Hendersons' relish Lucozade, Ribena Bricanyl, Pulmacort	Communal pride National pride (if we win) Good for running in Reliable old friend – soon must go Always reliable The computer I should have bought Used since I can remember For when I'm ill For when I have asthma
Brands I hate	McDonald's Anything with Posh and Becks on Anything with Murdoch or News International on it	Drab, cheerless Pseudo-media Unprintable
Brands I love to hate	Barclays Marlboro Nestlé Guinness British Royal Family	Ruthless, macho, couldn't care less Hate company; users are poseurs, hate smoking; smoke these when I do smoke Kills babies (Do they still? Didn't others do this too?) Just another multinational Kind of like them because its trendy not to
Brands I wouldn't be seen dead in	Nike, Adidas	Used to wear Nike – and a pair of 'Ron Hill's' for running – but now that slobs are wearing them I don't
Brands I might be seen dead in	Boeing, Aeroflot	
Anti-brands I love	Road protestors, tunnellers Reclaim the streets	Romantic, Robin Hood If I'm not driving at the time
Anti-brands I hate	Adbusters	Rarely witty, 'holier than thou', (though hate is too strong a word)
No brands (brands I won't buy)	Meat brands – Danepak etc. Nescafé	Vegetarian (part-time) Because it is
Brands I wish I didn't have to buy	Petroleum Car Pre-packed meals	Too many Hate driving Look great, taste like cardboard
Brands I use often	Muesli/oats PC Guinness, Whiskey/whisky Herbal tea/noodles Lacoste	Don't admit this publicly Not a Mac – but does the job You've got to drink something Good to have a blast – not so good for the liver To get over the whiskey/whisky How did that get in my wardrobe?
Generic hate	Multinationals	

does not know. This is constituted by the way in which these brands (and particularly those he favours) mark him out as a particular type of prospect and target for their marketing campaigns and the knowledge which they have of his purchasing patterns and preferences. Thus a large part of his identity is constituted from outside. However this constitution is not monolithic but is partial; what determines him as one thing in one context determines him in different ways in other contexts. To illustrate this point, consider the differential set of 'brand' determinations which are discussed below.

Brand/anti-brand as identifier

Brands are very useful to consumers as identifiers, as they are instantly recognizable and can save a person time and money in choosing between alternatives. Brands stand as a sign of consistent presentation and quality. Major companies expend considerable effort in ensuring these features. One principal way in which a brand may act as an identifier is when well-known brands are displayed openly by those who wear them.

The brand as a badge

You may remember that in Chapter 2 we discussed how rap band Run-DMC had begun to promote the Adidas brand in the mid 1990s. Adidas built on this unexpected boon through skilful marketing of its brand, by associating Adidas with those sports and pop celebrities which form youth affiliation groups. As a result it obtained a huge share of the dynamic and fickle youth clothing market. There are many examples of those such as 'Ryno' who became so devoted to Adidas that they constructed their websites as fan pages. The following is a detailed list of all the Adidas items owned by 'Ryno' as indicated on her website, in the year 2000 (see note vii):

> 15 pairs of shoes (basketball, leisure, turf training shoes, adventure boots, torsion trainers, 'response IV' running shoes, four types of socks, 21 T-shirts and other shirts, including basketball mesh tank tops, England and Bayern Munich football shirts, nine types of shorts, 8 types of hat, 3 bags and a range of diverse items such as watches, soccer balls, keychains and equipment bags.

What is interesting about the above is that 'Ryno's' loyalty is not to the soccer teams (England, Bayern Munich) or to the basketball teams so much as to Adidas. She can play with various identities such as 'runner', 'trainer', 'basketball player', 'football supporter' while all the time wearing the same identity, that of Adidas.

Branding the skin

A more recent development has been the remarkable growth in tattooing and body piercing, particularly among the youth in Western countries. In traditional societies, tattooing and piercing have long been associated with ritual **rites of passage**. Such rites publicly signify the transition from childhood to adulthood and often involve painful ceremonies which mark this transition. One line of argument to explain the growth of tattooing and piercing in Western countries is that as traditional rituals which mark such events have

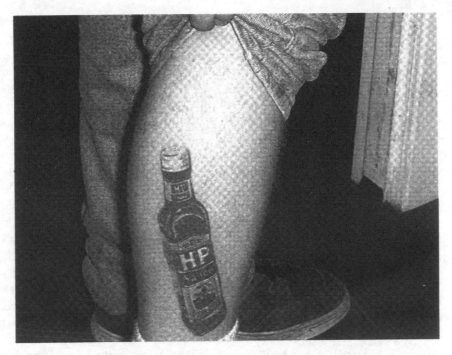

Figure 9.6 Branding the skin

declined to the point where they have virtually ceased to exist, such acts real-ize a person's desire to mark a significant personal event or transition on their own body, to place a seal as it were on the act itself. Recall John Schouten's discussion in Chapter 7, of people's reasons for undergoing cosmetic surgery. The reasons given by respondents to Schouten's study reinforce the view that the surgery marked an important transition for the person concerned. 'Joe', as we shall call him, decided that he was going to have a tattoo to mark each important event in his life. In looking back over the past eighteen years, the image that seemed to encapsulate everything is shown in Figure 9.6.

An alternative explanation for such practices is as a form of self-expres-sion and self-control. In this respect, tattooing may be construed as an act of defiance in what is seen to be a conflict between the individual and society with respect to the issue of control. One notable feature of body piercing is that it is reversible – if the rings are removed for long enough, the effects vanish. Similarly and perhaps learning from the lessons of skinheads, many people have their bodies tattooed, but only in places which would normally be covered by clothing. Such an act is construed as an outcome to maintain a private space, a place which can be known about and controlled by the self and by no-one else.

The person as brand

If the 'Hollywood' period from the 1920s to the 1990s can be thought of as the age of celebrity, where celebrities were chosen to signify particular attributes in competition with others, in order to appeal to a particular market segment, then nowadays everyone can be a celebrity. By this I do not mean to steal Andy Worhol's celebrated statement, that nowadays everyone can be famous for fifteen minutes, although there is some truth in this. Rather what is meant is that today ordinary individuals are subjecting themselves and their bodies to a similar brand discipline as that which has traditionally applied to products as things (brands) and people as products (celebrities).

Effectively this means that individuals are increasingly evaluating what they signify and how their 'offering' differs with respect to key competitors, whether this is in the world of work or of leisure. A similar 'brand development' cycle is followed to that outlined in section 9.3.2. People identify their brand position by consciously emphasizing something that is of value and unique to themselves, which acts as a positive generator of difference with others (competitors). A form of gap analysis is carried out whereby the person identifies the difference between where they are with respect to an ideal point and where they wish to be. Developing the 'brand' property may be expressed by increasing substance, for example through pursuing an educational qualification; however the ultimate aim is that it is displayed as a marker of competitive success and conveys badge value to others. Substance is thus subservient to style, and style can be worked on by focusing on a range of 'effective' self-presentation formats, from personal grooming to choice of clothes, deportment etc. The individual may also test several alternative propositions or persona, prior to making the go/no-go decision. The implementation plan consists of a detailed plan for securing advantage through brand leverage in the long term.

9.6   AND FINALLY – A WORD OF CAUTION

Much of the discussion in this chapter links the idea of branding to those of 'personality', 'identity' and brands. As Baudrillard noted, the fundamental reasoning behind this is that people in consumer societies tend to evaluate others on the basis of what they have and what they consume rather than in terms of what they do. However, having the brand is not enough, **style** is of crucial importance. For the same reasons that it was thought that Robin Cook would never make Prime Minister of the UK because he was too 'gnome-like', it is not just ownership of the brand that matters. As we discussed in Chapter 6, it is being able to carry it off – the ability to be able to 'wear' the expensive clothes, to be able to drive the expensive car. If one is not up to the task, one stands in danger of being branded as a fool. In any event only a very few of the many thousands of brands on offer matter sufficiently for us to invest our precious attention in. Andrew Ehrenberg (Ehrenberg, 2000; Kennedy and Ehrenberg, 2001) has for many years been like a voice in the wilderness in proclaiming that the vast majority of brands really don't matter that much to us.

9.7 CHAPTER SUMMARY

This chapter discussed the ways in which the histories of branding for people, products and companies intertwine with one another. First we looked at branding with respect to companies and brands, outlining why companies build brands; the relations between brands, market share and profits; brand leverage; sources of brand value; the relations between products and brands; and finally dealing with the brand development cycle. In considering the relations between people and brands we discussed how brands have meaning for people, and then turned to consider the ways in which people relate to brands involved in portraying the brand as stigma, product identifier and personal identifier, culminating in the situation where the person marks the self as a brand.

9.8 CASE STUDY: BARR'S IRN-BRU

Irn Bru was A.G. Barr's pillar brand. However by 1990, even in its Scottish heartland, Irn-Bru had lost its primacy in the Scottish market to soft-drinks giants Coca-Cola, which had recently begun to advertise heavily there, Pepsi and a growing number of other entrants into the market. As a result it was decided that if Irn-Bru was going to survive, the long-term future for it must be as a national (UK) and not a parochial (Scottish) brand.

For many years Barr's pop drink 'Irn-Bru' had occupied a special place in Scottish hearts. After all, nothing could be more Scottish than Irn-Bru. The links between Irn-Bru and the fabric of Scots' identity had been tellingly made in the advertising of the 1950s and 1960s. These ads had played on the theme that Irn-Bru was 'made frae girders' (constructed from girders). This idea linked Irn-Bru and Barr's, which connected it to the great iron, steel and shipbuilding industries of Scotland. Irn-Bru signified that the person who drank it was as 'hard as nails', a true Scot. Now the children of those who had first seen those ads were turning away from Irn-Bru towards substitutes.

Research indicated that awareness and the meanings associated with Irn-Bru were very different in Scotland and in England. The primary advertising appeal (based on 'Made in Scotland from Girders'), which focused on Irn-Bru's Scottish origins and metallic properties, was entirely product based. However in many ways this broke the rules of soft-drinks advertising where user values were seen to be the key ingredient. This had been apparent for many years. For example Coca-Cola was associated with the USA, and was advertised as 'The Real Thing', coming from the home of 'authentic' consumer culture. Its appeal, which was crafted over many years, was in many ways similar to that of the Disney Corporation, as represented by values of wholesomeness, mother, love and apple-pie. As such it represented a powerful appeal to the ideal values of many sections of youth both in the USA and abroad, particularly among those who wanted a piece of 'authentic' US culture – at an affordable price. Coke's rival, Pepsi, had adopted a different approach, which was to integrate the values of the brand with those of pop culture. This led to it signing a huge sponsorship deal with pop superstar Michael Jackson, which rebounded soon after when lurid details of Jackson's private life began to appear in the newspapers. Pepsi also sponsored the UK pop charts. In making such a huge commitment to pop culture, Pepsi executives realized that nowadays youth in relatively affluent consumer societies ate and drank things for their images, not for their use value (to quench thirst), nor for their exchange value (which isn't very much). In the 1990s, for teenagers to buy soft drinks they had to be 'cool', which did not mean to say that they had to be kept cool in a fridge. User values were not related to the drink's use value (its thirst-quenching quality) nor even to its exchange value (its cost) but rather to its image value – what it said about the person who drank it.

Research for Irn-Bru indicated that while the mainstream world of soft drinks is regarded as being fun, gregarious and attractive to teenagers, in contrast Irn-Bru was seen in England to be grey, tough, gritty and dull. Consequently the brand was regarded as being far removed from its core potential consumers – teenagers.

The task of the advertising was to make Irn-Bru part of the teenage world, but it was vitally important that the new identity did not in any way resemble the style of competitors. The advertising brief stressed that the bright, successful and rose-tinted view of the world presented by the giants was very attractive to teenagers. However while they found it attractive, they were not duped by it and could see through the flimsy, plastic values it portrays. Irn-Bru's 'Made in Scotland from Girders' epitomizes the tough, no-nonsense attitude that the brand has to the world. Based on this attitude, Irn-Bru can conspire with teenagers to see through the glossy world of Coke and thus position itself as the anti-hero of soft drinks. By using humour it was hoped that the brand could do this in a sympathetic rather than an openly confrontational manner (Figure 9.7).

Young boys had formed the target groups for previous campaigns. For the new campaign the target group was to be enlarged to include 15 to 19-year-old boys and girls. This group is very image conscious and highly advertising literate. Its favourite ads tend to be for lager. Its favourite style of humour is clever, quick witted and satirical. Its favourite heroes are cool, quirky anti-establishment figures like Indiana Jones, Crocodile Dundee, Eddie Murphy in *Beverly Hills Cop* or anyone from *Viz* (an irreverent magazine). Music is a very important part of its world.

In planning the campaign it was decided to avoid building images of Scotland. While the Scottishness of the brand was undeniable, it was felt that this should be kept at a level where people could find it if they were looking for it, but would not be bothered by it if they were not. In addition to this,

Figure 9.7 New-style Irn-Bru ad

the equating of Irn-Bru with anything metallic was to be avoided. This had to be interpreted as a character trait rather than as a physical property. The slogan 'Made in Scotland from Girders' should be retained but not explained.

Tracking survey data from the first 'connexions' campaign revealed that advertising awareness of Irn-Bru had grown significantly. More importantly, spontaneous recall had increased, which has the highest correlation with sales. In addition to this, more people claimed to drink the brand. The rate of sale in 1991 showed growth that was 30 per cent faster than its nearest rival. In the Thames region (around London in England), sales of Irn-Bru increased by 70 per cent year on year. This format is still being used by Barr's.

Case-study questions

1. Why is it important to establish brand values for soft drinks in consumer societies?
2. To what extent did the values associated with Irn-Bru stay the same and to what extent did they change with the introduction of the new campaign?
3. Try to think of how you can use water as an example to signify the relations between use value, exchange value and sign value?

END-OF-CHAPTER REVIEW QUESTIONS

1. What is meant by the following: 'brand mark', 'tangible brand', 'potential brand'?
2. Outline the relation between branding, market share and profits.
3. What is meant by 'brand leverage'?
4. What steps do companies and people follow in building brands?

REFERENCES AND FURTHER READING

Aaker, Jennifer (1995) Measuring the Human Characteristics of a Brand: A Brand Personality Hierarchy, *Advances in Consumer Research*, vol. 22: 393–4.

Allen, Douglas E. and Gerry Olson (1995) Conceptualizing and Creating Brand Personality: A Narrative Theory and Approach, *Advances in Consumer Research*, vol. 22: 392–3.

Bannister, Don and Faye Fransella (1980) *Inquiring Man: The Psychology of Personal Constructs*, 2nd edn, London: Penguin.

Buzzell, Robert D. and Bradley Gale (1987) *The PIMS Principles: Linking Strategy to Performance*, New York and London: Free Press and Collier Macmillan (now Palgrave).

Clark, Eric (1989) *The Want Makers*, London: Coronet Books.

Collin, Matthew (1998) *Altered State: The Story of Ecstasy Culture and Acid House*, London: Serpent's Tail.

Cornelissen, Joep and Phil Harris (2001) The Corporate Identity Metaphor: Perspectives, Problems and Prospects, *Journal of Marketing Management*, vol. 17: 49–71.

Davidson, H. (1987) *Offensive Marketing*, London: Penguin Business, pp. 293–304.

Douglas, Mary (1997) 'In Defence of Shopping'. In Pasi Falk and Colin Campbell (eds), *The Shopping Experience*, London: Sage.

Doyle, Peter (1997) *Marketing Management and Strategy*, London: Pearson Education.

Ehrenberg, Andrew (2000) Repetitive Advertising and the Consumer, *Journal of Advertising Research*, December: 39–48.

Elliott, Richard and Kertsadaeat Wattanasuwan (1998) Brands as Symbolic Resources for the Construction of Identity, *International Journal of Advertising*, vol. 17/2: 131–45.

Englis, Basil G. and Michael Solomon (1995) To Be and Not to Be: Lifestyle Imagery, Reference Groups, and the Clustering of America, *Journal of Advertising*, vol. 24 (Spring): 13–29.

Falk, Pasi (1997) 'The Genealogy of Advertising', pp. 81–108. In Pekka Sulkunen, John Holmwood, Hilary Radner and Gerhard Schulze (eds), *Constructing the New Consumer Society*, Basingstoke: Macmillan (now Palgrave).

Fournier, Susan (1995) The Brand-As-Relationship Partner: An Alternative View of Brand Personality, *Advances in Consumer Research*, vol. 22: 393.

Hebdige, Dick (1988) *Hiding in the Light*, London and New York: Comedia and Routledge.

Hogg, Margaret K. and Emma N. Bannister (2001) Dislikes, Distastes and the Undesired Self: Conceptualising and Exploring the Role of the Undesired End State in Consumer Experience, *Journal of Marketing Management*, vol. 17: 73–104.

Kelly, George A. (1955) *The Psychology of Personal Constructs*, vols I and II, New York: W.W. Norton.

Kennedy, Rachel and Andrew Ehrenberg (2001) There is no Brand Segmentation, *Marketing Research*, Marketing insights: 4–7.

Kitson, Harry D. (1921) *The Mind of the Buyer: A Psychology of Selling*, London: Macmillan.

Klein, Naomi (2000) *No Logo*, London: Flamingo.

Levitt, Theodore (1975) *Marketing Myopia*, Boston, Massachusetts: Harvard University Press.

McKay, George (1996) *Senseless Acts of Beauty: Cultures of Resistance Since the Sixties*, London: Verso.

McKay, George (1998) *DiY Culture: Party and Protest*, London: Verso.

Maffesoli, Michel (1997) 'The Return of Dionysus', pp. 21–38. In Pekka Sulkunen, John Holmwood, Hilary Radner and Gerhard Schulze (eds), *Constructing the New Consumer Society*, Basingstoke: Macmillan (now Palgrave).

Muniz Jr., Albert and Thomas O'Guinn (1999) 'Brand Community'. Unpublished paper presented as part of the Marketing Roadshow series, Edinburgh University, March 2000.

Murphy, J.M. (1992) *Brand Strategy*, Director Books.

O'Malley, Lisa and Caroline Tynan (1999) The Utility of the Relationship Metaphor in Consumer Markets: A Critical Evaluation, *Journal of Marketing Management*, vol. 15: 587–602.

Ries, A. and J. Trout (1986) *Positioning: The Battle for the Customer's Mind*, New York: McGraw-Hill.

Rogers, Carl (1981) *Client-Centred Therapy: Its Current Practice, Implications and Theory*, London: Constable.

Rudmin, F.W. and W.E. Kilbourne (1996) 'The Meaning and Morality of Voluntary Simplicity: History and Hypotheses on Deliberately Denied Materialism'. In R. Belk, N. Dholakia and A. Venkatesh (eds), *Consumption and Marketing: Macro-Marketing Dimensions*, Ohio: South-Western College Publishing and International Thomson.

Schouten, John and James H. McAlexander (1995) Subcultures of Consumption: An Ethnography of New Bikers, *Journal of Consumer Research*, vol. 22: 43–61.

Stern, Barbara B. (1988) How Does an Ad Mean?, *Journal of Advertising*, vol. 17, no. 2: 3–14.

Valentine, Virginia and Malcolm Evans (1993) The Dark Side of the Onion, Rethinking the Meaning of 'Rational' and 'Emotional' Responses, *Journal of the Market Research Society*, vol. 35/2: 125–44.

Williamson, Judith (1978) *Decoding Advertisements: Ideology and Meaning in Advertising*, London and New York: Marion Boyars.

NOTES

i   *Mail on Sunday*, 20 November 1983.
ii   *Sunday Express*, 18 October 1981.
iii *The Times*, 14 April 1984.
iv   *Guardian*, 17 February 1982.
v   Posted by lilly on 14 September 1998 at 13:09:11.
vi   See for example Collin (1998).
vii http://www.public.iastate.edu/~kicks/Adidas/a_collection.htm

CONSUMING ADDICTION

LEARNING OBJECTIVES

- To question the efficacy of the use of the word 'drug' given the vagueness of definition
- To discuss forms of association involving drugs at a number of different levels
- To discuss attempts to regulate business and consumer interests in relation to drug consumption
- To illustrate the means by which cigarette companies have sought to evade legislation over the years
- To describe behaviourist, cognitive–behavioural, economic–rational and psychoanalytic accounts of addiction

10.1   INTRODUCTION

On the evening before writing the first draft for this piece, BBC Radio 4 news reported a study that claimed to confirm suspicions that Ecstasy can cause long-term damage to the brain. Driving to work the next morning, the BBC 7.00 am news reported a House of Lords vote against a UK government bill to ban cigarette advertising. A number of arguments were deployed against the ban, for example in suggesting that dropping advertising would only serve to increase price competition, or would considerably reduce exposure to government health warnings, which must be shown in all cigarette advertising. Others took the view that a ban flew in the face of the cherished tradition of free speech or accused the government of inconsistency. Why ban tobacco advertising and not advertising for drinks? This claim was bolstered by another BBC report of the day, this time of a *Daily Express* investigation which claimed to prove that UK drinks companies were targeting children as young as eleven years old. Another BBC bulletin reported findings of the latest research into cancer which concluded that smoking contributes to most UK cancer deaths. Finally there was a report that Quaker Oats had axed pop band 'S Club 7' from advertising top brand Sugar Puffs after three of the group were found smoking cannabis. Switching briefly to Radio Scotland for the last few miles, there was a report that Hong Kong scientists claimed to have discovered a 'mutant' gene which indicated that 30 per cent of Asians, 10 per cent of Caucasians and 2 per cent of Afro-Caribbeans were biologically 'wired' to become addicted to heroin. By a coincidence on the day when the second draft began, the UK Government announced that it did not intend to introduce a bill to ban tobacco advertising for the current session of parliament. What a surprise!

The foregoing illustrates a small part of the daily debate over the use of a variety of legal and illegal substances which consumes legislators, regulators and marketers, and offers pointers to social and biological explanations for drug use. It also points up the incipient dangers inherent in the use and misuse of drugs. Sadie Plant (1999) notes that discussion of drugs is controversial and dangerous for academics. Not least of the problems is the act of definition of what a drug is. There are obvious difficulties of nomenclature; in the US the word 'drug', via the idea of the 'drug-store' can be linked generally to both legal and illegal drugs. In the UK on the other hand, where people visit the 'chemist' for a 'prescription', the mention of the word 'drug' is in many contexts regarded as instantly pejorative and stigmatic. As we shall see shortly, what counts as a drug can involve a vast range of sedatives, stimulants, depressants and hallucinogens. One quickly comes to realize that the meaning of a 'drug' is crucially dependent on the social context within which this is constructed. But this chapter is not just about drugs. The first section considers the diverse array of substances labelled as drugs within the social context of their consumption. The second part of the chapter focuses on explanations for drug addiction.

10.2   WHAT ARE DRUGS?

If one were to consider a drug at its simplest as a 'mood-enhancing substance' then the 'substance' contained in a drug could vary from something as 'hard' and tangible as heroin to something as 'soft' as a sunset. While some consider the 'substance' of a drug to be tangible, others label religion, ideologies and consumer society as constituting drugs. If one sticks to the idea that the substance of a drug is hard, this can in turn range from the organic, such as opium, to synthetic compounds, such as morphine and heroin. The distinction is complicated when one considers the nature of toxicity. Most 'naturally occurring' drugs come in a variety of forms. For example different varieties of hemp may by used in the production of paper and cannabis. Despite this, typologies of drugs have been developed which group these in terms of the likely effect which they will have on the mood-state of the consumer. Stimulants comprise a major organizing category of drug substances. No matter whether one snorts cocaine, smokes tobacco, swallows diet pills or over-the-counter stay-awake tablets, glugs caffeinated colas like Red Bull or sips the overpriced Triple Mocha Latté at the local espresso bar, the main role of the stimulant is to activate neurons in the central nervous system. These substances differ merely in the degree to which they increase alertness and confidence (or anxiety), decreasing appetite and fatigue. On the other hand alcohol and the opiates, including morphine and codeine derivatives, have the opposite effect in depressing the nervous system.

10.3   DRUGS AND SOCIETY

Wherever they are found, powerful substances play an iconic role in the central rituals around which human society is organized. The coca leaf played a central spiritual and healing role in Inca culture where it also eased the daily burden of manual labour and that of arduous treks in the mountains. Peyotl is known to have played a similar key role in Aztec civilization. In Asia and in the Indian subcontinent, cannabis and opium have been used as therapeutic agents for over a thousand years. Cannabis was also used by many African tribes. In East Africa and in the Yemen it is traditional to chew khat, whose role as a stimulant has been valued for many centuries. Chewing betel nuts has a long tradition in South and South-East Asia, while the drinking of the urine of reindeer which have consumed 'magic' mushrooms is traditional for northern nomads. There is also some evidence that mushrooms and other substances, including *belladonna* (deadly nightshade), played a role in the rituals of Celtic society.

One does not have to look far to detect the important symbolic aspects of the consumption of drugs in society. Traditionally they are marked by attachment to community or, more recently, to nation-state. For example traditionally the French drink wine and coffee, the British beer and tea (although the Irish have their whiskey, stout (and tea) and the Scots whisky, heavy (and tea)). An interesting phenomenon was the rise during the late 1990s of a new state of affairs whereby coffee began to supplant tea as the 'national' drink of the British.

10.3.1   Drug associations

Addictive substances are capable of forming associations at a number of levels: providing 'keys' to fit neuronal 'locks' within the central nervous system, flowing through the forms of association which connect groups, even matching the appropriate substance to enable humans to cope with the prevailing technology of the times.

10.3.1.1   Under lock and key: the neurobiology of drugs

A gruesome tale relates how, in 1964, Aryeh Routtenberg stuck electrodes into the brains of his experimental rats. The electrodes were placed such that current flowing through them caused a particular sensation of pleasure. For one hour each day, the rat could control this current by manipulating a lever in its cage. The rat had a choice. Another lever placed elsewhere in the cage controlled the food supply. But there was no contest. The researchers watched the rats slowly waste away to an ecstatic death (see note i). Such research raises a number of questions, not least of which is the point beyond which it is acceptable to torture animals. But what powerful motivation lay behind the rats' fatal fascination? In the mid-1970s evidence began to emerge that neurons themselves synthesize chemicals which numb the senses, dampen pain and create feelings of wellbeing and euphoria. Solomon Snyder, working at Johns Hopkins University, discovered a neuronal receptor for which heroin provided a rather crude 'key'. Working independently, Snyder, Kosterlitz and Hughes found the natural 'key' for this receptor, which they termed 'endorphin', a chemical which provides feelings of wellbeing. To persist with the rather crude analogy, while endorphins act as 'natural' opiates in responding to pain, heroin, which is a rather ill-fitting 'key', can open the lock but cannot then be withdrawn (by means of a transporter). As a result the overstimulated synapse, awash with chemicals, signals intensely pleasurable experiences through the 'pleasure centre' of the brain. In a similar way, nicotine mimics acetylcholine, caffeine, adenosine and marijuana, anadamide, while LSD is reputedly so similar to serotonin that it interferes with the serotonin system in the brain. Not all drugs bind to neuronal receptors. Cocaine works on those neurotransmitters which constitute the dopamine system. Rather than binding to the dopamine receptors, cocaine subverts the pathway by attaching itself to the dopamine re-uptake transporter. On the other hand amphetamines jam the re-uptake system open so that dopamine continually flows through it the wrong way, keeping the synaptic cleft suffused with the neurotransmitter. The above is of course a gross simplification of a reality rendered more complex by the fact that there are many neuronal subtypes and interactional effects between neurons. For example serotonin has a range of subtypes which play a role in a complex set of reactions to morphine, amphetamine, cocaine and ethanol, among others. Additionally serotonin receptors modulate the dopamine system while others have effects on acetylcholine receptors, related to nicotine (see note ii).

10.3.1.2 Drugs and technology: hand in glove?

Sadie Plant (1999) suggests a definite complementarity between the use of particular drugs and the challenges presented by new technologies to the cultures which they infuse. She suggests that one reason why opium dependence was so high in the nineteenth century was because the drug helped calm and numb the effects of the speedup of life and the attendant traumas associated with the early phase of industrialization. Cocaine came on line during the age of electricity and the development of new communications technologies in the late nineteenth and early twentieth centuries. Amphetamines enabled the twentieth century to keep up with its own speeds, particularly for military use; during the Second World War, speed (then known as 'blitz') 'made the Luftwaffe's pilots as high as the speeds at which their planes could fly' (Plant, 1999: 115).

10.3.1.3   Associations of people and drugs

Drugs bind individuals into groups of varying intensities of association. Below we consider a few instances of such association. While all substances are potentially addictive, it is argued that in some social situations the chances of not being addicted reduce almost to zero.

Egg-heads

Plant's excellent book *Writing on Drugs* (1999) is principally devoted to the use of drugs by the European intellectual elite. No matter what the substance was, one could argue that a primary motivation behind the use of drugs by intellectuals was to live life on the edge, to experience the completely new, to go where no man had gone before. For Coleridge and Edgar Allen Poe, opium produced the wonders of *Kubla Khan* and the *Murders of the Rue Morgue*; for de Quincey, opium became a technique for 'parting the veils between our present consciousness and the secret inscriptions on the mind' (1999: 57). Cocaine became the inspiration for a later generation where the experience formed the basis for Robert Louis Stevenson's *The Strange Tale of Dr Jekyll and Mr Hyde*; for Sigmund Freud, cocaine was a problem, a solution and a goal (1999: 77). Foucault used drugs as a means of personal enquiry and intellectual passion. Through drugs he followed a dangerous course in seeking to 'cut through the familiar categories that organize the self and the world' in order to free himself from categorization itself. The attendant danger was that, once freed of categories, one may find oneself immersed in the 'boundless monotony of a shapeless, meaningless reality' (1999: 157).

Poor cows

That is not to say that intellectuals did not also resort to drugs in order to escape tedium. Plant (1999) reproduces a fragment of a letter written by Freud where he complains about a boring dinner party where thankfully he had taken some cocaine beforehand. Escape from a life of tedium and drudgery provides a major motivation for the consumption of drugs by the poor. Recent UK studies suggest that while wealthier families reduced their consumption of cigarettes in the years since government has promoted the dangers of tobacco, poorer families showed less change (see note iii). A recent study suggests that for those at the bottom of the heap there has been no change in consumption. These are poorly qualified white, low-income lone parents (not widowed) who are council tenants. The authors of this study note that in this milieu, 'smoking among parents of young children seems almost inescapable':

> 'Britain's lowest income family now maintains a milieu wherein smoking remains a norm. Its association with disadvantage is more and more identifying smoking

as a compensation for disadvantage. Many lone parents identify smoking as their only compensation and they defend their habit assertively.'

[Marsh and McKay, 1994: 49]

The authors conclude that this all adds up to an 'extraordinary social and economic structuring of smoking in Britain at the moment'. There is something in some people's lives that causes them to need to smoke, to expect to smoke and not to give up. That thing is poverty.

Lager louts

Unlike smoking, there does not seem to be a social-class effect in relation to alcohol consumption in the UK. Here the most characteristic feature is that this decreases with age; the older a person is, the less alcohol he or she will tend to consume (see note iv). The mean alcohol consumption for the whole population is highest for people aged between 16 and 44. The mean consumption for men in this age group is around 20 units per week, falling to 15 units for those aged between 45 and 64. The mean consumption for women aged between 16 and 24 is 7 units per week, falling to 6 units between 25 and 44 and less than 5 units between 45 and 64. The heaviest drinkers are to be found among young men aged 16–24, 11 per cent of whom drink in excess of the safe limit of 50 units per week. From the above, despite the rise of 'dance' culture (see below), alcohol still forms the drug most likely to be associated with rites of passage for youth in the UK. The aspiration is simple – it is the preferred substance of most parents and it is prohibited. Given prohibition, the first encounter with alcohol is likely to be facilitated by an adult accomplice. Its surreptitious consumption will likely be with friends in a park or some other secluded spot; only then will its effects become clear.

10.4   DRUGS AND POPULAR CULTURE

It shouldn't be too improbable to claim that there has always been a symbiotic relationship between drugs and popular culture. The legal/illegal distinction has played an important role for those countercultural groups who are parasitical to the mainstream, such as disaffected youth and radical intellectuals (see note v). Generally discussion tends to focus on romanticizing associations between illegal drugs such as heroin, cocaine, cannabis, LSD and MDMA on particular variations of pop and dance culture, while ignoring the more mundane reliance on alcohol to 'tank up' prior to the late-night foray to the dancehall or club. Pop culture and drugs complement each other in the same way as love and marriage used to; changing fashions in the music and literary scenes are accompanied by changes in the preferred form of substance abuse (and vice versa). Sadie Plant (1999: 163) quotes the line attributed to Jill Jones that 'Jazz was born in a whiskey barrel, grew up on marijuana and is about to expire on heroin'. The word 'cool' sprang from the 'cool jazz' attitude and look, of drooped eyelids, the feeling of inviolability projected by Charlie Parker wannabees. Gradually the word spread through the jazz scene and was extended to 'any physically attractive male jazz musician or afficionado who patronized such clubs'. The 'cool' look was transformed and brought up to speed by James Dean and the 'Beat' generation, including Jack Kerouac and William Burroughs. According to Danesi (1994), coolness came to be extended to a set of discernible body movements, postures, facial expressions, voice modulations, dress-codes and hairstyles that coalesced in the 1950s with rock'n'roll. The 1960s presented an assortment of drugs of choice for the various tribes of hippies, yippies, Mods and Rockers with all the major bands (The Beatles, Stones, The Who, 'It's a beautiful day', the emergent Pink Floyd, Hendrix) stirring controversy with songs such as 'Lucy in the sky with diamonds', 'A day in the life', 'Brown sugar',[1] 'I can see for miles', 'Bulgaria' and 'Purple haze', among many others. Willis (1976) recounts how acid-heads in 1960s hippy culture used drugs as keys to unlock the door of the 'tight circle of apparent certainty' by facilitating new forms of experience: 'You can actually see, and I have seen, music', says Les, one of his informants: 'I have seen it bubbling out of the speakers'. If the emergence of reggae in the early 1970s brought a religious significance for some to the use of ganja, the availability of 'Columbian Gold' ensured its success. By the late 1970s heroin and speed were back in, as exemplified by the Stranglers 'Golden Brown' and Dexy's Midnight Runners. In contrast to punk and new romantic movements of the 1980s, the 1990s resounded to cries of 'acieed' and 'happy smiling people having fun'.

10.4.1   Acid House

The story of MDMA illustrates the complementarity between drugs and pop culture. While MDMA had been synthesized in the early 1900s, it was 'rediscovered' in the 1960s by Alexander Shulgin. In the UK it only came into its own in the late 1980s as part of 'Acid House' culture. Raves took place either in the open air or in huge stripped-out warehouses in industrial parks. The rave scene was perched on a knife edge between professional gangs that made hundreds of thousands of pounds per night and those enthusiasts who sought to organize it around the principles of a 'gift' community. In Essex, collectives such as Exodus began to organize impromptu open-air 'raves', which initially drew a hundred or so people but within one year were attracting thousands. The scene which developed around London's orbital motorway had all the ingredients for success: mystique, uncertainty, music, drugs and danger. The 'essential' mix soon spread to Blackburn, Lancashire, close to the reborn 'Madchester' scene peopled by the Happy Mondays, among others. Youth would drive in their thousands, waiting for the word to go to where the 'rave' was to be held that night. The opening pages of Collin's book on Acid House (1997) reads like a three-page ad for Ecstasy. On arrival at a warehouse at 10 pm, he and his friend are handed a gelatin capsule

---

[1] OK – so you're a purist – this was produced in the early 1970s.

which they swallow. For the next three-quarters of an hour or so they wait for something to happen, then:

> 'Almost imperceptibly everything shifted, like an elevator accelerating upwards. An overwhelmingly powerful charge surged through my body, rising through the veins and the arteries and the bones and the teeth, pushing me back into the plastic chair. Sit back . . . *fuuuuuck* . . . sit back and hold on, let it carry me . . . My mind begins to reassure my body; *ride it, ride it, go with it. You'll be alright, it's good, it's good, ride it.'*
>   [Collin, 1997: 2]

The effects ease slightly and he exchanges a few words with his friend. But the words are different, infused with an intensity of meaning accompanied by the warmth of the feeling that somehow 'Everything was going to be alright'. Then suddenly the music flashes into focus:

> 'It felt like the sound, each gorgeous slash of the riff, was slicing through every single cell in my body, transmuting its physiology. The drums seemed to sparkle into midair, reverberating as if in a cathedral, and the bass . . . it was as though I'd never heard it before. It resonated through to the core, pulsing from both inside and outside simultaneously.'

Next they rise somewhat unsteadily and move towards the dancing:

> 'And in a second we were amongst the throng, synched right into the matrix of bodies and sound; transported, transformed, together. *All right*, the feeling resonated through us as the drums thrashed upwards towards climax, *let's go* . . . .'
>   [1997: 2/3]

10.5   LEGAL ISSUES

Sadie Plant (1999) notes that drug legislation was originally enacted by the Chinese at the end of the nineteenth century as an attempt to control opium, which had been forced on them by the British and the Scots. In the UK during the early nineteenth century, opium was used by nearly everyone; workers in the foundries and factories of the new industrial cities such as Manchester used it in order to sleep at night and survive the working day, and mothers used it to soothe babies. Sigmund Freud helped popularize cocaine in the late 1880s in the (mistaken) belief that this non-addictive [*sic*] substance would aid in the recovery of opium and morphine addicts. (Incidentally, it is interesting to note that this 'spider to catch a fly' idea persisted into the next generation of substance development, where amphetamines were hailed as a new means for treating addictions.)

Regulation advanced with the development of the modern state. You may recall Foucault's research from Chapter 3, which discusses the new concern with the creation of healthy bodies through discipline, and which is also associated with filling the self up with the good things in life. It gradually became clear that opium derivatives and cocaine were not counted in the

---

latter category. The waning image of cocaine by the end of the nineteenth century led Coca-Cola to quietly substitute de-cocainized leaves for 'The Real-Thing' in 1902. Concern by the state for the creation of healthy bodies led to the proscription of all the opiates, and cocaine, amphetamines and an array of hallucinogens. Despite legislation, consumption of illegal substances rose during the course of the twentieth century, constituting a shadow economy of consumption whose fashions played off, mirrored and constantly fed into its mainstream counterpart.

The 'mainstream' development of drugs by the pharmaceutical industry grew rapidly during the course of the century and contributed many new substances to the shadow economy. The launch of Benzedrine ('speed') by Smith Kline in 1932 and the enthusiasm of the CIA for LSD in the 1950s, which prompted Eli-Lilly to produce an 'American' variant, ultimately boosted the shadow trade in drugs which the United Nations estimates is currently worth around 8 per cent of global GDP. Despite this, few 'neurotic' housewives or other sufferers of nervous ailments had the need to stray over the fence of legality in order gain comfort. From the late 1950s onwards a virtually unlimited supply of barbiturates and benzodiazepines was available through prescription to the masses of newly suburbanized nestmakers.[2] An alternative explanation to the 'comfortable, smooth, democratic unfreedom', which Marcuse attributes to the 'drug' of consumer society in relation to 1960s culture (see Chapter 3), might refer to the real drugs which were being ingested in record quantities on both sides of the legal divide during that period. Plant (1999) notes that legal production of amphetamine was maintained at around 10 billion doses per year during the 1970s. More recently, concerns have been raised at the number of US citizens in particular who are users of fluoxetene (Prozac) and of Ritalin.[3] One article discusses how a multitude of parents have bombarded high school counsellors in the USA, asking that their children be classified with ATHD (Attention Deficit Disorder), because of the benefits which 'victims' are entitled to under the Americans With Disabilities Act, 1990. The article suggests that despite scant evidence to support the disorder, some 2.5 million young Americans, who are mostly male, have been prescribed Ritalin which 'controls' it. The authors note wryly the irony of the use of a powerful amphetamine to slow down a hyperactive child (Machan and Kroll, 1996). Add to these the immense sales of drugs such as Viagra, Zantac, Tylenol, Advil and Zyprexa, and one can see that the decline in numbers taking illegal drugs (in the US, down from 29 million in 1979 to around 13 million at the turn of the millennium) has potentially been balanced from the other side of the seesaw (Economist, 1998). Despite this, reputedly half of the US 1.7 million prisoners are doing time for drug-related offences (1998: 23).

The question of government may be addressed from two broad directions;

---

[2] Reports suggest that 500,000 people in the UK are addicted to these substances, ten times that for opiods. Drugs include Valium and Diazepam. See http://www.benzodiazepines.net/

[3] Economist (2000) notes that, in its day, the brand equity of Prozac was immense. When on 9 August 2000 it was announced that Prozac would lose its patent protection two years earlier than hoped, shares of Eli-Lilly fell by 31 per cent or $38 billion.

first in relation to government attempts to regulate the propagation of legal drugs by business; secondly, with respect to government campaigns to restrict consumption of legal and illegal drugs.

10.5.1　Regulation and resistance to government control of business

Through the ages, governments have sought to regulate and control the supply of drugs for several ostensible reasons. One major motivation is the opportunity provided by regulation for raising revenue through taxation. Another is in maintaining the health of the social body. This can range from the repression of organized religion by successive Soviet governments to the forms of control of industry developed in Western societies. In relation to tobacco, attempts to legislate have constantly been frustrated. Cigarette advertising and promotion on television in the UK was banned in 1965 and the ban was extended to all tobacco products in 1991 by the European Broadcasting Directive. In 1987 a voluntary agreement was struck up between the cigarette industry and government to regulate tobacco-sponsored events by television. Over the years, tobacco advertisers developed a number of methods, some relatively crude, others ingenious, in seeking to get round the restrictions.

10.5.1.1　Changing the meaning of the 'health warning' on cigarettes

Common sense might lead one to imagine that from its inception, the idea of sticking a large 'health warning' on every cigarette pack and advertisement was anathema to the tobacco companies. Initially the aim of the health warning was simply to inform people of the health-risks endemic in smoking cigarettes. Voluntary agreements also meant that tobacco companies could not portray heroic images (for example the Marolboro Cowboy) in relation to their products. Gradually they began to realize that the less that was said in the ad, the more potential impact it had. Eventually some ads became so barren that they contained virtually no mention of the brand and the brand-user or the company which stood behind the brand. They contained so little information, perhaps a few splodges of the brand colours here and there, that often the only clue that this indeed was a cigarette ad was to be found in spotting the government health warning at the bottom of the otherwise incomprehensible space. The changing meaning of the health warning thus shifted from 'don't buy cigarettes, they are dangerous' to 'if you were too stupid to realize that this is a cigarette ad then this tells you that it is' – thus 'defusing' the original meaning of the health warning. Clever!

10.5.1.2　Advertising – on BBC?

On the other hand the industry could resort to cruder tactics. In 1990 the Health Education Authority of England produced a report on how cigarette companies managed to work around the ban on television advertising. The report cites breaches of the following aspects of the agreement:

- No location of static signs within camera sightlines for prolonged uninterrupted periods.
- No display of house or brand names or symbols on participants and officials, or on vehicles that are likely to come within the range of television cameras.
- The design or combination of colours used in the visual presentation of the set for small-arena sports should not resemble or depict the product of the sponsor.
- The use of the cigarette in the mouth is banned in tobacco advertising in the UK.

The report found that static signs were in fact used for considerable periods of time, that participants did display brand names and that colours used for small-arena sports often did resemble the products of the sponsor. In addition to this, there was evidence of smoking on camera by snooker players. The report also identifies defects in the agreement with respect to the legibility of health warnings (many tobacco-sponsored events did not have legible health warnings), and the exclusion from the agreement of events from abroad, including motor racing and football. The report is particularly scathing about the amount of coverage Formula One motor racing was receiving. Evidence from the Spanish Grand Prix indicated that:

> 'In this event tobacco name boards for the Marlboro, Camel and Gitanes brands were shown at a rate of 167 seconds per hour. The names and logos of the tobacco companies were also shown on the cars, and the participants in the race for 1177 seconds per hour. This together gave the equivalent of 40 advertisements lasting 30 seconds each per hour just showing tobacco names, so for more than one third of the BBC TV coverage of the event a tobacco name such as Marlboro, Camel, or Gitanes was shown on the screen.'   [Roberts, 1990 : section 28]

In light of this it is interesting to note the subsequent imbroglio which took place when it was revealed that the new Labour Government had awarded a specific exemption to advertising carried by Formula One, whose owner also happened to be a UK Labour Party benefactor. As the *Guardian* (see note vi): put it:

> 'Labour was deeply embarrassed by the disclosure, soon after it took office, that Formula 1 chief Bernie Ecclestone had donated £1m to the party. Quite coincidentally, of course, the government had exempted motor racing from the advertising ban for three years.'

10.5.1.3   The meaning of 'Lite'

The introduction of 'Lite' cigarette brands also enabled companies to promote products as being somehow better for you, when in fact the opposite is the case, as smokers of 'Lite' cigarettes tend to draw harder on the tip and thus ingest more harmful by-products than from conventional cigarettes. In constructing this favourable image, consider briefly the structural oppositions involved in providing the meaning of 'Lite':

'Lite' cigarettes – Light/Dark
Light/Heavy
Fun/Boring
Happy/Serious

The ultimate implication is: 'Lighten up, life's too short, you may as well enjoy yourself'. Surely this is contradictory? Above virtually any other consumption practice it is a proven fact that our lives will be shortened as a result of smoking tobacco. As we shall see in the next section, this statement appeals to the present orientation of the addict. Within the paradoxical experience of the addict there is no contradiction. The statement invites one to live for the moment, to consider that life is nasty, brutish and short, that there are very few pleasures in it, that we may as well die sooner rather than later, and that by implication, far from doing us harm, a cigarette may well do us some good.

10.5.1.4   Telling the truth as the ultimate lie?: 'Death' cigarettes

Perhaps the most disingenuous approach of all is that which was adopted by DEATH™ cigarettes whose campaign was developed in the 1990s. This marketing approach is similar to a contemporary campaign devised by the Coca-Cola brand Sprite which invited its (hyperimage-conscious) audience to 'Obey your thirst, not an image'. Under the skull and crossbones blazoned as its logo and entitled Welcome to DEATH™, Death cigarettes took transparency one stage further in its promotional material, which argued that:

'DEATH™ is a new brand of cigarettes using the underlying weakness of the cigarette industry as its fundamental strength and unique quality. The weakness I refer to is in my opinion the unwillingness or inability of the traditional cigarette companies to face up to the key issue in tobacco marketing. That is the association between smoking and health. The truth is smoking kills. Rather than face this issue the tobacco industry decided to close ranks, to evade, to concentrate on the less educated marketplaces in the Third World. Understandable, but nonetheless a mistake.

'In not confronting the issue, the industry left a door open for someone else to do so. Sadly, the first to take the opening were an even more conservative body, the 'anti-smoking' lobby. The tobacco industry has in effect given these fanatics a soap box from which to preach. Now this bum clenching minority of "Ashists" are trying to impose their anally retentive views on society as a whole. Their ultimate agenda to "ban smoking" – to make smoking illegal. Theirs is a regressive, blinkered and dangerously naive attitude. They are the cancer in a society that defends individual freedoms.'

The reader has no problems in decoding the meaning of the health warning:

'DEATH™ doesn't try to hide the health warning. 'DEATH™ is the health warning.'

While the aesthetics of the promotional material would probably have shocked most advertising creatives (because of the tacky imagery and fonts used), DEATH™ were in some ways ahead of the pack. The starkness and naivety of the message alone are disarming. Even more winning is the offer to donate a proportion of the price to a cancer charity. In another sense the DEATH™ promotion is the ultimate lie about advertising. For in saying that it is being totally honest and totally transparent, it invites the reader to believe that it and he or she are acting transparently and authentically. DEATH™ is thus asking us to believe that its appeal is beyond imagery, in other words, this is not an ad. But then of course, it is.

10.5.1.5　Targeting children

While the tobacco lobby has traditionally argued that advertising affects only the brands of cigarettes that are smoked and not overall levels of smoking, critics argue that as 120,000 smokers die each year in the UK, 120,000 more must be recruited if the market is to stay at the same level. While the UK voluntary advertising code specifically forbids targeting children, prominent academics argue differently. Through the 1990s a number of articles critically appraised children's perceptions of RJR brand 'Joe Camel' and other brands. Despite evidence from three studies published in 1991, which collectively argued for a total ban on all forms of cigarette advertising and promotion as a means to protect children from the dangers posed by tobacco, the US Federal Trade Commission vacillated and eventually decided not to impose a ban. Research carried out by Hastings et al. (1991) in the UK supported the view that school-age children (aged 11–14) recognize cigarette ads and interpret these positively. Furthermore they found that advertising has a reinforcing effect in encouraging child smokers to continue. A subsequent study carried out in the USA by Henke (1995) found that while 86 per cent of children (aged between 3 and 8 years) correctly identified 'Joe Camel' as a cigarette brand, they also identified a number of adult brand symbols. The authors found that, despite such high levels of brand recognition, attitudes towards smoking were universally negative among the sample. A major (800 interview) survey, reported by Mizerski (1995), studied product recognition among a much younger group of 3–6 year-olds, involving cartoon characters, including Joe Camel and the Marlboro Cowboy. He found that with the exception of the Marlboro Cowboy, character recognition improved with age. The level of product and trade recognition was generally high, with Mickey Mouse at 86 per cent, Joe Camel at 52 per cent and the Marlboro cowboy at 24 per cent. Recognition of Joe Camel was particularly high among older children. However even though he did not measure attitudes towards cigarette smoking, Mizerski concludes that 'cigarettes would be expected to be viewed unfavourably' given the prevalence of anti-smoking messages.[4] While Mizerski's study provides limited support to Henke (1995), Hastings and Aitken (1994) concluded unequivocally that advertising does encourage smoking, especially among the young. The authors also cite evidence that the tobacco industry itself did not believe in its own public pronouncements on this matter; a fact leant further weight given more recent revelations concerning the active suppression of evidence by the industry. In a further article, Hastings *et al.* (1995: 199) argued even more forcefully that 'there is clear evidence that tobacco advertising does influence levels of smoking, especially among children'. They argue against critics that such evidence will never amount to proof for the simple reason that proof is simply not possible in social research of this kind. In 1996 the FTC opened its own investigation of the use of Joe Camel, following the prompting of Congress members. Investigators considered evidenced provided by the FDA (Food and Drug Administration), including government statistics, showing that the Camel brand's share of the youth market jumped substantially after the popular ad campaign began. Additonally they found very high levels of awareness in 10 to 17-year-olds. The following year the FTC announced that it had charged R.J. Reynolds with unfair advertising practice and in particular with targeting children through Joe Camel. In November 1998 RJR dropped Joe Camel as part of a combined industry package, including billions of dollars in recompense for US government claims for treating sick smokers.

10.5.2	**Influencing drug consumption**

For many years, governments have sought to counter the appeal of legal and illegal drugs by devising their own information and prevention campaigns. This is a sensitive and controversial area which has seen right-wing libertarians make common cause with radical left-wingers in arguing against the perceived unwelcome extension of government into this area. The ostensible reason for government intervention is health. Since the 1960s, governments on both sides of the Atlantic have commissioned information campaigns which seek to balance the massive advertising spend of the tobacco companies. Reductions in the numbers of people smoking since the 1960s, in both the USA and the UK, suggest that such campaigns have played a part, at least in raising awareness of the issues, although knowledge of someone who died of cancer probably played a more powerful role.

Most anti-drugs campaigns tend to identify groups such as heavy users or those believed to be at-risk, which then form the basis for an information campaign, including mass advertising and support activities. Awareness levels, attitudes and propensity to quit are monitored through the course of

---

[4] It is puzzling how, given an otherwise impeccable study published in marketing's top journal, the author could reach the rather improbable conclusion that, even given anti-smoking messages from parents and teachers, the number of anti-smoking messages received by young children would outweigh the number of pro-smoking messages.

the campaign and in the time that follows it. One criticism of this approach is that while short-term effects in awareness levels and attitudes are often noted, this does not necessarily lead to long-term changes in behaviour. Another criticism relates to a lack of coherence across time and between campaigns. Inevitably the same target groups, the young and the poor, constitute targets for such campaigns, Yet the cumulative message transmitted across time may appear to lack coherence, as different campaigns not only utilize different appeals, but also adopt different approaches to classifying harmful behaviour and appropriate responses to this. Taking into account that messages involving alcohol and drugs are also aimed at the same groups, there is the distinct possibility that a cynical and blasé attitude can set in. Finally, there is the difficulty noted by Marsh and McKay (1994) that, for poor people, smoking is the only thing that keeps them going. The powerful argument which they provide is that it is poverty which keeps smokers chained to the habit. In this context, government promotional campaigns may increase anxiety more than anything else.

10.6	CONSUMING ADDICTION

'One thing you *can* hide is when you're crippled inside': Not-the-Beatles

Whether stigmatized by anti-drug campaigns or fashioned by some cool author into a wan anti-hero, the image of the addict stands like a shadow at the back of the entire discourse on drugs. One can follow several routes in seeking to understand addiction. Becoming addicted seems the most straightforward – although experience suggests that this doesn't necessarily add much insight. Another approach is to attend to the accounts of those addicts who can be bothered to tell their stories. These can form a useful backdrop to the more distant academic works. Consider the following excerpt from Caroline Knapp's autobiography:

> 'Beneath my own witty, professional facade were oceans of fear, whole rivers of self-doubt. I once heard alcoholism described in an AA meeting, with eminent simplicity as "fear of life" and that seemed to sum up the condition quite nicely. . . . Feelings of fraudulence are familiar to scores of people in and out of the working world – the highly effective, well defended exterior cloaking the small, insecure person inside – but they're epidemic among alcoholics. You hide behind the professional persona all day; then you leave the office and hide behind the drink.'
> [1997: 17]

For Knapp, the fraud lies in the body-armour of the 'professional persona' which she fabricates. In this sense she shares much in common with any other person who feels that there is a gap between the 'real' me (nobody) and the 'false' identity. As we shall see later, some academics might diagnose her situation by determining that her self-esteem is low and will seek to enable her to strengthen her ego-defences. Others, for instance those working from a 'Lacanian' perspective, could well deploy the opposite argument, that perceptions of inauthenticity may provide a unique form of insight, because the reality is that we are split inside and our constructed identities are fraudulent; the task here is to reconcile oneself to living in 'bits and pieces'. Fear of fraudulence threads through a number of accounts of addiction. One commentary argues that drugs offer an illusory 'quick fix' for those who falsely believe that they can bypass pain and suffering in the hope of gaining some form of transcendence or self-actualization. Plant (1999) talks of Baudelaire's argument that those who used hashish were cheating and cheated by their experiences of artificial and ersatz heavens.

Linked to the idea of fraudulence is deceit. While Coleridge said that he fashioned *Kubla Khan* from the fragments of an opiated dream, others questioned his account, suggesting that he may have made the story up to excuse the poem's brevity, or worse, that he had simply stolen the opening lines from the pages of the *Pilgrimage*. William Burroughs, a dedicated argonaut of addiction, wrote: 'There are degrees of lying, colloboration and cowardice – that is to say degrees of intoxication' (1978). Burroughs argues that lying and deceit are symptoms of the addict's possession by 'and dependency on' the drug, its total conditioning of their need.

Knapp (1997) recounts that at the time she had only 'small flashes' of insight into her condition. It did not seem to be like dependency at all; it was only when the world, and in particular the world around her, changed that this hazily came into perspective. Through the 1980s and into the early 1990s she drank 'socially' with the rest of her 'crowd', but then she observes that 'the culture swung in a new direction and I didn't swing with it'. The crowd and in particular the peer group have a deal of influence on consumption behaviour. Yet when the taste of the crowd swung round, Knapp didn't swing with it. Was there something unique about her, perhaps something in her family or even in her genetic inheritance which led to this? This raises the question of the degree to which she was not in control. We discuss several issues in relation to control in the next section.

10.6.1　Addiction or compulsion?

Powerful arguments have been developed which argue that addictive behaviour is nothing less than a form of compulsion; consumption is driven by social forces or by biology to the point where addiction is inevitable. Below we consider social determinist and biological determinist arguments.

10.6.1.1　Social determinist argument

The study carried out by Marsh and McKay (1994) on the situation of poor smokers in the UK, provides strong evidence of a link between smoking and social deprivation. But is this sufficient to prove that a person has no choice? The authors argue that while it is the case that members of low-income families will in all likelihood be smokers, this is not automatically the case:

'If they get some educational qualifications, become low cost owner occupiers, stay together, take lower paid nonmanual work, and shun all contact with the Department of Social Security, they are probably no more likely to smoke than are other men and women who share a similar lifestyle, but who have either more money or no children.'

While such aspirations may seem to be a pretty tall order for a young woman living alone apart from her child in an inner-city ratpit, they do allow some leeway for the exercise of choice.

10.6.1.2   Biological determinist argument

Following the mapping of the human genome, reports are emerging which link genetic mutation to the likelihood of addiction. Even if, as the result of a genetic mutation, some people are more predisposed to addiction than others, one would expect to see variations in relation to the social context in which the drug is (or is not) consumed. Becker (1996) suggests that it is necessary to look at the substances themselves, as these will be associated with different patterns of dependency. For example he argues that cigarettes and cocaine, which seem to be highly addictive for most people, tend to have a bimodal distribution of consumption with one mode close to abstention. On the other hand alcohol consumption tends to have a more continuous distribution, presumably because alcohol is not addictive for many people. Presumably he also means that alcohol is 'addictive' in the sense that some people may be predisposed to alcoholism through genetic variation.

Animal studies suggest that the nature of the substance itself plays a powerful role in the degree of compulsion felt. Carroll and Mattox (1997: 26) describe how animals with limited access to drugs generally self-administer more of the drug and exhibit more regular rates of self-administration than when access is unlimited. However this can depend on the drug itself. One experiment demonstrated that rats administered cocaine in a cyclic pattern with respites in-between periods of use; with heroin the self-administration was more invariable. The data for heroin were supported by a study where 15 rhesus monkeys were given the unlimited opportunity to self-administer several psychomotor stimulant drugs; 11 of the 15 died from overdose.

10.6.1.3   Shopping: compulsion or addiction?

Several marketing authors share the view that there is a compulsive dimension to consumption behaviour. O'Guinn and Faber define compulsive consumption (1989: 147) as:

'a response to an uncontrollable drive or desire to obtain, use or experience, a feeling, substance or activity that leads the individual to repetitively engage in behaviour that will ultimately cause harm to the individual and/or others.'

While acknowledging the repetitive element, Elliott (1994) and his co-researchers offer several reasons in support of their argument that it is better to conceptualize such behaviour as addictive. First, compulsion involves unwelcome pressure to do something against the individual's will, whereas an addiction involves the extension of a normal behaviour into a pathological habit. Elliott supports the idea that addiction is the more appropriate term to describe such behaviour, as it not only involves a degree of choice but also provides social utility to those who engage in it. There are positive aspects to such behaviour in gaining the attention of sales assistants, thus providing an emotional lift. In a later paper, Eccles and Hamilton (1999) argue that addictive consumption may be the only activity undertaken by these people where they do feel in control. This is not to say that compulsion is not seen as playing a role in addiction – far from it. Elliott's definition of addictive consumption behaviour explicitly includes the subjective experience of forms of compulsion:

> 'The definition of addiction as it is used here, involves a habitual behaviour pattern which is often experienced subjectively as a strong urge to perform the behaviour and often associated with a feeling of having limited control.'

We now turn to consider behavioural, cognitive–behavioural, rational and psychoanalytic theories of addiction.

10.6.2 Behavioural explanations of addiction

Behaviourist explanations place a great deal of reliance upon the environment as the key explanation of addiction. One of the most popular explanations is derived from B.F. Skinner's theory of operant conditioning which seeks to understand the operations of environmental stimuli in reinforcing drug-taking behaviour. As the environment is the main focus of the behaviourist explanation, such researchers have little time for subjective accounts of addiction such as Knapp's, arguing that there is no means of verifying such accounts. A fundamental assumption of the operant approach is that behaviour is lawful, that orderly relationships can be found between human drug-taking behaviour, drug-administration factors and environmental variables. For example studies have successfully demonstrated regular patterns of drug cost and the amount of a drug that is consumed. Once orderly relationships have been described, behaviour can be predicted and subsequently controlled. For example behaviour analysis predicts that smokers may increase their smoking when they switch from high to low nicotine concentration cigarettes so as to maintain desired nicotine levels, which is not a good thing as they will also inhale more toxic by-products of tobacco. As a result one can infer that encouraging smokers to switch from high to low nicotine products is not a desirable way to seek to control smoking. Behaviourists follow an experimental approach to analysing addictive behaviour which emphasizes the objective description of behaviour and explicitly omits reference to 'internal' states. This approach consists of the application of 'active' and 'placebo' drugs to experimental and control groups, and the observation and precise measurement of factors such as substance, dosage level and other factors that are thought to moderate reinforcement.

Carroll and Mattox follow a behaviourist view in seeking to understand the reinforcement of behaviour by drugs. Reinforcement is defined simply (1997: 3) as:

> 'A reinforcement occurs when the consequences of a response increases the future probability of the response.'

The authors argue that animal experiments can accurately mimic the effects of drugs on humans. As a result, experiments have been carried out on baboons, cats, dogs, mice, pigeons and squirrels, although rats and monkeys are the most common subjects. Experiments focus on a large number of aspects of drug self-administration reinforcement, including addiction, craving and withdrawal. For example researchers have explored the effects of variations in environmental conditions such as stress, social factors, feeding conditions and the availability of non-drug reinforcement. Animal research indicates that the physical stress associated with pinching rats' tails leads to greater ingestion of amphetamines, but that subjecting rats to repeated electric shocks or making them stand on hot plates has no effects on cocaine self-administration. However emotional stress created by making rats watch other rats being physically stressed increases cocaine self-administration (1997: 13, 28). Other research suggests that rats which are socially isolated will tend to self-administer cocaine at greater rates. Rats and rhesus monkeys deprived of food tend to self-administer drugs at a higher rate than those which are not. When rewards for food and cocaine are similar, rats tend to choose cocaine. However when the number of food pellets is increased, the number of cocaine choices decrease. Animals which have been forcibly pretreated with drugs tend to subsequently self-administer other drugs more rapidly than those which have not. Overall, the results show the consistent pattern that drugs which are self-administered by animals are also abused by humans, and drugs not abused by humans are not self-administered by animals.

In discussing reinforcement in relation to human self-administration of drugs, Spiga and Roache (1997) discuss relations between antecedents, behaviour and consequences in a relation to genetic, individual and social environments. Behaviour such as drinking, brought about by a specific antecedent (e.g a beer advertisement), is reinforced by the consequent drug effects. The genetic or behavioural history of an individual may act alone or in concert to influence drug-taking behaviour. For example individuals may drink excessively as the result of a behavioural history of reinforcement of alcohol drinking. Alternatively the authors argue that male children of alcoholics may be at greater risk of alcoholism through genetic factors than are men without a family history of alcoholism. The nature of 'setting factors', such as the characteristics of the physical and social surroundings, are also considered to be important. Spiga and Roache argue that drug-taking can be influenced by antecedent events. For example research evidence suggests that social isolation contingent on drinking alcohol (which you may remember is mentioned by Knapp in her account) acts to suppress alcohol self-administration (1997: 42) – although in the animal research discussed above, isolation increases self-administration. In the human context it thus appears that social isolation acts as a form of negative reinforcement or punishment. On the other hand research indicates that money may act as a positive reinforcer. For example one study showed that subjects tended to prefer cocaine over a placebo. However when offered money instead of the cocaine, cocaine self-administration decreased as a function of the increasing value of the money (1997: 45). Spiga and Roache argue that such studies illustrate the benefit of viewing substance abuse as an instance of operant behaviour, which highlights the implications of following different policies.

10.6.2.1 Addictive shopping[5]

While it is relatively easy to manipulate setting effects, substances and dosage rates for tangible drugs, the investigation of more ethereal but nonetheless addictive behaviours, such as addictive shopping, requires a modified methodology. Thus O'Guinn and Faber (1989) and Elliott (1994) have expressed the desire to understand the dynamics of 'negative' or 'abnormal' consumer behaviours and 'dysfunctional' consumer behaviour, respectively. The conceptualization of such behaviour is different, with O'Guinn and Faber labelling this as being compulsive while Elliott labels it as 'addictive'. Thus Elliott lends his support to a cognitive–behavioural view which does not see such behaviour as uncontrolled, but which focuses on a stepwise transition from normal through to problematic, then addictive behaviours, with different factors affecting different stages. The authors differ also in respect of the method followed, with Elliott following a more qualitative line of enquiry in supplementing his quantitative study. One could argue that these studies are behaviourist to the extent that they seek to understand the antecedents and consequences of addictive shopping; however they differ from the 'classic' behaviourist approach in that they place a great deal of emphasis on subjective accounts and seek to build models which lay out the processes at work inside the 'black-box' of subjective understanding.

With respect to similarities, the authors specify antecedent conditions to addictive buying behaviour. Faber and O'Guinn (1992) list factors such as low self-esteem, anxiety, depression and obsessions. Elliott (1994) also links anxiety/stress and low self-esteem as preconditions. He notes that while much research emphasizes the dysfunctional aspects of such behaviour, it does appear to fulfil some positive functions for the individuals concerned; for example gaining the attention of salespeople can make them feel important and gives them an emotional lift. While Elliott

[5] Some authors refer to compulsive consumption, others to addictive consumption. In the main they seem to be measuring something which is much more specific in relation to shopping behaviour. For this reason I use the term 'addictive shopping' to refer to all of the above in this section. Apologies to those who feel differently.

contends that an important function of 'normal' consumption is to maintain consumers in a positive mood and to 'repair' negative emotional states, he also argues that mood-repair is common across addictive appetitive consumption. Addictive buying is thus conceived of as a learned adaptive behaviour which may serve many different functions for individuals, or even for a single individual. However the short-term benefits of 'mood-repair' (positive reinforcers) tend to be outweighed by the long-term consequences (negative reinforcers), leading to a two-phase pattern which is initially positive, then negative. This explanation suggests that the effects of short-term reinforcement are very powerful for addicts who tend to privilege these over long-term consequences. Elliot's study confirms that there is a strong negative relation ($r = -0.44$; $p < 0.001$) between self-esteem and addictive shopping. There is also a relationship between addictive shopping tendencies and a scale designed to measure the extent to which people perceived that the shopping experience and the goods purchased would match their perceptions of socially desirable appearances ($r = 0.36$; $p < 0.001$). These were backed up by qualitative findings where 'nice clothes' play a role in making a respondent feel better. The study also confirms a relatively strong relation between addictive shopping tendencies and the extent to which shopping alleviated mood-repair ($r = 0.41$; $p < 0.001$), which was again supported by the qualitative research:

> 'I've suffered from anxiety for quite a few years ... It gave me pleasure to buy things and made me feel better. Now I look after my aged father and worry about his health and it makes me feel better if I buy a small thing.'   [1994: 169]

Elliot notes that changes in emotional experience before, during and after the shopping trip are also of interest – with excitement predominant before and during the trip, tempered by feelings of guilt and anxiety afterwards. This finding runs counter to that of O'Guinn and Faber (1989) whose respondents reported getting very little pleasure from the products which they bought, sometimes never unwrapping them. Roberts (1998) replicated many of the aspects of previous studies and included some new ones in his study of addictive shopping behaviour among the 'baby-buster' generation – those 44 million Americans born between 1965 and 1976. He argues that these young adults have been reared in a unique and radically changing environment where it was likely that many would show signs of addictive shopping tendencies. The antecedents which he measured included familial (similar behaviour by parents), psychological (esteem, perceived status and the ability to fantasize) and sociological influences (peer pressure, television-viewing, shopping frequency and credit-card use). Roberts found that 6 per cent of his sample could be identified as compulsive shoppers. Results supported a link between perceptions of parents' problems with the respondents' own compulsive buying. They also supported the negative relation with self-esteem, and positive relations with social status and television-viewing as reported in earlier studies. The number of credit cards owned was also found to be positively correlated with compulsion.

From the above, the results from studies in different countries show similar patterns. How are these interpreted and responded to? Elliott (1994) discusses a number of approaches. For example a cognitive–behavioural approach would be similar to addressing a 'controlled drinking' programme, whereby each individual's pattern of shopping would be subjected to a detailed functional analysis to explore the purposes that shopping behaviour might serve for the individual. Once identified, each precipitating problem is addressed through training by the substitution of alternative reinforcers, together with training in self-monitoring. Alternatively, cognitive therapy may be used to change the thought patterns that link mood with shopping behaviour, or may employ assertiveness training for those who have difficulty in coping with social influences. On the other hand Elliott develops the argument that the phenomenon of addictive-shopping behaviour may be an inevitable element of the postmodern condition, which is an argument that will be revisited below. Roberts (1998) discusses the implications from a public-policy perspective in linking addictive shopping with negative environmental effects, arguing for instance that, while the US population accounts for 6 per cent of the world's population, it consumes 33 per cent of the world's natural resources. Writing before George 'Dubya' Bush repudiated the Kyoto Protocol on global warming, Roberts placed his hopes on State intervention, arguing that it was useless to appeal to the altruism of an ingrained culture of consumption, exemplified by such high numbers of addicted shoppers. He also argues for restraint of financial services advertising, and reductions in credit-card limits, in the light of huge increases in credit-card use and debt. His own findings support the view that credit-card use accelerates spending.

10.6.3   Rational economic explanation of addiction

The rational economic account of addiction developed by Becker (1996) is partly indebted to behaviourism and in particular to the concept of reinforcement. In fashioning his theory, Becker argues that behaviour is rational to the extent that individuals maximize utility in a consistent way and that they consider the effects of their actions on future as well as present utilities. However he acknowledges a set of major constraints and limitations upon rationality: people make erroneous calculations, they can be influenced by how questions may be framed, their memories are imperfect, they may discount the future excessively, and their perceptions may be distorted by drugs and other influences. In order to come closer to reality, Becker modifies the classical economist's insistence that current preferences are independent of past and future consumption and of the behaviour of others:

> 'For example, whether a person smoked heavily or took drugs last month significantly affects whether he smokes or uses drugs this month. How a person votes depends very much on the way friends and others in the same peer group vote. Successful advertising for a product increases the desire for that product. The clothing people wear depends crucially on what other people wear.' [1996: 4]

The challenge for Becker lies in retaining the simplicity of the 'normal' economic explanation, while allowing for the substantial influences of a person's investments into consumption and of those others in a person's social network. He does so through the device of two basic capital stocks: personal capital and social capital. *Personal capital* includes relevant past consumption and other personal experiences that affect current and future utilities; *social capital* incorporates the influences of past actions by peers and others in a person's social network.

Becker does not attempt to pin the concept of addiction to a category of goods. Rather he argues that a good (whether this be cigarettes, cocaine, gambling, booze or jogging) may be addictive to some people and not to others. Addiction is a habit which involves an interaction between people and goods. The behaviourist concept of reinforcement plays a role here as:

> 'a person is potentially addicted to C if an increase in his current consumption of C increases his future consumption of C.'   [1996: 57]

Central to this is the idea that those who are addicted to harmful goods tend to become more present-oriented than future-oriented. This implies that a person is addicted to a good only when past consumption of the good raises the marginal utility of present consumption. This is similar to the behavioural psychological concept of reinforcement which holds that greater current consumption of a good raises its future consumption, which in turn implies that an addict will tend to build a level of tolerance towards a good over time. Tolerance means that given levels of consumption are less satisfying when past consumption has been greater. Rational harmful addictions imply tolerance because higher past consumption of harmful goods lowers the present utility from the same consumption level.

Key to Becker's argument are the related concepts of the depreciation of past consumption and the discounting of future consumption. The depreciation of past consumption relates to the exogenous rate of disappearance of the physical and mental effects of past consumption. Put more crudely, depreciation relates to the time it takes for the perceived beneficial effects of the good to wear off. Secondly, the less future-oriented the person is, the less likely he or she is to consider the full price of the consequences of his or her actions. Taken together, this implies that the more heavily past consumption depreciates and the more heavily the future is discounted, the more likely it is that consumption will increase and the person will become addicted.

10.6.4   Psychoanalytic explanations of addiction

Central to Freudian theory is the interaction between biology and environment. You should remember that this also played a key role in the explanation developed by Norbert Elias, which rests on the idea that changes in psychic structure are conditioned by changes in society. Others have developed this argument to suggest that as the environment changes, so the general character of society changes. Over the years, a number of theorists have used Freud's theories to discuss prevailing character types. Erich Fromm, Christopher Lasch and Teresa Brennan developed Freud's ideas in different directions to argue that the prevalent metaphor for describing the consumer is a narcissist. Explanations based on Lacan suggest either that this character has regressed to an imaginary form of identification with its mirror-image, or that it oscillates in an ambivalent fashion between the imaginary and the symbolic realms. In this text, Falk's (1994) approach comes close to the Lacanian explanation and one can also detect parallels in this to Cushman's (1990) concept of the 'empty self'. First we consider narcissism.

10.6.4.1 Narcissism and its discontents

In Freud's version, primary narcissism is linked to the earliest period of development, characteristic of the 'oral phase' where the infant does not differentiate 'self' from other aspects of the environment, including the mother. If anything, the mother is perceived to be an extension of the self. Explanations which claim that addiction is narcissistic thus claim that this is based on a form of secondary narcissism where the person's character-development regresses and is driven back to the earlier oral phase of development. For some psychoanalysts the entire consumer society and its creature, the consumer, are a means for a regression to an oral phase characterized by a desire to incorporate the whole world. For example Erich Fromm saw humanity as 'the freak of the universe', unique in being subject to nature yet at the same time transcending nature.

Erich Fromm: the marketing character

In 'To Have or To Be' (1978) Fromm reflected on what he considered to be the two basic modes of human existence: the 'having' mode, with its associations to the machine, destruction, alienation, mechanization and things; and the 'being' mode, which centred on the experience of being at one with, and centred on, persons. To Fromm, modern industrial society is centred on having.

Fromm claims that the 'having' mode is deeply etched into Western society, into customs, practices and language. One means of having is incorporation. This was a widespread practice in early societies where it was thought for example that by eating the heart of a brave warrior, one could incorporate the symbol of this bravery. Commenting on modern consumer society, Fromm says:

'The attitude inherent in consumerism is that of swallowing the whole world. The consumer is the eternal suckling crying for the bottle. This is obvious in pathological phenomena such as alcoholism and drug addiction'.   [1978: 27]

Fromm sees this 'having' mode as exemplified by the emergence of a new personality – the marketing character. The emergence of this character signalled a shift from the anal retentive 'hoarding' character to a new form which recalls Riesman's (1961) concept of the 'other-directed' character discussed in Chapter 6:

> 'The aim of the marketing character is complete adaptation so as to be desirable under all conditions of the personality market. The marketing character personalities do not even have egos (as people in the nineteenth century did) to hold onto, that belong to them, that do not change. For they constantly change their egos according to the principle: "I am as you desire me".'   [1978: 148]

Christopher Lasch: a Kleinian view of narcissism

Christopher Lasch develops his account of narcissism from Melanie Klein who disagreed with Freud on a number of points. It is thus unsurprising that Lasch should castigate Fromm's account of narcissism. First let us briefly outline Klein's theory. Unlike Freud, she felt that ego development begins at a very early age, even during that period when the child cannot differentiate himself or herself from the mother. In Klein's account, the baby is thought to be the bearer of two instinctual impulses – love and hatred. In the earliest phase of development which Freud calls the oral phase, the infant is in bits and pieces and does not differentiate between self and mother. The mother is thus not perceived as a totality which stands outside the self. Rather the mother's breasts are perceived as 'part-objects', as symbolized by the good breast and the bad breast. The good breast is an introjection of all the good features of contact with the mother; the bad breast on the other hand represents the introjection of all of the frustrations which the infant can only express by screams of rage. When the mother is absent, the fragile ego of the infant becomes anxious; however if a good internal part-object has been developed, the baby can hold onto this image by hallucinating it as a form of wish-fulfilment. In order to keep the negative feelings associated with the bad breast at bay, the infant splits the positive and negative images of the good and bad breast apart. This acts as a form of defence to protect the infant from anxiety. Eventually the infant's hatred is projected outwards to the external world. Once this happens, the bad feelings seem to be coming not from within but from the exterior, and the infant feels a persecutory anxiety. Klein referred to this state as the paranoid–schizoid position. In Klein's account, the child's life gradually becomes more complex so that by the age of six months or so the child begins to figure whole objects from what had been part-objects. He or she thus begins to develop a composite picture of 'mother' and of other significant objects such as the father and siblings (Klein retains the concept of objects to describe 'whole' people) as whole objects. At this stage, the child begins to recognize the disparity between the internal objects which he or she has created and the real person. Klein argues that all children move through this depressive stage where they must reconcile the real person with the love and hate images that they have constructed internally. The child enters the real social world when he or she confronts this ambivalence and copes with it by integrating the splits of the paranoid–schizoid position.

Christopher Lasch describes the narcissistic character as being ideally suited for a world which is based on 'warm' but fleeting relationships, bureaucratic organization and a world dominated by images. If, as Lasch suggests, 'every age develops its own particular forms of pathology which express in exaggerated form, its underlying character', then the dominant character of today is the narcissist. Lasch applies Klein's psychodynamic approach to 'borderline' narcissistic personality disorders, which he argues constitute the majority of cases seen by clinicians. Lasch then proceeds to describe an image-conscious hypochondriac who experiences violent oscillations in esteem, who is chaotic and impulse ridden, who describes vague feelings of emptiness and depression and who, although often ingratiating, cultivates a protective shallowness in emotional relations – in short, a thoroughly disagreeable personality. At the core of the narcissistic personality lies a potentially explosive bottled-up rage. Lasch argues that this is because it is no longer regarded as being socially permissible to express rage. It is the repression of rage which Lasch rails about most. He accuses Fromm of himself being a narcissist in seeking to 'sermonize about brotherly love' (1979: 72). In Lasch's account, narcissism has more to do with defences against aggression rather than with self-love. Narcissists lack the capacity to mourn because the intensity of their rage against love objects and in particular their parents prevents them from having happy experiences. They tend to avoid close relationships as these might release overpoweringly aggressive impulses. Their personalities largely consist of defences against this rage and against feelings of oral deprivation which originate in the pre-Oedipal stage of development. According to Lasch, such patients suffer from a 'pervasive form of emptiness and a deep disturbance of self-esteem'. They are also transfixed by images. The narcissist perceives the world as a mirror of himself and has no interest in external events other than the manner by which these reflect back on his own image. He is perfectly in tune with a world which is made up of the continuous transmission of images and behaves as if he were constantly 'on air', engaged in continuous self-surveillance, fronted by a fixed smile. Narcissists buy into the therapeutic ideology of the current age by constantly monitoring themselves for signs of ageing and ill-health which they seek to forestall. Why is it that narcissistic disorders are becoming more common? Lasch blames the stimulation of infantile cravings through advertising, the usurpation of parental authority by the media and schools, and the rationalization of inner life.

Discussion

The previous section outlines a range of psychoanalytic views of addiction. Fromm (1978) attributes this to what he describes as being the predominant personality of our time as evidenced by the 'marketing character', whose addictive personality is inherent in the desire to swallow the world. Against this, Lasch posits a different view of the narcissist, who exhibits severe oscillations in levels of esteem and who reports pervasive feelings of emptiness, all of which show similarities to the traits described by those such as Elliott (1994) who have researched addictive shopping behaviour. It is interesting that Lasch also mentions the 'therapeutic' concern of narcissists, implying that these might indeed be precisely the kind who would volunteer for such research. If Lasch's work seems to be rather outdated, it is worth noting that others, including Frosh (1991), continue to talk of the narcissist as one of the characteristic pathologies of our time. The dimension of the 'empty self' has been discussed in Chapter 7 in relation to the work of Falk (1994). It also features in the work of Cushman (1990) who like Falk situates his explanation in the retreat of community and the emergence of the modern isolated individual. For Cushman, this emerges as a form of compensatory consumption. However Elliott (1994) suggests that the work of Gergen (1991) might provide a better model for understanding his findings. The self postulated by Gergen is not empty but rather too full. While he agrees with Cushman that the common bonds of community have been lost, he argues that these have been replaced by all of the paraphernalia of modern technological consumption, including images from a mass of media. The 'postmodern' self which Gergen describes is not just saturated but overloaded. As a result the awareness of personal shortcomings in relation to the self can create negative emotional states such as anxiety or depression and, in order to escape these feelings, the individual may use a device known as 'cognitive narrowing'. In one response a person may narrow attention onto those immediate and pleasant experiences, and block out more unpleasant thoughts associated with the long term. This idea is similar to the notion of discounting the future described by Becker (1996) and discussed in the section on rational economic explanations of addiction. Elliott thinks that such narrowing may result in differences between addictive shoppers, with some being addicted to the symbolic consumption of the goods, while others are hooked on the shopping trip.

10.6.4.2 Freud: from Eros to Thanatos

A different perspective is provided when one considers the nature of Freud's own addiction. In his earlier career Freud wrote joyfully of cocaine's 'benign' effects and enthusiastically prescribed it to his patients. However through his life he struggled with cigarette addiction, which provoked several cancers and eventually led to his death. Sadie Plant argues that Freud's cigarette addiction played a role in a controversial revision to his theory which he formulated in later life. Freud's original theory argued that the human organism is driven by Eros, the life-principle, as expressed through the demand for the pursuit of pleasure and the avoidance of pain. However he found it difficult to reconcile this explanation with what he saw around him, particularly when he saw 'shell-shocked' soldiers returned from the First World War who had apparently lost the will to live. Rather than dwelling on this however, it is easier to illustrate Freud's change of position using the example of cigarettes (see note vii):

'Since the early nineteenth century, it has been recognized that the alkaloid of nicotine, administered to rats in pure form in minute doses, instantly produces death. No one who smokes fails eventually to get the signals that the body, with increasing urgency, sends as it ages; in fact every smoker probably intuits the poison from the instant of experiencing the first violent effects of lighting up, and probably confirms his understanding every day with the first puffs of the first cigarette. But understanding the noxious effects of cigarettes is not usually sufficient reason to cause anyone to stop smoking or resist starting; rather, knowing it is bad seems an absolute precondition of acquiring and confirming the cigarette habit.'

While the above statement would probably be challenged by those US legal syndicates currently stitching up 'Big Tobacco' interests who seem to assume that smoking 'victims' were cultural dopes unaware of the hazards of smoking, it rings true in my adolescent experience of the painful introduction to the noxious weed. The implications for Freud's theory are startling, for these imply that sometimes we actively desire and find a negative pleasure in that which is unwholesome – that we actively court the possibility of pain and thrill to its attendant dangers. Moral opprobrium in this context merely adds zest to the experience. In this light one can view Freud's conceptualization of Thanatos, the death drive, dominated by the nirvana principle, as a complement to that of Eros. In this more complex view, the human organism is continually pulled in two directions, with the sexual instinct striving for life, growth and development, and Thanatos or the nirvana principle working to restore this to an earlier state. While some authors such as Erik Erikson (mentioned in Chapter 6) portray these as evolving in an orderly fashion through the life-cycle, with the maturing adult gradually becoming taken over by the nirvana principle, others see them working in a dynamic relation to one another through the course of the life-span. Lacan takes this latter view (see note viii):

'The subject comes into being "barred" by the signifier and thereby injected with a sense of death. And this is poisoning rather than innoculation. The taste for death is not something that the subject acquires through experience, as one might say, or reaches towards as a last despairing manner of delectation, for it has been there from the start as a perilous gift of the signifier, and one that cannot be refused. The drive that circles round the excavated centre of being, is pulled outwards towards the objects that promise gratification, but inwards too towards the completest form of a loss that it already knows.'

Allow me to translate. The first part of the quotation repudiates Erikson's interpretation that the 'taste' for death comes with experience, instead death is there from the beginning. The 'excavated centre' of being is the hole created at the centre of the human subject as the result of the movement from the 'real' to the 'imaginary' and 'symbolic' realms. The intimation of death is coincident with the birth of subjectivity and occurs at precisely that point where the child identifies with its mirror image. At just the point where the child recognizes himself/herself ('that is me!'), he or she experiences a profound sense of loss and disconnection from the real. The resultant hole in the self provides the motor for a rootless desire which constantly reaches outwards in the (vain) search for gratification and fulfilment; however desire is also pulled 'inwards' towards the gap itself. In this explanation, addiction may be viewed in a number of ways: as an unrealizable bid to 'get back to the garden' of the pre-imaginary real, or as part of the oscillation in the subject between the imaginary and symbolic realms. This means that our desires often appear to be contradictory; what is 'life-affirming' is often simultaneously related to loss. Such a view prompts the researcher to explore the nature of 'perverse' pleasures, including smoking – to investigate the nature of the ecstasy in agony, the preoccupation with images of death in youth culture and other instances where Eros and Thanatos seek to work hand in glove.

Lacan would likely have been chary of the very term 'addiction', as his theory stresses the literally constitutive aspect of language which is never neutral and which is always related to power. In this view, language speaks through us, labelling us as 'normal' or 'deviant', 'addicts' etc., and such attributions work in the interests of power. In fact Lacan's critique of ego-psychology is based on this group's stress on adaptation to group norms. For example he criticized the ego-psychologists' insistence that heterosexual genital relations are the only 'wholesome' form, with the implication that other forms were deviant. In Lacan's view, psychoanalysis should not be used as a tool of social policy, for the purpose of social adjustment.

On the other hand Alastair McIntosh (1996), who dedicates his paper to the memory of his father who died from lung-cancer, is not so sanguine. He argues that a problem arises not just because people can become 'possessed' by, and addicted to, substances such as coffee, gin and cigarettes, but because the tobacco industry actively draws upon Thanatos in advertising its products. We described earlier how, in the UK, tobacco advertisers were driven to new heights of creativity when the voluntary code of practice, devised in the 1970s, insisted that advertisements should contain prominently displayed health warnings. It ultimately transpired that the only cue which a person could rely on to 'successfully' decode the meaning 'this is a cigarette ad' was the warning itself. But surely McIntosh's claim that advertisers actually seek to promote cigarettes through death imagery is a step too far? In fact it isn't. While McIntosh does not establish the universal use of death imagery in cigarette advertising, he describes many ads where such imagery has been used. Consider the following sample of descriptions:

'Silk Cut' ads (see note ix)

- A 1983 poster showing a length of purple silk with a scissors slit or knife slash across it. This pictorial image signifies 'cut silk' and so those who 'successfully' decode the meaning of the ad are primed for future visual puzzles relating to the Silk Cut brand. This ad obtained a high level of recall among the target market.
- A later award-winning poster which shows a woman showering behind a silk curtain. The curtain is not cut. But the image invites one to think that it might become so. A later group interprets this as corresponding closely to the 'shower scene' in the movie *Psycho*.
- Spring 1994. Poster depicting a Venus fly trap plant, which in nature slowly digests trapped flies. An oversize leaf appears to reach out with its jaws to rip out the crotch from a person's purple silk pants. The zip or 'fly' hangs surrounded by shredded purple silk, part consumed by the plant.
- Summer 1994. What looks like an Anopheles mosquito made out of purple silk thread wound round a proboscis-like steel needle. This cuts the surface on which it rests.
- From 1994. Poster depicting a purple-silk-gloved hand cuts off a telephone. In 1995 the same ad appears but this time drained of its colour to a 'deathly' white.
- From 1995. Poster showing a row of people lined up outside a toilet. They stand crouched, dressed in purple silk with chess pawns on their heads. A knife hangs on the door. When McIntosh described this to an M&C Saatchi staff member as 'dying for a fag', he was corrected – the intended meaning was 'dying for a slash'.

While the above descriptions 'fill-in' for the more diffuse meanings which were visually encoded in the real ads, it is not difficult to see the relations between sex and death. McIntosh (1996) uses these and others to argue that collectively these ads depict violated sexuality:

> 'The silk is not merely cut; it is knife-slashed. The erotic purple shower curtain triggers thoughts of rape and murder. The purple hand over the phone suggests cutting off communication in a vulnerable situation and the white version suggests the draining of life (I am told that a Hitchcock movie featured a man who you do not see cutting off the phone and attempting to strangle Grace Kelly, who stabs him with scissors). The mosquito sucks blood and gives cerebral malaria.'
>
> [1996: 12]

He suggests that at an unconscious level, the consumer is portrayed as having no real choice but to accept the brand; like rape fantasy, she might just lie back and accept it. However he argues that advertising creatives were not aware of what they were doing when they constructed these ads. As proof of this, he tells the reader that when he 'pointed out' the latent meaning of these ads to one creative who had been involved in their production, he quit. McIntosh's analysis isn't entirely one-way. He does appreciate that the destructive aspect of drugs constitutes a powerful appeal for the young.

However he interprets the ads as reinforcing a spritual vacuum where religion has largely failed in its role of providing emotional expression for matters of ultimate concern. In this light he asks whether modern cigarette advertising:

> 'is one of the most malevolent missionary endeavours of all time. Might the companies, nationally and transnationally, be seen as veritable Molochs: fiery tombs that consume the children for nothing but their own balance sheet salvation?'
> [1996: 24]

Strictly speaking, Richard Klein's (1993) argument is not psychoanalytic, however the main gist of his argument is that drug use is complex and is in effect an intimation of death. In this view, while cigarette smoking offers a range of utilities to smokers, utility alone fails to explain the power of cigarettes to attract the undying allegiance of billions of people who are dying from their habits. Instead, Klein resorts to the concept of the *sublime* first developed by the philosopher Immanuel Kant. Cigarettes are sublime because they propose a negative pleasure:

> 'a darkly beautiful, inevitably painful pleasure that arises from the same intimations of eternity; the taste of infinity in a cigarette resides precisely in the "bad" taste the smoker quickly learns to love.'

Because the motivations people have in smoking cigarettes are sublime, he argues, they in principle resist all arguments that are directed against them on the basis of health or utility. Klein goes further to suggest that perhaps we need more than a change of viewpoint to stop; perhaps people only stop smoking cigarettes when they start to love them. Klein pursues Foucault's arguments (discussed in Chapter 3) to suggest that nowadays society is obsessed with what he calls 'healthism'. By this he means the socially expressed concern of governments and of other social institutions to regulate the health of the population. However Klein notes that such concern may speak more to a strategy of power than to one of concern, for it is riddled with contradictions. He refers to Foucault's argument in the *History of Sexuality* that when nineteenth-century reformers, including pedagogues, doctors, priests and family moralists, sought to clamp down on masturbation, 'making it a vice did not cause it to diminish; on the contrary everything became masturbatory' (Klein, 1993: 182). In a similar fashion, he argues that what are called drugs have spread into every segment of society. While government and other organizations have been waging war on drugs for years, the problem appears to be worse now than ever. He argues that cigarettes are bad enough, they do not need to be demonized.

For me, Van Gogh's jaunty skull, staring boldly but blankly out on the world (Figure 10.1), as Yeats would put it 'casting a cold eye on life, on death' with a 'devil-may-care' attitude, sums up perfectly the frisson of the sublime in the aesthetic. How was it for you?

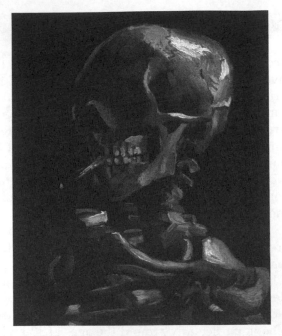

Figure 10.1 A terrible beauty: Van Gogh, *Skull with burning cigarette* [with thanks to the Van Gogh Museum]

10.7 CHAPTER SUMMARY

This chapter provided a brief introduction to the complexities surrounding drugs and addiction. The section on drugs dwells mainly on the cultural aspects of drug use and includes discussion of the ritual significance of drugs and of the role of marketers and government respectively in promoting, and seeking to regulate, drug consumption. The section on addiction is intended to act as a complement to earlier discussions on the body (Chapter 7) and eating disorders (Chapter 8) which feature different levels of theoretical explanation based upon control. Thus biologists, psychologists and social theorists discuss eating disorders as being centrally about control, in that they each highlight (quite different) aspects of control in explanations which focus on different levels of organization (neuronal, individual, dyadic, interpersonal and discursive). That control is a central concept in theories of addiction is illustrated by the debate as to whether chronic habitual shopping should be characterized as being compulsive or addictive. The section on addiction supplements the range of explanation by introducing behaviourist and rational views of addiction in addition to the accounts which are discussed in relation to eating disorders. In the chapter on addiction the psychoanalytic view is deepened by referring to Klein's theory and to the work of Christopher Lasch and also to Freud's later work which discusses the principle of Thanatos.

| 10.8 | CASE STUDY: SCOTLAND AGAINST DRUGS |

Scotland Against Drugs (SAD) was set up by the Scottish Office as an initiative to combat the growing consumption of illegal drugs in Scotland. The brief that was put out to agencies in Scotland was to devise a radical campaign which would seek to raise awareness of the dangers of taking drugs and to change attitudes towards drugs, particularly among youth. The anti-drugs brief created a lot of interest at Faulds advertising agency. Earlier campaigns which had been constructed on the platform 'Just Say No' and 'Heroin Screws You Up' had been a failure, and staff knew that considerable effort would need to be expended in creating an effective message.

The overall aim of the campaign was to raise awareness, create interest and change attitudes about soft drugs with the targets. Thus the campaign was aimed at *vulnerables*, or those who had not tried drugs yet, and those who were *experimenting* with drugs but had not become habituated to them. Research indicated that while primary school children aged under 11 years old tended to be anti-drugs, a change seemed to take place in secondary school, particularly around the ages of 13 and 14. In fact it turned out to be extremely difficult to locate 'vulnerables' among this group as most 13-year-olds had already experimented with drugs. Research suggested that 56 per cent of all 15-year-olds in Scotland had taken drugs, but only a tiny minority had experienced heroin or hard drugs. The campaign team decided that on this basis the campaign should not focus on 'hard' drugs such as heroin. Instead it would focus on 'soft' drugs, such as Ecstasy, Temazapan and glue-sniffing. One 'soft' drug, cannabis, was deliberately ignored as it was felt that so many parents took cannabis that an anti-cannabis campaign would not be credible.

Before making their pitch to the Scotland Against Drugs committee, Faulds' account-handler offered the brief to every creative team in a bid to look for ideas. The brief was to come up with a revolutionary campaign which would be thought of as 'mould-breaking'. This process generated about 140 visuals which were researched independently. The research phase was considered to be vitally important as the account-director for the campaign noted:

'People working in advertising agencies are all terribly middle class and we were using terminology such as "Ecstasy" but in actual fact it is difficult to find youth in Scotland who calls it this; they call it "Eccy". One of the key aims of the campaign has been to keep in touch with the kids to make sure we are on top of any changes in terminology, to make sure that we kind of reflect youth culture in our advertising.'

The researcher sought information as to how relevant these ideas were to those youth who formed the target group, the 13 to 15-year-olds. Previous research had shown that the 'Heroin Screws You Up' campaign had actively been used by heroin dealers to promote the drug (via the notion: 'If you want something which *really* screws you up then look no further). The research helped weed out some propositions that would not work with the target group. The idea 'Just Say No' was described as being 'like a red rag to a bull'. Another potential proposal which used a droopy condom to illustrate the effects of drugs on sex provoked great hilarity; members of the focus group requested a copy of the ad to show to friends – so this was dropped. It also became apparent that glue-sniffing had gone out of fashion and that instead younger people were 'buzzing' gas.

The main themes used in the campaign were heavily influenced by the research which had been conducted. In effect this represented recycling respondents' worst fears about drugs through the advertising vehicle. The research supported the view that young people were not motivated by the fear of death – 'at that age they think they are going to live forever'. However what did worry and annoy them was the fear of being ripped off by a dealer. Younger children were worried about the effects that drugs could have on their looks (rotting teeth) and emotions (paranoia, blackouts). Finally, older girls expressed fears that they could be sexually assaulted while under the influence of drugs. As a result of this process, the 140 propositions were refined to a list of 20, which eventually came down to a core of three television ads, four radio ads and four press/insert communications. The three television advertisements were based on themes identified in the research phase.

One, entitled 'Paranoid Instamatic' (Figure 10.2), was aimed at the younger audience who were concerned about the loss of their looks; a second showed a dealer who boasted about selling someone dog-worming tablets; the third advertisement showed a girl who is assaulted while under the influence of drugs. The ads were all researched again to ensure that the terminology used was correct.

The campaign utilized television, radio and press advertisements in addition to support material (see Figures 10.3 and 10.4). One form of support material was developed through a company called Convenience Advertising who pasted posters on the back of toilet doors in nightclubs. Post-campaign research was carried out with a sample of 1200 young people and indicated that overall the campaign achieved 80 per cent awareness. Even the radio campaign achieved 27 per cent.

An alternative view of SAD

A radically different view of the SAD Campaign is provided by Kevin Williamson in his book *Drugs and the Party Line* (1997). To summarize the key argument, Williamson suggests that the entire conception of SAD, which is centred around the concept of drug prohibition, is partial and doomed to failure, and that an alternative approach centred around 'harm reduction' and the eventual decriminalization of drugs offers a more feasible alternative. To support his argument, Williamson provides an historical

'I wouldn't take the stuff I deal.'

DEALERS ARE TAKING YOU FOR A CLASS 'A' MUG.

Figure 10.2 'Paranoid Instamatic' ad from SAD Youth Campaign

overview of attempts by governments to prohibit drugs such as alcohol, heroin and cannabis, arguing in each instance that prohibition has proved to be a failure. Williamson offers as evidence of the failure of drug prohibition, the continuing rise in numbers of drug seizures by UK customs and police, and the rapid rise in the numbers of people coming before the courts on drug-related offences. He also cites UK customs estimates which suggest that they apprehend only about 10 per cent of all illegal drugs entering the country.

Williamson next briefly reviews previous anti-drugs advertising campaigns such as the UK 'Heroin Screws You Up' and the US 'Just Say No' campaign, arguing that they achieved no lasting impact and claiming that for the duration of these campaigns drug use actually went up. He then describes the backdrop to the SAD Campaign as an opportunistic pre-election political stunt which for politicians could be explained as

Figure 10.3 Parent Campaign for SAD

a means to displace public attention from more fundamental issues, such as jobs, housing, education and health, rather than as a serious attempt to engage with the drugs issue. Williamson suggests that from its inception, the politicians involved with the SAD Campaign did not engage in an attempt to understand drug use but rather demonized all illegal drug use, irrespective of the different levels of harm that different individual drugs were doing to drug users and to society. Drug use was described as the 'enemy within', and members of organizations such as Crew 2000 and Enhance, which operated 'harm reduction' policies and offered advice on how to make drug use safer, were excluded from the

CLIENT: **SCOTLAND AGAINST DRUGS**
SUBJECT: **YOUTH CAMPAIGN : BOOKED MEDIA**

MEDIA SCHEDULE

PERIOD OF CAMPAIGN: **DECEMBER 1996–MARCH 1997**
DATE: 4th December 1996

15–24 YEAR OLDS
COVER: 30%
FREQUENCY: 1.6
SOURCE: CAA/NRS

PUBLICATION/MEDIUM	CIRCULATION	SIZE & POSITION	RATE CARD COST	COMM. %	ADJUSTED COST	NO. OF INSERTS	NET TOTAL
CINEMA							
CINEMA MEDIA	15+18 Cert Films Only	30"/40"				8 weeks	£ 30,259.96
PEARL & DEAN	15+18 Cert Films Only	30"/40"				8 weeks	£ 5,394.08
					SUB TOTAL		£ 35,654.04
RADIO							
SCOTTISH ILR - Clyde, Forth, Tay, Northsound, Moray Firth, Westsound, Central, Border, Shetland		2 x 40" / 1 x 30"				8 weeks	£ 22,224.94
SCOT FM		2 x 40" / 1 x 30"				8 weeks	£ 2,701.30
Forth FM: Steppin Out / Clyde 1: GB Experience / Moray Firth: Dance Zone / Northsound: The Party Zone / Border: The Dance Experience		1 x 40" / 1 x 20"				8 weeks	£ 868.70
					SUB TOTAL		£ 25,794.94
OUTDOOR							
ROCK BOXES	50 sites	4 sheets				4 weeks	£ 2,550.00
GLASGOW UNDERGROUND	31 sites	4 sheets				4 weeks	£ 1,445.00
EDINBURGH ARTS & ENTERTAINMENT	110,000	A5 leaflets				4 months	£ 2,932.99
	5,000	A2 Posters				4 months	£ 2,025.75
CONVENIENCE ADVERTISING	575 sites	A4 Posters				4 months	£ 20,000.00
HOGMANAY SCREENS EDINBURGH	3 screens						
	10 spots	1 x 30"				1	£ 1,890.00
					SUB TOTAL		£ 30,843.74

Calendar grid:

w/c Dec — January — February — March
Fri: 6 13 20 27 | 3 10 17 24 31 | 7 14 21 28 | 7 14 21 28

w/c Dec — JANUARY — FEBRUARY — MARCH
Mon: 2 9 16 23 30 | 6 13 20 27 | 3 10 17 24 | 3 10 17 24 31

Figure 10.4 Media schedule for SAD (excluding television)

council that was set up to provide advice for the Campaign. In particular Williamson attacked:

- The exclusion of drugs such as tobacco and alcohol from the campaign, which meant that it was seen by many young people as being hypocritical.
- The focus on mass-media advertising rather than support for 'harm reduction' agencies and other community-based initiatives.
- Employment of an advertising agency whose clients include whisky and beer producers.
- Inaccuracies in the ads themselves which stirred up unnecessary fears, for example that Ecstasy is cut with rat poison and that it makes women helpless and easy prey for rapists (see note x).
- The subsequent development of a war of words, which Williamson claims was initiated by SAD, between those who favoured the SAD approach and 'harm reduction' groups, which was conducted in public and which ultimately led to public confusion.
- That SAD would ultimately achieve nothing anyway.

Taking the last point, Williamson concludes that:

'It is likely that SAD will go the way of previous anti-drugs campaigns and be wound up. SAD has done nothing but damage to the important work done by people who have genuine experience in the drugs field.'   [1997: 62]

Williamson suggests that the lessons to be learned from SAD are that alcohol and tobacco should be included in any general anti-drugs exercise directed at young people, and that the advertising itself should not focus on shock treatment or 'worst-case scenarios', or put out inaccurate information. In a hard-hitting conclusion to his discussion of SAD, he adds:

'But most importantly of all, it has to be understood that expensive high-profile anti-drugs campaigns carried out in the media just do not work. In the SAD-sponsored survey published in the run up to their Drugs Awareness Week it was found that only 4 per cent of young people were actually likely to listen to the media when thinking about illegal drugs. Maybe SAD should have commissioned this survey before they wasted £900,000 of public money on media advertising, money which could have been better spent investing in drug support workers on the ground. Unfortunately they haven't learned from this. In October '97 SAD announced the launch of yet another high-profile – and no doubt just as expensive – advertising campaign planned for the media.'   [1997: 63]

Case-study questions

1. In your view, how appropriate was the SAD Campaign?
2. Discuss the pros and cons of using advertising in this manner.

END-OF-CHAPTER REVIEW QUESTIONS

1. How can semiotics be used to explain the means by which companies have sought to evade government restrictions in advertising? (Try to construct an explanation based on either a 'Saussurian' or a 'Peircean' point of view.)
2. How do substances appear to work on the brain?
3. Compare and contrast behaviourist and economic–rational ways of understanding consuming addiction.

REFERENCES AND FURTHER READING

Baker, Chris (1994) *Advertising Works 8: Papers from the IPA Advertising Effectiveness Awards*, Institute of Practitioners in Advertising, Henley-on-Thames: NTC Publications.

Becker, Gary S. (1996) *Accounting for Tastes*, Cambridge, Massachusetts: Harvard University Press.

Bowie, Malcolm (1991) *Lacan*, ed. Frank Kermode, Fontana Modern Masters, London: Fontana.

Burroughs, William (1978) *Nova Express*, London: Panther.

Carroll, Marilyn E. and Adnande J. Mattox (1997) 'Drug Reinforcement in Animals', pp. 3–39. In Bankole A. Johnson and John D. Roache (eds), *Drug Addiction and its Treatment*, Nexus of Neuroscience and Behavior, Philadelphia: Lippincott-Raven.

Collin, Matthew (1997) *Altered State: The Story of Ecstasy Culture and Acid House*, London: Serpent's Tale.

Crawley, Anne (1997) *Port Smoke Alert: Final Report of Smoking Prevention Project aimed at Young People in Port Glasgow*, Paisley, Glasgow: Argyll and Clyde Health Board, Health Promotions Unit.

Cushman, P. (1990) Why the Self is Empty: Towards a Historically Situated Psychology, *American Psychologist*, vol. 45, no. 5: 599–611.

Danesi, Marcel (1994) *Cool: The Signs and Meaning of Adolescence*, University of Toronto Press.

Eccles, Sue and Eleanor Hamilton (1999) 'Voices of Control. Researching the Lived Experience of Addictive Consumers'. Presented to the *First Critical Management Studies Conference*, UMIST, Manchester.

Eco, Umberto (1994) 'Does Counterculture Exist?', pp. 115–28. In Robert Lumley (ed.), *Apocalypse Postponed*, Bloomington: Indiana University Press.

Economist (1993) 'High and Hooked', Science and Technology Section, *The Economist*, 19 May, pp. 105–7.

Economist (1998) 'Give Them Pills, The Fuddled Masses; America's Addiction is Not Just to Illegal Drugs', *The Economist* (US), 2 May, vol. 47, no. 8066, pp. 23–5.

Economist (2000) 'Eli-Lilly's Drug-Induced Depression', *The Economist* (US), 12 August, vol. 356, no. 8, p. 55.

Elliott, Richard (1994) Addictive Consumption: Function and Fragmentation in Postmodernity, *Journal of Consumer Policy*, vol. 17: 159–79.

Faber, Ronald J. and Thomas O'Guinn (1992) A Clinical Screener for Compulsive Buying, *Journal of Consumer Research*, vol. 19: 459–69.

Faber, Ronald J., Gary A. Christenson, Martina De Zwaan and James Mitchell (1995) Two Forms of Compulsive Consumption: Comorbidity of Compulsive Buying and Binge Eating, *Journal of Consumer Research*, vol. 22, no. 3 (December): 296–305.

Falk, Pasi (1994) *The Consuming Body*, London: Sage.

Freud, Sigmund (1984) *On Metapsychology: The Theory of Psychoanalysis – Beyond the Pleasure Principle, the Ego and the Id, and Other Works*, Penguin Freud Library, vol. 11, London: Penguin.

Fromm, Erich (1978) *To Have or To Be?*, London: Abacus.

Frosh, S. (1991) *Identity Crisis, Modernity, Psychoanalysis and the Self*, London: Macmillan (now Palgrave).

Gergen, K.J. (1991) *The Saturated Self: Dilemmas of Identity in Contemporary Life*, New York: Basic Books.

Hastings, G.B., P.P. Aitken and A.M. MacKintosh (1991) *From the Billboard to the Playground*, August, Centre for Social Marketing, Glasgow: University of Strathclyde.

Hastings, Gerard B. and Philip P. Aitken (1994) Tobacco Advertising and Children: A Review of the Evidence, *European Journal of Marketing*, vol. 29, no. 11 (November): 6–18.

Hastings, Gerard B., Philip P. Aitken and Anne Marie MacKintosh (1995) Children, Smoking and Advertising: The Evidence is There for Those Who Wish to See It, *International Journal of Advertising*, vol. 13, no. 2: 195–202.

Health Education Authority (1990) *Beating the Ban: Tobacco Advertisements on BBC TV – A Threat to Our Children's Future Health*, AS82 [ISBN 1 85448 111 8], London: HEA.

Health Education Board for Scotland (1995) *Towards a Non-Smoking Scotland*, Edinburgh: HEBS.

Hemby, Scott E., Bankole A. Johnson and Steven Dworkin (1997) 'Neurobiological Basis of Drug Reinforcement'. In Bankole A. Johnson and John D. Roache (eds), *Drug Addiction and its Treatment*, Nexus of Neuroscience and Behavior, Philadelphia: Lippincott-Raven.

Henke, Lucy L. (1995) Young Children's Perceptions of Cigarette Brand Advertising Symbols: Awareness, Affect, and Target Market Identification, *Journal of Advertising*, vol. XXIV, no. 4: 13–28.

Hirschman, Elizabeth C. (1992) The Consciousness of Addiction: Toward a General Theory of Compulsive Consumption, *Journal of Consumer Research*, vol. 19, no. 2 (September): 155–80.

Klein, Melanie (1962) *Our Adult World and Its Roots in Infancy*, London: Tavistock.

Klein, Richard (1993) *Cigarettes are Sublime*, London: Picador.

Knapp, Caroline (1997) *Drinking: A Love Story*, London: Quartet Books.

Lasch, Christopher (1979) *The Culture of Narcissism: American Life in an Age of Diminishing Expectations*, New York: Warner Books.

McIntosh, Alastair (1996) *From Eros to Thanatos: Cigarette Advertising's Imagery of Violation as an Icon into British Cultural Psychopathology*, Centre for Human Ecology Occasional Paper, 22 August, Edinburgh: University of Edinburgh.

Machan, Dyan and Luisa Kroll (1996) An Agreeable Affliction, *Forbes*, 12 August, pp. 148–51.

Marsh, Alan and Stephen McKay (1994) *Poor Smokers*, London: Policy Studies Institute.

Mizerski, Richard (1995) The Relationship Between Cartoon Trade Character Recognition and Attitude Toward Product Category in Young Children, *Journal of Marketing*, October: 58–70.

O'Guinn, Thomas and Ronald Faber (1989) Compulsive Buying: A Phenomenological Exploration, *Journal of Consumer Research*, vol. 16: 147–57.

Plant, Sadie (1999) *Writing on Drugs*, London: Faber & Faber.

Roberts, James A. (1998) 'Compulsive Buying Among Students: An Investigation of its Antecedents, Consequences and Implications for Public Policy, *Journal of Consumer Affairs*, vol. 32, no. 2 (Winter): 295–307.

Roberts, J. L. (1990) *Beating the Ban*, London: Health Education Authority.

Spiga, Ralph and John D. Roache (1997) 'Human Drug Self-Administration: A Review and Methodological Critique', pp. 39–40. In Bankole A. Johnson and John D. Roache (eds), *Drug Addiction and its Treatment*, Nexus of Neuroscience and Behavior, Philadelphia: Lippincott-Raven.

Travers, Kathleen and David Liddell (1998) *Understanding Drug Use in Scotland: An*

Introduction for Health Professions, Edinburgh: Health Education Board for Scotland (HEBS).

UNDCP (1998) *World Drug Report*, Oxford University Press.

Wald, Nicholas, Stephanie Kimluk, Sarah Darly, Sir Richard Doll, Malcolm Pike and Richard Peto (1988) *UK Smoking Statistics*, Oxford Medical Publications, Oxford University Press.

Williamson, Kevin (1997) *Drugs and the Party Line*, Edinburgh: Rebel Inc., Canongate Books.

Willis, Paul (1976) 'The Cultural Meaning of Drug Use', pp. 106–18. In Stuart Hall and Tony Jefferson (eds), *Resistance Through Rituals*: Youth Sub-Cultures in Post-War Britain, London: HarperCollins Academic.

NOTES

i   *Source*: Economist (1993: 105).

ii   *Source*: Hemby *et al.* (1997: esp. 142, 145/6).

iii   One study indicated that smoking prevalence in social class I decreased from 64 per cent in 1958 to 30 per cent in 1985; equivalent figures for social class V indicated a shift from 72 per cent to 50 per cent. This study found that male smokers in social class V smoked 61 cigarettes per week while those in class I smoked an average of 29.

iv   *Source*: Elliott (1995: 202).

v   Such groups are parasitical to the extent that they rely on the mainstream for the 'daily-bread' of their sustenance – See Eco (1994).

vi   *Source*: http://www.guardianunlimited.co.uk/theissues/article/0,6512,332039,00.html

vii *Source*: Klein (1993: 1).

viii *Source*: Bowie (1991: 163).

ix   Source: McIntosh (1996: 10–12).

x   This claim may be as the result of publicity at the time concerning the effects of the Roche product Rohypnol which has led to a series of 'drug-rape' allegations in the USA and in Europe.

INDEX

About-Face   290, 291
Acid House culture   382–3
actualizers   244
adaptation   231
addiction   376–416
   behavioural explanations   393–7
   and compulsion   391–3
   psychoanalytic explanations   398–407
   rational economic explanation   397–8
Adidas   368
Adler, A.   318
adolescence   257, 321–2
adult   258
advertising   6, 65, 100, 353
   and body images   287–92
   cigarettes   385–9, 404–6
   genre in   206
   narcissistic ego   264–5
   structuralist analyses   201–5, 207–9
   subliminal   100–2
   use of metaphor and metonymy   191–4
   and women   7, 45–6, 115–17
aesthetics   167–8
affluence   149
Agassi, A.   214
aggression   11
Aitken, P.P.   389
alcohol   381
alienable objects   143
Allen, D.E.   359
Allport, F.H.   6
amphetamines   379–80, 384
amygdala   228
anal stage   252, 256
animal experiments   378–9, 392, 394

annihilation of space through time   57,
   59–60, 62, 73
anorexia nervosa (AN)   305–33
   discursive interpretation   323–31,
      332–3
   explanations of   306–22, 331–3
anthropology   151–3, 156–8
anti-consumerism   44, 45, 47–8, 383
   sovereign power   90–1
anti-drugs campaigns   389–90, 408–13
anti-globalization movement   120,
   129–30
anti-style   212
anti-trust   98–9
anxiety   69–70
appetite, disciplining of   281–3
aspirational groups   246–7, 363
attributions   359
augmented brand   355–6
authenticity   215–16, 265
autonomic nervous system   227
autonomy   256
AutoTrader   193, 211–12
avoidance groups   246–7, 363
AVP   316–17

Bachrach, P.   107–8
badge, brand as   368
Baratz, M.S.   107–8
Barclays Bank   89
Barr's Irn-Bru   371–3
Bartels, J.   92
barter   141
Barthes, R.   189, 199
Bartky, S.   126–7

Baudrillard, J.   36, 90, 171
    false needs   158–60
    simulation   216–18
    system of objects   190–1
Bauman, Z.   35, 69–70, 103, 104, 126
    peak experiences   172–4
Beck, U.   107
Becker, G.S.   397–8
behaviourism   393–7
Belk, R.   146
Berman, M.   56–7
Bilderberg group   112
binary oppositions   187, 202, 203–4, 326–8
biological determinism   392
biology
    and identity   227–36
    obesity   337–8
    starvation disorders   312–17, 332, 333
bitter experience   174
black youth culture   51, 169
Blue Grass   182–3
Blumberg, P.   165
body   276–303
    bodily strategies   285–300
    civilizing process   11–12, 17
    commodification   320
    fitness   126–7, 293–4
    future bodies   298–300
    identity and   278–85
    images and eating disorders   307–10
    and mind   19–20
    modern identity   283–5
    self-control/self-discipline   17, 280–3,
        327, 330
    self-expression   293–300
    self-fulfilment   292–3
    self-protection   286–92
    thinness   287–8, 300–1, 324–5
body-building   294
body mass index (BMI)   334
body piercing   368–9
Bond, J.   101
Boorstin, D.   217–18
Bordo, S.   336
Bouchard, T.   232
Bourdieu, P.   30–1, 152–3, 170, 281
    and distinction   237–9

bourgeoisie   16, 238
boycotts   89
boyish body   325
brain   227–31
brand communities   176–7, 365
brand development   356–8, 370
brand equity   349–50
brand extension   358
brand failure   350
brand image   355–6
brand leverage   349–50
brand persona   356–61
brand subcultures   364–5
brands   347–75
    brand values   348–54
    discourse and brand identity   366–70
    global   42–4
    'growing'   358
    managerial discourses   354–61
    popular brand discourses   361–6
    tribal icons   66–7
Branson, R.   195
Brennan, T.   63, 265
bricolage   200–1
Briscoe, J.   295–6
bulimia nervosa (BN)   305–22, 331–3
    explanations   306–22, 331–3
bureaucracy   37–8, 124–5
Burroughs, W.   391
Bush, G.   217
butter   202–4

Caillois, P.   261
calculability   38
Calvinism   33–7
capital
    cultural   170, 238–41
    economic   170, 238–9
    social and personal   398
    turnover time of capital   60
capitalism
    exercise of power   110–11
    spirit of   33–5
Carson, C.   182–3
'Cartesian' dualism   325–8
celebrity system   218
Chanel   195–6

change 56–72
children 259
  cigarette advertising 388–9
China 54–5
cigarettes *see* smoking
circuit of production 118–19
civilizing process 9–18, 25
class system *see* social class
cleanliness 163
clothing 189–90
Coca-Cola 53, 166–7, 371–2
Coca-colonization 53–4
cocaine 379, 380, 383–4
Coleridge, S.T. 391
collusion 98–9
commodities 159–60
  fetishism of 57–9, 72–3, 119
  marker goods 151–3, 282–3
  symbolic and diabolic devices 268
  see also objects; products
commodity exchange 141–7
  needs 147–61
community 176–8
  brand communities 176–7, 365
  commodity exchange and 143–4
  decline of 32, 54–5, 278–9, 283–5, 291
  gift exchange 139–41, 160
  place of community vs space of society 30–2
  postmodernism and neo-tribes 18–25
  primitive eating community 32, 278–9, 283–5, 291
  and society 269–70, 283–5
Community Organising Foundation (COF) 49–50
compensatory power 108
competition 84–6
  free between individuals 98–9
compulsion 391–3
concealment 58, 102
condign power 108
conditional power 109
conformity 106, 171
confusion marketing 101
connaissance 21
connotation 199–200
consensus 91

consequentialism 84
consumer goods *see* commodities; products
consumer society 1–28
  civilizing process 9–18
  Europe from Middle Ages to eighteenth century 3–5, 7–9
  postmodernism and neo-tribes 18–25
  US in 1920s 5–9
consumerism 5
consumers
  involvement and brands 354–61
  rationality 85, 102–5
  time-squeezed lifestyle 67–72
control
  civilizing process 10–16, 17
  internalization of 236, 286–7
  McDonaldization 38
  self-control *see* self-control/self-discipline
  social control 5–7
controlled de-control 25
convenience 161–3
conversation 285
Cooley, C. 247–8
core brand 355
Cornelissen, J. 358
corpus callosum 227
cosmetic surgery 295–8
cost–benefit analysis 146–7
Coupland, D. 153
court society 12–16, 18, 170
Cova, B. 66
credit 36
criminals 51–2
crises
  and the ego 255–8
  identity crisis 254, 258
Cross, G. 69
Crowther, C. 318, 319
Csikszentmihalyi, M. 265–8
cultural capital 170, 238–41
cultural consolidation 254–5
cultural individualism 23, 24
culture 25
  aesthetics 167–8
  brand subcultures 364–5

culture (*cont.*):
  needs and   151–3, 156–8
  popular   167–8, 381–3
  signs and identity   212–13
currency, products as   197
customer, as moral object   93–4

Dahl, S.   300
Dare, C.   318, 319
DDT   87–8
DEATH™ cigarettes   387–8
death drive (Thanatos)   249, 402–7
deceit   391
deception   102, 165
  signs and   213–18
decision processes
  gift exchange and commodity exchange
    146–7
  organizational   99–100
deficit   352–3, 354
democratic institutions   23, 24
Deneuve, C.   196, 199–200
denotation   199–200
dependence   143–4
Desmond, J.   193–4
despair   258
development
  and eating disorders   319–2
  Erikson   255–8
  Freud   251–3
  Lacan   261–4
dexfenfluramine   338, 339
diabolic devices   268
diachronic   187
diet
  disciplining of appetite   281–3
  and eating disorders   310–11
  and obesity   340–1
difference   183
  identity and   212–13, 255
  meaning as   186–7
differentiation   268
direct action   47, 88–91
disaffected consumers   44, 45, 46–7, 362–3
discipline
  body   17, 280–3, 327, 330
  disciplinary power   121–29

self-discipline   *see* self-control/self-
    discipline
discourse
  account of discipline   122–8
  and brand identity   366–70
  interpretation of anorexia   322–31, 332–3
  managerial discourses of brands   354–61
  popular brand discourses   361–6
disembeddedness   32, 70
Disney Corporation   41–2
displacement   250–1
distinction   152–3, 237–9
distortion   114–17
division of labour   35
Douglas, M.   157–8, 212–13
Drucker, P.   95
drugs   376–416
  anti-drugs campaigns   389–90, 408–13
  associations   378–81
  defining   377–8
  explanations for addiction   390–407
  legal issues   383–90
  and popular culture   381–3
  and society   378–81
Duesenberry, J.S.   152
Dukakis presidential campaign   217
duty, consumption as   35–7

early childhood   256
eating   327–8
eating community   32, 278–9, 283–5, 291
eating disorders   *see* anorexia nervosa;
    bulimia nervosa; obesity
Eco, U.   208, 213, 215
economic approaches to needs   148–9
economic capital   170, 238–9
economic individualism   23, 24
efficiency   38
  and convenience   161–3
ego   113, 249–50, 253–65
  narcissistic   253, 260–5
  realist   253–60
ego-identity   254–5
egoism   84
election campaigns   217–18
electronic herd   59–60
Elias, N.   33, 113, 121, 218

body   276–7, 278–9, 280
   civilizing process   9–18, 25
Elliott, R.   395–6, 397, 402
embarrassment   15
embeddedness   31
Emme, L.   300
emotions   17, 25
empowerment   328–9
empty self   283–5, 402
emulation   4
endorphin   379
England   3–4, 9, 18, 32
Englis, B.G.   246–7
enlightened self interest   86–7, 93
Enough   90–1
environment
   concern for natural environment   24–5
   costs of global trade to   63
   firms' attempts to control the
      consumption environment   100–2
Environmental Defence Fund (EDF)   88
EPA   52
Erikson, E.   254–60
Eros (life principle)   249, 402–4
erotogenic zones   251
Esso   351–2
esteem   169
Europe
   civilizing process   9–18
   consumption from Middle Ages to
      eighteenth century   3–5, 7–9
   early descriptions of anorexia nervosa
      323–4
European Values Study Group   23–4
Ewen, S.   5–7, 17, 45–6
exaggeration principle   294
examination   124
exchange   32
   forms of   138–47
   needs and commodity exchange
      147–61
exchange value   148–9
excluded identities   44, 45, 48–50
exhaustive common denominator (ECD)
   202, 204
externalities   94
Extropians   299

extroversion   233–5
Eysenck, H.J.   233–5

Faber, R.   395, 396
Falk, P.   54, 277, 278, 352, 353
   community and self   32, 278, 279, 283–6,
      291
false needs   115, 158–60
family   6–7
farming   74–7
fashion   4, 64, 65–7
   identity and   269–71
fasting   323–4
fat   328
fat-free fat   339, 341–3
fear of fatness   306–7
   see also obesity
Featherstone, M.   287
femininity, 'perfect'   325
fenfluramine   337–8, 339
fetishism of commodities   57–9, 72–3,
   119
Fidelity Brokerage Services   192
Fine, R.   2
firms   *see* organizations
fitness
   health and   126–7, 293–4
   organizations   127–8
fluoxetene (Prozac)   315, 338, 384
folk-tales   205–6
Fonda, J.   127, 297
food   328
   social marker   282–3
food industry   338–9, 341–3
Fordism   37–8
formal rationality   32–56
Formula One motor racing   386
Foucault, M.   277–8, 380
   discursive account of discipline   122–8
   'Foucauldian' interpretation of anorexia
      323–31, 332–3
Fournier, S.   359–60
France   5, 12–16, 18, 170, 238–9
fraudulence   390–1
Fredriksson, C.   52
freedom   269–71
Freud, S.   113, 380, 383

Freud, S. (*cont.*):
  cigarette addiction 402–3
  and psychoanalysis 249–53
Friedman, M. 84–5
Friedman, T. 59
Fromm, E. 114, 399–400, 401–2
'functional' signifier 239–40
fundamentalism 47, 174

Galbraith, J.K.
  needs 148–9, 153–5, 158
  power 108–12
games 248, 256–7
Ganetz, H. 65–6
Garner, D.M. 311
gender
  anorexia and discursive production of
    324–5
  and socialization 320–1
generativity 258
genetic inheritance 231–3, 337
genetic mutation 231, 392
genre 205–7
Gergen, K.J. 402
Germany 18
Giddens, A. 55–6, 70, 207
gift communities 139–41, 160
gift exchange 138–41
  comparison with commodity exchange
    142–7
global space, rationalization of 40–4
globalization
  anti-globalization movement 120,
    129–30
  of identity 52–5
  insecurity and risk 60–3
Goffman, E. 115–16
going with the flow 65–7
Grafton-Small, R. 145
Green, D.C. 85
Green Revolution 74–5
Grogan, S. 293, 309
Grönroos, C. 96
guilt 256–7
Guinness 355–6
Gulia, M. 176, 177–8
Gummesson, E. 96

habitus 237–9
Hall, S. 117, 118
Halmi, K.A. 306, 310–11
handkerchiefs 280–1
happiness 69–70
Harré, R. 294
Harris, P. 358
Harvey, D. 32–3, 56, 60, 62–4
Hastings, G.B. 388
'having' mode 399–400
Hawkes, T. 198
Hayek, F. von 84–5
hazards 104, 105
  see also risk
health 126–7, 293–4, 340
health inequalities 49
health warning, on cigarettes 385
Hebdige, D. 167–8, 212, 245–6, 364–5
hedonism 85
Hemingway, M. 196
Henke, L.L. 388
heroin 379
heroin chic 288
Hetzel, P. 218–19, 270, 271
hippocampus 228
Hirschman, E.C. 292–3
Hobbes, T. 82
Holt, D. 239–41
hormones 229–31
Hornbacher, M. 305
Horton, W. 217
hostility 212–13
Hot Topic 272–3
hunger 150
hunger-strikes 318–22
Hyde, L. 140–1, 143–5
hydraulic model of motivation 113
hyper-reality 215–18
hyperspace 62
hypochondria 324
hypothalamus 227
  eating disorders 313–17
hysteria 324

iconic signs 210–12
id 113, 249–50, 252–3
ideal woman 287–8

idealism   240–1
identifier, brand as   368–70
identity   225–75
    anorexia, power and   328–9
    and the body   278–85
    brand identity   366–70
    consumption-related identities   44–52
    creation of individual identities   247–8
    extension of self   265–8
    and fashion   269–71
    globalization of   52–5
    inside-out approaches   226, 227–36
    modern identity   283–5
    outside-in approaches   226, 236–48
    psychoanalytic theory   226–7, 249–65
    signs, difference and   212–13
identity confusion   257
identity crisis   254, 258
ideology   132–20
Ikerd, J.   75, 76, 77
images   72
    brand image   355–6
    and eating disorders   307–10, 325
    metaphor and metonymy in advertising
        193–4
    narcissistic ego   261, 262–4, 265
    self-protection and the body   286–92
imaginary order (stage)   261, 262–4
inalienable objects   143
independence   143–4
indexic signs   210–12
individualism
    and decline of community   32, 54–5,
        278–9, 283–5, 291
    discourse of   329–30
    growth in   23–5
individuals
    in brand discourse   365–6, 367
    creation of individual identities   247–8
    free competition between   98–9
    identity and lifestyle   242–4
industry   257
infancy   255–6
inferiority   257
information processing   102–3
initiative   256–7
inner-directedness   243

insecurity   60–3
institutional reflexivity   70
integrated consumers   44, 45–6
integration   268
integrity   258
intellectuals   380
interest groups   87–91
internalization of control   236, 286–7
internalized other   247–8
Internet communities   177–8
interpretant   209–10
intimacy   257–8
introversion   233–5
Irish 'theme' bars   41
Irn-Bru   371–3
irrationality of rationality   38, 39
Isherwood, B.   157–8
isolation   257–8
issue-based identities   46–7

Jhally, S.   58
'Jim Twins'   232–3
Joe Camel   388, 389

Kabyle people   30–1, 237
Ki-Zerbo, J.   54
Kilbourne, W.E.   50
Kirshenbaum, R.   101
Klein, M.   400–1
Klein, R.   339–41, 406
kleptomania   52
Knapp, C.   390, 391
knowledge, mediation of   103–5
Kotler, P.   95, 96–7
Kula exchange   139–40

labour-saving devices   163
Lacan, J.   403, 404
    narcissistic ego   261–5
Lane, R.E.   69, 70
language   184–8, 189, 207
langue, la   186–7
large-scale farming   74–7
Lasch, C.   400–1, 402
latency   252
legislation, drugs and   383–90
Leiss, W.   157

leisure time 34, 39, 70, 241
leptin 317, 337, 339
Levi-Strauss, C. 198–9, 200, 202
Levitt, T. 93
Leymore, V.L. 201–5
liberal pluralism 86–8
liberalism 82–108
   marketing theory 91–6
   questioning liberal assumptions 97–105
   view of power 86
libido 250, 260
life-cycle 255–8
   marketing and 258–60
life expectancy 49
lifestyle
   identity and 242–4
   time-squeezed 67–72
liminal identities 44–5, 50–2
'Lite' cigarettes 386–7
livestock farming 75–7
long-term 93
looking-glass self 247
love 260
Lukes, S. 112

machine bodies 289–90
Madden, O. 272–3
Maffesoli, M. 19–22, 24–5
male body 289–90
Malinowski, B. 139
malls 41
Malson, H. 323–31
managerialism 92
   discourses of brands 354–61
manners 15–16, 280–1
Marcuse, H. 112–14, 121–2
margarine 202–4
marginal utility 149
marker goods 151–3, 282–3
market 84, 118–19
market share 349–50
marketing
   and creation of false needs 158–60
   images and bodily self-protection 287–92
   liberal marketing theory 91–6
   and the life-cycle 258–60

making the market 65
proliferation of marketing discourse 127–8
scope of semiotic research 218–19
marketing character 399–400
marketing concept 92–5, 96–7
marketing myopia 93
Marsh, A. 391–2
Marx, K.
   annihilation of space through time 57, 59–60
   and fetishism of commodities 57–9, 119
   Marxist analysis of changing space–time relations 56–73
Maslow, A. 149–51, 155–6, 167, 171–2
Massim peoples 139
materialism 240–1
   marker goods 151–3
mature age 258
McCabe, M.P. 309–10
McCracken, G. 3–5, 16–17, 190
'McDonaldization' thesis 38–40
McIntosh, A. 404–6
McKay, S. 391–2
McKitterick, J.B. 92
McLuhan, M. 289
MDMA 382–3
Mead, G.H. 248
meaning *see* semiotics
mediation of knowledge 103–5
medical discourse 323–4
Mennell, S. 281–3, 306–7
mercantilist system 83
Merrill Lynch 192–3
metaphor 188, 191–4
metonymy 188, 191–4
Michman, R.D. 86
Middle Ages 11–12, 278–9, 281–2
Midland Bank 360–1
Miller, D. 53, 54
mimicry 261
mirror stage 262–4
misrecognition 263
Mizerski, R. 388–9
mobilization of bias 108
models 287–8, 300–1
modernity 18–19

Marxist analysis   56–73
modern identity   283–5
as rational ordering of space   32–56
'Mods'   245–6
money exchange   *see* commodity exchange
monoculture   74–5
Monteath, S.A.   309–10
Monterey tourist sites   220–1
mood-repair   396
moral agency   165
moral object, customer as   93–4
moral subjects   164–5
morality   164–5
More, M.   299
Morrison, S.   300
mourning   260
multinational corporations (MNCs)   40
Muniz, A.   176–7
music   51, 169, 381–3
mutation, genetic   231, 392
myth   200

Nader, R.   94, 95
narcissism   2–3
addiction   399–402
narcissistic ego   253, 260–5
needs   137–80
in commodity exchange   147–61
neo-tribes   18–25, 66–7
nervous systems   231
neurons   228–9, 230
neurobiology of drugs   378–9
neurotransmitters   229–31
news   216–17
'no-logo' identity   363
non-decisionmaking   107–8
non-places   62
Norkunas, M.   220–1
normality   122–3
nose blowing   280–1
novelty   4, 269–70

obesity   304–5, 333–41
biological explanations   337–8
eating disorders and fear of fatness   306–7
psychoanalytic explanations   336

social explanations   334–6
object–sign relations   210–12
objects   209–10
alienable and inalienable   143
extending the self into   266–7
symbolic and diabolic devices   268
system of   190–1
see also commodities; products
obsessive–compulsive tendencies   230–1
O'Donohoe, S.   207–8
Oedipus complex   252
O'Guinn, T.   176–7, 395, 396
olestra   341–3
Olsen, G.   359
operant conditioning   393–5
opium   379, 380, 383
oral stage   251–2, 255–6
Orbach, S.   319–22
organizations   111
attempts to control consumption environment   100–2
decision-making   99–100
fitness   127–8
rationality   99–102
responses to instability and flux   65–7
Orlan   297–8
other-directedness   243–4
and reference group influence   244–6
ownership   350–1

Packard, V.   94, 95
Pahl, R.   68, 69
paradigmatic relations   188
analysis of advertising   201–5
paradox of self-affirmation   297–8
paranoid–schizoid position   400–1
parenting   320–2
Parker, M.   55
parole   187
patina   3
patriarchy   325
peak experiences   171–4
Peirce, C.S.   184, 209–12
Pepsi   166, 372
person, as brand   369–70
persona
brand   356–61

persona (*cont.*):
  metaphor, metonymy and   192–3
personal capital   398
personal power   109
personality
  brands and   358–61
  ideology and   112–14
  introversion and extroversion   233–5
perspective   33
phallic stage   252, 256–7
pharmaceutical industry   384
phenteramine   337–8, 339
Philo, G.   216–17
physiological needs   148, 150, 154–5, 155–8
piercing, body   368–9
PIMS database   349
pituitary gland   227–8
place of community   30–2
Plant, S.   380
plastic surgery   295–8
play stage   248, 256–7
pluralism, liberal   86–8
politics   20, 23, 24
polysemy   208–9
popular culture   167–8, 381–3
position, brand   356
possessions   267
post-Fordism   63–5
postmaterialism   23
postmodernism   126–7
  and neo-tribes   18–25
poverty   157–8
  excluded identities   48–50
  and smoking   380–1, 391–2
  and time   71
power   81–136
  anorexia, identity and   328–9
  disciplinary   121–9
  sovereign   82–120
Precari Nati   129–30
preconscious   250–1
predestination   33–4
predictability   38
primitive eating community   32, 278–9,
    283–5, 291
production   36
  circuit of   118–19

creation of needs   158–60
products
  consumer goods and convenience   162–3
  consumer goods and saving labour   163
  generation of meaning   195–7
  system of   189–91
  see also commodities; objects
profits   349–50
property   109
Propp, V.   205
protectionism   83, 84
proxemics   21
Prozac (fluoxetene)   315, 338, 384
pseudo-events   217–18
psychic energy, investment of   265–8
psychoanalysis
  addiction   398–407
  approaches to identity   226–7, 249–65
  starvation disorders   317–22, 332, 333
psychogenesis   9
psychological needs   148, 150, 154–8
psychologization   14
psychology: approach to needs   149–51,
    155–6
psychoticism   235
Puritanism   33–7

qualitative relations   143
quality   165–7
quantitative relations   143

radical view of power   112–20
Radner, H.   127, 297
rage   401
railways   62
rational economics   397–8
rationality
  consumers   85, 102–5
  modernity as rational ordering of space
    32–56
  rational calculation of interests   99–105
rationalization   15, 36, 37
  global space   40–4
raves   51, 382–3
real order (stage)   261, 262
realist ego   253–60
reciprocity   138, 140, 141

recreation   34, 39, 70, 241
redundancy   203
reference group influence   244–7
referent   185, 197
reformism   107–12
regulation   385–9
reinforcement   393–5, 398
relationship marketing   96
relationships, brand   359–61
reliability   165–7
religion   23
    fasting   323–4
    peak experiences and   172–4
renunciation of the flesh   328
repression   250
    disciplinary power as   121–2
    ideology as   112–14
repressive desublimization   113–14
reputation   169
revised sequence   108, 111, 155, 158
revolutionary identity   47–8
revolutions   82
Riesman, D.   242–4
rights   82
risk   60–3
    modern hazards   104, 105
Ritalin   384
rites of passage   258
    branding the skin   368–9
    cosmetic surgery   296–7
ritual shared meals   284–5
Ritzer, G.   35, 38–40
Roberts, J.A.   396, 397
Rochberg-Halton, E.   265–8
'Rockers'   245–6
Rogers, M.   100–1
Rossi, J.   337
Rudmin, F.W.   50
'ruling ideas'   114–17
Run-DMC   51, 169

safety   164–7
Samms, C.   68
Sandikci, O.   208–9
Saussure, F. de   184–8, 207
school age   257
Schor, E.   67–8, 69, 70, 71, 163

Schouten, J.   296–7
scooters   245–6
Scotland Against Drugs (SAD)   408–13
sculpted body   295–8
self
    brands and filling the self with goods
        352–3
    concepts of   249–50
    empty self   283–5, 402
    extension of   265–8
    looking-glass self   247
    negative constructions of   330
    social self   6, 17, 248
self-affirmation, paradox of   297–8
self-control/self-discipline   34, 122
    and the body   17, 280–3, 327, 330
    civilizing process   10–16, 17
self-expression   293–300
self-fulfilment   292–3
self-gifts   140, 141
self-interest   86–7, 93
self-protection   286–92
selfishness   84
selling   93
semiotic square   44, 45
semiotics   181–224
    other sign systems   189–94
    Peirce   184, 209–12
    products and generation of meaning
        195–7
    scope of semiotic research   218–19
    semiological tradition of de Saussure
        184–8
    signs, identity and difference   212–13
    signs telling the truth and lying   213–18
    structuralism   198–209
senses   218–19
sentiment, shared   20–1
serotonin system   314–17, 337–8
services   64
sexuality
    and development   251–3
    disciplinary power   121–3, 125
shame   15, 256
Shell   351–2
Sherry, J.   146
shoplifting   52

shopping   392–3
  addictive   395–7
shopping malls   41
short-term   93
Sibley, S.D.   86
sign value   181
signified   185–6
  product as   195–6
signifier   185–6
signs   209–10
  arbitrary nature of   184–6
  identity and difference   212–13
  linguistics   184–8
  object–sign relations   210–12
  other sign systems   189–94
  telling the truth and lying   213–18
  see also semiotics
Silk Cut   405–6
simulacra   215–18
simulations   216–18
skin, branding   368–9
skinfold thickness measurements
    333–4
Smart, B.   35
Smith, A.   35, 83–4, 110
smoking   234–5, 380–1, 402–7
  cigarette advertising   385–9, 404–7
  gene for   235–6
social capital   398
social class   16, 49, 169–70
  and eating disorders   307
  identity   237–9
  measuring social classification   241–2
  needs and distinction   152–3
  obesity and   334–6
social control   5–7
social determinism   391–2
social self   6, 17, 248
socialization   247–8, 266, 320–1
societal marketing concept   95
society
  community and   269–70, 283–5
  drugs and   378–81
  space of society   30–2
sociogenesis   9
sociology
  explanations for obesity   334–6

explanations for starvation disorders
    306–12, 331–2, 333
  and needs   151–3, 156–8
Solomon, M.   246–7
sovereign power   82–120
  liberalism   82–107
  radical view   112–20
  reformism   107–12
space   29–80
  annihilation of space through time   57,
    59–60, 62, 73
  Marxist analysis of space and time
    56–73
  modernity as rational ordering of space
    32–56
  place of community vs space of society
    30–2
  separation of time from space   55–6
  speed-up and changing perceptions of
    space and time   71–2
  time–space compression   62–3
Spence, J.   320, 321
spirituality   171–4
stagnation   258
Stanford Research Institute (SRI)   244
starvation disorders   304–33
  biological explanations   312–17, 332, 333
  description and prevalence   306
  discursive explanation of anorexia
    323–31, 332–3
  psychoanalytical views   317–22, 332, 333
  social explanations   306–12, 331–2, 333
state, role of   87, 107
status   169–71
  exchange and   142
  objects and   190–1
Stelarc   298–9
Stern, B.   192–3
stigmatization   361–2
Stohr, O.   233
strangers   11
  identifying   236–41
stress   316–17
structuralism   187, 198–209
  analyses of advertising   201–7
style   51, 370
  anti-style   212

self-expression   293–300
subcultures, brand   364–5
sublimation   250–1
sublime   406
subliminal advertising   100–2
superego   113, 249–50, 252, 253
supermodels   288
surveillance   42, 123
symbolic interactionism   248
symbolic order   261, 264
symbols   210–12, 268
synapses   228–9
synchronic   187
synecdoche   188
syntagmatic relations   188
   analyses of advertising   205–7

tangible brand   355
taste   282–3
tattooing   368–9
technology   298–9
   drugs and   379–80
technostructure   110–11, 112
Thanatos (death drive)   249, 402–7
themed spaces   41–2
thin body   287–8, 300–1
   meaning of   324–5
Thompson, C.J.   292–3
throwaway society   65
time   29–80, 335–6
   annihilation of space through time   57, 59–60, 62, 73
   consumer goods and convenience   162–3
   Marxist approach to space–time relations   56–73
   modernity as rational ordering of space   32–56
   separation of time from space   55–6
   speed-up and changing perceptions of time and space   71–2
time–space compression   62–3
time-squeezed consumer lifestyle   67–72
Toffler, A.   65
tolerance   23, 24
tone   192
topology   278–9, 283–5
'totem' drinks   200

tourism   46
   tourist sites in Monterey   220–1
tradition   31
tradition-dominated person   242–3
'train' metaphor   207
tranquillisers   384
transportation   63
tribes, neo-   18–25, 66–7
Trinidad   53, 54
trust   255–6
Turner, B.   277
turnover time of capital   60
twin studies   232–3

unconscious   250–1
underclass   48–9
uneven development   17–18
Unilever   42–4
United Kingdom (UK)
   and American popular culture   167–8
   England   3–4, 9, 18, 32
United Nations Human Development Report   40
United States (US)
   consumption in the 1920s   5–9
   globalization of culture   53
   obesity   333, 334, 335, 337–8, 339, 340–1
   popular culture   167–8
   tourist sites in Monterey   220–1
use value   148–9
uses and gratifications research   117

value
   for money   167
   and worth   145–6
values   137–80
   aesthetics   167–8
   brand values   348–54
   brands, connotation of   350–2
   efficiency and convenience   161–3
   neo-tribes   21–2, 23–5
   reputation   169
   safety   164–7
   spirituality   171–4
   status   169–71
Values and Lifestyle Study (VALS)   244
Van Gogh, V.   406–7

INDEX

Veblen, T.   171
virtual communities   177–8
voluntary simplicity   50

Walmart   86
warriors   11
    transition to courtiers   12–16
waste disposal   59
Weberian analysis   32–56, 73
Wedgwood, J.   4
Wellman, B.   176, 177–8
Wensley, R.   96
Williamson, J.   117–18, 195–6, 197
Williamson, K.   409–13
Wilson, W.J.   48

women
    advertising and   7, 45–6, 115–17
    and body   126–7, 287–8, 289, 300–1
    ideal woman   287–8
    'perfect' femininity   325
work   68–9, 241
working class   238–9
worth   145–6

Yannacone, V.   88
young adult   257–8
youth   50–1
Yufe, J.   233
Yurok people   144